THE DECLINE
OF THE AGE OF LOUIS XIV

The

DECLINE OF THE
AGE OF LOUIS XIV

OR, FRENCH LITERATURE 1687–1715

by

ARTHUR TILLEY, M.A.

Fellow of King's College, Cambridge

BARNES & NOBLE, Inc.

NEW YORK

PUBLISHERS & BOOKSELLERS SINCE 1873

First published, 1929.
Reprinted, 1968 by Barnes & Noble, Inc.
By permission of the
Cambridge University Press

L. C. Catalog Card Number: 68-20701

Printed in the United States of America

PREFACE

THE subject of this book is French Literature from 1687 to
1715, but I have given it as its principal title *The Decline
of the Age of Louis XIV*, in order to emphasise the fact that
it is a study of that period of Louis's long reign when its glories
were losing their lustre, when Corneille and Molière were dead,
when Racine had renounced the stage, when the voice of
Bossuet was hushed, when the work of La Fontaine and Boileau
was nearly finished. The two figures, who principally represent
the literature of the period, La Bruyère and Fénelon, both rank
a little below the great writers who had passed or were passing
away, and if in spirit they are still of the classical age, they
wear their classicism with a difference. On the other hand,
Saint-Simon is not classical at all. If he belongs to any age,
it is to that of Louis XIII, but he is above all things himself,
and it is in his intense and vivid originality that his greatness
consists. It may be said, indeed, that his *Memoirs*, which were
not completed till after the middle of the eighteenth century,
do not really belong to our period, but they illuminate it with a
searching light, and though we cannot trust him unchecked for
historical facts, and though we have to make liberal allowances
for his prejudices, his picture of Versailles and the court remains
true in its main lines and is of unsurpassable interest.

In the field of purely creative literature our period is not
remarkable. In poetry it is represented only by society-verse
and the pretentious but empty odes of Jean-Baptiste Rousseau;
in fiction chiefly by fairy-tales and apocryphal memoirs; in
tragedy by Crébillon. Comedy, with Dancourt, Regnard, and
Lesage, makes a better show, but it is significant that its successes, especially its greatest success, *Turcaret*, are in the comedy
of manners and not in the comedy of character. For under the
influence of La Bruyère the study of man, which had been
the glory of the great age, was now diverted from character to
manners. In fact the only masters of psychological analysis who
appear prominently in these pages—Bourdaloue was still

preaching and confessing, but he belongs to the earlier generation—were two writers of "spiritual letters," Fénelon and
Mme de Maintenon.

But if our period is one of decline, it is also one of transition.
The old order is passing away, but a new order is beginning.
The seventeenth century is moribund, but the eighteenth is
being born. That this is more apparent in thought than in
literature will appear from my last three chapters. The case
for the "Moderns" was not only singularly weak from the
point of view of literature, but its success was largely due to
the aesthetic deficiencies of the reading public. Bayle and
Fontenelle are more important as thinkers and leaders of
thought than as writers. To both of these, to Bayle especially,
I have given much attention. Though I am far from satisfied
with the result of my efforts to understand Bayle, I present it
for what it is worth, hoping that it may serve as a starting-
point for some scholar better versed in theology and philosophy.

Besides the thought of the period I have taken into account
its social features, without a knowledge of which all literature
is apt to remain vague and unreal. Saint-Simon at Versailles,
Mme de Maintenon at Versailles and Saint-Cyr, La Bruyère
first in Paris and then at Chantilly, Fénelon at Cambrai, the
poets at Sceaux and the Temple, Fontenelle in the salon of
Mme de Lambert, the writers of comedy in the *bourgeois*
world, all have their appropriate setting, and an acquaintance
with this will help, I hope, to make their writings more
intelligible.

At the beginning of an article on Lesage, written more
than thirty years ago (*Études critiques*, vol. III), Brunetière
declared that the details of the period from 1688 to 1715 were
badly known, and in proof of this he alleged that it includes
some works of which Sainte-Beuve is apparently ignorant, and
some names which he does not even mention. As a matter of
fact, Sainte-Beuve has written more than thirty *causeries* on
the men and women of this period, and the only writers who
are practically passed over in his pages or not mentioned at
all are Dancourt, Mme d'Aulnoy and other women, like
Mme de Murat and Mme de La Force, who wrote fairy-tales

and apocryphal memoirs, and that industrious blender of history and fiction, Courtilz de Sandras.

But these omissions, which are not, after all, very serious, have been repaired since Sainte-Beuve's day. In 1882 Lemaître published an excellent book on Dancourt and comedy after Molière. Only two years ago M. Foulché-Delbosc published an admirable edition of Mme d'Aulnoy's *Relation du Voyage d'Espagne* and cleared up the mystery surrounding it. Other recent contributions to our period are Mr Woodbridge's thesis on Courtilz de Sandras, Mr Atkinson's three essays on the Extraordinary Voyage, and Miss Ruth Clark's excellent monograph on Hamilton.

As regards texts, it is a pleasure to record the approaching completion of M. de Boislisle's noble edition of Saint-Simon, begun nearly half a century ago. The *Textes Français Modernes* include Bayle's *Pensées sur la Comète*, edited by M. Prat, and Fontenelle's *Histoire des Oracles*, edited by M. Maigron, while in the useful and interesting *Collection des Chefs-d'œuvre méconnus*, edited by M. Gonzague Truc, will be found Regnard's *La Provençale*, Dufresny's *Amusements sérieux et comiques*, the *Vie de Monsieur du Guay-Trouin*, and some of Mme de Maintenon's letters. M. Lachèvre has printed in *Les derniers Libertins* considerable portions of the poetry of Mme Deshoulières, Chaulieu, and La Fare, and M. Georges Roth has edited for the *Bibliothèque Larousse* Baron's *L'Homme à bonne fortune*, two plays by Dufresny and three by Dancourt—but not *Les Bourgeoises à la Mode*. I should like to see the last omission made good, with the addition, perhaps, of *Les Curieux de Compiègne*, *Les trois Cousines*, and *Les Vacances*. Other *desiderata* are a selection from Fontenelle's *Éloges* and especially a new and definitive edition of Fénelon's letters.

The bibliographies at the beginning of the chapters speak for themselves. They do not pretend to be complete, but it has been my aim to mention the first edition of every work of any importance and to give all authorities that I have found helpful from the point of view either of biography or of criticism. There are bound to be some omissions, but I hope there are no serious ones. General works of reference are naturally not included, but I must acknowledge here my debt to two historical works, the eighth volume of the *Histoire de France*, edited by Lavisse, especially the chapters by M. Sagnac and M. Rébelliau, and the *Sources de l'Histoire de France* (1610–1715) by M. Bourgeois and M. André, frequent references to which will be found in the chapter on Prose Fiction. And the name of M. Bourgeois reminds me that in my list of authorities for Saint-Simon I ought to have mentioned his chapter on Memoirs in vol. v of Petit de Julleville's *Histoire de la Langue et de la Littérature française*, which contains, besides a sufficient account of the life and writings of the great Memoir-writer, a most just and impartial appreciation of the historical value of his work.

Finally, I should like to express my warm gratitude to two great Cambridge institutions, the University Library and the University Press. Without the former this book could never have been written; without the latter, it might never have been published.

A. T.

CAMBRIDGE

November 5, 1928

From an article in the *Times* of October 27, 1928, it appears that the great work of restoring the palace and gardens of Versailles to their pre-Revolution state, which was begun nearly six years ago, thanks largely to the princely generosity of Mr Rockefeller, is now more than half completed.

CONTENTS

CHAPTER I

LOUIS XIV AND VERSAILLES

I

II

CHAPTER II

SAINT-SIMON AND THE COURT

I

CHAPTER III

LA BRUYÈRE

CHAPTER IV

THE DRAMA

1. *The Stage and the Church*

2. *Tragedy*

3. *The minor successors of Molière*

4. *Dancourt*

5. *Lesage*

CHAPTER VI

PROSE FICTION

1. *Apocryphal Memoirs*

2. *"Extraordinary" Voyages*

3. *Fairy-tales*

4. *Oriental Tales*

5. *Anthony Hamilton*

CHAPTER VII

MME DE MAINTENON AND THE EDUCATION OF GIRLS

CHAPTER VIII
FÉNELON
I

II

III

CHAPTER IX
MASSILLON

CHAPTER X
THE QUARREL OF THE ANCIENTS AND THE MODERNS

CHAPTER XI

BAYLE

CHAPTER XII

FONTENELLE

EPILOGUE

CHAPTER I

LOUIS XIV AND VERSAILLES

I

THE personal rule of Louis XIV began with the death of Mazarin on January 9, 1661, and his own death took place on September 1, 1715. Thus, if you divide the period during which he really reigned into two equal halves, the middle point is March 7, 1688. Now it is precisely in the year 1688 that Saint-Simon puts the "apogee of the reign, the height of its glory and prosperity." From that date he counts its decline. "The great captains, the great ministers were no more; only their pupils remained." Condé and Turenne were dead; only Luxembourg and Villars remained. Of the great ministers Louvois alone was left, and he died, more or less disgraced, three years later.

Saint-Simon might also have noticed the disappearance of the great writers. In 1688 Molière had been dead for fifteen years, La Rochefoucauld for eight, Corneille for four. Mme de La Fayette lived till 1693, but she was in bad health, and after *La Princesse de Clèves* (1678) wrote nothing except some memoirs of the court. Her friend, Mme de Sévigné, was still writing her incomparable letters, but from the end of 1690 till her death in 1696 she was never separated from her daughter, the correspondent who called forth her best powers. Racine, though he was still to produce his masterpiece, had renounced the stage in 1677, and in the same year he and his friend Boileau were commanded by the king to "give up everything" in order to write a history of the reign. After this command practically all that came from Boileau's pen consisted of a few epistles and satires and the last two cantos of *Le Lutrin*. La Fontaine's work was nearly over by 1678; before his death in 1695 he only published one more book of *Fables* (1693). In 1688 Malebranche reached, in the words of M. Joly, "the apogee of his glory and reputation as a writer" by completing his *Entretiens métaphysiques*. In the same year Bossuet gave to the world his last work of first-rate importance, the *Histoire des variations des églises protestantes*. In March of the preceding year he had delivered the last and greatest of his funeral orations, that on Condé. It ends with the words, "Je reserve au troupeau que je dois nourrir avec la parole de la vie les restes d'une voix qui tombe, et d'une ardeur qui s'éteint," and Chateaubriand says with truth that in this peroration he seems to be burying the age of Louis XIV. Bourdaloue, indeed, lived and preached till 1704, but with Massillon we come to the age of transition.

Thus one by one the great writers of the school of 1660 were vanishing from the stage. "Tout est dit," sighs La Bruyère at the outset of *Les Caractères*, which appeared at the beginning of 1688, and the remark indicates a decline in the literature as well as in the general prosperity of the reign.

The year 1688 is also marked by another event, which, though not in itself significant, is at least symbolical of impending change. This is the practical completion of the great palace upon which Louis XIV, both in a material and in a spiritual sense, had stamped his masterful personality. "Among the causes of the French Revolution," says Lavisse, "one must number that fear of Paris and those promptings of pride which led Louis XIV to transform a château, once a secluded shooting-lodge, into the capital of France."

But before describing the stage upon which the later acts of the reign of Louis XIV were played, we must briefly consider the drama itself and the part played in it by its chief actor.

The Peace of Nymegen gave France, if you include Lorraine, almost the same frontiers as she had in 1792, and again in 1814. But this did not satisfy Louis XIV. He marked his discontent by dismissing Pomponne, his Minister for Foreign Affairs, the most honourable minister he ever had, and by appointing in his place Colbert's brother, Colbert de Croissy. With Croissy's help he proceeded to carry out by means of local *Parlements* or Courts of Justice created *ad hoc* a policy of "reunion," or, as a modern historian calls it, "clandestine annexation[1]." In accordance with the decisions of these courts various districts in Luxemburg, Lorraine, Alsace, and Franche-Comté were added to France, and without any judicial process the towns of Strasburg and Casale (on the Po) were occupied by French troops on September 30, 1681. Luxemburg was added on June 4, 1684. While Louis and Colbert de Croissy annexed, Vauban fortified. The gaps between the Meuse and the Moselle, and the Moselle and the Vosges, and that between the Vosges and the Rhine, known as the *trouée de Belfort*, were filled in, and the French frontier was thus considerably strengthened[2]. The Truce of Ratisbon (August, 1684) confirmed the annexations for twenty years.

Four years later the truce was broken. At the end of September, 1688, Louis, after issuing a manifesto, invaded the Empire at several points. For the moment he was only at open war with the Emperor, but before the end of the year the English Revolution deprived him of his only ally in Europe except the Turk. In May 1689 the new King of England declared war on France and already before this Louis had declared war on Spain and Holland. That criminal blunder of Louvois's, the devastation of the Palatinate (March—June 1689), did much to embitter European feeling, and before long Louis had a formidable coalition arrayed against him[3].

To meet the increased expenditure occasioned by the war and the ensuing financial distress Louis had to take extreme steps. By an edict of December 14, 1689, the fabrication and sale of gold and silver objects above a certain weight was forbidden and persons of every condition were ordered to sell any gold or silver plate which exceeded this limit. The king set

[1] É. Bourgeois in *Modern France*, Cambridge, 1922, p. 69. He points out that this policy was for a long time attributed to Louvois, but that its real author was Colbert de Croissy.

[2] See A. Longnon, *La Formation de l'Unité française*, 1922 (a posthumous publication of lectures given in 1889-1890), pp. 338-339.

[3] A treaty was ratified between the Empire and Holland at Vienna in May 1689, and in December of that year William, after concluding an alliance with Holland, gave his adhesion to the treaty. In June 1690 Spain, and in October Savoy, joined the coalition.

the example by stripping the state apartments at Versailles. Monseigneur and Monsieur followed suit, and Mme de Sévigné writes to her daughter from Brittany that her neighbours, the Duchesse du Lude, Mme de Chaulnes, and Mme de Lavardin, had all complied with the edict[1].

But France was still able to hold her own and to meet stroke with counter-stroke. The defeat of James II at the Boyne (July 1, 1690) was balanced by Tourville's victory over the English and Dutch fleets off Beachy Head on the preceding day, and by Luxembourg's victory over the allied forces at Fleurus on the day following. The crushing defeat of the French fleet off Cape La Hogue (May 29—June 3, 1692), which restored to England the command of the Channel and practically made the restoration of James II impossible, was followed on July 5 by the surrender of Namur, the great virgin fortress, to the French, and by the victory of Luxembourg over William at Steenkerke on August 3. In 1693 Luxembourg again defeated William at Neerwinden (July 29) and Tourville intercepted and partially destroyed the "Smyrna fleet," with cargoes estimated at many millions, in the Bay of Lagos (June 20).

But in 1693 France, though success had attended her arms, was exhausted. The crops, especially the grape and every kind of fruit, had failed, and it was not till the summer of 1694 that a good harvest relieved the situation. Moreover, taxation was becoming unendurable. Accordingly Louis entered into negotiations for peace, and though these were protracted for nearly four years, peace was signed at Ryswick on September 21, 1697, on terms very unfavourable to France[2]. It held for four years and then as the result of the momentous decision to accept the testament of the Spanish king, Charles II, in favour of Louis's grandson, the Duc d'Anjou, war broke out again. The decision was communicated to Madrid on November 12, 1700, and at first it appeared as if Europe, in spite of the Emperor's protests and warlike intentions, was prepared to acquiesce. But Louis XIV,

---

[1] Letter of December 18, 1689.

[2] "La malheureuse paix de Ryswick nous a extrêmement fait tomber de considération chez nos voisins et partout ailleurs" (Vauban, *Lettres intimes au Marquis de Puyzieulx*, ed. H. de Landosle, 1924, p. 71).

dazzled by the splendour of his position, made several blunders, with the result that on September 7, 1701, the Grand Alliance was formed at the Hague between the Empire (which was already at war), England, and Holland. Nine days later James II died at Saint-Germain and Louis gave fresh offence to this country by recognising his son as King of England, an act which, in spirit at least, was a direct violation of the Treaty of Ryswick. The death of William III (March 19, 1702) made no difference in English policy, and when the campaign opened in 1702 England and Holland took the field by the side of the Emperor.

The opposing forces were not unequally matched. France had as allies Spain, Portugal, Savoy, and Bavaria, and though Luxembourg was dead, she had generals of repute or promise in Villars, Vendôme, Boufflers, Catinat, and Berwick. Moreover, though he was now in his seventieth year, she still had her incomparable engineer, Vauban. But the fighting qualities of her opponents, especially of the British troops, were much higher than in the preceding wars, and before long the new Captain-General of the forces, created in this year Duke of Marlborough, revealed his superiority to the French generals by the crushing defeat of Blenheim (1704)[1]. Before this France had been deserted by two of her allies, Portugal and Savoy.

But it was the economical condition of France that more than anything else put her at a disadvantage in the long struggle. She was weighed down by a steady increase of debt and taxation, and of consequent misery in her people. Even in normal years the lot of the French peasant in the reign of Louis XIV was much as La Bruyère has depicted it. "If Paris and the court offer a prospect of wealth and pleasure," reports a Venetian ambassador in 1660, "the provinces are a sink of indigence and misery." "The provinces," says another ambassador in 1664, "are ruined by the poverty of the lower classes, who suffer less from the excessive weight of taxation

---

[1] "Pour moi, je vous avoue que je n'entrevois point par où nous pourrons nous relever d'une pareille perte, qui me paraît irréparable" (Vauban to Puyzieulx, *op. cit.* p. 129).

than from the greed of the tax-farmers (*les partisans*)[1]." A
year or two later La Fontaine drew his unforgettable picture
of the woodcutter:

> tout couvert de ramée,
> Sous le faix du fagot, aussi bien que des ans,
> Gémissant et courbé....
>
> Point de pain quelquefois, et jamais de repos.
> Sa femme, ses enfants, les soldats, les impôts,
> Le créancier et la corvée,
> Lui font d'un malheureux la peinture achevée[2].

This fable, first published in 1668, was probably written in
1666 or at any rate before the War of Devolution (May 1667)
had inaugurated the long series of Louis XIV's wars. By the
next decade the misery had considerably increased. In 1675 the
Governor of Dauphiné reports that "the greater part of the
inhabitants of this province have lived during the winter on
bread made of acorns and roots, and now they are eating grass
and the bark of trees." And in the same year the intendant of
Bourges says that "in the province of Berry and the neighbouring
provinces all the inhabitants, and particularly the agricultural
labourers, are more wretched than the slaves in Turkey or the
peasants in Poland[3]." In 1687 the truth of La Bruyère's picture
is confirmed by the report of two commissioners, D'Aguesseau
and D'Ormesson, who were sent to Maine and the Orléanais.
"The peasants," they say, "live on bread made with black
wheat; others, who have not even this, on roots of heather boiled
with the meal of barley or oats....But it is in their dwellings
that one sees most plainly their misery. They sleep on straw;
they have no clothes except what they have on; and no furniture[4]."

The same state of things is portrayed in an anonymous
pamphlet of 1689. After declaring that since the ravaging of

---

[1] Cited by Lavisse from *Relazioni degli ambasciatori Veneziani nel
secolo XVII*, III, 47 and 100.

[2] *Fables*, I, xvi.

[3] See Lavisse, VII, i, 341 and Lacour-Gayet, *Lectures historiques*,
1610–1789, pp. 383 ff. from vol. I of *Mémoires des Intendants sur l'état des
généralités*, ed. Boislisle in *Doc. inéd. sur l'hist. de France*.

[4] Lavisse, *ib*. 342.

the Palatinate Frenchman and cannibal have become synonymous terms, the writer draws a moving picture of the
miserable condition of the people, exhausted as they were by
the crushing burden of taxation and the harshness and dishonesty of the tax-farmers[1].

It was about the same year (1687) that Vauban began the
long investigations, founded partly on his own observations and
partly on the reports of his agents, which finally bore fruit in
his famous *Projet d'une dîme royale*.

In this treatise, the greater part of which was written in
1698, and to which I shall recur later, he says in an often-quoted
passage:

> As the result of inquiries carried on for several years I have come
> to the conclusion that nearly one-tenth of the people are reduced to
> beggary and actually live by begging; that of the other nine-tenths five
> are unable to give alms to the first tenth, because they are almost reduced
> to the same unhappy condition, three are very badly off, being embarrassed
> by debts and law-suits, and the remaining tenth only numbers some 100,000
> families, of which less than 10,000 are really in easy circumstances[2].

Vauban adds in a note that he estimated the population of
France after the Peace of Ryswick (1697) at 19 millions, and
he puts the loss of inhabitants between that date and 1707 at
from 400,000 to 500,000. M. Sagnac, though he points out that
owing to the absence of precise statistics it is impossible to
give authoritative figures, declares that the loss of inhabitants
from 1685 to 1715 cannot have been less than a million. It
was due not only to deaths from famine, which were far from
being confined to the years of special scarcity but in some
districts were of annual occurrence, but to a constant stream
of emigration. The revocation of the Edict of Nantes deprived
France of 200,000 Protestants, and economic distress drove
crowds of workmen into foreign countries.

[1] *Les Soupirs de la France esclave qui aspire après la liberté.*

[2] Vauban presented his book in manuscript to the king at the end of
1699. It was modified and completed in 1704 and published in 1707. See
for Vauban, Saint-Simon, *Mémoires*, V, 149–154. Boisguillebert in his
Détail de la France (1695) says in the chapter (vii) on *Richesse du petit
nombre et misère du grand* that "la plus grande partie est dans la dernière
indigence."

The causes of all this misery are admirably summed up by La Fontaine. They were, in his words, soldiers, taxes, creditors, and forced labour. The first and last causes were linked together by the labour which the peasant had to give for roads (generally for military purposes) and fortifications. But a far greater burden was the quartering upon him of the soldiers with their recognised right to pillage. As to the third cause, agricultural societies in all ages have suffered from the tyranny of creditors, and France was no exception. But in the reign of Louis XIV, especially during the latter part of it, the evil which weighed most heavily on the French peasant was the second of La Fontaine's causes—taxation. The chief taxes were the *taille*, the *gabelle* or salt-tax, the *traites* or *douanes* (customs), and the *aides* (chiefly excise duties of which the most important was the tax on liquors). Whether the *taille* or the *gabelle* was the best-hated tax of the *ancien régime* it would be difficult to say, but they were hated for different reasons, the *taille* because the liability to payment of it was a "social stigma," the *gabelle* because it lent itself to every sort of vexatious oppression. The custom-duties, though they grievously hampered commerce, being imposed on the transit of goods not only into France but from one part of France to another, hardly affected the peasant, but the *aides* hit him very hard, for it made it impossible for him to sell his wine or cider or oil (which he might have done with profit but for the tax) at a distance even of more than thirty miles from the place of production[1].

The taxation as a whole was not excessive in amount and, had the burden been fairly distributed, France could easily have borne it. It was the iniquitous system of exemptions which made the *taille* so crushing. These exemptions which were originally confined to the nobles and the clergy were always being extended, till they included nearly everyone who held a place, however subordinate, under government. An additional source of injustice was the unfair and arbitrary assessments of the local tax-collectors, and as fresh assessments were continually

[1] See Vauban, *La Dîme royale*, and cp. Taine, *L'ancien régime*, II, 249–253.

being made, there was no certainty as to the amount[1]. As is well known, the great majority of the taxes were let to *fermiers*, who were also called *traitants* or *partisans*. There were *fermes particulières* and *fermes générales* or *unies*, the latter comprising the *gabelle*, the *aides*, the five *grosses fermes* (i.e. the *douanes* or *traites* of Central France) and the *domaines*. In 1697 the number of *fermiers-généraux* was forty. As it was to the interest of the *fermiers* to extract as much as possible out of the pockets of the tax-payers, the whole system was thoroughly bad, and the *fermiers* became a byword for rascality and extortion. "The taxes," says Vauban, "have driven an infinity of people into the hospitals and the streets and have in part depopulated the kingdom; all to support armies of *traitants* and *sous-traitants* with their clerks of every kind; public leeches who are numerous enough to supply rowers for the galleys, but who after a life spent in criminal practices walk haughtily about Paris, decked with the spoils of their fellow-citizens, with as much pride as if they had saved the state."

It was a sign of the economic and financial distress of France that during the latter years of the reign of Louis XIV the revenue steadily decreased. According to Boisguillebert the total revenue from real and personal property diminished by 500 million *livres*, or about one half, from 1660 to 1695. In spite of the increase in taxation, the amount produced by it became less and less. In 1705 the *aides*, which barely exceeded half a million *livres* in 1604, and which had risen to 19 millions in 1695, dropped to less than 15 millions, and the five *grosses fermes*, which in 1691 had produced 11 or 12 millions, now only brought in 5 millions.

From about 1680 there was a yearly deficit. In 1697, after the war of the League of Augsburg, it amounted to 138 million *livres*, and in 1706 to 143 millions. In each of these years there was a serious financial crisis. Various expedients were resorted to, among the worst being the debasement of the coinage and the creation and sale of new offices. Far preferable

---

[1] "La Taille, étant entièrement arbitraire, n'a point de tarif plus certain que d'être plus haut plus on est pauvre...et plus bas plus on est riche" (Boisguillebert, *Le Détail de la France*).

were the new war-taxes—the *capitation* in 1695 and 1701 and the *dixième* in 1710. Both were excellent in intention, but, as they were largely evaded by the privileged classes, they produced far less than they ought to have done. There seemed to be nothing left but bankruptcy; indeed, after the death of Louis XIV various measures of partial bankruptcy were introduced. Saint-Simon, indeed, advocated general bankruptcy, and he argues for it with characteristic vehemence. His arguments are not convincing, but in the course of them he eloquently denounces the "spirit of conquest" with which Louvois, he says, inspired Louis XIV, the king's extravagant expenditure on buildings and other pleasures, and the cruel extortions of the tax-farmers and the tax-collectors[1].

In still plainer language Fénelon arraigned the king in the celebrated letter which he addressed to him anonymously about the year 1694, but which was probably never seen by the king, at any rate in the form in which it has come down to us. He begins by reproaching him with his love of war and he insists that the war with Holland was the source of all the misery which had come upon the country. And then he draws a terrible picture of the country's condition:

> Your people,…whom you ought to love as your children, and who up to now have been passionately devoted to you, are dying of hunger. The culture of the soil is almost abandoned; the towns and the country are being depopulated; every trade is languishing and no longer supports the workers. All commerce is destroyed.…The whole of France is nothing but a huge hospital, desolated and without resources[2].

Soon after Fénelon wrote this remarkable letter, a lieutenant-general of the *bailliage* of Rouen, named Pierre Le Pesant, Sieur de Boisguillebert, published in 1695 a treatise entitled *Le Détail de la France sous le règne présent*[3]; in which, after pointing out the evils of the existing economic system and especially the inequitable incidence of taxation, he makes certain proposals of reform, of which the chief were an equitable

---

[1] XI, 269–279.
[2] Fénelon, *Écrits et Lettres politiques*, ed. Ch. Urbain, 1921, pp. 143 ff.
[3] Printed in E. Daire, *Économistes-financiers du XVIIIᵉ siècle*, 1843–1846.

assessment of the *taille* among all classes, and the total abolition of the *aides* and all internal *douanes*. Chamillart, who
succeeded Pontchartrain as Controller-General in 1699, examined the book and thought well of it; but the *traitants* and
all those whose interests were bound up in the old system
were too powerful for a minister whose financial incapacity
was notorious.

A little later a man with a more varied and a more intimate
knowledge of the economic condition of the country, the great
engineer, Sébastien Le Prestre, Seigneur de Vauban (1633–
1707)[1], was moved to give expression to his long-meditated
projects of reform.

> The wandering life which I have led for forty years and more has given
> me the opportunity of visiting on several occasions and in several capacities
> the greater number of the provinces of this kingdom. I have thus often
> had occasion to give rein to my reflections and to notice what was good
> and what was evil in the various districts and to examine their condition
> and character. The poverty, too, of the inhabitants has often moved me
> to compassion and led me to investigate its cause.

The work of forty years, of which Vauban speaks in such
modest terms, was nothing less than the complete fortification
of the kingdom on all its frontiers; his chief periods of activity
were the intervals of peace between the great wars, from 1668
to 1672, from 1678 to 1688, and from 1698 to 1701. Beginning
with Dunkirk, his masterpiece, he fortified and enlarged nearly
every port from there to the Pyrenees, especially Cherbourg,
Brest, La Rochelle, and Bayonne. On the other sea his chief
work was at Perpignan and Toulon. He had a harder task on
the eastern and north-eastern frontiers. Here his great achievements were Belfort, Besançon, Strasburg, Metz, Montmédy,
Luxemburg (to be lost at the Peace of Ryswick), Maubeuge,
Condé, and Lille, besides many towns which were destined to
form a second line of defence. But the task which gave him
the greatest insight into the social and economic condition of
the French people was not a preparation for war but a work of
peace—the completion of the great *Canal des Deux Mers* or
du Midi, which goes from Toulouse on the Garonne to Agde on

[1] Fontenelle, *Éloge*; D. Halévy, *Vauban*, 1923.

the Mediterranean, a distance of 155 miles. It had been begun
by Paul Riquet in 1666 and was opened in 1681 the year after
his death. But there was still much to do, and Vauban, as
Commissioner-General of Fortifications, a post to which he
was appointed in 1678, had to superintend the work and took
a passionate interest in it.

In 1694 Vauban wrote in support of the proposed *capitation*
which, as we have seen, was introduced in the following year,
but only as a provisional war-tax. This was far from satisfying
him and five years later (1699) he presented and read to the
king the manuscript of his *Projet d'une Dîme royale*[1], in which
he proposed that the *taille*, the *aides*, and the *douanes provinciales*
should be abolished, and be replaced by a single tax, called
the *dîme royale*, on all income, whether from real or personal
estate. The reading of the manuscript occupied two hours and
a half for three evenings. The king listened to it attentively,
asked several questions, and finally praised it. It was also read
by Chamillart, the Controller-General. But it shared the fate
of Boisguillebert's treatise. Like Boisguillebert, Vauban found
arrayed against him a coalition of powerful interests—*traitants*,
intendants, and a whole army of secretaries and clerks—which
the Controller-General had neither the capacity nor the courage
to withstand. "So long as the war lasts," said the minister, "we
must think only of the war; with peace will come the time for
reform." Boisguillebert, whom Vauban had followed so far as
regards the abolition of the *taille* and the provincial customs,
was furious with this answer, and in a new edition of his *Détail
de la France*, published in 1707, he inserted an eloquent and
passionate reply to Chamillart, of which the burden was,
"Must we wait for peace to till the soil?" "Must we wait for
peace to ordain that the *taille* be fairly assessed?" "Must we
wait for peace to save the life of two or three hundred thousand
creatures who every year perish from want?" And then he turns
on the *traitants* who, he says, have received since 1684 200
millions for their share, and whose immense fortunes have
brought about the ruin of the state[2].

[1] Printed in Daire. *op. cit.* See above, p. 7.
[2] See Halévy, *op. cit.* pp. 190–192.

In the same year (1707) Vauban, who was as little disposed as Boisguillebert to postpone financial reform till the advent of peace, published his book anonymously—probably at Rouen. It was unfavourably received by the king and his ministers, and immediate steps were taken to suppress it. A few months later the great soldier died in disgrace, but "célébré par toute l'Europe...regretté en France de tout ce qui n'était pas financier, ou suppôts de financiers[1]." In an earlier volume Saint-Simon describes the personal appearance of perhaps "the most honest and the most virtuous man of his age, who for all his great reputation was also the most simple, the most sincere, and the most modest."

C'étoit un homme de médiocre taille, assez trapu, qui avoit fort l'air de guerre, mais en même temps un extérieur rustre et grossier, pour ne pas dire brutal et féroce. Il n'étoit rien moins; jamais homme plus doux, plus compatissant, plus obligeant, mais respectueux sans nulle politesse, et le plus avare ménager de la vie des hommes, avec une valeur qui prenoit tout sur soi et donnoit tout aux autres[2].

The years which immediately preceded the publication of Vauban's treatise were disastrous to France from the military point of view. Savoy and Portugal, as we have seen, deserted her in 1703; in 1704, as the result of the defeat at Blenheim, the French troops were driven out of Germany, and Bavaria lay at the mercy of the allies. In 1705 nothing decisive took place on the northern and eastern frontiers and there was no invasion of French soil. But in Spain, in spite of the efforts of Berwick, everything went amiss. Gibraltar was taken by the English on August 4, 1704; Barcelona capitulated in 1705 and the three Mediterranean provinces, Catalonia, Murcia, and Valencia, all recognised the Archduke Charles. In 1706 the disaster of Ramillies was followed by the loss of nearly the whole of Belgium. The frontier was in imminent danger and one of Vauban's last acts was the construction of two entrenched camps at Dunkirk (1706). In the same year the Milanese was evacuated as a consequence of the defeat of La Feuillade by Prince Eugène at Turin. In 1707 the French arms were

[1] Saint-Simon, *Mémoires*, V, 254.
[2] *Ib.* III, 379.

eminently successful in Spain, but Provence was invaded and Toulon was bombarded by land and sea. Vauban, who died in March 1707, was spared this last blow to his patriotism.

The year after his death was one of the most disastrous to France in the whole war. On July 11 came the crushing defeat of Oudenarde, and on October 22 the surrender, in spite of the stubborn defence of Boufflers, of the important town of Lille. And these reverses were followed by the terrible winter of 1709. Excessive cold began on the night of January 5–6, and this was the beginning of a winter for which they had to go back to the Great Winter of 1608 to find a parallel. There was a slight thaw from January 22 to 25, followed by two months of hard frost. In Paris and the neighbourhood above 30,000 persons are computed to have died of cold. At the beginning of spring there was another ten days thaw, followed by a fresh frost. All hope of a harvest was abandoned; the vines and fruit-trees were killed everywhere; Gascony lost its cork-trees and Provence its orange-trees and olives. To the tale of those who died of cold in the winter were now to be added those who died of famine in the summer[1].

Even more dangerous to the welfare of the country than military or economic disasters was the ever-growing absolutism of Louis XIV. His last powerful minister, Louvois, died in 1691. Colbert de Croissy, who had been Secretary of State for Foreign Affairs since 1679, lived, it is true, till 1696 and did excellent diplomatic work, but he kept in the background. From 1691, if not from 1689, Louis was not only his own First Minister but he dominated every department. The Council of State and the other Councils had gradually lost their importance, and for many years all real decisions had been made by the king in consultation with the Chancellor, the Controller-General, and the four Secretaries of State. But towards the end of the reign the ministers, even in their own departments, were overshadowed by the king, who more and more assumed

[1] See Saint-Simon, VI, 221 and 310; Madame's letters of Feb. 2, 9, 28, and March 2 (see below for bibliography); A. de Boislisle, *Le grand hiver et la disette de* 1709, in *Rev. des questions hist.* LXXIII (1903), 442 ff. and LXXIV, 486 ff.

the responsibility of the whole policy and administration of the kingdom. His industry was admirable : he worked regularly from eight to nine hours a day; he followed the details of all diplomatic questions and military operations; he read every dispatch; he dictated innumerable letters and sometimes wrote them with his own hand; he received deputations and he gave audiences on every sort of business. In this unceasing industry and in his belief in his own powers he resembles Catherine de' Medici, but, like Catherine, he lacked the qualities of the highest statesmanship—knowledge of men, moral courage, initiative, vision. An even worse feature of Louis's absolutism was his increasing interference with the liberty of his subjects, which he exercised chiefly through the lieutenant-general of police[1]. This office was originally a subordinate one, but in the hands of its first holder, La Reynie, it became in Saint-Simon's words a "sort of ministry[2]." Appointed in 1667 on the recommendation of Colbert, and with an express injunction from the king to provide for the better lighting and cleansing of his capital and the greater safety of its citizens, La Reynie gradually acquired other vaguely defined functions, which he exercised with great capacity and disinterestedness and with the complete confidence of Louis XIV. On his resignation in 1697 he was succeeded by Marc-René d'Argenson, who united to the intelligence and tact of his predecessor a courtier's suppleness and the determination of an ambitious man to succeed. Thus he readily lent himself to the inquisitorial tastes of his master, though he executed them, as a rule, with discretion and moderation[3]. But he used freely the worst absolutist methods, such as the opening of letters and other forms of espionage and the granting of *lettres de cachet*, without any form of inquiry.

Happily, there was another side to Louis's kingship. Amid the general panic of 1709 one man shewed firmness and dignity. This was the king. A stirring appeal to his people, helped by the exorbitant demands of the allies, met with a cheerful response, and though his opponents gained another victory at

[1] See P. Clément, *La Police sous Louis XIV*, 2nd ed. 1866.
[2] I, 394.
[3] *Ib.* XIV, 314.

Malplaquet (September 11, 1709), their losses were more than double those of the French. In 1710 the tide turned, and in spite of the captures of Douai and other of Vauban's fortresses Villars succeeded in checking the advance of the allies and the general conduct of the war was not unfavourable to France.

But, in Massillon's words, Louis's time of trial had not yet ended. "You have smitten him, O God! like David in his people; like David, you smite him in his children." And then the preacher recalls with touching eloquence the successive deaths of the Dauphin (1711), the Duc and Duchesse de Bourgogne (1712), their eldest son, the Duc de Bretagne (1712), and the Duc de Berry (1714). With the Duchesse de Bourgogne, says Saint-Simon, "joy, pleasure, amusement, and every kind of grace were eclipsed; darkness covered the whole surface of the court." The direct succession was only represented by "a feeble spark of life" (Massillon). But under these blows Louis shewed a real greatness of soul, and at this point Saint-Simon does him full justice[1]. If Louis XIV ever deserved the epithet of Great, it was, as Saint-Simon says, in the last days of his long and memorable reign.

II

The personality of Louis XIV found its most complete expression in his palace of Versailles, for here his autocratic spirit had full scope. From the time when by the death of Mazarin he became king in fact as well as in name Versailles was first his plaything and then his passion[2]. When on August 17, 1661, he visited Fouquet's sumptuous château of Vaux-le-Vicomte at

---

[1] XII, 150-154.

[2] My chief guide for this account of Versailles has been P. de Nolhac, *Versailles et la Cour de France* (*La Création de Versailles* and *Versailles, Résidence de Louis XIV*), 1925. See also A. Félibien, *Description sommaire du Château de Versailles*, 1674; J.-A. Piganiol de La Force, *Nouvelle description des châteaux et parcs de Versailles et de Marly*, 1701; L. Dussieux, *Le Château de Versailles*, 2nd ed. 2 vols., 1885 (requires some correction in the light of later evidence); A. Pérate, *Versailles*, 1912; G. F. Bradby, *The Great Days of Versailles*, 2nd ed. 1927 (a good popular account, chiefly founded on Saint-Simon).

the splendid entertainment given to celebrate its completion, it is easy to imagine that he felt this superb creation, to which Le Vau had contributed the building, Le Brun the decoration, and Le Nôtre the gardens, to be too magnificent for a subject, and that he determined to surpass it with one of even greater magnificence. The hunting-lodge of Louis XIII at Versailles was a beautiful little building of brick and stone with a steep slate roof, forming three sides of a court—the future *Cour de Marbre*—of which the fourth was a portico of seven arcades. This Louis XIV determined to enlarge, and accordingly after Fouquet's arrest he entrusted the work to the great triumvirate of Vaux-le-Vicomte. But no remonstrance on the part of Le Vau or his successors could ever persuade him to pull down his father's house. By May 1664 the work of transforming the gardens was sufficiently advanced to admit of the celebration of magnificent fêtes, nominally in honour of the queen and the queen-mother, but really in honour of Mlle de La Vallière[1]. One day was made especially memorable by the first production of *Tartuffe*. In July 1668, two months after the Peace of Aix-la-Chapelle, even more magnificent fêtes were held; the secret heroine was no longer Mlle de La Vallière, but Mme de Montespan. Molière's contribution was *Georges Dandin*. In the following autumn, a party of four friends, La Fontaine, Racine, Boileau, and Chapelle, visited the château and its gardens and took refuge from the heat in the Grotto of Thetis, and one of them, La Fontaine, has described the grotto in a charming mixture of prose and verse[2].

Meanwhile the work of adding to the old château went on under Le Vau, and, after his death in 1670, under his pupil, François Dorbay, in accordance with his plans. By 1671 the work of building was completed and handed over to the sculptors and decorators. The sculpture was almost finished when André Félibien wrote his *Description sommaire* in 1674. In the same year the king and his court resided at Versailles from the end of June to the end of October, the longest residence

---

[1] See Dussieux, *op. cit.* vol. I, frontispiece and p. 18, for prints of 1664 by Israel Silvestre.

[2] *Les Amours de Psyché et de Cupidon* was published in 1669.

that he had yet made there. Between July 4 and August 31, there were no less than six grand entertainments. At the third of these, on July 19, Molière's last comedy, *Le Malade imaginaire*, was performed, at the fifth (August 18) Racine's *Iphigénie* (the latter in a theatre erected in the *Orangerie*). During the next few years the court frequently visited Versailles, and by 1677 the idea of making it the seat of government was definitely matured in the king's mind[1]. In 1678 Louis found in Jules Hardouin-Mansart, great-nephew of the celebrated architect, François Mansart, a man well fitted to carry out his plans, and the Peace of Nymegen in August gave him the opportunity to push on the work with rapid energy. In 1680 the new design was completed in every detail, and a medal was struck with the legend *Regia Versaliarum*[2]. In the same year Mansart began to build the Great Gallery (*La Galerie des Glaces*) on the marble terrace between the pavilions of the king and queen. In 1682 the long South Wing, which changed the whole aspect of the château, was finished, and on May 16 Louis made his definitive entry into his transformed palace with more than usual pomp. Before the end of May the chapel, which Mansart had built in ten months, was consecrated. It was a provisional building, pending the erection of one more worthy of Louis and the palace, but it served till 1710, and there Bourdaloue, Massillon, and Fléchier —not Bossuet—preached their Advent and Lent courses[3].

Louis and the court were formally installed at Versailles, but the decorators were still at work. The private apartments, known as *Les Petits Appartements*, were not finished till 1684, and on November 15 of that year the Great Gallery, upon which Le Brun had been at work since 1680, was illuminated and revealed in all its splendour to the admiring courtiers. On the same night the "coucher du Roi" took place for the first

---

[1] Saint-Simon shrewdly conjectures the various causes which determined Louis to take this step. See *Mémoires*, XII, 67.

[2] Nolhac, *Versailles, Résidence de Louis XIV*, p. 8.

[3] It was situated immediately to the north of the *Salle d'Abondance*. The new chapel, further to the north, was begun by Mansart in 1698 and completed by his brother-in-law, Robert de Cotte, in 1710. The *Salon d'Hercule*, which occupied the place of the upper half of the old chapel, was not finished till 1736.

time in his new bedroom. In 1686 the *Salon de la Guerre* and the *Salon de la Paix*, at either end of the Great Gallery, received their final touches. Early in 1689 the North Wing, symmetrical with the South Wing, was finished, and the whole stately length of the façade towards the gardens was now complete[1]. On January 16 James II, the dethroned King of England, paid a visit to Versailles without ceremony and was shewn over the magnificent apartments by Loius[2]. Little did Louis know that the change in the English throne was the first step in the decline of his glory.

The rooms on the first floor of the central portion of the palace, in which the indoor life of Louis XIV was spent, were arranged on a simple and symmetrical plan[3]. The original "château de cartes" of Louis XIII, greatly transformed and embellished, provided the king's private apartments, all except two of which looked on the *Cour de Marbre*. On the south side were the Hall of the King's Guard and an ante-chamber, ordinarily called the *Salle où le Roi mange*, where the king's dinner was served when he dined in public. On the west side, with doors opening on the Great Gallery, were five rooms—an ante-chamber known as the *Salle des Bassans* from the Venetian painters, the Bassani, whose paintings hung there; the king's bedroom; the *Salon du Roi*, known also as the *Salle où le Roi s'habille*; the *Cabinet du Roi* or *du Conseil*, where the king presided over the *Conseil d'État* every Sunday, Wednesday and Thursday and every other Monday; and at the north-west corner, leading out of the *Cabinet du Roi* and without a window over the *Cour de Marbre*, the *Cabinet des Termes*[4], later called

---

[1] The length of the whole façade, including the central portion (320 ft.) and the wings, was about 1300 ft. The façades of Whitehall towards Charing Cross and Westminster in Inigo Jones's (or Webb's) plan are 1152 ft. The river front of the Houses of Parliament is 900 ft.

[2] Sourches, *Mémoires*, III, 22.

[3] See Saint-Simon, ed. Boislisle, XXVII, 254 for a plan of the first storey taken from the plans engraved by Demortin in 1714–1715, and Dussieux, *op. cit.* I, plan 7, after Blondel, *Architecture française*, 4 vols. 1752–1756, IV, book vi, no. 1, plan 8. I have reproduced part of the latter plan in my *Selections from Saint-Simon*, p. 66.

[4] So called because it was decorated with twenty figures of children in the form of *termini*.

the *Cabinet des Perruques*, where the king's wigs were kept and where he changed his wig several times a day. On the north side of the *Cour de Marbre* were the Billiard-room, where the king often played and where Chamillart, who was an excellent player, is said to have made himself so acceptable to his master that he became eventually Controller-General of Finance and Secretary of State for War[1], the *Cabinet des Tableaux* (called later the *Cabinet des Agates et des Bijoux*), and, adjoining it on the north, the *Salon Ovale*. This last led into what was known as *La Petite Galerie* with windows looking on to the *Cour Royale*. Its decoration was entrusted in 1685 to Le Brun's rival, Mignard. At each end it widened slightly into an almost square salon with a single window. In the western salon hung at one time Leonardo's *Mona Lisa*.

It would not have been like Louis XIV, whose passion for building was equalled by his extravagance, had he been content with the work already accomplished. But from 1689 to the Peace of Ryswick in 1697 he was not in a position to incur unnecessary expenditure at home, and no alterations were made in the private apartments. In that year, before the Grand Alliance had been formed and he had made England an active enemy by his recognition of the son of James II, he gave orders for throwing the *Salle des Bassans* and his bedchamber into one, so as to form a single large ante-chamber. It became known as *L'Œil de Bœuf* from the oval window which was made in the south wall, overlooking the *Cour de la Reine*[2]. Its decoration is chiefly celebrated for its beautiful frieze of stucco bas-reliefs which represent children in innumerable attitudes, leaping, dancing, running[3]. At the same time the *Cabinet du Roi* was enlarged at the expense of the *Cabinet des Perruques*, and the central room on this side, the *Salle où le Roi s'habille*, became the king's bedroom[4].

The *Grands Appartements*[5], or State Apartments, formed a

[1] Saint-Simon, *Mémoires*, II, 231.

[2] Opposite to it is a corresponding oval mirror.

[3] See Nolhac, *op. cit.* pp. 290–294, and for an illustration L. Hourticq, *Art in France*, 1911, p. 231.

[4] Nolhac, pp. 294–302.

[5] *Ib.* c. vii.

continuous suite along the north side of the château. Beginning at the west and opening out of the *Salon de la Guerre* was the *Salle du Trône* (the king's original bedroom[1]), where ambassadors were received in audience. It was called later the *Salle d'Apollon*. Then came in order the *Chambre du Lit* (later the *Salle de Mercure*); the *Salle des Gardes* or *des Festins* (later the *Salle de Mars*[2]); the Billiard-room (later the *Salle de Diane*); the *Grande Salle de l'Escalier du Roi* (later the *Salle de Vénus*); and the room which was called later the *Salle d'Abondance.* From this last apartment, which was added by Mansart, was the only entrance to the *Cabinet des Curiosités* or *des Médailles*, which however counted as one of the private apartments. It had twenty-four pictures, eight large and sixteen small, let into the wainscoting. The larger ones were Leonardo's *Virgin and St Anne*, Raphael's *La Belle Jardinière*, Mantegna's *Madonna of Victory*, four (unspecified) by Veronese, and one called *Tobit* and ascribed to Andrea del Sarto. Among the other treasures of the *Cabinet* was the famous cameo of sardonyx representing the *Apotheosis of Germanicus*, which Louis XIV bought in 1684 from the Abbey of Saint-Èvre (St Aper) at Toul for the enormous sum of 7000 gold crowns[3]. The *Grands Appartements* were approached by a magnificent staircase, begun in 1672 from plans left by Le Vau, and variously known as *Escalier du Roi, Le Grand Escalier*, and *Escalier des Ambassadeurs*[4]. It terminated in a double flight of stairs, leading in one direction to the *Salle de Diane* and in the other to the *Salle de Vénus* on the left, and to the salon at the east end of the Little Gallery on the right. Both staircase and gallery were destroyed by Louis XV, and we know them now only from Surugue's engravings of 1713.

---

[1] The *lit de parade* still remained after the king had moved into the bedroom which he occupied till 1697.

[2] In the *Salle de Mars* were Veronese's *Supper at Emmaus*, now in the Louvre, and Le Brun's *Family of Darius at the feet of Alexander*, described by Charles Perrault as "a true poem in which all the rules (action, place, and time) are observed." (See L. Hourticq, *De Poussin à Watteau* [1921], p. 66.)

[3] J. H. Middleton, *The Engraved Gems of Classical Times*, Cambridge, 1891, p. 6.

[4] For an illustration (after Surugue) see Dussieux, I, 299.

The decoration, of which we can also get an idea from the *Escalier de la Reine*, built rather later by Mansart, was begun in 1674 and completed in 1679. Four of the paintings on the walls celebrated Louis's victories over Spain in 1677; and the rest represented the four quarters of the world, personified as groups of men who had come to admire Versailles and the king. On the ceiling, which, says M. de Nolhac, may be regarded as a rehearsal for that of the Great Gallery[1], are painted various great episodes of the reign, both in war and peace. Four medallions represent Poetry, History, Art, and Sculpture writing the king's history. The whole work was the creation of Le Brun and its successful accomplishment set the seal to his reputation[2].

A greater work now awaited him. This was the Great Gallery, and especially the ceiling, which with the help of a few pupils he painted himself. The subject was naturally the glorification of Louis XIV; in a series of twenty-three pictures covering the immense vault—the gallery is about 240 feet in length—the history of the reign from 1661 to the Peace of Nymegen is set forth in mythological guise. The one recognisable figure everywhere is the king; the Duc d'Orléans, Condé, and Turenne are allowed to appear only in a single composition. The inscriptions beneath the pictures—for the allegories needed explanation—were composed, with true classical simplicity, by Boileau. The work, as we have seen, was completed in 1684, and two years later the decoration of the two salons at either end was also finished. In the northern one, the *Salon de la Guerre*, Germany, Holland, and Spain are represented as overwhelmed by the fury of Bellona; in the southern one, the *Salon de la Paix*, they are enjoying (thanks to Louis XIV) the blessings of peace. Thus the humiliation of the allies, as well as the glory of Louis, is the theme of all three ceilings. But Europe was preparing its revenge. In the very year (1686) in which Le Brun finished his work the League of Augsburg—at first only defensive—was being formed. Before long there was open war[3].

---

[1] *La Création de Versailles*, p. 203.

[2] For the staircase see *ib*. pp. 193–211.

[3] For the Great Gallery and the adjoining salons see Nolhac, *Versailles, Résidence de Louis XIV*, c. vi, and Pératé, *op. cit.* pp. 34–41.

Of all the splendour of the *Galerie des Glaces* only the ceiling remains[1]. But in the days of its greatness it was adorned in profusion with tapestries from the Gobelins, with mirrors polished at Saint-Gobain[2], with furniture by Charles Boule, made of rare woods and inlaid with gold or silver, and with the goldsmith's work of Claude Ballin.

The *Salon de la Paix* led into a suite of five rooms corresponding to the *Grands Appartements* on the other side of the central building. These were the queen's apartments, inhabited successively by Marie-Thérèse, the Dauphine, and the Duchesse de Bourgogne. They consisted of the queen's bedroom, the *Grand Cabinet de la Reine*, an ante-chamber, the Hall of the Queen's Guard, and the *Salon de Marbre*, which later became the *Grande Salle des Gardes*. The *Escalier de la Reine*, which was the staircase in ordinary use, corresponded to the *Escalier du Roi*, which was reserved for state occasions. From the landing three doors opened into the two *Salles des Gardes* and a vestibule respectively. East of the vestibule with windows looking on to the *Cour Royale* were the apartments of Mme de Maintenon, which will be described in a later chapter. The two great wings of the palace were inhabited by the royal family. In the North Wing, on the ground floor were the apartments of the Duc du Maine and the Comte de Toulouse, and on the first floor those of the Duc de Berry and the Prince and Princesse de Conti. In the South Wing, known later as *Aile des Princes*, were housed Monsieur, Madame, the Duc and Duchesse de Chartres on the first floor, and the Prince de Condé and the Duc de Bourbon and their wives on the ground floor. The Secretaries of State were lodged in the four pavilions of the wings of the front court. As for the mass of the courtiers they were crowded in small attics or in low and airless *entresols*, highly inconvenient for those who had not a private house in the town[3].

---

[1] It is so called from the mirrors which correspond to the seventeen windows looking on the gardens. The idea of the gallery, says M. de Nolhac, comes from that of the Palazzo Farnese at Rome, decorated by the Caracci, and that of the Palazzo Colonna, also at Rome, decorated in honour of Marcantonio Colonna, the Admiral of the Papal fleet at Lepanto.

[2] A factory near Laon.

[3] There are certain palatial houses in England, built round about the

There was, it is true, a certain amount of heating by mechanical methods, but the rooms of Versailles were very imperfectly warmed. They were often filled with smoke, and in severe winters the water and even the wine froze on the royal table. Worst of all was the primitive condition of the sanitary arrangements—one may almost say their complete absence.

One of the most difficult problems in connexion with Versailles was to provide a perennial supply of water for the great gardens which the genius of Le Nôtre had created. The first attempt to solve the problem was costly and disastrous in the extreme, and it vividly illustrates not only Louis's extravagance and love of the grandiose, but also his obstinacy and his callousness. Though Vauban strongly advised the employment of subterranean pipes, Louis, backed up by Louvois, insisted on a scheme diverting part of the water of the Eure, 30 miles distant, on a long aqueduct of arches, across the valley of Maintenon. Unfortunately the soil was marshy, which not only meant great difficulty with the foundations but caused an outbreak of malaria among the 40,000 soldiers who were employed on the work. In spite of the terrible mortality which ensued, it was carried on for four years, till the war of 1688 called away the soldiers to the trenches. The work was then abandoned, and the problem solved later by the installation of a hydraulic system at Marly. The aqueduct was partly pulled down to build the château of Crécy, near Dreux, for Mme de Pompadour, and all that now remains to recall this "cruel folly[1]" are fourteen arches.

year 1700, which in their size, their gardens, their avenues, and sometimes in their waterworks, shew plainly the influence of Versailles. The influence is the most striking in Boughton House in Northamptonshire, finished before 1695. Its builder was Ralph, Earl of Montagu, afterwards Duke, who was sent as ambassador to France in 1669 and 1676, and who lived in France from 1680 to 1685. Of about the same date are Easton Neston (1682–1702), also in Northamptonshire, built by Wren and Hawksmoor for William Fermor, the first Lord Leominster, and Chatsworth (1687–1706), built for the first Duke of Devonshire. A little later come the two great houses designed by Vanbrugh, Castle Howard for the third Earl of Carlisle, and Blenheim; the former was begun in 1701 and the latter in 1705.

[1] Saint-Simon, XII. And cp. the first paragraph of Mme de La Fayette's *Mémoires*: "On employait les troupes à ce prodigieux dessin pour avancer des quelques années les plaisirs du roi."

As for the gardens[1] with their *parterres* and *bosquets*, their fountains and basins and canals, the long *Tapis Vert*, opposite the centre of the palace, stretching from the *Bassin de Latone* to the *Bassin d'Apollon*, the new *Orangerie*, the famous Labyrinth and its groups of animals representing the principal fables of Aesop, the *potager* of Jean de La Quintinie, which became renowned throughout Europe, and the world of statues —gods, nymphs, tritons, symbolical figures of rivers and continents—which Coysevox, Girardon, Tubi, the brothers Marsy, and many lesser sculptors executed in marble or bronze after Le Brun's designs, this is not the place for a description of them. Though the glory of the palace itself has departed, the beauty of the gardens remains—an autumnal beauty, calling up a vision of all the vanished greatness.

> O Versailles, par cette après-midi fanée,
> Pourquoi ton souvenir m'obsède-t-il ainsi?
> Les ardeurs de l'été s'éloignent, et voici
> Que s'incline vers nous la saison surannée.
> Je veux revoir au long d'une calme journée
> Tes eaux glauques que jonche un feuillage roussi,
> Et respirer encore, un soir d'or adouci,
> Ta beauté plus touchante au déclin de l'année.
> Voici tes ifs en cône et tes tritons joufflus,
> Tes jardins composés où Louis ne vient plus,
> Et ta pompe arborant les plumes et les casques.
> Comme un grand lys tu meurs, noble et triste, sans bruit;
> Et ton onde épuisée au bord moisi des vasques
> S'écoule, douce ainsi qu'un sanglot dans la nuit[2].

But to people the solitude with living men and women, we must turn to the pages of Saint-Simon.

---

[1] See Nolhac, *Création de Versailles*, c. vi, and *Versailles, Résidence de Louis XIV*, cc. ii, iv, and v; Pératé, *op. cit.* c. v (with illustrations); Hourticq, *Art in France*, pp. 230–232.

[2] A. Samain, *Le Chariot d'Or*.

CHAPTER II

SAINT-SIMON AND THE COURT

I

IN July 1694, Louis, Duc de Saint-Simon, then in his twentieth year and in command of a regiment, began systematically to collect information and to make notes for the great memoirs which were to be the business of his life. After the Peace of Ryswick (1697) his regiment was disbanded, and five years later, on the outbreak of the War of the Spanish Succession, having failed to be nominated as a brigadier, he retired from the service. "Voilà encore un homme qui nous quitte," said the king. But the step enabled Saint-Simon to devote himself uninterruptedly to his work. In 1710, when his wife, having been appointed lady-in-waiting to the young Duchesse de Berry, was assigned a set of apartments between the two courts of the North Wing at Versailles[1], he established his "workshop" in one of them. It was an unrivalled post of observation for a writer of memoirs.

Saint-Simon's curiosity was unbounded, and he never lost a chance of obtaining information: "Je me suis toujours instruit journellement de toutes choses par des canaux purs, directs et certains." Among these channels were ministers, ladies-in-waiting, bedchamber-women, Maréchal the king's surgeon, and Bontemps the king's chief valet, a man of high character, who died in 1701 at the age of eighty. Nor did he confine himself to oral sources; he consulted histories, memoirs, genealogical works, and biographical dictionaries, with all of which his library was well stocked. But for many years he went on accumulating materials—notes of conversations, written portraits, detailed descriptions, essays on the history and genealogy of certain families—without attempting to produce a connected work. Then in 1729 his friend the Duc de Luynes procured for him the journal which the Marquis de Dangeau,

---

[1] Nolhac, *Versailles, Résidence de Louis XIV*, p. 123 n.

the Duke's grandfather, had kept from 1684 to his death in 1720 with amazing regularity and accuracy. It is little more than a court journal, noted up day by day, abounding in small details but with scarcely a single comment[1]. Saint-Simon speaks of it with superb contempt, but he recognised its helpfulness. So he had a copy made, and during the years 1729–1738 busied himself with adding notes, some of considerable length. At last, having arranged his long-accumulated materials, he began to write out his memoirs in full. In 1740 he reached the year 1701, and in 1751 the whole work, which ends with the death of the Regent, was completed. Four years later he died at the age of eighty.

It was many years before the finished work was printed—at first only in extracts or incomplete editions; then in a complete but badly edited edition (21 volumes, 1829–1830); then in two excellent editions without notes, of which the earlier, in 20 volumes, was edited by A. Chéruel and the later, in 22 volumes, by Chéruel and Ad. Régnier *fils*[2]. Finally in 1879 appeared the first volumes of a noble edition, edited and annotated by A. de Boislisle, which has now reached its thirty-ninth volume, bringing Saint-Simon's narrative down to the year 1721.

[1] *Journal de la cour de Louis*, 1684–1720, ed. Soulié, Dussieux, Chennevières, Mantz, Montaiglon, and Feuillet de Conches, 19 vols. 1854–1860. Sainte-Beuve, *Causeries du Lundi*, XI.

[2] 1873–1881. My references are to this edition, which has an excellent index, but I have greatly profited by the notes of Boislisle's edition and I refer to them when necessary. Vol. XXIX contains an index to all the preceding volumes.

There is a selection by C. de Lanneau under the title of *Scènes et portraits*, 2 vols. 1876, another in the Collection Nelson, entitled *La Cour de Louis XIV*, and I have edited a third (Cambridge, 1920).

There are two abridged translations in English, one by Bayle St John, 4 vols. 1857 and (New York) 1902, and the other, with notes, by Francis Arkwright, 6 vols. 1915–1918.

For biography and criticism see A. Chéruel, *Saint-Simon considéré comme historien de Louis XIV*, 1865; *Notice sur la vie et les Mémoires du Duc de Saint-Simon*, 1876. Sainte-Beuve, *Causeries du Lundi*, III (slight) and XV; *Nouveaux Lundis*, X. Taine, *Essais de critique et d'histoire*. G. Boissier, *Saint-Simon*, 1892. É. Faguet, *Dix-septième siècle*. A. Le Breton, *La "Comédie Humaine" de Saint-Simon*, 1914. C. W. Collins, *Saint-Simon*, Edinburgh, 1880. E. Cannan, *The Duke of Saint-Simon*, Oxford, 1886 (Lothian Prize Essay).

The author of the *Mémoires* was the representative of a younger branch of the ancient family of Rouvroy, a branch which had dropped its original name for that of Saint-Simon. His father, who was sixty-seven at the time of his birth, had been a favourite of Louis XIII, who created him a *duc et pair*. In consequence the son had grown up with an overweening sense of the importance of his order, and with a superstitious admiration for Louis XIII, whose portrait hung in every room of his château of La Ferté-Vidame, about 30 miles north-west of Chartres. He had also inherited from his father an un-reasoning antipathy for the families of Lorraine, Bouillon, and Rohan, and for all Secretaries of State—prejudices which must be taken into account in estimating his trustworthiness as a historian and a judge of character. His personal resentments, which were easily aroused when he imagined that a slight was being offered either to himself or to his order, also tended to warp his judgment and deflect his accuracy. He is careless too about figures and dates, and he makes little attempt to control the information that he collected. On the other hand his sources were generally good. "As for the exactitude and truth of what I relate one sees from the *Mémoires* themselves that the source of nearly everything is my personal experience, and that the rest is derived at first hand from the actors in the events that I narrate. I give their names, which as well as my intimacy with them are beyond all suspicion. When my information comes from a less sure source I call attention to it; and when I am ignorant, I am not ashamed to say so[1]." Finally, just before laying down his pen, he asks for indulgence for his style—for its negligences and repetitions, and for the obscurity which often arises from the length of his sentences. But his style needs no apology. His grammar and syntax may sometimes go astray, his language may be incorrect or collo-quial; but this is nothing compared with the impression of life that he gives to his record. He has the strong emotion and vivid imagination of a true creator. There are passages which literally vibrate with passion, and the stronger his passion the better he writes.

[1] Last chapter (XIX, 322).

The first event recorded in the *Mémoires* is the siege of Namur in 1792, but it is not till 1794 that the record of events becomes at all full. From that year onwards to the close of the reign it is of unsurpassed interest. It is true that the interest is not always sustained at the same high level; there are long accounts of minor squabbles about precedence and etiquette and elaborate chapters on genealogy, which the judicious reader will pass lightly over or even skip. But, as a picture of the court at Versailles, it is superb, and it is more than this; it is a picture of human life and character with Versailles for a background. Saint-Simon has peopled his stage with living beings, with men and women, whom we know from without and from within, whom we see acting and re-acting on one another, plotting, intriguing, loving, hating, moved by self-interest or public spirit. Above all we see the figure of Louis XIV, dominating the whole court with his personality. Saint-Simon is on the whole unjust to him, belittling his merits and exaggerating his defects, but he is too great an artist not to give him his proper place in the centre of the picture. Accordingly just after the account of his death he inserts a long digression on his character and reign, concluding with a valuable chapter on his daily life, as Saint-Simon knew it during his long connexion with the court[1]. The digression includes three chapters on Mme de Maintenon, of which the middle one, which relates to her daily life and habits, is of great value and interest. But her portrait as a whole is strongly coloured by prejudice. Saint-Simon and Mme de Maintenon were far from kindred spirits. She declared, with perfect truth, that he was "glorieux, frondeur et plein de vues," and he had an antipathy to her, which was all the more violent because it was caused not so much by her character as by her position. It was intolerable to the *duc et pair* that "la veuve Scarron," the ex-governess of Louis's bastards, should be the wife of the King of France.

The figure which is most in the picture after these two protagonists is that of the Duc d'Orléans. He is naturally prominent throughout the *Mémoires* and the general impression

[1] Ed. Chéruel, XII, cc. i–ix; ed. Boislisle, vol. XXXVIII.

that we get of his character is deepened by numerous touches. But just before the close of Louis XIV's reign he comes before us in a full-length and carefully drawn portrait, which is at once penetrating, life-like, and impartial[1]. Indeed there are more portraits in Saint-Simon's gallery which have the merit of impartiality than is generally supposed; and it is a merit, which, being the fruit of just and unbiassed observation, adds to, in fact crowns, the artistic achievement. Another full-length and impartial portrait, of great merit, though without the detail of that of the Regent, is that of the Prince de Conti[2]. His learning, his wit, his charm of manner, his popularity, are painted in brilliant colours, and then comes the *contre-coup*:

> Cet homme si aimable, si charmant, si délicieux, n'aimoit rien. Il avoit et vouloit des amis, comme on veut et qu'on a des meubles. Encore qu'il se respectât, il étoit bas courtisan; il ménageoit tout, et montroit trop combien il sentoit ses besoins en tous genres de choses et d'hommes; avare, avide de bien, ardent, injuste.

Hardly less remarkable is the portrait of Cardinal d'Estrées, who to Conti's learning, wit, and charm of manner added the advantage of a noble and majestic appearance.

> Il savoit haïr aussi et le faire sentir: mais il savoit encore mieux aimer. ...Avec beaucoup de politesse mais distinguée, il savoit se sentir; il étoit quelquefois haut, quelquefois colère; ce n'étoit pas un homme qu'il fît bon tâtonner sur rien[3].

Another Cardinal in the grand style was Cardinal de Rohan, a son of the famous Mme de Soubise:

> Né honnête homme et homme d'honneur, d'ailleurs d'un accès charmant, obligeant, d'une politesse générale et parfaite, mais avec mesure et distinction, d'une conversation aisée, douce, agréable. Il étoit assez grand, un peu trop gros, le visage du fils de l'Amour, et outre la beauté singulière, son visage avoit toutes les grâces possibles[4].

An even more favourable portrait of a prince of the Church is that of Cardinal de Janson, an intimate friend of Saint-Simon and his father, who died in 1713 at the age of eighty-three. He was Grand Almoner of France and Bishop of Beauvais,

---

[1] Ed. Chéruel, XI, 165 ff.   [2] VI, 271–275.
[3] X, 344 ff.   [4] X, 28–32.

and for two considerable periods was the French *chargé d'affaires*
at Rome[1].

> Il l'avoit l'âme et toutes les manières d'un grand seigneur, doux et
> modeste, l'esprit d'un grand ministre né pour les affaires, le cœur d'un
> excellent évêque, point cardinal.

This last portrait is perhaps coloured by affection, but Saint-
Simon is by no means blind to the limitations and defects of
his friends. He says at the beginning of the highly favourable
portrait of Maréchal de Boufflers[2], with whom he was extremely
intimate, and of whom he makes constant mention in the
Mémoires:

> Rien de si surprenant qu'avec aussi peu d'esprit, et un esprit aussi
> courtisan, mais non jusqu'aux ministres…il ait conservé une probité sans
> la plus légère tache.…Boufflers aimoit le Roi comme on aime un maître;
> il le craignoit, l'admiroit, l'adoroit presque comme un dieu.

Similarly he notes of his great friend, the Duc de Beauvillier,
whom he admired prodigiously, that he was too much afraid
of the king[3]; and of the Duc de Chevreuse, who was inseparable
from Beauvillier—they had both married daughters of Colbert
—that with a quicker intelligence than his friend he had a less
sound judgment, and that his optimism and the rapidity of his
reasoning often led him into false conclusions.

To another friend, Pontchartrain, who was appointed Controller-General in 1689, and Chancellor ten years later, Saint-
Simon is again perhaps too favourable, for though he was a
good administrator, he was not a successful financier. He had
a lively intelligence and a sincere love of letters, but on the
whole he was less remarkable than his wife. She was fat and
very ugly; but she was pious and charitable, equally intelligent
with her husband, and of sound judgment in the conduct of life.
"Jamais il n'y eut de meilleurs parents, ni de meilleurs amis
que ce couple, ni des gens plus polis[4]."

A more elaborate pair of portraits are those of the Duc and
the Duchesse de Bourgogne. That of the Duchess is life-like
and convincing; while it does not disguise her shortcomings, it

---

[1] X, 9–13.   [2] IX, 92–95.
[3] X, 276 ff.   [4] II, 226–228.

impresses one with her pervasive charm. Saint-Simon was deeply attached to the Duke, with whom he had been brought into relations through his intimacy with Beauvillier, who was the Duke's governor. After the Dauphin's death his relations became more intimate and he often discussed with him projects of political reform. When ten months later the new Dauphin followed his father to the grave, Saint-Simon was inconsolable. "La terre n'en étoit pas digne; il étoit mûr déjà pour la bienheureuse éternité[1]." As might be expected, the whole portrait is a highly laudable one, and, as Sainte-Beuve notes, it gives one a more favourable impression of the Duke than we get from Fénelon's letters. There was a certain want of balance and control in his character, which might have made his reign, had he lived, less admirable than Saint-Simon expected.

If Saint-Simon is sometimes biassed in one direction by affection or esteem, he is not unfrequently biassed in another by hatred or contempt, arising from personal resentment or class prejudice. His portraits of Père Le Tellier, Cardinal de Bouillon the Duc de Noailles(who married Mme de Maintenon's niece), and Maréchal de Villars are all coloured by the passion of a strong antipathy. His dislike of Villars and his consequent blindness to his high qualities as a commander were due to the fact that Villars, the great-grandson of a *greffier*, had been made a duke. Another commander whose merits Saint-Simon failed to recognise was Vendôme, but in this case his prejudice arose from a worthier motive, dislike of Vendôme's sloth and debauchery.

The portrait of Achille de Harlay, who was appointed First President of the Paris *Parlement* in 1689, is brilliant in its malignancy[2]. The truth about him appears to be that he was a man of great capacity and perfect integrity, but that he had a biting tongue and the reputation of a Tartuffe[3]. Saint-Simon hated him because he believed that he had shewn partiality to

---

[1] For these portraits of the Duc and Duchesse de Bourgogne see IX, 195 ff.

[2] I, 136–137; V, 166–171.

[3] See Boislisle's edition, XIV, 371 n.[2] and 617–622.

the Duc de Luxembourg in his case against his brother *ducs et pairs*. This is how he describes his outward appearance:

Pour l'extérieur, un petit homme vigoureux et maigre, un visage en losange, un nez grand et aquilin, des yeux beaux, parlants, perçants, qui ne regardoient qu'à la dérobée, mais qui, fixés sur un client ou sur un magistrat, étoient pour le faire rentrer en terre; un habit peu ample, un rabat presque d'ecclésiastique, et des manchettes plates, comme eux, une perruque fort brune et fort mêlée de blanc, touffue, mais courte, avec une grande calotte par-dessus. Il se tenoit et marchoit un peu courbé, avec un faux air plus humble que modeste, et rasoit toujours les murailles pour se faire faire place avec plus de bruit, et n'avançoit qu'à force de révérences respectueuses et comme honteuses à droite et à gauche, à Versailles[1].

The scale on which the portraits are drawn varies considerably. In contrast to the elaborate and leisurely presentments of protagonists like the Duc d'Orléans and Cardinal Dubois we have veritable miniatures of minor personages. A striking example is that of Mme de Castries—"un quart de femme, une espèce de biscuit manqué,"—in which in a few strokes he does full justice to her *esprit*, her learning, and her brilliant conversational powers, and at the same time notes that she was "glorieuse" and "cruellement méchante quand il lui plaisoit[2]." The following is from the portrait of Le Nôtre:

Le Nostre avoit une probité, une exactitude et une droiture qui le faisoit estimer et aimer de tout le monde. Jamais il ne sortit de son état ni ne se méconnut, et fut toujours parfaitement désintéressé. Il travailloit pour les particuliers comme pour le Roi, et avec la même application, ne cherchoit qu'à aider la nature, et à réduire le vrai beau aux moins de frais qu'il pouvoit. Il avoit une naïveté et une vérité charmante. Le Pape pria le Roi de le lui prêter pour quelques mois; en entrant dans la chambre du Pape, au lieu de se mettre à genoux, il courut à lui: "Eh! bonjour, lui dit-il, mon Révérend Père, en lui sautant au col, et l'embrassant et le baisant des deux côtés; eh! que vous avez bon visage, et que je suis aise de vous voir, et en si bonne santé!" Le Pape, qui étoit Clément X, Altieri, se mit à rire de tout son cœur; il fut ravi de cette bizarre entrée, et lui fit mille amitiés[3].

Other remarkable miniatures are those of Mme de Gesvres, Du Guet, Le Haquais, Toussaint Rose, one of the king's secretaries, and Bontemps his chief valet. The portrait of Catinat,

---

[1] I, 137.   [2] I, 390–391.   [3] II, 344.

for whose qualities as a commander and a patriot Saint-Simon had the highest regard, is like that of an ancient Roman from the pen of Plutarch[1].

The value of Saint-Simon's portraits as human documents, when they are not too much perverted by prejudice, is that they are largely founded on personal observation. They are not constructed after any particular formula; they begin, as a rule, with a description of the outward man, which is generally hit off with a few telling strokes; then follows the inner character, more or less elaborate, according as Saint-Simon had opportunities for studying it. When he is painting the chief actors in the drama, or his own personal friends, he fills out the picture with a considerable wealth of detail; for others he is content with a mere sketch. Sometimes, as we have seen, he gives us a full-length portrait, sometimes a miniature. But whether they are finished portraits or sketches, full-lengths or miniatures, they are all alive, all the work of a supreme artist.

But we do not know his men and women only from their obituary notices; we see them passing to and fro in the great panorama of Versailles; we note their movements, their gestures, their tricks of speech. But it is when he brings his actors together on the stage, when he reveals them to us in their relations with one another, conversing, disputing, intriguing, that he is most wonderful. His account of the "spectacle de Versailles" after the death of Monseigneur is surely one of the finest things in the whole of French literature[2].

Saint-Simon was not popular either with the king or with the majority of his fellow-courtiers. His faults and his virtues alike stood in his way. He was irascible, vain, and arrogant, and he criticised persons and institutions in season and out of season. We have seen that Mme de Maintenon called him "glorieux, frondeur et plein de vues (meaning 'chimerical views')." "Il faut tenir votre langue," was the king's remark to him, when his wife was given apartments in Versailles. D'Argenson in his *Mémoires* speaks of him as a "little saint without genius," and in the songs and satires of the Regency he is attacked under the

---

[1] IX, 188–189.

[2] VIII, cc. xii and part of xiii.

name of *boudrillon* (*bout d'homme*) and *petit furibond*. But with
all his faults he was essentially an honest man: his piety was
perfectly genuine, and he was a true patriot, keenly alive to
what was amiss in the political and social conditions of the time.
Like other patriots and reformers he viewed with apprehension
Louis XIV's increasing absolutism, and he recognised that the
unhappy condition of the French people was mainly due to the
king's love of war and glory and his boundless extravagance.
But his dislike of the king was partly founded on narrow prejudices, which often make him an unfair critic of his acts and
general policy. Moreover he lacked the trained accuracy, the
habit of controlling his information, and the sense of reality
which is as essential to the historian as it is to the practical
statesman. We go to the *Mémoires*, not for a political or military
history, but for a general picture of the Court of Versailles: and
this on the whole is as faithful as it is vivid.

II

Louis's choice of the sun for his device was peculiarly appropriate at Versailles, for there the whole court revolved
round him and "in the light of the king's countenance was
life."

Qui considérera que le visage du prince fait toute la félicité du courtisan,
qu'il s'occupe et se remplit pendant toute sa vie de le voir et d'en être vu,
comprendra comment voir Dieu peut faire toute la gloire et tout le bonheur
des Saints[1].

This was literally true of such typical courtiers as the Duc
d'Antin, son of M. and Mme de Montespan, or the Marquis
de Dangeau, or the Duc de La Rochefoucauld, the son of
the author of the *Maxims*, who sometimes, says Saint-Simon,
was ten whole years without spending a night away from the
court. "C'est un homme que je ne vois jamais," was Louis's
favourite comment on those who seldom came to court, and
in his eyes this was an unpardonable crime.

Saint-Simon's description of the "mechanism" of Louis
XIV's daily life at Versailles with its elaborate ritual and

[1] La Bruyère.

utter lack of privacy is too well known to need repetition here[1].
A good example, which will serve as an illustration of the whole
routine, is the king's dinner at one o'clock. He almost invariably
dined *au petit couvert*—alone, but in the presence of a crowd
of courtiers. As soon as the dinner was served in the ante-
chamber known as the *Salle où le Roi mange*[2]—it consisted
of three courses with five to seven dishes for each course—
the principal courtiers came in, followed by "tout ce qui étoit
connu," and the first gentleman of the chamber went to tell
the king. On rare occasions the Dauphin and his sons were
present, but they were never asked to sit down. Nor were the
princes of the blood, nor even cardinals. The only person thus
privileged was Monsieur, the king's brother, who was even
sometimes invited to share the king's dinner. His appearance
must have been a godsend to the courtiers, for he was cheerful
and conversational, while the king seldom opened his lips.
Dinner over, the king went back to his cabinet, and that was
the moment when courtiers of distinction might speak to him.
He remained standing by the door while he listened to what
they had to say, and only rarely did anyone ask permission
to follow him into the cabinet. Supper was at ten, *au grand
couvert*, with five courses, and all the royal family sat down
with the king. During this meal women, some of whom were
seated, formed part of the court circle. After supper the
king passed through his cabinet into the *Cabinet des Termes*
where he took his place in an arm-chair. Monsieur sat in
another, while Madame (but only after Monsieur's death),
the Duchesse de Berry, the Duchesse du Maine, and the
king's three illegitimate daughters sat on footstools. The
royal princes stood. The doors between the *Cabinet des Termes*
and the two adjoining rooms, the *Cabinet du Roi* and the
Cabinet du Billard or *des Chiens*, were left open so that the

---

[1] *Mémoires*, ed. Chéruel, XII, c. ix; ed. Boislisle, XXVIII, 330-381.
Boislisle (p. 337 n.[3]) points out that there was more variety in the routine
of Louis's daily life than Saint-Simon makes out.

[2] In January 1712 Louis for the first time had his dinner in Mme de
Maintenon's apartment, and after that he dined there regularly every
Sunday and Wednesday. (Sources, XIII, 272, cited by Boislisle.)

courtiers in either room could see the king and hear his conversation[1].

On three days of the week there was *appartement,* that is to say, from six to ten the state-apartments were thrown open and all those who had the *entrée* were admitted. Tables were set out for games of every sort and everyone might play at what he liked and with whom he liked. There were billiard-tables in the *Salle de Diane* and refreshments in the *Salle d'Abondance.* The king and queen and the royal family took part in the games, and the conversation was general[2]. But after 1691 Louis ceased to put in an appearance, and the Dauphin took his place. Then Monseigneur began to prefer Meudon to Versailles, and in his absence there was no *appartement.* Other amusements were theatricals and dancing, including *bals masqués.* The young Duchesse de Bourgogne with her love of amusement and her power of attracting men and women of every age, including the king, did much to enliven the court. At the beginning of 1700, from Candlemas to Lent, there were balls, or acting, or music nearly every night, and Saint-Simon declares that for the last three weeks before Lent he and his wife hardly ever saw the daylight. Another period of especial gaiety was the winter of 1710–1711, when, after a campaign which had not been unfavourable to France, the hopes of Louis XIV began to revive. At the beginning of December he announced that there would be *appartement* and *comédie* at Versailles even in Monseigneur's absence. Throughout the winter there were court-balls of every kind, and the wives of ministers gave magnificent entertainments[3]. "Mais Paris n'en demeura pas moins triste, ni les provinces moins désolées," is Saint-Simon's melancholy comment[4].

Theatricals and balls had a serious rival in gambling, which was a crying evil throughout the greater part of the reign. The

[1] Saint-Simon, *Mémoires,* VII, 297–299. See a letter of Madame, Sept. 20, 1714, for an account of how she spent her day (ed. Holland, pp. 450-451).

[2] See *Le Mercure galant* for December 1682 (Dussieux, I, 118 f.).

[3] *Mémoires,* II, 302.

[4] *Ib.* VIII, 167. He unkindly says that the king, contrary to his custom, thought the court ought to be kept amused, in order to conceal the disorder and serious condition of affairs.

favourite card games were *reversi, brelan, hombre, lansquenet*
and its varieties, *bassette* and *pharaon*. All except *hombre*, which
was extremely complicated, were childishly simple, demanding
neither skill nor judgment, nothing but a cool head. During
our period *lansquenet* was chiefly in vogue, but *brelan* ran it
close. Just before our period it was *reversi*. In 1686 the king
organised a great game of *reversi* for high points, and he repeated it in the following year. On Christmas Day 1678 Mme
de Montespan lost 700,000 crowns. Marie-Thérèse owed at her
death 100,000 crowns for debts at *bassette*. Monsieur and
Monseigneur were both great gamblers. So were Langlée
("un homme de rien") and Dangeau[1], both of whom owed
their high and influential position at the court largely to their
success, their good-temper, and their perfect probity in gambling[2]. They illustrate La Bruyère's remark in his chapter, *De
la Mode*:

> Il n'y a rien qui mette plus subitement un homme à la mode et qui le
> soulève davantage que le grand jeu; cela va de pair avec la crapule[3].

The *bourgeoisie* copied the court. Dufresny and Regnard
were confirmed gamblers; both made use of their personal
experience to write a play on the subject, and Dufresny
devotes a chapter to it in his *Amusements sérieux et comiques*.
It is interesting to contrast the nonchalance of Regnard's
hero with La Bruyère's picture of a gambling-table in *Des
biens de la Fortune*—"Toutes les passions, comme suspen-
dues, cèdent à une seule: le courtisan alors n'est ni doux, ni
flatteur, ni complaisant, ni même dévot"—or with those drawn
by Madame in her letters[4] or by Lesage in *Le diable*

---

[1] For Langlée see Saint-Simon, *Memoires*, II, 303–305; for Dangeau
see Mme de Sévigné, letter of July 29, 1676.

[2] See generally Dussieux, *op. cit.* I, 122–126.

[3] Cp. the portrait of a female gambler in Boileau, *Sat.* X, ll. 215–248.

[4] The principal letters of Madame written during the reign of Louis XIV
have been published as follows. Letters to her half-sister, the Raugrave
Louise, 1676–1722, ed. W. Menzel, *Bibliothek des literarischen Vereins in
Stuttgart*, vi, 1843. Letters to Louise and the other Raugraves, ed. W. L.
Holland, 1676–1706, *ib.* lxxxviii, 1867; 1707–1715, *ib.* cvii, 1871. Letters
to her aunt Sophia, Electress of Hanover (1672–1714), ed. E. Bodemann,
Hanover and Leipzig, 2 vols. 1891. French translation—*Correspondance*

boiteux[1]. The preachers were fully alive to the seriousness of this evil. In his sermon, *Sur la Pénitence*, Bourdaloue, addressing himself to men living in the great world—"Vous êtes un homme du monde, un homme distingué par la naissance"—inveighs first against their extravagance, and then against their love of gambling:

Vous aimez le jeu...qui n'est plus pour vous un divertissement, mais une occupation, mais une profession,...mais, si j'ose ainsi parler, une rage et une fureur.

He devotes to gambling the whole second part of the sermon *Sur les divertissements du Monde.*

But even the excitement of gambling could not dispel the atmosphere of *ennui* which clung to the court. "*Ennui* reigns here more than in any other place in the world," writes Madame in 1698[2]. "Toujours les mêmes plaisirs, toujours aux mêmes heures et toujours avec de mêmes gens," is the complaint of Mme de La Fayette. "La vie de la Cour est un jeu sérieux, mélancolique," observes La Bruyère. Even Louis XIV felt the irksomeness of that solemn etiquette which he had done so much to create. With a view to some escape from the ceremonial of Versailles he built as far back as 1670, near the end of the northern arm of the Canal and opposite the *Ménagerie*, the little "Trianon de porcelaine." It was merely a bungalow, but it was decorated with exquisite art, and it took its name from the tiles of Delft china with which the façade was covered.

extraite de ses lettres originales, ed. E. Jaeglé, 2nd ed. 3 vols. 1890 (this is more complete and more correct than the earlier translation by G. Brunet). English translation, with notes, by Gertrude Scott Stephenson, 2 vols. 1924–5. See G. Depping, *Rev. hist.* lv (1894), 308 ff. (history of the publication of her letters), lvi, lviii, 292 ff.; H. F. Helmolt, *Kritisches Verzeichniss der Briefe der Herzogin Elizabeth Charlotte von Orleans,* Leipzig, 1909 (gives a chronological list of her letters and a full bibliography); Arvède Barine, *Madame, Mère du Régent,* 2nd ed. 1909. For her descriptions of the gambling-table see a letter of 1695, Holland, p. 33; Jaeglé, I, 112; and one of 1699, Holland, p. 160.

[1] Two young men are mortally wounded after a quarrel at cards. The father of one, an only son, and the wife of the other arrive on the scene, and the wife pours curses on cards and their inventor, and on gambling-houses and everybody in them.

[2] Holland, p. 113; Jaeglé, I, 180.

Round it were four small pavilions similarly decorated and a beautiful garden, gay with jonquils, tuberoses, and other sweet-smelling flowers, the bulbs for which were specially sent from Provence.

But this was not enough. In 1679 Louis selected a spot about eight miles from Versailles in a shut-in valley without a view, close to a wretched village called Marly, on which to build a "hermitage[1]." Here with at most a dozen of his more important courtiers he would come from Wednesday to Saturday, two or three times a year. But, like all his buildings, the hermitage grew, till in 1686 it had become a toy Versailles with gardens, and sheets of water, and an aqueduct, and "forests of full-grown trees brought from Compiègne and beyond, three-fourths of which died and were at once replaced by others." "Telle fut la fortune d'un repaire de serpents et de charognes, de crapauds et de grenouilles, uniquement choisi pour n'y pouvoir dispenser," is Saint-Simon's expressive and entirely unfair comment, inspired by the hate with which he regarded everything connected with Versailles. Still Louis's passion for building was not satisfied. In 1687 he pulled down the "Trianon de porcelaine" and made Mansart erect on its site "a palace of marble, jasper, and porphyry, with delicious gardens." As time went on and he became more and more weary of Versailles, he made longer visits to Trianon and Marly, and every autumn he spent five to six weeks at Fontainebleau. At Marly, where etiquette was greatly relaxed, the accommodation was limited, and to be invited there was a coveted honour. The method of application was simple; the women had "to present themselves for Marly" at the king's supper, while the men had merely to say "Sire, Marly" in the morning.

The increasing gloom of the court in the latter part of the reign was partly due, it must be confessed, to a cause excellent in itself, the king's conversion. This was largely owing to the salutary influence of Mme de Maintenon, but partly also to his serious illness in 1686. The result was that he not only

---

[1] *Mémoires*, XII. The château was destroyed in the Revolution. The site is said to be charming.

abstained from innocent pleasures to which increasing years made him less and less inclined, but he encouraged, if he did not expect, his court to do the same. He also became extremely punctilious in the observance of religious ceremonies. Even in his unregenerate days he went to mass every day of his life— only missing once, says Saint-Simon—and he fasted strictly. After his conversion he seldom missed a sermon in Advent or Lent, and generally attended benediction (*salut*) on Sundays and often on Thursdays. He communicated regularly five times a year, on Easter-eve, on the eve of Pentecost, on the Assumption, on All-Saints'-eve, and on Christmas-eve, and after communicating he touched for the scrofula. In the afternoon he went to vespers and after consultation with his confessor filled up vacant benefices. He expected the court to be as strict as himself. "A l'heure qu'il est," writes Mme de La Fayette, "hors de la piété point de salut à la cour." Matthew Prior, when he went to France in 1698 as secretary to the Duke of Portland's embassy, was struck by the prevailing atmosphere of gloom and bigotry at the court:

Toute la Cour est sombre et triste; la bigoterie et le ménage y règnent à un point que les filles à genoux disent leur Patenostre dans les galeries, comme dans un couvent, et les gardes du corps, mettant leurs armes à part, nouent des franges comme les filles en Angleterre[1].

All this naturally led to hypocrisy. "Un (faux) dévot," says La Bruyère, "est celui qui, sous un roi athée, serait athée." In a well-known sermon on hypocrisy, preached on December 16, 1691, Bourdaloue inveighs against it as one of the worst evils of the day. "Les livres de dévotion," says the Abbé Du Bos writing to Bayle in 1696, "quoiqu'ils ne lisent pas plus que les autres, sont mieux vendus[2]." For beneath the veneer of piety free-thought and irreligion were rampant. "Faith is extinct in this country to such an extent," writes Madame in 1699, "that every young man is an atheist; but what is odd is that the same man who poses as an atheist in Paris plays at being devout at court[3]." In his funeral oration on the Prince de Conti, who

[1] Prior to E. of Albemarle, March 1, 1698 (*Calendar of the MSS. of the Marquis of Bath*, III, 195).

[2] See below, p. 43.   [3] Jaeglé, I, 202.

died in 1707, Massillon speaks of "un siècle, où la religion est devenue un jouet, ou de la débauche, ou d'une fausse science," and in one of his sermons of "la piété changée en gain et une indigne hypocrisie."

This hypocrisy is well illustrated by Saint-Simon's story of the trick played on the ladies of the court by M. de Brissac, major of the body-guard. On Thursday and Sunday evenings during the winter it was the king's habit to attend the service of benediction in the chapel at Versailles, which in consequence was always filled with ladies. But, if it became known that the king was not going to attend, the chapel was nearly empty. One evening Brissac, "an honest man, who hated shams," came into the chapel just after the prayers and before the service of benediction and said in a loud voice, "Guards, withdraw, the king is not coming." Thereupon all the ladies, except three or four, left the chapel, and when the king arrived he was surprised to find it empty[1].

We shall see in a later chapter how during the years of peace between 1697 and 1701 the *hôtel* in the Temple of the Grand Prior of Vendôme became a byword for drunkenness and debauchery and how its *habitués* made noisy professions of free-thought. Nor were the women better than the men. Mme de Maintenon, writing to the Princesse des Ursins in 1707, declares that "the women of to-day are unbearable; their absurd and immodest dress, their tobacco, their drinking, their gluttony, their coarseness, their idleness, are all so repugnant to my taste, and even so opposed to reason, that I cannot endure it." "Drinking (*das Saufen*)," says Madame in 1704, "is very fashionable among young women, and among those of the highest birth[2]." Eight years earlier she told her aunt, the Duchess of Hanover, that her daughter-in-law got as drunk as a tanner three or four times a week[3]. Of her daughter, the Duchesse de Berry, Saint-Simon says that "with the exception of avarice she was a model of all the vices." The sermons of Bourdaloue, with their attacks on luxury, extravagance,

---

[1] *Mémoires*, V, 423–424. Saint-Simon roughly indicates the date as about 1705.

[2] Holland, p. 348.   [3] Jaeglé, I, 125.

gambling, non-payment of debts, immorality, debauchery, and hypocrisy, are a heavy indictment of the later years of Louis XIV's reign[1]. It may be said of these witnesses, that Bourdaloue was an austere moralist and La Bruyère a morose one, that Mme de Maintenon was a prude, and that Madame and Saint-Simon were prone to exaggeration. But all were thoroughly honest, and all, except perhaps Madame, were observers of wide experience and remarkable penetration. Moreover their evidence is confirmed by that of a cool-headed and unbiassed witness, the Abbé Jean-Baptiste Du Bos (1670–1742), diplomatist and man of letters, and a future secretary of the Académie Française, whom we shall meet again in the chapter on the Quarrel of the Ancients and Moderns. Writing to Bayle in November 1696 he gives him a detailed account of "les mœurs et les manières d'aujourd'hui." Women, he says, appear to have forgotten that they are of a different sex to men. They behave like men, and they associate with them on a footing of complete equality and comradeship. They drink as much as men, and if they do not get drunk it is because getting drunk has gone out of fashion. Except for certain "women of quality," they do not smoke but they take snuff as freely as men. The love of gambling has been carried to such a point of refinement that it cannot go further. Everyone plays, and plays well. Everyone too speculates on the stock-exchange[2].

Eleven or twelve years later (1707 or 1708), when France had suffered disaster after disaster and death and misery had plunged the whole country into a state of profound depression, Massillon fulminated in burning language against the moral condition of the nation.

La colère de Dieu éclate sur nos crimes...il a vu les abominations qui sont au milieu de nous ; les fidèles sans mœurs, les grands sans religion, les ministres même sans piété ; le sexe sans pudeur et sans bienséance...

[1] See A. Feugère, *Bourdaloue, sa prédication et son temps*, 5th ed. 1889, pp. 397–454, and see, besides the sermons already referred to, the *Sermon sur l'Impureté* (1683), one of the three sermons edited by Gonzague Truc, 1921.

[2] E. Gigas, *Choix de la correspondance inédite de Pierre Bayle*, Copenhagen, 1890, pp. 283–285.

les débauches et les excès affreux autorisés par de grands exemples, un luxe monstrueux et insensé croître et augmenter avec la misère publique.

Then in a passage from which I have already quoted he inveighs against the prevailing hypocrisy[1]. As invariably happens, the fashion in morals and manners spread from the aristocracy to the middle class. Paris aped Versailles and the *bourgeoisie* aped the nobles. We shall see this when we come to the comedy of Dancourt. But while emphasising the shadows of the picture we must not shut our eyes to its relieving lights. There were sensible and virtuous men and women at Versailles, as we may learn from the pages of Saint-Simon; there were many families at Paris, especially among the professional classes, in which sobriety of conduct and a high moral standard were traditional; and in the provinces, too often ignored or ridiculed in French literature, there was much quiet devotion to duty, patriotism, and religion[2].

[1] Sermon on *Motifs de conversion* (cited by A. Bayle, *Massillon*, 1867, pp. 184–186).

[2] See F. Gaiffe, *L'Envers du Grand Siècle* [1924], esp. c. iv (*Le siècle des bonnes mœurs*), for a severe indictment of the age. His case would have been even stronger than it is, had he confined himself to really trustworthy evidence. On the other hand, M. Louis Bertrand's *Louis XIV*, 1923, is a fantastic panegyric, in which all evidence that makes against his hero or his age is contemptuously waived aside.

CHAPTER III

LA BRUYÈRE[1]

O N the very threshold of our period we meet with a new writer who was destined to become a classic—La Bruyère. But he introduces himself to us with the apologetic air of a late arrival. *Tout est dit*, he says at the outset of his book; everything that there is to say on the subject of human nature has been said already; the field has been thoroughly reaped; there is nothing left but to glean what has been left by the ancients and the cleverest moderns. The observation of human nature may still be carried on, but it must be on different lines. The great masters have explored the recesses of the heart; there remains the study of habits and manners, and generally of the outward man. The style of French prose has been brought to perfection,

[1] *Œuvres complètes*, ed. G. Servois, 3 vols. (vol. III in 2 parts), 1865–1878 (*Grands Écrivains de la France*). This is the classical edition; vol. III contains a bibliography. *Les Caractères*, edd. G. Servois and A. Rébelliau, 1893; 8th ed. revised, 1906. (A few passages of rather brutal realism about women, e.g. I, 178—character of Lélie—and 180 of the G.E.F. edition, are omitted.) For the editions (1st to 9th) published in La Bruyère's lifetime, see below, pp. 52–53, and the bibliography mentioned above. Notable later editions are those of Walckenaer, 1845 (the first critical edition), Hémardinguer, 1849, and Destailleur, 2 vols. 1854 (Bib. Elzévirienne).

All that is known of La Bruyère's life has been carefully collected by G. Servois in the biographical notice prefixed to vol. I (2nd ed. 1912) of his edition, pp. xv–ccxxx. See also P. Morillot, *La Bruyère*, 1904 (*Grands Écrivains français*), and a review of this by A. Rébelliau in *Rev. d'hist. litt.* XI (1904), 673 ff.

Sainte-Beuve, *Port. Litt.* I, 389 ff. (excellent); *Nouv. Lundis*, I, 122 ff. and X, 417 ff. G. Michaut, *La Bruyère de Sainte-Beuve* in *Rev. d'hist. litt.* 1906, pp. 505 ff. and 714 ff. (transcribes the notes which Sainte-Beuve had made in a copy of La Bruyère, evidently with a view to lectures). Taine, *Nouveaux Essais de Critique et d'Histoire*, 1865 (article of 1855). E. Allaire, *La Bruyère dans la maison de Condé*, 2 vols. 1886. Sainte-Beuve, writing in 1836, mentions "trois morceaux essentiels"—D'Olivet in his *Hist. de l'Académie* (1729), J.-B.-A. Suard, *Notice*, 1781 (reprinted in *Mélanges de littérature*, vol. II, and in several modern editions of La Bruyère), and Victorin Fabre, *Éloge*, 1810.

but it can be made more alert, more individual, more consciously
artistic.

> Qu'on ne dise pas que j'ai rien dit de nouveau; la disposition des
> matières est nouvelle. Quand on joue à la paume, c'est une même balle
> dont on joue, l'un et l'autre; mais l'un la place mieux.

Thus wrote Pascal at the opening of the great classical age
and La Bruyère says much the same thing when contemplating
its decline:

> Horace ou Despréaux l'a dit avant vous—Je le crois sur votre parole,
> mais je l'ai dit comme mien.

Literary formulas and literary dogmas may come and go, but
literature is for ever being renewed by individual genius.

Jean de La Bruyère, whose father held the office of Con-
troller of the *rentes de la ville*—or as we should say, Corporation
Stock—was born at Paris and was baptised in the Church of St
Christopher, near Notre-Dame, on August 17, 1645. Nothing is
known of his education, except that it included Greek, and the
first definite date in his career is his admission to the degree
of Licentiate of Laws in June 1665. He was also admitted
as an advocate, but we do not know whether he ever practised. At the age of twenty-eight he left the Bar and pur-
chased the office of Treasurer-General of Finance for the
district (*généralité*) of Caen. His duties did not involve
residence, and for the next eleven years he lived at Paris
with his mother. Their home from 1679 was in the Rue des
Grands-Augustins.

With his salary of about 2350 *livres* and with what he had
inherited from an uncle La Bruyère was comfortably off, and
in a tranquil fashion thoroughly enjoyed his studious and independent life[1]. We have no specific knowledge as to how he.passed
his time, but the first five chapters of his book throw considerable light on his tastes and occupations. He read widely, he
had a few friends of both sexes to whom he was warmly
attached, he delighted in congenial conversation and society.

---

[1] "La liberté n'est pas oisiveté; c'est un usage libre du temps, c'est le
choix du travail et de l'exercice: être libre, en un mot, n'est pas ne rien
faire, c'est être seul arbitre de ce qu'on fait ou de ce qu'on ne fait point.
Quel bien en ce sens que la liberté !" (*Des Jugements.*)

Above all, he observed and meditated, and probably he began to give a literary form to the results of his observations.

But in 1684 he gave up this free and pleasant life, which he valued so highly, to become tutor to the grandson of the great Condé, then a lad of sixteen. What determined him to sacrifice his independence? Was it loss of money, or disappointment in love, or the desire for change, or ambition? Or was it, as has been suggested, that he wanted to complete his book? His observations had hitherto been confined to the Paris *bourgeoisie*; now there was offered to him an unrivalled opportunity of studying at first hand great nobles, and great ministers, the court, and the world of fashion[1].

Since 1675 Condé, having fought his last campaign, had been living in retirement at Chantilly, entertaining his friends, embellishing his domain, and transforming the château built by Jean Bullant for the Constable de Montmorency into a comfortable modern residence. In 1684, the very year in which La Bruyère went to live there, the work was completed. But to this new-comer the interest of Chantilly must have been less in its buildings and its "superb alleys, where the sound of innumerable fountains was never silent[2]," than in the society which gathered there. In the pregnant phrase of the Duc d'Aumale, its last private owner, *toute Europe y passe*—generals, ambassadors, ministers, the *grand monarque* himself with his court. There La Bruyère could make at leisure his observations of *la cour, les grands*, and *le souverain*. Of the illustrious owner La Bruyère has drawn a portrait (Æmile) which is ostensibly a panegyric, but which ends with the words, "Nothing is wanting to him but the minor virtues[3]." The same defect is noted by Bossuet in his Funeral Oration, where he says that Condé sometimes behaved as if there were another man in his skin, to whom he abandoned, as too trivial for his great soul, the minor details of life. It was the "other man" who omitted the minor virtues, who neglected his person and his clothes and flew into violent rages. "In future," said Boileau, after a visit to Chantilly, "I shall take care always to agree with M. le Prince

[1] See E. Allaire, *La Bruyère dans la maison de Condé,* 2 vols. 1886.
[2] Bossuet, *Oraison de Condé.*   [3] *Du Mérite personnel.*

especially when he is wrong." But Condé was a good friend to
Boileau, as he had been to Molière, and at the time of the cabal
against *Phèdre* he sent a curt note to the Duc de Nevers,
who had threatened Boileau and Racine with a cudgelling, to
say that he should consider any insult to his two friends and
protégés as an insult to himself. Other men of letters who frequented Chantilly were Bossuet and Bourdaloue, Fénelon and
Malebranche. For Condé's swift intelligence was by no means
confined to the field of battle; he was widely read in philosophy
and theology, he was interested in science, and he was a recognised judge of literary merit.

Condé's son, Henri-Jules de Bourbon, known as M. le Duc
during his father's lifetime, was wholly without military talent,
but he had improved his natural intelligence by application,
and his knowledge and learning were remarkable. Unlike his
father he could be most agreeable when it suited him, combining charm with dignity, but he was "an unnatural son, a cruel
father, a terrible husband, a detestable master, a dangerous
neighbour, without friends, and incapable of friendship, jealous,
suspicious, uneasy...liable to the most violent outbursts of rage
even about trifles; never for two minutes in the same mind,
keeping his whole household in a tremor of agitation, a perpetual slave to his passions and his avarice[1]." Saint-Simon's
portrait is doubtless painted with an over-charged brush, but
it is confirmed in its main outlines by the Marquis de Lassay
who married Mlle de Châteaubriant, M. le Duc's natural
daughter. "M. le Prince (as he had now become) has not a
single virtue; his vices are softened only by his defects, and
he would be the most malignant man on earth, if he were not
the feeblest." Then Lassay goes on to speak of his outbursts of
fury, his avarice, his distrust of everybody—"his greatest expenditure is on spies"—and the fear that he inspired in his
wife and children. Like his father and mother he was small of
stature—"more like a gnome than a man" says Mme de
Maintenon's lively cousin, Mme de Caylus.

---

[1] In the admirable analysis of avarice in the chapter *De l'Homme* La
Bruyère has perhaps M. le Duc in mind.

This feature he handed down to his son, Louis, La Bruyère's pupil. "He was considerably smaller than the smallest man," says Saint-Simon; "he had an enormous head, a complexion of a livid yellow, and a face which inspired terror," and "he nearly always looked as if he were in a rage." Added to this unprepossessing appearance, he was extremely tactless, and addicted to brutal practical jokes. But both Mme de Caylus and Saint-Simon testify to his freedom from that self-seeking and love of money which were characteristic of his family. Nor was he, like his father, destitute of military talent. He behaved with great courage at Steenkerke and the siege of Philipps-bourg; and in the hard-fought field of Neerwinden, where he held a high command, he rendered distinguished service. Mme de Caylus, who was not blind to his defects, declares that his death, which took place in 1710, a year after his father's, was a loss to the State. Such in after life was the pupil whom it was La Bruyère's business to instruct in geography, history, and the institutions of France, the province of mathematics being left to the eminent physicist, Joseph Sauveur. The lad was far from a docile pupil, being often unruly and indolent, but under the new régime he made decided progress. "He was very intelligent and gave great promise," notes *La grande Mademoiselle* at this period. His marriage in the following year (1685), when he was seventeen, to the eldest daughter of Louis XIV and Mme de Montespan, Mlle de Nantes, who was only twelve, made at first no difference in La Bruyère's position. It was not till after the death of Condé, at the close of 1686, that the education of M. le Duc, as he was now called, was considered to be finished. But La Bruyère still remained attached to his household, with the title of "gentilhomme de la maison de Condé," and a yearly salary of 3000 *livres*. He gave lessons in heraldry to the Duke and in literature to the Duchess, and he probably also acted occasionally as librarian and secretary. The Hôtel de Condé at Versailles had been fitted up for the young couple, and here La Bruyère must have enjoyed excellent opportunities for observing the court.

The Duchess had inherited her mother's beauty—*belle comme les anges*, says Mlle de Montpensier—and the lively wit of her mother's family. But with all her gaiety and charm she could be unsparing with her tongue, and she shared her husband's unamiable propensity for practical jokes and for lampooning his friends in cruel verses. Her favourite butt was Jean de Santeul, Canon of Saint-Victor, who enjoyed a considerable reputation as the first Latin poet of his day. He was in great demand at Chantilly, where, like Boisrobert in the household of Richelieu, he fulfilled the double functions of man of letters and buffoon. His friend La Bruyère has drawn a not unkindly portrait of him under the name of Théodas, in which he dwells on the contrast between the folly of his behaviour and the intelligence of his remarks[1]. It is a well-known story how one day at Chantilly, having helped himself to a particular dish the moment that they sat down to table, the young Duchess gave him a resounding box on the ear, and how on his murmuring that it was not in this way that a queen of old had treated a poet (referring to the well-known but unfortunately apocryphal story of Margaret of Scotland and Alain Chartier), she flung a glass of water in his face with the words, "After the thunder, the rain." Even the victim laughed, and eventually commemorated the incident in a Latin poem. According to Saint-Simon he suffered worse at the hands of the Duke, who made him drink a tumbler of wine into which he had emptied his snuff-box[2].

La Bruyère had too much tact and self-respect to allow himself to be treated in this fashion, but Valincourt, the friend of Racine and Boileau, and the former's successor in the Académie Française, says that the Condé family always laughed at him, and La Bruyère in his chapter on *Les Grands* notes their "extreme propensity to laugh at the expense of others." There is no doubt that his highly sensitive nature suffered from the quasi-dependence of his position. He felt that he was the equal in heart and intelligence of *les grands*, but that under

[1] *Des Jugements.* Isaac Williams's well-known *Disposer Supreme and Lord of the Earth* is a translation of Santeul's *Supreme, quales, Arbiter.*

[2] Saint-Simon adds that he was seized with sickness and died forty-eight hours afterwards, but Bernard de La Monnoye, who gives a detailed account of Santeul's death, makes no mention of this.

the existing order of things personal merit (as he heads his second chapter) had not a fair chance[1].

He was prone to take offence and to think that he was being slighted. He was quick to resent a real or supposed insult, and, like Racine, he attacked his foes with shafts that were tipped with malice. In general society he was often silent and morose, but he would expand in the company of congenial spirits. If he was a good hater, he was also a good lover, and his heart warmed towards his real friends. Saint-Simon, who used to meet him at Versailles, and who appreciated his book as the work of a fellow-observer and fellow-pessimist, described him after his death as a "fort honnête homme, de très bonne compagnie, simple, sans rien de pédant et fort désintéressé." But the strongest testimony to his character will be found in his chapter (II) entitled *Du mérite personnel*, which could only have been written by a man of high aims, true modesty, and consistent self-respect.

We must now come to his book. As soon as he was freed from the task of educating the Duc de Bourbon, he began to prepare it for the press. It appeared at the beginning of 1688, under the title of *Les caractères de Théophraste traduits du Grec, avec les Caractères ou les Mœurs de ce siècle*. It was a small duodecimo volume of 360 pages, of which the translation of Theophrastus occupied the first 52 pages[2]. Thus La Bruyère's original work was modestly issued under the ægis of the Greek writer whom he had translated[3]. It contained 420 *remarques* or only about one third of the work as we know it in

[1] "I envy them their good fortune in having in their service persons who are their equals in heart and intelligence, and sometimes their superiors" (*Des Grands*).

[2] The privilege is dated October 8, 1687. There is no date of publication but some copies were circulating at the beginning of the year 1688. Bussy-Rabutin had a copy on January 26. There is a reprint of this original edition by D. Jouaust in the Cabinet des Bibliophiles. See J. Le Petit, *Bibliographie des principales éditions originales des écrivains français du XVe au XVIIIe siècle*, 1888, p. 428, for a reproduction of the title-page.

[3] M. Servois is convinced that La Bruyère did not translate Theophrastus till after he had written the "characters" contained in the first three editions, in none of which is there anything that recalls the Greek author (*Œuvres*, I, i, p. civ).

its final form. Its success was immediate, and a second and a third edition followed in the same year.

Favourable though its reception was by the reading public, it provoked, as Malezieu had foretold, considerable enmity in certain quarters. The praise of Racine in the first chapter and the even balancing of his merits with those of Corneille gave offence not only to Corneille and his brother, and their nephew, Fontenelle, but to the whole of their party in the Academy. Moreover Thomas Corneille, as one of the editors of the *Mercure galant*, and Fontenelle, as one of its chief contributors, had a special ground of complaint in the contemptuous remark that "Le H*** G*** (Hermès Galant) est immédiatement au-dessous de rien." In his fourth edition, which appeared in 1689, La Bruyère made this allusion still clearer by substituting M*** for H***, and he gave fresh offence by definitely ranging himself on the side of the Ancients in the great quarrel of the Ancients and the Moderns, and by introducing three malicious *remarques* at the expense of Charles Perrault, Fontenelle, and their allies. In his fifth edition (1690) he made a criticism of certain poets, which was manifestly aimed at Corneille, and in his sixth (1691) he inserted an unfriendly portrait of Benserade, that veteran of *précieux* verse, under the disguise of Théobalde, *bel esprit vieilli*. A few months later Benserade died, and La Bruyère had the imprudence to offer himself as a candidate for his vacant seat in the Academy, of which Fontenelle had been elected a member in the previous April. At the first scrutiny, or scrutiny by nominations (*bulletins*), he obtained only seven votes[1]. At his second attempt in 1693, when he was assisted by a letter written in his favour to Renaudot by Pontchartrain the Controller-General, he was successful. His *discours de réception*, which was novel, haughty, and unconciliatory, gave further offence to his opponents. After sounding the praises of Richelieu as the founder of the Academy, he proceeded to pass in review the individual mem-

[1] We know this from a letter of his to Bussy-Rabutin (*Œuvres*, II, 513). Among his supporters, besides Bussy, were Racine, Boileau, Bossuet, and Regnier-Desmarais. The other two were probably Segrais, and if not La Fontaine (whom he had possibly offended by his portrait of him), Rose or Renaudot.

bers—Regnier-Desmarais the secretary, Segrais, La Fontaine "more equal than Marot and more of a poet than Voiture," Boileau "superior to Juvenal, and the rival of Horace," Racine "who has planted himself by the side of Corneille," Bossuet "orator, historian, theologian, philosopher," Fénelon, their latest choice, whose "force and ascendancy are equally conspicuous in the pulpit and in conversation." And then, while thirty Academicians were anxiously awaiting to receive in their turn their due meed of praise, he stopped abruptly and with an apology for the pressure of time dismissed the rest with a few general and commonplace compliments. But there was worse than this, for he had wound up his praise of Racine with a hit at the conservative taste of a few old men, "to whom perhaps *Œdipe* (one of Corneille's least successful plays) is only dear as a memory of their youth." This provoked a malicious criticism of the *Caractères* from the pen either of Fontenelle or of the editor, Donneau de Visé, in the June number of the *Mercure galant*.

In his eighth edition (1693) La Bruyère delivered his counter-attack. He introduced into it the well-known portrait of Fontenelle as Cydias, and he printed with it his *discours de réception*, accompanied by a preface of remarkable vivacity, in which he defended his book against the malicious criticisms of the *Mercure galant* and exposed the machinations of Théobalde (who here stands for Fontenelle) and his allies, "faiseurs de stances et d'élégies amoureuses," "beaux esprits qui tournent un sonnet sur une absence ou sur un retour." This eighth edition was the last to receive additional matter. A ninth, without any new *remarques*, was published in 1696 shortly before his death.

During the last two years of his life (1694–1696) La Bruyère employed himself in writing dialogues on Quietism. Left unfinished at his death, they were published at the end of 1698 by the Abbé Ellies Du Pin, author of the *Bibliothèque des auteurs ecclésiastiques*, who completed the seventh dialogue and wrote the eighth and the ninth[1]. La Bruyère's authorship has been questioned on the ground that the style is different from

---

[1] *Dialogues posthumes du Sieur de La B*** sur le Quiétisme.* (*Œuvres*, II, 547–710, and see M. Servois's preliminary notice, *ib.* pp. 529 ff.)

that of *Les Caractères*, but this may be accounted for by the difference in the nature of the work. The dialogues were begun in the early summer of 1694, when Bossuet was busy examining the writings of Mme Guyon. When La Bruyère's death prevented their completion, Bossuet was at work upon his *Instruction sur les États d'Oraison*. It is quite possible that La Bruyère may have written the dialogues at Bossuet's suggestion. They represent the point of view of an orthodox layman who had little sympathy with mysticism, and who believed that there was no difference between the spiritual, if hysterical, mysticism of Mme Guyon and the gross perversions of the Spaniard, Molinos. La Bruyère had intended to finish the dialogues by way of justification with citations from Quietist literature—Molinos's *Guide spirituelle*, a letter by Falconi, Mme Guyon's *Moyen court, Explication du Cantique des cantiques*, and *Traité des Torrents* (manuscript)[1], and Malaval's *Pratique facile*, the Italian translation of which had been condemned by the Inquisition in 1688.

On May 8, 1696, La Bruyère read the dialogues to Antoine Bossuet, elder brother of the Bishop of Meaux, who was supping with him. Two days later (May 10) he died suddenly from a stroke of apoplexy[2].

We have seen that *Les Caractères*, as originally published, was a much smaller work than it finally became. From the fourth edition to the eighth La Bruyère, emboldened by success, and urged by his publisher, went on adding fresh *remarques*, or as he afterwards called them, *caractères*. Thus the fourth edition "corrected and augmented" contained 344 additional *remarques*, while in the eighth the number was finally brought up to 1120. But in spite of these additions the author adhered to his original sixteen chapters, though he often had considerable difficulty in finding appropriate places for the new *remarques*. This, coupled with his evident love of artistic

---

[1] Several manuscript copies were in circulation; Mme Guyon had supplied Bossuet with one for the purposes of his examination.

[2] "A neuf heures il soupa, en bonne santé: à dix il se sentit mal...et à onze heures il était mort. C'est dommage, il était bien intelligent. Mais il n'est pas étonnant qu'il ait eu une attaque d'apoplexie; il avait le cou fort court et une tête énorme" (*Correspondance de Madame*, I, 129).

workmanship, would seem to indicate that the arrangement of the chapters was the result of a certain plan. Sainte-Beuve, who was a warm admirer and a close student of La Bruyère, believes that his book is broadly divided into two parts, the first part (cc. i–x) leading up to the chapter on the Sovereign, and the second to that on Religion. M. Morillot suggests three divisions, the first (cc. i–vi) dealing with the sources of the social life of the period, the second (cc. vi–x) with society as observed from without, and the third (cc. xi–xvi) with the general study of man. As a variation on this I would suggest that La Bruyère's plan, so far as he can be said to have a plan, is to work in concentric circles of which the common centre is himself. Thus first he gives us his personal thoughts and feelings, with regard to books (c. i), ambition (c. ii), love and friendship (cc. iii and iv), and social intercourse (c. v). Then, combining observation from without with personal experience, he surveys the larger field of Paris *bourgeois* society (cc. vi and vii). Next, from his observation-post at Chantilly or Versailles, he passes in review the court (c. viii), the great nobles (c. ix), and the king (c. x). Finally, assuming the more detached attitude of a moralist and a philosopher, he treats of man in general (cc. xi–xiv) and of religion (cc. xv and xvi).

But if La Bruyère laid out his book on some such lines as these, he did not conform to them in any rigid or systematic spirit. It is only of a few of his chapters—e.g. *Des Ouvrages de l'Esprit, De la Cour, De la Chaire, Des Esprits forts*—that it can be said that all or nearly all the *remarques* relate to the subject indicated. Like Montaigne, whose *Essais* had evidently made a deep impression upon him, and whose example he was following in his adherence to his original chapters, he paid no strict observance to their titles. For, like Montaigne, he combined an artist's sense of composition with a hatred of even the appearance of system. A systematic treatise on morals or psychology was as alien to his intention as it was to that of his great predecessor.

He believed, modestly but erroneously, that everything that could be said on the subject of man had been said already, and that all that was left to a new writer was to tickle the jaded palates of surfeited readers. Therefore, for the sake of variety, he added to the ordinary fare of maxims and reflections short essays, dialogues, portraits, and even romances, each embodying the result of some particular observation or experience, and each chased and polished with the precision and delicacy of a goldsmith. It is not unlikely that in this departure from the established usage[1] he took a hint from Pascal, in whose fragments we find clear indications that he contemplated the admission of letters and dialogues into the framework of his Apology.

Brunetière has said that what La Bruyère's contemporaries chiefly admired in his book were the portraits. This is not altogether true, for the original success of *Les Caractères* was not due to the portraits, of which there were very few in the first three editions. But the portraits naturally appealed alike to good-natured curiosity and ill-natured malice. Keys to the originals began to circulate, first as oral rumours, and then in manuscript, the names being sometimes accompanied by malicious notes[2]. Finally in the tenth edition, published at the Hague in 1698, a key was added to the text. In the preface to his *discours de réception* La Bruyère hotly protested against the keys. In pointing out that they all differed from one another in their interpretations, and that many of the persons who were set down as the originals of the portraits were unknown to him, he had an easy task. It is also true, no doubt, that in many cases he has, as he says, "taken one trait from this man, and another trait from that man." But when, after stating that he has printed in capital letters the real names of those whom he praises, he adds that in the case of less favourable portraits he has used various means to put his readers off the scent, he is admitting that these less favourable portraits are also taken from life. Moreover, he protests too much, for none of his contemporaries could have failed to recognise either Lauzun in Straton, or Fontenelle in Cydias, or Benserade in Théobalde, or Santeul in Théodas.

The model for many of his portraits is obviously Theophrastus; that is to say, like his predecessor, he takes a single quality

---

[1] " Je sais même que j'aurai péché contre l'usage des maximes, qui veut qu'à la manière des oracles elles soient courtes et concises " (*Préface*).

[2] E.g. the *Clef de l'Arsenal* (1692), so-called from its existence in the Arsenal library.

as embodied in an imaginary type. Giton, the rich man, Phédon, the poor man, Gnathon and the other elderly egoists who are portrayed in the chapter *On Man*, Onuphre, the religious hypocrite, Démophile and Basilide, the pessimist and optimist, are all constructed after the plan of Theophrastus[1]. But while the pupil of Aristotle always starts from some abstract quality, La Bruyère in many cases is evidently inspired by some individual, though he may only borrow from him those characteristics which illustrate the quality that he is considering. Such are the portraits of Mopse, Celse, and Ménippe in the chapter *Du Mérite personnel*, which the keys are unanimous in referring to the Abbé de Saint-Pierre, the Baron de Breteuil, and Villeroy, respectively.

It was not only from Theophrastus that La Bruyère derived his love of portraits. These had been popular in France ever since the middle of the seventeenth century, when Mlle de Scudéry set the fashion in *Le Grand Cyrus* and continued it in *Clélie*. Mlle de Montpensier published through her secretary, Segrais, a collection of portraits in 1659, and one of the amusements of the *précieuses* and their admirers was to interchange portraits of themselves and their friends. But it was a rule of the game that the portraits of your friends should be highly flattering, and that in your own portrait the unfavourable element should be reduced to a minimum. The fashion spread to the memoir-writers, who, however, made no concession to the feelings of their sitters. Retz deals as faithfully with La Rochefoucauld as La Rochefoucauld deals with Retz. The fashion even reached the pulpit, and Bourdaloue's portraits, in which, as in those of La Bruyère, his hearers were too prone to recognise individuals, gave piquancy to his grave discourses[2].

---

[1] None of these appeared before the fourth edition.

[2]   " Nouveau prédicateur, aujourd'hui, je l'avoue,
         Écolier, ou plutôt singe de Bourdaloue,
         Je me plais à remplir mon sermon de portraits."
                                   Boileau, *Sat.* x.

In a sermon of Bourdaloue's, which we do not possess, *Sur la sévérité évangélique*, his audience thought they recognised the Comte de Tréville (La Bruyère's *Arsène*). " Il n'y manquait que le nom, mais il n'en était pas besoin," writes Mme de Sévigné (Christmas Day, 1671), but it is very doubtful whether she was right.

The author of *Les Caractères* differs from all his predecessors in the variety of his methods of portraiture. Biography (Chrysippe), romance (Émire), comedy (Nicandre and Élise), apostrophe (Zélie, Théobalde), dialogue (Philémon, Acis), dialogue and story combined (Irène), all take their place beside the Theophrastian pattern of which he has numerous variations. But, whatever the framework, all the portraits have this in common that they are the result of close and accurate observation of the outward man rather than of deep psychological insight. As M. Lanson says, La Bruyère is "a wonderful observer of the outward signs of the passions," or in other words, of manners and conduct. It is in the chapter on *La Mode* that some of his most finished portraits, namely those of the collectors, occur. All these are drawn wholly from the outside without any pretence at sympathy.

Moreover, accurate though his observation is of outward signs, he sometimes misses their true interpretation. He fails to realise that there are often mere tricks of manner which do not indicate, or indicate in an exaggerated degree, a man's real character. Persons who are shy or *gauche* often develop little tricks, which mislead the superficial observer; a haughty manner is not always the index of a haughty temper.

In his *causerie* on the Marquis de Lassay, Sainte-Beuve remarks that men are sometimes of greater worth when you know them intimately than they appear to be on a superficial acquaintance, and he cites as instances Lassay himself and the Duc d'Antin, two courtiers who are presented to us in no favourable light in Saint-Simon's gallery[1]. The same remark may be applied to Dangeau, the original of La Bruyère's Pamphile. For La Bruyère he is the typical courtier, puffed up with his own importance, and always seeking to ingratiate himself with great nobles and ministers. But he was also honest, trustworthy, and extremely good-natured, and of this La Bruyère says nothing. No doubt he would have pleaded, and with considerable justice, that Pamphile was the portrait, not of Dangeau, but of a typical courtier. He might also perhaps have pleaded that Cydias represents, not Fontenelle, but a typical

---

[1] *Causeries du Lundi*, IX, 165.

bel esprit. But it is at the same time, as we know from other sources, an extremely faithful portrait—so far as it goes—of La Bruyère's enemy. Its fault is that it is superficial and incomplete. It paints Fontenelle to the life as he appeared in the literary salons of his day, but it leaves out his better and more intrinsic qualities.

It is much the same with the portrait of a greater man of letters—La Fontaine. "Un homme paraît grossier, lourd, stupide; il ne sait pas parler, ni raconter ce qu'il vient de voir." This is no doubt a true description of the poet as he appeared in the company of strangers, and as he may have appeared, for instance, to La Bruyère at Chantilly. But in the society of his intimate friends, of Molière, or Boileau, or Racine, of Mme de La Sablière or Mme d'Hervart, the *bonhomme* was a charming companion and an excellent talker. The portrait of Corneille, which forms a pendant to this, is more faithful, for Corneille seems to have been "simple, timide et d'une ennuyeuse conversation" in every kind of society, but why add the malicious touch that "he only judged of the value of his piece by the receipts"? In dealing with a personal friend like Santeul (Théodas) La Bruyère shews greater sympathy, and for that reason more insight. He recognises his genius as well as his absurdities, his innate good sense as well as his outward buffoonery.

But by far the most sympathetic portrait in his gallery is that of Arténice in the chapter *Des Jugements*, of whom he says:

On ne sait si on l'aime ou si on l'admire: il y a en elle de quoi faire une parfaite amie; il y a aussi de quoi vous mener plus long que l'amitié.

Which was it in La Bruyère's case, love or friendship?

Vouloir oublier quelqu'un, c'est y penser. L'amour a cela de commun avec les scrupules qu'il s'aigrit par les réflexions et les retours que l'on fait pour s'en délivrer. Il faut, s'il se peut, ne point songer à sa passion pour l'affaiblir[1].

Is there a personal note in this, or are we to find it rather in the following?—

Les hommes souvent veulent aimer, et ne sauraient y réussir; ils cherchent leur défaite sans pouvoir la rencontrer; et, si j'ose ainsi parler, ils sont contraints de demeurer libres[2].

---

[1] *Du Cœur.*   [2] *Ib.*

Whatever were La Bruyère's feelings, they inspired him to draw a portrait which combines with even more than his usual delicacy of touch an unusual depth of penetration. The lady is depicted as young, radiant with health, modest, vivacious, witty without effort, well-read without the appearance of learning, an attentive listener rather than a brilliant talker, superior to vanity, absolutely sincere, eager to serve her friends. Who was the original of this charming portrait? Can we penetrate La Bruyère's secret? Are we to look for her in Catherine Turgot— Arténice is the anagram of Cat(h)erine—who at the age of thirteen married M. d'Aligre Boislandry, a councillor of the Paris *Parlement*? Alas! in the very year that La Bruyère published his fragment[1] she became the mistress of that selfish voluptuary, the Abbé de Chaulieu, who is the authority for this identification, and other lovers succeeded him[2]. Even granted that she was to some extent the victim of slanderous tongues, she cannot be said to have shewn *toute la sagesse* which La Bruyère prophesied for her[3].

On the whole La Bruyère's portraits, though by reason of their finished art they make a ready appeal to his readers, are not the most admirable part of his work. His true merit as an observer of society and a moralist rather lies in his general reflections, whether on particular classes—great nobles, courtiers, financiers—or on human nature in general.

It appears from the portrait of Arténice that he set a high value on conversation, not the conversation for effect of a iterary salon, but the quiet intercourse of two or three intimate friends. It is natural therefore that we should find some of his best thoughts in the admirable chapter *On Society and Conversation* (v), as for instance the following:

Le plaisir de la société entre les amis se cultive par une ressemblance de goût sur ce qui regarde les mœurs, et par quelque différence d'opinion sur les sciences.

[1] It first appeared in the eighth edition.

[2] Chaulieu was supplanted after four years by M. de Lassay, a son of the Marquis de Lassay.

[3] For Mme d'Aligre see La Bruyère, *Œuvres*, II, 322–337; Desnoireterres, *Les cours galantes*, 4 vols., II, 244–275; P. Janet, *Les passions et les caractères dans la littérature du XVIIe siècle*, 3rd ed. pp. 257–266. Allaire's conjecture that Arténice represents the Duchesse de Bourbon is most unlikely.

And is not the whole secret of real conversation contained in the *remarque* that, "l'esprit de la conversation consiste bien moins à en montrer beaucoup qu'à en faire trouver des autres"? La Bruyère evidently agrees with La Rochefoucauld that listening plays as important a part in conversation as talking. It is partly no doubt because women excel in the sympathetic function of a good listener that La Bruyère, in spite of the severe satire on them which his chapter *Des Femmes* (III) contains, evidently had a true and delicate appreciation of their better qualities.

Une belle femme qui a les qualités d'un honnête homme est ce qu'il y a au monde d'un commerce le plus délicieux.

Il y a dans quelques femmes...une grandeur simple, naturelle, indépendante du geste et de la démarche, qui a sa source dans le cœur, et qui est comme une suite de leur naissance; un mérite paisible, mais solide, accompagné de mille vertus qu'elles ne peuvent couvrir de leur modestie, qui échappent, et qui se montrent à ceux qui ont des yeux[1].

In the two chapters which succeed (vi, vii) *On Society and Conversation* the personal and intimate note largely disappears, and La Bruyère becomes more of an observer from the outside, an observer of a world with which he had little sympathy, the world of financiers and *bourgeois gentilshommes*. In the seventh, *De la Ville*, the satire is ill-natured rather than powerful, but the sixth, *Des Biens de Fortune*, contains an effective attack on wealthy *parvenus*, some severe and just remarks on gambling, the eloquent and highly finished picture of Zénobie[2], and the companion portraits of Giton, the rich man, and Phédon, the poor man. La Bruyère evidently disliked as much as Lesage the upstart financiers who were rapidly becoming such a power in France, and the whole chapter forms an interesting commentary on *Turcaret*, produced twenty years later (1709), when, owing to the unsuccessful conduct of the War of the Spanish Succession and the growing financial embarrassment of the government, the financiers had become almost a danger to the State.

[1] *Des Femmes.*

[2] It has been conjectured that Zénobie is Catherine de' Medici, and that the passage refers to her château and estate of Saint-Maur-les-Fossés, which by permission of the then owner, Condé, was at this time in the occupation of the quondam valet, Gourville.

In the chapter *On Society and Conversation,* there is a charming description of a small town on the side of a hill. A river bathes its walls, and a thick forest shelters it from the north winds.

Quel plaisir de vivre sous un beau ciel et dans ce séjour si délicieux!
Je descends dans la ville où je n'ai pas couché deux nuits, que je ressemble
à ceux qui l'habitent : j'en veux sortir.

Put by the side of this the concluding remark of the chapter *On the Court.*

La ville dégoûte de la province ; la cour détrompe de la ville, et guérit
de la cour. Un esprit sain puise à la cour le goût de la solitude et de la
retraite.

This is more or less La Bruyère's own history. Paris had spoilt him for provincial life; the court had disgusted him with Paris, but it had in the end given him a taste for solitude and retreat.

Qui méprise la cour, après l'avoir vue, méprise le monde.

La Bruyère was easily disillusioned, because, like nearly all the writers of the great age of Louis XIV[1], he saw the bad side of human nature more clearly than the good. Temperament, religious training literary influences, all combined to make him a pessimist. It is therefore little surprising if his picture of the court is as sombre as Saint-Simon's; indeed, if it lacks some of the darker shades of that Rembrandt among memoir-writers, it is more uniformly grey. The satire is gathered up and focussed in the long *remarque* beginning "L'on parle d'une région où les vieillards sont galants, polis et civils." Drunkenness, gambling, painted and immodest women, idolatry of the king, are the chief heads of the indictment, and for all of them, as we have seen, there is ample evidence in the memoirs, letters, and sermons of the time.

The chapter has also this merit that every remark bears directly on the main subject, which is continued in the latter part of the chapter entitled *De la Mode* (XIII). It is here that we have the pithy definition of a *faux dévot* as "celui qui, sous un roi athée, serait athée," and the long and elaborate portrait of Onuphre, the religious hypocrite, which is at once a criticism

---

[1] Malebranche is the exception.

of Molière's Tartuffe and an adaptation of that character to
the changed conditions of 1691[1].

The chapter, *Des Grands*, has a double interest. It is in the
first place the expression of La Bruyère's discontent, not to say
bitterness, arising from his position in the Condé family. But
it is more than this. In it we catch the first whisper of that
note which, nearly a century later, was sounded by Figaro in
his famous monologue. Compare

Les grands croient être seuls parfaits, n'admettent qu'à peine dans les
autres hommes la droiture de l'esprit, l'habileté, la délicatesse, et s'emparent
de ces riches talents, comme de choses dues à leur naissance.

with

Parce que vous êtes un grand seigneur, vous vous croyez un grand
génie! Noblesse, fortune, un rang, des places, tout cela rend si fier!
Qu'avez-vous fait pour tant de biens? Vous vous êtes donné la peine de
naître de plus. Du reste, homme assez ordinaire ; tandis que moi, morbleu!...

In both cases this explosion of revolutionary sentiment was
mainly the outcome of personal dissatisfaction, of the feeling
that in the world as organised in their day personal merit was
of less account than hereditary rank. If La Bruyère does not
say "tandis que moi, morbleu!" he certainly thinks it. But he
is also inspired by a real touch of democratic feeling. After
comparing the condition of the great with that of the people,
he says in often-quoted words, "Faut-il opter? Je ne balance
pas, je veux être peuple," and in three remarkable passages he
gives expression to sympathy, rarely found in the literature
of his day, with the sufferings of the poor.

Il y a six-vingts familles indigentes qui ne se chauffent point pendant
l'hiver, qui n'ont point d'habits pour se couvrir, et qui souvent manquent
de pain[2].

Il y a des misères sur la terre qui saisissent le cœur[3].

And finally there is the well-known *remarque* beginning,

L'on voit certains animaux farouches, des mâles et des femelles[4], répan-
dus par la campagne, noirs, livides et tout brûlés du soleil.

---

[1] It was not introduced till the sixth edition.
[2] *Des Biens de Fortune.*   [3] *Ib.*
[4] *Des Hommes*; this *remarque* first appeared in 1690.

La Bruyère has no suggestions to make for the amelioration of the people's condition, but, so far as his sympathies go, he deserves an honourable place besides Fénelon and Vauban and Boisguillebert.

The chapter on *Du Souverain ou de la République*, the latter part of the title having been added in the sixth edition, may be regarded as the coping-stone of La Bruyère's observations and reflections at Chantilly and Versailles. It is a curious mixture of panegyric and criticism, of panegyric of Louis XIV and criticism of the policy of conquest which marked his reign.

> Que sert en effet au bien des peuples et à la douceur de leurs jours que le prince place les bornes de son empire au delà des terres de ses ennemis ; qu'il fasse de leurs souverainetés des provinces de son royaume?...Que me servirait, en un mot, comme à tout le peuple, que le prince fût heureux et comblé de gloire par lui-même et par les siens, que ma patrie fût puissante et formidable, si, triste et inquiet, j'y vivais dans l'oppression et dans l'indigence?

And earlier in the chapter he declaims against the iniquity of war.

> La guerre a pour elle l'antiquité ; elle a été dans tous les siècles : on l'a toujours vue remplir le monde de veuves et d'orphelins, épuiser les familles d'héritiers, et faire périr les frères à une même bataille....De l'injustice des premiers hommes, comme de son unique source, est venue la guerre, ainsi que la nécessité où ils se sont trouvés de se donner des maîtres qui fixassent leurs droits et leurs prétentions. Si, content du sien, on eût pu s'abstenir du bien de ses voisins, on avait pour toujours la paix et la liberté.

This is plain speaking, but on the other hand the panegyric on Louis XIV, to which the whole leads up, is a strange blend of just and discerning praise with excessive flattery. Sainte-Beuve's explanation that under Louis XIV no book was complete, or even secure against attack, unless it contained a portrait of the king, may be the correct one[1], but it will hardly

---

[1] Cp. the following passage in a letter of Madame written Dec. 15, 1701: "Je demandais un jour à quelqu'un de raisonnable pourquoi dans tous les écrits on louait toujours le Roi. On me répondit qu'on avait expressément ordonné aux imprimeurs de n'imprimer aucun livre qui ne contînt son éloge, et cela à cause des sujets" (*Correspondance*, I, 255).

cover the flattery of Monseigneur which appears in *Les Jugements*.

In chapters II–IX La Bruyère's mordant and unsparing criticism is, as we have seen, chiefly directed against certain classes—financiers, lawyers, courtiers, great nobles. But in chapter X, *On Man*, he aims his shafts at humanity in general, and his pessimism is more pronounced than ever. The opening remark is exactly in the spirit of Philinte when he says to Alceste that knavery, injustice, and self-interest are as natural to man as the love of carrion to a vulture[1].

Ne nous emportons point contre les hommes en voyant leur dureté, leur ingratitude, leur injustice, leur fierté, l'amour d'eux-mêmes, et l'oubli des autres ; ils sont ainsi faits, c'est leur nature.

This is the key-note of the whole chapter, but at the end one asks oneself whether this expression of undiluted pessimism with regard to the human race is wholly genuine, and whether La Bruyère, like so many satirists, is not to a considerable extent carried away by literary tradition and his love of artistic effect. Close observer of outward details and patient collector of "little facts" though he was, it may be doubted whether his knowledge of the more hidden places of human nature was not largely formed and coloured by the study of his predecessors, Montaigne, Pascal, La Rochefoucauld. This suspicion finds support in what he says about children. He begins with a sweeping and, in this instance, manifestly calumnious attack.

Les enfants sont hautains, dédaigneux, colères, envieux, curieux, intéressés, paresseux, volages, timides, intempérants, menteurs, dissimulés ; ils rient et pleurent facilement ; ils ont des joies immodérées et des afflictions amères sur de très petits sujets ; ils ne veulent point souffrir de mal, et aiment à en faire : ils sont déjà des hommes.

Yet in most of the *remarques* that follow this morose and elderly bachelor shews not only a considerable knowledge of children but a real sympathy with their ways. Does not the explanation of this inconsistency lie in the fact that while in his initial *remarque* he is merely giving a rhetorical form to

---

[1] *Le Misanthrope*, Act I, Sc. i, 173–178.

a well-worn commonplace of literary pessimists, in the succeeding ones he is recording his personal experience? After
all, his pessimistic attitude towards man in general is much
the same as that of his contemporaries, especially of Boileau
in his eighth Satire, of La Fontaine in his fable, *Les Compagnons d'Ulysse* (XII, i), and of Fontenelle in his *Dialogues
des Morts*. Moreover it would be unfair to set La Bruyère
down as a complete pessimist. He is very far from disbelieving
in virtue, and he is now and again sincerely eloquent in its
praise.

Le seul bien capable de le [le sage] tenter est cette sorte de gloire qui
devrait naître de la vertu toute pure et toute simple ; mais les hommes ne
l'accordent guère, et il s'en passe.

Celui-là est bon qui fait du bien aux autres ; s'il souffre pour le bien
qu'il fait, il est très bon ; s'il souffre de ceux à qui il fait ce bien, il a
une si grande bonté qu'elle ne peut être augmentée que dans le cas où ses
souffrances viendraient à croître ; et, s'il en meurt, sa vertu ne saurait
aller plus loin ; elle est héroïque, elle est parfaite.

Such is the noble conclusion of the chapter *On Personal
Merit*.

The chapter, *Des Jugements*, is composed, like its predecessor,
of miscellaneous thoughts on human nature, but it is not so
uniformly pessimistic. Moreover, if, on the one hand, it is
disfigured by the violent and unjust attack on William of
Orange, on the other, it is adorned by the charming portrait
of Arténice, to which reference has already been made. Another
pair of chapters is formed by XIII (*De la Mode*) and XIV (*De
quelques Usages*), which deal chiefly with the follies of passing
fashion.

On the threshold of his book as well as on its title-page,
La Bruyère proclaims that his subject is human conduct
(*mœurs*), and in his preface, moved by certain criticisms, he
insists that the title of his book, *Les Caractères ou les Mœurs de
ce siècle*, implies that its scope is not confined to the French
court or the French nation. He thus claims to be a moralist in
the widest sense of the term. He offers, he says, to the public
a portrait of itself, in order to enable it to correct its defects.
Corriger les hommes, this is the only aim in his opinion worthy

of a writer, and, whether by satire or ridicule, whether by exhortation or psychological analysis, it was the aim of practically every writer of the great age of Louis XIV.

Up to this point there has been nothing distinctively Christian about La Bruyère's moral instruction. Indeed, it may be said, and it was said in his day, that many of his portraits and reflections shew a conspicuous lack of Christian charity. But in his last two chapters he definitely takes up a Christian attitude. Chapter XV (*De la Chaire*) consists chiefly of criticisms on the pulpit oratory of the day, and may be compared with Fénelon's *Dialogues sur l'Éloquence*, which, though they were not published till after their author's death, date from about 1683. It is well written, even eloquent in parts, but there is nothing particularly original in its ideas. The last chapter of all (*Des Esprits forts*) was in its first form as short as the preceding one, but La Bruyère made considerable additions to it in his seventh edition (1692), partly perhaps in order to meet the criticism that he was incapable of developing a connected argument (*pas capable de faire rien de suivi*).

It is an ambitious chapter and often rises to a high pitch of eloquence. But it is La Bruyère's misfortune that he inevitably owes much to Pascal, and that, as Chateaubriand has pointed out in the *Génie du Christianisme*, alike in his argument and in his language he falls short of his model[1]. It is, however, no reproach to La Bruyère that he is not a Pascal, and that he does not bring to the discussion of religious problems the passion and insight of that intense and profound spirit. His whole attitude towards religion is that of a man who has never known doubt: " I feel that there is a God. I do not feel that there is no God: that is enough for me; all the reasoning in the world is of no use to me. I conclude that God exists. This conclusion is in my nature; I was imbued with its principles too easily in infancy, and I have preserved them too naturally in advanced age to suspect them of falsity. But there are some thinkers who have abandoned their

---

[1] 3rd part, book II, c.v. He compares the long passage beginning, "Vous êtes placé, ô Lucile, quelque part sur cet atome": with Pascal's famous, "Qui est-ce qu'un homme dans l'infini? etc."

principles. It is a great question whether such people exist. If possibly they do, that only proves the existence of monsters."

If La Bruyère as an apologist for the Christian Faith is inadequate, as a critic of books and style he deserves the closest consideration, and his first chapter (*Des Ouvrages de l'Esprit*) is among his very best. The first thing in it that strikes the reader is his knowledge and appreciation of sixteenth-century literature. For him French literature begins, not with Malherbe, but with Marot. If he is too severe in his condemnation of Rabelais's indecency—for there is nothing corrupt in Rabelais—he gives full recognition to his merits:

> Où il est bon, il va jusques à l'exquis et à l'excellent, il peut être le mets des plus délicats.

He has read Amyot, and he admires his style. He has closely studied Montaigne at a time when Montaigne's readers in France were decreasing, and he has paid him the compliment of a formal imitation[1]. One can hardly expect a contemporary of Boileau to be just to Ronsard, but though he is blind to his immense services to style and versification, he recognises that he is "plein de verve et d'enthousiasme." As was natural in a French critic of the latter part of the seventeenth century, he is a far better judge of prose than of verse. But it is something that he ventures to speak of Théophile de Viau in the same breath with Malherbe, though in contrasting their treatment of nature he fails to observe that Théophile with all his negligences was a real lover of nature, while Malherbe only uses it as a theme for rhetorical commonplace.

In that very difficult task in which not a few great critics have failed, the task of appreciating his contemporaries, La Bruyère is at his best. His comparative estimate of Corneille and Racine has won universal praise. In contrasting the idealism of Corneille's characterisation, the richness and variety of his action, the inequalities in his style, with the realism, the simplicity, and the even merit of Racine, he is merely expressing in admirable form what was more or less the common opinion. But in noting

---

[1] In *De la Société.*

that Racine can be "grand and sublime (merveilleux)" and
Corneille "touching and pathetic," he contributes a fresh observation of his own[1]. It is not only in this chapter that we must
look for his judgments on his contemporaries. His *discours de
réception* contains, as we have seen, short but admirable appreciations of La Fontaine ("il élève les petits sujets jusqu'au
sublime"), Boileau, Racine, Bossuet, and Fénelon.

As for the "rarest genius" of all the writers of the reign of
Louis XIV, La Bruyère's praise of him is warm and just—
"quelle source de la bonne plaisanterie, quelle imitation des
mœurs, et quel fléau du ridicule"—but both here and elsewhere
he introduces an element of censure. "Il n'a manqué à Molière
que d'éviter le jargon et le barbarisme, et d'écrire purement[2],"
while his portrait of Onuphre is a direct criticism of Tartuffe[3]
and that of Timon an indirect one of Alceste[4]. The criticisms
are those of a man who had read Molière's plays, but who
had never seen them acted, or at any rate had little experience
of the stage. It may be a just criticism that a typical religious
hypocrite would not refer to his *haire* and his *discipline*, but
"Laurent, serrez ma haire et ma discipline" is one of the
finest entries in all the history of the stage. The observations
which are strung together to form the portrait of Onuphre may
be all true, but Onuphre is at the best only a type. Tartuffe is
an individual and he is alive.

The charge of writing incorrectly has been brought against
Molière by Fénelon and Vauvenargues as well as by La Bruyère,
and again in our own day by Schérer; but it has never been made
by any dramatic writer or critic, or indeed by anyone who is
at all conversant with the requirements of the stage[5].

---

[1] It is interesting to compare Vauvenargues's letter to Voltaire on Corneille
and Racine (1743) and Voltaire's answer; also Voltaire's letter to Mme du
Deffand (1764), and her answer (see G. Lanson, *Choix de Lettres du
XVIIIe siècle*, pp. 66, 115, 153, 381).

[2] M. Servois suggests that "le jargon et le barbarisme" refers to
Molière's peasants, but this does not seem at all likely.

[3] *De la Mode.*

[4] *De l'Homme.*

[5] See Brunetière, *Études critiques*, VII, 85–132, for a full discussion of
the question.

La Bruyère's *remarque* on the epistolary art is of great interest. In it he proclaims the superiority of women in this branch of literature, a verdict for which there was ample justification in his day, and for which in spite of Voltaire, and Horace Walpole, and Gray and Cowper, there is much to be said even now. He was doubtless thinking in the first place of Mme de Sévigné's letters, which had a certain circulation in manuscript, and copies of which had possibly been sent to him by Bussy-Rabutin. He may also have received from the same source copies of the admirable letters of Mme de Scudéry. At any rate he felt himself warranted in coming to the following conclusion:

> Si les femmes étaient toujours correctes, j'oserais dire que les lettres de quelques-unes d'entre elles seraient peut-être ce que nous avons dans notre langue de mieux écrit[1].

The three writers to whom with Montaigne he was the most indebted were Pascal, La Rochefoucauld, and Malebranche. Though he does not mention Malebranche by name, he criticises him by implication, and he refers to Pascal and La Rochefoucauld to point out the difference between his book and theirs:

> Moins sublime que le premier et moins délicat que le second, il ne tend que rendre l'homme raisonnable, mais par des voies simples et communes [2].

La Bruyère's remarks on style have a peculiar interest, in the first place because he was an accomplished practitioner of his art, and in the second because he had a decided influence on the development of French prose. Of its history during the twenty years which preceded the publication of his book he has given a brief sketch:

> L'on écrit régulièrement depuis vingt années; l'on est esclave de la construction; l'on a enrichi la langue de nouveaux mots, secoué le joug du latinisme, et réduit le style à la phrase purement française; l'on a presque retrouvé le nombre que MALHERBE et BALZAC avaient les premiers rencontré, et que tant d'auteurs depuis eux ont laissé perdre; l'on a mis

---

[1] Sainte-Beuve in his annotated copy of La Bruyère appends the remark, "Mme de Maintenon est correcte."

[2] *Discours sur Théophraste.* Pascal's name occurs only once in *Les Caractères*, in the chapter *De l'Homme*, as an example of a *grande âme*.

enfin dans le discours tout l'ordre et toute la netteté dont il est capable: cela conduit insensiblement à y mettre de l'esprit[1].

According to M. Servois the last phrase simply means that the improvement in style has worked a corresponding improvement in thought. This seems rather a tame conclusion and one hardly warranted by the words. According to the more usual interpretation they furnish us with a key to La Bruyère's own aims with regard to style. Great writers like Pascal, La Rochefoucauld, Bossuet, Malebranche, followed by men of lesser genius such as Le Père Bouhours and Bussy-Rabutin[2], have brought, he says, French prose almost to perfection. In the matter of construction, vocabulary, harmony, order, and polish there is little room for improvement. The one thing left for a writer who wishes to obtain a hearing is to spend more thought upon his style, to concentrate on it the full play of his intelligence, to make it a more exact reflection of his own thoughts and personality. La Bruyère is not thinking, if I may differ from Sainte-Beuve, of the *esprit* of Pellisson and Fléchier[3]. Nothing was more hateful to him than that cheap and conventional display of *esprit* which was dear to the *précieux* society[4]. He has, in fact, told us what his meaning is:

> Tout l'esprit d'un auteur consiste à bien définir et à bien peindre. Moïse, Homère, Platon, Virgile, Horace, ne sont au-dessus des autres écrivains que par leurs expressions et par leurs images : il faut exprimer le vrai pour écrire naturellement, fortement, délicatement.

The same thought is expressed by Pater, another careful artificer of style. "In the highest, as in the lowliest literature, the one indispensable beauty is, after all, truth," and its principle is the "absolute accordance of expression to idea," "the word's adjustment to its meaning[5]."

---

[1] *Des Ouvrages de l'Esprit*; see Sainte-Beuve's comments (*Port. litt.* I, 407).

[2] *Des Ouvrages de l'Esprit*.

[3] Sainte-Beuve couples with them Bussy and Bouhours, but both these writers are free from any affectation of *esprit*.

[4] Occasionally, however, he descends to a tasteless play upon words (see Rébelliau, *Notice littéraire*, p. xxii n.[2]).

[5] *Style* in *Appreciations*.

La Bruyère, then, aimed in the first place at *bien définir*. Thus he is the ancestor of all those choice and delicate spirits who have been tormented by the search for the right word and the right expression, of Marivaux and Flaubert, of Pater and Henry James. "Il y a dans l'art un point de perfection." "Il faut toujours tendre à la perfection." "Entre toutes les différentes expressions qui peuvent rendre une seule de vos pensées, il n'y en a qu'une qui soit la bonne." "Les esprits médiocres ne trouvent point l'unique expression et usent de synonymes."

But La Bruyère also aimed at *bien peindre*. He was not content with the more or less abstract style that prevailed in his day. He strove to give concrete form to his ideas. "Les esprits justes," he says, "et qui aiment à faire des images qui sont précises, donnent naturellement dans la comparaison et la métaphore." He evidently regarded himself as an *esprit juste*, and he had, as M. Rébelliau claims for him, a "very vivid and a very inventive imagination"—but an imagination which was more alive to the world of the senses than to the world of the spirit, and which saw things in detail rather than as a whole. His portraits, as M. Lanson points out, instead of being mere abstract analyses, like the fashionable portraits of the day, are often real sketches of visible beings, firmly drawn, and sometimes even coloured[1]. One of the most striking is that of a doctor of the Sorbonne:

Un homme à la cour, et souvent à la ville, qui a un long manteau de soie ou de drap de Hollande, une ceinture large et placée haut sur l'estomac, le soulier de maroquin, la calotte de même, d'un beau grain, un collet bien fait et bien empesé, les cheveux arrangés et le teint vermeil, qui avec cela se souvient de quelques distinctions métaphysiques, explique ce que c'est que la lumière de gloire, et sait précisément comment l'on voit Dieu, cela s'appelle un docteur[2].

His little pictures of life have all the vigour and animation of an engraving by Callot. To obtain his effects he does not shrink from the use of technical terms—"Diognète sait d'une médaille le *fruste*, le *flou* et la *fleur de coin*"—or of familiar words—"Il y a des âmes sales, pétries de boue et d'ordure."

---

[1] *L'Art de la Prose*, pp. 119–123.   [2] *Du Mérite personnel*.

His portraits of Giton, the rich man, and Phédon, the poor man, and still more that of Gnathon, the glutton, might be signed by a modern "naturalist."

But *bien définir et bien peindre* was not the sole aim of La Bruyère's innovations in style. It is unfair to say with Taine that "his talent consists chiefly in the art of arresting attention." Rather, to quote his own words :

Il donne quelque tour à ses pensées, moins par une vanité d'auteur, que pour mettre une vérité, qu'il a trouvée, dans tout le jour nécessaire pour faire l'impression qui doit servir à son dessein.

"Donner quelque tour à ses pensées"—that is a modest way of putting it, for Chateaubriand does not exaggerate in the least when he says of him that "no one has given greater variety to his style, more diverse forms to his language, more movement to his thought." And this variety, M. Rébelliau points out, is partly obtained by minute attention to the construction of each phrase. There is no known rhetorical artifice—inversion, interrogation, repetition, enumeration—to which he does not have recourse. And he invents new ones. Sometimes he begins his sentence with an arresting expression, such as, "Tout est dit"; sometimes he keeps the arresting phrase or word till the very end of the sentence.

Like all conscious innovators in style, especially those who strive after originality, La Bruyère has been reproached with various defects, with jargon (to use his own term), with obscurity, with affectation, with bad taste. From not one of these defects is it possible wholly to acquit him[1]; but they are not of the essence of his style. They are occasional blemishes on a beautiful raiment, but they are not interwoven into the texture. In spite of them La Bruyère will always be honoured as a great artist of prose. If in the opinion of the best judges he stands a little lower than the greatest prose-writers of the classical age, it is because he lacks the art to conceal his art. The sense of effort is seldom absent from his pages. His most perfect expressions, those in which he has found the one word which most adequately expresses the thought, are the result of patient search, rather than of happy inspiration.

[1] See Rébelliau, *Notice littéraire*, pp. xxi–xxii.

One of the methods employed by La Bruyère for giving variety to his style is the judicious blending of the long oratorical phrase of the seventeenth century with the short broken phrase of the eighteenth. In this as in other ways La Bruyère is of both centuries. On the one hand, he follows the great tradition of the classical age, on the other, he prepares the way for Montesquieu and Voltaire. But his influence on the eighteenth century was not confined to style. It affected whole departments of literature. It was most marked in comedy. The transition from the comedy of character to the comedy of manners, from Molière to Dancourt and Lesage, is largely due to *Les Caractères*. The light which *Des Biens de Fortune* throws on *Turcaret* has already been pointed out. *De la Ville* throws a similar light on Dancourt's plays, and there is a close correspondence between many of La Bruyère's characters and those of Dancourt. Régnard's *Le Distrait* is manifestly inspired by Ménalque, and the remarks on gambling in *Des Biens de Fortune* may have helped him in writing *Le Joueur*. Destouches's *Le Glorieux, Le Médisant, Le Dissipateur* are all studies of secondary characters such as abound in La Bruyère.

In the novel too the same influence was all-important. "Lesage is La Bruyère in action," says Sainte-Beuve, and this is as true of his novels as of *Turcaret*, conspicuously so of *Le Diable boiteux*, and hardly less so of *Gil Blas*. "In the character of Onuphre," says M. Morillot, "there are four or five novels in germ," while the story of Émire, remarks the same writer, which is told by La Bruyère in three pages, might be expanded into a romance of three hundred[1].

Finally it is pointed out by Sainte-Beuve that the women of the eighteenth century who lived before the days of Jean-Jacques Rousseau, Mme de Lambert and Mme de Staal-Delaunay at their head, were "exclusively pupils of La Bruyère; they read him when they were young, and they made haste to verify him by experience[2]." "Heureux homme que La Bruyère! Son talent regarde deux siècles; sa figure appartient à tous les deux. Il termine l'un; on dirait qu'il commence et introduit l'autre[3]."

---

[1] In *Hist. de la Langue et de la Littérature française*, v, 594–596.
[2] *Port. litt.* III, 440–441.   [3] Sainte-Beuve.

CHAPTER IV

THE DRAMA

1. *The Stage and the Church.*

IN 1673, the year of Molière's death, the Théâtre du Marais was closed, and by the king's orders Colbert chose its best actors and actresses for Molière's company, while the rest went to the Hôtel de Bourgogne. About the same time Molière's company, having been ousted from the Palais-Royal by the grasping and intriguing Lulli, bought from the Marquis de Sourdéac the lease of a theatre which he had made out of a tennis-court in the Rue Mazarine. It became known as the Hôtel Guénégaud from the street which runs into the Rue Mazarine just opposite to it. In 1679 the company was joined by the great actress Mlle de Champmeslé and her husband, and the Hôtel de Bourgogne, from which they had seceded, being now left without a tragic actress, the king ordered the two companies to be united into one.

Thus in 1688, when our period opens, Paris had only a single theatre in which French drama (as distinguished from opera) was habitually performed by French actors[1]. It is true that the Italians, who from 1673 to 1680 had shared the Hôtel Guénégaud with the Palais-Royal company and in 1680 had found a home in the vacant Hôtel de Bourgogne, not only introduced scenes spoken in French into their Italian plays but often acted entire French comedies[2]; but the Comédie-Française, as we must now call the united company, regarded this as an infringement of their privileges and it was only after Louis XIV had heard the arguments of Baron on one side and Domenico[3], the Harlequin of the Italian company, on the other, and had decided in favour of the Italians, that the controversy ceased. Another

---

[1] In 1688 there were two theatres in London, the Theatre Royal in Drury Lane, and the Duke of York's in Dorset Garden, but from 1682 to 1695 the two companies were united.

[2] Gherardi prints fifty-five for the years 1682–1697.

[3] His real name was Giuseppe Biancolelli.

rival was the opera, which, as we have seen, had been installed by Lulli in the Palais-Royal.

In June 1687 the Comédie-Française received notice to quit the Rue Guénégaud within three months, the reason being that the Sorbonne, which was on the point of opening the Collège des Quatre Nations (now the Palais de l'Institut[1]), objected to the proximity of the impious play-actors. Then began a long search for a theatre, a search which was greatly lengthened by the objections of the *curés* of the various parishes in which the actors proposed in turn to establish themselves. At last after many disappointments they were permitted to buy a tennis-court in the Rue Neuve des Fossés-Saint-Germain-des-Prés, now the Rue de l'Ancienne Comédie, and the new theatre opened on April 18, 1689, with *Phèdre* and *Le Médecin malgré lui.*

The opposition of the Church, which had so greatly hampered the comedians in their search for a new home, would have been less successful but for the changed attitude of Louis XIV. Since he had become devout, he no longer looked with favour on the stage, and he readily listened to churchmen, when they objected to the establishment of a theatre in their neighbourhood. Moreover this change of attitude on his part was shared by many courtiers, who, as La Bruyère says, became devout because it was the fashion. "The best actor," writes Madame on November 1, 1691, referring to Baron, "is leaving the stage. The devout party have frightened him by saying that all the actors will be dismissed and that a pension will be given to the first who retires voluntarily[2]." "We have nearly had the theatre closed," she writes again on December 23, 1694, "but the Archbishop of Paris and Père La Chaise are said to have told the king that it would be too dangerous to forbid respectable entertainments[3]." Then she goes on to relate how Mascaron had recently preached against the drama, saying that "it excited

---

[1] The building, which was on the site of the old Hôtel de Nesle, was begun by Le Vau in 1664.

[2] *Correspondance de Madame*, I, 88. The story that Baron was frightened into leaving the stage by the devout party rests no doubt only on gossip.

[3] *Ib.* I, 106.

the passions," and how the king turned towards her and said, "He is not preaching against me, for I no longer go to the theatre, but he is preaching against you, who love the theatre and go to it."

If it be true that the Archbishop of Paris and Père La Chaise dissuaded the king from closing the theatre, they did not represent the sentiments of the great majority of the clergy. These had been expressed by Bossuet earlier in the same year (1694) in his well-known treatise, *Maximes et Réflexions sur la Comédie*[1]. Its occasion was a letter which had appeared during the preceding Lent at the head of an edition of Boursault's *Œuvres dramatiques* and which was generally attributed to a Théatin, named Père Caffaro. The scandal was great. The Paris preachers outvied one another in denouncing the stage and the "illustrious theologian" who had dared to write in its defence. Bossuet read the letter with indignation, but instead of fulminating against the writer in an official document he wrote privately to Père Caffaro, denouncing his whole argument and bidding him either recall his letter or disavow it (May 9, 1694)[2]. This produced an immediate reply from Père Caffaro, in which he solemnly declared that he had not written the letter and that he agreed with Bossuet in everything that he had said about the stage. A month or two later Bossuet published the *Maximes et Réflexions sur la Comédie*.

This is not the place to discuss Bossuet's treatise. It is sufficient to say here that it is marked by his usual lucidity, eloquence, and orderly arrangement of his arguments, and that on the other hand it betrays the tendency to exaggerate the case against his opponent and the occasional lack of Christian charity which are regrettable features in nearly all his controversial pamphlets. Both these features are prominent in his attack on Molière, of whom Fénelon wrote, "Encore une fois, je le trouve grand." The cruel reference to Molière's death is too well known to be repeated, but it may be noted that when Bossuet quotes against him the saying of Our Lord, "Woe unto you that laugh now! for ye shall mourn and weep," he is reflecting a view which many of the French clergy of his

[1] Ed. A. Gazier, 1881.   [2] Bossuet's letter was first printed in 1771.

day shared with the English Puritans, namely that all laughter is sinful. As for the other feature, it is a gross exaggeration to say that in Molière's plays "virtue and piety are always made ridiculous, sinfulness (*corruption*) always excused and made amusing." The first part of the treatise (chapters I–XI) is of considerable importance and interest, because it expresses in masterly language the ideas which prevailed among the stricter French ecclesiastics in Bossuet's day and which continued to prevail well into the nineteenth century. It is to be noted that the Church objected to tragedy almost as much as to comedy, because, in the words of Mascaron, "it excited the passions." The supporters of the stage defended the representation of love on the ground that it generally ended in marriage. But marriage, argues Bossuet, "pre-supposes concupiscence, which, according to the rules of the faith, is an evil which must be resisted"—an idea which he develops much more completely in his *Traité de la Concupiscence*, shewing thereby a profound ignorance of the subject—perhaps permissible in a celibate priest.

In December 1695 the Abbé Du Bos writes to Bayle that the clerical campaign against the stage has made the theatres more popular, but a year later we find Madame writing to her aunt, the Electress of Hanover, who had asked for some good actors to be sent to her, that "since the clergy have taken to preaching with such fury against the stage, there are fewer good actors than formerly." In the following year the Italian actors were summarily ordered to close their theatre and to leave the kingdom. The ostensible reason was their continued violation of decency and morality, but the real reason was their production of a play entitled *La fausse Prude*, in which everyone recognised Mme de Maintenon[1].

2. *Tragedy.*

In spite of the attacks of the clergy and the disapproval of Louis XIV, the Comédie-Française continued to flourish. So far as tragedy was concerned, it still depended mainly upon the masterpieces of Corneille and Racine. Of the older men who had

---

[1] Saint-Simon, *Mémoires*, I, 427.

aspired to be their rivals, Quinault died in 1688 and Pradon's least bad tragedy, *Régulus*, appeared in the same year. In 1695 the Abbé Boyer, then in his seventy-eighth year, with fifty years of continuous production behind him, scored a success with *Judith*. By reason of its unimpeachable morality it was welcomed by playgoers as an answer to Bossuet's treatise of the preceding year, but even its name is only known at the present day from Racine's crushing epigram[1].

The most successful of the younger men was Jean-Galbert de Campistron (1656–1723)[2], a native of Toulouse, who prided himself upon being Racine's favourite disciple. One of his most successful plays, *Andronic* (1685)[3], is founded on Saint-Réal's historical novel, *Don Carlos*, though the scene of the story is transferred to Constantinople; it is inferior to the plays of Alfieri and Schiller on the same subject. Campistron wrote eight other tragedies, of which *Tiridate* (1691)[4] had a prodigious and to us inexplicable success. This may have been due largely to the acting of Baron, who retired from the stage at the end of the year in which it was produced. But Campistron was also popular with the reading public, for a seventh edition of his works was issued in 1707. Of his two comedies one, *Le Jaloux désabusé*[5], had only a moderate success when first produced in 1709, but it was revived with much greater success in 1724 and it kept the stage for another century. Its fault is that it has little

---

[1] A financier is represented as sitting next to Boyer at a performance, and saying to him through his tears,

"Je pleure hélas! de ce pauvre Holopherne
Si méchamment mis à mort par Judith."

[2] *Œuvres*, 2 vols. 1739; 3 vols. 1750; *Chefs-d'œuvres*, 1820. See for the rest of the chapter the indispensable *Histoire du théâtre françois depuis son origine jusqu'à présent*, 15 vols. 1734–1749 (carrying the history down to 1721), by François (1698–1753) and Claude Parfait, vols. XII–XV. The elder brother and principal author had close relations with the stage, and was the friend of many actors and actresses.

[3] *Œuvres*, 1739, vol. I; *Répertoire du théâtre françois ou Recueil des tragédies et comédies restées du théâtre depuis Rotrou* (Corneille, Molière, Racine, Regnard, and Crébillon are not included), ed. Pétitot, 1817, vol. I.

[4] *Œuvres*, vol. II. Victor Fournel in *Contemporains et Successeurs de Racine*, *Rev. d'hist. litt.* I (1894), 233 ff., regards *Tiridate* as Campistron's masterpiece, but this opinion is not generally shared.

[5] *Œuvres*, vol. II; *Répertoire*, vol. IX.

or nothing of the comic spirit and is often positively tedious. Dorante, the jealous husband, is Alceste without his attractiveness and strong individuality. His wife, Célie, is much better. She is honest and tender like Éliante, but she has enough of Célimène's coquetry to give her the charm that her husband lacks. Among the foolish or designing women who figure so largely in the comedies of our period she stands forth as a rare and distinguished figure.

> Elle est jeune, elle est belle et sage. Ah, quelle femme!
> Quel sens, quelle droiture, et quelle grandeur d'âme!
> Exemple dans ce siècle et bien rare et bien beau!
> Elle va s'enfermer dans le fond d'un château.

François-Joseph de La Grange-Chancel (1677–1758) was a still feebler follower of Racine. His first tragedy, *Adherbal* (originally called *Jugurtha*), was produced in 1694, when he was only just seventeen. It is said that Racine helped him with advice and the play met with complete success. During the latter part of his dramatic career, which terminated long before his death, he devoted himself almost entirely to Greek subjects, but he made very little advance on his first attempt. *Amasis* (1701), which is generally regarded as his best tragedy, furnished some hints to Voltaire for his *Mérope*. The part of Iphigénie in *Oreste et Pylade* (1697), his first Greek play, was the last creation of Mlle de Champmeslé, who died in the following year. Her successor, Mlle Duclos, had the advantages of a majestic appearance and a superb voice, but she was ignorant and unintelligent. Thanks to her and Beaubourg, who succeeded Baron in most of his parts, the declamatory style of acting, which Baron had done so much to discountenance, reigned supreme at the Comédie-Française for the next twenty years.

Like Campistron, Antoine de La Fosse (1653–1708) owed his best play, *Manlius Capitolinus* (1698)[1], to a historical romance —*La Conjuration de Venise*—by Saint-Réal, and just as Campistron had transferred the scene of *Andronic* from Spain to Constantinople, so La Fosse, taking his story from Livy, substituted Rome for Venice. His immediate model, however, was not

---

[1] *Répertoire*, vol. I. This was his second play; his first, *Polyxène*, appeared twelve years earlier, his fourth and last in 1703.

Saint-Réal's novel, but Otway's tragedy of *Venice Preserved* (1682), though in conformity with the traditions of classical tragedy he discarded the comic scenes, which are the worst part of that play. In other respects he is far inferior to his model. His plot is uninteresting, his characters are lifeless, and his style, though dignified, is monotonous and dull. The part of Servilius, the friend of Manlius, was a favourite one with Talma, and, thanks largely to his acting, the play kept the stage till his death in 1826.

The *Médée*[1] of Hilaire-Bernard de Longepierre (1659–1721), a native of Dijon, who was well versed in Greek literature, has at least the advantage of an interesting subject. As in *Phèdre*, the interest is concentrated on the title-rôle, so much so that Jason is represented as a sorry scoundrel, and the rest are mere puppets. Médée herself, who, as Longepierre acknowledges, owes something to Euripides and Seneca, is an arresting figure and it is not surprising that the part was a favourite one with actresses. However, the play when it was first produced in 1694, was coldly received, and it was not till after the author's death that it was revived in 1728 with triumphant success. Médée was later one of Mlle Dumesnil's most effective parts.

We may now pass to the only important figure in French tragedy between Racine and Voltaire. It is true that Crébillon is no longer acted or even read, but his name at any rate is known beyond the narrow circle of professed students. For he was not content to follow humbly in the footsteps of Corneille and Racine. He had two definite aims, one to introduce more incident and greater complication into tragedy, and the other to make it more tragic. The first aim, however, cannot be said to be a new one; it was rather a reaction from Racine to the Corneille of *Rodogune*, *Héraclius*, and the plays of his declining years. As regards the second aim Crébillon was more in accord with Racine than with Corneille, for Racine's plays are, with one or two possible exceptions, definitely tragic, while Corneille prefers a happy ending and fails to be truly tragic, because his hero, whatever his fate, is the sole arbiter of it. But Crébillon's theory that tragedy can be made more tragic by

[1] *Répertoire*, vol. I.

exciting horror rather than fear will be best tested by a consideration of his plays.

Prosper Jolyot de Crébillon (1674-1762)[1] was, like Longepierre, a native of Dijon and, like so many of the great writers of the seventeenth century, a pupil of the Jesuits. He seems to have been an unruly pupil, and to have shewn no disposition for classical or indeed other learning. Even in after life his reading consisted chiefly of novels and especially of those of La Calprenède. Having abandoned law for literature, he made his *début* as a dramatist in 1705 with the tragedy of *Idomenée*. In this he follows closely in the paths of Corneille and Racine. There are three principal characters and three confidants. The main subject, which is the sacrifice of Idamante by order of the gods, recalls *Iphigénie*, while the idea of making Idamante and his father Idomenée both in love with Erixène is borrowed from *Mithridate*. Idomenée again is a Racinian character, but on the other hand Idamante is almost a Cornelian superman. The play, in spite of severe criticisms of the last act, was a decided success, partly because it seemed to promise a much-needed revival in French tragedy. In his next play, *Atrée et Thyeste* (1707), Crébillon proceeded to put his ideas into execution. Having chosen the repulsive story of Atreus and Thyestes, he works up its horrors till they culminate in Atrée offering to Thyeste, as a pledge of reconciliation, a cup filled with his son's blood. This Crébillon justified by saying that his Atrée was not so cruel as the Atreus of Seneca, and by a reference to Corneille's *Rodogune* in which Rodogune, after ordering one of her sons to be assassinated, tries to poison the other. But Corneille's *dénouement*, though terrible and melodramatic, is not horrible or repulsive. As for Crébillon's idea of substituting horror for fear in Aristotle's famous definition of tragedy, it is incompatible with the definition, for there can be no purgation of horror. In short, horror has not the effect of making tragedy more tragic, for it repels the spectator instead of arousing his pity. The self-blinding of Oedipus in

---

[1] *Œuvres Complètes*, 3 vols. 1824. There were numerous editions before this: the most recent is of 1885, with a notice by A. Vitu. See F. Brunetière, *Les Époques du théâtre français*, pp. 205 ff.

Sophocles's masterpiece, to which Crébillon might have referred, though it is not so repulsive as his own *dénouement*, is certainly open to criticism.

Crébillon's other aim was to make the plot more complicated. He does this in his new play by making Plisthène, who is really the son of Thyeste, the supposed son of Atrée. It is a favourite contrivance in melodrama, but one which the reader, if not the spectator, finds extremely tiresome. In the preface to his next play, *Électre* (1708)[1], Crébillon frankly says that the subject is too simple. So by way of complicating it he makes Électre in love with Égisthe's son and Oreste in love with his daughter. He is especially pleased with the idea of making Électre in love. This makes her, he thinks, more deserving of pity, and gives him the advantage over Aeschylus, Sophocles, and Euripides, and all who have treated the subject. As a matter of fact the greater part of the earlier acts of the play, owing to the love-scenes, is a failure. In the later acts there are two decidedly good scenes, that between Oreste and his governor, Palamède (III, v), and the recognition of Oreste by Électre (IV, ii). Finally the play has this merit, that Palamède and Électre are the only two of Crébillon's characters who are alive. Palamède is a man of action inspired by noble sentiments. Électre, in her lonely austerity, her indomitable resolution to avenge her father, which is unshaken by either love or fear, is a striking figure. Adrienne Lecouvreur made a brilliant *début* in the part in 1717.

Crébillon's fourth tragedy, *Rhadamisthe et Zénobie* (1711), is regarded as his masterpiece. The story is founded on a long romance entitled *Bérénice*, which appeared from 1648 to 1651 and is generally attributed to Segrais. But Crébillon has once more gone to *Mithridate* for his central situation, and has made Pharasmane and his two sons Rhadamisthe and Arsame, in love with the same woman, Zénobie. The plot, which is bewildering in its complications, is carried out by the help of strong situations and improbable incidents, including

[1] Produced December 14, 1708, and played for the fourteenth and last time, January 12, 1709. The brothers Parfait say that it would have had a longer run, but for the excessive cold (see above, p. 14) which caused the theatre to be closed from the 14th to the 22nd of January.

those favourite expedients of romantic melodrama, the mis-understanding and the recognition. The play is a melodrama too in its complete lack of psychology. Its only merits are a general air of grandeur and heroism, not unworthy of Corneille, and one scene at least, the meeting of Rhadamisthe and Zénobie (III, v), which is of real pathos. With Mlle Duclos as Zénobie and Beaubourg as Rhadamisthe, both of whom with their decla-matory style were just suited to this type of melodrama, the play had a great success. It ran for thirty-two performances—a very long run in those days—and it was no less successful when printed. Two editions in eight days and four in the course of the year attest to its popularity with the reading public.

Rhadamisthe et Zénobie was the high-water mark of Crébillon's success. His next play, *Xerxes* (1714), which has a highly complicated and badly constructed plot, had to be withdrawn after a single performance, and *Sémiramis* (1717) was equally a failure. It was severely criticised and after seven performances was withdrawn by the author himself. It deserved its fate, for it is founded on the repulsive theme of a mother (Sémiramis) falling in love with her son, believing him to be a stranger. Discouraged by these checks, Crébillon kept silence for nine years and then produced *Pyrrhus* (1726), a play of a wholly different type from its predecessors. Nobody dies and the play ends happily; it is in fact a tragi-comedy. It pleased the public but not the author, who had only abandoned his theory of horror as a concession to "the feebleness" of his audience. He now retired from the stage for twenty-two years, and only re-appeared in 1748 with a tragedy entitled *Catilina*, which was received with enthusiasm and ran for twenty performances. But this success was almost entirely due—for the play is a poor one—to jealousy of Voltaire, who had achieved two striking successes with *Zaïre* and *Mérope*, and whose enemies, with Mme de Pompadour at their head, had egged on the septua-genarian poet to re-enter the lists. He lived to produce yet another play, *Le Triumvirat* (1754), and he did not die till eight years later, at the age of eighty-eight.

Such was French classical tragedy during the latter half of the personal rule of Louis XIV. With the exception of *Athalie,* which was presented twice only in Mme de Maintenon's apartments at Versailles and not at all in Paris till 1716, it did not produce a single masterpiece, nor has it produced one since *Athalie*. It cannot be said that with the death of Racine the mould was broken; the mould was there, but there was no one to fill it with life. With all his cleverness, with all his love of the stage, Voltaire could not rise above *Zaïre* and *Mérope*. Yet classical tragedy was still produced in France and still attracted aspirants to literary fame. Marmontel, La Harpe, and others made brilliant *débuts*, but the promise of their first plays was never realised. La Touche's *Iphigénie en Tauride*, Saurin's *Spartacus*, and De Belloy's patriotic play, *Le Siège de Calais*, had each a phenomenal success, but the success was not repeated. "Tous les ressorts de notre système dramatique semblent usés," writes Grimm in 1778; "après deux ou trois mille pièces jetées pour ainsi dire dans le même moule. Comment ne le seraient-ils pas[1]?"

Yet tragedies constructed after the same pattern continued to appear till they were finally driven from the field by the advent of the Romantic drama. But, when ten years later a great actress of classical tragedy, Rachel, helped to bring about a fresh reaction, it was Corneille and Racine alone who held aloft the classical standard. It is a wonderful testimony at once to the consummate skill with which Corneille constructed the pattern and to the equally consummate skill with which Racine adapted it to his different ideals, that, in spite of the fact that they had no real successor, classical tragedy should have reigned in France for nearly two hundred years.

3. *The minor successors of Molière.*

Every classical tragedy, whatever its contents, had to conform in structure to a rigid pattern. But classical comedy, as it left Molière's hands, was much more flexible. It is true that Molière kept fairly strictly to the accepted rule of five acts of verse for the highest kind of comedy and of three acts or one act of prose for comedy of a lower type. But *L'École des Maris* has only three acts of verse and *L'Avare*—possibly because Molière was

---

[1] *Correspondance*, XII, 49.

pressed for time—is a prose-comedy in five acts. In the twelve *comédies-ballets* there is more variety. Nine are in prose, *Les Fâcheux* and the unfinished *Mélicerte* are in verse, and *La Princesse d'Élide* was begun in verse and finished, for want of time, in prose. Some are in five acts, some in three, and some in one. Nor did Molière confine himself in his verse-plays to the customary Alexandrine; in *Le Sicilien* he uses *vers blancs*, in *Amphitryon* and *Psyché vers libres*. Of greater importance is the variety of forms which his comedy assumes—high comedy, tragi-comedy, pastoral comedy, mythological comedy, romantic drama, farce, *comédie-ballet*. Yet through all these experiments he never after *Les Fâcheux* deviated far from the type of comedy which he loved best, the social comedy of character.

Molière's immediate successors, some of whom were little junior to him, while one, Hauteroche, was his senior, subsisted chiefly on imitations and borrowings from his lighter plays. There was little originality either of observation or treatment in their work, but their knowledge of the stage—for the great majority of them were actors—enabled them to produce some agreeable light comedies, which hit the fancy of the day. Some were no longer alive at the beginning of our period. Mont-fleury and Brécourt had both died in 1685; Raymond Poisson lived till 1690 but wrote nothing after 1680. Donneau de Visé (1640–1710), who as a young man had produced three or four successful comedies, especially *Les Dames vengées* (1675), had long ago ceased to write for the stage and was chiefly occupied in editing *Le Mercure galant*. Of those who were still at work Charles de Champmeslé, husband of the great actress, whose last comedy, *La Veuve* (never printed), appeared in 1699, two years before his death, had many years earlier produced a few pieces which have a certain merit as amusing and satirical pictures of *bourgeois* society, but which are ill-constructed and carelessly written. There remain Hauteroche, Boursault, and Baron[1].

---

[1] See E. Lintilhac, *Histoire générale du théâtre en France*, vol. III, 1908, pp. 366–395; L. Petit de Julleville, *Le théâtre en France*, 1901, pp. 213–219; J. Lemaître, *La Comédie après Molière et le théâtre de Dancourt*, 2nd ed. 1903, c. ii.

Noël Le Breton, Sieur de Hauteroche (1617–1707)[1], was nearly five years older than Molière, but he did not produce his first comedy till 1667, when Molière was already famous. Though of good family, he became an actor and after a short engagement at the Marais joined the Hôtel de Bourgogne, where he excelled in tragic parts of the second or third rank. As Pompée in Corneille's *Sertorius* he is imitated by Molière in *L'Impromptu de Versailles*. His *Crispin médecin* (1670) which is regarded as his best play, his *Crispin musicien* (1674) and his *Le Cocher supposé* (1685)[2], are all strongly reminiscent of Molière; *Les Bourgeoises de qualité* (1691), his last comedy and the only one which belongs to our period, is a combination of *Les Femmes savantes* and *Les Précieuses ridicules*. Hauteroche is an unequal writer, but he has the merits of gaiety and stage-craft.

Edme Boursault (1638–1701)[3] has neither style nor gaiety nor dramatic sense, and his comedies only deserve consideration by reason of their extraordinary success and of their interest, slender though it may be, as social documents. He is probably best known at the present day as the author of *Le Portrait du Peintre* (1663), that malicious attack on Molière which as a young man he was commissioned to write by the Hôtel de Bourgogne. In spite of this and in spite of his later encounters with Racine and Boileau, he was really a kind-hearted and honourable man, who had a real desire to reform society. The three comedies in which he gave expression to this desire were all works of his maturity and they appeared at fairly long intervals—*Le Mercure galant* in 1683, *Ésope à la Ville* in 1690 and *Ésope à la Cour* in 1701, soon after the author's death. They are all what the French call *pièces à tiroirs*, that is to say, they are composed of organically disconnected scenes strung together by a slender thread of plot. His model, of course, was Molière's *Les Fâcheux*, that brilliant little example of social satire. In *Le Mercure galant* Boursault is more satirist than moralist; in the other two comedies he is a moralist pure and simple. Donneau de Visé's attempt to stop the production

---

[1] *Théâtre*, 3 vols. 1772.
[2] *Rép. du théâtre françois*, 3me *ordre*, vol. III.
[3] *Théâtre*, 3 vols. 1746.

of *Le Mercure galant* was ill-advised[1], for it was in no sense an attack on his popular and successful journal. Rather, it was a first-rate advertisement of its influence. A *bourgeois* who wishes to be ennobled in order to marry a young *marquise*, a tax-collector who has embezzled 200,000 francs, a couple of inventors, a would-be professor of Norman, an attorney of the Châtelet and an attorney of the Court—all these appear in turn in the editor's office and solicit the support of his powerful journal. There is little that is new in these types, and the great success of the play, like that of a modern revue, must have been due to its actuality. Probably it portrayed not only general types, but living individuals and actual incidents. It is thus a feeble forerunner of *Les Caractères* and of that form of comedy which owed so much to La Bruyère—the comedy of manners[2].

Boursault's two other comedies *à tiroirs* are weighed down by the character of Aesop, who wearies us with his superhuman wisdom and virtue, and still more with his intolerable habit of solving every question and difficulty that is submitted to him by means of a fable. "Ésope," says Lemaître, "is not a man, but a moralising machine." The earlier of the two plays, *Ésope à la Ville*[3], calls for no remark, but in *Ésope à la Cour* (1701)[4] there are two characters of some interest. These are M. Griffet, a farmer of taxes, and Iphicrate, a retired general, who disbelieves in the existence of God. Referring to these, Lemaître reminds us that we are at the dawn of the eighteenth century[5]. La Bruyère had already pilloried the *partisans* and other contractors for taxes and had drawn the portraits of Sosie and Crésus, but the *fermier* was a new character in comedy[6] and precedes by eight years his great successor, Turcaret. Iphicrate is

---

[1] It was so far successful that the play appeared under the title of *La Comédie sans titre*.

[2] *Le Mercure galant* was revived in 1889, but with only moderate success.

[3] *Répertoire*, 3me ordre, 1819, vol. III. Vanbrugh produced an English version of it.

[4] *Répertoire*, vol. IX.

[5] See J. Lemaître, *op. cit.* pp. 76–79.

[6] M. Harpin, who appears in a single scene of Molière, *La Comtesse d'Escarbagnas*, is only a tax-collector.

naturally a very poor second to Don Juan, and Aesop for all his gravity and sententiousness is a less effective defender of religion than Sganarelle. His only good point, which, as usual, he supports with an apologue, is that the free-thinkers generally sent for a priest when they thought they were dying. In spite, however, of Aesop's feebleness as a reasoner, Iphicrate confesses to being moved by his arguments—but not before he has uttered half-a-dozen lines, which faithfully depict the court of Louis XIV at the time the play was written.

> A parler sans contrainte et d'un cœur ingénu,
> Quel dieu, hors la fortune, à la cour est connu?
> Pour peu que l'on y prie, on est toujours en garde;
> On observe avec soin si le prince y regarde;
> Et lorsque par hasard on rencontre ses yeux,
> C'est lui que l'on invoque encor plus que les dieux[1].

There is yet another passage, not mentioned by Lemaître, in which Boursault appears as a follower of La Bruyère and as a herald of the eighteenth century. It occurs in the scene (Act I, Sc. iii) in which Croesus appoints Aesop to be his minister of state, and like the passage just cited is an indictment of the court. In it Aesop contrasts the prevailing honesty of the people with the dishonesty, the hypocrisy, the dissimulation, the flattery, the love of gambling, and dissipation of the court. Thus Boursault falls into line with La Bruyère and Fénelon and Saint-Simon.

The most interesting of the actor-playwrights who followed in Molière's footsteps is his favourite pupil, Michel Boyron, called Baron (1653–1729)[2]. His connexion with Molière's company began when he was a boy of twelve, but owing to a quarrel with Mlle Molière, who, it is said, boxed his ears at a rehearsal, he left the company and did not return to it till 1669. He was at once restored to Molière's favour and under his careful tuition made such rapid strides in his profession that seven days after his master's death, when he was only nineteen, he appeared

---

[1] Act III, Sc. iii.
[2] *Théâtre*, 2 vols., Amsterdam, 1736; 3 vols. 1759. B. E. Young, *Michel Baron, acteur et auteur dramatique*, 1905; G. Roth, *Chefs-d'œuvre comiques des successeurs de Molière* (Bibl. Larousse), vol. I.

successfully in the difficult part of Alceste. In spite of this
success he deserted to the Hôtel de Bourgogne in the Easter
vacation, probably because the rival theatre offered him a better
opportunity for tragic parts. For Baron's range in acting was
different from his master's. They both excelled in high comedy,
but Molière, while equally good in all kinds of comedy—"il
était tout comédien," says *Le Mercure galant* just after his death,
"depuis les pieds jusqu'à la tête"—did not succeed in tragedy.
Baron, on the other hand, with his noble presence[1] and fine
natural voice, was a great tragic actor, but was out of his
element in low comedy and farce. He introduced to the Hôtel
de Bourgogne that natural style of acting in which he had
been so carefully trained by Molière.

The playwright was very inferior to the actor, for Baron was
too much absorbed in himself to be a close observer of others
or to be able to create a living character. If *L'Homme à bonne
fortune*[2] (January 1686) is the only one of his comedies that
survives, it is because the coxcomb of a hero is more or less
Baron himself—Baron with his cold-blooded libertinism and
his overweening belief in himself[3]. But the plot lacks interest,
and the dialogue point and vivacity. Pasquin and Marton are
the regular valet and *soubrette* of French comedy, but Pasquin
is less resourceful than his compeers and Marton is often prosy.
The best that can be said for the play is that certain scenes
testify to its author's knowledge of the stage and to his eye for
a comic situation[4]. The play, however, was a decided success,
and "Moncade" became a recognised term for a *bel ami*. Before
the end of the year Baron produced another comedy—*La
Coquette et la fausse Prude* (December 1686). It is, as Lemaître
says, a mosaic put together out of borrowings from Molière.
In particular the coquette is a coarsened Célimène and the prude
a vulgarised Arsinoé. It was even more successful than its

---

[1] His portrait by Largillière, painted about 1720, is in the Foyer des
artistes of the Comédie-Française. M. Roth reproduces an engraving of a
painting by Troye (p. 12).

[2] *Répertoire*, vol. X; *Chefs-d'œuvre comiques*, vol. I.

[3] He thought himself the greatest actor since Roscius.

[4] Some competent French critics, e.g. Petit de Julleville and M. Roth,
think much better of it than I do.

predecessor. Baron's next venture, *Le Jaloux* (1687), was in verse, but though it met with a fairly good reception on the stage, it was not printed till after his death. After this play, except for three little prose-comedies in one act, which were never printed, he produced nothing till 1703, twelve years after his retirement from the stage. His new piece, *L'Andrienne*, was a verse translation, with a few changes to suit modern manners, of Terence's *Andria*[1]. A similar rendering of the *Adelphi* followed in 1705.

In his preface to *L'Andrienne* Baron says that he believed Terence had never been presented before on the French stage. But there had been numerous French translations, in particular, the recent one by Mme Dacier of all the plays (1688). Three years later, following in Baron's footsteps, the Abbé David-Augustin Brueys (1640–1723), a native of Aix, and Jean Palaprat (1650–1721), a native of Toulouse, produced an adaptation of the *Eunuchus*, a play which required more drastic handling than the *Andria* "pour l'accommoder à nos mœurs." The result was a French play (entitled *Le Muet*[2]) instead of a Roman one, and the credit for its skilfully conducted plot belongs as much to its adapters as to the original author[3]. The two friends also collaborated in *Le Grondeur*, produced four months before *Le Muet*, which Voltaire strangely declares to be "superior to all Molière's farces." Brueys himself said of it, "C'est une bonne pièce. Le premier acte est excellent; il est tout de moi. Le

[1] *Répertoire*, vol. x.

[2] *Ib.*

[3] In 1679 Bossuet, in a letter to Innocent XI, giving an account of the Dauphin's education, wrote that the poets whom the Dauphin liked best were Virgil and Terence, and that the pleasure he derived from Terence was combined with profit. For he had seen "the deceitful allurements of voluptuousness and women, and the blind passions of young men, whom the flattery and intrigues of a valet had drawn into difficult and slippery places." But Terence read to the accompaniment of a moral commentary was a very different matter in Bossuet's eyes from Terence acted on the stage, and in his letter to Père Caffaro he points out that though Terence is more decorous than Aristophanes or Plautus, he is not on that account more chaste. In neither letter does Bossuet notice that according to Christian ethics Terence is immoral as well as unchaste even from a pagan point of view, as for example in the treatment of the parasite at the conclusion of the *Eunuchus*.

second, cousi cousi, Palaprat y a travaillé. Pour le troisième, il ne vaut pas le diable. Je l'avais abandonné à ce barbouilleur" —a verdict which the reader will endorse. Palaprat, who was present when it was delivered, merely roared with laughter, for the two men in spite of frequent disputes over their respective merits, were fast friends, and were both of a gay and easy temper. Palaprat, who was in the services of the Grand Prior of Vendôme, followed his patron to Italy in 1693 and wrote no more for the stage. Brueys, however, continued to produce plays—in December 1693 *L'Important*, in 1706 a modernised rendering of the famous *L'Avocat Pathelin*, which was only superseded in comparatively recent times by a translation of the old play, and in 1722, a year before his death, *L'Opiniâtre*[1]. Brueys was brought up as a Protestant, and as such engaged in a controversy with no less an opponent than Bossuet, with the result that he became a convert and an active controversialist on the Romanist side. His theological writings, which fill ten volumes, are naturally dead, and both he and Palaprat have disappeared from histories of French literature as writers of comedy—perhaps, remembering *Le Muet*, not altogether deservedly.

It will have been seen that there was very little originality in these successors of Molière. They borrowed characters and scenes from his plays, and helped by a considerable knowledge of the stage, for they were for the most part actors, and blessed with a careless gaiety, they produced some actable and successful comedies. Baron and Brueys also followed Molière's example by making a particular type of character the central figure, and thus we have *L'Homme à bonne fortune* and *Le Jaloux*, *Le Grondeur* and *L'Important*. But they never get beyond the type, and even the type is never really alive. The only writer in the whole group, whose work shews any originality or any attempt to strike out a fresh path is Boursault, and he unfortunately lacked dramatic instinct. Not one had any gift for style, either in verse or in prose.

It is a relief to turn to four men of a higher order of merit— Dancourt, Lesage, Regnard, Dufresny. Each has some distinctive

---

[1] *Théâtre*, 3 vols. 1735.

quality; all may be read with pleasure, and the plays of two at least still keep the stage. Dancourt began his long dramatic career in 1685 and did not end it till 1717. Dufresny, the eldest of the four, wrote for the Théâtre-Français from 1692 to 1721 and Regnard from 1694 to 1708. Lesage's connexion with the same theatre was a short one, for, not counting two earlier failures, it was confined to the years 1707 and 1709. All four were, as we shall see, largely influenced by La Bruyère.

4. Dancourt.

Florent-Carton Dancourt[1] (1661–1725) was born at Fontaine-bleau of a good Picard family. His father, who was originally a Protestant and had become a Catholic, sent him to the Jesuit college of Louis-le-Grand, where the famous preacher, Père de La Rue, impressed by his aptitude for study, tried in vain to make him a Jesuit. His humanities completed, he read law and was received as an advocate, but, falling in love with a daughter of the actor La Thorillière, abandoned all thoughts of a legal career, carried off the lady, married her in spite of his family's opposition and after Easter 1685 made his *début* on the boards of the Théâtre-Français. Two months later he produced successfully his first comedy, *Le Notaire obligeant*, afterwards called *Les Fonds perdus*, and for the next thirty-two years he only allowed three to pass without providing his fellow-actors with at least one piece annually. Indeed in two years (1692 and 1695) he produced no less than four. In 1718 he left the stage and, retiring to a property which he had in Berry, devoted himself to religious practices and meditation[2]. He died in 1725 at the age of sixty-four. As an actor he had the advantages of good looks, a good figure, and a good voice, and, contrary to what one might expect from his plays, he excelled in the

---

[1] *Œuvres*, 12 vols. 1760; *Théâtre choisi*, ed. F. Sarcey, 1884. J. Lemaître, *op. cit.*

[2] There is a manifest allusion to this in the chapter (II, i) of *Le Diable boiteux* entitled *Des Tombeaux*. The devil shews Don Cléofas "un monument qu'un auteur dramatique a fait construire dans l'église d'un village, où il s'était retiré après avoir mené à Madrid une longue et joyeuse vie. Cet auteur a donné au théâtre de comédies pleines de gravelures et de gros sel; mais il s'en est repenti avant sa mort."

graver parts of comedy, or what were called *rôles à manteau.*
One of his best rôles was Alceste.

In his first piece he revealed a talent for easy and natural
dialogue, and he followed up his initial success with two one-
act parodies of operas, *Angélique et Médor* and *Renaud et
Armide.* His next attempt, *La Désolation des Joueuses* (1687),
inspired by the recently published edict against *lansquenet,* was
a brilliant success, but it was *Le Chevalier à la Mode* (October
1687) that made his reputation.

In this play, which is in five acts of prose, Dancourt had as
collaborator a certain M. de Saint-Yon, who two years earlier
had produced a comedy entitled *Les Façons du Temps.* Judging
from the long extracts, some of which are complete scenes,
given by the brothers Parfait[1], it has little merit beyond the
liveliness of its dialogue. It has no real plot and the characters
—a young man and his creditors, a valet and a *soubrette,* a *femme
intrigante* and an attorney—are mere sketches of familiar types.
Le Chevalier à la Mode[2], which had a prodigious success when
first produced, is of much higher quality. The *Chevalier* himself
is a variety of that unpleasant type of rascal which Molière
had portrayed with a light hand in Dorante of *Le Bourgeois
gentilhomme* and which Molière's pupil Baron had drawn more
elaborately only the year before as the hero of his *L'Homme à
bonne fortune.* But whereas Molière had brought out the pre-
datory side of his *chevalier d'industrie,* Baron had laid greater
stress on his love-making propensities. The *Chevalier* of Saint-
Yon and Dancourt, as Lemaître says, "manque de relief." He is
more akin to Moncade than to Dorante, but he lacks the fatuity
of Moncade and the aristocratic impertinence of Dorante, and he
is altogether of coarser clay than either. Indeed, his attraction
for even such foolish women as Mme Patin, the *Baronne,* and
the *petite brune,* Lucile, is not very comprehensible. Mme Patin
is a more impressive figure. From her first appearance in the
first scene, breathless and almost speechless from the affront
which she had received from a "marquise de je ne sais comment," to the very last, in which she dismisses her faithless

---

[1] *Hist. du théâtre françois,* XII.
[2] *Répertoire,* vol. VIII.

Chevalier with "Tu n'épouseras pas ma nièce, perfide!" she dominates the play. The widow of a financier or, to be more particular, of a *partisan* or tax-contractor, she is a new type in literature. She is vulgar and snobbish to the core—"Il faut que je devienne marquise, quoi qu'il en coûte,"—but she can hardly be called a caricature. Nor is she merely a type of her age: she might easily pass for the wife or widow of a modern profiteer. The other characters are of lesser calibre, but Lisette the maid, with her humour and irony, who flatters her mistress and then betrays her, has a touch of real individuality, while M. Migaud, the staid lawyer, who marries Mme Patin for her money, and M. Serrefort, her brother-in-law, who protests against her ostentation and extravagance and finally secures the reversion of her 40,000 *livres* a year by marrying his daughter to the son of M. Migaud, are sufficiently good sketches. The Baroness is less successful, and the episode of her bursting into Mme Patin's salon with two swords in order to force her to fight a duel is none the less improbable from the point of view of art because it was founded on an actual occurrence. Finally, the plot, though it drags in the last two acts, is fairly well worked out.

Five years later, Saint-Yon and Dancourt collaborated again in another five-act prose play, *Les Bourgeoises à la Mode* (November 1692)[1], which is generally regarded—I think rightly —as the high-water mark of Dancourt's achievement. In this play the ambition of the two *bourgeoises*, Angélique, the wife of M. Simon, a notary, and Araminte, the wife of M. Griffard, a commissioner of police, is to become women of fashion, to associate with *femmes d'épée* (wives of nobles) rather than with *femmes de robe* (wives of lawyers), to ride in a handsome coach, and to have gambling parties of *hombre* or *lansquenet* in their houses. As each of their husbands wants to make love to the other's wife, the two ladies conspire to extort money from them. In this perhaps pardonable object they have the assistance of Lisette, Angélique's maid, the *Chevalier*, who is in love with Marianne, Angélique's step-daughter, Frontin, the *Chevalier's*

---

[1] *Répertoire*, vol. IV. It ran to 25 performances.

accomplice who passes for his valet, and Mme Amelin, a pawn-broker and dealer in old clothes who turns out to be the *Chevalier's* mother. All these characters, with the exception of M. Griffard and Marianne, who do not appear till the Second Act, are firmly outlined in the First Act, and though they never become markedly individual, they develop into excellent types. The two *bourgeoises* are less extravagant than Mme Patin; Frontin and Lisette, in their audacity, their alertness, and their eye to their own interests, more than dimly foreshadow the Frontin and Lisette of *Turcaret*; and Marianne, who is bored with her music-lessons, and her history-lessons, and her geography-lessons, and who, when she is alone, "dreams of many things," especially of matrimony, is not a bad type of the *ingénue* as conceived by Dancourt[1]. But the most individual character of all is Mme Amelin. She is of the same family as Frosine in *L'Avare*, Mme Thibaut in Dancourt's *La femme d'Intrigues*, Mme La Ressource in Regnard's *Le Joueur*, and Mme Jacob in Lesage's *Turcaret*. But she does not, as they do, combine with her business as a dealer in old clothes and a pawnbroker that of an *entremetteuse et intrigante*. Though she only appears in eight scenes, and though in these she confines her remarks to what is strictly necessary, she makes a favourable impression on us by her directness, her clear vision, her honesty (so far as her trade permits), and above all by her love for her rascal of a son. "A cela près, Jeannot est bon garçon, et je ne puis m'empêcher de l'aimer." This maternal affection at once makes her true to nature and raises her from the type to the individual. Nor is it an exaggeration to say that she, and she alone, saves the play from the unrelieved sordidness of its predecessor. The plot is too complicated for a comedy of manners, and its working out leaves much to be desired. On the other hand, the dialogue marks a decided improvement on that of *Le Chevalier à la Mode*. It is crisper, more to the point, truer to nature, and in consequence more dramatic[2].

---

[1] The minor character of M. Josse, *orfèvre*, may be regarded as a tribute to Molière.

[2] Vanbrugh produced an English version of *Les Bourgeoises à la Mode* in 1705. Except for three additional scenes he follows the original pretty

The only five-act comedy in prose which Dancourt wrote without the help of a collaborator is *La Femme d'Intrigues* which appeared in the same year as *Les Bourgeoises à la Mode*, but nearly ten months earlier (January 1692)[1]. With its feeble and barely existent plot and its twenty-eight characters, the majority of whom have nothing to do with the main action, it shews Dancourt's incapacity to construct a long play. But as a document bearing on the social conditions of the day it is of considerable interest. The chief character, Mme Thibaut, is a Mme Amelot in a large way of business, "a power," as Lemaître says, in Paris life. She is not only a money-lender, a pawnbroker, and a buyer of old clothes, but she carries on an agency for every kind of shady transaction. The magnitude of her business may be gathered from the fact that she has in her employ three dozen maid-servants, thirty coachmen, and over a hundred lackeys[2].

Of Dancourt's prose plays in three acts, six in all, two were produced in 1700. The earlier of the two, *La Fête du Village* (better known by its later title of *Les Bourgeoises de Qualité*[3]), though it kept the stage for a century, is very inferior to *Les Bourgeoises à la Mode*. Mme Blondineau, the wife of a Paris attorney, and her sister, the widow of a *greffier*, are more or less caricatures, and the *dénouement*, which is brought about by

closely, but he has adapted his version to the coarser and more realistic tastes of the aristocratic audience which patronised the English drama. Hazlitt praises it highly, without mentioning its origin, and later English critics are almost unanimous in regarding it as an improvement on the original. I cannot agree with this. By coarsening the characters and introducing licentious passages which do not exist in the original—the long scene between Dick (the *Chevalier*) and Brass (Frontin), which Hazlitt quotes in full, will furnish an instance—Vanbrugh has produced a play, which may have been more suited to English tastes than Dancourt's, but which is on a distinctly lower plane of art. Particularly offensive is the transformation of the *ingénue* Marianne into another Miss Prue. But I am amazed at the statement in the *Dictionary of National Biography* that *The Confederacy* "has been described as the lowest point of morality to which English comedy ever sank."

[1] *Théâtre*, vol. II. And see Lemaître, *op cit.* pp. 170–174.

[2] One remark by a minor character is worth preserving. "J'en suis à ma cinquième édition," says a *précieuse* when asked whether she is married.

[3] *Répertoire*, vol. XIX; reprinted separately in 1888.

the parties to two marriage-contracts signing them without having read them, has the improbability which is permissible in a farce but not in a play which pretends to be a representation of real life. *Les trois Cousines*[1] is a much better play. It is thoroughly gay without being farcical, and the characters, who are all drawn from village life, are natural, alive, and distinct. The scene in which the three girls, played by Dancourt's two daughters and Mlle Desmares, the niece of Mlle de Champmeslé, form a plot for securing their respective lovers, is particularly successful. Other good characters are *la meunière*, her man Blaise, and the bailie.

In the same volume (XIX) of *Le Répertoire* as these last two plays will be found five of Dancourt's one-act comedies in prose, and of these three are of decided merit. *Les Vacances* (1696) is another representation of village life and a particularly good one. As in *Les Bourgeoises de Qualité* and *Le Prix de l'Arquebuse*, the village in which the scene is laid is in La Brie, that wooded table-land between the Seine and the Marne which travellers to the south have on their left soon after leaving Paris[2]. The lack of logical sequence in the conduct of the play is atoned for by several well-drawn characters—an attorney named Grimaudin, who has become the *seigneur* of the village; a schoolmaster; Grimaudin's housekeeper; a rascally ex-valet (Lépine); his former master, Clitandre, a cavalry officer, whose company has been quartered in the village; Angélique, the attorney's daughter, with whom Clitandre is in love; and Maugrebleu, the attorney's drunken son, who is a soldier in Clitandre's company. Grimaudin is described in the opening scene as "un honnête homme qui a gagné du bien," but in the next scene he frankly explains to Lépine, who is his god-son, that he had made his money out of a law-suit "which he had had the wit to prolong for seventeen years," and which was not yet decided. In *L'Été des Coquettes* (1690) there is another Clitandre, whose character of *homme à bonnes fortunes* is more clearly indicated

---

[1] *Répertoire*, vol. XIX. The brothers Parfait were told that the piece was written by one Barrau, and revised by Dancourt.

[2] Mme de Sévigné spent her childhood at Sucy-en-Brie, about 12 miles from Paris, in the home of her guardian the Abbé de Coulanges.

than in *Les Vacances*. Like Baron's Moncade, he has been making love to three women at once, and a similar exposure awaits him. The play is founded on the idea that in the summer, when officers are all on active service, Paris coquettes have to put up with civilian admirers, and as with so many of Dancourt's plays this actuality greatly contributed to its success. *Le Mari retrouvé* (1698)[1] is founded upon an actual event, recorded in *Les Causes célèbres*, the disappearance of a gentleman and the trial of his wife for his murder. On his re-appearing in order to establish her innocence, he was treated by the judges as an impostor and not till three and a half years later was his identity established by the Paris *Parlement*[2]. Dancourt, who wrote his play while the case was still undecided, has turned the gentleman into a miller and the judge of Châtillon-sur-Indre into a bailie. The first scene, between the lover (another Clitandre) and his valet, is of great promise and all the earlier scenes have the spirit of true comedy. But the later ones, as so often with Dancourt, degenerate into extravagance and farce. On the other hand, the *dramatis personae* are more varied than usual, and they include types of character as well as social types. Besides Clitandre, who, like his two namesakes, is a reformed rake, we have Charlot, a good-looking and rather fatuous peasant, and Colette, the miller's niece, an *ingénue* who in two excellent scenes with Charlot shews that she combines *esprit* and frankness with innocence and simplicity. Of the two remaining plays in vol. XIX of *Le Répertoire, Les Vendanges de Suresnes* (1695) was extremely successful. It was often revived during the first half of the eighteenth century and still survived in the early part of the nineteenth. It is a pure farce and must be judged as such, but though it might be highly amusing on the stage, its subject, the baiting and mystifying of a foolish provincial squire, leads us inevitably to compare it to its disadvantage with the immortal *Monsieur de Pourceaugnac. La Maison de Campagne* (1688), another farce, seems to me the weakest play in the volume, and I am surprised that

---

[1] A separate edition was published in 1878.
[2] *Hist. du théâtre françois*, XIV, 105.

Vanbrugh should have selected it for production on the English stage[1].

Of the three plays which accompany *Les Bourgeoises à la Mode* in vol. IV of *Le Répertoire, troisième ordre, Le Tuteur* (1695), which was highly successful, has the well-worn plot of a guardian (M. Bernard) who intends to marry his ward, but who is frustrated by the machinations of a lover, disguised as a journeyman painter, and his valet, disguised as a gardener, aided and abetted by the girl and her maid. The conduct of the plot is more logical and more natural than usual with Dancourt, except for the *dénouement*, in which an uncle of the girl suddenly appears as a *deus ex machina*. The only noteworthy character is that of Lucas, M. Bernard's gardener. In *Le Galant jardinier* (1704), which has a similar and equally conventional plot, the lover is disguised as an under-gardener and his valet as a sergeant of militia. Lucile resembles Colette of *Le Mari retrouvé* in being more of a true *ingénue* than most of Dancourt's young girls, and the long scene between her and Marton (ix), her maid, is admirable. "Si j'en crois ses yeux et mon cœur," she says to Marton in explanation of how she came to be in love. Whereupon Marton cuts her short with "Ses yeux et mon cœur! Comment diantre, voilà du style le plus tendre, le plus délicat. S'expliquer ainsi en sortant du couvent. Ah! nature, nature!" There is also an amusing scene between two stutterers (xvii), and Lucas, the head-gardener, is a good example of a greedy peasant. *Les Curieux de Compiègne*, produced on October 4, 1698, is a reminiscence of the great review held with unparalleled magnificence at Compiègne from August 30 to September 22 of that year[2]. The visit of two shopkeepers, one with his wife and daughter, and of the delightful Mme Robin, a Paris *bourgeoise*, to the camp, and their encounter with two officers, one of whom is in love with the shopkeeper's daughter, furnishes the occasion for some amusing scenes and for a good portrayal of *bourgeois* manners and sentiments.

---

[1] *Plays*, 2 vols. 1776, vol. II. An edition of *La Maison de Campagne* was published in 1878, and M. Roth has included it in his selection; "cet excellent vaudeville," he says, "est un modèle du genre."

[2] See Saint-Simon, *Mémoires*, ed. Chéruel, II, c. viii; ed. Boislisle, V, 348–375.

From the foregoing account of Dancourt's comedies it is clear that the chief interest is not so much in the individual plays as in the picture of contemporary society which they afford as a whole. It is in the main a picture of Paris *bourgeois* society. The *noblesse* is only represented by a few stray and shady specimens, whom the need of money has brought into relations, more or less discreditable, with the business world. Country-folk play a larger part, but even they figure in connexion with some retired professional or business man. Chief among the types who fill the picture are the *bourgeoises*, such as those of *Le Chevalier à la Mode, Les Bourgeoises à la Mode,* and *Les Bourgeoises de Qualité.* Their great ambition is to be regarded as *femmes de qualité,* to give gambling-parties and suppers, and above all to have their carriage. Their husbands are less ambitious. They usually belong to *la petite robe* or even to a lower professional class; bailies, attorneys, notaries, registrars, commissioners of police[1]. Of *la grande robe,* of the young magistrates "qui prennent de la cour ce qu'elle a de pire," and who become "des copies fidèles de très méchants originaux[2]," there are, so far as I can recollect, no examples. Nor is there any full-length portrait of a financier. To draw that was left to Lesage. However, after the production of *Turcaret,* Dancourt made a serious attempt with Trapolin in *Les Agioteurs*[3], a play in three acts, which he produced in 1710[4]. Trapolin, whose character is highly praised—too highly, to my mind—by Lemaître, was five or six years back a mere peasant, but when the play opens he is doing a large business as a bill discounter, money-changer, and money-lender. This business, which is described in great detail and in too technical language, affords the only interest in the play, for the plot, as too often with Dancourt, is very poor, indeed is barely existent. It may be noticed that there are as many as nineteen characters, and that generally in Dancourt's drama there is a tendency to increase the number of characters beyond what was customary in Molière's time[5].

[1] See especially *Les Bourgeoises de Qualité* and cp. Lemaître, *op. cit.* pp. 143–148.

[2] La Bruyère, *De la Ville.*

[3] See Lemaître, *op. cit.* pp. 148–164.

[4] *Théâtre,* vol. X.

[5] There are, however, 17 in *Le Bourgeois Gentilhomme* and 16 in *Don Juan.*

To the mixture of classes, which was becoming more and more common in Dancourt's day, there are scattered references. The Count in *Les Bourgeoises de Qualité*, who is in love with Angélique, but who is almost on the point of marrying the rich widow of a registrar, says to M. Naquart the solicitor, "Je me mettrai dans les affaires."—"Un homme de votre qualité dans les affaires?"—"Pourquoi non? Les gens d'affaires achètent nos terres, ils usurpent nos titres et nos noms même: quel inconvénient de faire leur métier, pour être quelque jour en état de rentrer dans nos maisons et dans nos charges[1]?"

That unpleasant person, the *chevalier d'industrie*, one of whose chief industries consists in sponging on the women to whom he makes love, is a fairly common figure and, as we have seen, furnishes the title-rôle in *Le Chevalier à la Mode*. Closely allied to him, for both alike are *hommes à bonnes fortunes*, is the noble rake, generally a gambler, who seeks to repair his broken fortunes by marriage—whether with an elderly widow or with a young girl is more or less a matter of indifference, provided that she has money. It will be remembered that in three comedies, *Les Bourgeoises de Qualité, L'Été des Coquettes*, and *Le Mari retrouvé*, he bears the name of Clitandre —an insult to the honest man and true gentleman whom we admire as the lover of Henriette in *Les Femmes savantes*.

The young girls, whose fate it is to marry these adventurers and rakes, are generally *ingénues*, fresh from the convent. They are ignorant of life, but they have a precocious curiosity to explore it. If Dancourt is to be trusted, the *jeune fille* has changed considerably since Molière's day. She is more independent, more inclined to revolt against parental control, and above all more ready to meet half-way the advances of an admirer. The three girls in *Les trois Cousines* are innocent enough at heart, but they do not hesitate to plan an elopement with their lovers. It is only the exceptions such as Lucile in *Le Galant jardinier* and Colette, the miller's niece, in *Le Mari retrouvé* who are intelligent without being forward or unmaidenly. But these are country girls. Angélique, the heroine

---

[1] Act III, Scene iv.

of *La Parisienne*[1] (a poor play), is, as her maid says, "une petite personne qui ira loin." Her parents have arranged for her a marriage with a well-to-do elderly *bourgeois*, but she has provided herself with a lover of her own and, in case he fails, with a couple of provisional suitors. In *La Foire de Bezons*[2], a lively bustling play, Chonchette is similarly described by Frosine, the *intrigante*, as "une enfant qui promet beaucoup," and she suggests the commentary that "aujourd'hui les filles naissent avec tant d'esprit que la plus jeune est quelquefois la plus habile."

Dancourt's valets and *soubrettes* conform pretty closely to the type which served Molière in his earlier comedies. But Frontin is a more cynical observer of life than Mascarille or Scapin and has a much keener eye to his own interests. Lisette is equally intelligent and equally alive to the main chance. She gives her young mistress shrewd advice and is ready to help her in her love affairs, but she is not really attached to her, like Dorine or Nicole or Toinette. Thus the new names stand for new types[3]. Another character, who is prepared to give her services in love affairs, especially when they are of a questionable nature, is the familiar *entremetteuse*, of whom we have a conspicuous example in Mme Thibaut. Dancourt has several varieties of the type, and to one of them, a character of *La Foire de Bezons*, he has given the name of their prototype, Molière's Frosine.

There is a special interest in types not represented in Molière, for instance, the officers in *Les Curieux de Compiègne*, *Le Retour des Officiers* (1697), and *La Foire de Bezons*, and the cleverly sketched *abbé* in *L'Été des Coquettes*, who is what Furetière in *Le Roman bourgeois* calls "un jeune abbé sans abbaye, c'est-à-dire un tonsuré de bonne famille," and belongs to the same type as La Bruyère's "jeune abbé avec des mouches et du rouge comme une femme." In Dancourt's

---

[1] One act, 1691 (*Théâtre*, vol. II).

[2] One act, 1695 (*Théâtre*, vol. IV). Marotte, in *Le Moulin de Javelle* (one act, 1695, vol. V), is equally precocious.

[3] See Lemaître, *op. cit.* pp. 182–185. He cites two significant passages from *Les Bourgeoises à la Mode* (I, iii and xiii).

comedy he wears a violet-blue doublet, an embroidered waist-coat, and lace ruffles, and he is powdered with Cyprus-powder. In *La Foire de Bezons* an *abbé* attends the fair in the company of a notary and a chorus girl. Other types which do not figure in Molière's gallery are the *cocher*, of which there is a notable example in *Le Moulin de Javelle*[1], and the female inn-keeper, who is well represented by Mme Bertrand in the same play and by Mme Pinuin in *Les Curieux de Compiègne*.

Another novelty in Dancourt's drama is the part played in it by peasants and village life. Several of his *bourgeois* have houses in the neighbourhood of Paris, and, as we have seen, La Brie is the scene of three plays[2]. In these we make the acquaintance of the village schoolmaster, the notary, and other local functionaries. In *Le Charivari* (1697)[3], *Les Vendanges de Suresnes*, *Le Galant jardinier*, and *Le Tuteur* an important part is played by the gardener—Thibaut in the two former plays, and Lucas in the two latter[4]. He speaks in the dialect of the neighbourhood of Paris, the dialect of the peasants of *Don Juan*. The majority of Dancourt's peasant characters—there are no less than three in *Le Mari retrouvé*—use the same dialect. They are generally represented as greedy of money, and shrewd where their own interests are concerned. One type of French country life is poorly represented, that is, the *hobereau* or small noble who lives on his estate. The three *hobereaux* who make a fugitive appearance in *La Maison de Campagne* (scenes xxix and xxx) are not even thought worthy of a name. It is a type which has not fared well in French comedy, for has it not been held up to eternal ridicule by Molière in M. de Pourceaugnac? But M. Halévy in his delightful little book on Vauban points out that the small rural nobles, both as landlords and soldiers, had deserved well of France. He declares that M. de Pourceaugnac merits our esteem; that he had been a brave officer, and that his real fault was that he was too poor to go to Versailles. He was in Louis XIV's words "un homme que je ne vois jamais,"

---

[1] See Lemaître, *op. cit.* p. 186.
[2] See above, p. 98.   [3] *Théâtre*, vol. VI.
[4] In *Le Médecin malgré lui* there is a Thibaut (a peasant) and a Lucas (a servant). Both speak in dialect.

and, as I have said, in the eyes of the Roi-Soleil he could have no graver fault.

Dancourt had not only a great knowledge of the stage, but he knew his public, and the success of many of his plays was due to their actuality. He had the instinctive *flair* of a journalist or a writer of revues. We have seen that *Les Curieux de Compiègne* and *Le Mari retrouvé* were founded upon actual events. So was *La Loterie* (1697), while *La Gazette de Hollande* (1692) was inspired by an anecdote of the time. *Le Moulin de Javelle, La Foire de Bezons, Les Vendanges de Suresnes, Le Retour des Officiers, Les Vacances*, are all concerned with topics of contemporary interest. *L'Opérateur Barry* is named after a popular charlatan of the day[1], and *L'Opéra de Village* (1692) was a satire on Pécourt, the composer of ballets for the Opera. *La Foire de Saint-Germain* (1696) was an attempt to rival a piece which Regnard and Dufresny had produced with great success the year before. *Le Diable boiteux* and *Le second Chapitre du Diable boiteux* followed closely—in the same year (1707)—on Lesage's story.

Dancourt's picture of society is, it must be confessed, a sordid one. Of course, it is not a complete picture. No dramatist or novelist—not even Balzac with all his pretensions—ever gives us a complete picture. They can only describe the world they know, and even their picture of this limited world is liable to be coloured by their own temperament. Some are optimists, some are pessimists; one man is a satirist, another a sentimentalist. Further, it is easier for a writer of comedy to excite laughter by portraying vice than by portraying virtue, and Dancourt was indolent and his morals were easy and accommodating. But, says Lemaître, "it is the business of the stage to concentrate in a few characters, and at the same time exaggerate, the vices and defects of an age; for it is almost entirely by its vices that one age is distinguished from another." There is something of a fallacy in this. Each age has its fashions and oddities, even its minor vices, but the more glaring vices are not peculiar either to ages or to countries, and the

---

[1] One act, 1702. *Théâtre*, vol. VIII (a poor play).

fundamental sins of human nature exist always and everywhere. However, allowing for the exaggeration inevitable to comedy we may accept Dancourt as an accurate observer and faithful reporter as far as he goes. We may accept as characteristic of his age the ignorant, dishonest and ostentatious *traitants*, the *bourgeoises* who wish to be thought *femmes de qualité*, the elderly women of doubtful character, and their gallants, the *chevaliers d'industrie* and *hommes à bonnes fortunes*. We may perhaps accept also, but with some reserve—for here stage-convention certainly plays a part—the rascally valets and self-seeking *soubrettes*, and the *ingénues* with their thinly-veiled immodesty. But we must not forget that there is another side to the picture. In his Septuagesima sermon *On Idleness* Bourdaloue declares that "you will find innocence only among those middle classes who live by work...shopkeepers engaged in a legitimate business, and artisans who reckon their days by the work of their hands, servants who fulfil literally the divine precept, 'Thou shalt eat the labours of thy hands[1].'"

Such is the comedy of Dancourt—interesting from the variety of social types to which he introduces us, and meritorious from the natural ease of his dialogue and his feeling for dramatic movement. It marks the vigorous beginnings of the comedy of manners, but it can shew no real masterpiece. For that we must turn to a dramatist of greater powers of concentration, a more industrious worker and a more conscientious artist.

5. Lesage[2].

The life of Alain-René Lesage (1668–1747) was an uneventful one, and may be briefly told. He was born at Sarzeau, an obscure Breton town in the peninsula of Rhuys, which with that of Locmariaquer protects the sea of Morbihan from the Atlantic. His father, who was a notary and registrar, died when

---

[1] *Œuvres*, ed. le Père Bretonneau, 16 vols. 1707–1734, vol. IV.

[2] *Œuvres*, 12 vols. 1821; *Le Théâtre de la Foire*, 10 vols. 1721–1737. *Hist. du théâtre françois*, XV, 6 ff. Brunetière, *Études critiques*, III; *Époques du théâtre français*. E. Lintilhac, *Lesage*, 1893 (*Les Grands Écrivains français*). Sir W. Scott, *Miscellaneous Prose Works*, 6 vols. 1827, vol. III.

he was nine, and his mother five years later. At fourteen he was sent to the neighbouring Jesuit College at Vannes, and then to Paris to study law. Like Dancourt, he was received as an advocate, and after marrying the pretty daughter of a master-joiner (1694) he, again like Dancourt, deserted the law, though not for the stage, but for literature. Before long he had the good fortune to find a patron in the Abbé de Lyonne (a son of Hugues de Lyonne), who paid him a pension of 600 *livres*. With this assistance Lesage was able to support his family by his pen, and for nearly half a century led a quiet *bourgeois* life in the *faubourg* Saint-Jacques. His marriage was a thoroughly happy one, and it was blessed with three sons and a daughter, whom he carefully educated to be good citizens and Christians. Of his sons, the eldest and the youngest went on the stage[1]— greatly to his annoyance—while the second took Orders and became a Canon at Boulogne. It was in this son's house, where he and his wife had gone to live about five years previously that he died in 1747 at the age of seventy-eight.

The Abbé de Lyonne did Lesage another good turn by directing his attention to Spanish literature. The first result of this was a volume entitled *Théâtre Espagnol* (1700), which contained translations of two plays, a drama by Francisco de Rojas Zorrilla (*Le Traître puni*[2]) and a comedy by Lope de Vega (*Garder et se garder*). In 1702 Lesage made his *début* at the Théâtre-Français with *Le Point d'honneur*, translated from another comedy (*No hay amigo para amigo*) by Rojas Zorrilla. The piece was a failure and its author, leaving the drama for the novel, produced in 1704 a translation of the spurious continuation of *Don Quixote* which had appeared in 1614 under the pseudonym of Avellaneda. Fitzmaurice-Kelly describes it as "a clever, brutal, cynical, amusing book," and Lesage adapted

---

[1] The eldest, whose stage name was Montmény (not Montmesnil), acted at the Théâtre-Français. He was first-rate in the parts of valets and peasants, and he was also excellent as Turcaret. He predeceased his father in 1743.

[2] Dancourt produced a version of Rojas Zorrilla's drama in verse under the title of *La Trahison punie* (1717). Vanbrugh's *False Friend* (1702) is a free version of Lesage's play, but he has restored some of his cuts, probably from a literal French translation of the Spanish original (*D.N.B.*).

it to the taste of the French public with such skill that it went through four editions in his lifetime. In fact, throughout the second half of the work he is less an adapter than an original author.

In the summer of 1707 he again had recourse to a Spanish author for the ground-work of a story. His original this time was *El Diablo cojuelo* (1641) by Luis Vélez de Guevara, and he gave the same title, *Le Diable boiteux*, to his version of it[1]. The account of how a scholar of Alcala, named Don Cléofas, released a lame devil from a bottle is taken from the Spanish story with little alteration, but, whereas *El Diablo cojuelo* is mainly a novel of incident, Lesage treats the adventures of the scholar and his guide in such a way as to make them a series of observations on the society of Madrid (Paris), and, following the pattern of La Bruyère, gives them the form either of portraits, characters or anecdotes. These fill six of the original sixteen chapters (iii, vi, xi, xii, xiv, xvi), the remainder consisting of the two introductory chapters, *Les Amours du Comte de Belflor*, a well told romantic story (iv and v), *La Force de l'Amitié* (xiii and xv), three short stories (viii–x) and the account of how the devil avenged Don Cléofas on his faithless mistress (vii). The stories are translated or imitated from other Spanish sources than Guevara, but Lesage has largely drawn on him for the portraits and anecdotes. He has also borrowed freely from *Les Caractères* and from the comedy of the seventeenth century, partly from the common stock of conventional types, and partly from particular writers—Molière, Quinault, Dancourt, Dufresny. There is very little of first-hand observation, Lesage's originality, as M. Vic points out, consisting in the number of his portraits and the rapidity with which they are drawn. By this means he produces the illusion of a crowd and of movement and gives us a well-filled and living picture of the Paris society of his day. On the other hand, many of the portraits are drawn too rapidly and not a few lack significance. The satire is sometimes too bitter and the general effect is too uniformly sordid. Lesage has not yet attained to the concen-

---

[1] See for the title-page *Le Petit*, p. 477. The Spanish work is divided into ten *trancos* or strides ; Lesage only borrows from the first four of these.

tration and selective power of *Turcaret*, or to that large toler-ance and psychological insight which distinguish *Gil Blas*.

Whatever may be the defects of *Le Diable boiteux*, it ob-tained an instant and phenomenal popularity—partly owing to the personal allusions which it was supposed to contain. A second edition was at once put in hand and appeared, with a good many alterations in unimportant details, in the autumn. A third followed in October, but though fresh editions were issued at Lyons and Amsterdam, there was no further Paris edition till 1726, when Lesage made considerable changes and added six new chapters[1].

Shortly before the publication of *Le Diable boiteux* Lesage had returned to the stage with *Don César Ursin* (March 15, 1707), a free rendering of Calderón's *Peor esta que estava*, but the public of the Théâtre-Français received it badly. On the other hand, they welcomed with applause a little one-act piece which accompanied it, which was entirely the work of Lesage. *Crispin Rival de son Maître*, as the piece was called, has the rapidity of movement, the skill in ravelling and unravelling a plot, the fidelity to nature, which its author had learnt from his Spanish models. It is also full of gaiety, and the gaiety is pointed by keen satirical hits at society, which give a foretaste of *Le Mariage de Figaro*.

The success of *Crispin Rival de son Maître* encouraged Lesage to offer two more comedies, both in one act, to the Comédie-Française. The first, which he called *Les Étrennes*, hoping that it would be produced on January 1, 1708, was refused outright. The second, *La Tontine*, was read and accepted at the end of February for performance after Easter, but, probably for reasons of State—for Lesage had represented the tontine as a gambling transaction—it was not played till twenty-four years later. *La Tontine* out of hand, Lesage set to work upon *Turcaret*; it was

---

[1] The above account is founded on the exhaustive and admirable article, *La composition et les sources du Diable boiteux de Lesage* by M. Jean Vic in the *Rev. d'hist. litt.* XXVII (1920), 48 ff. The 2nd and 3rd editions are only known to him by one copy of each, that of the 3rd edition being in the *Bibliotheca Nacional* of Madrid. The 1726 edition is in 2 vols. of 11 and 10 chapters respectively, the new chapters being I, xi and II, vi–x, while I, vii corresponds to chapters vi and vii of the original edition.

read before the company on May 15, 1708, and accepted. But the *traitants*, when they learnt the import of the new piece, brought all their influence, backed no doubt by solid arguments, to bear upon the comedians, to induce them to postpone its production, and it was not till the Dauphin issued an order that the piece should be rehearsed and played without delay that the opposition was overcome. On February 14, in the terrible winter of 1709, *Turcaret* was presented to the public. It ran for seven performances, the receipts at the last performance amounting to 653 *livres* and 4 *sols*. This cannot be accounted a success, but it was not, as it has sometimes been represented to be, a complete failure. Lesage, however, must have remembered La Bruyère's saying, "Un projet assez vain serait de vouloir tourner un homme fort sot et fort riche en ridicule; les rieurs sont de son côté."

The plot of *Turcaret*[1] is very simple, if, indeed, it can be said to have any plot at all. The Baronne de Porcandorf (her name is mentioned casually in the Fourth Act), the young widow of a foreign colonel who had been killed in Flanders, has designs on M. Turcaret, a rich *traitant*, and he has promised to marry her. But he is in no hurry to fulfil his promise, nor is she in any hurry to hold him to it, for she is quite content with the considerable presents which he daily makes her. Meanwhile, she is infatuated with a certain *chevalier d'industrie*, who dissipates the fruits of her conquest at the gambling-table. At the end of the First Act Frontin, the *Chevalier's* valet, puts the situation in a nut-shell:

J'admire le train de la vie humaine! Nous plumons une coquette, la coquette mange un homme d'affaires; l'homme d'affaires en pille d'autres: cela fait un ricochet de fourberies le plus plaisant du monde.

At this point Frontin takes command; he finds a new maid for the *Baronne* in the person of his pupil and confederate Lisette, and he himself enters the service of M. Turcaret. As the play develops we learn more about Turcaret. The son of a pastry-cook, he began life as a lackey. He carries on usury in the name of one of his clerks. He has persuaded a young cashier,

[1] I have used the edition of Mr A. Hamilton Thompson (Cambridge 1918) which follows the text of 1821.

who owes his post to him, to lend him 20,000 *francs* out of his partner's funds. A dealer in old clothes, who comes to see the *Baronne* on business, reveals that he is her brother and that he has a wife. Finally he is arrested on a writ issued by his partners for the cashier's embezzlement. His exposure involves that of the *Chevalier*, for the *Baronne* discovers that he has been swindling her. So she loses both prospective husband and lover. Frontin alone triumphs, for he has secured 40,000 *francs* with which to start life with his Lisette. "Voilà le règne de M. Turcaret fini; le mien va commencer." On this note the play ends.

It must not be supposed that, because *Turcaret* has practically no plot, it is badly constructed. It is true that the technique is less strict than that of the older comedy—eight, for instance, of the thirteen characters are not even mentioned in the First Act—but it is of much more importance that the play goes steadily forward without any diminution of interest to its appointed end, which is the downfall of Turcaret. This is partly due to the thoroughly business-like and effective character of the dialogue. Nearly every speech, nearly every word even, bears on the action. There are no long *tirades*, no scintillating interchanges of wit, there is nothing to distract the reader or spectator from the interest of the drama. But the dialogue is neither dull nor commonplace. It is as easy and as natural as Dancourt's, and, as M. Lintilhac has admirably pointed out[1], it is seasoned with dramatic *esprit*, that is to say, with the *esprit* which lights up with a flash of wit or humour the true inwardness of a situation or a character. M. Lintilhac gives, as instances of this quality, Marine's "Il ne se tuera point, madame, il ne se tuera point" (of the *Chevalier*) and her "Ils n'ont pas de quoi la payer," when Frontin says, "Nous allons prendre la poste." Here and there, indeed, the *esprit* takes a form which is not suited to the particular speaker, as when Marine says, "Cette approbation vaut mieux . que celle de l'Académie." But when Mr Hamilton Thompson objects that the *Baronne* is incapable of the *esprit* which she shews in her dialogue with Turcaret and the *Chevalier*[2], he forgets that a

[1] *Lesage*, pp. 154–158.　　　　[2] *Turcaret*, p. xli.

woman may be vain, infatuated, and even credulous, and yet be alert in her conversation. Many a fool is a good talker. *Turcaret* is a remorseless attack on the *traitants* or farmers of the taxes. At the time that Lesage wrote it, they were at the height of their power. The disasters of the war since the battle of Blenheim and its ever-increasing expenses compelled Louis and his ministers to turn more and more to them for financial assistance. And as a natural consequence they drove harder and harder bargains. A special cause of their unpopularity with the *bourgeois* class to which Lesage belonged was the issue of paper money in the form of notes for which the holders could not obtain payment, even in part, from the Treasury. This drove them to the money-lenders—and nearly every *traitant* was under the rose a money-lender—who discounted their notes at higher and higher rates of interest. Thus, at the end of 1706 the rate was 54 per cent., and in spite of all Chamillart's efforts to reduce the amount of paper money, 173 million *francs* of it was still in circulation at the end of 1707[1].

One of the objections to Lesage's play was that the portraits were too life-like. As a matter of fact, probably none of his characters were portraits, and except for Turcaret it does not appear that any original was suggested. The *traitant* of the time who comes nearest to Lesage's hero was Paul Poisson, who was originally a lackey, like Turcaret, and who when he became rich assumed the aristocratic surname of Bourvallais. He was very ignorant and often made himself ridiculous, but he had a remarkable aptitude for finance. In 1705 he narrowly escaped sharing in the bankruptcy of another financier and ex-lackey, La Noue. But he survived the crisis and in 1708 he was fabulously rich with a superb *hôtel* in the Place de Vendôme and a charming country house at Champ on the Marne[2]. Even richer and of a higher character for probity was Samuel Bernard, whom Saint-Simon describes as "the most famous and the richest

---

[1] *Histoire de France*, ed. E. Lavisse, VIII, i. 180 f.

[2] He owned fifteen *seigneuries* in La Brie, and his fortune was estimated at about 15 million *livres* (see Saint-Simon, ed. Boislisle, XVI, 685 ff.). Yet another ex-lackey was Raymond, who died a *fermier-général* (Gaiffe, *L'Envers du Grand Siècle*, p. 120).

banker in Europe." Nine days before Lesage's play was read
before the Comédie-Française Desmarets presented him to the
king at Marly. Louis received him most graciously and personally conducted him round the gardens. Saint-Simon and
others wondered at "the king's prostitution, as it were, to a
man like Bernard[1]," but they soon learnt the reason. The
banker, enchanted by the king's graciousness, furnished the
Exchequer with a much larger sum than Desmarets had hoped
for, with the result that in the following January, a month
before the production of *Turcaret*, he had to suspend payment.
He was extremely insolent, arrogant, and vain, but he was
generous and charitable, and his house at Paris, where he kept
great state, was frequented by the best society. Hénault, who
was a visitor there in his youth, and who gives a graphic
description of Bernard's character, says expressly that "he was
not M. Jourdain and not M. Turcaret[2]."

We have seen that the world of finance is represented in
Dancourt's comedy by a few rapidly sketched figures, of whom
the most memorable are M. Patin in *L'Été des coquettes*, Trapolin
in *Les Agioteurs*, and Rapineau in *Le Retour des Officiers*, but
that he has not given us a full-length portrait of a financier.
This we have for the first time in Turcaret[3]. In the first scene
in which he appears (I, vi) he is represented as ignorant, vain,
and credulous (so far resembling M. Jourdain). Then, when
Marine has informed him of the *Baronne's* relations with the
Chevalier, he becomes insolent, abusive, and violent (II, iii)—
"J'ai déjà cassé la grande glace et les plus belles porcelaines."
But after the *Baronne's* lying explanations he is again credulous,
infatuated (II, v, vi), and boastful (III, iv), till the *Marquis's*

---

[1] *Mémoires*, V, 457-458.

[2] Hénault, *Mémoires*, ed. F. Rousseau, 1911. The passage is translated
by Mr Hamilton Thompson, *Turcaret*, pp. xxvi f. MM. Bourgeois and
André suggest that the portrait of Turcaret may have been inspired by
certain pamphlets which appeared in the years 1706-1708—*Nouvelle école
publique des finances ou l'art de voler sans ailes*, 1706; *Les partisans
démasqués*, 1707 ; *Pluton maltôtier, nouvelle galante*, 1708 (Bourgeois and
André, *op. cit.* IV, No. 3095). Gaiffe, *op. cit.* pp. 119-132, quotes from the first
and last. I have only seen the last.

[3] Griffet in Boursault's *Ésope à la Cour* (1701) is only a sketch.

revelations threaten to undermine his position (III, v, vi).
Hitherto he has appeared as a fool, but in the famous scene
with his clerk, M. Rafle, who carries on his money-lending
business for him, he shews that he has all the qualities necessary
for success in his profession. He is cool-headed, bold, unscru-
pulous, merciless. In this scene we recognise the truth of two
remarks of La Bruyère: "Il faut moins d'esprit que d'habitude
ou d'expérience pour faire sa fortune," and "Un bon financier
ne pleure ni ses amis, ni sa femme, ni ses enfants[1]." The rest of
the play does not add much to our knowledge of Turcaret, but
we learn that he has agreed to make his wife an allowance on
condition that she does not come to Paris and that he owes her
for five quarters (V, x).

Turcaret is firmly and admirably drawn. He is a type rather
than a strongly-marked individual, but as a type he is a masterpiece, for he is not only the type of the *traitant* as he existed
in France during the last twenty years of the seventeenth
century and the first twenty or more of the eighteenth, but he
is the type of the man in every age who, starting from nothing,
has risen by ignoble and dishonest methods to wealth and
position. The modern profiteer in his ignorance, his ostentation,
and his greed is a living incarnation of Turcaret.

The picture of Turcaret is completed by the addition of his
clerk, M. Rafle, *qui tient son bureau d'usure*, and of his foolish
valet, Flamand, for whom he procures a snug post at Falaise
with plenty of opportunity for making money dishonestly. But
the finishing touch is given by the *Baronne*. The ex-lackey,
the ex-usurer on a small scale, makes up for many years of
hard work and privation by indulgence in every kind of extravagance and luxury, and not the least expensive of his
luxuries is "gallantry." Turcaret, if we may believe his wife,
has several mistresses. To the *Baronne* he is apparently laying
siege in a more regular fashion, but his love-making consists
chiefly in giving her costly presents both of money and

---

[1] *Des biens de fortune.* Cp. Turcaret's own view: "Un bel esprit n'est
pas nécessaire pour faire son chemin. Hors moi et deux ou trois autres,
il n'y a parmi nous que des génies assez communs. Il suffit d'un certain
usage, d'une routine que l'on ne manque guère d'attraper" (II, vi).

jewels. This exactly suits her, for she is a typical adventuress. The widow of a foreign colonel, she has spent the little money that he left her, and her only resource is M. Turcaret. "You must either marry him, or ruin him," says the candid Marine. "At the worst you will retrieve from his shattered fortune enough to set up your carriage and to figure brilliantly in society. Thus, whatever people may say, they will unconsciously fall into the habit of regarding you as a woman of quality."

But this admirable programme will fail, Marine goes on to point out, if the *Baronne* persists in her infatuation for the *Chevalier*[1]. He is less interesting and less powerfully drawn than the other two. He lives by his wits, but he is not witty; he makes love to most women that he comes across, old or young, but he does so chiefly for the profit that he gets out of them. He is in fact a *chevalier d'industrie* rather than an *homme à bonnes fortunes*. A more original character, but equally typical of the age, is the Marquis de La Tribaudière, the one tolerably good fellow in the play. Not that he is an ornament of society. He sleeps all the day and drinks, except when he is dancing, all the night. Consequently he is seldom seen sober, and his appearance in that condition in the Fifth Scene of the Third Act provokes a comment from the Baroness. Among the other minor characters are Mme Turcaret, who calls herself a Countess and gives herself the airs of a woman of quality, and M. Turcaret's sister, Mme Jacob, *revendeuse à la toilette* and *entremetteuse*. Both are familiar types, but a delightful touch is given to the portrait of Mme Turcaret by her description of the society at Valognes (a small town near Cherbourg) of which she is the chief ornament. "J'ose dire que ma maison est une école de politesse et de galanterie pour les jeunes gens" (V, vii). Moreover when she adds, "On joue chez moi, on s'y rassemble pour médire....J'y donne aussi quelquefois des fêtes galantes, des soupés-collations," she might be describing the salon of a

---

[1] The relations between the three recall, as has been frequently pointed out, those between M. Jourdain, Dorante, and Dorimène, but Dorante has the impertinence of a fine gentleman, and I doubt whether Dorimène is an adventuress.

bourgeoise at Paris who aspired to be a *femme de qualité*, and weare at once reminded of Dancourt's *Les Bourgeoises à la Mode*.

Of M. Rafle and M. Furet Mr Hamilton Thompson says truly that "their names are guides to their occupations." They must be most amusing figures on the stage, and Turcaret rightly describes M. Furet, a rascally friend of Frontin's, who pretends to be a sheriff's officer, as "un plaisant original." Of M. Rafle, Turcaret's clerk for his business as a usurer, it need only be said that he represents to the life one's conception of the type.

There remain three characters who figure more prominently in the play, and they are all servants. It is true that Marine disappears after the First Act, but during that act she is seldom absent or silent. She is perfectly ready to aid and abet her mistress in plundering Turcaret—"Il a de l'argent, il est prodigue et crédule; c'est un homme fait pour les coquettes"— but the *Baronne* must play the game fairly; she must not spend on the *Chevalier* the plunder that she gets out of Turcaret. Marine is candid and vivacious. "Elle a des reparties brillantes qui m'enlèvent," says the *Chevalier*, when he suffers from her tongue. Indeed, as I have observed above, her mordant wit is sometimes too brilliant for her station. Frontin is her equal in wit and humour and irony. He has all the resourcefulness of Mascarille and Scapin and their many descendants. But he differs from these in his outlook on life. He is not content to be a valet all his days. His ideal, which is less vague, more positive than Hector's in *Le Joueur* or Valentin's in *Les Ménechmes*, is to make money quickly and dishonestly and then settle down as a respectable citizen. "Après quelque temps de fatigue et de peine, je parviendrai enfin à un état d'aise. Alors quelle satisfaction! quelle tranquillité d'esprit! Je n'aurai plus à mettre en repos que ma conscience." He has no intention of becoming, like other valets in the service of financiers, a clerk or a revenue-officer; he will continue to make money dishonestly, but he will make it in the world of high finance, and he and his Lisette will be respected in their quarter. Lisette will make him an admirable helpmeet. She does not make witty speeches; she does not even talk much; but whatever she says is to the point. She is quite as wideawake as Frontin, and she has the same ambitions. She is tired of being a *soubrette*. So she keeps Frontin up to the mark, and she has a secret presentiment that with him for a husband she will become one day a *femme de qualité*.

I have dwelt in some detail on the characters of Lesage's play, because it is only by so doing that we can fully realise why it is generally regarded as the first great French comedy of manners. It is so by its careful selection of types and by the creative force which embodies these types in characters that live. It brings to the light with completeness and fidelity a dangerous and growing plague-spot in Parisian society—the power of money[1]. It is therefore natural to compare it with *Le Chevalier à la Mode* and *Les Bourgeoises à la Mode* of Dancourt and Saint-Yon, in both of which money plays a conspicuous part, especially in *Le Chevalier à la Mode*. The inferiority of Dancourt's play to *Turcaret* lies partly in the unsatisfying representation of its central character, and partly in the lack of precision and firmness with which the other characters, except Mme Patin, are drawn. *Les Bourgeoises à la Mode* has a far better claim to be called a great comedy, for the types portrayed in it stand out in much greater relief on the canvas. Araminte and her step-daughter, the *ingénue*, are delicately as well as firmly drawn; Mme Amelin is a masterly portrait of which Mme Jacob is but a slighter reproduction; finally, Frontin and Lisette, as I have already said, are worthy forerunners of the same-named pair in Lesage's play. The dialogue too is worthy to be compared with that of *Turcaret*. But, in spite of these merits, Dancourt's comedy, with its complicated plot of many threads, and the suddenness with which these threads are cut rather than disentangled, is far less effective as a comedy of manners than *Turcaret*. The very absence of plot (in the narrower sense of the term) in Lesage's masterpiece, leads us to concentrate all our attention on the characters and on the social conditions of which they are the results. It has been said that the play lacks a moral purpose

---

[1] M. Lintilhac refers to Ponsard's *L'Honneur et l'Argent* and Augier's *La Question d'argent* as descended from *Turcaret* (*Lesage*, pp. 196–198).

and that Lesage regards the corrupt society, of which he draws the picture, with tolerant and amused eyes. But the thoroughness and the fidelity with which the picture is drawn, and then left without any comment to our contemplation, is more effective as a moral lesson than if it were dinned into our ears by preaching or indignation. One may prefer the method of Molière—though his morality too has been called in question —who matches vice with virtue and mingles honest folk with his rascals, but one must admit that Lesage's simpler method has its merits. If he paints for us a vicious world, he neither exaggerates nor extenuates its viciousness.

The hindrance which the comedians had offered to the production of *Turcaret* and the very moderate success which it had when produced disgusted Lesage with the Théâtre-Français, and accordingly he devoted his dramatic activities in the future to the theatres of the fairs, of which the chief at this time were the Foire Saint-Germain held from February 1 to Palm Sunday on the site of the Marché Saint-Germain, and the Foire Saint-Laurent, held from August 9 to September 29 on the site of the Gare de l'Est. At each of these fairs a considerable number of small theatres provided variety entertainments, and these included in their programme farces and comedies, partly in French and partly in Italian, and interspersed with songs and dances. The expulsion of the Italians in 1697 was the signal for greatly increased activity on the part of the *forains*, who regarded themselves as inheritors of the Italian *répertoire*. But there were great difficulties in their path. Dialogue was forbidden them as infringing the privileges of the Comédie-Française and singing as infringing those of the Opera. But at last thanks to the great perseverance and ingenuity of their actor-managers they succeeded in establishing on their boards two kinds of drama, *comédie en vaudevilles* and *comédie en ariettes*, the only difference between them being that the songs in the former were sung to old airs and those in the latter to new ones. The second kind developed into the *opéra comique* and both kinds were sometimes called by that name[1].

[1] See for the above Lintilhac, *op. cit.* pp. 11–20. Favart, the famous director of the *Opéra comique*, whose *Les trois Sultanes* (1761) achieved so

Lesage, with his dramatic skill and especially his gift of pointed dialogue and rapid movement, was a godsend to the *forains*. In 1712 he gave them a piece, which was never printed, called *Les Petits-Maîtres*, and in the following year he wrote for them two farces, *Arlequin, Roi de Serendib*, and *Arlequin invisible*, to both of which he gave an Oriental setting. But of the hundred pieces or more with which he and his collaborators, Fuzelier and Dorneval, enriched the *Théâtre de la Foire* only these two belong to the reign of Louis XIV. In 1714 he was engaged upon a greater work, which appeared at the beginning of 1715[1]. It was the first two volumes of *Gil Blas*. But as this was only the first part (books I–VI) of a work which was not completed till 1736 and which marks a new and important development in the history of the French novel, I shall say nothing about it here, but shall go on at once to consider the work of our two remaining writers of comedy—Regnard and Dufresny.

6. *Regnard*[2].

Jean-François Regnard (1655–1709) was, like Molière and Dancourt, the son of a well-to-do Paris *bourgeois*, and like them he received a good education, without, however, applying himself very seriously to his studies[3]. Having lost his father when he was only two, he found himself, on coming to man's estate, master of a considerable fortune. Being now independent,

---

remarkable a success, is a direct descendant of Lesage, Fuzelier, and Dorneval.

[1] Some copies of the first edition bear the date of 1714.

[2] *Œuvres*, 2 vols. 1708 (some copies are dated 1707; see Le Petit, pp. 471–472); 2 vols. Brussels, 1711; 5 vols. 1731 (the first edition to include the *Voyages*, *La Provençale*, and the *Poésies diverses*); 6 vols. 1789–1790 (the first complete edition, with good introductory prefaces by C.-G.-T. Garnier), reprinted 1810 and 1820; 6 vols. 1820 (Didot); 6 vols. 1822 (Crapelet); 2 vols. 1854 (Delahays). *Théâtre*, ed. G. d'Heylli, 2 vols. 1876 (7 plays). Sainte-Beuve, *Causeries du Lundi*, VII, 1 ff. J.-J. Weiss, *Essais sur l'histoire de la littérature française*, 1891. F. Sarcey, *Quarante ans de théâtre, Molière et la comédie classique*, 1900, pp. 225–251. P. Toldo in *Rev. d'hist. litt.* 1903, 25 ff.; 1904, 56 ff.; 1905, 424 ff. (a laborious investigation into Regnard's sources).

[3] The father called himself Renard. Jean-François, like Molière, was baptized in the Church of Saint-Eustache.

he set out on his travels and paid two visits to Italy. But on his return from his second visit he was captured by pirates and carried off to Algiers, and thence to Constantinople. Here he spent two years in rigorous captivity, till he was ransomed for 10,000 *livres*. The episode, which incidentally shews that the *dénouement* of *L'Avare* (produced ten years earlier) with its story of shipwreck and corsairs was not so improbable as might be supposed, was made more romantic by a love affair with a charming Arlésienne who was his fellow-captive. Regnard has himself recounted the story, with some alterations, in *La Provençale*[1]. The husband of the lady—Mme de Prade in real life, Elvire in the story—was left at Algiers when she and Regnard were taken to Constantinople, and Mme de Prade, having had news of his death, was prepared to marry Regnard on their return to Arles. Unfortunately M. de Prade, who had also been ransomed, suddenly appeared at Arles, and Regnard lost his bride. As a cure for his disappointment he set out again on his travels in April 1681, and with two companions visited Holland, Denmark, Sweden, Lapland, Poland, Turkey, Hungary and Germany.

Returning to Paris in December 1682, he settled in a comfortable house at the top of the Rue Richelieu, where he entertained his friends with generous prodigality. Among his more illustrious guests were the Duc de Bourbon, La Bruyère's pupil, and the Prince de Conti.

> Conti, le grand Conti, que la gloire environne,
> Plus orné par son nom que par une couronne.

The house and its hospitality are well described by Regnard himself in the epistle—an invitation to a friend—from which the above lines are taken[2]. He also acquired a country house at Grillon, near Dourdan, about 35 miles south-west of Paris, where he dispensed good cheer on the same generous scale.

> Grand'chère, vin délicieux,
> Belle maison, liberté tout entière,
> Bals, concerts, enfin tout ce qui peut satisfaire
> Le goût, les oreilles et les yeux.

> .　　.　　.　　.　　.

---

[1] Ed. E. Pilon (*Chefs-d'œuvre méconnus*), 1920.
[2] *Épître* vi. A M*** (printed by Pilon).

> Les dames, le jeu, ny le vin,
> Ne m'arrachent point à moy-même;
> Et cependant je bois, je joue et j'aime.
> Faire tout ce qu'on veut, vivre exempt de chagrin,
> Ne se rien refuser, voilà tout mon système;
> Et de mes jours ainsi j'attraperai la fin[1].

Regnard proved a true prophet, for less than six years after he wrote this frank exposition of his "system" of life, he died suddenly at Grillon—it is said from the results of too much good cheer—on September 5, 1709.

Regnard's connexion with the stage began in 1688, when, at the age of thirty-three, he produced *Le Divorce* at the Italian theatre. Six other pieces, all of a broadly farcical character, followed, but not even the latest and best, *La Coquette*, has much attraction for the modern reader[2]. In 1692 he made acquaintance at the gambling-table with a kindred spirit in the person of Charles Dufresny and for four years the pair collaborated in writing pieces for the Italians. It was just the kind of work to suit their indolent, easy-going temperaments, for the plays were made up of more or less detached scenes, with little or no attempt at characterisation. Their joint production amounted to four plays, of which *La Foire de Saint-Germain* (1695)[3] had an enormous success. A year later the partnership was abruptly ended by a quarrel which arose out of the production of Regnard's *Le Joueur* at the Comédie-Française. His connexion with that theatre had begun two years earlier with *Attendez-moi sous l'Orme* (May 1694), a clever and bright little prose-comedy in one act[4]. It was followed in July by *La Sérénade*[5], which though more successful than its predecessor, is a poorer play. It is said to have been

---

[1] *Œuvres*, 1820, II. Compare *Chanson faite à Grillon en* 1703 (*Œuvres*, IV, 428), in which he describes Grillon as a true Abbey of Thelema.

[2] For the titles of these pieces with references to the volumes of Gherardi in which they are to be found, see Lintilhac, *op. cit.* IV, 36 n.[1]

[3] Regnard, *Œuvres*, VI; the play is very dull to read.

[4] The brothers Parfait, who shew a strong bias in favour of Dufresny and against Regnard, attribute this play to the former, but Dufresny never claimed it. The confusion arose from the fact that Dufresny produced at the Italian theatre in 1695 a play which has the same title (a proverbial saying), but which is totally different. (See Regnard, *Œuvres*, II, 429–441.)

[5] *Œuvres*, II.

originally destined for the Italian theatre, as, indeed, is evident from the nature of the piece. In his next play, *Le Bourgeois de Falaise*, or *Le Bal*[1] (as it is generally called), Regnard adopted verse as his medium. It has hardly any plot and is not particularly amusing.

Of the remaining seven plays—*La Critique du Légataire* is negligible—that Regnard wrote for the Comédie-Française four have kept their place—or had until recently—in the *répertoire*. Of the three that have dropped out, *Le Distrait* (1697)[2] in five acts of verse is founded upon one of La Bruyère's least successful "characters," Ménalque. Léandre, whose eccentricity gives his name to the play, is a complete failure; his blunders are not merely unnatural and meaningless but they are not even amusing. But Clarice, with whom he is in love and who returns his love, is a charming type of a sensible and virtuous girl—a type all too uncommon in the comedy of our period— and the *Chevalier* is a really original creation. "Égoïste avec naïveté,...étourdi, abandonné, sans principes, sans scrupule, avec cela toujours prêt à devenir sage et toujours vivant à la dérive." Such is Weiss's happy description of him, and he adds, "Il faut l'insouciance du caractère français pour qu'un si franc libertin ne soit pas un homme perdu, et pour que ses maximes n'en fassent pas un fripon[3]."

Le Retour imprévu (February 1700)[4], in one act of prose, is founded, like Larivey's *Les Esprits*, on the *Mostellaria* of Plautus. It is lively and amusing enough, but except in the last two scenes, the scenes with the drunken *Marquis*, it is devoid of humour. *Démocrite* (January 1700), a verse play in five acts, has more real merit. It is agreeable to read, well constructed, and carefully written. Its best known and most successful scene, however, that between Strabon and Cléanthis (Act IV, Sc. vii), was invented by Mlle Beauval and La Thorillière.

The four plays that are still in the *répertoire* are, in order of production, *Le Joueur* (1696), *Les Folies amoureuses* (1704), *Les Ménechmes* (1705), and *Le Légataire universel* (1708).

---

[1] *Œuvres*, II.   [2] *Théâtre*, I.
[3] *Essais*, p. 260.   [4] *Théâtre*, I.

Les Folies amoureuses[1] has been highly praised by Sainte-Beuve, but it seems to me no better and no worse than *Le Retour imprévu*. Its plot is the old one of the elderly guardian who wants to marry his ward, and the other characters—her maid, Lisette[2], her lover and his valet—are equally conventional. The chief fun is when the ward, Agathe, pretends to be mad, and dresses up in various characters. This is excellent fooling, no doubt, on the stage, but it does not provoke much mirth in the study. *Les Ménechmes*[1], a five-act comedy in verse, was revived with great success at the Odéon in 1884. The theme of twins who cannot be distinguished apart is an old one and offers an easy opportunity for a series of laughable misunderstandings; Regnard has managed these with his usual gaiety and knowledge of the stage. There is nothing remarkable about the characters. Valentin and Finette are like nearly all the other valets and *soubrettes* in Regnard's comedies. They combine head with heart; they have *esprit* and even a touch of humour; they are alive to their own interests, but they have a certain attachment to their employers, and they are frankly in love with one another. The two Ménechmes, though exactly alike in appearance, are a complete contrast in character and manners. The *Chevalier*, amiable, witty, and charming, is at bottom a true *chevalier d'industrie*. Sarcey rightly calls him "le dernier des hommes," but Regnard, with his characteristic outlook on life, evidently regards him with some sympathy. His twin is passing honest, but he is rude in manner and brutal in speech, and his willingness to marry the elderly aunt, Araminte, who at the opening of the play is her niece's rival with the *Chevalier*, shews a complete bluntness of sensibility. Araminte herself, though a well-worn type, is a spirited sketch. But the chief merit of the play is in the sustained vivacity of the dialogue and the brilliance of the verse[3].

I have left to the last *Le Légataire universel* and *Le Joueur*, partly because they are generally acclaimed as Regnard's masterpieces, and partly because they best represent the two

[1] *Théâtre*, II.
[2] This part was Mlle Beauval's last creation; she had acted with Molière.
[3] Sarcey, *op. cit.* pp. 229–244.

different types of comedy which he cultivated—the lively and often rollicking farce and the comedy of character. Forty years ago when Regnard was still regarded as second—*longo intervallo*, but still second—to Molière as a writer of comedy, it was a common opinion among critics that *Le Légataire universel* was more in accord with Regnard's genius than *Le Joueur* and therefore to be preferred. This was the view alike of J.-J. Weiss, a brilliant, if erratic critic, and of Francisque Sarcey, who represented so admirably the common sense of the average playgoer. I venture to differ from this view. To my mind, not only does *Le Joueur* belong to a higher type of comedy than its rival, but it is a more successful example of its *genre*. The fault of *Le Légataire universel*, *pace* Weiss and Sarcey, is that it is not laughable enough. It is no doubt full of gaiety, but only some of the scenes are provocative of real laughter. The first funny scene is that with the apothecary, M. Clistorel (Act II, Scene x). With the masquerading of Crispin, first as Géronte's nephew (III, ii) and then as his widowed niece (III, vi), the fun becomes more hilarious, and in the scene (IV, vi) in which Crispin counterfeits the dying Géronte and dictates to the notary a will in favour of his master, Ergaste, not forgetting himself and Lisette, and in that in which the notary reads the will to the resuscitated Géronte (V, vi) the fun reaches its climax. But these are only five scenes out of nearly forty. Compared with *Le Chapeau de Paille*, *La Cagnotte*, and *L'Affaire de la rue Lourcine*, *Le Légataire universel* is but meagre fare. In fact in none of his plays does Regnard offer us so rich a feast of unreason as Labiche.

If *Le Légataire universel* has been overpraised, *Le Joueur* has had less than its due. One criticism is that Regnard does not attempt a serious study of the psychology of a gambler. But, in the first place, *Le Joueur* is not a tragedy but a gay comedy, and secondly, gambling in its initial stages does not necessarily produce tragic consequences. Charles Fox was regarded as the type of an unlucky gambler, but it was not till he had lost over £100,000 that he began, in his friend Lord Carlisle's words, "to be unreasonably impatient at losing." Regnard himself was an ardent gambler all his life, but he

never lost his gay temper. His hero, Valère, is the son of a
rich man, and though, being dependent on his father, he has
some difficulty in raising money, he evidently does not regard
his losses as serious[1]. He is not really in love with Angélique's
person, and it is because she at last realises this, and not because
she is piqued at his pawning her portrait, that she breaks with
him and accepts Dorante. This is true to nature. Of the other
characters the *Comtesse* and the *Marquis*, both of whom owe
not a little to Molière, are amusing and humorous and have a
certain individuality. Here is the *Marquis's* portrait of himself:

> Il craint. Je suis pourtant fort connu dans la ville,
> Et si vous l'ignorez, sachez que je faufile
> Avec ducs, archiducs, princes, seigneurs, marquis,
> Et tout ce que la cour offre de plus exquis;
> Petits-maîtres de robe à courte et longue queue,
> J'évente les beautés et leur plais d'une lieue.
> Je m'érige aux repas en maître architriclin;
> Je suis le chansonnier et l'âme du festin.
> Je suis parfait en tout. Ma valeur est connue;
> Je ne me bats jamais qu'aussitôt je ne tue:
> De cent jolis combats je me suis démêlé;
> J'ai la botte trompeuse et le jeu très-brouillé.
> Mes aïeux sont connus; ma race est ancienne;
> Mon trisaïeul était vice-bailli du Maine.
> J'ai le vol du chapon; ainsi, dès le berceau,
> Vous voyez que je suis gentilhomme manceau[2].

M. Toutabas, the professor of backgammon, is an original
knave, and Mme La Ressource, pawnbroker, dealer in old
clothes and *intrigante*, is a good example of a familiar type:

> C'est une illustre au moins, et qui sait en secret
> Couler adroitement un amoureux poulet:
> Habile en tous métiers, intrigante parfaite:
> Qui prête, vend, revend, brocante, troque, achète,
> Met à perfection un hymen embauché,
> Vend son argent bien cher, marie à bon marché[3].

Hector and Nérine are as gay and witty as the rest of
Regnard's valets and *soubrettes*; they are also honest after

---

[1] Sarcey sees this (*op. cit.* p. 227).
[2] Act III, Sc. xi. Compare Acaste's speech in *Le Misanthrope*, III, i.
[3] Act V, Sc. ii.

their fashion, and Hector is really attached to his master and Nérine to her mistress. The soliloquy with which Hector opens the play is one more example of Regnard's dexterous verse:

> Il est, parbleu, grand jour. Déjà de leur ramage
> Les coqs ont éveillé tout notre voisinage.
> Que servir un joueur est un maudit métier!
> Ne serai-je jamais laquais d'un sous-fermier?
> Je ronflerais mon soûl la grasse matinée,
> Et je m'enivrerais le long de la journée.
> Je ferais mon chemin; j'aurais un bon emploi;
> Je serais dans la suite un conseiller du roi,
> Rat-de-cave ou commis; et que sait-on? peut-être
> Je deviendrais un jour aussi gras que mon maître.
> J'aurais un bon carrosse à ressorts bien liants;
> De ma rotondité j'emplirais le dedans;
> Il n'est que ce métier pour brusquer la fortune;
> Et tel change de meuble et d'habit chaque lune,
> Qui, Jasmin autrefois, d'un drap du Sceau couvert,
> Bornait sa garde-robe à son justaucorps vert.

And as a pendant to this we have Valentin's similar vision of a happy life in *Les Ménechmes*:

> Devant qu'il soit deux ans,
> Je veux que l'on me voie, avec des airs fendants,
> Dans un char magnifique, allant à la campagne,
> Ébranler les pavés sous six chevaux d'Espagne.
> Un suisse à barbe torse et nombre de valets,
> Intendants, cuisiniers, rempliront mon palais;
> Mon buffet ne sera qu'or et que porcelaine;
> Le vin y coulera comme l'eau dans la Seine;
> Table ouverte à dîner; et, les jours libertins,
> Quand je voudrai donner des soupers clandestins,
> J'aurai vers le rempart quelque réduit commode,
> Où je régalerai les beautés à la mode:
> Un jour l'une, un jour l'autre, et je veux, à ton tour,
> Et devant qu'il soit peu, t'y régaler un jour[1].

It will be seen from the above quotations that Regnard had a real genius for dramatic verse.

Purists have objected that his style is often careless and incorrect, and that it abounds in *chevilles* and impossible rhymes. But all critics, especially dramatic critics, and the great majority

---

[1] Act IV, Sc. ii.

of readers are agreed that it is admirable for the purpose of gay comedy—easy, vivacious, pointed, picturesque, graceful, lucid, and, above all, thoroughly French. This is not to say that it is the highest kind of dramatic style, for it does not vary with the characters of the speakers[1]. It is the style of Molière's *L'Étourdi*, brilliant, but too uniformly brilliant; dramatically inferior to that of *Le Misanthrope* and the other great comedies, in which Nature takes the pen into her own hand. But the natural style is also to be found in Regnard, as for instance in the following passage from Crispin's reminiscences

> Certain jour, me trouvant le long d'un grand chemin,
> Moi troisième, et le jour étant sur son déclin,
> En un certain bourbier j'aperçus certain coche.
> En homme secourable aussitôt je m'approche,
> Et, pour le soulager du poids qui l'arrêtait,
> J'ôtai des magasins les paquets qu'il portait.
> On a voulu depuis, pour ce trait charitable,
> De ces paquets perdus me rendre responsable.
> Le prévôt s'en mêlait. C'est pourquoi mes amis
> Me conseillèrent tous de quitter le pays[2].

Regnard has other merits besides style and gaiety. His plays are well constructed, he has a strong sense of the stage, and above all he has a feeling for movement. But when all is said he is not of the first rank. His observation is seldom original and never deep; he cannot create a great character; and though he weaves his borrowings into his work with remarkable skill, he can neither conceal them nor improve upon them, as great borrowers do. A large proportion of his characters owe their being to Molière, and even his language is reminiscent, not only of Molière, but also of Racine, whom he evidently greatly admired. Regnard, in short, was content to be a faithful disciple of Molière, following him where he could with great deftness, but making no effort to climb the higher paths of his master's art—his power of characterisation, his insight into social relations, his innate moral seriousness.

---

[1] It is a great merit in *The Way of the World* that the style varies with the characters. The brilliance of Millamant and Mirabell stands out in relief.

[2] *Les Folies amoureuses*, I, v.

Regnard's literary activity was not confined to comedy and
La Provençale. He wrote a feeble Racinian tragedy, *Sapor*,
which was never put on the stage, narratives of his travels, of
which the longest, *Le Voyage de Laponie*, is of considerable
interest, a few miscellaneous poems, six epistles in verse, and
two satires, of which the first, *Satire contre les Maris*, is an
answer—not very effective and poorly versified—to Boileau's
Satire contre les Femmes, and the second, *Le Tombeau de M.
Boileau Despréaux*, is a tasteless and malignant attack on the
great critic. Regnard, however, was too good-natured to persevere in a quarrel and he made honourable amends in the
dedication which he prefixed to *Les Ménechmes*:

> Qui connaît mieux que toi le cœur et ses travers?
> Le bon sens est toujours à son aise en tes vers ;
> Et, sous un art heureux découvrant la nature,
> La vérité partout y brille toute pure.

7. *Dufresny*.

Charles Dufresny, Sieur de La Rivière (1648–1724)[1], was the
great-grandson of Henri IV and the "Belle Jardinière" of
Anet, and Louis XIV tacitly acknowledged the relationship
by giving him a post of *garçon de chambre* and later (1682) a
dowry on his marriage. The favour, however, which he continued
to shew him was also due to the fact that Dufresny was excellent company, being a man of lively conversation and various
accomplishments. But he loved gaiety and pleasure and hated
restraint and monotony, and so when the court became
intolerably austere and gloomy he threw up his post and
escaped to Paris and freedom. We have seen how he fell in
with a kindred spirit in Regnard, and how from 1692 to 1696
the pair collaborated in writing plays for the Italian theatre, and
how their partnership and friendship were abruptly terminated
on the production of *Le Joueur* (February 1697). The quarrel

---

[1] *Œuvres*, 6 vols. 1731 ; 4 vols. 1747 (best edition). Gherardi, *Le théâtre
italien*, vol. VI. *Théâtre choisi*, ed. G. d'Heylli, 1882; *Chefs d'œuvres
comiques*, vol. I. *Hist. du théâtre françois*, XV, 397 ff. E. Fannière, *The
Modern Language Review*, VI (1911), 335 ff.

arose because Dufresny accused his associate not only of appropriating ideas common to both but of stealing Dufresny's plot and characters. Unfortunately for Dufresny, when, two months later, he produced *Le Chevalier joueur* in proof of his assertion, it was incontinently damned.

Discouraged by this failure, following as it did the very moderate success of the first play, *Le Négligent* (1692), that he wrote for the Théâtre-Français, he abandoned the stage for a time. He made his next appearance in public at the beginning of 1699 with an anonymous work entitled *Amusements sérieux et comiques*[1]. Though La Bruyère's name is never mentioned, it is evidently inspired by *Les Caractères* and shews direct traces of its influence[2]. But it lacks the patient accumulation of material, the deliberate judgments, and above all the consummate art of its model. And if the general plan of La Bruyère's work is not easy to detect, the twelve *Amusements* which take the place of La Bruyère's fourteen chapters follow one another merely at haphazard, and the contents are not always what one would expect from the titles. *Le Voyage du Monde* (ii) treats solely of the court, for the reason no doubt that a post at court was Dufresny's first introduction to the world. *Le Pays des Promenades* (vi) is chiefly concerned with women. *Le Jeu* (x) includes such various matter as Academies, *cafés,* and shops. The longest chapter, *Le Cercle bourgeois* (xi), which was evidently suggested by La Bruyère's *De la société et de la conversation* and *Des biens de fortune*, is even more varied. It contains several portraits—*la joueuse, le joli homme, le grand parleur* (compare La Bruyère's Théodecte), the elaborate portrait of *l'homme de probité* which Dufresny repeated and developed in his comedy of *Le Faux honnête homme* (1703), and *l'homme doré et le valet*, which recalls La Bruyère's well-known "character" of Sosie. Moreover, in this *Amusement* will be found the story of the diamond ring which

---

[1] The *achevé d'imprimer* is dated December 6, 1698; the publisher was Claude Barbin. 2*me édition revue corrigée et augmentée*, 1707; ed. Jean Vic (with an introduction), 1921.

[2] For example, "Est-il donc vrai qu'on ne puisse plus rien inventer de nouveau?"—"Celui qui peut imaginer vivement avec goût et justesse est original dans les choses mêmes qu'un autre a pensées avant lui."—"La cour est un pays très amusant."

furnished Balzac with the plot and central scene of his *La Paix du ménage*.

In order to provide a thread on which to string his scattered observations, Dufresny in his third *Amusement* introduces a Siamese traveller, who comments on the strange usages that he encounters in Paris. Thus the book forms a link between *Les Caractères* and *Les Lettres persanes*. As M. Vic points out, *Le Cercle bourgeois* seems to have directly inspired the 48th Persian letter, in which Usbek recounts his experiences of a visit to a *grand cercle*. At an early stage, however, Dufresny warns his readers that "he shall drop his Siamese when he finds him in his way," and in *Le Cercle bourgeois* he says, "Frankly, I don't very well remember where I left him." In justification of this casual method he declares that he would rather his *Amusements* were irregular than tedious. But his imaginary companion has his uses, as in the chapter on Gambling, a subject on which Dufresny was well qualified to speak. He quotes a fragment from a letter to Siam, which contains an accurate description of the fashionable game of *lansquenet* under the guise of a religious ceremony. The Siamese believes the cards to be badly painted representations of gods, and the banker to be the priest who presides over the sacrifices.

If Dufresny can neither claim to be a moralist like the author of *Les Caractères* or a thinker on political and social questions like the author of *Les Lettres persanes*, his observations not only on the manners of his day but also on human character in general are distinguished by common sense, discrimination, and subtlety. Especially, his remarks on women in the sixth *Amusement* with their delicate sympathy and appreciation confirm what Collé says with reference to his plays that he was in a sense a forerunner of Marivaux[1].

Dufresny's dramatic production was intermittent, and only the pressure of his creditors seems to have roused his activity. The publication of *Amusements sérieux et comiques* was followed by the appearance of five plays in four years (1699–1703).

---

[1] Collé, *Journal et Mémoires*, ed. H. Bonhomme, 3 vols. 1868, III, 57–58.

During 1707 and 1709 he produced four more[1], and then he rested for six years. For part of the time (1710–1713), however, he was occupied with *Le Mercure galant,* the privilege for which had been granted to him by the king on Donneau de Visé's death. His next play, *La Coquette de Village* (1715), and the three which followed (1719 to 1721), were all in verse. In 1721 he had another spell as editor of *Le Mercure,* and in 1724 he died. He was a true *panier percé,* he could keep neither posts nor money. But he was a man of great charm and versatility, and, if his life was disorderly, it was not vicious.

Dufresny's comedies were but moderately successful. Two were withdrawn after the first performance, and only three, *Le Mariage fait et rompu* (1721), *La Réconciliation normande* (1719), and *La Coquette de Village,* exceeded the mark of ten performances. The fact that all these were in verse seems to shew that Dufresny, who in the preface to his early play, *Le Négligent,* had maintained the superiority of prose to verse for comedy, and whose verse is very decidedly inferior to his prose, had correctly gauged the taste of the public when he abandoned prose for verse. Dancourt, it may be noted, began to write verse plays in 1707. It was not only the public of Dufresny's day that preferred his plays in verse, for of his six plays that are included in *Le Répertoire* four are in verse, and this is certainly not due to the quality of the verse.

All critics agree that though Dufresny's comedies contain some excellent scenes, they are, as a rule, badly constructed, the scenes not being linked together to form an organic whole. This disorder is generally regarded as symptomatic of Dufresny's disorderly life. But his weakness as a dramatist lies deeper than this. Even his best scenes fail to bring out their dramatic possibilities. His dialogue, though often nimble and witty, does not carry the action forward, or, at best, it does

---

[1] His second marriage with his washerwoman, in order to pay her bill, is related by Lesage in c. x of *Le Diable boiteux.* As this work was published in 1707, the marriage, if the story is true, was probably a recent event. It is said that Dufresny's new wife insisted on his working, and his literary activity during the following years—indeed, during the rest of his life—bears out this statement.

so, not by a gradual progressive movement but by sudden jerks. Further, his language is seldom that of true comedy; it lacks the raciness and the comic turns of farce, neither has it the humour or the characterising power of great comedy. Yet Dufresny has some real merits. It is to his credit that at a time when the French stage was over-shadowed by the great figure of Molière he dared to break away from the beaten paths. "Molière a bien gâté le théâtre," he says in the prologue to *Le Négligent*: "si l'on donne dans son goût: Bon, dit aussitôt le critique, cela est pillé, c'est Molière tout pur; s'en écarte-t-on un peu: Oh! ce n'est pas là Molière[1]." He shewed his originality in the choice both of his plots and his characters. Take as an example *Le Mariage fait et rompu* (1721)[2], the most successful of his plays when produced, and the one which some critics—rightly, I think—regard as his masterpiece. Nearly all the characters—a judge (*le Président*) and his wife, an ex-corsair (*le faux Damis*), a Gascon who is cool-tempered and a man of his word (Gracignac), the landlady of a hotel at Marseilles—are original, and the fact that the heroine is a widow, not an *ingénue*, and that there is no valet and no *soubrette* adds to the originality. The plot, too, is original. *La Présidente* is anxious for a marriage between the widow and her brother, but the other characters combine to thwart her. The ex-corsair personates Damis, the widow's late husband, and confounds *La Présidente* by producing some compromising letters which the lady, who passes for a severe prude, had written in her less prudish days to the real Damis. Moreover, the plot is worked out much more successfully than in Dufresny's other plays, and the interest is sustained to the end. Finally it is the best versified of his plays; probably because he had realised that in his earlier verse plays he had mistakenly tried to make his verse as much like prose as possible.

The most read and the most generally admired of Dufresny's comedies is *L'Esprit de Contradiction* (1700), which is in one act and in prose[3]. Mme Oronte, who represents the spirit of

---

[1] Quoted by F. Brunetière in *Les Époques du théâtre français*, p. 203.

[2] *Répertoire*, vol. xx.

[3] *Ib.* Separately printed 1878, 1890, and 1906.

contradiction, is Dufresny's most ambitious attempt in the portrayal of character, but she is a type rather than an individual; she is the study of a single trait or humour and not of a complete character. Nor, though she is the occasion for comedy, is she herself comic. Of the other characters, Lucas, who talks in dialect, has too much *esprit* for a gardener and M. Thibaudois too little for a wealthy business man. Both, however, are comic figures. The chief defect of the play is that the plot is too ingenious; it is by no means easy to follow the labyrinth of deception into which the plan for foiling Mme Oronte leads the conspirators. Similarly, *Le double Veuvage* (1702)[1], a prose play in three acts, suffers from a too artificial and too symmetrical plot. But Gusmand, the Countess's steward, is an original, and the contrast between the two lovers, the serious and sentimental Dorante, and the gay and lively Thérèse, is in the spirit of true comedy.

Of the three remaining plays of Dufresny's which are included in *Le Répertoire*, *Le Dédit* (1719)[2] is slight and unimportant, shewing evident signs of hurry, and *La Coquette de Village* (1715)[3], save for the spirited but caricatured sketch of the farmer, Lucas, is little better. *La Réconciliation normande* (1709)[4], which is also in verse, but which is in five acts, has greater pretensions. The leading idea, that of a brother and sister who hate one another, is a promising subject for comedy. But the two principal characters are no more than sketches, and the others have even less individuality. There are one or two good scenes, especially one between the brother and sister, which begins with a forced reconciliation and ends with a renewed enmity. But Dufresny is at his worst in five acts; he becomes long-winded and tedious. Nérine is a particularly tiresome character, and, though she is almost always on the stage, it is not clear whether she is a maid or a housekeeper.

Dufresny was a shrewd and tolerant observer of life, and like Molière, but unlike Dancourt, he took greater interest in character than in manners. He worked also on original lines and he especially prided himself on his originality in the

---

[1] *Répertoire*, vol. XX. [2] *Ib.*
[3] *Ib.* [4] *Ib.* vol. X.

choice of characters and plots. But his characters are either
clever sketches, sometimes bordering on caricature, or not very
impressive types. Partly from indolence, partly because he
lacked a natural gift for drama, he failed in the construction
of his plays, and above all he had not the knack of easy,
natural, and dramatic dialogue.

It will have been noticed that four of Dufresny's comedies (not
including one which was produced some years after his death)
were written after the death of Louis XIV. During the last five
years of the reign he had besides Dancourt, whose best work
was done, a rival in Philippe Néricault Destouches (1680–
1754), who produced four plays during that period, the last,
Le Médisant (1715), being a real success. But, as Destouches's
dramatic career was interrupted for several years by a diplomatic mission to London, and as his two best plays, *Le Glorieux*
(1732) and *Le Philosophe marié* (1727), belong to the latter half
of his career, and as, moreover, he is to be regarded rather as
a forerunner of Nivelle de La Chaussée than as a true follower
of the school of Molière, I shall say nothing about his work.
It may, however, just be noted that all his four earlier plays
were in verse and in five acts, and that their titles at any rate—
Le Curieux impertinent, L'Ingrat, L'Irrésolu, Le Médisant—
indicate an intention to carry on the study of character. But
though these titles recall *Le Misanthrope, L'Avare,* and *Le
Malade imaginaire,* the influence of La Bruyère is far more
perceptible than that of Molière in the plays themselves.

It remains to say a few words by way of retrospect. As I
said at the outset, the influence of La Bruyère on all the four
dramatists that we have been last considering is palpable. It
makes itself felt in both the extent and the quality of their
observation. For, like La Bruyère's, it is just, accurate, and even
subtle, but it does not go deep; it does not penetrate to the
springs of character; it is content to paint men as the world
sees them. And this is just as true of Dufresny, who, as I have
said, is more interested in character than in manners, and of
Regnard, who is not a close observer of either, as it is of Dancourt and Lesage, who are before all things observers of manners

Further, seeing that Dancourt has to his credit more than twice as many plays as the other three together, and that the one really great play is *Turcaret*, it is the comedy of manners that gives the dominant note. On the other hand, in our Restoration comedy—to call it by a well-established if inaccurate name—the comedy of manners is represented by only about 20 comedies (including half-a-dozen by Rawlins, Sedley and Shadwell) out of the 182 produced between 1660 and 1700[1].

It is characteristic of the French comedy of manners that it never has that underlying suggestion of tragedy that we find in *Le Misanthrope, L'Avare,* and *Le Malade imaginaire,* and perhaps in *Tartuffe*. The reason of course is that it does not probe deep enough; it stops short of the fundamental seriousness of life. Dancourt, Regnard, and Dufresny were all men of pleasure, and they made their art subordinate to their pleasure. Regnard wrote when it pleased him, Dufresny when his creditors pressed him. Dancourt, though far more productive, was a hasty and careless writer. A *dancourade* was probably the affair of only a week. Lesage, sober liver and industrious worker, was a deeper observer and a more conscientious artist. But he can hardly be called a severe moralist; he was content to laugh at the world with kindly laughter. If in *Turcaret* he wields once or twice the lash of the satirist, it is because financiers, like actors, were special objects of his dislike. But in all the comedies of our period no other character than Turcaret, and he only in one or two scenes, ever rouses our indignation and hardly any character excites our sympathy. There is no Dorimant and no Mirabell; on the other hand there is no Fidelia, no Valentine and Jeremy, no Millamant[2].

It is perhaps only because the French comedy of manners

---

[1] Allardyce Nicoll, *A history of Restoration Drama*, 1660–1700, Cambridge, 1923.

[2] I suggest that the comedy of Etherege and Congreve is less "artificial" than is generally supposed. Dorimant and Mirabell are true portraits of heartless rakes. Mr Allardyce Nicoll is right in saying that "faithful reflections of upper-class social life" were among "the things demanded by the audience of the Restoration." But he regards *The Country Wife* as "a bright and glorious farce." Is it not rather a turbid mixture of fantasy and realism?

is less realistic than its English rival that it is far more decent both in action and speech. But, whatever the reason, it shews that the manners of the middle-class audience of the Théâtre-Français were far superior to that of the aristocratic wits and fops who patronised the Theatre Royal or the Duke's Theatre. Moreover, it is noticeable that what Dryden in *Marriage à la Mode* calls "the difference betwixt the sexes" plays a comparatively minor part in French comedy, and the relations between *chevaliers d'industrie* and silly and often elderly women are left to the imagination. Not much attention is paid to plot, and in *Turcaret*, as we have seen, there is practically no plot at all. This is all to the good in a comedy of manners. *The Way of the World*, brilliant though it is, would be a better play if it were not weighted with a complicated intrigue, which none of its ardent admirers have ever attempted to unravel. Finally, the dialogue of the French dramatists is easy, natural, and often pointed; Dancourt's no doubt is conversational and sometimes incorrect, but Lesage's prose and Regnard's verse have made them classics and given them an immortality which Regnard might otherwise have missed.

APPENDIX TO CHAPTER IV

LA BRUYÈRE AND LESAGE ON BARON

According to all the keys the last part, at least, of the paragraph in *Des Ouvrages de l'Esprit* which begins, "Ce n'est point assez que les mœurs du théâtre…" (No. 52), refers to Baron's *L'Homme à bonne fortune*. It first appeared in the fifth edition of *Les Caractères* (1690). The keys are also unanimous in giving Baron as the original of Roscius in the 33rd paragraph of *Des Femmes* (first published in the seventh edition, 1692)[1].

Baron is satirised by Lesage in *Gil Blas* under the name of Carlos-Alonzo de La Ventoleria. He is represented as "plus vieux que Saturne," with dyed hair and eyebrows (Baron was only 60 when this was written), and as having spent the first 60 years of his life "dans une ignorance crasse" (Baron was in fact well educated). Laura, who is describing him to Gil Blas, goes on to say that she does not like his acting, and that, among other defects, he has an affected pronunciation and a shaky voice—which is quite untrue of Baron. It should be noted that Don Mathias, to whom a few chapters earlier Gil Blas is acting as secretary, is given to bragging of "good fortunes" of his own invention, and that the name of the host at the dinner-party which, as the result of his bragging, involved him in a fatal duel, was Don Juan de Moncade.

It is also said that Baron is referred to in *Le Diable boiteux*, vol. II, c. v (*Des Songes*):

Cet acteur est si vieux qu'il n'y a tête d'homme à Madrid, qui puisse dire l'avoir vu débuter. Il y a si longtemps qu'il paraît sur le théâtre, qu'il est pour ainsi dire théâtrifié. Il a du talent, et il en est si fier et si vain, qu'il s'imagine, qu'un personnage tel que lui est au-dessus d'un homme[2].

---

[1] This paragraph, with several others in the same chapter, is omitted from the edition of Servois and Rébelliau in the *Classiques français*.
[2] This passage first appears in the edition of 1726.

CHAPTER V

POETRY

THE drought which impoverished the sources of poetry in France after the death of Malherbe, and which persisted for nearly two hundred years, was caused not so much by the fetters of language and metre as by the spirit which made the fetters possible. The age of reason had little understanding of an art which is essentially the expression of individual emotion and imagination. "Nous aimons les vérités déclarées," said Saint-Évremond in 1685, "le bon sens prévaut aux illusions de la fantaisie; rien ne nous contente aujourd'hui que la solidité et la raison[1]."

When Malherbe died, there were still living two men who had a genuine, if slender, lyrical gift—Saint-Amant and Tristan L'Hermite. But neither of these any more than Théophile de Viau, whose death had preceded Malherbe's by two years, possessed the faculty of self-criticism and the sustained interest in their work which distinguish the true artist from the gifted amateur. Moreover, Tristan's last lyrical volume was published as early as 1641[2] and Saint-Amant's in 1649[3]. During the rest of the reign of Louis XIV the silence was not broken by a single poem of real lyrical inspiration.

There was, it is true, plenty of verse, but it was seldom of a higher type than what is known as occasional verse, destined to be read aloud in *précieux* salons or to adorn the letters of literary correspondents. Much of this verse—*bout-rimés*, madrigals, epigrams, enigmas, sonnets, epistles, portraits—was collected in various *Recueils*, a form of publication which had a tremendous vogue from 1652 to 1668. After that the production began to slacken considerably, but it revived again to some

[1] *Sur les poèmes des anciens* (*Œuvres choisies*, ed. Gidel, p. 378. As a modern writer says, "C'était bien sonner le glas de la poésie." R. Bray, *La Formation de la Doctrine Classique en France*, 1927, p. 121).

[2] *La Lyre*. In 1648 he published *Vers Héroïques*.

[3] *Œuvres*, III*ᵉ partie*.

extent in the last decade of the century. The longest-lived of these *Recueils* was first published in 1663 as a single volume with only twenty-two pieces. It was known as "La Suze-Pellisson," though it contained but a single piece by each of these authors. It went on expanding till 1674, when it appeared in four volumes with 349 pieces and in this form it reappeared several times down to the middle of the eighteenth century[1].

Henriette de Coligny, Comtesse de La Suze (1618–1673), who with Pellisson gave her name to this *Recueil*[2], figures with Mlle de Scudéry and Mme Deshoulières as one of the three Graces in Titon Du Tillet's monument of *Le Parnasse français*, of which he conceived the idea in 1708. In the quarrel between the Ancients and the Moderns she is recognised both by Boileau and by François de Callières, who may be regarded as a neutral in the great controversy, as one of the chief elegiac poets of France, so that she retained her reputation for a considerable time. Like the other two Graces of *Le Parnasse français* she had a *précieux* salon.

Mme Deshoulières is better known, and one or two of her poems have kept a place in modern anthologies. Born on the last day of the year 1637[3], Antoinette Du Ligier de La Garde was married at the age of thirteen to an officer in high favour with Condé, who followed the fortunes of that illustrious rebel when he entered the service of Spain (1652). During the first year of her husband's absence the young wife, who was intelligent, well-educated, and beautiful, continued to live with her parents, but, in September 1653, having joined Deshoulières at Rocroy, which Condé had retaken for the King of Spain, she lived first there and then at Brussels for three years. But when her husband, having made his peace with Louis XIV, was

---

[1] See F. Lachèvre, *Bibliographie des Recueils collectifs de Poésies publiées de 1597–1700*, 3 vols. 1901–5.

[2] A selection of her poems was published in 1666.

[3] She was baptized on January 2, 1638. See, for a notice of her life, F. Lachèvre, *Le libertinage au XVIIe siècle*, XI, *Les Derniers Libertins*, pp. 25–63, and for a rapid appreciation of her poetry, Sainte-Beuve, *Portraits des Femmes*, pp. 365–382. There is a supposed portrait of her as a shepherdess, attributed to Mignard, at Chantilly.

appointed governor of Cette, she remained at Paris, and her house became a *bureau d'esprit*, at which might be found Pellisson, Conrart, Lignières, and other frequenters of *précieux* salons, and free-thinkers like Dehénault, Mitton, and the Chevalier de Méré. She figures as Dioclée in the second edition of Somaize's *Dictionnaire des Précieuses* (1660) and she carried out her free-thought so thoroughly that her third child (a son, born in 1666) was not baptized—a most unusual thing in those days and one to be kept secret from all but the most intimate friends. Though many men, including Condé and the younger Loménie de Brienne, fell in love with her, she had an un-blemished reputation, for she was a virtuous woman and she loved her husband[1]. But she did not see much of him, for he was constantly on service, and in 1671 he was sent to Bayonne and employed for ten years on the task of fortifying Guyenne. She herself spent two and a half of these years in Dauphiné (1672–1674) and then returning to Paris made her house, which was now in the Rue de l'Homme Armé, once more an active literary centre. It became the headquarters of the opposition to the party of Boileau and Racine, and she played a leading part in the cabal against *Phèdre*. This was in 1677, and about the same time she began a long and assiduous correspondence with Fléchier, carried on in accordance with the rules of the game as played by the *précieuses* and their admirers. But after he became a bishop (1685) the tone of *galanterie* was exchanged for a sincere expression of real friendship[1]. A change, too, had taken place in Mme Deshoulières's religious opinions. Her old friend, Jean Dehénault, who had helped to form her "libertine" opinions, died in 1682, after having been reconciled with the Church; she herself was suffering from cancer in the breast; and her daughter came under the influence of Fléchier. So she too made her peace with the Church, and as a proof of her good faith persuaded her son, aged nineteen, to be privately baptized. She also wrote a poem of congratulation to Louis XIV on his revocation of the Edict of Nantes. Though she was well known as

[1] See L'Abbé Fabre, *De la correspondance de Fléchier avec Mme Des Houlières et sa fille*, 1871.

a poetess, she had as yet published nothing but occasional poems in *Le Mercure galant* and *Le Nouveau Mercure galant* and a feeble tragedy called *Gesneric* (1680). However, in 1680, when she was fifty, she published a collected edition of her poems[1]. In January 1693 her husband died and Louis XIV conferred on her a pension of 1000 *livres*. She only enjoyed it for thirteen months, as she followed her husband to the grave in February 1694. Her friend Mlle L'Héritier, who also achieved a considerable reputation as an authoress, commemorated her in a little volume entitled *Le Triomphe de Madame Deshoulières, receue dixième Muse au Parnasse.* It was dedicated to Mlle de Scudéry. In the same year (1694) Boileau published his Tenth Satire, written in 1692, in which he attacked Mme Deshoulières and her salon in the well-known lines which begin with "C'est une Précieuse" and end with,

Là, du faux bel-esprit se tiennent les bureaux;
Là, tous les vers sont bons pourvu qu'ils soient nouveaux.

Most of Mme Deshoulières's pieces are album verses or other occasional poems suggested by some simple incident or commonplace thought. Her longer and more serious poems have a note of persistent melancholy. She is fond of comparing unfavourably the lot of man with that of the rest of creation: as in two of her best-known pieces, *Moutons* and *Le Ruisseau*[2]. An Ode written during a severe illness in 1686 is a sincere expression of religious feeling, but, though its technique is adequate, it nowhere rises to the level of true poetry. Of the

---

[1] A second part, which also contained poems by her daughter, was published in 1695. The chief later editions, most of which have some additional poems, are those of 1705, 1707–11, 1725 and 1747 (all in two volumes). I have used the last, to which a notice by La Boissière de Chambors, a friend of her daughter's, is prefixed. A selection of her poetry was edited by M. de Lescure in 1882 and M. Lachèvre prints her *poésies libertines philosophiques et chrétiennes* in *Les Derniers Libertins.*

[2] " Ruisseau, nous paraissons avoir un même sort.
D'un cours précipité nous allons l'un et l'autre,
Vous à la mer, nous à la mort."

same date is one of her most ambitious efforts, entitled *Diverses réflexions*. I will quote the best stanza:

> Misérable jouet de l'aveugle Fortune,
> Victime des maux et des lois,
> Homme, toi qui, par mille endroits,
> Dois trouver la vie importune,
> D'où vient que de la Mort tu crains tant le pouvoir?
> Lâche, regarde-la sans changer de visage;
> Songe que si c'est un outrage,
> C'est le dernier à recevoir[1].

In *Le Temple du Goût* Voltaire represents "le doux mais faible Pavillon" as humbly paying court to Mme Deshoulières, who is placed far above him. Étienne Pavillon (1632–1705), nephew of Nicolas Pavillon, the austere and saintly Bishop of Aleth, wrote madrigals and stanzas to Iris, which, thanks largely to his amiability and charm of conversation, were highly popular in the Paris salons. He was regarded as the Voiture of his day and was chosen to succeed Voiture's rival, Benserade, in the Academy. But when his poems were published, which was not till 1715, ten years after his death, it was discovered that his reputation had greatly exceeded his merits. The same kind of light verse was also represented by Philippe-Emmanuel, Marquis de Coulanges (1631–1716), whose *Recueil de Chansons* was published, without his authority and much to his annoyance, in 1698[2].

Both these last-named poets, as well as Mme Deshoulières, were past fifty when our period opens, so that the greater part of their work belongs to an earlier age. But they still continued to write their facile and uninspired verse, and in 1691 the *Recueils* which had been so popular in the palmy days of the *précieuses* began once more to appear. The same slender verse also received encouragement from two new literary centres,

---

[1] Quoted by Sainte-Beuve, a fact of which I was not aware when I copied it from the 1747 edition.

[2] "Toujours aimé, toujours estimé, toujours portant la joie et le plaisir avec vous, toujours favori et entêté de quelque ami d'importance, un prince, un pape (car j'y veux ajouter le saint-père pour la rareté), toujours en santé, jamais à charge à personne, point d'affaires, point d'ambition; mais surtout quel avantage de ne point vieillir! voilà le comble du bonheur." (Mme de Sévigné to Coulanges, January 8, 1690.)

which took the place of the vanished *précieux* salons. The most conspicuous was the Court of Sceaux, where the Duc and Duchesse du Maine established themselves in 1700, with the intention—so it appeared—of making it a complete contrast to the dullness of Versailles. The Duchess's entertainments were of the most varied description; lectures on the Cartesian philosophy, astronomy, the immortality of the soul, Greek tragedy, and Plato alternated with allegories, impromptus, songs and comedies[1]. Her chief organiser was the Duke's former tutor, Nicolas de Malezieu[2], and he was ably assisted by the Abbé Genest, a writer of tragedies and light verse, "homme simple et vrai," whose monstrous nose inspired endless jests without ruffling his imperturbable temper[3]. Among the other toilers in the "galères du bel esprit" were the Cardinal de Polignac, who gave evidence of his scholarship and his Cartesianism in a much-admired Latin poem, *L'Anti Lucrece*; Jean-Baptiste de Valincour, the friend of Boileau and Racine, and the latter's successor in the Academy; the Marquis de Sainte-Aulaire (1643–1742)[4] who, when he was over sixty, discovered that he had a gift for writing songs, and on the strength of them, much to Boileau's disgust, was elected to the Academy; and (more occasionally) his fellow-poets the Abbé de Chaulieu, the Marquis de La Fare, and the Irishman, Anthony Hamilton.

These last four form a link between Sceaux and the society over which the Duc de Vendôme (1654–1712), great-grandson of Henri IV and Gabrielle d'Estrées, and his brother Philippe,

---

[1] See the *Memoirs* of Mme de Staal-Delaunay who became *femme de chambre* to the Duchess in 1711; Hamilton, *Œuvres*, III, 149–153 (for the account of a *fête* held in 1705); C. Hénault, *Mémoires*, ed. F. Rousseau, 1911, c. xi; Sainte-Beuve, *Causeries du Lundi*, III, 206 ff.; Arvède Barine, *Princesses et grandes dames*, 3rd ed. 1893; G. Desnoiresterres, *Les Cours galantes*, 4 vols. 1859–1864, vol. IV; A. Jullien, *Les grandes nuits de Sceaux* (nocturnal entertainments in the park).

[2] Fontenelle, *Éloge*, *Œuvres*, VII, 252–281. The name is sometimes wrongly written Malézieux.

[3] Pellisson and Olivet, *Hist. de l'Academie Française*, II, 369; D'Alembert, *Hist. des membres de l'A. F.* III, 437 ff.

[4] " L'aisé, le tendre Sainte-Aulaire
　　Plus vieux encor qu'Anacréon."
　　　　　(Voltaire, *Le Temple du Goût.*)

Grand Prior of France (1655–1727), presided at the latter's
hôtel in the quarter of the Temple[1]. The Duke had considerable
military talents, marred, however, by sloth, neglect of discipline,
and carelessness about details. Having distinguished himself
at Steenkerke and in Piedmont, he was given the command of
the army of Catalonia (1695), and the capture of Barcelona by
his troops was an important factor in bringing about the Peace
of Ryswick (1697). He was less successful in the war of the
Spanish Succession, and after the defeat at Oudenarde and the
capitulation of Lille he remained at home more or less in disgrace. But in 1710 he was sent as general to Spain, where he restored the fallen fortunes of Philip V[2]. Though he was governor
of Provence, he lived chiefly at Anet, near Dreux, in the château
which Philibert de L'Orme had built for Diane de Poitiers, or
at his brother's *hôtel* in Paris[3]. During the years of peace
(1678–1688 and 1698–1702) the two brothers collected round
them at Anet and especially at the Temple a congenial society of
free-livers and free-thinkers, whose sole watchword was pleasure.
But the Duc de Vendôme had been imbued by his aunt, the
Duchesse de Bouillon, the youngest and not least attractive of Mazarin's five Mancini nieces, with a certain love of
literature, especially of songs and epigrams and other forms
of light verse. So among his guests were to be found the
Duc de Nevers, Mme de Bouillon's brother, Sainte-Aulaire,
the Duc de Saint-Aignan (1607–1687), Chapelle (1626–1686),
La Fontaine[4], Hamilton, and that strange Damon and Pythias,
Chaulieu and La Fare.

In their taste in verse Sceaux and the Temple had much in
common. In the *Divertissements de Sceaux*, as the volume was
called in which the Abbé de Genest collected in 1712 the verse
of himself and his fellow-workers[5], *chansons* and *rondeaux*

---

[1] At the corner of the Rue du Temple and the Rue de La Corderie.
[2] Prejudice blinds Saint-Simon (*Mémoires*, ed. Chéruel, II, 344–5; ed.
Boislisle, VII, 190–194) to his military talent. For a fair appreciation see
M. Boislisle's edition, XIII, 564–567.
[3] In 1685 he sold his own *hôtel* to the king, who pulled it down to make
the Place de Vendôme.
[4] See La Fontaine's *Épître à Vendôme*, written in September 1689.
[5] A *Suite des Divertissements* was published in 1726.

predominate, and the incense which is offered with an unsparing hand to the Duchess is seasoned with wit. Voiture is often the model, but in obedience to the Duchess's commands the *style marotique*, which had become so fashionable at the Temple, is also cultivated.

Except during the thirty years from 1550 to 1580 when the Pleiad was at the height of its popularity Marot never lost favour in France. Both burlesque and the poetry of the *précieux* salons were largely inspired by him. Voiture brought back the *rondeau* into honour, and Benserade, who carried on the *précieux* tradition in poetry till his death in 1694, turned—by order of the king and for the use of the Dauphin—Ovid's *Metamorphoses* into *rondeaux*, saying in his preface that he was endeavouring to follow in Marot's footsteps. The *Recueil de Barbin* (1692) contained no less than seventy poems by Marot. In 1700 an edition of his works—the first since 1615—was published by Moetjens at The Hague, and it was followed by three others before the end of the reign. Moreover it was the fashion to write not only *rondeaux*, but *ballades*, epigrams, and epistles in the *style marotique*, which consisted in the employment of archaic expressions, inversions, and the suppression of articles and personal pronouns. Hamilton in an epistle to his brother-in-law, Gramont, makes fun of this fashion as practised at the Temple.

> Il est un lieu près du Marais,
> Où depuis quelque temps le genre marotique
> Se renouvelle avec succès.
> Emprunter les nouveaux attraits
> Que l'on trouve à son aire antique:
> De Ronsard ou de Rabelais
> Instruisez-vous dans la boutique,
> Il ne faut que cinq ou six traits
> D'un langage obscur et gothique
> Pour divertir à peu de frais[1].

He was answered by his friends, Chaulieu and La Fare[2], who both followed the fashion, as did Mme Deshoulières and even Hamilton himself. But the influence of Marot on all of these

---

[1] *Épître à Gramont* (*Œuvres*, III).
[2] See G. L. Van Roosbreck, *Un débat sur Marot au XVIIIᵉ siècle* in *Rev. du XVIᵉ siècle*, IX (1922), 281 ff.

was in form and not in substance. The only poet who caught the true spirit of Marot, his gay mockery, his blend of simplicity and malice, was the veteran La Fontaine[1].

The *Épître à Gramont* was written in what was known as *le genre mixte*, that is to say, half in prose and half in verse. This kind of epistolary composition is said to have been made popular by the famous *Voyage de Chapelle et Bachaumont*, which appeared in 1663. In the very same year La Fontaine wrote to his wife—that much neglected lady—half-a-dozen charming letters in verse and prose, in which he describes his journey from Paris to Limoges. But these were not La Fontaine's first experiments in *le genre mixte*, for there are earlier ones addressed to Fouquet (1661) and to his friend, Maucroix (1662). He continued the practice throughout his life. In 1687 he sent one to the Duchesse de Bouillon in London, and this having been answered by Saint-Évremond, he wrote to him in the same fashion. It is in this last letter that occurs his often-quoted remark, "J'oubliais maître François, dont je me dis encore le disciple, aussi bien que celui de maître Vincent, et celui de maître Clément." In 1689 he wrote three "mixed" letters to the Prince de Conti.

But we must not linger over La Fontaine, who belongs to an earlier age. The chief poetic figure of our age is unquestionably Chaulieu, for though he was past fifty when it opens, being rather older than Mme Deshoulières, his best poetry was written during the later years of his life, when, chastened by gout and old age, he became at once more serious and more sincere.

Guillaume Amfrie de Chaulieu (1636–1720)[2] was a Norman, the son of a councillor of the Rouen *Parlement*. Having completed his humanities at the College of Navarre in the

---

[1] See W. de Lerber, *L'influence de Clément Marot aux XVIIᵉ et XVIIIᵉ siècles*, 1920.

[2] He died June 28, 1720, at the age (according to his death certificate) of about 84. *Poésies* (with a few by La Fare), Amsterdam [Lyons], 1724. *Œuvres*, ed. Saint-Marc, 2 vols. 1750; ed. Fouquet, 2 vols. 1774 (most complete and best edition). *Poésies libertines* in F. Lachèvre, *Les Derniers Libertins*, with a biographical notice. See Sainte-Beuve, *Causeries du Lundi*, vol. I (an admirable and sagacious appreciation).

University of Paris, he became, thanks to his lively wit, shrewd
good sense, and amiability, a welcome figure in society. About
1675 the Duchesse de Bouillon introduced him to the Duc de
Vendôme with the result that the Duke and his brother, whose
affairs were in great disorder, made him their man of business.
At Anet he met Chapelle, his master in the art of writing
gay and easy verse, and he rapidly acquired the reputation of
a poet.

> Libertin et voluptueux,
> Vif par tempérament, par raison paresseux,
> Plongé dans les plaisirs, mais capable d'affaire,
> Accort, insinuant, et quelquefois flatteur,
> J'ai su d'un discours enchanteur
> Tout l'usage que pouvait faire
> Beaucoup d'imagination,
> Qui rejoignît avec adresse,
> Au tour précis, à la justesse,
> Le charme de la Fiction.

These lines from an epistle to his friend, La Fare, who had
asked him for his portrait, are no bad description of his character and life. Pleasure was his main object, and as he had an
income of nearly 30,000 *livres* from the abbey and four priories
which, not being in Orders, he held *in commendam*, he was able
to indulge his tastes. Among his many loves was Mme d'Aligre,
the original of La Bruyère's Arténice[1], and towards the end of
his life, when he was blind and crippled by gout, "he had as
lively a passion" for Mlle Delaunay, the *fille de chambre* of
the Duchesse du Maine, "as one can have at the age of eighty."
But this idyll was cut short by the conspiracy of Cellamare.
The lady was confined in the Bastille, and soon after her release
Chaulieu died, "fortified by the Sacraments of the Church"
(1720)[2].

For Chaulieu, like nearly all the French free-thinkers of the
latter half of the seventeenth century, had been reconciled to
the Church before his death. His free-thought had never been

---

[1] See above, pp. 59–60.
[2] "C'était un agréable débauché de fort bonne compagnie, qui faisait
aisément de jolis vers, beaucoup du grand monde, et qui ne se piquait pas
de religion" (Saint-Simon).

of an extreme type. We can estimate its different phases from three poems to which he calls special attention in a preface that he wrote for an edition of his works, and which he entitles *Trois façons de penser sur la Mort*. The earliest, written in 1695, and the latest, written in 1708, are addressed to La Fare, the third, written in 1700, to the Duchesse de Bouillon. The first, he says, was written " on Christian principles...je l'ai faite sans être, par malheur, dévot," the latest " on the principles of Deism, without being Socinian," the third " on the principles of Epicurus, without being impious or atheistical." This, however, is not an altogether correct account. The earliest poem has nothing distinctly Christian about it, and differs hardly at all in sentiment from the latest. Both express a firm belief in a beneficent God, and the later one ends with these lines:

> Mais, plein d'une douce espérance,
> Je mourrai dans la confiance
> De trouver, au sortir de ce funeste lieu,
> Un asyle assuré dans le sein de mon Dieu.

The intermediate poem is certainly Epicurean, but, though it is not " impious," there is no trace in it of a belief in God. It is the poem of a sage who accepts with gratitude the gifts of nature, and who is ready to enjoy life while it lasts and to depart without murmuring when the feast is over. " Death is simply the end of life,...a peaceful sleep,...the beginning of an eternal rest."

The majority of Chaulieu's poems are of a lighter character, consisting for the most part of epistles interchanged with his friends or songs inspired by some supper-party. A whole group is entitled *Divertissement de Sceaux* in which the Duchesse du Maine and her *habitués*—Malezieux, the Abbé Genest, the Duc de Nevers—all play a part. Later young M. Arouet comes on the scene with a poetical letter beginning,

> A vous, l'Anacréon du Temple,

and Chaulieu replies (July 1716) with a flattering answer, mostly in prose, to " la plus jolie lettre du monde," in which he disclaims the honour of being M. Arouet's master, and M. Arouet writes again and insists that he is his master for all his disclaimer. In fact Voltaire has given in *Le Temple du Goût* a fairly just, if over-friendly, appreciation of Chaulieu's qualities as a poet.

> Je vis arriver en ce lieu
> Le brillant abbé de Chaulieu,
> Qui chantait en sortant de table.
> Il osait caresser le dieu
> D'un air familier, mais aimable.
> Sa vive imagination
> Prodiguait, dans sa douce ivresse,
> Des beautés sans correction,
> Qui choquait un peu la justesse,
> Mais respirait la passion.

"Passion" is hardly the word for the sober emotion which Chaulieu at times displays, and his imagination cannot be said "to be prodigal of beauties." But "dans le pays des aveugles le borgne est roi," and Chaulieu is, as I have said, the best poet of our period; two at least of his poems have real poetic merit and deserve a place in any anthology of French poets. Both sing the praises of his Norman home at Fontenay near Les Andelys and the superiority of country life to that of Paris. The earlier of the two, *La Retraite*, was written in 1698, the later one, *Les Louanges de la Vie champêtre à Fontenay, ma maison de campagne*, in 1707. On the whole, I prefer *La Retraite*, but there is not much to choose between them, and I will give some stanzas from both that the reader may judge for himself.

> Ma retraite aux neuf Sœurs est toujours consacrée,
> Elles m'y font encor entrevoir quelquefois
> Vénus dansant au frais, des Grâces entourée,
> Les Faunes, les Sylvains, et les Nymphes des bois.
>
> Mais je commence à voir que ma veine glacée
> Doit enfin de la rime éviter la prison:
> Cette foule d'esprits dont brillait ma pensée
> Fait au plus maintenant un reste de raison.
>
> Ainsi pour éloigner ces vaines rêveries,
> J'examine le cours et l'ordre des saisons,
> Et comment tous les ans à l'émail des prairies
> Succèdent les trésors des fruits et les moissons.
>
> Je contemple à loisir cet amas de lumière,
> Ce brillant tourbillon, ce globe radieux;
> Et cherche s'il parcourt en effet sa carrière
> Ou si, sans se mouvoir, il éclaire les cieux.

Puis delà tout-à-coup élevant ma pensée
Vers cet Etre, du monde et Maître et Créateur,
Je me ris des erreurs d'une secte insensée
Qui croit que le Hazard en peut être l'Auteur.

Ainsi coulent mes jours, sans soin, loin de l'Envie:
Je les vois commencer et je les vois finir.
Nul remords du passé n'empoisonne ma vie,
Satisfait du présent, je crains peu l'avenir.

Heureux qui, méprisant l'opinion commune
Que notre vanité peut seule autoriser,
Croit, comme moi, que c'est avoir fait sa fortune,
Que d'avoir, comme moi, bien su la mépriser.

The above are the last seven stanzas of *La Retraite*; the following are the last six of the poem in praise of Fontenay.

Fontenay, lieu délicieux,
Où je vis d'abord la lumière,
Bientôt, au bout de ma carrière,
Chez toi je joindrai mes ayeux.

Muses, qui dans ce lieu champêtre
Avec soin me fîtes nourrir;
Beaux arbres, qui m'avez vu naître,
Bientôt vous me verrez mourir.

Cependant du frais de votre ombre
Il faut sagement profiter,
Sans regret, prêt à vous quitter
Pour ce manoir terrible et sombre,

Où de ces arbres dont exprès,
Pour un doux et plus long usage,
Mes mains ornèrent ce bocage,
Nul ne me suivra qu'un cyprès.

Mais je vois revenir Lisette,
Qui d'une coiffure de fleurs
Avec son teint à leurs couleurs
Fait une nuance parfaite.

Égayons ce reste de jours
Que la bonté des Dieux nous laisse;
Parlons à Lisette d'amours:
C'est le conseil de la sagesse[1].

---

[1] Mr Lucas prints this poem in the *Oxford Book of French Verse*, but he omits the last two characteristic stanzas, as well as the first three of the whole poem.

Another poem, *Complainte sur la Mort de La Fare* (1712), is worthy of honourable mention by virtue of its sincerity and its felicity of expression. In his portrait Chaulieu had described himself as "l'ami le plus fidèle que Nature eût jamais formé," and certainly his friendship for La Fare goes far to justify his boast.

Charles-Auguste, Marquis de La Fare (1644–1712)[1], began his career both at court and in the army with every advantage and every prospect of success. Like his father, he served with distinction, especially at the battle of Senef (1674), but on Louvois refusing to make him a brigadier and otherwise turning a cold shoulder on him, he retired from the army (1677) and devoted himself to Mme de La Sablière. How he deserted her for the combined attractions of *bassette* and Mme de Champmeslé is described in a well-known letter of Mme de Sévigné's (July 14, 1680). A few years later he attached himself to Vendôme and his brother, and became one of the society of the Temple. This proved his undoing, for the indolence which was at the root of his character led to increasing sloth, gluttony, and intemperance. It was fitting that his best poem should be *Sur la paresse* and that another of some merit should be addressed to *La Volupté*.

> Ame de toute la Nature,
> Reine de la terre et des Cieux[2].

His poetry is little more than a paler reflection of his friend Chaulieu's, and Voltaire judges it correctly in *Le Temple du Goût*:

> La Fare, avec plus de mollesse,
> En baissant sa lyre d'un ton,
> Chantait auprès de sa maîtresse
> Quelques vers sans précision
> Que le plaisir et la paresse
> Dictaient sans l'aide d'Apollon.

"Il dormait partout les dernières années de la vie," says Saint-Simon, and he died, according to the same authority, of

---

[1] *Poésies*, 1755; M. Lachèvre, *op. cit.* pp. 215 ff. He prints from a MS of the *Bib. Nat.* several unpublished poems, which he attributes with great probability to La Fare.

[2] From the MS in the *Bib. Nat.*

acute indigestion caused by a surfeit of cod. In spite of his failings, "everybody loved him, except Louvois," and his Memoirs[1],
written in his later years, shew that his sloth had neither in-
jured his style nor impaired his intelligence. He did not like
Louis XIV and he found much to criticise in his reign, but his
reflections are often shrewd and to the point, and though his
portraits make no pretension to be complete, they often hit off
a character, or at least one side of it, with happy brevity. Thus
Lauzun is "le plus insolent petit homme qu'on eût vu depuis
un siècle," La Rochefoucauld is "l'homme de son temps le plus
galant, le plus délié, le plus poli," and his son, the favourite of
Louis XIV, is "homme de mérite, poli et sage de bonne heure."
But his hero is Turenne—"non seulement le plus grand homme
de guerre de ce siècle et de plusieurs autres, mais aussi le plus
honnête homme et le meilleur citoyen." Finally, it must be
noted in La Fare's favour that he was one of the very few men
of his day who disapproved of the revocation of the Edict of
Nantes[2].

Reserving Hamilton, whom Voltaire groups in *Le Temple
du Goût* with his friends Chaulieu and La Fare, for the next
chapter, I pass on to another friend of theirs, who differs from
all the writers of verse previously mentioned in that he was a
poet by profession, instead of an amateur who wrote poetry
only when it pleased him.

In the eighteenth century and for the first thirty years of
the nineteenth Jean-Baptiste Rousseau (1671–1741)[3] was regarded as a great lyrical poet, and his *Ode à la Fortune* was
learnt by heart in every school in France. In 1820 a standard

---

[1] *Mémoires et réflexions sur les principaux évènements du règne de
Louis XIV et sur le caractère de ceux qui y ont eu la principale part*,
Rotterdam, 1716; Petitot, 2ᵉ série, vol. LXV; Michaud and Poujoulat, 3ᵉ série,
vol. VIII; ed. E. Raunié, 1884. See E. Bourgeois and L. André, *Les sources
de l'histoire de France*, II, No. 838. The Memoirs end abruptly at the year
1693.

[2] *Mémoires*, ed. Raunié, pp. 284–285. See for La Fare, Sainte-Beuve,
Causeries du Lundi, X, 389.

[3] The date of his birth is also given as 1669 and 1670, but the true date
is 1671 (see Jal, who prints his certificate of baptism). *Œuvres*, Soleure,
1712; 2 vols. London, 1723; ed. Amar, 5 vols. 1820. Sainte-Beuve, *Portraits
littéraires*, vol. I. *Nouv. Biog. Gén.* (a good article by V. Fournel).

edition of his works in five volumes was edited and annotated, with an introductory notice, by J.-A. Amar, who becomes at times quite ecstatic in his admiration. Nine years later (1829) Sainte-Beuve attacked Rousseau's reputation in a severe article, the bitter tone of which he afterwards regretted, but which he reprinted as an example of a Romanticist pamphlet. Rousseau, however, has been treated no better by later critics, and in histories of French Literature he fills a continually decreasing space. Thus his interest at the present day is chiefly historical, in that he serves to shew us what the eighteenth century regarded as great poetry.

He was of humble origin, but his father, who was a Paris shoemaker, had saved enough to give him a good education. His Jesuit teachers found him a brilliant pupil, and in 1694, full of ambition, he began his literary career, like so many others of his time, with a play at the Théâtre-Français. But *Le Café*, a comedy in one act, was a failure, and his subsequent dramatic attempts—two operas and two more comedies—were hardly more successful. After *Le Capricieux* (1700) he gave up the stage and his other published pieces were never acted. Meanwhile he had been acquiring a growing reputation as a poet. His acknowledged masters were Marot, Malherbe, and Boileau, the last of whom gave him personal encouragement. He aspired to be the poet of a transitional age, combining the sound traditions of the seventeenth century with the experiments of the eighteenth. He neglected no means of success; he paraphrased Psalms for the Duc de Bourgogne, and wrote obscene epigrams for the Temple; he accompanied Maréchal Tallart on his embassy to London, and he found a Maecenas in Rouillé Du Coudray, the director of finance[1]. Unfortunately he had a gift for satire, and, believing that he owed the failure of his comedies to a cabal of certain men of letters, he scattered satirical couplets about the Café Laurent, which they frequented[2].

[1] He was intelligent, honest, capable, and learned, but of brutal manners and incredibly debauched. See Saint-Simon, III, 52 and XII, 371 and Duclos, *Mémoires*, ed. Barrière, p. 133. The latter describes him as "parfaitement honnête homme avec beaucoup d'esprit et de littérature, mais aimant le vin jusqu'à l'ivresse, et débauché jusqu'au scandale."

[2] Antoine Galland, the translator of the *Thousand and One Nights*,

The *café* at this time was a new institution, taking the place
of the *cabaret* as a rendez-vous for literary men, who were
no longer patronised by the court or the salons. We first hear
of coffee being drunk in France soon after the middle of the
seventeenth century. In 1658 the younger Thévenot, the well-
known traveller, who had recently returned from Cairo, gave
coffee to his friends after dinner. Ten years later a Turkish
ambassador at Paris made it fashionable[1], and in 1672 the first
débit de café was opened there. In spite of Mme de Sévigné's
prediction—"cela passera comme le café"—Bayle, writing in
1685, says that coffee was drunk after dinner at Paris and
Lyons by nearly every one above the position of a tradesman[2].
The most famous of the Paris coffee-houses were the Café
Procope, established by a Sicilian of that name in 1690 in the
Rue Neuve des Fossés-Saint-Germain-des-Prés, immediately
opposite to the Théâtre-Français[3], the Café Laurent or Laurens
in the Rue Dauphine, and the Café Gradot on the Quai du
Louvre.

Though Rousseau's couplets were naturally anonymous,
there was no doubt as to their author, and at last the widow
Laurent had to beg him to leave off coming to her *café*. He
then took to sending his couplets to her address by post, till this
too was stopped. His chief enemy was Houdar de La Motte;
both were candidates for the Académie Française. La Motte was
elected and Rousseau failed, and soon after La Motte's reception (1710) couplets of a still more atrocious character were
found on the staircases of those *habitués* of the Café Laurent
who were most strongly opposed to Rousseau. Rousseau thereupon received a public castigation at the hands of a frequenter

said of him, "M. Rousseau ressemble aux mouches qui laissent de l'ordure
partout où elles se passent."

[1] D'Israeli, *Curiosities of Literature*, IV, 95 (from Le Grand, *Vie privée
des François*).

[2] In a review of a treatise on coffee, tea, and chocolate (*Nouv. de la Rép.
des lettres*), 1685, pp. 497 ff. According to this treatise there were at this time
3000 coffee-houses in London.

[3] The Café Procope is referred to in the well-known passage of the *Lettres
persanes*—"Il y en a une (maison) où l'on apprête le caffé de telle manière
qu'il donne de l'esprit à ceux qui en prennent" (*Lettre* XXXVI).

of the Café, a poet and ex-soldier, named La Faye[1], but he
denied the authorship of the couplets and declared that the real
author was the geometrician, Joseph Saurin. The case came
before the law-courts and in the upshot Rousseau was sentenced
to perpetual banishment from France both for "his impure
satirical, and defamatory verses" and for his calumnious accu-
sation of Saurin.

It is doubtful whether Rousseau was guilty on the first
charge, but, except for a short visit *incognito* to France in 1738,
he spent the remaining twenty-nine years of his life in exile—
at Soleure in Switzerland, where the French ambassador, the
Comte du Luc, gave him hospitality, at Brussels, in London,
where he published an edition of his works, and again at
Brussels, where he died in 1741.

Rousseau was an adept in the technique of verse composition.
He could construct a strophe with considerable skill; he could
write in dignified, correct, and appropriate language; he had a
good ear for harmony; he had carefully studied Horace and
Pindar; and he had all the mythological tags at his fingers'
ends. Indeed so well planned and smooth is the mechanism of
his odes that on a first and hasty reading one is almost persuaded
that they are the real thing. But a second reading dispels the
illusion. Even his most admired odes, *A la Fortune, Sur la mort
de Conti, Sur la naissance du Duc de Bretagne, A M. le Comte
du Luc*, even his famous cantata, *Circé*[2], are but examples
of cold and empty rhetoric. Behind the imposing façade of
their verse you find nothing but commonplace ideas clothed in

---

[1] Jean-François Leriget de La Faye distinguished himself as a diplomatist in the negotiations for the Peace of Utrecht. He wrote light verse
of considerable charm, but it was rather for his general distinction and his
generosity towards artists and men of letters than for his poetry that he
was elected to the Academy in 1730. A letter to him from Voltaire (dated
1716) is printed in *Voltaire: choix de lettres*, ed. L. Brunel, pp. 4–8. The
lines at the head of the letter begin with "La Faye, ami de tout le monde,"
and end with "Quand vous alliez sur le Parnasse Par le café de la Laurent."
The letter contains some violent abuse of Rousseau's writings and character.
Six years later Voltaire wrote to Rousseau a letter full of the grossest flattery
(*op. cit.* pp. 14–17).

[2] "C'est un des chefs-d'œuvre de la poésie française," says La Harpe, who
was in general a severe critic of Rousseau.

commonplace and conventional language. Moreover the pervading tone is one of flattery, exaggeration, and insincerity. For Rousseau is seldom sincere, except when he is bemoaning his misfortunes or proclaiming his merits and the wickedness of his enemies. His best lyrical work is to be found in his paraphrases of the Psalms and Hezekiah's prayer, which form book I of the Odes, for in these he finds thoughts and images ready to his hand. I will quote the first three stanzas of Hezekiah's prayer:

> J'ai vu mes tristes journées
> Décliner vers leur penchant;
> Au midi de mes années
> Je touchais à mon couchant:
> La Mort, déployant ses ailes,
> Couvrait d'ombres éternelles
> La clarté dont je jouis;
> Et, dans cette nuit funeste,
> Je cherchais en vain le reste
> De mes jours évanouis.
>
> Grand Dieu, votre main réclame
> Les dons que j'en ai reçus;
> Elle vient couper la trame
> Des jours qu'elle m'a tissus:
> Mon dernier soleil se lève,
> Et votre souffle m'enlève
> De la terre des vivants,
> Comme la feuille séchée,
> Qui, de sa tige arrachée,
> Devient le jouet des vents.
>
> Comme un lion plein de rage,
> Le mal a brisé mes os;
> Le tombeau m'ouvre un passage
> Dans ses lugubres cachots.
> Victime foible et tremblante,
> A cette image sanglante
> Je soupire nuit et jour;
> Et dans ma crainte mortelle,
> Je suis comme l'hirondelle
> Sous les griffes du vautour[1].

---

[1] *Œuvres*, I, x; a paraphrase of Isaiah, xxxviii, vv. 10–14. See Sainte-Beuve's criticisms.

I must also in justice to Rousseau quote some stanzas from his non-religious odes. Here is a much-admired one from the famous *Ode à la Fortune*:

> Montrez-nous, guerriers magnanimes,
> Votre vertu dans tout son jour:
> Voyons comment vos cœurs sublimes
> Du sort soutiendront le retour;
> Tant que sa faveur vous seconde,
> Vous êtes les maîtres du monde,
> Votre gloire nous éblouit:
> Mais, au moindre revers funeste,
> Le masque tombe, l'homme reste,
> Et le héros s'évanouit[1].

The next quotation is from the ode on the death of the Prince de Conti, to whose portrait by Saint-Simon I have referred in an earlier chapter[2].

> Peuples, dont la douleur aux larmes obstinée
> De ce prince chéri déplore le trépas,
> Approchez, et voyez quelle est la destinée
> Des grandeurs d'ici-bas.
>
> Conti n'est plus. O Ciel! ses vertus, son courage,
> La sublime valeur, le zèle pour son roi,
> N'ont pu le garantir, au milieu de son âge,
> De la commune loi.
>
> .   .   .   .   .   .
>
> Aussi la renommée, en publiant ta gloire,
> Ne sera point soumise à ces fameux revers;
> Les Dieux t'ont laissé vivre assez pour la mémoire,
> Trop peu pour l'univers[3]!

Both La Harpe and Amar have called attention to the happy choice of metre. I forbear to quote from the ode to M. le Comte du Luc[4], because, in spite of the praises of La Harpe, it seems to me to have most of Rousseau's worst faults. But I will end by giving the first stanza of Circe's complaint in his famous cantata of that name:

---

[1] II, vi.   [2] See above, p. 30.   [3] II, x.
[4] III, i.

Cruel auteur des troubles de mon âme,
Que la pitié retarde un peu tes pas :
Tourne un moment tes yeux sur ses climats ;
Et, si ce n'est pour partager ma flamme,
Reviens du moins pour hâter mon trépas[1].

Besides dramas, odes, and cantatas, he wrote twelve dull epistles, of which two, including one to Clément Marot, are in the *style marotique*, two books of "allegories," and four books of epigrams[2]. His correspondence with Brossette[3], the Abbé d'Olivet, Rollin, Louis Racine, Crousaz, the Swiss mathematician and philosopher, and others is his best certificate of character. The style of his letters is sober and dignified and they shew a many-sided interest in literature and affairs. But he never forgives an enemy, and when an enemy publishes anything he has not a good word to say for it. Among his enemies was Voltaire, whom he met at Brussels and quarrelled with in 1722. The quarrel was unfortunate, for Voltaire never lost the chance of a stinging epigram or a malicious phrase.

The popularity of Rousseau's poems, which, as we have seen, lasted well into the nineteenth century, is evidence of the low condition into which French poetry had fallen. It was a thoroughly unpoetical age. This will appear even more unmistakeably when we come to the Quarrel between the Ancients and the Moderns. Perrault and Fontenelle, the protagonists in that Quarrel, though they both wrote much verse, were essentially prosaic souls, who had no conception of poetic values. The only pleasure that poetry gave them was that of a difficulty overcome. Perrault translated Homer and Virgil into prose and believed that his translations gave the reader as good an idea of Homer and Virgil as the originals. Fontenelle said that poetry was not of much importance, and regarded Aeschylus as "une manière de fou." Fontenelle's friend La Motte, the champion

---

[1] IV, vii. Circe's complaint consists of only three stanzas, of which the third is a repetition of the first.

[2] The fourth book by reason of its obscenity is not contained in the edition of 1820.

[3] The correspondence with Brossette has been edited by M. Paul Bonnefon (2 vols. 1910–1911) in the *Textes français modernes*. It begins in April 1715.

of the Moderns in the second phase of the Quarrel, who wrote every kind of poetry with equal facility but of whom not a line has survived, has given us his views in a *Discours sur la poésie* which he published with his Odes in 1707. Adopting Boileau's

Chez elle un beau désordre est un effet de l'art

from his not too happy appreciation of Pindar in the *Art poétique*, he defines *beau désordre* as a "succession of thoughts linked together by a common relation to the subject, but freed from the grammatical connexions and careful transitions which enervate lyrical poetry." And in two odes, one of which appeared in the volume of 1707, and another in a later volume of 1711, he appeals to Reason as the true guide and beacon of poetry[1]. In fact under the impulse of Fontenelle and La Motte there developed a regular campaign against poetry and especially against rhyme. La Motte, indeed, went to such extremes in the defence of his paradox that he actually wrote an ode in prose[2] and spoke of versification as "mechanical and ridiculous labour," a remark which Voltaire completely refuted in the preface to the 1730 edition of his *Œdipe*.

---

[1] *Les poètes ampoulés* (*Odes*, 1707) and *L'Enthousiasme* (*Odes et autres ouvrages*, 1711). See Vial and Denise, *Idées et Doctrines littéraires du XVIIIe siècle*, pp. 323–325.

[2] *Ode à M. de La Faye.*

CHAPTER VI

PROSE FICTION

BETWEEN *La Princesse de Clèves* (1678) and *Gil Blas* (1715) there are no conspicuous landmarks—unless you count *Télémaque* as a novel—in the history of the French novel. But there was a plentiful supply of minor and hybrid forms of fiction, which may be roughly classified under two heads, (1) works which more or less pretend to be records of fact, (2) works which are content to be pure fiction. Under the former head come Apocryphal Memoirs and Extraordinary Voyages; under the latter Fairy-tales and Oriental tales.

1. *Apocryphal Memoirs.*

The first of these four classes is by far the most complex, for in France in the seventeenth century there was no fixed border-line between history and romance. Mézeray is more concerned with his form than with his matter; and his successors write to entertain rather than to instruct, and deliberately interweave fiction with fact. Saint-Réal's *La Conjuration de Venise* and Vertot's *La Conjuration de Portugal* are excellent narratives, but untrustworthy histories. The title of Saint-Réal's other work is *Dom Carlos, nouvelle historique*[1]. But if the public demanded the introduction of fiction into history, on the other hand, ever since the success of La Calprenède's *Cassandre* it had insisted on a historical background for fiction. In *Le Grand Cyrus*, indeed, and still more in *Clélie* this background is little more than a pretence, but in *La Princesse de Clèves* Mme de La Fayette keeps close to

---

[1] For the relations between history and fiction in the seventeenth century in France see G. Dulong, *L'Abbé de Saint-Réal*, 2 vols. 1921–1922. In the preface to his *Histoire de France* (1713) the Père Daniel insists upon the virtues of sincerity and truth in a historian. "Mais ce qu'on a le droit d'exiger de lui, c'est qu'il ne s'abandonne point à son imagination, et surtout qu'il ne s'émancipe pas jusqu'à feindre des épisodes romanesques pour égayer sa narration et varier son histoire."

historical fact, so far as her authorities represent it. Her main concern, however, is not with historical fact but with psychological truth, and in this she had no immediate successor. On the other hand, a work like the *Histoire amoureuse des Gaules* of Bussy-Rabutin (1665) was followed by a whole crop of *Annales Galantes* and *Nouvelles Galantes* and *Histoires Secrètes*[1], while so-called histories and memoirs, highly spiced with scandalous and libellous anecdotes, became increasingly popular.

The most prolific producer of this class of literature, which blended fiction with fact and romance with history, was Gatien de Courtilz, Sieur Du Verger, generally known as Courtilz de Sandras (1644–1712)[2], who, after retiring from the army with the rank of captain, adopted the profession of a journalist and pamphleteer[3]. His writings, all of which were anonymous, vary in range from more or less serious history, such as *Mémoires contenant divers évènements remarquables arrivés sous le règne de Louis le Grand*[4] or *Annales de la cour de Paris pour les années 1697 et 1698*[5], to scandalous stories about Louis XIV like *Les Conquêtes amoureuses du grand Alcandre* and *Le grand Alcandre frustré*[6], and pure romance with a more or less historical background like the *Mémoires* of Rochefort and D'Artagnan.

---

[1] Miss R. Clark, *Anthony Hamilton* [1921], gives a list of twenty-one *histoires galantes* relating to the Court of England alone.

[2] Sandras was his mother's name; he dropped it after 1684.

[3] Lelong, *Bibliothèque historique*, 4 vols. (under titles of each work—see index); Niceron, *Mémoires des hommes illustres*, II, 165 ff.; [Lenglet Dufresnoy,] *Bibliothèque des Romans*, II, 88–92; P. M. Woodbridge, *Gatien de Courtilz*, 1925. See also A. Le Breton, *Le Roman au dix-huitième siècle*, 1898, c. i.

[4] Cologne, 1683, 1684. See E. Bourgeois and L. André, *Les Sources de l'Histoire de France—XVIIe siècle*, IV, No. 3081. There is a fairly long critical notice of this by Bayle in the *Nouvelles de la République des Lettres* for March 1684, pp. 41 ff. Bayle controverts the author's assertion that Louis XIV was badly educated.

[5] Cologne [perhaps Rouen], 1701, 1702, 1711; Amsterdam, 1702, 1703, 1706. See Bourgeois and André, IV, No. 3092.

[6] *Ib.* Nos. 2999 and 3013. Reprinted at San Remo in 1874 with notes by Paul Lacroix and in vol. IV of *L'Histoire amoureuse des Gaules*, ed. Boiteau and Livet. Mr Woodbridge questions the authorship of Courtilz. Lelong accepts it. Bayle declines to pronounce an opinion. Courtilz was in the Bastille when it was published.

It was natural that a writer of this character should be looked
on unfavourably by the government of Louis XIV, and consequently Courtilz spent nearly all the last forty years of his
life either in Holland or in the Bastille. He was in Holland
from 1683 to 1689 and many of his books were printed in that
country. He was in the Bastille from 1693 to 1699 and again
from 1702 to 1711, his second imprisonment being due, it is
said, to the *Annales de la Cour et de Paris*, in which more or
less trustworthy information, especially as regards social and
economic conditions, is interspersed with gossip and scandalous
stories.

It is by his apocryphal memoirs that Courtilz has a place in
the history of French fiction. His first experiment under this
head appeared in 1687 and was entitled *Mémoires de M^r
L.C.D.R.*[1] The initials have always been accepted as standing
for Le Comte de Rochefort, but whether Courtilz's hero is to
be identified with the Marquis de Rochefort, who was made a
Marshal of France in 1675 and died in the following year[2],
or whether, as seems much more probable, he is a purely
imaginary person, is a matter of no moment, for the story of
his life is certainly fictitious. Courtilz, however, tells us that
his friend, as he calls him, had entrusted his memoirs to him,
and that he has published them without additions or omissions. Judged as fiction, which it really is, the book is of
slender merit. Rochefort is far from an impressive creation; he
has no distinctive characteristics except a love of adventure,
and adventures we have in plenty. Unfortunately Courtilz is
an indifferent story-teller. Before the reader has time to become interested in one adventure he is switched off to another.
Indeed, after the first third of the book it trails off into a
succession of disconnected episodes.

---

[1] Cologne, 1687; *seconde édition revuë et corrigée, ib.* 1688, 1692.
Numerous editions were published at The Hague. There is an English
translation, of which there is a copy of the 3rd ed. (1705) in the Cambridge
University Library, and of the 4th ed. (1707) in the British Museum, but
I can find no trace of the first or second edition. See Bourgeois and
André, *op. cit.* II, No. 732.

[2] It is against this that they have different Christian names.

Courtilz, however, scored a popular success, but in spite of this he did not repeat his experiment till eleven years later, when he produced *Mémoires de J.-B. de La Fontaine*[1]. His new hero was a real person, who, after a highly adventurous career in France, was sent by Louvois as a spy to England. Returning to France he also acted as a spy for William, but his double treachery was detected and he was confined for several years in the Bastille, where Courtilz made his acquaintance and doubtless obtained much information about his life. In his preface, however, he frankly admits that it is impossible to say precisely whether he is giving to the public romance or history.

And now we come to the one book by which this once popular writer is known to any but a few students, and that because it is the source and origin of a famous work of genius. It appeared in 1700 and was entitled *Mémoires de M^r D'Artagnan Capitaine Lieutenant de la premiere Compagnie des Mousquetaires du Roi, contenant quantité de choses particulieres et secrettes qui se sont passées sous le Regne de Louis le Grand*[2]. Its nominal author was Charles de Baatz (1611–1673), a younger son of the Marquis de Castelmore, who took the name of his mother's family and after rising to the rank of brigadier was killed at the siege of Maestricht. Courtilz says in his preface that he has put together several fragments which he found amongst D'Artagnan's papers, "en leur donnant quelque liaison," but, knowing his methods, we may be fairly sure that no such papers existed. The *Mémoires d'Artagnan* have more or less the same defects as the *Mémoires de Rochefort*. As in the earlier book the interest soon dies away. In the second and third volumes the personality of the hero, which gives a sort of unity to the first volume, becomes fainter and fainter; and indeed in the third volume he hardly appears at all. Even in

[1] Cologne [The Hague], 1698, 1699, 1701. An English translation under the title of *The French Spy* appeared in 1700. See Bourgeois and André, *op. cit.* II, No. 756.

[2] Cologne, Pierre Marteau [Rouen], 3 vols. 1700, 1701, 1704; Amsterdam, 4 vols. 1704; 3 vols. 1715; Paris, 1896 (incomplete). English translation by Ralph Nevill, 3 vols. 1898. See Bourgeois and André, *op. cit.* II, No. 776.

the first volume his adventures are too often interrupted by historical digressions or by incidents and anecdotes which have nothing to do with him. If in the *Mémoires de Rochefort* the adventures are not sufficiently developed, here they are related at too great length. Moreover, Courtilz's style, which in the earlier work was, though slipshod, at any rate easy and lucid, has now become diffuse and cumbrous. But with all its defects the book appealed to the imagination of Dumas and inspired him to write his great trilogy. His debt is mainly to the first volume, the first fifty pages of which correspond fairly closely to the first six chapters of *Les trois Mousquetaires*. But Dumas has given life and individuality to Athos, Porthos and Aramis, of whom we hear very little in Courtilz's book, and he has transformed the equally colourless figure of Milady into a dangerous and impressive criminal. Even D'Artagnan gains considerably. In Courtilz's hands he is a typical Gascon—brave, adventurous and boastful. But he is not a sympathetic character; he is wanting in self-respect, and as a lover he is insincere, hardhearted, and mercenary. Moreover, as he grows older, he sensibly deteriorates, while Dumas's hero consistently improves.

Though Dumas does not mention it, he has also borrowed from the *Mémoires de Rochefort*. It was there that he found the dramatic incident of the discovery of the *fleur de lis* on Milady's shoulders and he adopts Rochefort as a historical character, calling him *l'âme damnée du Cardinal*, and giving him a not inconspicuous part in his narrative. It must have been with a sense of dramatic fitness that at the close of *Vingt ans après*[1] he makes him fall by the hand of D'Artagnan, with whom he had had three previous encounters.

In the year following the publication of the *Mémoires d'Artagnan* Courtilz published *Mémoires de M. le Marquis de Montbrun*[2] and *Mémoires de Madame la Marquise de Fresne*[3], the former being unfinished. Montbrun was a natural son of the Duc de Bellegarde, and Mme de Fresne was also a real

---

[1] *Les trois Mousquetaires* and *Vingt ans après* together cover the same period as the first volume of *Les Mémoires d'Artagnan*.

[2] Amsterdam, 1701, 1702, 1708.

[3] *Ib.* 1701, 1702, 1722, 1734.

person. The memoirs of Montbrun conform to the pattern which Courtilz had found so successful, but those of Mme de Fresne form a highly romantic narrative in which corsairs and crime and bloodshed play a prominent part. Lastly, in the year before Courtilz's death there appeared *Mémoires de M. de B*** secrétaire de L.C.D.R.* (le Cardinal de Richelieu)[1], which is pure fiction and which, like its predecessor, is romantic in character.

M. Le Breton in the first chapter of his *Le Roman au XVIII* *siècle* and Mr Woodbridge in his excellent monograph both claim for Courtilz that he has had a considerable influence on the development of the French novel. In particular they claim that he gave it a definitely realistic character and so prepared the way for Lesage and Marivaux and the Abbé Prévost[2]. There is no doubt some truth in this. The autobiographical form of *Gil Blas*, the choice of a picaresque hero, the introduction of historical characters, the far-ranging observation of men and manners—all these are foreshadowed by Courtilz de Sandras. But there is a vast difference between the fumbling and careless prentice-work of the *Mémoires* of Rochefort and D'Artagnan and the finished art of *Gil Blas*. Memoirs are not the same thing as autobiography, and they lack the unity which genuine autobiography ensures; Rochefort and even D'Artagnan are but shadowy figures; Courtilz's observation of society and manners though the result of personal experience, especially of the army and the law-courts, is hurried and superficial, and the whole texture of his work is loose and uneven. Moreover he does not, as a good historical novelist should, use history merely as a background for his hero's adventures, but, as I have said, he digresses into historical events with which his hero has nothing to do.

His history, however, such as it was, helped to win popularity for his books and it was as history that Bayle criticised them.

[1] Amsterdam, 2 vols. 1711. According to Bourgeois and André, *op. cit.* II, 703, this was really published at Rouen.

[2] M. Le Breton makes it clear that the opening of the *Vie de Mariane* is taken from the *Mémoires de M. de B**** and he finds traces of Courtilz in the novels of Prévost.

"C'est un livre plein de faussetés," he says of the *Mémoires de Rochefort* with reference to Courtilz's slanderous reflection on the character of that most virtuous lady, Marie de Hautefort, Duchesse de Schomberg[1], and after making a detailed criticism of the *Vie de Turenne*, one of Courtilz's more serious works, he comes to the conclusion that it is not to be trusted[2]. Yet in his account of Louis XIII in the *Dictionnaire historique* he quotes several passages from *Le Testament politique de M. Louvois*, which is ascribed to Courtilz. Evidently Bayle in his search for historical truth did not know what to make of the strange blend of fact and fiction, of history and romance, which found such favour with his contemporaries.

Another work which perplexed him in a similar way[3] was Mme d'Aulnoy's *Mémoires de la Cour d'Espagne*[4], which together with her *Relation du Voyage d'Espagne*[5] had achieved great popularity when he published his Dictionary. Her methods of mystification were bolder and simpler than those of Courtilz de Sandras, and were so successful that they escaped complete detection till three years ago. As regards the *Mémoires* it had long been known that they included a transcript of the memoirs attributed to the Marquis de Villars (known as "le bel Orondate" and father of the Maréchal de Villars), who was

---

[1] *Dict. hist.* art. Schomberg.

[2] *Réponse aux questions d'un provincial*, I, xxvii. Twenty years earlier he reviewed Courtilz's *Vie de Coligny*, which is mainly fictitious, as a serious biography (*Nouvelles de la République des lettres*, 1686, pp. 278 ff.).

[3] *Dict. hist.* art. Nidhard (the German Jesuit who was confessor to Queen Mariana), note C, where Bayle makes some very sensible remarks on the subject.

[4] *Mémoires de la Cour d'Espagne*, 2 vols. Paris, 1690; *ib.* 1692; The Hague, 1691; *ib.* 1692 (twice); Lyons, 1693; E. T. 2 vols. 1692; Amsterdam, 1716.

[5] *Relation du Voyage d'Espagne*, 3 vols. Paris, 1691, 1697, 1699; The Hague, 3 vols. 1691, 1692, 1693, 1705, 1712, 1715; Amsterdam, 1716. E. T. *The Lady's Travels into Spain* [1691?]; 2nd ed. 1692; 10th ed. 1735–1736. Both works have been edited (defectively) by Mme B. Carey, in 1874 and 1876 respectively, under the common title of *La Cour et la Ville de Madrid vers la fin du XVIIᵉ siècle* and recently the *Relation* has been admirably edited and annotated by R. Foulché-Delbosc, *Revue hispanique*, vol. LXVII (1926). See also a full review of this last by Jeanne Mazon in *Rev. de littérature comparée*, 1927, pp. 724–736.

ambassador in Spain from 1671 to 1673 and again from 1679 to 1681[1].

But M. Foulché-Delbosc has now shewn that Mme d'Aulnoy also used other sources, namely the *Gazette* and two translations of Spanish works relating to Father Nidhard. He has in fact accounted for the whole of her narrative except some sixty or seventy pages. The result of his inquiry is that the *Mémoires de la Cour d'Espagne* do not fall within the category of fiction.

It is otherwise with Mme d'Aulnoy's far more entertaining work, the *Relation du Voyage d'Espagne*, for which she adopted the form of letters, purporting to have been written by her between February 1679 and September 1680 from various places in Spain to a cousin in France. It is doubtful whether Mme d'Aulnoy ever was in Spain, and certainly her information is chiefly derived from the memoirs attributed to Villars, from various printed sources, from the letters either of her mother Mme de Gudannes, referred to in the book as "a near relation," who was living in Spain, or of her daughters who paid long visits to their grandmother. It is possible also, says M. Foulché-Delbosc, that she was acquainted with the letters which the Marquise de Villars wrote in 1679–1681 to Mme de Sévigné, Mme de Coulanges and other friends, and which, like those of Mme de Sévigné, passed from hand to hand and were sometimes copied. But she supplements these borrowings with romantic stories of her own invention, is greatly given to exaggeration and indulges plentifully in embroidery. The part played by fiction in the *Relation* is thus fairly considerable,

---

[1] The Memoirs, which were in manuscript when Mme d'Aulnoy appropriated them, were first printed in 1733, and then again in 1861 in a limited edition published in London and edited by William Stirling (Sir W. Stirling-Maxwell), who was ignorant of the earlier edition. There is a longer and a shorter form of the manuscript; both these editions were printed from the shorter form. In 1893 A. Morel-Fatio blended the two forms in a composite edition. The attribution to Villars was doubted by Mme Carey, and her doubts are confirmed by M. Foulché-Delbosc, who believes that the author was an attaché or secretary who had an intimate knowledge of Spanish affairs and the society of the court.

and much of what she relates must be received with caution[1]. Four years later she published a corresponding work on the English court, which is almost wholly fictitious and is of no value[2].

Of all Mme d'Aulnoy's writings her first attempt, *Histoire d'Hypolite, Comte de Duglas,* had the most lasting popularity, for it was reprinted no less than 38 times from 1690 to 1875[3]. It is pure fiction, as is her last work, *Le Comte de Warwick,* the only one which gives her name in full on the title-page. Of her *Contes des Fées,* which are her real title to fame, I shall speak later. The little that is known of her is not to her credit[4]. Whatever truth there may be in the stories of her life, it is certain that she and her mother, who had married M. de Gudannes as her second husband, suborned two men to bring a charge of treason against M. d'Aulnoy, and that as the result of a trial he was acquitted and the two men were executed.

About the disorderly lives of two other successful lady-writers of fiction in the form of biographies and memoirs there is no room for doubt. Both bore highly distinguished names. Charlotte-Rose Caumont de La Force (1650–1724), granddaughter of Jacques-Nompar, Duc de la Force and a Marshal of France, the original of La Bruyère's Césonie[5], specialised in *Histoires secrètes,* one of which, *Histoire secrète de Navarre,* was

---

[1] Taine greatly admired the *Relation* and accepted it at its face value (*Essais de Critique et d'Histoire,* 7th ed. 1906, afterwards included in the *Derniers Essais*). Martin Hume speaks of Mme d'Aulnoy's evidence as "very untrustworthy," and has "grave doubts whether she went to Spain at all," but he quotes her nevertheless in his *Spain* (Cambridge, 1898). See for illustrations of her untrustworthiness, Foulché-Delbosc, *op. cit.* pp. 93–104.

[2] There is a recent English translation by Mrs W. H. Arthur, annotated and edited by G. D. Gilbert, 1913.

[3] The 2nd edition, however, did not appear till 1708. There is a modern edition of 1875.

[4] Her maiden name was Marie-Catherine Le Jumel de Barneville; she was born in 1650 or 1651 and died in 1705. In 1666 she married François de La Motte, Baron d'Aulnoy, a man of forty, who had been valet to César, Duc de Vendôme.

[5] *Des Femmes.*

often reprinted[1]. She also wrote a historical novel called *Gustave Vasa, histoire de Suède.* Henriette-Juliette de Castelnau, Comtesse de Murat (1670–1716), wrote *Le Comte de Dunois* and other fictitious biographies, and also *Mémoires de Mme la Comtesse de M****, which purports to be her own autobiography, but is for the most part a romance[2].

Of greater merit as a writer, but with hardly a better reputation, was Anne de Bellinzani (*c.* 1657–1740), daughter of an Italian clerk of Mazarin's, and wife of the Président Ferrand. A love affair with the Baron de Breteuil (the original of La Bruyère's Celse[3] and the father of Voltaire's Mme Du Châtelet) led to her being confined in a convent, where she beguiled her time by editing her tender, not to say passionate, correspondence with her lover and publishing it under the title of *Histoire nouvelle des amours de la jeune Belise et de Cléante* (1689). The book became popular and was often reprinted[4], as was a volume of her other letters (1691)[5].

2. *"Extraordinary" Voyages.*

The "Extraordinary" Voyage—to use a term which was, I believe, invented by M. Lanson, and which has been adopted by an American writer who has made a special study of the subject[6]—is a fictitious narrative, which purports to be the

[1] Also *Hist. secrètes* of Marie de Bourgogne and Catherine de Bourbon, Duchesse de Bar (sister of Henri IV).

[2] See for both these ladies, F. Brunetière, *Études critiques*, V, 203–207; for Mlle de La Force, the letter of Du Bos referred to above (p. 250); and for Mme de Murat, F. Gaiffe, *L'Envers du Grand Siècle*, 1924, pp. 221–222. Both Brunetière and Gaiffe quote from the report of D'Argenson (lieut.-general of police) for the year 1700.

[3] *Du Mérite personnel.*

[4] In 1704 it was printed in a volume with the famous letters of the Portuguese Nun.

[5] *Lettres de la Présidente Ferrand* followed by *Histoire des amours* (*Lettres du XVIIe et du XVIIIe siècle*), ed. E. Asse, 1880. See M. Langlois, *Souvenirs d'une Précieuse, Rev. d'hist. litt.* XXXII (1925), 497 ff. He prints some reminiscences (anonymous but evidently by Mme Ferrand) for the years 1656 to 1691. Their chief aim is to defend Colbert against Le Tellier and Louvois.

[6] G. Atkinson, *The Extraordinary Voyage in French Literature before*

account of a real voyage to some distant and little-known country or countries. It is often enlivened by thrilling adventures, and it invariably presents the picture of an ideal society which serves as a pretext for criticism—social, political, religious—of the European world in general and of the writer's own country in particular. In nearly every case, it may be added, the writer's point of view is that of a rationalist and a socialist. It is as a sign of the increasing discontent with the government of Louis XIV and with the prevailing ideas on politics and religion, and not as literature, that these voyages deserve our attention. The writers may be third-rate figures in literature, but they are interesting as precursors of the eighteenth-century spirit.

The Extraordinary Voyage of the later seventeenth century is distinguished from earlier works like More's *Utopia*, the Fourth and Fifth Books of *Pantagruel*, Bacon's *New Atlantis*, Campanella's *City of the Sun*, and the *Histoire comique* of Cyrano de Bergerac, by the fact that it takes elaborate pains to have an air of reality. It furnishes documentary details of events, dates, and places, and it borrows largely from real voyages or from the actual experience—if he has any—of the writer.

I have shewn in another place[1] that Rabelais's interest in geographical discovery was stimulated by the numerous accounts of voyages that appeared during the first half of the sixteenth century. Towards the close of that century, namely in 1590, the engraver, Theodore de Bry, began the publication, at Frankfort, of that great series of voyages which by maps and hundreds of other engravings did so much to impress upon the public the wonders of the new world. His own share of the work, entitled *Grands Voyages*, which was not completed till 1634, was concerned with America and the West Indies; that of his two sons which was published in twelve parts at intervals from 1598 to 1628 and was entitled *Les Petits*

1700, New York, 1920; *The Extraordinary Voyage in French Literature from 1700 to 1720*, Paris, 1922; *Les Relations de Voyage du XVIIe siècle et l'évolution des idées*, [1924].

[1] *Studies in the French Renaissance*, Cambridge, 1922, c. iii.

Voyages, dealt with the East Indies. In 1616[1] Jean Mocquet, apothecary to Henri IV and successor of André Thevet as *Garde du Cabinet des singularitez du Roy*, who had taken part in no less than six expeditions, published a narrative of his experiences, which by its realistic and picturesque descriptions and its thrilling illustrations must have done much to kindle interest in unknown or little-known countries[2]. Though Mocquet's gift of detailed observation does not prevent him from introducing a certain amount of fiction into his narrative, he does not "lie flamboyantly"—the expression is Mr Atkinson's— like Vincent Le Blanc, the records of whose voyages (made from the age of twelve to that of sixty) were "faithfully" edited by a lawyer named Pierre Bergeron in 1648[3]. To what extent this "editing" was carried is difficult to determine, but it seems clear that while Le Blanc was a born lover of adventure, and was ready not only to believe everything that was told him but to invent the most blood-curdling incidents, Pierre Bergeron was capable of improving upon him. Moreover, by his philosophic comments and his comparisons between Europe and the little-known lands visited by Le Blanc, he foreshadows the later Extraordinary Voyage.

The man who, according to M. Chinard, contributed as much as anyone to fixing the type of "the child of nature," as described by Rousseau, was the Dominican father, Jean-Baptiste Du Tertre[4], who published a short sketch of the history of the Antilles in 1654[4], and a far more extensive work on the same subject in four volumes from 1667 to 1671[5]. This is not the

---

[1] Parts I–IX of the *Grands Voyages* were published from 1590 to 1602, parts X–XIII from 1619 to 1634. Parts I–X of the *Petits Voyages* appeared from 1598 to 1613, part XI in 1619, and part XII in 1628. (See *Bibliotheca Sunderlandiana*, Nos. 2052, 2053.)

[2] *Voyages en Afrique, Asie, Indes Orientales et Occidentales*, 1616; 1617; Rouen, 1645; *ib.* 1665; E. T. 1696. (See G. Chinard, *L'Amérique et le rêve exotique dans la littérature française au XVIIe et XVIIIe siècle*, 1913, pp. 24–29; Bourgeois and André, *op. cit.* I, No. 449.)

[3] 2nd ed. 1649; 3rd ed. Troyes, 1658; E. T. *The World surveyed*, 1660. See Chinard, *op. cit.* pp. 79–83; Atkinson, *The Extraordinary Voyage before 1700*, pp. 25–33.

[4] *Bib. Sund.* No. 12187.

[5] *Histoire Générale des Antilles*, 4 vols. 1667–1671.

place to give an account of his book; it is sufficient to say
that Chateaubriand speaks of it with high praise, quoting a
passage which he compares to Amyot's Plutarch[1], and that
M. Chinard devotes to it twenty-five pages, in which he com-
mends the father as the predecessor of Bernardin de Saint-
Pierre in his descriptive powers, and of Jean-Jacques in his
admiration of the untutored savage as the happiest and most
virtuous of mankind[2].

Du Tertre's experience was confined to the Antilles, and
neither he nor his book seems to have been well known. But there
were four Frenchmen of the seventeenth century who travelled
extensively in the East whose records were widely read and
still occupy a distinguished place in the annals of travel. These
were François Bernier, who spent twelve years in India—
eight as physician to the Emperor Aurangzeb—and who published in 1670–1671 two volumes on the Mogul Empire[3]; Jean
Thévenot, who visited Turkey, Egypt, Arabia, Palestine, Persia,
and India, and who died at Miana in Armenia at the early
age of thirty-four[4]; Jean Chardin, a Protestant jeweller, who
travelled in the East, chiefly in Persia, more or less con-
tinuously from 1665 to 1677, and, having come to reside in
England in 1680, was made a member of the Royal Society,
and knighted by Charles II[5]; and lastly, Jean-Baptiste Tavernier, who in six voyages from 1630 to 1668 visited Turkey,

---

[1] *Le Génie du Christianisme*, 4ᵐᵉ *ptie*, liv. IV, c. vii.

[2] Chinard, *op. cit.* pp. 39–54.

[3] Often reprinted; the most recent English translation is by A. Constable
(*Constable's Oriental Miscellany*, vol. I, 1891).

[4] *Relation d'un voyage fait au Levant*, 1664; *Suite du même voyage*,
1674; *Relation de l'Indostan*, 1684; *Voyages de M. de Thévenot*, 5 vols. 1689
and often reprinted; E. T. 1686–1687.

[5] See Evelyn's account of his visit to him, accompanied by Sir John
Hoskins and Sir Christopher Wren, to invite him to honour the Royal
Society with his company (*Diary* for August 18, 1680). Evelyn became
godfather to his son, and his daughter married Sir Christopher Musgrave
of Edenhall. The original edition of Chardin's travels (London, 1686) only
contains his journey to Ispahan. It is reviewed by Bayle in the *Nouv. de
la Rép. des Lettres* for 1686, pp. 1061 ff. and 1124 ff. In 1711 Chardin
published a fuller but still incomplete edition of his travels (3 vols.
Amsterdam). The best of the older editions, *Voyages du chevalier Chardin*

Persia, India, Sumatra, Batavia, and Celebes and died on his
seventh voyage, either at Moscow or Smolensk, in 1689, at the
age of eighty-four. Tavernier, who, like Chardin, was a jeweller,
was much less learned, especially in the matter of languages,
than the other three travellers (all of whom he came across
during his travels), but his *Six Voyages*, which first appeared
in 1676, had an immediate success, and was reprinted about
a dozen times before the end of the reign of Louis XIV[1].

Of less importance was C. Dellon, a physician, who visited
Madagascar, Isle-Bourbon, Surat, Calicut, and Goa, at which
last place he spent two years in the prison of the Inquisition
(1674-1676), being finally released at Lisbon. He wrote two
accounts of his experiences—*Relation d'un voyage fait aux
Indes Orientales*[2] and *Relation de l'Inquisition de Goa*[3].

On the other hand, Melchisedech Thévenot, uncle of Jean
Thévenot and a keeper of the royal library, though he was
deeply interested in geographical discovery, and, for the time,
a considerable Orientalist, never travelled beyond Europe. But
the great collection of voyages, mostly translated from various
languages, which he published, with maps, in four parts from
1663 to 1672[4], helped greatly to spread the knowledge of distant

en Perse et autres pays de l'Orient, was published at Amsterdam in 1735.
A new English edition, a reprint of that of 1720, with an introduction by
Sir P. Sykes, was published in 1928. Lord Curzon in his *Persia* (2 vols.
1892) speaks very highly of his merits. See D. C. A. Agnew, *Protestant
exiles from France in the reign of Louis XIV*, 3 vols. 1871, II, 140 ff.;
Bourgeois and André, *op. cit.* I, No. 488.

[1] An English translation of the *Six Voyages*, by John Phillips, Milton's
nephew, was published in 1677 and often reprinted. See Bourgeois and
André, *op. cit.* I, No. 462, and also for bibliography V. Ball, *Travels in
India by J.-B. Tavernier*, 2nd ed. (by W. Crooke), 1925, I, pp. ix ff.
Tavernier's work was rather severely criticised soon after its appearance
and some of his information is at second-hand, but Lord Curzon is on the
whole favourable to him (*op. cit.* I, p. 24 n.[1]).

[2] 2 vols. 1685; 1689; Amsterdam, 1699; Cologne, 2 vols. 1709; *ib.*
3 vols. 1711; E. T. 1698 and 1699.

[3] Leyden, 1687; Paris, 1688; E. T. by H. Wharton, 1688. *Voyages de
M. Dellon*, Amsterdam, 1709. See Bourgeois and André, *op. cit.* No.
501.

[4] *Relations de divers voyages curieux qui n'ont pas été publiées* (often
bound up together in 2 vols. fo.). Many of the translations are made from

countries and to stimulate the curiosity of the public. One of the maps in the first part represents a large imaginary continent called *La Terre Australe*, of which there had been rumours ever since the publication of the travels of Marco Polo, and it is this imaginary continent that is the scene of the two earliest apocryphal or "extraordinary" voyages that appeared in French literature.

La Terre Australe inconnue appeared in 1676. Its nominal author was "Mr Sadeur," and its nominal place of publication was Vannes[1]. But it was printed at Geneva, and its real author was Gabriel Foigny, a disreputable person, who, after being a Franciscan monk, became a Protestant and then again a Catholic. The *Histoire des Sévarambes* was first published at London in English (1675), and then at Paris (1677–1679) in French. Though no name appears on the title-page, its author was undoubtedly Denis Veiras or Vairasse of Alais, another Protestant[2]. As neither of these voyages belongs to our period, I must refer my readers for an account of them to Mr Atkinson, M. Chinard, and M. Lachèvre. Both contain the two elements which I have noted as a constant characteristic of the Extraordinary Voyage, a narrative of adventure (which in

the collections of Hakluyt and Purchas. In 1681 Thévenot published a volume in small 8vo entitled *Recueil de Voyages*. It was reprinted in 1682 (*Bib. Sund.* No. 12409). Before his death in 1692 he printed several new pieces, destined to form a fifth part, and after his death these were published together with the original four parts in 1696. See A.-G. Camus, *Mémoire sur la collection des grands et petits voyages et sur la collection des voyages de M. Thévenot*, 1802.

[1] Reprinted under the title of *Les Avantures des Jacques Sadeur*, 1692, 1693 and 1705; E. T. 1693. The original text is reproduced by F. Lachèvre in *Les Successeurs de Cyrano de Bergerac*, 1922. See Atkinson, *op. cit.* pp. 15–19; Chinard, *op. cit.* pp. 195–210. Also Bayle, *Dict. hist.* art. Sadeur; A. Lichtenberger, *Le Socialisme au XVIIIe siècle*, 1895, pp. 38–40, and *Le Socialisme utopique*, 1898, pp. 37–40.

[2] The first part of the English text appeared in 1675, the second part, which is abridged from the French version, in 1679. part I of the French version was published in 1677, and part II in 1678–1679. Part II was reviewed as an authentic record of travel in the *Journal des Savants* for March 7, 1678 (p. 91). Later editions of the whole work were published at Brussels, 1682, and at Amsterdam, 1682, 1702, 1715, 1716. A Dutch translation appeared in 1683 and a German one in 1689. M. Lachèvre gives two short extracts.

Foigny's book is largely fantastic), and a Utopian account of the country visited, which serves as an excuse for a trenchant criticism of the institutions and religion of Western Europe. Vairasse's ideal government is a paternal despotism; Foigny's is one of complete liberty; but in both Utopias life is ordered with such machine-like regularity that it becomes at once repulsive and ridiculous. Both authors are Deists.

Only one Extraordinary Voyage of any importance was published during our period, but before coming to it mention must be made of another work of genuine travel. For it has one feature of the Extraordinary Voyage, namely exaggerated praise of a savage community coupled with malicious criticism of European civilisation in general and of that of France in particular. The author was a certain Baron de La Hontan (*c.* 1666–1715?), a Gascon gentleman who went as a soldier to Canada in 1683, and his book was entitled *Nouveaux voyages de Mr le baron de La Hontan dans l'Amérique septentrionale*[1]. The original two volumes were speedily followed by a third, entitled *Supplément aux Voyages du Baron de Lahontan où l'on trouve des Dialogues curieux entre l'auteur et un sauvage de bon sens qui a voyagé*[2]. The work proved immediately popular; two more editions appeared in the same year, and a third in 1704[3]. Then in 1705 an ex-Benedictine of Saint-Maur, who had abjured Catholicism for Protestantism, by name Nicolas Gueudeville (*c.* 1650–*c.* 1720), brought out a revised edition[4],

---

[1] The Hague, 2 vols. 1703 (B.M.). See for the work and its author, J. E. Roy, *Proceedings and Transactions of the Royal Society of Canada*, vol. XII (1894), pp. 63–192 (with a bibliography); Bourgeois and André, *op. cit.* I, No. 585; Chinard, *op. cit.* pp. 167–187; A. Lichtenberger, *Le Socialisme utopique*, pp. 32–41.

[2] The Hague, 1703 (B.M.); re-issued separately, Amsterdam, 1704.

[3] These early editions are very rare.

[4] 2 vols. The Hague, 1705. There is also an Amsterdam edition of the same date, which I have used.

The *Dialogues* are generally supposed to be the work of Gueudeville, but M. Chinard thinks that he merely revised them. In his preface to the edition of 1705 Gueudeville says that he has made many alterations in both the matter and the language of Lahontan's work, but M. Chinard, who has carefully compared his edition with the original one, declares that the changes do not amount to much except in the Third Dialogue. Gueudeville translated the *Moriae Encomium* and the *Colloquia*, More's *Utopia*, and the Comedies of Plautus.

which became the basis of many subsequent ones. In all there were twenty-two (including English, Dutch, and German translations), from 1703 to 1741[1].

The only chapter in Lahontan's travels proper with which we need concern ourselves is that in which he describes the religion of the Indian savages. They believe, he tells us, in the immortality of the soul and in a Great Spirit who is everywhere and in everything. They object to Christianity because it is contrary to Reason, and they treat with ridicule both the Fall of Man and the Incarnation. At the same time they reproach Christians with habitually violating the precepts of that Son of God in whom they profess to believe.

In the first of the dialogues between Lahontan and a Huron named Adario, which were added as a supplement, this attack on Christianity is developed at greater length and with increased acrimony. The two other dialogues are more interesting. In the second the Huron compares the "incomparable liberty" which he enjoys with the "vile slavery" of the French, and he recommends revolution as the obvious cure for tyranny. In the last dialogue he declares that all private property or "Le Tien et le Mien" is an abuse. He compares the manners and customs of the Indians with those of the French, greatly to the disadvantage of the latter. He is eloquent on the absurdities of dress and on the tyranny of fashion. In words which recall La Bruyère he describes the condition of the poor in France:

> Pâles, maigres, décharnés, enfin de vrais squelettes vivants, et d'ailleurs tout nus, à quelques haillons près....Voilà donc notre homme qui meurt de faim pendant que les Commis et les Financiers se regorgent de sa substance.

In conclusion he draws a Utopian picture of Huron society— a society which has for its sole and only good the observance of Natural Law. The Huron has not only the last word in these dialogues but it is clear throughout that Lahontan's sympathies are with him. To make this clearer, in all the editions of the work there is an engraving of a "noble savage," brandishing a spear,

---

[1] An English translation, 2 vols. appeared as early as 1703. It has been reprinted by R. G. Thwaites, Chicago, 1905.

with one foot on a book[1] and the other on a sceptre and a crown. Above is inscribed, "Et leges et sceptra terit[2]." It matters little, says truly M. Chinard, whether Lahontan or Gueudeville is the author of the dialogues. The remarkable thing is that the writer, ten years before the death of Louis XIV, "announces not only Jean-Jacques Rousseau, but the *Père Duchesne* and modern revolutionary socialists[3]."

Of the two Extraordinary Voyages which belong to our period the earliest—in fact earlier than the *Voyages de Lahontan* —is the *Histoire de Calejava* of Claude Gilbert[4]. But it needs only a brief notice here, for, unlike the other works of its class, its interest is wholly didactic and the element of adventure is almost entirely lacking. The voyage of four Europeans to

[1] M. Chinard says "a bible," but is it not rather a book of laws?

[2] This engraving forms the frontispiece of vol. I of the original edition. In the Amsterdam edition of 1705 it is placed opposite to p. 104 of vol. II.

[3] *Op. cit.* p. 185. M. Chinard couples with the travels of Baron de Lahontan those of another popular writer, the Flemish Récollet father, Louis Hennepin—*Description de la Louisiane*, 1683; *Nouvelle découverte d'un très-grand Pais situé dans l'Amérique*, Utrecht, 1697; *Nouveau voyage d'un Pais plus grand que l'Europe, ib.* 1698. But it seems to me that M. Chinard is mistaken in thinking that the religious and social opinions which the father attributes to the Indian savages have a malicious intention or that his work is "injurious rather than useful to religion and society." It may be added that the works have no independent value as records of travel. The second and its continuation, the third, are merely an amplification of the first, and all three are copied largely from the writings of Cavelier de La Salle and Chrétien Le Clercq, another Récollet father. Hennepin was in Quebec from 1674 to 1680; he made his voyage down the lower Mississippi in 1679–1680. See Chinard, *op. cit.* pp. 160–167; Bourgeois and André, *op. cit.* I, Nos. 578, 594 and 595; Parkman, *La Salle and the Discovery of the Great West*, 1899, p. 247 n.[1].

[4] *Histoire de Calejava ou de l'isle des Hommes raisonnables. Avec le paralelle de leur Morale et du Christianisme.* MDCC. There is no name of author, or printer, or place, but it was printed at Dijon by Jean Ressayre. The author, who was an advocate of Dijon (1652–1720), fearing a prosecution, burnt all but one copy, which is now in the *Bibliothèque Nationale* (D². 7939 Rés.). See G. Lanson, *Rev. des Cours et Conf.* 1908–1909, pp. 219– 221 (I have not seen this); G. Atkinson, *The Extraordinary Voyage in French Literature from 1700 to 1720*, pp. 27–30; Lachèvre, *Les successeurs de Cyrano de Bergerac*, pp. 210–234: Lachèvre reproduces the last books (XI and XII). I have not seen the unique copy of the original.

Calejava (the land of Ava), which is reached in a little over two months from the coast of Lithuania, is briefly related in the first book, while the remaining eleven consist chiefly of dialogues, in which the travellers and a native of Ava discuss such subjects as reason, God, the immortality of the soul, and the customs, morality, and religion of the Avaïtes. Like most Utopian societies, they have all things in common. They believe in God, the soul, and reason, that all men are equal, that it is God's will that man should be happy in this world, and that the golden rule is to love your neighbour as yourself. These three precepts, declares one of the Europeans, Alatre, whose name signifies "Without worship," contain all that is essential in the teaching of the Gospel.

If we were to accept the contention of Mr Atkinson, the next Extraordinary Voyage to be noticed would be the *Voyage et Avantures de François Léguat*, which was published in London in French and English in 1708[1]. The most interesting portion of the book—the only one which need concern us—is the author's account of the residence for two years of himself and seven companions in the small uninhabited island of Rodriguez, which lies about 330 miles to the eastward of Mauritius[2]. His narrative is remarkable for his careful and detailed observations on the natural history of the island, and especially for his account of the famous extinct Solitaire, a cousin to the Dodo of Mauritius[3]. The first to question the genuineness of his story was his contemporary, Bruzen de La Martinière, who in his Dictionary of Geography (1726–1730) classes it among "fabulous travels." But this view, though it has found supporters from time to time,

---

[1] *Voyage et Avantures de François Leguat et de ses compagnons en deux isles desertes des Indes Orientales*, 2 vols. London, 1708 (it was reviewed in journals for the year 1707); *ib.* 1711; *ib.* (really Rouen), 1720; *ib.* 1721. There is a counterfeit Amsterdam edition of 1708. Translations: English, *A new Voyage to the East Indies by Francis Leguat*, 2 vols. 1708; ed. Pasfield Oliver for the Hakluyt Society, 2 vols. 1891. Dutch, Utrecht, 1708. German, Leignitz (really Frankfort and Leipzig), 1709. See Bourgeois and André, *op. cit.* I, No. 528; G. Atkinson, *op. cit.* pp. 35–65, and 113–135.

[2] Original French edition, I, 59–164; ed. Oliver, I, 50–137.

[3] Orig. ed. I, 98–103; ed. Oliver, 77–81.

has never been altogether accepted, and during the latter half of the last century Leguat's veracity was established in the eyes of scientific naturalists by his precise and accurate descriptions of the fauna and flora of Rodriguez. So strong was this conviction that the text of his narrative, transcribed from the first English edition, was edited by Captain Oliver for the Hakluyt Society in 1891. Quite recently, however, the question has been again raised by Mr Atkinson, who contends that Leguat's story is based on an engraving in the *India Orientalis* of the brothers De Bry[1], with judicious additions from the writings of various travellers.

But Mr Atkinson is wrong. It happens that Mr Stanley Gardiner, the Professor of Zoology in the University of Cambridge, has visited Rodriguez, and he says that he is "quite sure the writer was at Rodriguez," and he adds that he "bases this view on references to topography, nature of land, caves, soil and so on, not on the animals and plants in the first instance." Leguat's narrative, therefore, does not belong to the category of Extraordinary Voyages[2].

There is no question as to the *Voyages et Avantures de Jaques Massé*[3] being a work of fiction, for its authorship is

[1] Reproduced in the Hakluyt edition of Leguat, II, 371. For the brothers De Bry see above, p. 170.

[2] After reading the account of the Solitaire in Alfred Newton's *Dictionary of Birds*, I came to the conclusion that Leguat's description of it was made from personal observation. Prof. Gardiner, however, tells me that he might have seen a specimen either in Paris or in Holland. There is a practically perfect skeleton in the Museum of Zoology at Cambridge. Neither Cauche nor Carré nor Du Bois, from whom Mr Atkinson thinks that Leguat borrowed his description, visited Rodriguez, the only home of the bird known as the Solitaire. The Solitaire described by Carré and Du Bois is a different bird.

It is agreed that the preface to Leguat's Voyage is by Maximilien Misson, who, like Leguat, was a Protestant, and who died in London in 1722, and it is probable that he edited the book. He may have introduced some matter of his own, but the jaunty and self-conscious style of the preface is totally different from the naïve simplicity of the main text.

[3] A Bourdeaux, chez Jaques l'Aveugle, 1710. Bordeaux is no doubt not the real place of printing. I have used an edition from the Acton collection of the Cambridge University Library, with the imprint, L'Utopie, chez Jaques l'Aveugle, 1760. There is an English translation of 1733 by

acknowledged by Simon Tyssot de Patot (1655—after 1727), whose family moved from Rouen to Delft, and who became a professor at Deventer. His other writings include a second Extraordinary Voyage, *Le Voyage de Groenland* (1720), and *Lettres Choisies* (1727), which led to his dismissal from his professorship. The story of Jacques Massé is as follows. He was a surgeon by profession and in that capacity he joined a ship which was sailing from Dieppe to Martinique. The ship foundered off Cape Finisterre, but the crew were picked up by an English vessel and landed at Lisbon. Here Massé spent nearly a year and then joined a Portuguese vessel bound for the East Indies. On nearing St Helena, he encountered a violent storm, which blew for twenty-two days and finally drove his ship on an unknown and apparently uninhabited coast about Latitude 44° S. and Longitude 60° E. His adventures now began in earnest. Setting out with two companions to explore the country, he marched for nearly four hundred miles, until, after losing one of his companions, he reached a fertile valley, where, with his remaining companion, La Forêt, he was hospitably received by the inhabitants. This newly-discovered country is, as one might expect, a sort of Utopia; at any rate it is organised with that mathematical precision and regularity which is so tiresome a feature of many Utopias. It is divided into villages or cantons, perfectly square in shape, and consisting of twenty-two houses, eleven on one side of a canal and eleven on the other. In each canton there is a Judge and a Priest, and one of the Judges acts as host to the two travellers and briefly expounds to them the laws and religion of the country. "I believe," he says, "in an increate Substance, a Universal Spirit, supremely wise and perfectly good and just, who has made heaven and earth and all things therein, who upholds, governs, and animates them." This Being they honour with worship and thanks, but they do not pray to Him, and they do not believe in immortality. There

Stephen Watley. See G. Atkinson, *op. cit.* c. iv; Lanson (*loc. cit.* pp. 258–270); Le Breton, *op. cit.* pp. 359–363. Voltaire in his *Lettres Philosophiques* refers to "l'auteur déguisé sous le nom de Jaques Macé" (ed. Lanson, I, 175).

follows the account of a "curious conversation," in which the
Priest of the canton, who has been dining with the Judge,
attacks Christianity with singularly crude and puerile criticisms.

After a time La Forêt's skill as a maker of clocks and
watches comes to the ear of the king of the country and the
two Europeans are summoned to court. The account of their
sojourn there is not particularly interesting, and the long discourses which Massé makes to the king on astronomy and
religion are decidedly tiresome. At last their residence at the
court is brought to an abrupt termination, owing to the king's
favourite wife—he has twelve wives—having made midnight
assignations with the inflammable La Forêt, in order to get
him to make her a watch. On one of these occasions La Forêt
is observed by an officer of the court, and he accordingly
persuades his friend, greatly against his inclination, that they
had better make a hasty escape. After some thrilling adventures they find themselves back at the point of the sea-coast
from which they had started five years before. Here after a
time they fall in with their former companions, who had built
a fort with a stockade to defend themselves against savages.
These had attacked them on several occasions and in large
numbers, but they had been successively repelled. The account
of two of these attacks will be read with delight by those who
remember the part played by savages and stockades in the
favourite books of their childhood[1]. After this it is a considerable bathos to come to the mathematical and scientific studies
with which the united companions occupy themselves during
the next twelve years.

But there are other adventures to follow. Four of the company embark on a Spanish ship bound for Goa, where Massé
is imprisoned by the Inquisition and sent to Lisbon to serve a
life-sentence with hard labour. The ship is attacked by pirates,
and Massé is sold for a slave and taken to Algeria. After thirty
years of slavery he is at last ransomed through the good offices
of the British Consul, who had known his younger brother,

[1] Mr Atkinson points out that similar accounts are to be found by
dozens in the voyage literature of France in the seventeenth century.

and he arrives in London just fifty years after he had sailed from Lisbon on his second voyage.

There is considerable merit in this novel of adventure. It is written in a good narrative style—simple, straightforward, clear—and the realistic details, which are introduced casually and without undue emphasis, help to create the illusion of truth. Nor is this illusion disturbed by the adventures being wildly improbable. Mr Atkinson indicates as the chief sources of Tyssot de Patot's information, Mocquet, Tavernier, Dellon, and Lahontan[1], and he points out that there are clear reminiscences of the *Histoire des Sévarambes* and the *Terre Australe inconnue*. One defect of the book is that the hero is perfectly colourless. Another is that the narrative is too often interrupted by scientific and religious digressions, introduced partly to shew off the author's knowledge of science, and partly to air his free-thinking opinions. Mathematics, astronomy, and the history of the formation of the earth, are all the subjects of tiresome disquisitions[2], and the *post-mortem* dissections of two of Massé's companions are carefully described.

In the religious discussions, while Massé retains his rôle of good Catholic and La Forêt that of fervent Protestant, the attacks on Christianity are assigned to others—to the Judge and the Priest of the unknown country, to a Chinese fellow-prisoner at Goa[3], and to a renegade Christian in Algeria[4]. "Je suis Universaliste," says the Chinaman, "ou de la religion des honnêtes gens; j'aime Dieu de tout mon cœur...et je tâche de faire aux hommes, sans exception, ce que je souhaite que l'on me fasse à moi-même." But he does not believe in the Divinity of Christ, or in the Virgin Birth, or in miracles. The Christian renegade, a Gascon by birth, is described by Massé as "the boldest Atheist or Deist I have ever seen." The two had long discussions and finally the renegade, who had found no religion which could satisfy a reasonable man, relates to Massé

---

[1] For all these see above, pp. 171–173 and 175–177.

[2] See especially part II, pp. 105–119. "Nous nous exerçâmes des années (twelve years) dans ces belles sciences."

[3] Part II, pp. 137–153.

Part II, pp. 178–200.

the Fable of the Bees, which is a transparent satire on the Christian story of the Incarnation and the Crucifixion.

Tyssot de Patot's second Extraordinary Voyage, *Le Voyage de Groenland*, falls outside the limits of my period, and as, according to Mr Atkinson, it is "poorly constructed, badly written, and tiresome to read," with no new elements but "the polar setting and a psychological interest in sorcery and miracles," I need do no more than refer the reader to Mr Atkinson's competent account of it[1].

3. *Fairy-tales.*

We learn from a letter of Mme de Sévigné's to her daughter that as early as 1677[2] the telling of fairy-tales was a fashionable pastime at court. But it was not till nearly twenty years later that they assumed a written form and that, thanks to the genius of Perrault, they became a highly popular branch of literature[3]. "Les Contes des Fées ont été longtemps à la mode," writes the Comte de Caylus, who was born in 1692, "et dans ma jeunesse on ne lisait guères que cela dans le monde[4]."

Charles Perrault (1628–1703)[5], who was the initiator of this new *genre*, was the youngest of five brothers, of whom three, besides himself, made some mark in the world—Pierre, the eldest, as a dabbler in letters, Nicolas, as a Doctor of the Sorbonne and a Jansenist theologian, and Claude, who was a physician by profession, as the architect of the noble colonnade (eastern front) of the Louvre. Charles began life as an advocate, but gave up the bar to become clerk to his brother Pierre, who was Receiver of the Finances for Paris. The post gave him

---

[1] *Op. cit.* pp. 99–110.

[2] August 6, 1677. Lang gives the year wrongly as 1676.

[3] See G. Saintsbury, *History of the French Novel*, I (1917), 245–272 for an excellent account of the French fairy-tales of this period.

[4] *Le Cabinet des Fées*, XXV, 379.

[5] See P. Bonnefon, *Charles Perrault, Essai sur sa vie et ses ouvrages* in *Rev. d'hist. litt.* XI (1904), 365 ff.; XII (1905), 549 ff.; XIII (1906), 606 ff.; Arvède Barine in *Rev. des Deux Mondes* for December 1, 1890; A. Hallays, *Les Perrault*, 1926. Perrault's agreeable *Mémoires de ma vie* (Avignon, 1755; ed. Bonnefon, 1909) were written in 1702, but they do not go beyond 1688.

ample leisure for literary work, and he made a reputation as a
writer of light verse, especially of a celebrated *Portrait d'Iris*[1].
He was a frequenter of *précieux* salons and an active opponent
of Boileau and his friends. In 1663 on the recommendation of
Chapelain he was employed by Colbert as *Contrôleur des
bâtiments royaux.* Having gained the minister's confidence, his
functions rapidly extended, and he became the intermediary
between Colbert and the numerous body of artists, men of
letters, actors, booksellers, and workmen, who worked for the
king. He was also a member of Colbert's Petite Académie—
a small body, which later developed into the Académie des
Inscriptions et Belles-lettres—and from 1671 of the Académie
Française. In this latter capacity he shewed great activity,
urging on the work of the Dictionary, introducing the ballot
into the elections, and generally improving the organisation and
consequently the influence of this honourable but easy-going
assembly.

About 1681 he resigned his post under Colbert and returned
to the world of letters. He was once more active in opposition
to Boileau and the classical school, and he produced much
literature including a long Christian epic entitled *Saint-Paulin*
(1684), "which," he says, "had a fair success in spite of the
criticisms of a few wits." One of these wits was of course
Boileau. Three years later, as will be recounted in its proper
place, he began his celebrated campaign on behalf of the
Moderns against the Ancients. But the only writings of his
that are read at the present day are those of his old age—his
Mémoires and his immortal *Contes du temps passé.*

He began with three tales in verse, of which the first, *La
Marquise de Sallusses ou la patience de Grisélidis*[2], was published
in 1691. It was reprinted with the other two—*Peau d'Asne* and
Les Souhaits ridicules—in 1694, but this is stated to be the
second edition[3]. It is therefore often supposed that the two later
contes first appeared in the *Recueil de pièces curieuses et nouvelles
tant en prose qu'en vers* of the bookseller of the Hague, Adrian
Moetjens. But as Moetjens only published pirated works, it is

---

[1] Printed in *Portraits de Mlle Montpensier.*
[2] Le Petit, *op. cit.* p. 436.   [3] *Ib.* p. 438.

much more probable that *Peau d'Asne* and *Les Souhaits ridicules* were published, either together or separately, in 1693 or early in 1694. *Peau d'Asne* shews a marked improvement on *Grisélidis* and was so greatly appreciated that a fourth edition of the three *contes* was published in 1695.

In these verse tales Perrault appears as a facile and agreeable follower of La Fontaine, but in the following year he struck out a line of his own by contributing to *Le Mercure galant* for February 1696 a fairy-tale in prose, entitled *La Belle au bois dormant*. It was reprinted in the second part of the fifth and last volume of Moetjens's *Recueil*[1]. Seven more prose tales by the same hand were published in the fourth part (1697) of the same volume, but all eight had already appeared at Paris earlier in the year as *Histoires ou Contes du temps passé*[2]. A Dutch reproduction bears the alternative title of *Contes de ma mère loye*. The privilege for the Paris volume was granted to P. Darmancour, Perrault's youngest son, aged nineteen, and the dedication was signed by him, but there is no good reason to question Perrault's authorship. He no doubt associated his son with the tales, because he had been one of the children to whom they were told[3].

Of these celebrated fairy-tales there is no need to speak at length. It is now recognised that the tales themselves are as old as the hills and common to countries widely remote from one another. Perrault used nothing but oral sources, and he had probably never heard either of the *Notti* of Straparola or of the *Pentamerone* of Basile, to which Dunlop supposed that he was indebted. It was just because his sources were oral and not

---

[1] Each volume of the *Recueil* contained six parts.

[2] See Le Petit, *op. cit.* p. 439. The best modern editions are those by Ch. Giraud, 2nd ed. 1865; A. Lefèvre, 1875; A. Lang, Oxford, 1888.

[3] See Bonnefon, *Rev. d'hist. litt.* XIII (1906), 628–634. Marty-Laveaux, *op. cit.* VII (1900), thinks that, with the exception of *Le Petit Chaperon rouge*, they were written by the son and revised by the father. This last view has been recently supported by M. Émile Henriot in the *Rev. des Deux Mondes* for January 15, 1928. On the other hand, M. André Hallays (*Journal des Débats* for January 22, and February 5, 1928) is still a firm believer in the authorship of the father (see *Chronique des Lettres françaises*, No. 32, pp. 172–174).

literary that he tells his stories to his readers as he had told them to his children, with a brevity, directness, and simplicity which give them a singular impression of reality. They also shew a remarkable dramatic instinct. Indeed, in this combination of simplicity with dramatic power Perrault is a prose La Fontaine. He also resembles the great fabulist in the touches of archaism in his language and in his sly asides of wit or humour. Finally, it is interesting to note that this champion of the Moderns is in his brevity and his self-restraint a thorough classicist.

The greatest favourites among these immortal tales are *Le Petit Chaperon rouge*, which is a model of brevity; *La Barbe-bleue*, which, except for the enchanted key, is not a fairy-tale; *Le Maître Chat ou Le Chat botté*, the most humorous of all; and *Cendrillon ou la Petite Pantoufle de verre*. The least popular is certainly *Riquet à la Houppe*, which is only partly traditional and is not simple enough for a child. *La Belle au bois dormant* is charming as far as the awakening of the princess, but there it should have ended, as it does in Grimm. Perrault had already revised the story as it appeared originally in *Le Mercure galant* by the omission of certain passages[1], but he might have carried his revision further with advantage. The story of *Tom Thumb* is deservedly popular with boys, but whether in Perrault's version or in the numerous other versions it is difficult to say. *Les Fées*, or the story of the two sisters, from the mouth of one of whom came pearls and diamonds and of the other toads and vipers, appears in Grimm as *The three little men in the wood*. Perrault's version is very short, but its moral is a little too obvious. Fairy-tales though they are, Perrault's stories represent the manners and the daily life of his time, and they are drawn from all classes of society. Only the Sleeping Beauty and Riquet of the Tuft are born in a palace. Bluebeard is a wealthy lord, but, in spite of the popular tradition current in Brittany and La Vendée, he is not to be identified with the historical monster, Gilles de Rais, who was executed in 1440. Cinderella is of noble birth, and

---

[1] See Bonnefon, *op. cit.*; *Rev. d'hist. litt.* for 1906, pp. 623–626.

the two sisters of *Les Fées* are apparently of the *bourgeois* class. But Tom Thumb is the son of a woodcutter, the master of Puss in Boots is the son of a miller, and Little Red Riding Hood is a poor village maiden.

On the other hand the stories of Mme d'Aulnoy, who ranks next to Perrault as a writer of fairy-tales[1], begin almost invariably with, "There was once upon a time a King and a Queen." Fortunée, who is the daughter of a poor labourer, is quite an exception. Other marked differences between her tales and Perrault's are their prolixity and their love of exaggeration. In *Finette Cendron*, which is a version of *Cinderella*, there is a magic ball of thread which guides Finette for 3000 leagues, the ogre's palace has walls of emeralds and rubies and a roof of diamonds, the ogre's wife is fifteen feet in height and thirty in girth, and the ogre swallows fifteen children as if they were fifteen fresh eggs. In the *Blue Bird*, one of Mme d'Aulnoy's best-known stories, the order of the Knights of Love, which the wicked Queen has made for King Charming, is composed of jewels so large and wonderful that "since the beginning of the world a like thing had never been seen." But, in spite of exaggerations, the best of her tales, which include *The White Cat*, *The Yellow Dwarf*[2], *Fortunée*[3], *Gracieuse et Percinet*, *La Belle aux cheveux d'or*[3], *Le Mouton*[3], *La Biche au Bois*, and *Le Prince Lutin*, deservedly take high rank in the nursery.

Mme de Murat's fairy-tales[4] are hardly less extravagant in incident and detail than Mme d'Aulnoy's and they are far less

---

[1] *Contes de Fées*, 4 vols. 1697 (a conjectural first edition the existence of which is proved by a reference to it in *Le Mercure galant*); *Les Illustres Fées*, 1698 (*Bib. Nat.*); *Contes nouveaux ou Les Fées à la mode*, 2 vols. 1698 (*Bib. Nat.*); *Suite des contes nouveaux*, 2 vols. 1698 (see Foulché-Delbosc, *op. cit.* pp. 120–124); *Nouveaux contes de Fées*, 1708, Amsterdam; *Cabinet des Fées*, 41 vols. 1785–1789, II–IV and part of VI; E. T. with an introduction by Lady Ritchie (illustrated), 1895.

[2] As regards *The Yellow Dwarf*, I agree with Prof. Saintsbury that fairy-tales should not end tragically. Perrault's version of *Little Red Riding Hood* has not kept the field.

[3] Translated in the *Blue Fairy Book*.

[4] *Contes des Fées*, 1697 ; *Nouveaux contes de Fées*, 1698 ; *Le Cabinet des Fées*, vol. I (six selected tales).

interesting. Moreover, as they are all sentimental love-stories, even the fairies not being exempt from the tender passion, they are quite unsuited to children. The tales of Mlle de La Force[1] are of much the same character, but one of them, *La Bonne Femme*, is not without charm. Lastly there is Mlle L'Héritier (1664–1734), the friend of Mme Deshoulières[2], and a connexion of Perrault's, who wrote much miscellaneous prose and verse, including a few fairy-tales, of which one, *L'Adroite Princesse ou Les Aventures de Finette*, was generally included in editions of Perrault from 1742 onwards, and attributed to that writer[3]. It is inconceivable how such a mistake can have been made, for nothing can be more unlike Perrault in treatment or style. The only resemblance is that, just as Perrault appends to his tales a *moralité* in verse, Mlle L'Héritier founds her tale on two proverbs, "Idleness is the mother of all vices," and "Mistrust is the mother of safety." The story, which has a touch of eighteenth-century *grivoiserie*, is quite as unsuitable to children as those of Mlle de La Force and Mme de Murat, to the latter of whom it is dedicated. Mlle L'Héritier also wrote *La Tour Ténébreuse et Les Jours lumineux, Contes anglois* (1705), which consists of two stories supposed to be told by Richard Cœur de Lion in his Austrian prison to his faithful Blondel[4]. When one considers the great inferiority of these later fairy-tales to Perrault's, and especially their unsuitability for children, one is not surprised that Mme de Maintenon, in a letter to the Comte d'Ayen (her niece's husband) asking him to find someone to write short stories for young persons, should declare roundly that she does not want fairy-tales or tales like *Peau d'Asne*[5].

[1] *Les Contes des contes*, 2 vols. 1698; *Les Fées*, 1708; *Le Cabinet des Fées*, vol. VI.

[2] See above, p. 141.

[3] For instance in vol. I of *Le Cabinet des Fées* and in Giraud's edition of Perrault (1864). It first appeared in print in the *Œuvres meslées* of Mlle L'H***.

[4] *Le Cabinet des Fées*, vol. XII.

[5] P. Jacquinet, *Mme de Maintenon, Choix de ses lettres*, p. 112. The letter was written in March 1700.

4. *Oriental Tales.*

The vogue of the fairy-tale prepared the way for what the Comte de Caylus calls the "succès prodigieux" of *Les Mille et Une Nuits* and *Les Mille et Un Jours.* Antoine Galland (1646–1715), to whom "wholly and solely," says Sir Richard Burton, Europe owes its knowledge of the *Arabian Nights*, was the youngest child of poor parents, who moved to Noyon from another part of Picardy when he was six months old[1]. From an early age he shewed a strong bent towards learning, and judicious help enabled him to accomplish his desires. He became fairly competent first in Latin and Greek, and then in Hebrew, Arabic, Persian, and Turkish. Five years of travel in the East (1670–1675), followed by short visits to Smyrna (twice), Lesbos and Constantinople and by another three years (1685–1688) of travel, gave him an intimate knowledge of Oriental life as well as of Oriental languages. In 1709 he was appointed Professor of Arabic at the Collège de France, his colleague being François Pétis de La Croix. Among his friends were the most learned men in the kingdom—Barthélemy d'Herbelot, Professor of Syriac at the Collège de France, Étienne Baluze, Colbert's librarian, the foremost man of his time for general learning, the two great Benedictines, Dom Mabillon and Dom Montfaucon, and the Bishop of Avranches, Pierre-Daniel Huet.

It was, we may conjecture, the popularity of the fairy-tale that suggested to him the idea of introducing the great Arabian collection of *The Thousand and One Nights* to his fellow-countrymen. However this may be, in 1704 he published the first four volumes of his famous translation. It is in reality not a translation but an adaptation, made with rare skill and literary tact, to suit the taste of his French readers. "It suppresses much of the local colour," says Burton, "it expunges the childish indecencies," "it rejects the proverbs, epigrams, and moral reflections which form the pith and marrow of the book,"

---

[1] All the various biographical notices of Galland seem to have as their ultimate source the short autobiography which he wrote in 1711. See *Journal Parisien d'Antoine Galland (1708–1715), précédé de son autobiographie*, ed. H. Omont, 1919.

and "it disdains the finer touches of character[1]." Moreover, it contains only a quarter of the original work. However reprehensible this treatment may seem to modern Orientalists, it was completely justified. If *The Nights* lost their Oriental character, they commended themselves not only to the French public, but, through translations, to the whole Western World. Had M. Mardrus's scholarly translation in sixteen volumes appeared in 1704, it would not have had more than half-a-dozen readers, but Galland's adaptation achieved immediate success and within a few years was often reprinted. The success encouraged him to continue his work and in 1705 he published a fifth and sixth volume, and in 1706 a seventh[2]. The eighth volume did not appear till 1709, the ninth and tenth in 1712, and the eleventh and twelfth, after Galland's death, in 1717[3]. But, with three exceptions—*Ganem, The Sleeper awakened,* and *The Magic Horse*—none of the stories in the last five volumes, not even *Aladdin* and *Ali Baba,* though they are all genuine Oriental tales, are in the original text of *The Thousand and One Nights.* One of the great merits of *Les Mille et Une Nuits* is its style. It is simple, limpid, straightforward, without digressions, and with few reflections—the style of the born story-teller.

Galland's example was shortly followed by his colleague, Pétis de La Croix (1653–1713) who, though a Professor of

[1] See Burton's *Arabian Nights,* Library edition, 1894, vol. VIII, p. 101, and generally for Galland's translation, *ib.* pp. 86–101. Similarly the most recent French translator, J. C. Mardrus, speaks of Galland's stories as "écourtés, déformés, expurgés de tous les vers, poèmes et citations des poètes" (*Le livre des Mille et Une Nuits,* 16 vols. 1912, p. xiii).

[2] Fontenelle's approbation is dated April 4, 1705. Vol VII contains the stories of *Nur Al Din,* but it is not clear whether they were in the manuscript from Syria which Galland used, as the fourth and last volume of this has been lost.

[3] See Galland's *Journal Parisien* and Appendix I (by W. F. Kirby) to vol. VIII of Burton's *Arabian Nights.* The *Bib. Nat.* has copies of all the original editions except of vols. II and III, vol. II being represented by an edition of 1705. The principal later editions are those of A. Caussin de Perceval, Professor of Arabic at the Collège de France for nearly forty years, 9 vols. 1806; E. Gauttier, 7 vols. 1822–1824; E. Destains, 6 vols. 1823–1825, with an introduction by Ch. Nodier; A. L. A. Loiseleur-Deslongchamps (in the *Panthéon littéraire*), 1838.

Arabic, was better versed in Persian and Turkish. In 1710 he published the translation of a Turkish work by Sheikh Zadah, the tutor of Amurath II—*L'Histoire de la Sultane de Perse et des Visirs. Contes turcs.* In the same year he began a translation of *The Thousand and One Days*, which his Persian friend Moclès or Mukhli, chief of the Sufis of Ispahan, had composed in imitation of *The Thousand and One Nights*, taking his material from certain Indian comedies[1]. In this latter work Pétis de La Croix was assisted by Lesage, thanks to whom, the style has the classical simplicity of Galland's work.

5. *Anthony Hamilton.*

I have purposely left to the last a writer of considerable interest and some importance, who represents nearly all the different kinds of literature—*vers de société*, biographical memoirs, fairy-tales, Oriental tales—that have been noticed in this and the previous chapter. Anthony Hamilton (1644 or 1645–1719)[2], who gave to France a classic which French critics have described as characteristically French, was the grandson of the first Earl of Abercorn, a Scottish nobleman who settled in Ulster at the time of the Great Plantation in 1610. In 1651 he went with the rest of his family to France, where they lived for the next ten years, at first (almost certainly) at Caen and later in Paris. When they returned to England in 1661, Anthony was fifteen or sixteen, too young to have acquired any definite literary tastes, and it was doubtless under the auspices of Saint-Évremond, to whom he was introduced two years later by his future brother-in-law, the Chevalier de Gramont[3], that he made acquaintance with the literature of the country in which he had passed the greater

---

[1] 5 vols. 1710–1712. There is a recent English translation, by J. H. McCarthy, 2 vols. 1892. See *Le Cabinet des Fées*, XXXVII, 266, 274, 278.

[2] *Œuvres*, 3 vols. 1812. See Ruth Clark, *Anthony Hamilton*, 1921 (an admirable piece of work); Sainte-Beuve, *Causeries du Lundi*, vol. I; A. Sayous, *Hist. de la littérature française à l'étranger*, 2 vols. 1853, II, c. VI (excellent); G. Saintsbury, *Essays on French Novelists*, 1891; *History of the French Novel*, I (1917), 305–324; S. Gwynn, *Macmillan's Magazine*, May 1898.

[3] The Chevalier married Elizabeth Hamilton in December 1663.

part of his life[1]. Saint-Évremond's judgment on French literature carried great weight with the English courtiers and men
of letters, but though he possessed a real critical gift, he had
strong prejudices, and he was especially prejudiced against
the great writers who had helped to make illustrious the reign
of the monarch who had banished him from France. Even
Molière and La Fontaine, with whom he had much in common,
he only tolerated. He still clung to the favourites of his youth—
Montaigne, Malherbe, Corneille, Voiture. We may conjecture
then, with some confidence, that it was Saint-Évremond who
inspired Hamilton with a taste for Voiture. Hamilton found
in him a kindred spirit—frivolous, witty, sociable—and he
learnt from him to admire Voiture's contemporaries, Sarasin
and Benserade, and even the ponderous Chapelain.

For his life during the thirty years which elapsed between
his return to England and his final settlement in France, we
have very few facts. "It is more than likely," says Miss Clark,
that he accompanied his brother George to France in 1668,
and he certainly served in the "régiment d'Hamilton," which
George raised in Ireland in 1671 for service with the King
of France. After the Peace of Nymegen (1678) he seems
to have left France, and in 1681 we find him established at
Dublin. He fought in the army of James II at the battle of
the Boyne (1690), retired to France after the defeat, and, being
outlawed in the following year, attached himself to the gloomy
court of the exiled monarch at Saint-Germain, of which he
has written a well-known description—not to be taken too
seriously—in his unfinished tale of *Zeneyde*[2].

But Hamilton was not dependent on this little court for
society. He was a welcome guest at Sceaux and the Temple,
and at both his gift for writing facile verse was frequently
called into requisition. In these productions, which are in a
literal sense *vers de société*, he is content to follow the fashion.
He is particularly fond of writing letters half in verse and
half in prose, but he also writes *rondeaux*, after the manner of
"the great Voiture," *chansons* set to well-known airs, and what

---

[1] See the *Épître à Gramont* (*Œuvres*, I, I ff.).
[2] *Œuvres*, II, 399 ff.

he calls *bouquets*. He has wit, gaiety and charm, but he is too facile and careless ever to reach a high level. His best-known poem may be quoted as a favourable example.

> Celle qui adore mon cœur n'est ni brune ni blonde;
> Pour la peindre d'un seul trait,
> C'est le plus charmant objet
> Du monde.

Only three of his poems have any pretensions to seriousness, but one of these, entitled *Réflexions*, shews real feeling. This is the first stanza:

> Grâce au ciel! je respire enfin
> Au bord fatal du précipice,
> Où m'avaient entrainé le désordre et le vice,
> Qui règnent dans le cœur humain;
> Le Sauveur m'a tendu la main,
> Et j'ai senti cette bonté propice
> Qu'on n'invoque jamais en vain.
> Idole que mes vœux n'ont que trop encensée,
> Volupté! vif objet de nos désirs errants,
> Ivresse d'une âme insensée,
> Ne troublez plus de tranquilles moments.
> Fuyez, spectacles séduisants,
> Fantômes qui teniez ma raison balancée,
> Entre vos vains engagements;
> Éloignez de mes yeux tous ces enchantements,
> Et n'offrez plus à ma pensée
> Vos frivoles amusements[1].

Among his earliest pieces, if not absolutely his earliest, are two songs on the birth of James II's daughter (June 28, 1692) but it was the *Épître à Monsieur le Comte de Gramont*, half in prose and half in verse, which made his reputation. In this epistle, written in 1704 or early in 1705, he announces his intention of writing a memoir of his celebrated brother-in-law, now in his seventy-eighth year. At first he had thought—so he says with delightful gravity—of entrusting the task to some learned and serious person, as, for instance, Rollin or Mabillon or even Boileau. But it occurred to him that they might be wanting in sympathy for his hero, so he decided upon applying to Gramont's

---

[1] *Œuvres*, III, 308.

friends, Chaulieu and La Fare. Then the shade of the "inimitable" Saint-Évremond appeared to him and urged him to take the work in hand himself, and by January 1707, when Gramont died, the *Mémoires* were nearly, if not entirely, completed. Hamilton, however, had no intention of publishing them, and it was greatly to his annoyance that they appeared in 1713 under the title of *Memoires De La Vie Du Comte De Grammont* (Gramont is the correct spelling); *contenant particulierement l'histoire amoureuse de la Cour d'Angleterre sous le regne de Charles II* and with the well-known fictitious name of Pierre du Marteau of Cologne as publisher[1].

In reading the book, one asks oneself whether Hamilton's admiration for his hero is altogether sincere. He is certainly not presented to us in a very favourable light. He cheated habitually at cards and won large sums which provided for his reckless and ostentatious extravagance; he was an inconstant lover both before and after his marriage, and he often made love for the sole pleasure of supplanting another man[2]. In spite of these unpleasant defects—cheating at cards was not regarded in those days with the same disapproval as now—the Chevalier de Gramont was in high favour both at the English and the

---

[1] See for the title-page Le Petit, *op. cit.* p. 478. Editions are numerous; the best is that by G. Brunet, 1859, with a full commentary. My quotations are from M. de Lescure's edition in the *Librairie des Bibliophiles*, 1876. The *Mémoires* were translated in 1714 by the Huguenot refugee, Abel Boyer, but his translation is slovenly and incorrect. It has, however, been frequently re-published in a revised form, notably in 1811, with full notes and illustrations by Sir Walter Scott. This edition formed the basis for the two best modern editions, both copiously annotated—that of H. Vizetelly, 1889, and that of G. Goodwin, 2 vols. 1903. Another translation was published in 1794 by the brothers, Edward and Silvester Harding, with 76 portraits, poorly executed, by Silvester.

[2] See for both counts the report of his conversation with Saint-Évremond (*Mémoires*, ed. Lescrie, pp. 94-98). For cheating at cards see also the story of how he plucked the Comte de Caméran at Lyons (c. iii), and compare "il jouoit gros jeu et ne perdoit que rarement" (p. 93) with Sourches, *Mémoires*, I, 313, and the addition of the anonymous annotator that he made by gambling at the English court fifty to sixty thousand crowns a year. Once only he lost heavily and this was at basset, a game in which, says the annotator, *industrie* does not help you. For his inconstancy in love see the last sentence of the *Mémoires*.

French courts. Sourches, no doubt, gives the true reason when he says, "La cour perdit en lui l'homme du plus agréable esprit qu'il a eu depuis longtemps." He was attractive, especially to Charles II and Louis XIV, because he was not only witty but frank—a quality, which, when exercised with tact, is much appreciated by monarchs. Moreover, what he said was made more attractive by the way in which he said it. Recognising this, Hamilton is very chary of quoting his witty remarks or reproducing his stories of his adventures. "It would be idle to write down word for word his diverting narratives: their savour evaporates on paper, and whatever form you give to them the life that lies behind them is absent[1]." The only stories therefore that Hamilton relates in the Chevalier's own words are those of his valet, Termes, and the quicksands of Calais[2], and of two amusing incidents of the campaign of Catalonia in which he played a leading part[3].

The *Mémoires* fall into two parts, of which the first, only about a quarter of the whole, relates Gramont's adventures, chiefly in Piedmont, before he came to England, while the second is the well-known account of the English court. The first part is decidedly the more entertaining of the two, thanks partly to the delightful character of Matta, who is almost as prominent as the Chevalier himself. On the other hand, the second part, the *Histoire amoureuse de la Cour d'Angleterre*, as it is called in the original edition, has attracted the most attention, both as a record of social life under Charles II and as a rich pasture for lovers of gossip and scandal. Horace Walpole declared that he knew the *Mémoires* by heart; he made elaborate notes with a view to a new edition, and he spent much time in hunting for portraits of the more important characters[4].

---

[1] *Mémoires*, p. 62.   [2] *Ib.* pp. 119–121.

[3] *Ib.* pp. 140–144. See for a concise notice of the Chevalier Saint-Simon, *Mémoires*, ed. Boislisle, XIV, 559–567.

[4] In 1772 he printed at the Strawberry Hill press a hundred copies of a new edition, with three portraits (Anthony and Elizabeth Hamilton and the Chevalier de Gramont). It was dedicated to Madame ——, but in the reprint by Dodsley in 1783 the blank was filled in with the name of Mme Du Deffand, who had died three years previously (R. Clark, *Modern Language Review*, X (1915), 58–63).

At the outset Hamilton says frankly that he will be troubled neither by chronology nor by the arrangement of his facts, but frequent and minute examination has shewn that the facts themselves may be accepted in the main as trustworthy. The social historian then will find in the *Mémoires* a true, if slightly coloured, picture of the Court of Charles II—a picture which corresponds closely both with the statements of contemporary historians and memoir-writers and with the comedies of the Restoration dramatists. But the ordinary reader grows tired of this monotonous record of frivolity and amorous pursuit. Miss Clark has rightly called attention to the brilliance of the portraits. Except for the full-length portrait of Elizabeth Hamilton they are only vignettes, but they are drawn with a consummate hand. One of the most famous is that of Mrs Wetenhall (*née* Bedingfield). Even in a line or two Hamilton can hit off a likeness. Miss Clark gives several instances, of which among the most striking are the description of Cerise, the host of the inn at Lyons, as "suisse de nation, empoisonneur de profession et voleur d'habitude," and that of M. de Sénantes, as "fort en généalogie comme sont tous les sots qui ont de la mémoire."

The first of Hamilton's *Contes, Le Bélier,* was probably written in the early summer of 1705. Its ostensible purpose was to explain why his sister, Mme de Gramont, had changed the name of the small property which Louis XIV gave to her in 1703 from Les Moulineaux to Pontalie, but its real object was to satirise the fairy-tales which Perrault and his imitators had made so popular. Moreover in 1704, as we have seen, there had appeared the first volumes of *Les Mille et Une Nuits* and these also have their share of Hamilton's ridicule. This object is openly avowed by him in the verse with which *Le Bélier* opens[1]:

> Et je fourrai dans cet ouvrage
> Ce qu'a de plus impertinent
> Des contes le vain étalage,

and the *Arabian Nights* are spoken of with equal disrespect as *fatras*.

---

[1] *Œuvres*, II, 115 ff.; the verse occupies 18 pages.

The chief characters of *Le Bélier* are a druid and his beautiful daughter Alie, a hideous and stupid giant named Le Moulineau, and a wonderful ram, who is the giant's trusted adviser and who entertains him with stories after the manner of Scheherazade. Their adventures are told with much gusto, and the giant's constant interruptions of the ram's stories, which always begin with "Bélier, mon ami," are highly amusing. But the numerous complications and the general incoherence, which Hamilton has purposely introduced by way of satire, do not make the tale easy reading. It should be added that the ram turns out to be the Prince de Loisy, Alie's lover, and that after being mortally stabbed by her (through a misunderstanding of her father's directions) he recovers his life, overthrows the giant, and is happily married to his lady-love. And this was why the name of Les Moulineaux was changed to Pontalie.

Hamilton's other two completed stories were written some ten to fifteen years later, between 1710 and 1715, that is, after the publication of the tenth volume of Galland's translation of the *Arabian Nights* and when Pétis de La Croix and Lesage were producing, if they had not actually completed, their translation of *Les Mille et Un Jours*. Both stories, *Fleur d'Épine*[1] and *Les Quatre Facardins*[2], are not only burlesques of the *Arabian Nights* but they are closely connected with it. *Fleur d'Épine* is the thousand and first night and is told by Scheherazade's sister Dinarzade; *Les Quatre Facardins* is the thousand and second night and is told by Dinarzade's lover, the Prince of Trebizond. Some very good judges, including Professor Saintsbury, prefer *Les Quatre Facardins*, but I confess myself unable to cope with the extreme intricacy of its narrative. Hamilton himself seems to have been baffled by it, for he left it unfinished. *Fleur d'Épine*, on the other hand, has a certain unity of action, and Fleur d'Épine herself is of remarkable charm. Montégut, indeed, calls it the most charming fairy-tale ever written in France. It should be noted that in both stories most of the characters are purposely made

[1] *Œuvres*, II, 1 ff.
[2] *Ib.* 257 ff.; Facardin is the popular spelling of the name of the celebrated Emir, Fakhr-ed-Din (R. Clark, *op. cit.* 244 n.[1]).

ridiculous and the adventures purposely extravagant; in *Les Quatre Facardins* the satire is directed not only against the Oriental tales but against the western romances of chivalry and particularly against *Amadis*. Moreover, in both stories, and also in *Le Bélier* there is, as Professor Saintsbury points out, "a perpetual undercurrent of satirical criticism of life." For Hamilton was not merely a wit but also a shrewd observer of his fellow-men. He often preferred solitude to company and there was a vein of melancholy in his composition. Indeed in one of his shorter writings, *Relation d'un voyage en Mauretanie*, he figures as "le triste Marc-Antonin."

None of Hamilton's stories were printed till 1730, but they circulated in manuscript among his friends, who were doubtless entertained, not only by the stories themselves, but also by thinly-disguised allusions to contemporary persons and events. The first publisher, for instance, tells us that *Le Bélier* contains "mille petits faits déguisez."

Finally, we come to the important question of Hamilton's prose style. Like his verse it has wit, gaiety, ease, and grace. The *Mémoires*, it is true, are not wholly free from *préciosité*. Perhaps the most glaring instance is the description of Jermyn as "un trophée mouvant des faveurs et des libertés du beau sexe," but others, less glaring, are scattered over the whole work. It was not for nothing that Hamilton was an admirer of Voiture. He was also addicted to certain mannerisms, such as the over-employment of antithesis, in this resembling Fléchier, and the occasional use of forced metaphor. These blemishes, however, are confined to the second part of the *Mémoires* and a possible reason is that in this record of frivolity and scandal Hamilton felt the need of an artificial reinforcement for his natural *esprit*. Certainly the first part of the *Mémoires* and all the tales are almost entirely free from any sort of affectation. In the tales especially we realise that the style is that of the eighteenth century[1]. It is no longer transitional like that of La Bruyère; it definitely renounces the long oratorical period of the seventeenth century for the short broken period of the eighteenth.

---

[1] M. Lanson in his *L'Art de la Prose* quotes a fairly long passage from *Fleur d'Épine* (pp. 145–147).

If it has not the gravity of Montesquieu or the nervous strength of Voltaire, it at least anticipates their directness, simplicity, clarity, and grace. "De tous les livres," says Voltaire of the *Mémoires*, [c'est] "celui où le fonds le plus mince est le plus paré du style le plus gai, le plus vif et le plus agréable," and the testimony is important as coming from Voltaire. For Voltaire, not only in his style, but also in his light verse and his tales, came in some measure under the influence of Hamilton, and it is this influence which makes Hamilton, a foreigner, an amateur, who wrote for his friends and not for the public, and whose works may seem to some austere readers wholly frivolous, a figure of considerable importance in the history of French literature.

CHAPTER VII

MME DE MAINTENON AND THE
EDUCATION OF GIRLS[1]

MADAME DE MAINTENON, without being a figure of the
first importance, has an assured place in the history of French
literature, first as a letter-writer, and secondly for her services
to the education of women.

[1] The letters of Mme de Maintenon were first published by La Beaumelle
at Nancy in 2 vols. in 1752, and then at Amsterdam in 8 vols. (with a supplementary volume containing letters from the Bishop of Chartres, Godet Des
Marais) in 1755–1756. But over eighty of the 2500 letters were fabricated by
the editor, and most of the rest were falsified or altered by him, in concert
with the ladies of Saint-Cyr. A hundred years later Théophile Lavallée,
one of the professors at the military school of Saint-Cyr, began a publication of Mme de Maintenon's works, which, at his death in 1867, comprised
the following volumes: *Lettres sur l'Éducation des Filles*; *Entretiens
sur l'Éducation des Filles*; *Lettres historique set édifiantes*, 2 vols.;
Conseils et Instructions aux Demoiselles pour leur conduite dans le monde,
2 vols.; *Correspondance générale*, 4 vols. The 4th vol. carries the correspondence down to the end of 1701; a 5th vol. which was printed, but
never put into circulation and is very rare, stops at 1705. Selected letters
have been published by O. Gréard, *Mme de Maintenon, Extraits de ses
lettres sur l'éducation*, 1884; A. Geffroy, *Mme de Maintenon, d'après sa
correspondance authentique*, 2 vols. 1887; P. Jacquinet, *Mme de Maintenon
dans le monde et à Saint-Cyr*; *Choix de ses Lettres et Entretiens* [1888];
Lettres à D'Aubigné et à Mme des Ursins, ed. G. Truc (*Chefs-d'œuvres
méconnus*), 1921. For various publications of unpublished letters see
Bourgeois and André, *op. cit.* II (1913), pp. 359 ff.

D'Haussonville and Hanotaux I, *Mémoire et Lettres inédites de Mlle
d'Aumale*, 1902; II, *Les Cahiers de Mlle d'Aumale*, 1903; III, *Mme de
Maintenon à Saint-Cyr, Dernières Lettres à Mme de Caylus*, 1905. Mme
de Caylus, *Souvenirs*, 1770; ed. É. Raunié, 1889. Duc de Noailles,
Histoire de Mme de Maintenon, 4 vols. 1848–1858. Lady Blennerhasset,
Louis XIV and Mme de Maintenon, 1910 (competent and trustworthy).
Mme Saint-René Taillandier, *Mme de Maintenon*, 1920 (a study of re-
markable delicacy and insight; there is an English translation by Lady
Mary Loyd, 1922). *Lettres de Paul Godet des Marais à Mme de Maintenon*,
ed. l'Abbé Berthier, Brussels, 1755; reprinted Paris, 1908. See also

Her life, so far as it is known—for there are still dark places in it—has been told so often, that it is unnecessary to tell it over again here, and, at any rate for the earlier part of her career, a brief summary will suffice. Françoise d'Aubigné was born November 27, 1635, in the prison of Niort, where her father Constant d'Aubigné, the unworthy son of the stout Huguenot leader and distinguished writer Agrippa d'Aubigné, was incarcerated. She was baptized as a Catholic, but she was brought up in the Protestant faith by her aunt the Marquise de Villette, the favourite daughter of Agrippa d'Aubigné. In 1645, her father having been released on the death of Richelieu three years previously, she went with her parents to Martinique. She returned with them to France in 1647, and, on her father's death towards the end of that year, was again entrusted to the care of Mme de Villette. But by order of Anne of Austria she was handed over to her godmother, Mme de Neuillant, who tried in vain to convert her to Catholicism. She was then sent to an Ursuline Convent in Paris, where, harshness and persecution having failed, she finally yielded to gentler methods. She now rejoined her mother and shared her poverty till her death in 1650.

In 1652 Mme de Neuillant arranged for her a marriage with the poet Scarron, who was forty-two and a helpless cripple. He died in 1660, leaving debts which nearly swallowed up his small estate, and all that his widow had to live on was a pension of 2000 *livres* bestowed on her by the queen-mother. As Scarron's wife she had played hostess to many people of wit and fashion, and with these she kept up her relations. Especially she frequented the salons of Mme d'Albret and Mme de Richelieu. With both these ladies she was a great favourite, and her good looks, her quick intelligence, her gaiety, her readiness

Sainte-Beuve, *Causeries du Lundi*, IV, VIII, and XI; É. Faguet, *XVIIᵉ Siècle*, 1887.

Th. Lavallée, *Histoire de Saint-Cyr*, 1856. P. Rousselot, *Histoire de l'Éducation des Femmes en France*, 2 vols. 1883. O. Gréard, *L'Éducation des Femmes par les Femmes, Études et Portraits*, 1886; 7th ed. 1907. G. Compayre, *Histoire critique des doctrines de l'Éducation en France*, 1879, I, 359–384.

to help others, and her uprightness made her also a general favourite[1]. Her chief beauty was in her bright almond-shaped black eyes; she had a good complexion, an aquiline nose, a large mouth with red lips, fine teeth, and a charming smile. Her hands and arms were well modelled and she had a noble presence, which with the brightness of her eyes she still retained in extreme old age[2]. A portrait of her by Mignard, painted in 1659, the year before Scarron's death, bears testimony to the general accuracy of this description[3].

The first nine years of Mme Scarron's widowhood were the happiest of her whole life. But this life was now to undergo a great change. In Mme d'Albret's salon, she had made friends with Mme de Montespan, who was a relative of M. d'Albret's, and when the royal mistress was about to become a mother and was at her wits' end to know how the child was to be born and brought up in secrecy, she turned to Mme Scarron for help. It was a strange service to ask of a religious woman. In her perplexity Mme Scarron consulted her spiritual director, the Abbé Gobelin, an ex-officer of saintly character, who had a reputation for severity and strictness. His decision was that if the king would avow his paternity and personally request her to become governess to his child, the request should be obeyed. Accordingly when the child, a girl, was born (1669)[4], Mme Scarron, concealed by a mask, was present at its birth, and carried it off then and there to a small house in the outskirts of Paris. With all deference to the Abbé Gobelin, she made a false step.

---

[1] See A. de Boislisle, *Le Veuvage de Françoise d'Aubigné* in *Rev. des questions hist.* LVI (1894), 48 ff.

[2] See *ib.* p. 54.

[3] This is the only portrait of her in her young days. It is the property of M. Penjon and is reproduced as the frontispiece to the *Mémoire de Mlle d'Aumale*. The two best-known portraits of her are that by Ferdinand Elle at Versailles with her niece, Mlle d'Aubigné, painted about 1696 (see Mme Saint-René Taillandier, *Mme de Maintenon*, p. 168), and that by Mignard, as S. Frances of Rome, the foundress of the community of the Oblates, in the Louvre. There are more han 30 portraits of her in the Cabinet des Estampes, and 20 at Saint-Cyr. One of the former, engraved by Giffart in 1687, is reproduced by Faguet, *Hist. de la litt. française*, II, 158.

[4] She died in 1672.

If it left her conscience untroubled, it led her from one false position to another, and finally condemned her to a life of semi-servitude.

For the second child, the Duc du Maine (*b.* 1670), another small house was taken, thus making the arrangements for secrecy more complicated. But on the birth of the third child in 1672 the whole nursery was established in a larger house at the far end of the Saint-Germain quarter, near the barriers and Vaugirard[1]. In the winter of 1671–1672 Mme de La Fayette, who lived in the Rue Vaugirard, and her friend Mme de Sévigné, who had known and liked Mme Scarron in the old days, met her frequently. "We sup every evening at Mme Scarron's," writes Mme de Sévigné to her daughter on January 13, 1672; "her mind is amiable and wonderfully upright." "Mme Scarron sups here every evening," she writes again on February 26, "and she is delicious company."

In December 1673 Louis XIV, with Oriental arrogance, legitimised his bastards, and there being no longer any need of secrecy Mme Scarron was openly installed in Mme de Montespan's apartments at Saint-Germain as governess to her children. The change, if anything, increased the difficulties of her position. She was now under Mme de Montespan's orders and subject to the vagaries of her capricious temper. "The days pass in a slavery which prevents me from doing what I should like to do," she writes to her director (July 10, 1674). But one hope sustained her. She had "an immense longing to buy a landed property," and the king had promised her a reward for her services. On the last day of September 1674 she wrote to her director that the king had given her 200,000 *francs*, and before the end of the year she signed a contract for the purchase of an estate at Maintenon, 30 miles from Versailles and 12 miles from Chartres[2]. In a letter of January 15, 1675, she signs herself "Maintenon" for the first time; in 1680 the title of *Marquise* was granted her, and in 1688 her estate was made a Marquisate.

---

[1] It was on the site of 25 Boulevard Montparnasse.

[2] The price was 250,000 *francs*, the balance of 50,000 *francs* being provided out of her savings.

The royal gift relieved Mme de Maintenon from the poverty which had been her lot nearly all her life, but it riveted her chains all the more firmly. Moreover at this time the religious party at the court were doing their utmost to separate the king and Mme de Montespan. At Easter 1675 Bossuet thought that his admonitions had proved successful, for both the sinners professed repentance and consented to a voluntary separation. But when the king, according to his custom, returned from the wars in July, with three Flemish towns to his credit, his promises of amendment were forgotten. Mme de Montespan bore him more children, the last—the Comte de Toulouse—in 1678. Mme de Maintenon's letters to her director, who wished her to remain at court, are full of complaints. "God knows the bottom of my heart," she writes from Versailles in October, "and I hope that He will break my chains, if it is necessary for my salvation." Meanwhile the haughty mistress was losing her hold over Louis XIV. Seven children—four died in childhood—in nine years had told upon her complexion and her figure, and she was growing more and more irritable. At the end of 1679 she was supplanted by a new mistress *en titre*, Mlle de Fontanges.

In January 1680 Mme de Maintenon was appointed second bedchamber-woman to the Dauphine, and soon afterwards the king began to shew a marked liking for her society. "Elle lui fit connaître un pays tout nouveau, je veux dire le commerce de l'amitié et de la conversation sans chicane et sans contrainte; il en paraît charmé," writes Mme de Sévigné in July, and in September the same witness reports that the courtiers call her "Mme de Maintenant," and that she passes every evening from eight to ten with His Majesty. Some months earlier Mlle de Fontanges, after being created a Duchess, had been packed off to the Abbey of Chelles, to die there in the following year, and the door had been finally shut, not to say banged, in the face of Mme de Montespan. The coveted post of mistress to the king was vacant. It was never again filled. Louis returned to the queen, and she recognised gratefully that she owed his return to the influence of Mme de Maintenon.

The years 1680–1683 were spent by Mme de Maintenon in peace and tranquillity, and freed from the tyranny of Mme de

Montespan she no longer wished to leave the court, of which, in Mme de Sévigné's words, she had become the "soul." But on July 30, 1683, the queen died after a short illness, and Mme de Maintenon went through a fresh period of agitation. The scrupulous care with which she suppressed every direct proof of her marriage deprives us of definite information about this crisis in her career. But stray allusions in her letters and the statements of Saint-Simon and Mme de Caylus, though they were both children at the time, point to the probabilities that her marriage with Louis XIV was decided on in September 1683, and that it took place some time in January 1684.

It will be seen from the foregoing brief narrative that, except on the hypothesis that she was a female Tartuffe, Mme de Maintenon cannot be fairly accused of having supplanted Mme de Montespan. The connexion between Louis XIV and Mme de Montespan ended in as ordinary and commonplace a fashion as it had begun, with the declining attractions of the lady and the satiety of the gentleman. It was only when the king's passion was growing cold that Mme de Maintenon began to urge them both to sever the connexion[1]. Nor is it possible to suppose that she ever contemplated either succeeding Mme de Montespan as mistress, or, seeing that she was older than the queen, who was apparently in perfect health, the queen as wife. The task that she had set herself, at the instigation of her spiritual director and the religious party at the court, was the salvation of the king's soul, and so far as this consisted in his return to decent living, she had succeeded. But with the death of the queen a fresh crisis arose, a crisis which could only be averted by the king's marriage to Mme de Maintenon. It was a wonderful position for the daughter of a small noble and the widow of Scarron, but it was a position of servitude— of a servitude which was to last for more than thirty years. Mme de Maintenon dearly loved esteem and respect, and a sphere for the exercise of influence, but she must often have sighed for the liberty and independence of her château at Maintenon.

[1] For her justification of her conduct see *Lettres historiques et édifiantes*, II, 73.

Fortunately we possess a full record of her daily life and habits, for in addition to Saint-Simon's account of what he calls her *mécanique*[1]—and on this subject his testimony may be accepted—we have the detailed narrative of an ordinary day at Versailles which she gave to Mme de Glapion, one of the ladies of Saint-Cyr, in 1707, and which the latter recorded in writing[2].

Mme de Maintenon rose at six, made a partial toilet, said her prayers, attended Mass, and then returned to the room which served her as bedroom, sitting-room, and dining-room. At about half-past seven a stream of visitors began to arrive—the king's first surgeon, his first physician, and his first valet de chambre. Then, after a short interval, during which she wrote a few pressing letters, came various high officials—the Minister for War, the Archbishop of Paris, and possibly a general on the eve of departure for the front. Next would appear, perhaps, the Duc du Maine, to be followed by the king, and it was not till His Majesty went to Mass that the poor lady was left alone to finish her toilet and replace her night-cap by a more becoming head-dress. With the king's return from Mass the procession began again. The king was succeeded by the Duchesse de Bourgogne and a large number of ladies, who did not even allow Mme de Maintenon to dine in peace—she dined at noon—with her friends Mme d'Heudicourt and Mme de Dangeau. At last they went off to their own dinner and Mme de Maintenon was left to talk to her old friends or play a game of backgammon. But often the Dauphin would drop in, and, as he never had anything to say, it was hard work to entertain him. The afternoon began with the return from dinner of the king and all the princesses with their ladies-in-waiting, filling the room and making it insufferably hot. After half-an-hour the king retired, but the rest remained for a long time and, being freed from the restraint of the king's presence, overwhelmed Mme de Maintenon with their conversation.

---

[1] *Mémoires*, XII, c. vii; ed. Boislisle, XXVIII, 242–281. The chapter will also be found in my selections from Saint-Simon, with the addition of a passage from VI, 203–204.

[2] Geffroy, II, 43 ff.

Moreover, one of them invariably remained behind the rest in order to pour out her family troubles or appeal to Mme de Maintenon for her good offices with the king. "C'est à moi qu'il faut s'adresser, par qui tout passe."

The next event in the day was the king's return from hunting, when he confided to her his worries and difficulties, sometimes even being moved to tears. "Conversation he had none." At seven a minister would arrive, often with bad news, and the king would settle down to serious work.

Mme de Maintenon's apartments were separated from the king's by the *Salle des Gardes du Roi*, and to reach her bedroom from his own he had to traverse first the large antechamber known as the *Salle des Bassans*, then the antechamber in which he dined in public, then the *Salle des Gardes du Roi*[1] and finally the vestibule and two small narrow ante-chambers of Mme de Maintenon's apartments. From the second of these ante-chambers a door opened into her bedroom. Between the door and the fireplace of the bedroom, which was 40 feet long by 20 broad, was placed the king's arm-chair, its back to the wall, with a table in front of it and a folding-chair for the minister in attendance. On the other side of the fireplace was Mme de Maintenon's arm-chair, and beyond it a deep narrow alcove in which her bed was placed. Opposite to the foot of the bed was another door, leading into a larger room—*le grand Cabinet*—which Mme de Maintenon hardly ever entered, and which was used in the evening for cards and other games by the Duchesse de Bourgogne and those ladies who had the *entrée*[2].

While the king did business with his minister, Mme de Maintenon read or worked. Often he would ask her advice—"What does your Solidity think?"—and then she would give it. The extent of her political influence has often been discussed, but the general opinion now is that, in spite of the protestations of the ladies of Saint-Cyr and other of her admirers, and of the deprecatory statements in her letters, Saint-Simon's

[1] See above, p. 19.
[2] Mme de Maintenon's apartments were greatly altered when Louis-Philippe transformed Versailles into a National Museum.

account of her share in affairs is not greatly exaggerated[1]. She was certainly much interested in the relations of France with Spain, as her correspondence with Mme des Ursins shews, and she wrote regularly to Villars during all his campaigns from 1703 onwards. But her influence made itself by suggestion and by advice, when it was asked for, and never by open interference or underhand intrigue. Nor did her advice always prevail. She was opposed to the acceptance of the King of Spain's will, and when the war brought disaster upon disaster, especially in the terrible year 1709, she was all for peace.

In the sphere of religion there is no question as to her influence, and Mme Saint-René Taillandier is not far wrong in saying that the central object of her religious policy was the king's salvation. She has been made responsible by her enemies, above all by Michelet, for the revocation of the Edict of Nantes. But though, like every Catholic in the kingdom, except a few individuals of unusual enlightenment and tolerance, she certainly approved of it, she had nothing to do with the actual repeal, and she cordially disliked the policy of wholesale and enforced conversions. She detested Louvois, the author of the *dragonnades*, as much as he detested her. What appealed to her most in the wretched business was the restoration of unity to the Church, that ideal which blinded Bossuet by its splendour, and pleased Louis XIV by its appearance of order and symmetry. Mme de Maintenon too was inclined by nature to set a high value on order and orthodoxy and to dislike any religious views which shewed any variation from the established pattern. Her church

---

[1] See H. Baudrillart in *Rev. des questions hist.* XLVII (1890), 101 ff. and Saint-Simon, *Mémoires*, ed. Boislisle, XXVIII, 254 n.[5] In Mme Glapion's report the printed text runs, "Si on veut que je suis en tiers dans ce conseil, on m'appelle," but the manuscript has, "Quand il travaille avec ses ministres et on ne m'appelle pas, *ce qui est très rare*, je me retire." This was one of the alterations which La Beaumelle made in concert with the good ladies of Saint-Cyr, who in their devotion to Mme de Maintenon's memory forgot the *droiture* and *simplicité* which she was for ever commending to them. (A. Taphanel, *La Beaumelle et Saint-Cyr*, 1898, p. 215.)

policy and her recommendations to appointments proceeded on these lines. When the Archbishopric of Paris, the most important see in the kingdom, became vacant by the death of Harlay (1695), she procured the nomination of Noaille:, the Bishop of Châlons, a man of saintly but far from strong character, whose intelligence lagged behind his virtues. Did she prefer him to Bossuet because she thought he would be more accessible to her influence? At any rate she trusted greatly in him, and in the campaign against Quietism he was her firm ally. But as soon as she found that he was tainted with that other heresy, Jansenism, she abandoned him, with hardly a struggle, to the king's displeasure.

But we must go back to Mme de Maintenon's bedroom, where she has supper with her two friends, while the king goes on working. It is a hurried and uneasy meal, for the king is always interrupting her and begging her to make haste. At about nine o'clock, she looks so tired, that even the king, who was peculiarly unobservant of the sufferings and discomforts of others, says that she ought to go to bed. So her women come in and undress her in a great hurry—she hates hurry—for His Majesty is impatient of their presence. At last she is in bed and her women are dismissed, though often she has further need of their services. The king stays till supper-time, the Dauphin, and the Duc and the Duchesse de Bourgogne having meanwhile come in to say good-night. At ten or soon after they all go, and Mme de Maintenon is left alone for the first time since half-past seven in the morning.

Such was a normal day of Mme de Maintenon's life at Versailles, but it must be remembered that the irksome monotony of her existence was relieved by frequent visits to Saint-Cyr.

To obtain a more intimate knowledge of Mme de Maintenon's character we must go to her letters, and we may take as a starting-point a letter written to her by Fénelon (probably at the beginning of 1690), in answer to a request that he would tell her of her faults—a letter which is as remarkable for its frankness as for its insight.

"Vous êtes née," he says, "avec beaucoup de gloire, c'est-à-dire de cette gloire qu'on nomme bonne et bien entendue, mais qui est d'autant plus

mauvaise qu'on n'a point de honte de la trouver bonne....Vous tenez encore
à l'estime des honnêtes gens, à l'approbation des gens de bien, au plaisir
de soutenir votre prospérité avec modération[1]."

Mme de Maintenon recognised that this was one of her
chief faults, and in a conversation with Mme de Glapion, which
is of great importance for a knowledge of her character[2], she
declared that during the first years of her widowhood her great
wish was to have the approbation of *les honnêtes gens*, and that
later when she was at court she desired the esteem and praise
of everybody, from the king to a street-porter, and that there
was nothing that she would not have done or suffered in order
to be well spoken of. "Une belle réputation"—that was her
one aim. "I did not care in the least for riches, I was in a position far too high to need interest, but I wanted honour....Is
not this the sin of Lucifer?"

Presently Fénelon puts his finger on another defect.

Vous êtes naturellement bonne, et disposée à la confiance, peut-être
même un peu trop pour des gens de bien dont vous n'avez pas éprouvé
assez à fond la prudence. Mais quand vous commencez à vous défier, je
m'imagine que votre cœur se serre trop.

Saint-Simon similarly accuses her of taking sudden likes
and dislikes, "both often without cause or reason[3]." This last
remark is unfair. Mme de Maintenon was not capricious, but,
as Fénelon justly says, she was prone to give her confidence
too rashly and then abruptly to withdraw it. She was decidedly
engouée, to use Saint-Simon's expression, with Fénelon himself,
with Cardinal de Noailles, and with Mme de Brinon, the first
Superior of Saint-Cyr. And then when she found these *gens
de bien* wanting in prudence and consequently mistrusted
them, she tightened her heart-strings. We see this in a letter
which she wrote to Cardinal de Noailles, after learning of
his Jansenist sympathies[4]. Three years later, she writes to
his nephew, the Duc de Noailles, who had married her niece:
"M. le cardinal de Noailles et moi nous brouillons tous les jours

---

[1] *Corr. générale*, I, 399 ff.; Fénelon, *Œuvres choisies*, IV, 131 ff.
[2] *Lettres hist. et édifiantes*, I, 211 ff.; the conversation was held in
1707.
[3] *Mémoires*, XII, 102.   [4] Geffroy, II, 13.

de plus en plus....Ma destinée est de mourir par les évêques, vous savez ce que M. de Cambrai m'a fait souffrir[1]." Her change of attitude towards these prelates arose partly because, as has been said, she shared Louis XIV's love of order and orthodoxy, and partly because she lacked the courage to displease him. Up to a certain point she would support a losing cause or a falling individual, but, when once either had definitely lost the king's favour, she abandoned the contest as hopeless. Yet Saint-Simon is grossly unfair when he accuses her, first of procuring the appointment of his friend, Chamillard, and then of plotting his downfall[2]. She had nothing to do with his appointment, and he fell because, though an honest and kindly man, he was an incompetent minister.

Fénelon's next criticism is that she is unsympathetic (*sèche*) and severe, that she does not permit people to have any defects, and that when she discovers any failing in those whom she had hoped to find perfect she turns against them too suddenly and too entirely. The last part of this criticism is more or less a repetition of what Fénelon had said before, and the first part is only partially true. Mme de Maintenon may have had too high a standard of human nature, but she had a patient and kindly temper, and, judging by her letters to the ladies of Saint-Cyr, though she certainly could be severe she was never hard or unsympathetic.

It has been suggested with probability that Mme de Maintenon's request to Fénelon was prompted not merely by a desire to know her faults, but in order to test him as a possible successor to the Abbé Gobelin, who was growing old and who was too much impressed by her exalted position to be able to direct her with sufficient authority. Fénelon continued to write to her spiritual letters down to May 1694[3], but she did not choose him for her director. Possibly she was unwilling "to submit herself entirely to the advice of a single director[4]."

---

[1] Geffroy, II, 77.   [2] *Mémoires*, VI, cc. xxiii–xxvi.

[3] Twenty-four letters from Fénelon to Mme de Maintenon are printed in his *Lettres et Opuscules*, 1850, and some of his *Instructions ou Avis* are evidently addressed to her.

[4] Cp. Gréard, *L'Éducation des Femmes*, pp. 64–65.

Possibly she realised that Fénelon's letter was coloured by that exaggerated view of Pure Love with which Mme Guyon had indoctrinated him. Exaggeration in religion was as little to Mme de Maintenon's taste as a dominating influence.

It is a pity that we have so few letters for that happy period of Mme de Maintenon's life after the death of Scarron, when, free from the restraint and secrecy which were afterwards imposed upon her, she could indulge in her natural propensity to mirth and gaiety. But except for a few mere notes, written soon after Scarron's death, there are only four letters for this period—two to her brother[1], one to her cousin, M. de Villette (lively and affectionate), and one to her cousin's wife. The only really entertaining letter that we have for the whole first thirty-four years of her life is one to Mme de Villarceaux, a little more than a month before Scarron's death, in which she gives a lively account of the triumphal entry of Louis XIV and his bride, Marie-Thérèse, into Paris.

An important group of letters, some hundred and forty in all, ranging (except for the two letters above mentioned) from 1671 to 1693, is formed by her correspondence with her brother, Charles d'Aubigné[2]. He was an amusing fellow and not a bad one at bottom, but he was in Saint-Simon's words a *panier percé*, for ever dissipating his money, his health, and his opportunities. One cannot sufficiently admire the inexhaustible patience and good sense with which his sister gets him out of scrapes, procures him appointments, and gives him good advice. Finally, when in middle life he married an insignificant *petite bourgeoise* of fifteen, only to neglect her, she educated his wife and took entire charge of his only daughter. Her tone throughout the correspondence is that of an elder sister, though she was in fact a year younger. She never shrinks from telling him home-truths—"I do not understand how one can be a gentleman at heart and behave to him (M. de Villette) as you do"—and in her first letter to him after making the acquaintance of his wife she says with excessive candour that she is ugly,

---

[1] One of these, assigned to 1660–1663, is not in Lavallée, but is printed by Geffroy, I, 16 ff. and by Truc, pp. 57 ff.

[2] M. Truc prints twenty-four.

insupportably rude, and of untidy habits, and that she talks like a woman of the *Halles*[1]. Another letter illustrates Mme de Maintenon's remarkable gift for details, for she calculates to the last *sou* what ought to be the daily expenditure of her brother's household on food, wood, and candles, and she frames for him a budget with the precision of a Chancellor of the Exchequer[2].

The terms in which she announces his death to his son-in-law, the Comte d'Ayen, no doubt faithfully represent her feelings towards him:

> J'ai pleuré M. d'Aubigné; il était mon frère et il m'aimait fort; il étai bon dans le fond, mais il avait vécu dans de si grandes désordres que je puis dire qu'il ne m'a donné de joie que dans la manière dont il est mort.... Il a tenu des discours très-édifiants et qui partaient de son cœur[3].

To Philippe de Villette, who became a distinguished sailor, as well as to his wife, she wrote from time to time, with cousinly affection, and though during his absence in America she played him the mean trick of carrying off his little daughter and making her a Catholic, he soon forgave her, and eventually, following the example of his two sons—his wife had always been a Catholic—was himself converted. The daughter, who was known as Mlle de Mursay, was married by her aunt (*à la mode de Bretagne*) before she was fifteen to the Comte de Caylus (in 1686), who proved to be a confirmed drunkard. She became one of the most attractive women of her day[4], and her memoirs are a lively source of information for Mme de Maintenon and the court generally.

Mme de Maintenon's correspondence with the Abbé Gobelin is naturally of the greatest interest, for, as we have seen, he was her spiritual director and adviser all through the most difficult years of her strange career[5]. But the interest is practically

---

[1] *Correspondance générale*, I, 91 ff.; Truc, pp. 69 ff.

[2] *Corr. gén.* I, 104 ff.; Truc, pp. 80 ff.

[3] Geffroy, II, 18.

[4] "Les Jeux et les Ris brillaient à l'envi autour d'elle; son esprit était encore plus aimable que son visage, on n'avait pas le temps de respirer, ni de s'ennuyer quand elle était quelque part" (Choisy, *Mémoires*, ed. Petitot, 2ᵈᵉ série, LXIII, 298).

[5] He became her director about 1666.

confined to the years 1674–1677; of the more crucial period which followed only a few letters survive. For the Abbé was ordered to give up or destroy all the letters in which there was any reference to Mme de Maintenon's marriage, and consequently the letters which he sent to Saint-Cyr just before his death only form a small proportion of the whole correspondence. From those which relate to the years 1674–1677, when Mme de Maintenon was openly established at court as the governess of the royal children, we can follow, beneath the reserve which her prudence dictated, the perplexed workings of her troubled mind. We see conscience, self-interest, pressure from without, resistance from within, all striving for mastery, and we get glimpses of what she had to endure at the hands of Mme de Montespan, now repentant, now triumphant, now clinging with despair to her last foothold. "Il est impossible que je soutienne longtemps la vie que je mène," she writes in December 1676[1]. One letter of the later years which has escaped destruction is especially noteworthy.

"Je suis dans une paix dont je prendrais plaisir de vous entretenir," she writes on September 20, 1683, from Fontainebleau; and she ends her letter with "Ne m'oubliez pas devant Dieu, car j'ai grand besoin de forces pour faire un bon usage de mon bonheur[2]."

This can only mean that the question of her marriage with the king had been definitely decided.

The Abbé Gobelin's successor was Paul Godet Des Marais, who had been Fénelon's fellow-student at Saint-Sulpice, and who by Mme de Maintenon's influence was appointed Bishop of Chartres. Two days after his appointment (February 8, 1690) he wrote to her his first letter of direction[3]. Saint-Simon speaks in terms of the warmest praise of his character, his intelligence, and his work as a bishop, but his letters to Mme de Maintenon do not give one a high idea of his qualities as a director. He is conventional and commonplace, and the commendations which he bestows upon her so liberally would have

---

[1] *Corr. gén.* I, 321; Geffroy, I, 83.   [2] *Corr. gén.* II, 222.
[3] *Ib.* III, 213. Godet Des Marais's letters to Mme de Maintenon were published by the Abbé Berthier at Brussels in 1755; none of them is dated.

turned the head of a less sensible woman. He is always telling her that she is "au premier rang des justes," and in a letter which begins with " Il est vrai que votre état est une énigme," he exalts her as "the light of the world and the salt of the earth[1]." Only one of Mme de Maintenon's letters to her director has escaped destruction, but he often refers to and sometimes quotes from her monthly *renditions de conscience*, in which with what he calls her "natural candour and truthfulness" she accuses herself of various faults and shortcomings[2]. Impatience is the fault which recurs most frequently. But, though she may have been impatient in small things, in things that really matter she seems to have possessed an inexhaustible stock of patience. Without it she could never have endured, much less have carried on with so much skill and smoothness, the daily round that she described to Mme de Glapion.

Another ecclesiastic besides Godet Des Marais who owed his advancement to Mme de Maintenon was Louis-Antoine de Noailles, who, to the indignation of the Jesuits, was translated from Châlons to Paris in 1695. From 1694 to 1700 he was in frequent correspondence with Mme de Maintenon, who shews her interest not only in the great Quietist controversy but in all religious questions. In fact, she writes like a Minister of Public Worship to the head of the National Church, even employing a cypher to indicate the names of persons. But these harmonious relations came to a sudden end. The publication of the *Cas de Conscience*, and the consequent recrudescence of the Jansenist controversy, were followed by an ordinance of the Archbishop, now a Cardinal, in which he plainly revealed his long-suspected Jansenist sympathies (1703). From that moment Mme de Maintenon, whose director, Godet Des Marais, was almost as ardent an opponent of Jansenism as his fellow-Sulpician, Fénelon, withdrew her confidence from Cardinal de Noailles and her letters to him become few and far between. In 1709 she writes to him as follows:

Je ne puis jamais cesser de respecter mon archevêque, d'estimer vos vertus, et, si je l'ose dire, d'aimer votre personne ; mais il est vrai que tous ces sentimens ne me causent plus que de l'amertume.

[1] *Lettre* XLI   [2] See particularly *Lettre* XXXV.

Meanwhile a close friendship had been growing up between Mme de Maintenon and the Cardinal's young nephew, the Comte d'Ayen (Duc de Noailles from January 1704), to whom she had married her niece, Mlle d'Aubigné, in 1698, and from December 1700 to the end of the reign she kept up a regular correspondence with him. Saint-Simon has left two portraits of the Duke, in which his passionate hatred finds expression in strongly-contrasted lights and shadows[1]. He exaggerates his superficial attractions in order to make his fundamental villainy appear the blacker. When you have said of a man that "the serpent which tempted Eve is the original of which he is the most exact, the most faithful, the most perfect copy" you can hardly carry invective further. Saint-Simon's exaggeration is here gross and palpable, but as Sainte-Beuve says in his judicious estimate of the Maréchal de Noailles, as he became in 1712, you cannot neglect Saint-Simon's moral portraits altogether[2]. "Il a du flair." The truth seems to be that Noailles was exceedingly ambitious and not over-scrupulous, and that in the pursuit of his ambition he was all things to all men, devout with Mme de Maintenon and a debauchee with the Regent. But though he was not a great commander in the field[3], and though he was too incapable of sticking to a given line of policy and conduct to be an efficient minister, he was a hard worker and a good servant of his country. He apparently learnt from periods of temporary disgrace to set bounds to his ambition, and his failures neither cooled his ardour nor soured his temper[4].

At any rate the Duc de Noailles, whose versatility, accomplishments, and charm of manner were undeniable, made his way without difficulty into the good graces of Mme de Maintenon. Her letters to him shew real cordiality and liking, and on the whole give a higher estimate of her powers as a letter-writer than any other letters of the last twenty years of her

---

[1] *Mémoires*, IX, 147 ff.; XI, 227 ff.   [2] *Nouveaux Lundis*, vol. x.

[3] He commanded the French army at Dettingen, and served under Maurice de Saxe at Fontenoy.

[4] See A. Chéruel, *Saint-Simon considéré comme historien de Louis XIV*, pp. 536–540.

life. She chats to him about trivial incidents, she tells him the gossip of the court and the doings of their common friends. She is sometimes serious and intimate, as in the letter above referred to on her brother's death. At the end of 1705 Noailles was sent to Spain, and for the next six years he served either in Catalonia or in Roussillon, commanding the French in the indecisive battle of Villaviciosa. "Je m'ennuie ici [Fontainebleau] à la mort," she writes in October 1705, and in July 1707 she says, "Je suis plus que jamais hermite à la cour. Il n'y a personne sans exception à qui je puisse parler." "Votre absence me paraît bien longue," she writes in September 1709, "vous me seriez un secours et une consolation. Dieu ne le veut pas; mais il veut bien que je vous aime avec une grande estime et beaucoup de tendresse."

When the Duc de Noailles went to Spain, Mme de Maintenon already had a correspondent there in the person of the celebrated Princesse des Ursins (Anne-Marie de La Trémoille), widow of Flavio Orsini, Duke of Bracciano, who after a short period of disgrace had returned to Spain in triumph in June 1705. A correspondence at once began between her and Mme de Maintenon, whom she had met in the old days at the Hôtel d'Albret, and it was carried on with great regularity till a year after her summary dismissal in December 1714[1]. The contrast in character between these two women, who were drawn to one another by the similarity of their position, is well brought out by Sainte-Beuve. It is the contrast between a woman who was before all things a politician, and one whose interest in politics was secondary to her interest in religion; between a woman of high courage and bold and hopeful disposition, and one whose ambition had long been satisfied, who was now disillusioned, and whose prudence and timidity had

---

[1] *Lettres inédites de Mme de Maintenon et Mme des Ursins*, 4 vols. 1826, carelessly edited by Bossange from a copy in the British Museum. The first part of the correspondence, down to May 1, 1676, has been lost. The first letter printed by Geffroy (II, 84) is dated June 5, 1706. Geffroy published 180 new letters in 1859. Sainte-Beuve has three articles on her (*Causeries du Lundi*, V, 401 and XIV, 260 ff.). Her most recent biographers are Mme Saint-René Taillandier (1926) and Maud Cruttwell (1927).

increased with years[1]. In a letter of January 1708, Mme de Maintenon herself points out the contrast between the optimistic
opinions of her correspondent and her own pessimistic ones,
and in the dark year, 1709, she writes, "Vous pensez qu'il faut
périr plutôt que de rendre; je pense qu'il faut céder à la force
au bras de Dieu, qui est visiblement contre nous, et que le
Roi doit plus à ses peuples qu'à lui-même." But the Princess
never lost courage and the result shewed that she was right.
Mme de Maintenon's letters are by no means confined to political and military matters. She relates the news of the court,
even chronicling the arrival of the Duc de Bretagne's teeth[2], and
though she writes with a certain reserve, the letters are easy
in tone and of considerable interest for their comments on the
society of the court.

Another friend with whom Mme de Maintenon corresponded
on intimate terms during the last twenty years of her life was
Mme de Dangeau (*née* Sophie-Marie Löwenstein, of the family
of the Electors of Bavaria), who in 1686 had married, as his
second wife, the Marquis de Dangeau, the well-known courtier
and memoir-writer, and who, thanks to the charm of her person
and character, was a general favourite[3]. She often dined or
supped with Mme de Maintenon, and the latter's letters to her
reveal a very genuine affection. The following charming note
is probably the one referred to by Dangeau as accompanying
a lottery-prize which had been won by Mme de Maintenon and
sent as a present to her friend.

Trouvez bon, madame, que je répare l'aveuglement de la fortune, qui se
déclara hier pour moi dans la seule dispute que je puisse jamais avoir
avec vous[4].

[1] Mme de Maintenon was seven years older than the Princesse des
Ursins.

[2] "Pourquoi craignez-vous tant les dents à votre prince?...Le nôtre en a
huit" (April 22, 1708). The Duc de Bretagne was born in January 1707 and
died in March 1712.

[3] "Elle était belle comme les anges dans une jeunesse riante, une taille
fine, les yeux bleus et brillants, le teint admirable, les cheveux du plus
beau blond du monde, un air engageant, modeste, et spirituel" (Choisy,
Mém. p. 299).

[4] Geffroy, II, 336 and note 1. Unfortunately Mme de Maintenon destroyed

We have seen Mme de Maintenon as revealed in her letters to her family, her spiritual director, and her friends; but it is in the group of letters addressed to the ladies of Saint-Louis, who formed the educational and administrative staff of Saint-Cyr, that we find the fullest and freest expression of her remarkable personality. Here we see her firm grasp of policy, her passion for details, her deep-seated and somewhat anxious religion, her combination of sternness with inexhaustible patience and kindness, her austerity tempered by sympathy with innocent pleasures, her energy, and her enthusiasm for her work.

The letters not only deal with questions of education or administration, but they contain much spiritual advice. For in the difficult art of spiritual direction Mme de Maintenon, woman though she was, was superior to most priests, and hardly inferior to the great Fénelon himself[1]. In consequence the letters are valuable not only for the light they throw on the writer's character, but because they introduce us to some interesting personalities. There is Mme de Brinon, the first Superior of Saint-Cyr, something of a *précieuse* and a *femme savante*, whose head was turned by the attention paid to her at court, and who had to be summarily dismissed, without, however, putting an end to the friendship between her and Mme de Maintenon[2]. There is Mme du Pérou, who was elected no less than eight times to the office of Superior, and who ended her last term only a year before her death in 1748 at the age of eighty-two. Of all the ladies she was the one who best understood Mme de Maintenon's aims and who carried them out with the greatest smoothness and efficiency. A letter of

her letters to Mme de Montchevreuil, who, according to Saint-Simon, was her most intimate friend. She looked like a witch, he says, and was "dévote à l'outrance." She died in 1699.

[1] "Elle eut la maladie des directions," says Saint-Simon (*Mémoires*, XII, 103), who is particularly unfair and ill-natured on the subject of Mme de Maintenon's relations with Saint-Cyr.

[2] "Mme de Brinon, l'âme de Saint-Cyr, l'amie intime de Mme de Maintenon, n'est plus à Saint-Cyr....Elle ne paroît point mal avec Mme de Maintenon, car elle envoye tous les jours savoir de ses nouvelles; cela augmente la curiosité de savoir quel est donc le sujet de sa disgrâce (Mme de Sévigné to Mme de Grignan, December 8, 1688).

February 27, 1693, is a good example of the confidence which
Mme de Maintenon placed in her, while another, written in
June 1697, contains a remarkably clear and succinct account
of the Quietist controversy. There is Mme de Fontaines, who
was elected Superior in 1694 and 1703 and who was general
mistress of the classes at the time of the reform. She was so
beautiful that people who saw her for the first time gave an
involuntary cry of admiration, while her uprightness, her simple
piety, and her gentle firmness made her an ideal mistress and
Superior. The only criticism that Mme de Maintenon makes
on her régime is that she is too economical, and that the sisters
are not well enough fed[1].

Mme de Veilhan was a more difficult character. She carried
her piety to excess and Mme de Maintenon had great difficulty
in bringing her to a more reasonable frame of mind. One letter
especially is a model of frankness and wisdom[2]. It was part
of Mme de Veilhan's singularity that she took the keenest interest in politics and war and was always anxious to hear the
latest news. One of the few letters of Mme de Maintenon which
is written in a really playful tone and which shews any power
of description is addressed to this devout and warlike lady
from Dinant, where Mme de Maintenon and other ladies of
the court were established while the king was besieging
Namur[3]. In a very different tone is the extremely severe letter
which she wrote to Mme de Berval for having made a satirical
remark on one of the confessors attached to Saint-Cyr. "You
make fun of your neighbour, you make fun of a priest, and of
a priest who has been given to you for a spiritual father[4]." She
was only twenty-two, poor young Mme de Berval, when she
committed this dreadful sin, and she became an excellent
member of the community.

Of all her dear ladies the one perhaps who filled the warmest
spot in Mme de Maintenon's heart was Mme de Glapion. As
a child she had been Mme de Maintenon's most cherished
pupil, and even when she was still a novice she was regarded

---

[1] *Lettres hist. et édifiantes*, I, 353.   [2] *Ib.* I, 159.
[3] *Ib.* I, 218.   [4] *Ib.* I, 197.

by her as a treasure. Tall, pale, blue-eyed, Mme de Glapion[1] had a singularly graceful and gracious presence. She was well read and, as was natural in a pupil of Saint-Cyr, her favourite authors were Racine and Fénelon. She adored music, was a good musician, and had a beautiful voice. She had a passion for geography and geographical discovery. She also had a passion for nursing and, having learnt pharmacology and a little surgery, made an admirable and devoted head of the infirmary. But with all these gifts she was restless and unsatisfied. Partly as the result of bad health, she had fits of lassitude and religious depression, and she passed long hours in melancholy meditation[2]. Fortunately she carried her troubles and perplexities to Mme de Maintenon, and nothing gives one a better idea of that lady's skill and tact as a spiritual director than the letters in which she strengthens and admonishes the uneasy spirit of her pupil. All are worth reading, and one in particular has become deservedly celebrated. It was first published by Louis Racine in his edition of his father's works, and Voltaire in his *Siècle de Louis XIV* quotes from it a pathetic passage in which the writer refers to her own experience:

Que ne puis-je vous donner mon expérience! que ne puis-je vous faire voir l'ennui qui dévore les grands, et la peine qu'ils ont à remplir leurs journées! Ne voyez-vous pas que je meurs de tristesse dans une fortune qu'on auroit peine à imaginer? J'ai été jeune et jolie; j'ai goûté les plaisirs; j'ai été aimée partout: dans un âge un peu plus avancé, j'ai passé des années dans le commerce de l'esprit; je suis venue à la faveur, et je vous proteste, ma chère fille, que tous les états laissent un vide affreux[3]. Une inquiétude, une lassitude, une envie de connaître autre chose, parce qu'en tout cela, rien ne satisfait entièrement; on n'est en repos que lorsqu'on s'est donné à Dieu, mais avec cette volonté déterminée dont je vous parle quelquefois; alors on sent qu'il n'y a plus rien à chercher, qu'on est arrivé à ce qui seul est bon sur la terre; on a des chagrins, mais on a une solide consolation et une paix au fond du cœur au milieu des plus grandes peines[4].

[1] *Ib.* I, 379[2] and II, 101 n.[2] There is an exquisite portrait of Mme de Glapion by Comte d'Haussonville in his introduction to the *Mémoire de Mlle d'Aumale*, pp. xlii–lvi.

[2] "Vous buvez à longs traits les choses mélancoliques," writes Mme de Maintenon to her.

[3] Voltaire stops here.

[4] *Lettres hist. et édif.* II, 101 ff. The latter part of the letter contains an

Mme de Maintenon's loving care and patience bore fruit. After four troubled years Mme de Glapion, at the age of thirty-two, attained resignation and serenity. Ten years later (1716), when Mme de Maintenon was living at Saint-Cyr, having retired there on the king's death, she was elected Superior, and she was still Superior when Mme de Maintenon died in her arms. She lived for another ten years, and so closely did she model herself on the pattern of her friend and benefactress that they declared at Saint-Cyr that while she lived Mme de Maintenon seemed still to live in her.

Another of Mme de Maintenon's treasures was Mme de La Maisonfort, but unfortunately very little remains of their long correspondence[1]. Born in 1660, she taught first at Noisy and then at Saint-Cyr with brilliant success. She became the ardent disciple of her relative, Mme Guyon, and it was mainly through her apostleship, helped by the approval of Fénelon, that the doctrines of Quietism spread rapidly among teachers and pupils. The *Chanoinesse*, as she was called—she had been provided with a canonry in her childhood—for all her religious ardour, had little inclination to take religious vows. But pressed by Mme de Maintenon and Fénelon, who was her director, she agreed to abide by the decision of the five priests who watched over the spiritual welfare of Saint-Cyr. She received their verdict with tears, but fifteen months later (March 1692) she took her simple vows, and in April 1694 her perpetual vows. Meanwhile she continued to be the apostle of Quietism, till on May 10, 1697, she and two other ladies were summarily expelled by an order of the king and sent to other convents[2]. On the following day Mme de Maintenon wrote thus to Mme de Radouay:

Vous ne pleurerez jamais tant vos sœurs que je les ai pleurées depuis quatre ou cinq ans, et encore plus depuis deux ou trois mois que je croyais qu'il en faudrait venir à ce qui s'est fait ; je les aimais par inclination et par

interesting reference to Racine's death. See *ib.* between pp. 95 and 193 for the letters generally ; they range from 1702 to 1706.

[1] *Lettres hist. et édifiantes*, I, 135, 193 and 266; Geffroy, I, 218.

[2] Before this (in 1696) she had begun a spiritual correspondence with Bossuet (see Bossuet, *Correspondance*, VII, 311) and after his death she sent all his letters to her to Fénelon to read.

estime les voyant très vertueuses; mais je dois préférer le bien de la maison à toute autre considération, et j'espère de la bonté de Dieu pour Saint-Cyr, qu'il vous donnera des supérieurs et temporels incapables de tolérer la moindre nouveauté sur la religion[1].

Je dois préférer le bien de la maison à toute autre considération. With one addition the words are literally true. For the good of the king or for the good of Saint-Cyr Mme de Maintenon was prepared to sacrifice everything and everybody—including herself. *Incapables de tolérer la moindre nouveauté sur la religion.* That too is characteristic. She could not bear any deviation from the straight and narrow path of conservative orthodoxy. And none the less—or perhaps rather all the more—because she still retained a decided flavour of Calvinism in her religion —not in doctrine, but in practice. For she was austere, almost ascetic, and, to the end of her life, though she was a frequent communicant, she preferred the quiet office of vespers to the pomp of high mass.

With her large correspondence, Mme de Maintenon, as was common in those days, dictated most of her letters. Indeed her autograph letters came to be so rare that they were cherished at Saint-Cyr as precious treasures. She had a succession of secretaries, for whom she found suitable husbands, but the only one who is at all well known was the last—Mlle d'Aumale. Born in 1683, she came to Saint-Cyr when she was seven, and remained there till she was twenty. Two years later (1705) she became Mme de Maintenon's secretary and was with her till her death. She was ugly, as she cheerfully acknowledged, but she was capable, attractive, and amusing, and the lively letters which she wrote on her own account—mostly, indeed, by Mme de Maintenon's orders or under her eyes, but with full liberty of expression—are excellent reading. Some of the best are written to Mme de Glapion. Some time between 1721 and 1729 she wrote a memoir of Mme de Maintenon[2], and, as Mme de Caylus was at this time writing her *Souvenirs,* the two

[1] *Op. cit.* I, 481. For Mme de La Maisonfort and Saint-Cyr see Lavallée, *Hist. de Saint-Cyr,* c. x.

[2] Published by D'Haussonville and Hanotaux under the title of *Les Cahiers de Mlle d'Aumale* (see above, p. 200). It is more complete and methodical than the *Mémoire,* which was written in 1725 or 1726.

friends communicated to one another the results of their labours. Thus there are certain resemblances not only of subject-matter but of form between the two narratives. After the death of her patroness Mlle d'Aumale went to live with her mother at Vergie, a small village in Picardy, and this remained her head-quarters for several years. She died at Soissons in 1756, having survived all Mme de Maintenon's correspondents at Saint-Cyr except Mme de Vandam, who died in 1768 at the age of ninety.

The variety and extent of Mme de Maintenon's correspon-dence, the business character of many of her letters, the hurry in which they were often written, and the fact that she employed a secretary, make it unfair to compare her with Mme de Sévigné, who wrote at leisure two letters a week to her daughter and a few more to her friends. But Mme de Maintenon had not Mme de Sévigné's natural aptitude; she lacked her imagination, her gift for picturesque description, her spontaneity, the apparent impulse of her pen to run away with her while all the time she had it under her artistic control. It is the want of spontaneity that one misses most in Mme de Maintenon's lighter correspondence, for one feels that she has been deprived of it by the necessities of her position. Her best letters on the whole, apart from the spiritual letters, are those to the Duc de Noailles; she is under less constraint with him than with the Princesse des Ursins. But after all the chief interest of her letters is in the writer herself. From her letters we learn to know her real goodness of heart, her womanly tenderness, her love of influence and authority, her stern, even ruthless, subordination of individuals to causes, and, above all, the shaping and sustaining force of all her actions, her deep-rooted and profoundly sincere religion.

One merit no one can deny her letters—that of being well written. She is clear, correct, and brief. Like La Bruyère and Fontenelle and Anthony Hamilton she represents the transition from the long phrase of the seventeenth century to the short phrase of the eighteenth. But while La Bruyère's style is varied, concrete, and alert with *esprit*, Mme de Maintenon's is uniform, even monotonous, abstract, and simple. As Sainte-Beuve notes, it just stops short of the tension and the dryness of eighteenth-century prose. From these Mme de Maintenon was saved by a natural warmth of heart, which devotion to reason never wholly chilled. I have already quoted a passage from one of her best-known letters; I will add two letters in full, one written to the Comte d'Ayen in December 1701, about rehearsals at Versailles for some private performances of *Athalie* which took place before the king on February 14, 23, and 25, 1702, and the other written to Mme de Caylus in June 1717, giving an account of Peter the Great's visit to Saint-Cyr.

Mme la duchesse de Bourgogne m'a dit qu'elle ne voyait point qu'*Athalie* réussît, que c'est une pièce fort froide, et plusieurs autres choses qui m'ont fait pénétrer, par la connaissance que j'ai de cette cour-là, que son personnage lui déplaît. Elle veut jouer Josabeth, qu'elle ne jouera pas comme la comtesse d'Ayen; mais, après avoir reçu ses honnêtetés là-dessus, je lui ai dit que ce n'était pas à elle à se contraindre dans une chose qui ne se fait que pour son plaisir; elle est ravie, et trouve *Athalie* une fort belle pièce. Il faut la jouer, puisque nous y sommes engagés; mais en vérité il n'est pas agréable de s'ingérer de rien, non pas même pour eux. Vous faites aussi ces sortes de choses-là trop parfaites, trop magnifiques, et trop dépendantes d'eux. Si on y retourne l'année qui vient, il faudra à donner un autre tour. Il faut donc que la comtesse d'Ayen fasse Salomith; car, sans compter l'honnêteté qu'on doit à Mme de Chailly, qu'on a fait venir exprès pour jouer Athalie, je ne puis me résoudre à voir la comtesse d'Ayen jouer la furieuse. Bonsoir, mon cher neveu, que de dégoûts se trouvent en tout! que vous êtes heureux d'être sage! Mais il faudra encore renoncer à votre sagesse, qui, telle qu'elle est, ne vous satisfera jamais entièrement[1].

J'envoie savoir de vos nouvelles, ma chère nièce, et de celles de mes bons amis. Je n'ai rien à vous dire de nous; je ne vois personne. Mlle Gaudry vient de me dire que le czar traîne avec lui une fille, au grand scandale de Versailles, de Trianon et de Marly. Je ne puis ajouter foi à ce discours-là. Notre supérieure retombe de temps en temps; elle est assez mal aujourd'hui. Je viens de recevoir une lettre de la mère de Mlle d'Aumale, qui me mande que le pays est déjà édifié de sa sainteté. Adieu, Madame, je crains toujours d'apprendre de mauvaises nouvelles de Mme de Dangeau et de l'affaire des princes.

---

[1] Geffroy, II, 1. In one performance the Duc d'Orléans played the part of Abner and the Comte d'Ayen that of Joad; in another the Comte d'Ayen was Abner, while the celebrated actor, Baron, who had retired from the stage, took the part of Joad.

Dans ce moment, M. Gabriel entre, et me dit que M. de Bellegarde me mande qu'il veut venir ici après dîner, si je le trouve bon, c'est-à-dire le czar. Je n'ai osé dire que non, et je vais l'attendre sur mon lit. On ne me dit rien de plus et je ne sais s'il faut l'aller recevoir en cérémonie, s'il veut voir la maison, les demoiselles, s'il entrera au chœur, etc.; je laisse tout au hasard.

Le czar est arrivé à sept heures, et s'est assis au chevet de mon lit; il m'a fait demander si j'étais malade; j'ai répondu que oui. Il m'a fait demander ce que c'était que mon mal. J'ai répondu : "Une grande vieillesse avec un tempérament assez faible." Il ne savait que me dire, et son truchement ne me paraissait pas m'entendre. Sa visite a été fort courte ; il est encore dans la maison, mais je ne sais où. Bonsoir, ma chère nièce, je m'en vais prendre mon lait. M. du Plessis, que le maréchal de Villeroy m'a envoyé ce matin, m'a fait dire qu'il avait passé chez vous, que vous n'étiez pas éveillée, et que vous étiez mieux ; c'est donc que vous avez été malade : j'en suis bien fâchée.

J'oubliais de vous dire que le czar a fait un peu ouvrir le pied de mon lit pour me voir; vous croyez bien qu'il en aura été satisfait[1].

It is possible that La Bruyère, when he said that women were naturally better letter-writers than men, may have had Mme de Maintenon, among others, in his mind[2]. For even though he may not have seen her letters, she may have had some reputation as a letter-writer. At any rate it is interesting to note that Sainte-Beuve wrote in the margin of his copy of La Bruyère, opposite to the remark, "Si les femmes étaient toujours correctes, j'oserais dire que les lettres de quelques-unes d'entre elles seraient peut-être ce que nous avons dans notre langue de mieux écrit," the words, "Mme de Maintenon est correcte." Mme de Maintenon's own recipe for writing well was a very simple one, "Le principal pour bien écrire est d'exprimer clairement et simplement ce qu'on pense." This was the advice she gave one day at Saint-Cyr, after correcting the letters of several of the pupils[3].

For Mme de Maintenon was not only the "Spiritual Superior" (her official title) of Saint-Cyr but she was also its "Governess" (*Institutrice*), and it is of this side of her work,

---

[1] Geffroy, II, 388. [2] See above, p. 70.

[3] Jacquinet, *op. cit.* p. 311 (from *Lettres et Entretiens sur l'Éducation des Filles*).

especially in its relations to the general education of women in her day, that I must now speak.

Well-educated women were rare in France in the seventeenth century, rarer than in the sixteenth. Mme de Sévigné and her daughter, Mme de La Fayette, Mme de Maintenon herself, the Abbess of Fontevrault (Gabrielle de Rochechouart, sister to Mme de Montespan), and Mme de La Sablière were among the exceptions, and to these we must add a few like Mlle Dupré, Mlle de La Vigne, and Mme Dacier, who were true *femmes savantes*. But, as Rousselot points out, all these ladies, except Mme Dacier, who was born in 1651, had finished their education well before 1672, the year of Molière's *Les Femmes savantes*, which, according to Mme de Lambert, did not a little harm to the education of women. "Depuis ce temps-là on a attaché presqu'autant de honte au savoir des femmes qu'aux vices qui leur sont les plus défendus."

If this was so, it was the result of a misunderstanding. Molière's comedy is a satire first on the affectation of learning, and secondly on women, whether *savantes ridicules* like the three ladies of his play, or really learned women, who for the sake of learning or science neglect their children and their household duties.

Exceptional cases apart, the standard of women's education in France in the seventeenth century was very low. The unhappy wife of the great Condé, who was married to him in 1641 and who had a son in 1643, was sent to a convent the year after her marriage to learn to read and write. This was perhaps a rare case, but the great majority of women in the upper classes, if they could write, certainly could not spell. The following specimens are given by Rousselot: "J'ai cru que Votre Altesse serét bien ése de savoir sete istoire" (Mlle de Montpensier); "Il lia sy lontant que je n'ay antandu parler de vous" (Mme de Montespan). The ordinary governess in a nobleman's family was a peasant, or at best a *petite bourgeoise*, whose chief business was to keep her charges clean and tidy. Nor was monastic education, at any rate in the latter half of the century, much better. The Ursulines, who had been established in Paris in 1610 as a teaching Order for women, had greatly declined in efficiency. "Vos mères," wrote Mme de Maintenon in 1682 to her Ursuline friend, Mme de Brinon, "sont les plus sottes créatures que j'ai jamais vues." Much had been done by Port-Royal for the education both of boys and girls, but so far as girls were concerned, it was confined almost entirely to moral and religious instructions, and though the *pensionnaires* at Port-Royal-des-Champs still remained after their dismissal in 1661, they were educated under great difficulties. In his *Avis à une dame de qualité* Fénelon indeed says, "J'estime fort l'éducation des bons couvents," but he had previously qualified his praise by indicating that good convents were very rare.

Fénelon was the real pioneer of female education in France. His classical treatise, *De l'Éducation des Filles*, though not published till 1687, was written about 1680[1]. It was written at the instance of his friend, the Duchesse de Beauvillier, who was the mother of eight daughters. It has two superlative merits: it is founded upon a solid psychological basis, and it never loses sight of the fact that education is a preparation for life, and not for a degree or an examination. The very titles of the first two chapters—*De l'importance de l'éducation des filles* and *Inconvénients des éducations ordinaires*—are a sign that Fénelon is breaking fresh ground. For hitherto the education of women had been neglected because it was considered of no importance. In his very first words he sounds the note of reform: "Rien n'est plus négligé que l'éducation des filles," and then he points out how far less important the education of girls is considered than that of boys. "Girls," they say, "must not be learned; curiosity makes them vain and precious; it is enough that they should know how to manage their households and obey their husbands without reasoning about it." This is the very language of Chrysale. But Fénelon agrees with Molière that "il faut craindre de faire des savantes ridicules," and that they are not required to know political or military science, or jurisprudence, or philosophy, or theology.

---

[1] With this should be read *Avis à une dame de qualité sur l'éducation de sa fille*, first printed in 1715. It is sometimes said that the lady addressed is Mme de Beauvillier, but Fénelon writes to her as the mother of an only daughter.

In the second chapter he shews that remarkable insight into character, especially into female character, which made him so admirable a director. "L'ignorance d'une fille est cause qu'elle s'ennuie et qu'elle ne sait à quoi s'occuper innocemment." Here again Fénelon is at one with Molière:

> Mais comment voulez-vous, après tout, qu'une bête
> Puisse jamais savoir ce que c'est d'être honnête?
>
> . . . .
>
> Une femme d'esprit peut trahir son devoir;
> Mais il faut pour le moins qu'elle ose le vouloir:
> Et la stupide au sien peut manquer d'ordinaire,
> Sans en avoir l'envie et sans penser le faire[1].

The following passage might have served Flaubert as a text for *Madame Bovary*:

> Au contraire, les filles mal instruites et inappliquées ont une imagination toujours errante. Faute d'aliment solide, leur curiosité se tourne en ardeur vers les objets vains et dangereux. Celles qui ont de l'esprit s'érigent souvent en précieuses, et lisent tous les livres qui peuvent nourrir leur vanité; elles se passionnent pour des romans, pour des comédies, pour des récits d'aventures chimériques, où l'amour profane est mêlé. Elles se rendent l'esprit visionnaire, en s'accoutumant au langage magnifique des héros de roman; elles se gâtent même par là pour le monde: car tous ces beaux sentiments en l'air, toutes ces passions généreuses, toutes ces aventures que l'auteur du roman a inventées pour le plaisir, n'ont aucun rapport avec les vrais motifs qui font agir dans le monde, et qui décident des affaires, ni avec le mécompte qu'on trouve dans tout ce qu'on entreprend.
> Une pauvre fille, pleine du tendre et du merveilleux qui l'ont charmée dans ses lectures, est étonnée de ne trouver point dans le monde de vrais personnages qui ressemblent à ces héros: elle voudroit vivre comme ces princesses imaginaires, qui sont, dans les romans, toujours charmantes, toujours adorées, toujours au-dessus de tous les besoins. Quel dégoût pour elle de descendre de l'héroïsme jusqu'au plus bas détail du ménage!

The next six chapters (iii–viii) are concerned with the education (including religious instruction) of boys and girls alike, up to the time of their first communion. Then follow two chapters on the characteristic failings of girls. They talk too much and with too great vehemence. They are by nature artificial and they love duplicity (*finesse*). They are timid and

---

[1] *L'École des Femmes*, Act I, Sc. i.

full of false shame, and this is another source of dissimulation. But the most dangerous fault in women is vanity; they are born with a desire to please. Hence a passionate love of personal adornment, which, helped by the constant change of fashions in France, leads to extravagance.

Having thus prepared the way, Fénelon proceeds in two important chapters (xi and xii) to consider the instruction of women in detail. This instruction, he begins by pointing out, must be determined by their duties in after life. These are the education of their children—of their sons up to a certain age, and of their daughters till they marry or enter a convent—and the management of their servants and household expenses, and, very commonly, the granting of leases and the receiving of rents. Domestic economy therefore fills a large place in Fénelon's programme, and he is particularly good on the treatment of servants. Then he comes to education in the more special sense of the term. A girl must first be taught to read and write—to read with a correct pronunciation and in a simple and natural tone, and to write a neat and legible hand. She must be able to spell, she must have a practical knowledge of grammar, and she must learn to express herself with brevity and precision. She must also know the four rules of arithmetic. This will enable her to practise the keeping of accounts, an occupation which many people find *fort épineuse*, but which tends to the orderly conduct of a household. An elementary knowledge of law is also desirable, enough to know the nature of a contract and the difference between a will and a donation. Girls who will have property of their own should have an acquaintance with the duties and rights of landed proprietors. These are the indispensable subjects of instruction, but "it will not be useless," he adds, to allow girls to read profane works that are not dangerous for the passions. Let them read Greek and Roman history and that of France and other modern countries. It is generally supposed, he says, that a well-brought-up girl should learn Italian and Spanish; but he thinks the study of them useless, in fact harmful, for it will lead to the reading of dangerous and undesirable books. Latin is better, for it is the language of the Church; moreover the beauties of

Latin literature are far more solid than those of Italian or Spanish. But even Latin should only be taught to girls of sound judgment and modest conduct. Fénelon would also allow those who have a taste for it to read poetry and "works of eloquence." Only these must be very carefully selected; anything which hints of love is dangerous. Music should, as far as possible, be confined to church music, and painting is chiefly desirable because it is useful for tapestry-work.

In criticising this educational programme it must be remembered that Fénelon's one object was to fit a girl for her vocation, that in Fénelon's day there were only two possible vocations—marriage and a convent—and that girls were married at a very early age, even at twelve or thirteen. Bearing these points in mind, it will be admitted that a girl educated on Fénelon's lines, especially if she had included the studies that are "not useless," would make an excellent wife, and would be in some respects better educated than many girls are to-day. Notably, she would speak and read with a proper intonation, she would write a fair and legible hand, and she would have some knowledge of general history, and not merely that of a particular period in the history of her own country.

The weak spot in Fénelon's scheme is his mistrust of imagination, though, as a matter of fact, the author of *Télémaque* was less mistrustful of it than many of his contemporaries. Antiope, his ideal woman, the bride of Télémaque, had, we are told, a lively imagination, which she held in check by her discretion. But it is these "lively imaginations" that Fénelon fears to excite by imaginative literature, whether poetry or prose. Especially he dreads anything which may rouse the sentiment of love. It was before he became a confessor at Saint-Cyr that the pupils acted *Andromaque*. It seems absurd to us that a girl should know nothing about love before her marriage, but in those days love was not the basis of marriage, and Mme de Maintenon handed over her young cousin to M. de Caylus in complete ignorance of his character or his habits. Fénelon's preference of Latin to Italian or Spanish on account of its "more solid beauties," can hardly be defended, for Dante is as solid as Virgil and, from Fénelon's point of view, less dangerous, and St John of the Cross (with whom as a great mystic he should have been acquainted) is a far safer author to put in the hands of a young girl than Fénelon's favourite Horace.

We have seen that Fénelon wrote *De l'Éducation des Filles* about 1680, the year in which Mme de Maintenon began her first educational experiment at Montmorency; and seeing that Mme de Beauvillier, for whom Fénelon's treatise was written, was also the friend of Mme de Maintenon, it is highly probable that the latter read the treatise before it appeared in print (1687), and during the period that she was herself making practical experiments in the field of education. First a few poor girls at Montmorency, then sixty at Reuil, four miles from Saint-Germain, then a hundred daughters of poor nobles at Noisy on the outskirts of Versailles, these were the successive stages which led up to the crowning accomplishment, the inauguration of Saint-Cyr on August 2, 1686. The buildings were the work of the younger Mansart, and the "Constitutions" were drawn up by Mme de Maintenon in concert with Mme de Brinon, and submitted for final revision to Louis XIV[1], who took the deepest interest in the scheme and gave it the benefit of his aptitude for minute details. "We have founded in this house of Saint-Cyr," he says in the letters-patent, "a community which shall be composed of thirty-six professed sisters (*Dames*), two hundred and fifty *demoiselles* of noble birth, and twenty-four servants." The official title was "Maison et Communauté de Saint-Louis," and that of the professed sisters, "Dames de Saint-Louis."

It was not a monastic institution. Louis XIV disliked convents, and Mme de Maintenon had a very poor opinion of them as places of education. The professed sisters—at first twelve in number besides the Superior—only took simple vows—the three ordinary vows of Poverty, Chastity, and Obedience, and a special vow to devote themselves to the teaching of the *demoiselles*. It was Mme de Maintenon's aim that the education should be such as to fit the pupils to take their place in society. Accordingly, with her memories of the salons of Mme de Richelieu and Mme d'Albret, she set to work to

---

[1] The language was revised by Boileau and Racine.

cultivate their *esprit*. The mistresses composed ingenious conversations for them, or made them compose these themselves;
they discussed with them the subjects of their reading, whether
in history or in other works; they made them write letters in
the manner of Balzac and Voiture, and recite passages from
the best poets[1]. As we have seen, Mme de Brinon, the first
Superior, lent herself only too readily to this kind of instruction.
She talked and wrote with great facility and she fancied herself
as a theologian and a *bel esprit*. She even made her pupils
declaim scenes of a religious tragedy which she had composed
herself in a style redolent of *préciosité*. Thereupon Mme de
Maintenon, whose classical taste was offended, substituted the
plays of Corneille and Racine, with the result that the pupils
entered too thoroughly into the spirit of Racine, and their
success in *Andromaque* was so complete that it was never
repeated. But Mme de Maintenon begged Racine to write "a
kind of poem on a moral and religious subject, in which song
should be mingled with narrative, and the whole should be
linked together by action[2]." So after some hesitation and
reflection Racine agreed, and *Esther* was produced before the
king on January 26, 1689. The part of Élise, the *confidente* of
Esther, was played by Mlle de La Maisonfort, a younger sister
of "the Canoness," and that of Mardochée by Mlle de Glapion,
whose voice, Racine declared, "went straight to the heart."
The prologue was written expressly for Mme de Caylus, who
was a born actress, and who in subsequent performances took
the part of anyone who happened to be indisposed[3].

Esther was a huge success. The king especially was delighted,
and it was largely to please him that there were six more
representations. At the second Mme de Caylus played Esther.
The most brilliant was the fourth (February 5, 1689), which
was honoured by the presence of James II of England and
Mary of Modena, who just a month ago had found a hospitable
refuge at Saint-Germain. The last representation (February 19)
has been immortalised by Mme de Sévigné's enthusiastic
account of it and her amusing report of her conversation with
the king, which consisted of three short sentences on either

[1] Preface to *Esther*.   [2] *Ib.*   [3] *Souvenirs*, p. 144.

side. "Et puis Sa Majesté s'en alla et me laissa l'objet de l'envie." On the king's return to Versailles he heard of the sudden death of his niece, the Queen of Spain, and the performances came to an end. But next year (1690) they began again; there were five in January and two in February. The king was as well pleased as before, and he invited Racine to write a new play on a religious subject. But *Athalie* was produced under very different conditions from those of *Esther*. It was played in an ordinary class-room, without any scenery, and the *demoiselles* acted in their ordinary clothes. There was a rehearsal on January 5, 1691, at which the king and Monseigneur were present, and a performance on February 22, which was witnessed also by the ex-King and ex-Queen of England, and five or six other persons, including Père La Chaise and Fénelon. They found the great tragedy cold and uninteresting, but Mme de Maintenon, to her eternal honour, declared it to be the finest play she had ever seen.

The production of *Athalie* in so meagre a fashion was due largely to Mme de Maintenon's recognition that her plan of making Saint-Cyr a college for girls who would take their place in society was in many respects a failure. It had failed chiefly by reason of its close proximity to Versailles. If to Mme de Maintenon it was the chief work of her life, to the court it was a plaything. The girls were spoilt by the attentions of the king and the court. They became conceited and insubordinate, and the success of *Esther*, coinciding as it did with the advent of Quietism, brought matters to a head. A change in the system of education was inevitable, and under the influence of her director, Godet Des Marais, Mme de Maintenon reluctantly came to the conclusion that the mundane spirit could only be exorcised by transforming Saint-Cyr into a religious community. To this Louis XIV at first strongly objected, but he finally gave way, and on December 1, 1692, the House of Saint-Louis was made into a regular monastery of the Order of St Augustine.

The *Dames* had now to assume the humble rôle of novices, with the result that by the end of the year 1694 twenty-one out of twenty-eight had taken solemn vows. But in accordance with the king's wish they were still called by their family names.

The 250 pupils were divided into four classes, distinguished by the colour of the ribbon which they wore on a black dress. The red class, which consisted of children from seven to ten, had 56 pupils, and there were the same number in the green class (aged eleven to thirteen). The yellow class (aged fourteen to sixteen) had 62 pupils and the blue class (aged seventeen to twenty) 76. The classes were divided into *bandes* or *familles* of eight to ten pupils each with a *mère de famille* at the head. Each class had four mistresses and five monitresses. The latter were chosen from the two upper classes and were distinguished by a black ribbon. It is hardly necessary to say that the yellow class was the most difficult to manage.

The instruction in the red class consisted of reading, writing, arithmetic, the elements of grammar, a little church history, and the catechism. To this was added in the green class music and a very little geography, mythology, and history. In the yellow class the chief subjects were the French language, music, and religion; they also learnt drawing and dancing. In the blue class the instruction was confined to the French language and music, but very great attention was paid to moral education.

Mme de Maintenon attached great importance to the study of language, and this was taught not so much by grammatical rules, as by actual practice and by explanation of the meaning of words. The pupils no longer had to write essays or conversations, but letters, in which, as we have seen, simplicity and brevity were the qualities chiefly recommended. Judging by the specimens sent to Mme de Maintenon for correction, the standard of orthography was not high.

On the subject of religious instruction Mme de Maintenon shewed her usual good sense. It was her aim, she said, to make her pupils good Christians and not prospective nuns, and in order to render their instruction more agreeable she wrote for them dialogues and conversations on various points of conduct, morals, or religion. The prominence given to music was largely due to Louis XIV, who loved it passionately and was a good musician. The books of music preserved in the municipal library of Versailles cover a fairly wide field—motets and other church music by Lulli, Campra, and Clérambault, harpsichord music by the brothers Couperin, selections from Lulli's operas of *Atys*, *Roland*, and *Armide*. The majority of the *Dames* played the harpsichord, and some the violin.

Manual work was another prominent feature, especially in the two upper classes. The girls sewed, knitted, embroidered, and worked at tapestry; they made dresses both for themselves and for the *Dames*, and all the linen for the house, the infirmary, and the chapel. They dusted, washed, and swept; they made the beds and in fact did nearly all the service of the house. The big girls dressed and brushed the hair of the little ones. They washed in cold water, slept in hard beds, sat on hard chairs, and seldom saw a fire. The food was plain but wholesome, and they had plenty of it.

Thus Saint-Cyr was a practical application of Fénelon's principle that education should be a preparation for life. The programme was even more severely practical than Fénelon's. While Fénelon's treatise was written for the special benefit of a Duchess, the majority of Mme de Maintenon's girls who did not take vows could only look forward to a modest position as the wives of poor men, or possibly to remaining unmarried; for, though a few dowries were provided, the money set apart for this purpose did not amount to much. In the matter of literature Mme de Maintenon was decidedly less liberal than Fénelon. Under the influence of the reaction from the performances of *Esther* and *Athalie* she condemned all profane literature[1]. Later, she regarded all novels as bad, "because they dealt only with vices and passions," and Roman history as dangerous, "because it puffed up the mind." Remembering perhaps the enthusiasm for ancient history which was so marked a feature of the Hôtel de Rambouillet and the novels of Mlle de Scudéry, she was afraid that "all these grand examples of generosity and heroism would uplift the minds of the pupils too much, and make them as conceited and precious as they were before." Thus she would have the mistresses give them mere "notions," as she called them,

[1] *Entretiens sur l'Éducation des Filles*, VIII (June 1896), 20–26.

of history, as for instance that Alexander was a king of Mace-
donia and a great conqueror[1]. She thought that the Lives of
the Saints and the Acts of the Martyrs, if properly explained,
would provide them with all the mythology, philosophy, and
history that they needed.

Mme de Maintenon's distrustful attitude towards literature
was largely the result of the failure of her first experiment.
In her anxiety to guard against intellectual vanity and idle
curiosity she went to the opposite extreme. But her good sense
partially restored the balance, and her practice was more liberal
than her precepts. She did not proscribe plays altogether,
but she substituted Duché de Vancy for Racine and *Jonathas*
for *Athalie*, and she wrote, as we have seen, "conversations"
which provided parts for five or six pupils. Highly characteristic is the Conversation on Reason, in which the chief
speaker, Adelaïde, extols its virtues in language evidently
inspired by St Paul's famous chapter on Charity[2]. In harmony
with this panegyric is the statement that at Saint-Cyr "everything serves to form their reason—even games." For, besides
the outdoor games, of which the chief were prisoner's base and
skittles, they played chess and draughts, and what Mme de
Maintenon called "jeux d'esprit."

Even as modified by the relaxations in practice Mme de
Maintenon's reformed scheme of education is defective on the
intellectual side. Looking at it only from her own point of view,
as a preparation chiefly for married life, it is open to criticism.
It is not good for any woman to have no intellectual occupation.
The management of a household, the education of children, the
writing of letters, needlework and tapestry, take up a considerable part of a woman's day, and, if she is a musician as well,
may fill it. But most women have some time for reading, and,
even if they have not, it is well for them to have acquired, when
young, a sufficient fund of knowledge to enable them to take

---

[1] A frequently reprinted little text-book, *Instruction sur l'histoire de
France et sur l'histoire romaine, par demandes et par réponses* (1684) by
the Abbé Le Ragois, a nephew of the Abbé Gobelin, and tutor to the
Duc du Maine, was in use at Saint-Cyr. It was used in schools down to
about 1840.

[2] Jacquinet, *op. cit.* pp. 465 ff.

an interest in current intellectual topics. Would a pupil of Saint-Cyr have *des clartés de tout*? Would she come up to Clitandre's modest ideal? In other words, would she make a true companion for a man of intelligence and culture?

Whatever criticisms may be made on this scheme of education, there is no question as to its success. Several new communities were established on similar lines—by the Ursulines at Mantes and Niort, by the Benedictines at Moret and Bisy, and by the Bernardines at Gomerfontaine. Mme de Maintenon took a particular interest in this last, the Abbess of which was an old pupil of Saint-Cyr. Some of the pupils made brilliant marriages, and there was a general belief that a wife who had been educated at Saint-Cyr was a real prize. Boileau expresses this belief in the well-known lines:

> Mais eût-elle sucé la raison dans Saint-Cyr,
> Crois-tu que d'une fille, humble, honnête, charmante,
> L'Hymen n'ait jamais fait de femme extravagante[1]?

That Fénelon was in complete sympathy with Mme de Maintenon's reformed scheme of education may be judged from an admirable discourse which he gave at Saint-Cyr towards the end of 1691, when he was at the zenith of his popularity and influence in that community and was still in high favour with Mme de Maintenon. The discourse, which is entitled *Entretien sur les avantages et les devoirs de la vie religieuse*, contains the following passage:

Il me semble que je vous entends dire: Puisque nous sommes destinées à l'instruction, ne faut-il pas que nous soyons exactement instruites? Oui, sans doute, des choses dont vous devez instruire ces enfants. Vous devez savoir les vérités de la religion, les maximes d'une conduite sage, modeste et laborieuse; car vous devez former ces filles ou pour des cloîtres, ou pour vivre dans des familles de campagne, où le capital est la sagesse des mœurs, l'application à l'économie et l'amour d'une piété simple. Apprenez-leur à se taire, à se cacher, à travailler, à souffrir, à obéir, à épargner. Voilà ce qu'elles auront besoin de savoir, supposé même qu'elles se marient. Mais fuyez comme un poison toutes les curiosités, tous les amusements d'esprit; car les femmes n'ont pas moins de penchant à être vaines par leur esprit que dans leur corps. Souvent les lectures qu'elles font avec tant d'empressement se tournent en parures vaines et en ajustements immodestes de leur esprit: souvent elles lisent par vanité, comme

---

[1] *Satire* x (*Les Femmes*, 1693).

elles se coiffent. Il faut faire de l'esprit comme du corps; tout superflu doit être retranché: tout doit sentir la simplicité et l'oubli de soi-même. O quel amusement pernicieux dans ce qu'on appelle lectures les plus solides! On veut tout savoir, juger de tout, parler de tout, se faire valoir sur tout: rien ne ramène tant le monde vain et faux dans les solitudes que cette vaine curiosité des livres. Si vous lisez simplement pour vous nourrir des paroles de la foi, vous lirez peu, vous méditerez beaucoup ce que vous aurez lu[1].

It will be noticed that Fénelon speaks of the pupils as being destined either for the cloister, or for a life in the country as wives of poor nobles. For that reason, as I have already said, the education at Saint-Cyr is more practical and less liberal than that prescribed by Fénelon.

Fénelon's own treatise, which was several times reprinted and of which he published a revised edition in 1696, found an echo in the *Avis à sa Fille* of La Marquise de Lambert, which, though not printed till 1728, was written in 1709 and circulated among her friends[2]. We shall meet with this lady in a later chapter, as the founder of the first eighteenth-century salon, but it may be said here, that she was not only a well-educated and well-read woman, but that she had considerable influence in the intellectual world. For that reason her views on education are of considerable importance.

In a letter written to Fénelon in the early part of 1710 she acknowledges her debt to him, or, as she calls it, "her theft." "You have taught me," she says, "that my first duty was to set about forming the minds and hearts of my children: I found in

---

[1] Fénelon, *Œuvres*, XVII, 420; the discourse is printed in part by Jacquinet. Deforis printed it as Bossuet's (1778), but it is undoubtedly by Fénelon, as Mme de Maintenon refers to it and quotes from it in one of her *Avis aux maîtresses des classes* (1692). See E. Griselle, *Fénelon*, pp. 15–22.

[2] *Avis d'une Mère à son Fils et sa Fille*, 1728. The *Avis à son Fils* first appeared in an unauthorised edition. It was written in 1701 or 1702 (while the French arms were still unsuccessful in Italy). There are English translations of the two *Avis* by W. Hatchet (London, 1729; Dublin, 1731), T. Carte (1737), Rowell (1749), and A. Haggard (1885). Fénelon read the *Avis à son Fils* in January 1710 and in a letter to Mme de Lambert's friend, Louis de Sacy, the translator of Pliny's *Letters*, highly commended it. This led to an interchange of letters between Fénelon and the authoress (Fénelon *Œuvres*, VII, 667 ff.).

Télémaque the precepts that I have given my son, and in *L'Éducation des Filles* the counsels that I have given my daughter." Her modesty has led her to exaggerate the amount of her debt. It is true that like Fénelon she begins her treatise with the complaint that the education of girls has been neglected, that she repeats verbally his statement that "girls are born with a violent desire to please," that she follows him in regarding a knowledge of Italian as dangerous, and that her advice to her daughter as to the treatment of servants is evidently inspired by his treatise. But her attitude towards literature and the higher education generally is decidedly more liberal than Fénelon's. This is only natural. For while Fénelon's advice, though given to an individual mother and to a mother whom he knew would give the most careful attention to her daughters' education, is more or less general in character, Mme de Lambert's is addressed to her own daughter, with whose character she was presumably acquainted, and who was on the eve of her entry into the world. It is therefore natural that she should take a bolder line.

In the first place, she is not afraid of curiosity. "N'éteignez point en vous le sentiment de curiosité; il faut seulement le conduire et lui donner un bon objet." "C'est un penchant de la nature," she truly says, "qui va au-devant de l'instruction." As for the subjects of instruction, she first recommends Greek and Roman history, and for the very reason for which Mme de Maintenon distrusts it. "Il élève l'âme et nourrit le courage par les grandes actions qu'on y voit." Then comes the history of France, "for it is not permissible to ignore the history of one's country." She would add a little philosophy, especially the new philosophy of Descartes; also ethics, to be read in Cicero, Pliny, and other writers. As for languages it is enough for a woman to be able to speak her own, but she may study Latin, if she has an inclination for it. Italian is dangerous; it is the language of love, and Italian writers have an ill-regulated imagination. Poetry may be harmful, but she would not like to forbid the fine tragedies of Corneille. The reading of novels is more dangerous; "ils mettent du faux dans l'esprit."

A taste for unusual branches of knowledge must be kept

within bounds. "Les filles doivent avoir sur les sciences une pudeur presque aussi tendre que sur les vices[1]." Women are ordinarily governed by their imagination, but it must be regulated and made submissive to truth and reason. In order to be happy, you must think sanely. It is good from time to time to be alone. Set apart certain hours of the day for reading and reflection.

Mme de Lambert's distrust of poetry and novels would seem to be the logical outcome of her views on the subject of love. "Si votre cœur a le malheur d'être attaqué par l'amour, voici les remèdes pour en arrêter le progrès." There is evidently no connexion in her mind between love and marriage. Yet in her *Réflexions nouvelles sur les Femmes*[2] she devotes thirty pages out of fifty to a long digression on the art of honourable love. "L'amour est le premier plaisir....Il ne le faut pas bannir de la Société; il faut seulement apprendre à le conduire."

When Mme de Lambert's three little treatises appeared in print, the eighteenth century was already well advanced, and many of the characteristics which we associate with it were fully developed. Among these was the influence of woman.

---

[1] Women attended Carré's lectures on mathematics (Fontenelle, *Éloges*, *Œuvres*, vol. VI). When Mlle Delaunay went to Sceaux at the age of eighteen, in 1711, she was regarded as a prodigy of learning (*Mémoires*, p. 53). She had read the works of the great anatomist, Duverney, and had no doubt attended his famous lectures, for he told them at Sceaux that she "knew the human body" better than any girl in France (*ib.* p. 77).

[2] *Par une Dame de la Cour*, Paris, 1727—an unauthorised edition which Mme de Lambert did her best to suppress; *Nouv. édition corrigée*, Londres, 1730. There is an English translation by F. Lockman (1729; 1737). It is accompanied by the two *Avis* in an Amsterdam edition of 1732. All three, together with *Traité de l'Amitié* and *Traité de la Vieillesse*, are included in *Œuvres morales de la M^{ise} de Lambert*, ed. M. de Lescure, 1883. The *Réflexions* begin with a reference to certain novels by women which had been recently published. If Mme de Lambert is thinking of novels by Mme d'Aulnoy and Mlle Bernard, which appeared in 1690 and 1692 respectively, or of the *histoires secrètes* and the *Mémoires*, which contain more fiction than fact, of her friends, Mlle de La Force (1692–1698) and Mme de Murat (1697), we may infer that the *Réflexions* were written during the last decade of the seventeenth century, or, at latest, in the early years of the eighteenth. Mention is made of Saint-Évremond, who died in 1703.

This is not the place to attempt an estimate of that influence, but it may be said at any rate that the woman who influenced French society and literature in the eighteenth century was very far from realising the ideal either of Fénelon or of Mme de Lambert. Whatever may be said for her intellectually, she fell very short of it on the moral and religious side. The education in convents of the worldly type went from bad to worse. Even those that took Saint-Cyr for their model often copied its organisation but neglected its spirit. The task of finding a good governess was no easier than when Fénelon wrote, and the neglect of children by their mothers, which he pointed out was at the root of the whole evil, increased at an alarming rate[1].

But the eighteenth-century woman, as we chiefly know her, the woman who held a salon and wrote memoirs and letters and generally promoted the cultivation of *esprit*, the woman, in short, of Paris society, represented, after all, only a small minority of the nation. In the provinces there were wives of poor or moderately well-to-do nobles, in Paris there were wives of professional men and other members of the higher *bourgeoisie*, who managed their households and educated their children, who kept their accounts and wrote simple and correct French, who performed, humbly and austerely, their religious duties— and of all these it may be said that they owed much to the example of Saint-Cyr, and to the precepts and practical wisdom of Mme de Maintenon.

It was at her beloved Saint-Cyr that her last years, the years after Louis XIV's death, were spent. A short letter which she wrote to the Princesse des Ursins, ten days after the "great event," is worth quoting in full:

> Vous avez bien de la bonté, Madame, d'avoir pensé à moi dans le grand événement qui vient de se passer; il n'y a qu'à baisser la tête sous la main qui nous a frappé.
>
> Je voudrais de tout mon cœur, Madame, que votre état fût aussi heureux que le mien. J'ai vu mourir le roi comme un saint et comme un héros. J'ai

---

[1] "Souvent une mère qui passe sa vie au jeu, à la comédie, et dans des conversations indécentes, se plaint d'un ton grave qu'elle ne peut pas trouver une gouvernante capable d'élever ses filles. Mais qu'est-ce que peut la meilleure éducation sur des filles à la vue d'une telle mère?" (*De l'Éducation des Filles*).

quitté le monde que je n'aimais pas; je suis dans la plus aimable retraite que je puisse désirer[1].

As it happened this letter was written from Marly, but Mme de Maintenon practically never left Saint-Cyr during her widowhood. Her faithful secretary, Mlle d'Aumale, remained still with her, but except for Mme de Caylus and Mme de Dangeau, and very occasionally the Maréchal de Villeroy, "le refuge de tous les misérables," she practically saw no one but the ladies of Saint-Cyr and their pupils. Once, as we have seen, the Tsar came and peeped at her in her bed, and they exchanged a sentence or two[2]. On February 9, 1719, she wrote to Mme de Dangeau begging her to put off a promised visit. "Je suis dans une faiblesse qui me rend incapable d'une attention de suite. Venez aux jours gras[3]." She died on April 15, the Saturday in Easter-week. She was in her eighty-fourth year.

[1] Jacquinet, *op. cit.* pp. 186–187.
[2] The Tsar's visit to Saint-Cyr was on June 11, 1717. See the letter to Mme de Caylus printed above, p. 226. Saint-Simon's account (*Mémoires,* XIV, 30) is inaccurate.
[3] Jacquinet, *op. cit.* p. 191.

CHAPTER VIII

FÉNELON[1]

LA BRUYÈRE'S attitude towards his predecessors of the Classical Age was one of respectful admiration. If he ventured to introduce certain novelties into literature, it was because he

[1] The earliest edition of Fénelon's works which is at all complete is that of Versailles, 35 vols. 1820–1830 (*Œuvres*, I–XXII, *Correspondance*, XXIII–XXXIII, *Table*, XXXIV, Supplementary volume, XXXV), edited by the Abbé Gosselin, Superior of the Seminary of Issy, with the assistance of his fellow-Sulpician, the Abbé Caron. Eighteen years later Gosselin brought out a new edition in 10 vols. Paris, 1848–1852 (variously known as the edition of Paris, the edition of Saint-Sulpice, and the *édition* Gaume), which reproduced the text of the Versailles edition with a few modifications and the addition of some letters and minor pieces. Other letters were published in 1850, 1853, 1874, 1904. Nearly all Fénelon's important writings will be found in *Œuvres choisies*, 4 vols. Hachette, 1862 (frequently reprinted).

The chief authority for the history of Fénelon's writings is the *Hist. littéraire de Fénelon*, 1843, in which the Abbé Gosselin collected the various notices and analyses interspersed in the Versailles edition of his works. He revised it in 1850 and published the revision as vol. I of the Saint-Sulpice edition. See also A. Cherel, *Fénelon au XVIIIe siècle en France: Tableaux bibliographiques*, Fribourg, 1917.

Ramsay, *Hist. de la vie et des ouvrages de Fénelon*, 1723. The life by the Marquis de Fénelon, published in 1747, is merely an abridgement of this. Card. de Bausset, *Histoire de Fénelon*, 3 vols. 1808–1809; 3rd ed. 1817; new ed., "revised, corrected, and considerably augmented" by the Abbé Gosselin, 4 vols. 1850. Viscount St Cyres, *Life of François de Fénelon*, 1901. Miss E. K. Sanders, *Fénelon, his friends, and his enemies*, 1901.

Éducation des Filles, 1687; revised and corrected by the author, 1696 (3 editions); 1699; 1715; 1885 (with an introduction by O. Gréard).
Explication des Maximes des Saints, 1698; ed. A. Cherel, 1911.
Suite du quatrième livre de l'Odysée, ou les Avantures de Télémaque, fils de l'Ulysée, 12mo, Veuve Barbin, 1699, 208 pp. containing 4¼ books; 4 vols. 12mo, Moetjens, 1699 (*Bib. Nat. Rés.* 3086–9; this is apparently the first complete edition); 2 vols. 12mo, Brussels, Foppens, 1699; 2 vols. 12mo, Moetjens, 1701 (the first with Fénelon's name); *première édition conforme au manuscrit original* (ed. by the Marquis de Fénelon), 2 vols. 12mo, 1717 (in 24 books); ed. A. Cahen, with a full commentary, 2 vols. 1920 (*Grands Écrivains de la France*).

felt as a late-comer that this was his only chance of being heard. In the Quarrel of the Ancients and the Moderns he was whole-heartedly on the side of the Ancients. Fénelon, on the other hand, though he was steeped in ancient literature, though he was as familiar with Homer and the Greek tragedians as Racine, though he knew Virgil and Horace almost by heart, preserved a dignified neutrality in the great quarrel; for he judged litera-ture not as a partisan, but in accordance with his own indi-vidual taste. Even more markedly individual was his attitude in politics and religion. In *Télémaque* and the *Examen de Conscience*, both written for the benefit of the Duc de Bourgogne, he con-demned in no measured terms that love of war and personal glory which was so conspicuous in the Duke's grandfather, Louis XIV. Not content with this indirect criticism he addressed, as we have seen, a letter to the king himself, which was a severe and even violent arraignment of his whole government[1]. It was the same in religion and in Church policy. At a time when the mysticism of the preceding generation had fallen out

Dialogues des Morts, 12mo, 1712 (45 dialogues); *avec quelques fables* (67 dialogues, 25 fables), ed. Ramsay.

Démonstration de l'existence de Dieu, 1712 (disavowed by Fénelon); complete edition with both parts, 1718.

Dialogues sur l'éloquence...avec une lettre à l'Académie française, ed. Ramsay, 1718; *Lettre à l'Académie*, ed. A. Cahen, 1902.

Examen de conscience pour un Roi...avec la vie de l'auteur, by the care of John Carteret, Lord Granville, London, 1747.

D. Nisard, *Hist. de la littérature française*, XII, 396 ff., 1849. Sainte-Beuve, *Causeries du Lundi*, II, 1850; *ib.* X, 1854 (review of *Correspondance spiri-tuelle*). M. Matter, *Le Mysticisme en France au temps de Fénelon*, 1865. F. Brunetière, *Études critiques*, II, 1881 (with his article in the *Grande Encyclopédie* as an appendix). É. Faguet, *Dix-septième siècle*, 1890. P. Janet, *Fénelon*, 1892 (*Les Grands Écrivains français*). M. Cagnac, *Fénelon, Directeur de Conscience*, 1901; *Fénelon, Études critiques*, 1910. A. Del-planque, *Fénelon et ses amis*, 1910 (detached from a larger work, *Fénelon et la doctrine de l'amour pur*, Lille, 1907). H. Bremond, *Apologie pour Fénelon*, 1910. J. Lemaître, *Fénelon*, 1910. E. Griselle, *Fénelon, Études historiques*, 1911. Works which deal with some special feature in Fénelon's career are referred to in the text below.

The best portrait of him is that by Vivien at Munich.

[1] See above, p. 10. "The true originator of the opposition in literature was Fénelon" (Acton).

of favour he was a convinced mystic; and, while the majority of his fellow-Churchmen were Gallicans, he was an Ultramontane. Thus he found himself in disagreement with the three great representatives of the reason and common sense of his age, with Boileau, with Louis XIV, and with Bossuet.

Partly owing to this disagreement, partly owing to an exaggerated idea of his tolerance in matters of religion, helped too by the biographies of the Chevalier de Ramsay, a Boswell without his genius (1723), and of the Marquis de Fénelon, his favourite great-nephew (1747), there grew up by the middle of the eighteenth century a legendary Fénelon, who was honoured by the Philosophers as an enlightened friend of humanity, and even as a precursor of themselves. Their admiration was expressed with enthusiasm at a sitting of the Academy on August 25, 1771, when La Harpe's prize *éloge* was read aloud by the Director, D'Alembert, and "the hall was transformed into a temple in which all were of Fénelon's religion." Christians of every shade vied with the Philosophers in their veneration, and under the Empire the *imprimatur* of the Church was set on Fénelon's reputation by the publication in 1808 of an official biography, written by a loyal Sulpician, Cardinal de Bausset.

It was not till near the middle of the nineteenth century that the reaction began. Désiré Nisard was too jealous a guardian of the classical tradition not to be aware that Fénelon, whose writings he greatly admired, was far from being a true representative of the great Classical Age. Taking as his text the well-known saying of Louis XIV that Fénelon was "l'esprit le plus chimérique" in his kingdom, he confirmed it by an examination of Fénelon's views on politics, religion, spiritual direction, and literary criticism, in all of which he declared that Fénelon aimed at an impossible perfection[1]. In 1872 a staunch Protestant, Onésime Douen, attacked the legend of Fénelon's tolerance in a volume which would have been more effective if it had been more temperate[2]. A few years later a more formidable adversary, Ferdinand Brunetière, who disliked

[1] *Hist. de la litt. française*, XII (1849), 396 ff. The criticism of Fénelon first appeared in the *Rev. des Deux Mondes*, 1845 and 1846.
[2] *L'Intolérance de Fénelon*, 2nd ed. 1875.

Fénelon as an aristocrat, an individualist, a mystic, and an opponent of Bossuet, wrote an unfriendly but discriminating and not altogether unfair account of him for *La Grande Encyclopédie*; and he followed this up in 1881 with an article, "étincelant de verve et d'injustice," on M. Guerrier's thesis, *Mme Guyon, sa vie, sa doctrine et son influence*. The next attack was delivered by M. Lanson, "le plus savant et le plus intelligent des *bossuétistes*[1]," in his *Bossuet* (1891), which contains a thoroughly unfair account of the Quietist controversy. Then came M. Crouslé with his *Fénelon et Bossuet, Études morales et littéraires* (1894), "la plus énorme des massues qu'on ait jamais branlées contre Fénelon." It was time for a *fénelonien* to take the field, and one appeared in the person of the Abbé Bremond, who in his *Apologie pour Fénelon* gave the *bossuétistes* no quarter, and shewed that a rapier is a more formidable weapon than a club. Happily, however, there are admirers and students of Fénelon who have not thought it incumbent on them to attack Bossuet—Mgr Moïse Cagnac, M. Albert Delplanque, and M. Eugène Griselle, editor of the *Revue Fénelonienne*. Moreover the short biographies and criticisms of Faguet, Janet, Thamin[2], and Lemaître are to be as much commended for their impartiality as for their insight.

In this country Fénelon's reputation stood as high as ever it did in France and it was maintained at its zenith till a later date. He was admired for various reasons—as a Greek scholar, as the author of *Télémaque*, as a liberal, and as a man of saintly life. Professor Saintsbury, writing in 1882, was only expressing the general opinion of Englishmen when he said in his *History of French Literature* that "to Fénelon every virtue under heaven may be assigned." Miss E. K. Sanders in her *Fénelon* (1901) is a decided *fénelonienne*, admirable in her sympathetic understanding of Fénelon's mysticism, but unfair to

---

[1] "J'appelle 'bossuétiste' non pas celui qui préfère Bossuet à Fénelon, mais celui qui fait siennes les préventions de Bossuet à l'endroit de Fénelon, et qui, pour mieux exalter le premier, croit nécessaire d'humilier le second." This definition of M. Bremond's will, with the names transposed, serve for that of a *fénelonien*.

[2] In Petit de Julleville, *Hist. de la langue et de la littérature française*, v, viii (1898).

Bossuet[1]. Lord St Cyres in his *François de Fénelon,* which appeared in the same year as Miss Sanders's book, is better informed and more critical than his rival, but he is unsympathetic not only in his treatment of mysticism, but towards Roman Catholicism and the Roman Church in general, and in points of detail he is too much under the influence of Brunetière and other *bossuétistes.*

I.

François de Salignac de La Mothe-Fénelon was born on August 6, 1651, in his father's château of Fénelon, which stands on a steep rock overlooking the Dordogne, at the extreme limits of Périgord, where it borders on Quercy. Partly owing to the fact that after the expulsion of the English from Guienne it enjoyed greater peace than other provinces, and partly owing to its distance from the capital, which prevented the "new rich" from pulling down the old châteaux and replacing them by classical buildings, Périgord has preserved more of its ancient châteaux than any French province except Touraine[2].

In after life Fénelon recalled with pride that the family of Salignac and its junior branch of La Mothe-Fénelon had been distinguished in arms and diplomacy and the Church. But the only other member of his family who is known to history is Bertrand de Salignac de La Mothe-Fénelon, Fénelon's great-great-uncle, who wrote an account of the siege of Metz by Charles V in 1552 and was sent as ambassador to England in 1572.

Fénelon's parents were for their station in life extremely poor. The fourteenth child of his father (by his second wife), he was sent at the age of twelve to the nearest University, that of Cahors, and three years later (1666) to the College of Du Plessis at Paris. At these two seats of learning he laid the

---

[1] In her *Bossuet* (1921), on the other hand, she inclines towards Bossuet.

[2] See J. de Foville and A. Le Sourd, *Les Châteaux de France* (1913). They give photographs of nineteen châteaux for the department of Dordogne, which represents Périgord, and mention eighteen more. Few of these—the chief exception is Montaigne—are later than the sixteenth century. Fénelon is of the fifteenth and sixteenth. It is six miles from Sarlat, the birthplace of Étienne de la Boétie. Another Périgord château is Bourdeilles, the birthplace of the Abbé de Brantôme.

foundation of that intimate knowledge of Greek and Latin literature which distinguished him beyond nearly all his contemporaries. At Paris he was under the guardianship of his uncle, the Marquis Antoine de Fénelon, an ex-duellist, who had become a devoted supporter of the Church, and it was by his uncle's advice that in 1668 he entered the Seminary of Saint-Sulpice, which had been founded in 1641 by the Marquis's intimate friend, Jean-Jacques Olier. Olier died in 1657, but his spirit survived in his successor, M. de Bretonvilliers, and in M. Tronson, who directed Fénelon's theological studies, and for whom throughout his life he felt the affection and devotion of a son for a father. It was doubtless at Saint-Sulpice, imbued as it was with the mystical spirit of M. Olier, that Fénelon learnt the first lessons of mysticism and "pure love[1]."

Fénelon left Saint-Sulpice in 1676, took Orders soon afterwards, and in 1678 was appointed Superior of the Congregation of *Les Nouvelles-Catholiques*, which had been instituted for the instruction of Protestant women who had been converted to Catholicism. But when Fénelon was appointed, the so-called "New-Catholics" included a considerable proportion of young women and children who had been carried off by force from Protestant homes, and had still to be converted. Fénelon brought to this task all his persuasiveness and tactful skill, and in recognition of his services he was, seven years later, after the revocation of the Edict of Nantes (October 1685), sent on a mission to Poitou and Saintonge to bring about the conversion of the Protestants of those provinces.

It is in connexion with this mission that the question of his tolerance was raised by M. Douen. The truth appears to be that in his religious opinions Fénelon was neither more nor less intolerant than his brother Churchmen and the great majority of his lay contemporaries. It is clear from the letters in which he gave an account of his mission to Seignelay, the Secretary of State for *La Marine et la Religion prétendue réformée*, and from a similar letter addressed to Bossuet, that he entirely approved of the Revocation and that he recognised the right of the government to employ force as well as persuasion in certain cases. On

[1] See A. Delplanque, *op. cit.* pp. 282–286.

the other hand he greatly preferred persuasion to violence, and he clearly recognised that conversion by force could lead to nothing but indifference or hypocrisy[1]. The letter to Bossuet reveals his distaste for his task and his longing to return to Paris.

Fénelon had been introduced to Bossuet by his uncle soon after he was appointed to the *Nouvelles-Catholiques,* and he paid frequent visits to him at Germigny, the country house of the Bishops of Meaux. His friendship with the Duc de Beauvillier and his Duchess, which lasted throughout their lives, dates from about the same time. It was for the Duchess that he wrote about 1680 his *Traité de l'Éducation des Filles,* which was the first of his writings to appear in print, namely in 1687.

In 1689 a great change took place in Fénelon's life. On August 16 of that year the Duc de Beauvillier was appointed governor to the Duc de Bourgogne, and on the following day he proposed the Abbé de Fénelon to the king for the post of tutor, and his proposal was accepted. Bossuet was delighted at the appointment and wrote a charming letter of congratulation to Mme de Laval, a daughter of his old friend, the Marquis de Fénelon. An admirable letter of encouragement and warning, inspired by true Christian sentiment, was addressed to Fénelon himself by M. Tronson. With Fénelon were associated his nephew, the Abbé de Beaumont, and the Abbé Fleury as assistant-tutors, and his old friend, the Abbé de Langeron, as reader[2].

The Duc de Bourgogne, says Saint-Simon in his famous portrait of that prince,

naquit terrible, et sa première jeunesse fit trembler. Dur et colère jusqu'aux derniers emportements, et jusque contre les choses inanimées; impétueux avec fureur, incapable de souffrir la moindre résistance, même des heures et des éléments, sans entrer en des fougues à faire craindre que tout ne rompît dans son corps; opiniâtre à l'excès; passionné pour toute espèce de volupté,... souvent farouche, naturellement porté à la cruauté; barbare en railleries et à produire les ridicules avec une justesse qui assommoit. De la hauteur des cieux il ne regardoit les hommes que comme des atomes avec qui il n'avoit aucune ressemblance quels qu'ils fussent.

[1] Acton both in his *Lectures on Modern History* and in his *French Revolution* exaggerates Fénelon's tolerance.

[2] See Cte d'Haussonville, *La Duchesse de Bourgogne,* 4 vols. 1898–1908, I, c. v.

On the other hand his intelligence was of a high order:

> L'esprit, la pénétration brilloient en lui de toutes parts: jusque dans ses furies ses réponses étonnoient; ses raisonnements tendoient toujours au juste et au profond, même dans ses emportements. Il se jouoit des connoissances les plus abstraites. L'étendue et la vivacité de son esprit étoient prodigieuses, et l'empêchoient de s'appliquer à une seule chose à la fois, jusqu'à l'en rendre incapable.

Such, according to Saint-Simon, was the seven-year-old pupil who was put in the hands of the Duc de Beauvillier and Fénelon. The transformation that they brought about was astonishing.

> De cet abîme sortit un prince affable, doux, humain, modéré, patient, modeste, pénitent, et, autant et quelquefois au delà de ce que son état pouvoit comporter, humble et austère pour soi....Cette grande et sainte maxime, que les rois sont faits pour leurs peuples, et non les peuples pour les rois ni aux rois, étoit si avant imprimée en son âme qu'elle lui avoit rendu le luxe et la guerre odieuse[1].

Anyone familiar with Saint-Simon will suspect that he has forced the note in the first two passages in order to heighten the contrast between the Duke as a child and the Duke as a young man. As a matter of fact we have only to turn to a letter which Fénelon wrote to Père Martineau, the Duke's confessor, after the Duke's death, to see that Saint-Simon has given an entirely false impression of the boy's character[2]. He was certainly subject to tempests of ungovernable rage, and they sometimes lasted a whole day[3]; but when the storm died down he was repentant and submissive, and grateful to those who corrected him. In his ordinary moods he shewed no trace of that haughtiness of which Saint-Simon accuses him[4]. He was always sincere and ingenuous; he did not even wait to be interrogated to confess his faults. As to his precocious intelligence Fénelon is in full agreement with Saint-Simon[5].

---

[1] *Mémoires*, IX, 209 ff.

[2] *Œuvres*, VIII, 123.

[3] For his fits of rage see Fénelon's portrait of *Le Fantasque* (*Œuvres choisies*, II, 161). "En se levant, le pli d'un chausson lui a déplu: toute la journée sera orageuse et tout le monde en souffrira. Il fait peur, il fait pitié: il pleure comme un enfant, il rugit comme un lion."

[4] See Fénelon's fable of *Le jeune Bacchus et le Faune*.

[5] See generally for the Duke's education D'Haussonville, *op. cit.*

Like Bossuet, Fénelon wrote for the benefit of his pupil books which, going beyond their immediate purpose, have taken their place in French literature. They differ however from Bossuet's more ambitious works—the *Discours sur l'histoire universelle*, the *Politique tirée de l'Écriture Sainte*, and the *Traité de la connaissance de Dieu et de soi-même*—in being strictly educational, that is to say, in being adapted to the comprehension of the pupil.

Of the thirty-six so-called *Fables* only about half are proper fables, and not all of these are beast-fables; the rest are either fairy-stories, or Oriental tales, or classical tales written in the manner of *Télémaque*. Fénelon was a great admirer of La Fontaine; he made his pupil translate his fables into Latin prose and write original fables on the same subject[1]. La Fontaine, on his side, dedicated to the young prince his twelfth book (1694) as well as three of its separate fables (i, ii, and iv)[2]. On La Fontaine's death Fénelon wrote for his pupil's benefit a charming little Latin theme, which begins:

Heu! fuit vir ille facetus, Aesopus alter, nugarum laude Phaedro superior, per quem brutae animantes, vocales factae, humanum genus edocuere sapientiam.

Fénelon's own beast-fables are written to point a moral, and except for their easy and graceful style have no particular artistic merit. Between his *Le Pigeon puni de son inquiétude* (xx) and La Fontaine's *Les deux Pigeons* there is a world of difference. Some of the fables have a direct reference to the prince's character: *L'Abeille et la Mouche* to his outbursts of anger, *Le jeune Bacchus et le Faune* to his haughtiness when reproved. Better than the beast-fables are the little stories, especially the *Histoire d'Alibée Persan* (xxxiii), *Les Aventures de Mélésicthon* (xxxv), and the last and longest, *Les Aventures d'Aristonon* (xxxvi). The two latter, with their classical tone

[1]   Ce qui m'étonne est qu'à huit ans
             Un prince en fable ait mis la chose.
                            (*Le Loup et le Renard*, XII, ix.)
    [2] One of these, *Les Compagnons d'Ulysse* (XII, i), was first published in 1690.

and their graceful but conventional descriptions of scenery, resemble *Télémaque.*

The *Dialogues des Morts*[1] even more than the *Fables* have that *lactea ubertas* which Quintilian found in Livy. They make no attempt to portray character, but they are interesting as expressions of Fénelon's ethical and political opinions and they help to throw light on his pupil's character. In the very first dialogue (*Mercure et Charon*) we have a portrait of him as *le jeune Picrochole,* thus giving him the name of Rabelais's swashbuckling monarch, who might have said himself, like Louis XIV on his death-bed, "J'ai trop aimé la guerre."

> MERCURE. Je crois qu'il aimera la paix et qu'il saura faire la guerre. On voit en lui les commencements d'un grand prince, comme on remarque dans un bouton de rose naissante ce qui promet une belle fleur.
> CHARON. Mais n'est-il pas bouillant et impétueux?
> MERCURE. Il l'est étrangement....Il est impétueux, mais il n'est pas méchant: il est curieux, docile, plein de goût pour les belles choses; il aime les honnêtes gens, et sait bon gré à ceux qui le corrigent. S'il peut surmonter sa promptitude et sa paresse, il sera merveilleux, je te le prédis.

In the third dialogue (*Chiron et Achille*) Chiron points out that the true remedy for the violent transports and indocile temper of youth is to be afraid of oneself and to be guided by wise men. And then he ends with a prophecy:

> You will come to life again, after long centuries, with genius, elevation of character, courage and a love of the Muses, but with an impatient and impetuous temperament; you will have Chiron at your side; we shall see what use you will make of him.

All the first six dialogues are inspired by Greek legend and literature. The sixth, in which the speakers are Ulysses and Grillus (whom Circe changed into a pig), is on the same subject as *Les Compagnons d'Ulysse* (XII, i), which La Fontaine dedicated to Fénelon's pupil. "Foible, vain, léger, malin, trompeur et injuste"—Grillus's opinion of man is no higher than that of La Fontaine's wolf. And this agrees with what Fénelon says elsewhere in his own person:

---

[1] First published in an unauthorised edition in 1712 (45 dialogues). Sec Le Petit, *op. cit.* p. 453.

Laissez couler l'eau sous les ponts; laissez les hommes être hommes, c'est-à-dire, foibles, vains, inconstants, injustes, faux et présomptueux. Laissez le monde être toujours monde: c'est tout dire: aussi bien ne l'empêcheriez-vous pas. Laissez chacun suivre son naturel et ses habitudes: vous ne sauriez les refondre; le plus court est de les laisser, et de les souffrir. Accoutumez-vous à la déraison et à l'injustice[1]!

In the majority of the dialogues the speakers are taken from Greek or Roman or French history, but it is as a moralist rather than as a historian that Fénelon criticises their actions. And the lesson that he strives to impress upon his pupil is that a prince should prefer peace to war, and justice and humanity to glory. With this aim he passes in review the kings of France from Charles VII to Louis XIII (Charles VIII, Henri II, and Charles IX are omitted) and for none of them except Louis XII and Henri IV has he a good word. He has an even worse opinion of Richelieu and Mazarin, and has nothing to say in favour of their successful foreign policy. Was this because he regarded them as having inspired Louis XIV with his love of war and conquest?

Perhaps the best and most interesting dialogue is that between Socrates, Alcibiades, and Timon (xviii), in which Socrates declares that the misanthropy of Timon and the philanthropy or self-interested popularity of Alcibiades are equally to blame. When we remember that Saint-Simon said of Fénelon that "jamais homme n'a eu plus que lui la passion de plaire" and that Mme Guyon in the early days of their friendship told him that "l'envie de plaire" was one of his chief faults, it is a fair conjecture that, when he makes Socrates say, "Il y a deux manières de se donner aux hommes. La première est de se faire aimer, non pour être l'idole des hommes, mais pour employer leur confiance à les rendre bons," he is defending, not without justification, his own love of popularity[2].

We do not know the precise date at which *Télémaque* was written, but it was probably during the years 1695 and 1696[3]. In

---

[1] *A une demoiselle* (Cagnac, *op. cit.* pp. 243–244).

[2] The first authorised edition of the *Fables* and the *Dialogues des Morts* was published by Ramsay in 1718 (2 vols. 12mo); it contained 25 fables and 67 dialogues.

[3] See *Télémaque*, ed. Cahen, I, xlii–xliv.

1699 the first part of it—four and a quarter books—was printed
without Fénelon's authority from a copy of his manuscript,
which the copyist had sold to the printer as his own work[1].
When it became known that the real author was Fénelon, the
king at once stopped the publication, and, though numerous
more or less complete editions were surreptitiously printed at
Paris and elsewhere before the end of the year, it was not till
1717 that Fénelon's great-nephew gave to the world the first
really complete and authorised edition.

The phenomenal success of *Télémaque* on its first appearance
was due largely to the fact that it was supposed to be a satire
on Louis XIV and his government. Later, it obtained a more
durable vogue on its own merits, especially as a work for
young persons, for whom it was the gate through which they
entered into the magic realm of fiction. Whether in a translation or in its original tongue, it penetrated into nearly every
country of Europe[2]. But with the development of the novel in
the nineteenth century and the increasing crowd of competitors
it was read less and less, even as a school-book. Yet an unprejudiced reader will find in this now rather neglected classic
much that is attractive, not only to his moral but to his aesthetic
judgment. The imitations of Homer and Sophocles and Virgil
may not have the same charm for us that they had for our
ancestors; we may criticise the descriptions of scenery as too
general and too conventional; but we must admit that the
story is well managed, that Télémaque, in spite of his difficult
rôle as a virtuous young prince, is not an unsympathetic figure,
and that the different forms of love—sensual love, passionate
love, and the reasonable love which ends in a happy marriage—
are delicately symbolised by Calypso, Eucharis, and Antiope[3].

But like the *Dialogues des Morts* the book has a special
interest in the light that it throws on Fénelon's views of
government. He no doubt thought he was sincere in his assertion that no satire was intended in his book, and that none of
his characters was a portrait; but it was only natural that his

---

[1] See Le Petit, *op. cit.* p. 451.
[2] In the catalogue of the *Bib. Nationale* it comprises 741 items.
[3] D'Haussonville, *op. cit.* I, 378–379.

contemporaries should see Louis XIV in the ruler (Idomenée) whom Mentor addresses in the following words:

Une vaine ambition vous a poussé jusqu'au bord du précipice. A force de vouloir paroître grand, vous avez pensé ruiner votre véritable grandeur. Hâtez-vous de réparer ces fautes; suspendez tous vos grands ouvrages; renoncez à ce faste qui ruineroit votre nouvelle ville; laissez en paix respirer vos peuples; appliquez-vous à les mettre dans l'abondance, pour faciliter les mariages[1].

Happily Idomenée repents of his former errors and under the guidance of Mentor transforms his kingdom of Salente[2] into a model society. The laws and regulations introduced by Mentor are of the most drastic and paternal character. "He regulated dress, food, furniture, and the size and decoration of houses, for all the different social scales." He even prescribed the colour of their dress, white for those of the first rank, blue for those of the second, and so on to the seventh rank. The slaves—it is not after all a perfect society—are to wear grey-brown. Their food is to be of the best, but it must be prepared *sans aucun ragoût*. I need not refer to the other regulations, which would certainly have confirmed Louis XIV in his opinion that Fénelon was the *esprit le plus chimérique de son royaume*. But Salente was a great success; when Télémaque returned there later, he was surprised to find what a change for the better had taken place.

The account is interesting, not so much as a picture of a paternal Utopia but for its stinging criticisms on the government and policy of Louis XIV. First for his wars:

Les maux de la guerre sont encore plus horribles que vous ne pensez. La guerre épuise un État et le met toujours en danger de périr, lors même qu'on remporte les plus grandes victoires[3].

Next for his buildings:

Lequel vaut mieux, ou une ville superbe en marbre, en or et en argent, avec une campagne négligée et stérile; ou une campagne cultivée et fertile avec une ville médiocre et modeste dans ses mœurs[4]?

Lastly for his absolutism and luxury:

Souvenez-vous, ô Télémaque, qu'il y a deux choses pernicieuses dans le gouvernement des peuples, auxquelles on n'apporte presque jamais aucun

---

[1] Book X.   [2] See books X, XI and XVII.   [3] Book XI.   [4] Book XVII.

remède; la première est une autorité injuste et trop violente dans les rois; la seconde est le luxe qui corrompt les mœurs[1].

The other Utopia that is portrayed in *Télémaque* is the exact antithesis of Salente[1]. If Salente, according to modern ideas, is over-governed, in La Bétique there is no government at all. Here are "les délices de l'âge d'or"—-a perfect climate, double harvests, evergreen trees, sheep with the finest wool, and mines of gold and silver, which are left unworked. Land and all things are held in common; each family is ruled by its head; they live in tents lined and roofed with waxed skins or the bark of trees. "Innocence, good faith, obedience, and horror of vice dwell in this happy land." There is no need of judges, for everyone is judged by his own conscience." They are never ill and they live to a great age, without loss of gaiety or vigour. They are as difficult to subjugate as they are incapable of wishing to subjugate their neighbours. Hence they dwell in profound peace.

In this description of La Bétique Fénelon is evidently inspired by the classical tradition of a golden age. But he borrows little from any of the *loci classici* on the subject[2]. He owes nothing to Hesiod or Virgil and only a hint or two to Ovid[3]. M. Chinard, however, recalling the fact that his elder brother was a missionary in Canada for twelve years (1667–1679), detects a possible source of his description in the accounts of the New World[4]. There is certainly one touch that supports his suggestion. For we read in the Père Sagard's history of Canada that the cabins of the Hurons are covered with the bark of trees and that the bark is prepared by women just as in La Bétique[5]. In La Bétique too the women make shoes out of sheep-skins, which may be another Canadian reminiscence. Mr Atkinson agrees with M. Chinard, but when he goes further

[1] Book XVII.
[2] Hesiod, *Works and Days*, ll. 109–126; Virgil, *Ecl.* IV and *Georg.* I, 125–129; Horace, *Epod.* XVI; Ovid, *Met.* I, 89–112.
[3] He has borrowed some touches from Strabo, III, ii, 4–14.
[4] G. Chinard, *L'Amérique et le Rêve exotique dans la littérature française au XVIIe et au XVIIIe siècle*, 1913.
[5] G. Sagard, *L'Histoire du Canada*, Tross, 4 vols. 1866, pp. 235 and 257. The original edition is of 1636.

and sees a "definite kinship" between *Télémaque* and the two
Extraordinary Voyages, the *Terre australe* and the *Histoire des
Sévarambes*, I cannot follow him[1]. Throughout the work Fénelon
is never weary of pressing home his lessons to princes, of
pointing out the evils of war and extravagance and arrogant
display, and of insisting that "kings do not reign for their own
glory but for the good of their people." The whole duty of
kings is summed up in Mentor-Minerva's parting admonition
to Télémaque:

> Fuyez la mollesse, le faste, la profusion; mettez votre gloire dans la
> simplicité; que vos vertus et vos bonnes actions soient les ornements de
> votre personne et de votre palais; qu'elles soient la garde qui vous environne,
> et que tout le monde apprenne de vous en quoi consiste le vrai bonheur.
> N'oubliez jamais que les *rois ne règnent point pour leur propre gloire, mais
> pour le bien des peuples.*

And then follows a special warning addressed to his pupil:

> Surtout soyez en garde contre votre humeur: c'est un ennemi que vous
> porterez partout avec vous jusqu'à la mort.... Défiez-vous de cet ennemi.

In Fénelon's judgment few kings have had a satisfactory
record. When Télémaque visits the kingdom of the dead[2], he
is astonished to find how many kings there are in Tartarus,
and how few in the Elysian fields. For "good kings are very
rare, and the majority are so bad, that the gods would fail in
justice, if after allowing them to abuse their power when they
lived they did not punish them after death." This descent of
Télémaque into hell is modelled on Homer and Virgil, but
Fénelon has coloured it with the spirit of Christianity. The
bad kings are punished for their sins not by physical but by
spiritual sufferings; the avenging Fury holds before them a
mirror which reveals to them their past vices. The good kings
live in the light of a heavenly glory, and are wrapped in a
felicity which comes from within. "They feel pity for the
sorrows of the living; but it is a sweet and peaceful pity which
in no wise diminishes their immutable felicity."

---

[1] G. Atkinson, *The Extraordinary Voyage in French Literature*, 1922.
See below, chapter VII, for the two voyages referred to.

[2] Book XIV.

Fénelon's description of the Elysian fields, in which the good kings have their reward, may be cited as a typical example of his descriptive style:

Télémaque s'avança vers ces rois, qui étoient dans des bocages odoriférants, sur des gazons toujours renaissants et fleuris. Mille petits ruisseaux d'une onde pure arrosoient ces beaux lieux, et y faisoient sentir une délicieuse fraîcheur; un nombre infini d'oiseaux faisoient résonner ces bocages de leur doux chant. On voyoit tout ensemble les fleurs du printemps, qui naissoient sous les pas, avec les plus riches fruits de l'automne, qui pendoient des arbres. Là jamais on ne ressentit les ardeurs de la furieuse Canicule; là jamais les noirs aquilons n'osèrent souffler, ni faire sentir les rigueurs de l'hiver. Ni la Guerre altérée de sang, ni la cruelle Envie, qui mord d'une dent venimeuse et qui porte des vipères entortillées dans son sein et autour de ses bras, ni les Jalousies, ni les Défiances, ni la Crainte, ni les vains Désirs, n'approchent jamais de cet heureux séjour de la paix. Le jour n'y finit point, et la nuit, avec ses sombres voiles, y est inconnue: une lumière pure et douce se répand autour des corps de ces hommes justes, et les environne de ses rayons comme d'un vêtement.

Fénelon is said to be the inventor of this "poetic" prose, a name which may be justified by the use of such words as *bocage, onde, aquilon*, which are ordinarily confined to poetry, and by the rhythmical balance of the sentences. But poetic prose is only a variety of picturesque prose, the prose which aims at presenting a picture to the reader and which appeals to his imagination through his senses. As a writer of such prose Fénelon is some way behind the great masters of the art. He has not the marvellous eye for details of form and colour which give Bernardin de Saint-Pierre's descriptions of land and sea, of sunrise and sunset, the precision of a painter's note-book. He has not the magic strokes by which Chateaubriand, while hardly less precise than Bernardin, conjures up some scene or landscape before the reader's imagination. His epithets—*beaux, délicieuse, doux, riches, noirs*—are vague and general; he mentions the flowers and the fruits, but he does not know their names; his personifications of War and Envy are conventional and unimpressive; the only really imaginative touch in the whole passage—*les environne de ses rayons comme d'un vêtement* —is borrowed from the Psalms.

No—it is not in the ambitious descriptive passages that Fénelon's style is at its best; it is rather in Mentor's political and moral exhortations and in Télémaque's simple outbursts of warm and generous feeling. In these conversations between tutor and pupil we have the true Fénelon—the warm heart and the clear brain expressing themselves naturally in easy, lucid, graceful, and harmonious language.

II.

While Fénelon was playing Mentor to the Duc de Bourgogne's Telemachus and was exercising upon his pupil all his persuasive influence, he himself was subjected to an influence which affected his character as well as his whole future career—the influence of that extraordinary woman, Mme Guyon.

Married before she was sixteen to a man of thirty-eight, whom she saw for the first time two days before the marriage-ceremony, Mme Guyon (Jeanne Marie Bouvier de La Motte) had to endure for twelve years the violent temper of a gouty husband and the persecution of an odious mother-in-law[1]. Left a widow in 1676 with two boys and an infant daughter, she became more and more drawn to a religious life, and in 1681, having given up her boys and her large income (with the exception of a small annuity), she went to Gex in Savoy, where she fell in with Père La Combe, a Barnabite Father whose acquaintance she had made some years before. Appointed by the Bishop of Geneva to be her spiritual director, he imbued her with the doctrines of exaggerated mysticism. Two years later, the disciple having now become the teacher, the pair began a wandering life together, visiting and preaching at Turin, Grenoble, Genoa, and other places. On their arrival at Paris in 1687 they were followed by malicious reports of their doctrines and their morals, and by order of the Archbishop of Paris the Father was sent to the Bastille and Mme Guyon was confined in a convent (January 1688). She was released after eight months of captivity through the intervention of Mme de Maintenon and Mme de Miramion, and thanks to her piety, her intelligence, her obvious sincerity and her singular powers of fascination, she gradually made her way into the little circle

---

[1] L. Guerrier, *Mme Guyon, sa vie, sa doctrine et son influence*, 1881. The American life by T. C. Upham (1848; new ed. 1905) is wholly uncritical.

of devout men and women with whom Mme de Maintenon was associated.

It was in October 1688, at the country house of the Duchesse de Béthune-Charost, a daughter of the famous *surintendant*, Nicolas Fouquet, that Fénelon first met her. He was, he says, prejudiced against her, but they happened to return to Paris in the same coach, and eight days later Mme Guyon "found herself," as she says in her *Life*, "united to him"—this was the mystical term for spiritual union—"without any obstacle," or, as Saint-Simon puts it, "leur esprit se plut l'un à l'autre; leur sublime s'amalgama."

They did not often meet, but they carried on an unflagging correspondence, of which Mme Guyon's share was by far the larger[1]. Of this correspondence only an expert in advanced mysticism can form a competent judgment, but it is difficult to understand how Fénelon, who after all had a large reserve of prudence and common sense, could have been so powerfully affected by a woman whose sentiments and language were so crudely exaggerated, sometimes even to the verge of blasphemy. But he assures her that "rien me scandalise en vous, et je ne suis jamais importuné de vos expressions." Indeed, throughout the correspondence it is Mme Guyon who appears as the director, and Fénelon as the directed. She points out his faults: "l'habitude de raillerie et l'envie de plaire," above all his *amour-propre* and his preoccupation with himself. And he in his turn deplores his frequent *sécheresse* towards others and his sensitiveness where his reputation is concerned[2]. In fact, the impression

[1] "Je n'ai vu ni pu voir bien souvent Mme Guyon. Mon principal commerce avec elle a été par lettres" (Fénelon to M. de Noailles, at this time Archbishop of Paris). The correspondence down to December 26, 1689, has been edited by Maurice Masson, *Fénelon et Mme Guyon*, 1907. The thirty-eight letters of Fénelon were rejected by Gosselin as apocryphal, but Masson has, I think, demonstrated their authenticity. The correspondence continued till the attacks on Mme Guyon began in 1693 (Fénelon to M. de Noailles). Fénelon's letters after 1689 are missing, but M. Seillière thinks with great probability that many of Mme Guyon's *Lettres spirituelles* may form part of her later correspondence with him (see Seillière, *Mme Guyon et Fénelon, précurseurs de Rousseau*, p. 192).

[2] See Letters X, XVI and XCIV (Mme Guyon), and XXXIX, LXXXV and XCIII (Fénelon).

that one gets from the letters hardly bears out the account which Fénelon gave of their relations to Mme de Maintenon six years later. But let him speak for himself:

Je dois savoir les vrais sentiments de Mme Guyon mieux que tous ceux qui l'ont examinée pour la condamner; car elle m'a parlé avec plus de confiance qu'à eux. Je l'ai examinée en toute rigueur, et peut-être que je suis allé trop loin pour la contredire. Je n'ai jamais eu aucun goût naturel pour elle ni pour ses écrits. Je n'ai jamais éprouvé rien d'extraordinaire en elle, qui ait pu me prévenir en sa faveur. Dans l'état le plus libre et le plus naturel, elle m'a expliqué toutes ses expériences et tous ses sentiments. Il n'est pas question des termes, que je ne défends point, et qui importent peu dans une femme, pourvu que le sens soit catholique. C'est ce qui m'a toujours paru. Elle est naturellement exagérante, et peu précautionnée dans ses expressions.

Il est vrai qu'elle a parlé quelquefois comme une mère qui a des enfants en Jésus-Christ, et qu'elle leur a donné des conseils sur les voies de la perfection; mais il y a une grande différence entre la présomption d'une femme qui enseigne indépendamment de l'Église, et une femme qui aide les âmes en leur donnant des conseils fondés sur ses expériences, et qui le fait avec soumission aux pasteurs.

La plupart de ces expressions pleines de transport sont insoutenables, si on les prend dans toute la rigueur de la lettre. Il faut entendre la personne, et ne se point scandaliser de ces sortes d'excès, si d'ailleurs la doctrine est innocente et la personne docile[1].

In the year 1689 Mme de Maintenon, prompted by Fénelon, introduced Mme Guyon to Saint-Cyr and allowed her to give *conférences*, with the result that both teachers and pupils were filled with enthusiasm for Quietism and Pure Love. This went on for five years, till at last the Bishop of Chartres (M. Godet Des Marais), who was Mme de Maintenon's director and a profound theologian, took alarm, and after carefully reading Mme Guyon's writings denounced them to Mme de Maintenon as full of dangerous errors. Bossuet and the Bishop of Châlons (M. de Noailles)[2], whom she also consulted, were of the same opinion, and so was Bourdaloue. Thereupon, by Fénelon's advice, Mme Guyon submitted to Bossuet not only her printed works—*Le Moyen court et très facile de faire oraison*

---

[1] Letter of March 7, 1696.

[2] See a letter to Noailles from Mme de Maintenon written in June 1694 (Geffroy, *op. cit.* I, 245).

(Lyons, 1686; Paris, 1686) and *Le Cantique des Cantiques interprété selon le sens mystique* (Grenoble, 1685)[1]—but all her manuscripts including *Les Torrents spirituels* and her autobiography[2]. Bossuet spent four or five months in examining them, and in January 1694 he had a long interview with the writer. Finally, at her request, a commission of three, consisting of Bossuet, the Bishop of Châlons, and M. Tronson, was appointed to make a more formal examination. Owing to M. Tronson's infirmities they held their meetings at Issy, a house of the Seminary of Saint-Sulpice, of which he was now Superior, and on March 10, 1695, they signed their report in the form of thirty-four articles. Fénelon, having obtained their consent to certain modifications, including the addition of the last four articles, also signed it. Five weeks earlier he had been nominated to the Archbishopric of Cambrai, the king stipulating that he should spend three months of every year at Versailles—the canon law required nine months' residence—and that for the rest of the year he should superintend the Duc de Bourgogne's education from Cambrai. Fénelon accepted the appointment with reluctance, for it took him away from the capital and the court, the two great centres of influence.

On April 16 Bossuet and M. de Noailles published an ordinance which included the articles of Issy, and a condemnation of Mme Guyon's printed works, and soon afterwards Mme Guyon signed a declaration of her submission. Here the whole affair might have ended. But Bossuet was not satisfied, and he determined to make a thorough study of the whole question. Learned theologian though he was, he had little acquaintance with the history and practice of mysticism, and

[1] These and other of Mme Guyon's writings were reprinted in *Les opuscules spirituels*, Cologne, 1712; Paris, 1790. *Le Moyen court* is written in a simple and clear style with an effective use of simile.

[2] The published *Life* (3 vols. Cologne, 1720; 3 vols. Paris, 1790) does not contain a passage relating to the beginning of Mme Guyon's friendship with Fénelon which she begged the Duc de Chevreuse to remove from the manuscript submitted to Bossuet. The latter, however, had previously copied passages from it. The missing five leaves are almost certainly those printed by Masson in his *Fénelon et Mme Guyon*, pp. 1–12, from a MS of Saint-Sulpice. The last leaf is so extravagant as to make one doubt of her sanity.

he confessed to Fénelon at the beginning of the controversy that he had never read either St François de Sales or St John of the Cross[1]. He now gave many months to the careful study of the whole subject, and towards the close of the year 1695 he wrote to Fénelon that he was working at an *Instruction sur les États d'Oraison* and that he proposed to submit it to him for examination. Fénelon, who was still on perfectly friendly terms with him, promised that he would give his approval to it after examination. But when the manuscript was put in his hands and he saw that the margins were filled with citations from Mme Guyon's writings, handled, he thought, with flagrant unfairness (*des réfutations atroces*), he returned it to Bossuet without reading it through and without his approval (August 1696).

At this point the question arises: What is there to account for the change in Bossuet's attitude towards Mme Guyon and her doctrines which took place between the articles of Issy and the *Instruction*? Apparently his study of mysticism had convinced him that the Church was in danger, and, whereas in the articles he had carefully distinguished between Mme Guyon and Molinos, he now, under the influence perhaps of the latter's recent condemnation (1687), regarded Mme Guyon's indifference to the practice of the virtues as a stepping-stone to the grosser doctrines of the Spanish mystic. He felt that he represented the sovereign authority of the Church, and that the party of Fénelon were supporting Mme Guyon against that authority, and, whereas he had formerly treated Mme Guyon with mildness and consideration and had admitted her to Holy Communion, he now passionately desired to make her confess not merely to errors of expression, but to those of a fundamental nature[2].

In a passionate and injudicious, but admirably written, memorandum Fénelon set forth his reasons for withholding his approval from Bossuet's *Instruction*[3]. He acted, he says, partly

---

[1] Fénelon to Bossuet, Feb. 9, 1697 (*Œuvres choisies*, IV, 70 ff.), and again in the *Réponse à la Relation*. Bossuet never denies it.

[2] See H. Delacroix, *Études d'histoire et de psychologie du mysticisme*, 1908, pp. 276–278.

[3] *Hist. de Fénelon*, II, 331 ff.; *Œuvres choisies*, IV, 62 ff. The whole is quoted by Bossuet, with comments, in his *Relation sur le Quiétisme*.

out of consideration for his friend Mme Guyon, " une pauvre femme captive"—she had been in prison since Christmas, 1695— "accablée de douleurs et d'opprobres," and partly from the feeling that "he could not impute to her such horrible doctrines without traducing himself and doing himself irreparable injustice." The only course left to him was for himself to write a work explaining the whole system of the inward life (*les voies intérieures*) and this work was nearly ready. He would not, however, publish it until it had been approved by M. de Noailles (now Archbishop of Paris) and M. Tronson. In October, therefore, he sent them copies of the work, and by M. de Noailles's advice also submitted it to M. Pirot, a doctor of the Sorbonne. He further agreed to the Archbishop's request that it should not appear in print before Bossuet's treatise. The Duc de Chevreuse, however, who had undertaken to see it through the press, obtained permission from the Archbishop to publish it at once if he thought fit, and thus Fénelon's *Explication des Maximes des Saints sur la Vie intérieure*[1] appeared in January or February 1697, more than a month before Bossuet's *Instruction sur les États d'Oraison*[2].

It was badly received. Friends and foes, clergy and laity, criticised alike its substance and its form[3]. Arranged in forty-five articles, each with *vrai* and *faux* as sub-headings, it is, unlike all Fénelon's other writings, devoid of all literary charm. It was now for the first time that Fénelon's relations with Mme Guyon were revealed by Mme de Maintenon[4] to the king. He was filled with indignation, and though he gave Fénelon permission to appeal to the Pope (April 27), when he asked for leave to defend his book in person, he forbade him to leave his diocese, thereby exiling him from the court (August 1). Finally, in

[1] Ed. A. Cherel, 1911; *Œuvres choisies*, III, 180-239. Owing to the Pope's censure, it is not included in either of the official editions of Fénelon's works.

[2] The printing was finished January 25. Bossuet writing on February 3 says he received it two days before.

[3] See a letter to Fénelon from M. Brisacier, a faithful admirer (*Hist. de Fénelon*, II, 33 ff.). Fénelon, however, believed that this unfavourable reception was engineered by Bossuet and his party.

[4] *Hist. de Fénelon*, III, 22.

January 1699, the king with his own hand struck Fénelon's
name off the list of officers of the young prince's household[1].

The scene of the great controversy now shifts to Rome.
Forbidden to go himself, Fénelon sent in his place his *vicaire-
général* and old friend, the pious and high-minded Abbé de
Chantérac. Bossuet was represented by his nephew, the Abbé
Bossuet, who happened to be in Rome at the time, and this
"little nephew of a great man" did much to envenom the weapons
with which the two adversaries fought in this unhappy duel.
It was largely as the result of his suggestions that Bossuet
wrote his famous *Relation sur le Quiétisme*[2], in which, making
unfair use of more or less private documents[3], he heaped ridicule
upon Fénelon and Mme Guyon. It was a cruel book, but it was
powerfully written and it was eagerly read.

> Le livre de M. de Meaux fait un grand fracas ici. On ne parle d'autre
> chose. Les faits sont à la portée de tout le monde. Les folies de Mme Guyon
> divertissent. Le livre est court, vif et bien fait. On se le prête, on se l'arrache,
> on le dévore[4].

"Ma *Relation* sera foudroyante," Bossuet had said, and for
the moment Fénelon at Cambrai and his friends at Rome
seemed crushed by the blow. But Chantérac urged Fénelon to
reply, and he did so with such promptitude and effect in the
Réponse à la Relation de M. de Meaux that public opinion underwent a complete change, and, as if "by enchantment," says
Cardinal Bausset, serenity and confidence were restored to
Fénelon's supporters. Well might Bossuet exclaim, "Qui lui
conteste l'esprit? Il en a à faire peur[5]."

For the rest of the year the contest was waged with increasing
bitterness—manœuvres and intrigues at Rome, pamphlets and
counter-pamphlets at Paris. M. Lanson may call it a "delicious
comedy," but to unprejudiced friends of the Church it is a pitiful

---

[1] The Duc de Bourgogne married Marie-Adelaïde of Savoy in December 1697, but they did not live together till October 1699.

[2] *Œuvres*, XXIX, 521–625.

[3] I.e. Mme Guyon's autobiography and Fénelon's *Mémoire* of August 2,
1696.

[4] Mme de Maintenon to the Cardinal de Noailles (June 29, 1698).

[5] Fénelon first saw the *Relation* on July 5, and his *Réponse* reached
Rome on August 30.

tragedy. Fénelon and Bossuet were no doubt fighting in the first instance for truth, Fénelon for the due recognition of mysticism by the Church, Bossuet against its exaggerated development. But two such masterful spirits could not help also fighting for personal victory, and their animosity was inflamed by the radical difference in their temperaments. Bossuet, as he says of himself, was "the simplest of men"; Fénelon was complex and subtle. Fénelon was peculiarly sensitive, while Bossuet, at any rate in controversy, had no mercy for the feelings of his opponents.

At last, Innocent XII, brow-beaten by Louis XIV, delivered judgment on March 12, 1699, the day before his eighty-fifth birthday. In the form of a brief, drawn up by four of the cardinals, it condemned Fénelon's book as containing rash, scandalous, and erroneous propositions, and these it proceeded to set out to the number of twenty-three. Bossuet and his friends, who had been becoming less confident of the result, received the judgment at first with complete satisfaction, but this was greatly diminished when they reflected that the obnoxious work had not been declared heretical and that no censure had been passed on Fénelon's other writings on the subject.

Fénelon on his side rose nobly to the occasion. In a *mandement* addressed to his diocesans he signified his submission to the papal brief, "simply, absolutely and without the shadow of a restriction." But he subsequently declared that his submission was not to be termed a "retractation." He admitted that some of his propositions and expressions, though they were to be found in writers who had been canonised, were unsuited to a dogmatic work and were therefore rightly censured. But the Pope, he said, had not condemned any part of his real doctrine, "but only the expressions of his book *in the sense they naturally bore, which was a sense he never intended*[1]."

This is certainly over-subtle, but it is not insincere. The fact is that Fénelon was embarrassed by his desire to defend Mme Guyon. He had rashly encouraged her to communicate to him all her experiences of the interior life, and he had made little or no attempt to correct or moderate her expressions. Then, as soon

[1] *Hist. Litt.* (*Œuvres*, I), p. 211, citing a letter of October 2, 1699.

as the attacks on her began, he had with excessive prudence
ceased all intercourse with her and had signed the articles of
Issy. Perhaps his conscience reproached him for what must
have seemed to her the desertion of her cause. At any rate, when
she was imprisoned, and when Bossuet followed up the articles
of Issy with a carefully prepared attack on her whole system,
Fénelon abandoned his prudent attitude and made a chivalrous
but hopeless attempt to reconcile his friend's doctrines with
common sense and the orthodox teaching of the Church.

This is not the place, even if I had the necessary knowledge,
to enter into the general question of Quietism or to consider
how far the mysticism of Mme Guyon, whether as expressed
by herself or as interpreted by Fénelon, goes beyond that of
the great mystics such as St Teresa and St John of the Cross[1].
But it may be pointed out that the papal censure of Fénelon's
book is almost entirely concerned with the question of Pure
Love. On the far more difficult question of Quietism in the
narrower sense of the term, that is to say of passivity, and on the
doctrine of the One Act, it says very little. It merely condemns
the proposition that "there is a state of contemplation" (i.e. contemplative prayer) so perfect that it becomes habitual (XVI) and
the proposition that "in the passive state one practises all the
distinct virtues without thinking that they are virtues." With
regard to Pure Love it condemns numerous propositions which
under different aspects uphold the chimerical doctrine that the
ideal of Pure or disinterested Love is indifference to salvation.
This is just as repugnant to common sense as the true doctrine,
of which it is an exaggeration, namely that the Love of God
must be pure and disinterested, is in accordance with it.

That Fénelon was justified in his contention that the propositions condemned by Innocent XII did not represent his real
opinions is shewn by comparing the *Maximes des Saints* with
his later teaching, which, as Baron von Hügel points out, became

---

[1] See the careful analysis of the controversy by the Abbé Gosselin in
Œuvres, I, 177–254, esp. pp. 204–211 ; F. von Hügel, *The mystical element
of religion as studied in St Catherine of Genoa and her friends*, 2 vols.
1908, II, 129–174; H. Delacroix, *op. cit.* 1908, esp. pp. 118–307 ; E.
Underhill, *Mysticism*, 1911, pp. 375–426.

increasingly clarified and improved, as for instance in his *Instruction Pastorale* of September 15, 1697[1], in his *Première Réponse aux difficultés de M. de Chartres* (printed February 1698)[2] and in two letters to Bossuet on Charity (October 1698[3], and January 1699[4]). In all of these treatises Fénelon deals almost exclusively with the question of Pure Love, and, carrying the war into the enemy's camp, insists, as against Bossuet, that " Charity" or the Pure Love of God is not merely the desire for eternal bliss.

For his views on the Prayer of Quiet a letter of March 6, 1696, to the Carmelite Sister, Charlotte de Saint-Cyprien, is of great importance. In this he says that "contemplation" does not dispense with distinct acts of virtue, that "silence" (i.e. the Prayer of Quiet) is not an inactive and idle condition of the soul, but a cessation of every unquiet and busy thought, that "contemplation in this life is never continuous and uninterrupted," and that "in the intervals one can and must practise distinct acts of all the virtues[5]."

While Fénelon, on the one hand, corrected the exaggerated expressions which in his eagerness to defend Mme Guyon he had used concerning Pure Love in the *Maximes des Saints*, Bossuet, on the other, in his till recently unpublished *Instruction sur les États d'Oraison—second traité*[6], abandoned his view that an element of self-interest is involved in the love of God. Thus on the only question on which the Pope pronounced a decision there was practically no difference of doctrine between them. The real difference was, as I have said, one of temperament. Temperamentally Fénelon was far more of a mystic than Bossuet. There is truth in M. Seillière's view that Bossuet represents masculine mysticism and Fénelon feminine mysticism, and in the saying of M. Delacroix that Bossuet stands for ordinary reasonable Christianity as against extraordinary Christianity. The Duchesse d'Orléans was not far wrong when she spoke of *querelle d'évêques*; she was altogether right when

[1] *Œuvres*, III, 186 ff.
[2] *Ib*. pp. 124 ff.
[3] *Ib*. pp. 215 ff.
[4] *Ib*. pp. 354 ff.
[5] *Ib*. VIII, 449 ff.; *Œuvres choisies*, IV, 99 ff.
[6] Written in 1695. Ed. E. Levesque, 1897.

she said: "Je suis avec M. de Cambrai et M. de Meaux comme les enfants qui aiment papa et maman: je fais grand cas de l'un et de l'autre[1]."

III.

Louis XIV and Bossuet had triumphed. Fénelon had been banished to his diocese, and his book had been censured by the Pope. But Fénelon after the censure held a higher place than he did before in the public estimation, and it is the last sixteen years of his life that have especially endeared him to posterity[2].

The see of Cambrai was a peculiar one, in that it consisted partly of territory which had been given to France by the Peace of Nymegen (1678) and partly of territory which was still subject to Spain. It was of large extent, comprising in all 764 villages; it included the dioceses of Arras, Saint-Omer, Tournai and Namur, and it stretched from east of Namur nearly to Ypres and from south of Cambrai nearly to Brussels[3]. The population was largely Flemish, and it required all Fénelon's tact and charm to win their affections. But he succeeded.

Ses aumônes, ses visites épiscopales réitérées plusieurs fois l'année, et qui lui firent connoître par lui-même à fond toutes les parties de son diocèse, la sagesse et la douceur de son gouvernement, ses prédications fréquentes dans la ville et dans les villages, la facilité de son accès, son humanité avec les petits, sa politesse avec les autres, ses grâces naturelles qui rehaussoient le prix de tout ce qu'il disoit et faisoit, le firent adorer de son peuple, et les prêtres dont il se déclaroit le père et le frère, et qu'il traitoit tous ainsi, le portoient tous dans leurs cœurs[4].

The difficulties of Fénelon's administration were greatly increased by the fact that for twelve years (1701–1713) Flanders was the theatre of war. Victorious and vanquished armies, plundering as they went, advanced and retreated; the country was depopulated and the land was left uncultivated. The worst years were from 1706 to 1709, from Ramillies to Malplaquet.

---

[1] *Corr. de Madame*, I, 176 and 179.

[2] See E. de Broglie, *Fénelon à Cambrai d'après sa correspondance, 1699–1705*, 1884.

[3] *Gallia Christiana*, vol. III. [4] Saint-Simon, *Mémoires*, XI, 61.

In 1708 the Archbishop wrote to Prince Eugène to demand his protection for the churches at Tournai or in the neighbourhood. During the terrible winter of 1708–1709 he provided corn for the French armies, and in the following autumn, when the battle of Malplaquet rolled the tide of war ever nearer to Cambrai, he turned his seminary into a hospital for the wounded and kept an open table in his palace for officers and soldiers. Happily the revenues of his see were large—nominally 200,000 *livres*—and this Archbishop-Duke and Prince of the Empire lived with great personal simplicity. Moreover, like his spiritual teachers St Teresa and St John of the Cross, he had a remarkable faculty for organisation and his huge diocese was a model of order and good government.

All this is told with picturesque details by Saint-Simon in the famous obituary-portrait from which I have already quoted and which begins with the following description of Fénelon's person[1]:

Ce prélat étoit un grand homme maigre, bien fait, pâle, avec un grand nez, des yeux dont le feu et l'esprit sortoient comme un torrent, et une physionomie telle que je n'en ai point vu qui y ressemblât, et qui ne se pouvoit oublier, quand on ne l'auroit vu qu'une fois. Elle rassembloit tout, et les contraires ne s'y combattoient pas. Elle avoit de la gravité et de la galanterie, du sérieux et de la gaieté; elle sentoit également le docteur, l'évêque et le grand seigneur; ce qui y surnageoit, ainsi que dans toute sa personne, c'étoit la finesse, l'esprit, les grâces, la décence, et surtout la noblesse. Il falloit effort pour cesser de le regarder. Tous ses portraits sont parlants, sans toutefois avoir pu attraper la justesse de l'harmonie qui frappoit dans l'original, et la délicatesse de chaque caractère que ce visage rassembloit. Ses manières y répondoient dans la même proportion, avec une aisance qui en donnoit aux autres, et cet air et ce bon goût qu'on ne tient que de l'usage de la meilleure compagnie et du grand monde, qui se trouvoit répandu de soi-même dans toutes ses conversations; avec cela une éloquence naturelle, douce, fleurie, une politesse insinuante, mais noble et proportionnée, une élocution facile, nette, agréable, un air de clarté et de netteté pour se faire entendre dans les matières les plus embarrassées et les plus dures; avec cela un homme qui ne vouloit jamais avoir plus d'esprit que ceux à qui il parloit, qui se mettoit à la portée de chacun sans le faire jamais sentir, qui les mettoit à l'aise et qui sembloit enchanter, de façon qu'on ne pouvoit le quitter, ni s'en défendre, ni ne pas chercher à le retrouver.

[1] *Mémoires*, XI, 58–66.

As a portrait of Fénelon as he appeared to the world this could not be bettered. But Saint-Simon expressly says that he knew him only by sight, and that he had not seen him since his exile. He therefore makes little attempt in his long notice to give us the inner man. The one fault of which he accuses him, and on this he is insistent, is ambition. He says that Fénelon's great aim was to return to the court and become a member of the *Conseil d'État*, that, when the Duc de Bourgogne became Dauphin, his ambition, which was by no means dead, reawakened with force, and that even after the sudden extinction of his hopes, it "surnageoit à tout, se prenoit à tout," leading him even to cultivate the friendship of the Duc d'Orléans.

For the last of these charges at any rate there is no evidence. That Fénelon loved to influence both persons and affairs and that he would gladly have played Mentor to his pupil as King of France may be freely admitted; but that he aspired to be the Richelieu of the future monarch is very doubtful, and it is quite possible that Saint-Simon has credited Fénelon with ambitious dreams which his friends Beauvillier and Chevreuse cherished on his behalf.

Saint-Simon's notice may be supplemented by the account which Bossuet's secretary, the Abbé Le Dieu, gives of his visit to Cambrai six months after Bossuet's death[1]. The chief impression that we get from his graphic narrative is, first, the marked consideration and courtesy which Fénelon shewed to his guest, and, secondly, the harmonious blending of profusion and magnificence with simplicity and homeliness which proclaimed the Archbishop as a *grand seigneur* of the most authentic type. The description of the mid-day dinner is particularly pleasing. In the dining-room were three tables, with places for over fifty. At Fénelon's own table there were sixteen—secretaries, chaplains, and nephews. Le Dieu had his special place on the Archbishop's right; the Abbé de Chantérac, the *grand vicaire*, was on his left; the others sat where they pleased. There was abundance of food—several kinds of soup, beef and mutton, every sort of *entrée* and *ragoût*, partridges

---

[1] Le Dieu, *Mémoires et Journal sur la vie de Bossuet*, 4 vols. 1857, III, 153–171.

and other game, magnificent fruit (peaches, grapes, pears) and excellent red wine, but no beer. The table linen was clean and the silver was heavy and in the latest taste. There were a great many servants in livery, who waited admirably, and the butler was of the true episcopal type ("homme de bonne mine, entendu et autorisé dans la maison"). The Archbishop himself ate very little, but with his own hand he helped his guest to all the most dainty dishes, and each time that Le Dieu took off his hat to thank him—in those days they wore their hats at meals—the Archbishop uncovered in response. The conversation at the table was easy and gay, and all took part in it except the young nephews. After dinner they adjourned to the Archbishop's state bedroom, in which he did not sleep, but in a small room, very simply furnished.

Fénelon was assisted in the administration of his diocese by his two *grands vicaires*, the Abbé de Chantérac and the Abbé de Beaumont. Chantérac, who, as we have seen, was his representative at Rome in the Quietist controversy, was eleven years his senior. He was a distant relative, belonging, like Fénelon, to a noble family of Périgord. A Sulpician and skilled theologian, he was remarkable for his piety and his wisdom. Fénelon's name for him was *le vénérable* and sometimes *le subtil*. The other *grand vicaire*, Pantaléon de Beaumont, a much younger man, having been born in 1660, was Fénelon's nephew. Tall of stature, he was called "le grand abbé" (to distinguish him from the Abbé de Langeron) or "le grand Panta." He was an excellent man of business, and in the Archbishop's absence he managed the household. He was gay and cheerful, and his uncle's letters to him point to a common interest in literature, especially in ancient literature. The Abbé de Langeron, *le petit abbé*, was a year or two senior to *le grand abbé*. On his death in 1710 Fénelon wrote that he had lost an intimate friend, who for thirty-four years had been the delight of his life and his greatest help in the service of the Church. Singularly intelligent and cultivated, he was the sharer of Fénelon's literary and intellectual activities, and beneath his wit and love of a joke there was great seriousness and good sense[1].

[1] For the three *abbés* see A. Delplanque, *op. cit.* pp. 199–306, and E. de Broglie, *op. cit.* pp. 21–33.

Among the nephews whom the Abbé Le Dieu records as dining at the Archbishop's table was Gabriel-Jacques, Marquis de Fénelon, the second son of the eldest son of his eldest brother, who was brought up by his great-uncle at Cambrai, and who was sixteen at the time of Le Dieu's visit. We shall meet *le très cher Fanfan* again when we come to Fénelon's correspondence[1]. He was the future head of the family, since his elder brother was destined for an ecclesiastical career. He too was often at Cambrai, and other brothers—for they were fourteen in family—came and went.

Fénelon's one recreation was walking; accompanied by a *grand vicaire* or a nephew he took long walks in the neighbourhood of Cambrai, and his love of nature, which, if not that of a close observer, was perfectly genuine, helped his appreciation of his favourite Virgil. No slight portion of his time was given to writing. The Jansenist controversy, fanned to fresh life by the celebrated *Cas de Conscience* (1702), occupied him till the publication of the Bull *Unigenitus* in 1713, and his writings on the subject fill no less than seven volumes (IX–XVI) of the Versailles edition of his works and two (part of III, IV, and part of V) of the Paris edition. However severely Fénelon attacked the Jansenist doctrines with his pen, he treated the Jansenists personally, of whom there was a very considerable number in his diocese, especially in Hainault, and many even in Cambrai itself, with marked toleration and kindness. One cannot, however, but regret that Fénelon gave so much time to controverting doctrines which, whatever their merits or demerits, portended, as Bossuet saw, no danger to the Church.

On the other hand, his political writings have a real interest, at any rate for students of French history. To the letter to Louis XIV and to the later *Examen de Conscience sur les Devoirs de la Royauté*, which chiefly confine themselves to general principles and those of a moral order, I have already briefly referred in this and a previous chapter[2]. In the *Plans de Gouvernement*, known also as the *Tables de Chaulnes*[3], from the small town

---

[1] Delplanque, *op. cit.* pp. 167–198. [2] See above, pp. 10 and 245.
[3] *Écrits et lettres politiques*, pp. 97 ff.; *Œuvres choisies*, IV, 399 ff. First printed in the *Hist. de Fénelon*, 1808 (see ed. of 1817, IV, 411 ff.).

in Picardy, nine miles south-east of Péronne, where they were
concerted by Fénelon and the Duc de Chevreuse in November
1711, with the view of presenting them to the Duc de Bourgogne, now Dauphin, Fénelon enters into details of practical
politics, and one cannot fail to be struck by the enlightened
breadth of view with which he surveys the whole field of
government.

In Fénelon's eyes the two radical maladies from which the
French monarchy was suffering were absolutism and over-
centralisation, and to provide a cure for these maladies was
the main object of his projected reforms. He proposed, therefore, that "Particular" Estates, as he terms them, should be
established in every province on the model of those in Languedoc, and that the States-General should meet every three
years. The administration of the provinces should be made
more efficient by increasing the number of the governments
and diminishing their extent. The intendants should be
abolished. A large proportion—nearly half—of these heads of
reform—they are no more than heads—relate to the Church,
and of these it may be briefly said that Fénelon's ideal was
the reciprocal independence of Church and State. A characteristic head is "Plan pour déraciner le Jansénisme." Fénelon's
proposals as regards the nobles are all in the direction of increasing their prestige and influence and of preserving the
purity of their race. They were to be at liberty to engage in
trade without loss of nobility, but *mésalliances* were to be
forbidden. In the matter of finance Fénelon is vague and un-
practical. The salt-tax, the *grosses fermes*, the capitation tax,
and above all the tax-farmers, should be abolished, and it
should be left to the Provincial Estates to raise their share of
the sum required. Finally, it is interesting to notice, as an
instance of Fénelon's liberalism, that this intimate friend of
Colbert's family was in favour of free trade[1].

The keen interest that Fénelon took in the foreign policy
of his country is shewn by the various *mémoires*, eight in all,

---

[1] During the later years of Louis XIV's reign Colbert's system was
keenly criticised, especially by the Council of Commerce, which was re-
established in 1700 (see Ph. Sagnac in *Modern France*, p. 200).

which he wrote on the war of the Spanish Succession. In two
of these, the first written in the winter of 1709–1710, and the
second about August 1710, he is insistent on the need for peace,
and more than one modern critic has pointed out that in this
case it was Fénelon who was practical and Louis XIV who
was chimerical—but that Louis was right[1].

The *Traité de l'Existence de Dieu* is only a sketch for a
large work which Fénelon had planned on the subject[2]. The
first part[3], which he wrote in his young days, was published
without his authority in 1712. It was widely read, and amongst
its admirers was Leibniz. It is popular in character, being a
development of the famous argument from final causes, and
is more remarkable for eloquence and lucidity of exposition
than for precision of thought or scientific knowledge. The
second part, which he wrote much later, and which was published with the first part after his death, in 1718, is very
different in character, being purely metaphysical[4]. It follows
closely the lines of Descartes's argument—the methodic doubt,
the *Je pense, donc je suis,* the criterion of certainty, the necessary existence of God, the conception of an infinite being by
the mind of a finite being. This last proof had already been
adumbrated in the first part in words which recall Montaigne
and Pascal: "Voilà l'esprit de l'homme, faible, incertain, borné,
plein d'erreurs. Qui est-ce qui a mis l'idée de l'infini dans un
sujet si borné et si rempli de l'imperfection?" So far Fénelon
merely develops Descartes, but M. Paul Janet points out that in
the last two chapters—*Nouvelles preuves de l'existence de Dieu,
tirées de la nature des idées* and *De la nature et des attributs de
Dieu*—he is largely influenced by Plato and Neo-Platonism,
and that it is to the latter source that his argument on the

---

[1] *Mémoires* I–IV are printed in *Œuvres choisies,* IV, 366 ff. For the
others see *Œuvres,* vol. VII.

[2] *Hist. de Fénelon,* IV, 278 ff.; *Œuvres,* I, 1 ff.; *Œuvres choisies,* III,
1 ff.

[3] *Démonstration de l'Existence de Dieu, tirée du spectacle de la Nature
et de la connoissance de l'homme.*

[4] *Démonstration de l'existence et des attributs de Dieu, tirée des idées
intellectuelles.* The edition of 1718, which was the work of Ramsay and
he Marquis de Fénelon, is incomplete and inexact.

absolute unity of God must be referred. Here M. Janet makes
the criticism that it is difficult to reconcile this doctrine of the
Unity of God with the Christian dogma of the Trinity[1], and
it is characteristic of Fénelon that he should be so deeply
absorbed in his proof of the One and Indivisible God as
to leave out of sight the Three Persons of the Trinity.
Another criticism is that of Mgr Cagnac, who, on the strength
of certain passages, accuses Fénelon of a strong tendency
towards pantheism, which, he says, ill accords with his refutation of Spinoza in chapter III[2]. But passages like "Ainsi je
vois Dieu en tout, ou, pour mieux dire, c'est en Dieu que je
vois toutes choses," and "Je vois le fini dans l'infini" are far
less suggestive of Spinoza than of Malebranche (whose views
on Nature and Grace Fénelon had refuted in an early treatise)
and his vision of all things in God.

For a modern reader Fénelon as a philosopher has far less
interest than Fénelon as a critic of literature. At a meeting of
the French Academy on November 23, 1713, it was agreed
that each member should set forth his views as to the kind of
work which the Academy might suitably undertake. Accordingly, Fénelon, who had been elected to that august body in
1693 in place of the worthy Pellisson, the historian of the
Academy, wrote a memorandum[3], in which he suggested:
first, that the Dictionary should include "a full and exact
collection of all the possible remarks on the French language...which was perhaps the only thing it wanted, in
order to become the language of all Europe, and, so to speak,
of the whole world"; secondly, that after the completion
of the Dictionary, the Academy should publish (1) editions
of every good French author with notes on their language,
their sentiments, and their art, each Academician, without
exception, to choose an author, (2) a Rhetoric, (3) a Poetic.
This memorandum was followed in the autumn of 1714 by a

---

[1] In this very brief account of Fénelon's treatise, I am largely indebted
to M. Janet, *Fénelon*, pp. 151–163.

[2] *Études critiques*, p. 295.

[3] *Mémoire sur les occupations de l'Académie françoise*, first published in
1787; *Œuvres choisies*, II, 301 ff.

letter on the same subject addressed to M. Dacier, the Secretary of the Academy[1]. First printed in 1716, it ranks with *Télémaque* and *L'Éducation des Filles* in the general estimate of Fénelon's writings, and at the present day it is perhaps more interesting than either. It is by way of being an amplification and development of the memorandum, but it is very far from being a formal treatise. It shews knowledge, taste, breadth of mind, and an independent judgment, but it makes no pretence to thoroughness or depth of thought. It simply gives the critical views of a refined and cultivated man, who has been nourished on the best classical literature, but who does not on that account despise the moderns.

Fénelon's first criticism is that the French language as the result of the efforts to purify it during the last hundred years had been constrained and impoverished. "Le vieux langage se fait regretter quand nous le trouvons dans Marot, dans Amyot, dans le cardinal d'Ossat: il avoit je ne sais quoi de court, de naïf, de hardi, de vif et de passionné." It is true that Ronsard "parloit grec en françois," but he was right in trying to enrich the language. Fénelon pleads also for greater simplicity of speech; the *genre fleuri* is out of place in the language of passion; real grief does not express itself in points, and plays on words are ill suited to the denunciatory accents of a preacher. There is too much *esprit* in French poetry: how far better is the natural language of Virgil and Horace! Then follow many quotations from these writers to illustrate their simplicity, their passion and their truth to nature. He quotes two lines from Catullus, "qu'on ne peut nommer sans avoir horreur de ses obscénités," as an example of passionate simplicity, and points out their superiority to the ingenious and artificial touches of Ovid and Martial. He finds little to admire in French poetry: he thinks that the laws of French versification are too rigorous, that greater freedom should be allowed in the matter of rhyme, and that inversion should be introduced with discretion.

Fénelon's observations on tragedy and comedy are mainly interesting for his criticisms on the three chief French

---

[1] *Lettre sur les occupations de l'Académie* (*Œuvres choisies*, II, 306 ff.).

dramatists. Corneille and Racine, he says, deserve the highest praise, but in introducing an episode of love into *Œdipe* and *Phèdre* respectively they have yielded to the fashion of the day for romance and *bel-esprit*. This is certainly true of *Œdipe*, but Hippolyte's love for Aricie may be defended on the ground that by arousing Phèdre's jealousy it leads to the catastrophe. Fénelon finds the celebrated monologue of the *Cid*—"Percé jusques au fond du cœur"—pompous and affected (*ampoulé et fleuri*) and the long narrative of the death of Hippolyte in *Phèdre* as unnatural and out of place—and here modern criticism is with him. Finally he complains that Corneille's Romans speak with too great emphasis, especially Augustus in *Cinna*.

In comedy it is not perhaps surprising that this mystical and refined churchman should find Aristophanes farcical, and should prefer Terence to Plautus. In the latter judgment nearly all Frenchmen—wrongly I submit—would agree with him. Then, after praising Terence unreservedly, he says abruptly, " Il faut avouer que Molière est un grand poëte comique." He has represented a greater variety of characters than Terence, and he has penetrated deeper into some of them. But he has faults. He sometimes uses a "multitude of metaphors"—or, as we should say, mixed metaphors—and generally his prose is better than his verse, though even his prose is not always simple enough[1]. Secondly, he often forces his characters, in order to please the *parterre* (evidently broad comedy is not to Fénelon's liking). Thirdly, he makes vice graceful and virtue ludicrously and unpleasantly austere ("il a donné un tour gracieux au vice, avec une austérité ridicule et odieuse à la vertu").

Fénelon's views on history are sound and enlightened. The perfect historian must be impartial; he must give breadth and unity to his narrative by the omission of unimportant details and by linking events to one another in a continuous chain of cause and effect; he must be picturesque like Froissart, he must make his characters live, and he must set them against a background which faithfully represents the manners of their

---

[1] For a masterly defence of Molière against this charge, see Brunetière, *Études critiques*, VII, 85–132.

age. The last section of his letter deals with the great Quarrel of the Ancients and the Moderns, which had recently broken out afresh with the dispute between Mme Dacier, the wife of his correspondent, and La Motte. Fénelon seemingly holds the scales even: he finds imperfections even in the most perfect of the ancients; and he would gladly see the moderns surpass them; it is far from his wish to pronounce a judgment; only he would counsel those writers who are the ornaments of their century not to despise those whom so many centuries have admired. La Motte, who was a fellow-Academician, wrote to him that he was delighted with this expression of his views[1]. But he failed to notice that the many quotations with which the whole discourse is so delightfully illustrated are with hardly an exception taken from the ancients. The correspondence with La Motte arose out of the latter's miserable abridgement in verse of the *Iliad*, a copy of which he sent to Fénelon. The Archbishop's letters to him are models of diplomacy, in which the Gascon, the *grand seigneur*, and the cultivated humanist all play their parts[2].

Fénelon's letter to M. Dacier contains a section on rhetoric, but rhetoric is dealt with at much greater length in the *Dialogues sur l'Éloquence*, of which it will be more convenient to speak in the next chapter.

It will be gathered from the above that Fénelon was a letter-writer of much charm and urbanity. In fact the Abbé Gosselin in his *Histoire littéraire de Fénelon* is unusually eloquent on the subject of his correspondence. "To penetrate to the depths of his beautiful soul and discover all its great and amiable qualities, we must study him above all in his letters....It is in these that he discloses himself, so to speak, in his entirety." Then he becomes almost ecstatic in his praise and finally declares that the reader will find in them the delicate touches and the lively graces which distinguish the letters of Mme de Sévigné. A modern critic, M. Lanson, is of much the same opinion. "It is possible," he says, "that Fénelon's masterpiece is his vast correspondence....It is in his letters that we must

[1] Letter of November 3, 1714.
[2] See below, p. 346.

look for Fénelon in his entirety, just as we look for Voltaire in his."

The correspondence is vast indeed, for it comprises over two thousand letters, and it forms about a third of his whole literary work. In both the edition of Versailles and that of Paris, the latter of which adds some unpublished letters, it is divided into six sections, as follows: (i) correspondence with the Duc de Bourgogne, the Ducs de Beauvillier and de Chevreuse, and their families; (ii) correspondence with his own family; (iii) divers letters; (iv) letters on the jurisdiction of the Archbishop of Cambrai; (v) spiritual letters; (vi) correspondence on Quietism[1]. No doubt when the much-to-be-desired new edition of the correspondence makes its appearance[2], the whole series of letters will be arranged in chronological order; but meanwhile the present arrangement has its advantages. It enables us at any rate to study the *Spiritual Letters* by themselves. Ever since the first collected edition, which was published in 1718, they have been widely read for devotional purposes, but they have far more than a devotional interest. They are of first-rate importance as psychological documents, and that not only by reason of Fénelon's wonderful insight into the character of his correspondents—only a few were his penitents—but also for the light that they throw on his own character[3].

The natural starting-point for their study is the *Letter on Direction*[4]. After quoting with approval the saying of St François de Sales in the *Introduction à la vie dévote*, "Choisissez un confesseur entre mille, dit Avila, et moi je vous dis entre

---

[1] To these must be added the letters published in 1853, 1863, and 1874 respectively.

[2] E. Griselle, *op. cit.* pp. 267 ff. suggested that Fénelon's second centenary in 1915 should be the signal for such an edition.

[3] Mgr Cagnac has published an admirable selection—*Lettres de Direction*, 5th ed. 1920—which includes a certain number of letters not comprised in the *Lettres Spirituelles* of the Versailles and Paris editions. See also *Fénelon, Directeur de Conscience*, by the same writer. There is a rather fuller selection in *Œuvres choisies*, IV, 95–273. There is an English translation in two volumes (*Letters to Men*; *Letters to Women*) by Mrs Sidney Lear.

[4] *Œuvres*, V, 72–78; *Œuvres choisies*, IV, 250 ff.

dix mille," Fénelon proceeds to draw a picture of the ideal
director:

Il faut le chercher sage, éclairé, mortifié, expérimenté, détaché de tout,
incapable de nous flatter, exempt de tout soupçon de nouveauté sur la
doctrine et de tout excès dans ses maximes, mais pourtant droit, ferme,
prêt à compter pour rien le monde et les grandeurs les plus éblouissantes ;
en un mot, qui, étant le vrai homme de Dieu, ne cherche que lui seul dans
tous les conseils qu'il donne.

When you have found this marvel, he adds, he will have his
faults like other men, but you must not be scandalised by them;
you must submit your will entirely to his. Finally, he completes
the picture by saying that the director must be reserved, serious,
simple, gentle, accommodating, and even, in a modest fashion,
gay. Such a director was Fénelon himself, and as an example
of his methods we may first take his correspondence with the
Comtesse de Gramont, sister of Anthony Hamilton and wife
of the Chevalier, afterwards Comte de Gramont, whose memoirs
were written by Hamilton. She was brought up at Port-Royal
and throughout her life retained her Jansenist sympathies. There
is a charming, if flattering, portrait of her as a young girl in the
Mémoires de Gramont, but to complete it we must turn to Saint-
Simon's obituary notice, written forty-six years later:

C'étoit une grande femme, qui avoit encore une beauté naturelle sans
aucun ajustement, qui avoit l'air d'une reine, et dont la présence imposoit
le plus....C'étoit une personne haute, gracieuse, mais sans prétention et
sans entreprise, qui se sentoit fort, mais qui savoit rendre, avec beaucoup
d'esprit, un tour charmant, beaucoup de sel, et qui choisissoit fort ses
compagnies, encore plus ses amis....Ses dernières années furent uniquement
pour Dieu[1].

Fénelon, who was her director for eleven years, from 1686
to 1697, is fully alive to her faults, her pride, her fastidiousness,
her sharp tongue. "Vous ne pouvez dompter votre esprit
dédaigneux, moqueur et hautain, qu'en le tenant comme en-
chaîné par le silence." In another letter he says with great
insight into human nature:

Tout air de mépris et de hauteur, tout esprit de critique et de moquerie
marque une âme pleine d'elle-même, qui ne sent point ses misères, et qui

[1] *Mémoires*, v, 474. Mme de Caylus, reflecting no doubt Mme de
Maintenon's dislike of her, says that she was sometimes "dénigrante,
hautaine et rampante" but she admits that she had "beaucoup d'esprit."

se livre à sa délicatesse, qui met tout son plaisir dans le mal d'autrui. Rien ne devrait être si propre à nous humilier, que ce genre d'orgueil facile à blesser, moqueur, dédaigneux, fier, jaloux de vouloir tout pour soi, et toujours implacable sur les défauts d'autrui. On est bien imparfait, quand on supporte si impatiemment les imperfections du prochain[1].

And in a still more remarkable letter he points out that *amour-propre* is the root of the jealousy, hatred, and enmity that exist not only between individuals but between communities and nations:

De là vient qu'on est dans le commerce du prochain, comme les malades qui ont langui longtemps dans un lit : il n'y a aucune partie du corps où l'on puisse les toucher sans les blesser. L'amour-propre malade, et attendri sur lui-même, ne peut être touché sans crier les hauts cris....L'unique remède est donc de sortir de soi pour trouver la paix.

At one time Mme de Gramont had scruples about remaining at court, and Fénelon shews her how she may carry on her devotions and religious meditations amidst the turmoil of a court life. But at a later date, when she and her husband were at Bourbon drinking the waters, he sympathises with her delight in her freedom, and he draws a picture of the court worthy to stand by La Bruyère's:

Versailles ne rajeunit pas de même ; il y faut un visage riant, mais le cœur ne rit guère. Si peu qu'il reste de désirs et de sensibilité d'amour-propre, on a toujours ici de quoi vieillir : on n'a pas ce qu'on veut ; on a ce qu'on ne voudrait pas. On est peiné de ses malheurs, et quelquefois du bonheur d'autrui ; on méprise les gens avec lesquels on passe sa vie, et on court après leur estime. On est importuné, et on serait bien fâché de ne l'être pas et de demeurer en solitude. Il y a une foule de petits soucis voltigeants, qui viennent chaque matin à votre réveil, et qui ne vous quittent plus jusqu'au soir ; ils se relaient pour vous agiter. Plus on est à la mode, plus on est à la merci de ces lutins. Voilà ce qu'on appelle la vie du monde, et l'objet de l'envie des sots[2].

Fénelon had a far more difficult task with the Comtesse de Montbéron, the wife of the Governor of Cambrai, a woman of

[1] He makes the same remark to the Duchesse de Mortemart (a daughter of Colbert) : "C'est par imperfection qu'on reprend les imparfaits."
[2] For the letters to Mme de Gramont see *Œuvres*, VIII, 593–615 ; *Œuvres choisies*, IV, 169–177 ; Cagnac, *Lettres de Direction*, 52–80 ; also Sainte-Beuve, *Causeries du Lundi*, X, 23–29 (from two articles on *Fénelon, sa correspondance spirituelle et politique*).

about Fénelon's age and a grandmother. In his earliest letters to her he recommends for her daily reading the New Testament, the historical books of the Old Testament, the *Psalms*, *Proverbs*, *Ecclesiastes*, *Wisdom*, passages from the Prophets, the *Imitation*, St Catherine of Genoa, and especially the works of St François de Sales. Very soon he discovers that she is that most difficult of persons to direct, a woman tormented with over-scrupulousness, and one cannot sufficiently admire the untiring patience, sympathy, and insight with which for fourteen years he combats this fault. He points out how her too lively imagination exaggerates unimportant trifles to the neglect of matters which are really important. The only remedy is simple and unreasoning obedience. As in the case of Mme de Gramont, he finds the source of her disease in excessive *amour-propre*:

Dieu a réduit votre amour-propre à crier les hauts cris, à se démasquer, à découvrir l'excès de sa jalousie. O que cette impuissance est douloureuse et salutaire tout ensemble! Tant qu'il reste de l'amour-propre, on est au désespoir de le montrer; mais tant qu'il y a encore un amour-propre à poursuivre jusque dans les derniers replis du cœur, c'est un coup de miséricorde infinie que Dieu vous force à le laisser voir. Le poison devient un remède. L'amour-propre poussé à bout ne peut plus se cacher et se déguiser. Il se montre dans un transport de désespoir; en se montrant, il déshonore toutes les délicatesses et dissipe les illusions flatteuses de toute la vie: il paraît dans toute sa difformité. C'est vous-même idole de vous-même que Dieu met devant vos propres yeux. Vous vous voyez, et vous ne pouvez vous empêcher de vous voir[1].

Le fonds que vous avez nourri dans votre cœur depuis l'enfance, en vous trompant vous-même, est un amour-propre effréné et déguisé sous l'apparence d'une délicatesse et d'une générosité héroïque; c'est un goût de roman, dont personne ne vous a montré l'illusion. Vous l'aviez dans le monde, et vous l'avez porté jusque dans les choses les plus pieuses. Je vous trouve toujours un goût pour l'esprit, pour les choses gracieuses et pour la délicatesse profane, qui me fait peur. Cette habitude vous a fait trouver des épines dans tous les états. Avec un esprit très-droit et très-solide, vous vous rendez inférieure aux gens qui en ont beaucoup moins que vous. Vous êtes d'un excellent conseil pour les autres; mais pour vous-même les moindres bagatelles vous surmontent. Tout vous ronge le cœur; vous n'êtes occupée que de la crainte de faire des fautes ou du dépit d'en avoir fait. Vous vous les grossissez par un excès de vivacité d'imagination,

---

[1] *Œuvres*, VIII, 660; Cagnac, pp. 212 ff. M. Seillière rightly calls this letter magnificent.

et c'est toujours quelque rien qui vous réduit au désespoir. Pendant que vous vous voyez la plus imparfaite du monde, vous avez l'art d'imaginer dans les autres des perfections dont elles n'ont pas l'ombre. D'un côté, vos délicatesses et vos générosités, de l'autre, vos jalousies et vos défiances, sont outrées et sans mesure. Vous voudriez toujours vous oublier vous-même, pour vous donner aux autres ; mais cet oubli tend à vous faire l'idole de vous-même et de tous ceux pour qui vous paroissez vous oublier. Voilà le fond d'idolâtrie raffinée de vous-même que Dieu veut arracher[1].

To cure this she must forget herself and drive out *amour-propre* by means of the love of God:

L'amour-propre ne parle que du *moi*, qui, selon lui, n'est jamais assez bien traité; il n'est question que d'amitié, d'égards, d'estime; il est au désespoir de tout ce qui ne le flatte pas. Au contraire, l'amour de Dieu veut que le *moi* soit oublié, qu'on ne le compte pour rien ; que Dieu seul soit tout ; que le *moi*, qui est le dieu des personnes profanes, soit foulé aux pieds ; que l'idole soit brisée, et que Dieu devienne le *moi* des âmes épouses, en sorte que Dieu soit ce qui les occupe, comme les autres sont occupées du *moi*.

And in the last letter of the series he says, "C'est dans l'oubli du *moi* qu'habite la paix[2]."

In more than one letter Fénelon encourages her by a relation of his own psychological experiences. For instance he writes on November 7, 1700:

Pour moi, je suis dans une paix sèche, obscure et languissante ; sans ennui, sans plaisir, sans pensée d'en avoir jamais aucun ; sans aucune vue d'avenir en ce monde ; avec un présent insipide et souvent épineux ; avec un je ne sais quoi qui me porte, qui m'adoucit chaque croix, qui me contente sans goût. C'est un entraînement journalier ; cela a l'air d'un amusement par légèreté d'esprit et par indolence. Je vois tout ce que je porte ; mais le monde me paraît comme une mauvaise comédie qui va disparaître dans quelques heures.

With this passage may be compared others in which he speaks of the mental and spiritual lassitude and discouragement from which he at times suffered: "Je suis dans une honteuse

---

[1] *Œuvres*, VII, 680; *Œuvres choisies*, pp. 218 ff. (another magnificent letter).

[2] We have 225 letters from Fénelon to Mme de Montbéron (*Œuvres*, VIII, 616–710; *Œuvres choisies*, IV, 178–228; Cagnac, pp. 194–219. And see E. Seillière, *Mme Guyon et Fénelon*, pp. 307–319).

lassitude de la croix" and "Je sais par expérience ce que c'est d'avoir le cœur flétri et dégoûté de tout ce qui pourroit lui donner de soulagement[1]." In a remarkable letter to the Duchesse de Mortemart he draws a most unflattering portrait of himself, which must be given in full:

Je ne veux jamais flatter qui que ce soit; et même dès le moment que j'aperçois, dans ce que je dis ou dans ce que je fais, quelque recherche de moi-même, je cesse d'agir ou de parler ainsi. Mais je suis tout pétri de boue, et j'éprouve que je fais à tout moment des fautes, pour n'agir point par la grâce. Je me retranche à m'apetisser à la vue de ma hauteur. Je tiens à tout d'une certaine façon, et cela est incroyable; mais, d'une autre façon, j'y tiens peu, car je me laisse assez facilement détacher de la plupart des choses qui peuvent me flatter. Je n'en sens pas moins l'attachement foncier à moi-même. Au reste, je ne puis expliquer mon fond. Il m'échappe, il me paroît changer à toute heure. Je ne saurois guère rien dire qui ne me paroisse faux un moment après. Le défaut subsistant et facile à dire, c'est que je tiens à moi, et que l'amour-propre me décide souvent. J'agis même beaucoup par prudence naturelle, et par un arrangement humain. Mon naturel est précisément opposé au vôtre. Vous n'avez point l'esprit complaisant et flatteur comme je l'ai, quand rien ne me fatigue ni ne m'impatiente dans le commerce. Alors vous êtes bien plus sèche que moi; vous trouvez que je vais alors jusqu'à gâter les gens, et cela est vrai. Mais quand on veut de moi certaines attentions suivies qui me dérangent, je suis sec et tranchant, non par indifférence ou dureté, mais par impatience et par vivacité de tempérament.

On the strength of these and similar passages M. Seillière contends that Fénelon was a constitutional neurasthenic and as such a precursor of Rousseau. But there are a great many persons who are subject to fits of severe depression without being neurasthenics, and moreover Fénelon's many-sided nature lends itself particularly ill to the dangerous method of constructing a character from isolated utterances. Nor must it be forgotten that Fénelon's model as a director was François de Sales, of whom he says that "he made himself all things to all men, not to please all, but to gain all, and to gain them, not for himself, but for Jesus Christ."

It would swell this already long chapter beyond due proportion, if I referred to all the points of interest in these remarkable letters. But I cannot entirely pass over those which

[1] *Œuvres*, VIII, 568.

Fénelon wrote to his dear friends, the Ducs de Beauvillier and
de Chevreuse and their families. There are only about half a
dozen letters to the Duc de Beauvillier and some of these as well
as the greater number of the numerous letters to the Duc de
Chevreuse are in no sense letters of direction. But others are
primarily concerned with their spiritual welfare, and it is of
interest to compare them with the full and admirable portraits
which Saint-Simon has drawn of these common friends of
himself and Fénelon[1]. Beauvillier's faults, according to Saint-
Simon, were over-caution, a shrinking from publicity, and an
excessive fear of the king. Chevreuse was a man of keener
intelligence, greater knowledge, and wider interests, but his
judgment was less sound. He was an incurable optimist; he
had an exaggerated and restless curiosity; and above all things
he loved an argument, reasoning with unanswerable logic, but
more often than not from false premisses. This is how Fénelon
deals with him:

> Souffrez que je vous représente que vous suivez, sans l'apercevoir, très
> souvent votre pente naturelle pour le raisonnement et pour la curiosité.
> C'est une habitude de toute la vie qui agit insensiblement et sans
> réflexion, presque à tout moment.
>
> Votre état augmente encore cette tentation subtile: la multitude des
> affaires vous entraîne toujours avec rapidité. J'ai souvent remarqué que
> vous êtes toujours pressé de passer d'une occupation à une autre, et que
> cependant chacune en particulier vous mène trop loin. C'est que vous
> suivez trop votre esprit d'anatomie et d'exactitude en toute chose. Vous
> n'êtes point lent, mais vous êtes long.

One of Chevreuse's sons, the Vidame d'Amiens, afterwards
Duc de Chaulnes, was hardly less dear to Fénelon than were
his parents, and his letters to him are models of wise advice
and encouragement. The young soldier, weary of frivolity and
dissipation, was trying to lead a sober and religious life amid the
distractions of camp and court, and under Fénelon's patient
guidance he succeeded in his object[2]. His elder brother, the
Duc de Montfort, was killed in action in 1704, and it is probably

---

[1] *Mémoires*, X, 276 ff.
[2] Born in 1676, he died a Marshal of France in 1744. The letters, forty-
seven in number, range from 1704 to the end of 1714. See Cagnac, pp. 220 ff.;
the most important letter is that on pp. 223 ff.

to him that a remarkable letter, written in 1689, is addressed. The young man's director begins by pointing out that his two chief dangers are softness (*mollesse*) and the love of amusement ("un homme mou et amusé ne peut jamais être qu'un pauvre homme"), and he proceeds to give him much detailed and practical advice how to combat these faults[1].

But of all Fénelon's letters of direction of this type, that is to say, of letters written to men who had recently turned to religion, the one perhaps that shews the greatest insight into human nature is that addressed to the Marquis de Seignelay, the son of Colbert, and the brother-in-law of Chevreuse. As Minister of Marine he carried out his father's ideas with brilliance and capacity, but he was worn out by hard work and the excesses of his youth. It was to a man struck with mortal illness that Fénelon wrote in July 1690, and he died in the following November at the age of thirty-nine. It is difficult to recognise the *doux* Fénelon in these stern and outspoken letters, of which the following passages may serve as specimens:

Gardez-vous donc bien de vous inquiéter sur la confiance de votre conversion, et sur les moyens de la cacher, de peur qu'elle n'éclate, et qu'ensuite elle ne se tourne en scandale. Cela arriverait infailliblement si vous comptiez sur vos forces. Votre courage, tout grand qu'il est, serait ce roseau brisé dont parle l'Écriture; au lieu de vous soutenir, il percerait votre main. Mais abandonnez-vous à Dieu: ne faites rien d'éclatant; mais aussi ne rougissez point de l'Évangile: cette mauvaise honte empêcherait que Dieu ne bénît votre retour; je la craindrais cent fois plus que votre fragilité.

Ce qui m'embarrasse le plus n'est ni votre promptitude contre vos domestiques, ni vos oppositions pour les gens qui vous traversent; ce que je crains pour vous, c'est votre hauteur naturelle et votre violente pente aux plaisirs.

Vous êtes environné de gens de plaisir; tout ne respire chez vous que l'amusement et la joie profane: tous les amis qui ont votre confiance ne sont pleins que de maximes sensuelles, ils sont en possession de vous parler suivant leurs cœurs corrompus.

---

[1] Cagnac, pp. 33 ff. There is a charming portrait of the Duc de Montfort by Saint-Simon (*Mémoires*, IV, 143), who was his intimate friend. Born in 1669 he was twenty at the date of Fénelon's letter. "Une éducation beaucoup trop resserrée et trop longtemps l'avoit jeté d'abord dans un grand libertinage."

Il n'est pas question de prêcher ni de baisser les yeux; mais il s'agit de se taire, de tourner ailleurs la conversation, de ne témoigner nulle lâche complaisance pour le mal, de ne jamais rire d'une raillerie libertine ou d'une parole impure[1].

Fénelon was never Mme de Maintenon's director, but from 1689 to 1694 she consulted him from time to time on spiritual matters, and his answers are full of good sense and sound advice. He does not forget the difficulties of her position, and he is particularly solicitous for her health, knowing no doubt the insensibility of Louis XIV to the discomfort and sufferings of those about him, even of his own wife. The most famous of Fénelon's letters to her is the long one in which, in compliance with her request, he points out her faults. The result is the masterly portrait to which I have referred in the previous chapter[2].

If Fénelon was an incomparable director, he was a sure and delightful friend. His letters to the Abbé de Beaumont, the Marquis de Fénelon, and the Chevalier Destouches are a charming blend of gaiety, simplicity, and affection. Those to the Abbé de Beaumont were written for the greater part between October 1701 and October 1705, generally during the Archbishop's absence from Cambrai on episcopal visitations. The prevailing tone is one of playful gaiety, but they end on a note of deep affection, such as, "Je suis tout à toi, Mon cher et unique Panta," "Tout à mon fils Panta"; "Tout au cher Panta, au vénérable (the Abbé de Chantérac) et aux ex-bambins (the great-nephews). Vous seriez un grand homme, si vous datiez vos lettres. Samedi nous nous embrasserons." These last sentences are the conclusion of a letter dated from Bavai, "où se trouvent aqueducs et médailles antiques[3]." In the next,

---

[1] Cagnac, pp. 120 ff.; Œuvres, VII, 202–213; Œuvres choisies, IV, 258 ff.

[2] Œuvres, VIII, 483 ff. See above, pp. 209–211. It is generally recognised that many of the Instructions ou avis sur différents points de la morale et de la perfection chrétienne (VI, 72 ff.) are addressed to Mme de Maintenon.

[3] There were remains of a Roman amphitheatre and circus at Belges or Bavai (Bagacum Nerviorum) in Hainault. It was the birthplace of Jean Lemaire.

written from Le Quesnoi six months later, occurs the following often-quoted passage:

Il y a sous mes fenêtres cinq ou six lapins blancs qui feroient de belles fourrures: mais ce seroit dommage; car ils sont fort jolis et mangent comme un grand prélat. Je vois aussi deux petits coqs, l'un noir, et l'autre à plumage de couleur d'aurore. Ils sont comme la France et l'Empire: le noir est Achille, et l'aurore est Hector.

> Ludus enim genuit trepidum certamen et iram,
> Ira truces inimicitias, et funebre bellum[1].

Fénelon is fond of quoting Virgil or Horace, especially the latter, in his letters to the Abbé de Beaumont, who evidently shared his uncle's classical tastes. Except for a few letters written in October and November 1710, there is an interval in the correspondence till May 1714. The remaining letters are grave in tone, but equally affectionate. "J'ai senti, mon cher enfant, combien je vous aime, et c'est ce qui m'a le plus alarmé, car Dieu m'ôte les personnes que j'aime le plus" (November 26, 1714).

The first letter to the Marquis Gabriel-Jacques de Fénelon, Fénelon's great-nephew, is dated January 7, 1709, when the young man, now in his twenty-first year, was a captain in the regiment of Royal Cuirassiers. There are no letters between November 1710 and August 1712. During that interval the Marquis was severely wounded in the leg at Landrecies (1711), and with the renewal of the correspondence Fénelon's affection is expressed with increased warmth and tenderness. "Mon cher neveu" now becomes "mon cher fanfan" and the *vous* is generally replaced by *tu*. Fénelon does not forget his nephew's moral and spiritual welfare, and, experienced man of the world that he was, he warns him of his faults—brusqueness, stiffness, and unsociability.

Je veux que tu te fasses aimer; mais Dieu seul peut te rendre aimable, car tu ne l'es point par ton naturel roide et âpre. Il faut que la main de Dieu te manie pour te rendre souple et pliant; il faut qu'il te rende docile, attentif à la pensée d'autrui, défiant de la tienne, et petit comme un enfant: tout le reste est sottise, enflure et vanité.

[1] Horace, *Ep.* i, xix, 48 f.

The Marquis's wound having failed to heal properly, an operation became necessary (February 1713), and during the next four months Fénelon's letters are frequent and full of anxiety. One marvels how he found time to write so many letters—sometimes two on the same day—and is it profane to wonder whether the young man was not sometimes just a little bored by the surgical advice which his good uncle showered upon him? The last letter is dated December 14, 1714, twenty-four days before Fénelon's death. We have seen how the Marquis, who became a distinguished diplomatist and soldier and was killed in action at Raucoux in 1746, collaborated with the Chevalier de Ramsay in honouring the memory of the uncle who had been to him as a father.

Fénelon's most uniformly gay letters are those which he wrote to the Chevalier Destouches, who commanded the artillery in Flanders and like many other officers enjoyed the hospitality of the Archbishop of Cambrai[1]. The correspondence begins on July 31, 1711, when Destouches was forty-three and Fénelon sixty. Destouches was an amiable pagan, who indulged freely in the pleasures of the table, a weakness for which his correspondent alternately reproves him and laughs at him, and Fénelon was well aware of the incongruity of the warm friendship which had sprung up between them.

Si vous alliez montrer ma lettre à quelque grave et sévère censeur, il ne manqueroit pas de dire: "Pourquoi si vieil évêque aime-t-il tant un homme si profane?" Voilà un grand scandale: je l'avoue; mais quel moyen de me corriger? La vérité est que je trouve deux hommes en vous: vous êtes double, comme Sosie, sans aucune duplicité pour la finesse; d'un côté vous êtes mauvais pour vous-même; de l'autre vous êtes vrai, droit, noble, tout à vos amis.

That was the secret of the attachment. Destouches was sincere and honest and a true friend[2]. Moreover he loved his

---

[1] He was the father of D'Alembert (born 1717), who was exposed by his mother, Mme de Tencin, on the steps of Saint-Jean-le-Rond. Destouches was absent on a mission to the Antilles, but on his return he found out the child, looked after his education, and left him an annuity of 1200 francs.

[2] "Il dort. Il mange. Il digère comme il peut. Il chante. Il rit. Il a beaucoup de grâces dans l'esprit, et beaucoup de noblesse dans le cœur.

Virgil and his Horace. So Fénelon's letters to him sparkle with gaiety and *esprit* and are interspersed with citations from their favourite authors. And if sometimes the gaiety becomes frivolous and the *esprit* is a little forced, only a morose censor will forget that *dulce est desipere in loco*[1].

When sentence of exile was passed on Fénelon, the Duc de Bourgogne was forbidden to communicate with him, but at last, after a silence of four years, he found means to send him a letter (December 22, 1701). Fénelon's reply is followed in his published correspondence by two magnificent letters, both undated. The first is a homily on the love of God and the love of one's neighbour. The love of God, he says, does not demand the austerities, the solitude, or the contemplative life of the hermits of old; it does not ask for heroic actions, or the re-nunciation either of property or position. It only asks for innocent morals and well-regulated conduct, for justice, so-briety, and moderation in the use of everything. You must love your friends, not from *amour-propre*, but "in the order of God" and for God. You must not expect to find them perfect; you must love them with their imperfections. And the letter con-cludes with a beautiful passage on love, inspired by St Paul's famous chapter. The second letter begins with the noble exhortation: "Enfant de Saint-Louis, imitez votre père: soyez, comme lui, doux, humain, accessible, affable, compatissant et libéral": and continues throughout in the same lofty strain[2].

In 1702 the Duc de Bourgogne, by the king's permission, had two interviews with his former tutor. From 1702 to 1708 we have no letters, but in the autumn of the latter year the severe criticisms that were made on the Duc de Bourgogne's conduct as joint-commander with Vendôme of the army in Flanders led Fénelon to write several letters to him[3]. The

Mais il ruine sa santé, et ne songe point à son salut. Il me réjouit et il m'afflige" (Fénelon to Mme de Chévry, July 1714—*Lettres inédites de Fénelon*, ed. X. Barbier de Montault [1863]).

[1] The letters to Destouches, between 50 and 60 in number, will be found in vol. VIII of the *Œuvres* in the section, *Lettres diverses*. See Delplanque, *Les amis de Fénelon*, c. ii, and Sainte-Beuve, *Causeries du Lundi*, vol. II.

[2] Cagnac, pp. 84 ff.   [3] Eight in all (*Œuvres*, VII, 268 ff.).

second of these (September 16th)[1] and a rather later one
(October 15th)[2] are remarkable for the frankness with which
Fénelon recounts the reports that have reached him, and the
sternness with which he rebukes the Duke's shortcomings and
admonishes him on his future conduct.

On April 11, 1711, the Dauphin died from small-pox, and
Fénelon's pupil became Dauphin in his stead. It was only
natural that Fénelon should cherish high hopes—the hopes,
not of a mere self-seeking politician, but of a sincere and
enlightened patriot. We have seen how after counsel taken with
his friend, the Duc de Chevreuse, he drew up plans for the
reform of the government, and we know how ten months later
his hopes were frustrated. On February 18, 1712, the new
Dauphin followed his father to the grave. "Hélas, mon bon
duc," Fénelon writes to the Duc de Chevreuse, "Dieu nous a
ôté toute notre espérance pour l'Église et pour l'État" (February
27), and six days later he writes to Chevreuse's son, the Duc
de Chaulnes, "Je ne puis, mon bon et cher duc, résister à la
volonté de Dieu qui nous écrase. Il sait ce que je souffre."
But other trials awaited him. Chevreuse died in November of
the same year; Beauvillier in August 1714. In a letter of this
year, but with no further indication of date, he writes in a strain
of disconsolate pessimism:

Je ne suis plus qu'un squelette qui marche et qui parle, mais qui dort et
quimange peu....Un vaste diocèse est un accablant fardeau à soixante-trois
ans....Les jours sont longs, quoique les années soient courtes....Le monde ne
donne que des plaisirs de vanité. D'ailleurs il est plein d'épines, de troubles,
de procédés lâches, trompeurs et odieux[3].

In November 1714, he had a carriage accident of which he
gives a lively and graphic account to his friend Destouches.
Though he received no outward injuries, his constitution
suffered a severe shock. On January 1st of the following year
he was taken ill. On January 6th, after receiving extreme
unction, he wrote to Père Le Tellier urging him to represent
to the king that he had accepted the condemnation of his
book with absolute simplicity, and that there had never been
a moment in his life in which he did not have the most profound

[1] *Ib.* p. 268; Cagnac, p. 93.   [2] *Œuvres*, VII, 277 ff.   [3] Cagnac, p. 260.

respect and the most inviolable attachment for His Majesty's person[1]. On the following day, January 7, 1715, he died.

Fénelon had a richly endowed nature. He was a philosopher, a theologian, an educationalist, a political thinker, and the author of a phenomenally successful work of fiction; he organised his diocese and his household with remarkable efficiency; and above all he had an almost unrivalled knowledge of the human heart. He threw himself with eager intensity into everything that he undertook. He was a creature of moods; sometimes gay and easily amused, sometimes in the depths of depression[2]; generally urbane, courteous, and charming, but on occasions unsympathetic and sarcastic. This points to a sensitive and highly strung temperament, but to describe him as a neurasthenic is a misnomer. He has been accused of insincerity, but it must be remembered that he was a Gascon, and that, being a Gascon, his emotions were quickly stirred and words came to him easily, that his subtle brain saw distinctions not very obvious to plain men, and that the prudence which never wholly deserts a Gascon inclined him to withdraw from positions into which he had too rashly advanced. At the outset of his career, the Abbé Fénelon, the Superior of the New Catholics, had a decided air of worldliness and ambition. Then came his intercourse with Mme Guyon and his tutorship of the Duc de Bourgogne, and into both he threw himself heart and soul. To his work as tutor he brought all his knowledge of human nature, his singular power of influence, and his literary facility. Of his relations with Mme Guyon it is not easy to form a judgment. Probably his interest in mysticism impelled him to make the most of this unrivalled opportunity of observing at first-hand the working of the inward life of a pronounced Quietist. Probably also he welcomed Mme Guyon's doctrines, grossly exaggerated in expression though they were, as a cure for that *amour-propre* which he knew to be his besetting sin. Then when the clouds gathered, the adventurous and chimerical half of his nature beat a retreat, and the prudent

---

[1] *Œuvres*, VIII, 282.

[2] "Souvent la mort me consolerait; souvent je suis gai, et tout m'amuse."

and practical half assumed control. But the severity of Bossuet's attack on Mme Guyon's doctrines aroused at once his chivalry, his self-love, and his conviction of the essential justice of his cause, and he flung himself into the contest with Bossuet with characteristic energy. He was defeated, and to a lesser man defeat would have meant humiliation. But he bore himself with such dignity that in the eyes of the world his defeat seemed a victory. What was far more admirable, he gained a victory over himself. In the work of his large diocese, in innumerable acts of charity, in measures of relief for the French army, in care for individual officers and soldiers, in the society of beloved friends and relatives, in the companionship of nature and books, he found a cure for his *amour-propre*, and he learned that the love of man is a true form of Pure Love, and that for the great majority of devout souls action is as necesssary as contemplation. Thus he proved by one more example that the truest mystics are those whose mysticism goes hand in hand with practical genius.

However ambitious Fénelon was, he was certainly not ambitious of literary fame. Unlike his fellow-Perigordian, who said in the *envoi* to the first edition of his *Essays* that he was " moins faiseur de livres que de nulle autre besogne," but who revised his latest edition with almost meticulous care, Fénelon remained all his life supremely indifferent to the publication of his writings. The only works of his that appear to have been written without a definite practical object are the *Dialogues sur l'Éloquence* and the unfinished *Traité de l'Existence de Dieu*. The only important work that was published with his authority in his lifetime is the *Traité de l'Éducation des Filles*[1]. Like George Sand, Fénelon began to write at no very early age, and, like George Sand, he revealed himself at once as the possessor of an easy and graceful style, which he retained unchanged throughout his life. Critics of his style have been too apt to found their remarks upon *Télémaque*. But as I have already pointed out, it is not in his descriptive passages, written

[1] Neither the *Traité du Ministère des Pasteurs* (1688) nor the *Explication des Maximes des Saints* (1698) is important from the literary point of view.

in so-called poetic prose, that Fénelon is at his best, but in exposition and argument. Here his clear thought finds expression in a flowing and harmonious style. Indeed it often flows so smoothly as to become monotonous. But, when it is quickened by deep emotion, as in the *Traité de l'Existence de Dieu*, or warmed by controversy, as in the *Réponse à la Relation* or in the *Mémoire* addressed to Mme de Maintenon, it soars or swells with his theme. So too in the *Spiritual Letters*, under the influence of sternness or tenderness it takes on stronger or softer accents, while in the letters to his intimate friends it becomes gay, playful, and of an irresistible charm. Yet, this style, with all its undoubted merits, is, like La Bruyère's, a little below that of the great masters of French prose, and for the opposite reason. If La Bruyère gives too much thought to his style, or at least does not sufficiently conceal that thought, Fénelon gives too little. He charms and soothes us, but he seldom grips us with an arresting phrase or a striking image. He writes well by instinct: he has an artistic sense of proportion and harmony, and the feeling of a classical scholar for correct and polished diction. But he is always the *grand seigneur*, writing without effort and without desire for literary fame. It is as a man and not as a writer that he is of surpassing interest.

CHAPTER IX

MASSILLON[1]

W E have seen that in March 1687, not long before the opening of our period, Bossuet, at the close of his funeral oration on Condé, bade a touching farewell to the Paris pulpit. Three years later, Fléchier[2], who belonged to Bossuet's generation, also preached his last funeral oration—on the Duc de Montausier. Before this he had been appointed to sees far distant from Paris—to Lavaur in 1685 and to Nîmes in 1687. Earlier still, Mascaron[3], who, like Fléchier, had made his reputation by his funeral oration on Turenne (1675), had been made Bishop of Agen, and after his appointment only preached once before the court—in the year 1694. Thus of all the preachers who had made a name in the first half of the reign of Louis XIV only Bourdaloue[4] was left. The period of his greatest prominence was from 1677 to 1693, during which years there were only two, 1677 and 1687, in which he did not give a course of sermons in Paris. His last course before the court was during Advent, 1697. After that he only preached occasionally in Paris.

[1] During Massillon's lifetime several unauthorised editions of his sermons were published at Trévoux—4 vols. 1705; 5 vols. 1708; 5 vols. 1714—without his name, and mixed with the sermons of other preachers. Massillon, to protect himself, obtained a privilege in 1706, but never availed himself of it. After his death his *Œuvres* were published by his nephew, Père J. Massillon, in 15 vols. 1745–1748, and this edition, in the absence of the manuscripts, has been followed by subsequent editors. The latest edition is that of the Abbé Blampignon, 4 vols. 1865–1868 ; 1886. His *Œuvres choisies* (Garnier) include the *Petit Carême* in full, and nine other sermons, and his *Oraisons funèbres* have been published with those of Fléchier and Mascaron.

See D'Alembert, *Éloge de Massillon*; Sainte-Beuve, *Causeries du Lundi*, IX (1853); L'Abbé Bayle, *Massillon, étude historique et littéraire*, 1867 ; L'Abbé Blampignon, *Massillon, d'après des documents inédits*, 1879, and *L'Épiscopat de Massillon suivi de sa correspondance*, 1884 ; F. Brunetière, *Études critiques*, II.

[2] 1632–1710.　　　　[3] 1634–1703.　　　　[4] 1632–1704.

Thus, when Fénelon wrote, probably between 1678 and
1685[1], his *Dialogues sur l'Éloquence,* the only great representative of pulpit oratory in Paris was Bourdaloue. Bossuet had
not preached there regularly since 1669, when he was nominated to the see of Condom. As in most things, so in the
matter of pulpit oratory, Fénelon was a rebel against prevailing traditions. His criticisms may be summed up as being
chiefly directed against four defects: (1) the abuse of divisions,
(2) the abuse of learning by heart, (3) the abuse of keeping
too closely to the theme of a single text, and (4) the prominence given to morals at the expense of doctrine. Though
Fénelon does not mention him by name there is no doubt
that these criticisms were to some extent aimed at Bourdaloue, who with his love of order and method strictly adhered
to the traditional practice in the arrangement of his sermons.
This practice was as follows: after giving out his text, the
preacher indicated his proposed treatment of it in a short
exordium and announced the divisions or points (almost invariably three in number), into which he intended to divide
his discourse. Then followed the body of the sermon, in which
each point was developed in turn. Often the divisions were sub-
divided, and the process then became artificial and wearisome;
but there seems no good reason for objecting, as La Bruyère
does in his chapter *De la Chaire,* even more unreservedly than
Fénelon, to the simple divisions, to which great preachers
like Bossuet and Bourdaloue conformed as easily and naturally
as Corneille and Racine to the five acts of a tragedy[2].

On the nature of the text Fénelon and La Bruyère hold
rather different views. La Bruyère thinks that a preacher
should choose a single truth, "capital, terrible, or instructive,"
and should treat it thoroughly until he has exhausted it.
Fénelon, on the other hand, objects to the preacher confining
himself to the explanation of a single passage, without reference to what goes before or after. Above all he objects to

---

[1] According to Ramsay and the Marquis de Fénelon, a work of his
youth. They were first published in 1718.

[2] Liddon, who was a close student of Bossuet, almost invariably has an
exordium and three divisions.

ingenuity in the choice of a text or to the arbitrary interpretation of it. His *Dialogues* open with a severe criticism on a preacher who had taken for his text on Ash Wednesday the words from Psalm CII, "I have eaten ashes like bread," and had introduced into his exordium the story of Artemisia who mixed the ashes of her husband Mausolus with her daily drink. We shall see that Massillon is rather too fond of making a refrain of his text and of isolating it too entirely from its context.

Another practice to which Fénelon objects is that of learning the sermon word for word by heart. On the other hand he says that the majority of speakers who do not learn by heart do not sufficiently prepare their speeches. A speaker ought to meditate profoundly on his subject, to prepare all the movements likely to affect his audience, and to arrange his speech on a careful and orderly plan. Bossuet, it may be pointed out, went considerably further than this in his earlier days. He wrote his sermons in full, and then carefully revised them. But he did not take his manuscript into the pulpit nor did he learn it by heart. Of Demosthenes, to whose example Fénelon appeals, we are told by Plutarch that he never spoke in the assembly unless he had prepared and meditated over his speech, but that he used to say in conversation that, though he never spoke without notes, he often spoke without having written down everything that he was going to say. Fénelon also refers to the practice of Cicero, in whose speeches, he says, there are evident signs of improvised passages. But one of the most eloquent of Cicero's forensic speeches, that on behalf of Milo, was composed, at any rate in the form in which it has come down to us, in the seclusion of his study.

The speakers in Fénelon's *Dialogues* had been led to consider the question of learning by heart by a reference to Bourdaloue's habit of preaching with his eyes shut. The speaker, A., who represents Fénelon himself, says that Bourdaloue did it to help his memory. Though it is very doubtful whether this was the real reason, the fact remains that Bourdaloue learnt his sermons by heart, as did Massillon. Bourdaloue is not mentioned by name, but it is evident from the criticisms that follow that he

is "the preacher whom we heard together a fortnight ago."
The chief faults that Fénelon finds in him as an orator are a
monotonous voice, "which is naturally melodious but which is
not well managed"; the uniform rapidity of his diction, and the
equally uniform vehemence of his gestures; and a style which
always aims at convincing the reason and never at touching
the heart[1]. But Fénelon does Bourdaloue the justice to say
that "the pulpit was under great obligations to him, for he had
rescued it from its slavery to declaimers and had invested it
with great force and dignity." And in the memorandum on the
occupations of the Academy, written about 30 years later than
the *Dialogues*, he declares that Bourdaloue's style "has effaced
all the other styles and has perhaps reached the highest
perfection of which our language is capable in this kind of
eloquence."

Another complaint which Fénelon makes against the preachers
of his day is that "they are too much concerned with moral portraiture and do not pay enough attention to the explanation
of evangelical doctrine." Here again he is possibly thinking of
Bourdaloue, but though morality fills a much larger place in
his sermons than dogma, his morality, as Feugère observes, is
always closely connected with dogma, and it may be added
that it is always founded upon purely Christian principles.

It is evident that the kind of sermon which commended
itself both to Fénelon and La Bruyère was one in which the
preacher expounded to his hearers the simple truths of the
Gospel, and held their attention not by rhetorical artifices or
closely-reasoned argument but by the force of a natural and
sincere eloquence. It is interesting to see how far Fénelon's
practice conformed to his precepts.

Fénelon had no great reputation as an orator. It appears
from the *Liste des Prédicateurs* that his preaching in Paris
churches was confined to the years 1680–1688 and that in no
year did he deliver a complete course of sermons for either
Advent or Lent[2]. Only ten of his sermons have come down to

---

[1] For a good defence of Bourdaloue against some of Fénelon's criticisms
see A. Feugère, *Bourdaloue* 5th ed. 1889, cc. i and ii.

[2] E. Griselle, *Fénelon*, pp. 10–14.

us and of these three are called *Entretiens* and one—that for
the consecration of the Elector of Cologne at Lille—a *Discours*.
In addition, however, to these complete discourses we have
heads for sixteen sermons and two panegyrics. The greater
part—so we are told by the Abbé Gosselin—are "early
examples of his talent," and may therefore be assigned to the
years 1680–1688, during which he occupied Paris pulpits. It is
interesting to notice that in spite of Fénelon's criticisms of his
contemporaries he strictly adheres to tradition in the arrangement of his sermons. Text, exordium, division into points—
they are all there. Generally he contents himself with two
points, but sometimes he has three, and in the *Entretien sur
la Piété* he even introduces sub-divisions.

The best-known of his sermons[1], the only one which has
achieved fame, is that preached on the Feast of the Epiphany,
1685, in the Church of Foreign Missions before the ambassadors
of the King of Siam. Much of it is extremely eloquent,
especially the references to the work of the Jesuits in the
Indies and China, and to that of François Pallu, Bishop of
Heliopolis, in Siam, Cochin-China, and China, in which last
country he had died in the previous year. But it is emphatically
a sermon for a special occasion, and the preacher in his efforts
to be eloquent has not altogether avoided the pitfalls of
exaggeration and bad taste. Of the sermon for the consecration of the Elector of Cologne (1707), it may be similarly said
that it is eminently suited to the occasion—eloquent and full
of good advice, but without much depth of thought. In the
sermons which Fénelon preached on more ordinary occasions
the eloquence is less studied, but there is the same appeal to
the emotions rather than to the intellect. That preached for
the festival of St Teresa has been singled out by Bourgoin for
special praise, and it deserves it, for in the great mystic, in the
adept of Pure Love, Fénelon had a theme dear to his heart.
La Bruyère would have preferred the sermon for the Assumption
of the Virgin Mary, for here we have a simple exposition of
the Gospel story and teaching, the homily of a true pastor of

[1] For an appreciation of Fénelon's sermons see A. Bourgoin, *Les Maîtres
de la Critique au XVIIe siècle*, 1889, pp. 297–304.

his flock. The noble *Entretien sur les Avantages et les Devoirs de la Vie religieuse* is also practical and homiletic; notably it contains, by way of an attack on *amour-propre*, one of those *peintures morales* which Fénelon thought were too frequent in the sermons of his day, and in which Bourdaloue so greatly excelled[1].

Shortly before La Bruyère published his *Caractères* and just after Fénelon wrote his *Dialogues* some new preachers made their *début*, either at the court or in one of the Paris churches. The three perhaps who obtained the greatest fame in their day, though now they are almost forgotten, were the Oratorian Jean Soanen, afterwards Bishop of Senez, whom Fénelon couples with Bourdaloue as the best model for a beginner, and the Jesuits, Honoré Gaillard and Charles de La Rue. The latter preached no less than four Advent and nine Lenten courses before the court and several funeral orations, of which that for the Maréchal de Boufflers (1711) was considered to be his masterpiece[2]. To his brother Jesuit was entrusted the difficult task of performing the same service for the Archbishop of Paris, Harlay de Champvallon, whose unedifying life had been terminated by a sudden death.

Le 6 août, il passa la matinée à son ordinaire jusqu'au dîner. Son maître d'hôtel vint l'informer qu'il étoit servi. Il le trouva dans son cabinet, assis sur un canapé et renversé : il étoit mort. Le P. Gaillard fit son oraison à Notre-Dame : la matière étoit plus que délicate, et la fin terrible. Le célèbre jésuite prit son parti : il loua tout ce qui méritoit de l'être, puis tourna court sur la morale. Il fit un chef-d'œuvre d'éloquence et de piété[3].

Rather earlier in date than any of these was the Père Séraphin, a Capuchin, who began to preach in Paris in 1671, but who did not become famous till 1692, when he preached the *carême* in the parish church of Versailles. "Cet homme que je souhaitais impatiemment, et que je ne daignais pas espérer de notre siècle, est enfin venu," wrote La Bruyère, evidently

---

[1] For this sermon see above, pp. 238–239.
[2] For these preachers see A. Hurel, *Les Orateurs sacrés à la cour de Louis XIV*, II, 136–190.
[3] Saint-Simon, *Mémoires*, I, 278.

from a quite recent impression of this Versailles course, in a *remarque* which was first printed in the eighth edition of *Les Caractères* (1694). And he goes on to say that the courtiers deserted the royal chapel "in order to hear the word of God from the lips of this apostolic preacher." Two years later the Père Séraphin preached the *carême* in the royal chapel of Versailles and again in 1696[1], not long before La Bruyère's death. His characteristics, as one may infer from La Bruyère's remarks, were great simplicity, both of thought and style, and the liberal use of texts, which he always cited in French[2].

During Lent, 1699, when the Père Séraphin was giving his last course of sermons before the king, a new preacher was making a great reputation in Paris, and on the strength of it was commanded to preach the following Advent course at Versailles. The new preacher was Jean-Baptiste Massillon, born in 1663 at Hyères in Provence. He joined the Oratory in 1681 and, after teaching the humanities and rhetoric successively at Pézenas, Marseilles, and Montbrison (Loire), he was sent in 1689 to Vienne, where he took Orders and held chairs first of philosophy and then of rhetoric. In 1695 he was transferred to Lyons and a year later to the Oratorian Seminary of Saint-Magloire in Paris. In 1698 he preached, with great success, the *carême* at Montpellier, and in the following year, as we have seen, he was chosen to preach for the same season in the church of the Oratory in the Rue Saint-Honoré. His first appearance before the court was on All Saints' Day of the same year, the customary beginning of the Advent course. On its conclusion Louis XIV paid him a happily-turned compliment. "When I have heard other preachers," he said, "I have

---

[1] "Jamais succès ne fut égal à celui du père Séraphin," writes Mme de Maintenon to the Archbishop of Paris after his sermon for the Purification in 1696, and at the end of the course she says, "Le père Séraphin a soutenu son carême, et le finit hier à faire pleurer bien des gens" (Lavallée, *Corr. gén. de Mme de Maintenon*, IV, 65 and 91).

[2] Hurel, *op. cit.* pp. 186–189; Saint-Simon, I, 308. The story is told that on one occasion when he was preaching before the court the Père Séraphin apostrophised Fénelon, who had fallen asleep (La Bruyère, *Œuvres*, II, 419 n.[1]).

been greatly pleased with them. When I hear you, I am greatly
displeased with myself." Yet Massillon only preached two other
courses before Louis XIV, the *carêmes* of 1701 and 1704[1]. Two
years after the king's death he was appointed to the see of
Clermont and in the following year (1718) he was chosen to
preach a special Lenten course before the eight-year-old prince,
Louis XV. In 1719 he was elected a member of the Académie
Française. In 1720 he was one of the two bishops who acted
as assistants to the Cardinal de Rohan in the consecration of
the Abbé Dubois to the see of Cambrai—the see which Fénelon
had adorned. The appointment was scandalous in the extreme.
Apart from the grave irregularities of Dubois's life, he was not
in Orders, all of which were conferred on him within the space
of eight days[2]. On Massillon's share in the proceedings let us
hear Saint-Simon:

Il (Dubois) voulut Massillon, célèbre prêtre de l'Oratoire, que sa vertu,
son savoir, ses grands talents pour le chaire, avoient fait évêque de
Clermont, parce qu'il en passoit quelquefois, quoique rarement, quelque
bon parmi le grand nombre des autres qu'on faisoit évêques. Massillon,
au pied de mur, étourdi, sans ressources étrangères, sentit l'indignité de
ce qui lui étoit proposé, balbutia, n'osa refuser. Mais qu'eût pu faire un
homme aussi mince, selon le siècle, vis-à-vis d'un régent, de son ministre
et du cardinal de Rohan? Il fut blâmé néanmoins, et beaucoup, dans le
monde, surtout des gens de bien de tout parti[3].

And the "gens de bien" were right. Moreover, it is difficult to
see how the Regent and his Minister could have effectively shewn
their disapproval. They could not have deprived Massillon of
his see, and he wanted no more favours at their hands. As a
matter of fact, save for one visit to Paris in 1723, when he
pronounced the funeral oration for the Regent's mother, he
spent the rest of his life, which ended in 1742, in the diligent
administration of his see.

It will help us to arrive at a fair-minded judgment of Massillon's merits as a preacher, if we begin by considering the

---

[1] He preached the *carême* of 1699 in the Church of Saint-Gervais in
Paris.

[2] Not, as is often said, in the same morning (Bayle, *op. cit.* pp. 329–
330).

[3] *Mémoires*, XVII, 32–33.

earliest of his sermons that have come down to us, the "Advent" of 1699. The opening sermon, *Sur le Bonheur des Justes,* the text of which is taken from the Sermon on the Mount, begins with a bold and striking contrast between the world's ideal of a fortunate prince and that of Christ as expressed in the beatitudes. In the body of the sermon he paints a picture of the world—the world of the court, as he is careful to explain—in colours far blacker than La Bruyère's. It must have required some courage for this comparatively young man of thirty-five, with his modest bearing, downcast eyes, and general air of simplicity, to face soldiers and courtiers and fine ladies with denunciations of their passions and jealousies and criminal attachments, of their love of gambling and immodest spectacles. There is, however, a certain exaggeration in his picture, which must have tended to lessen its effect, and to make his audience, while admiring and enjoying his oratory, indifferent to his moral lessons. It was the preacher's business, they might say, to denounce the world; but it was theirs to make the best of it.

The sermon[1] which follows this in Père Joseph's edition was preached on the following day—All Souls' Day. It is one of Massillon's more famous sermons, for, besides containing the often-quoted companion pictures of the death-beds of the sinner and the just man, it is throughout a striking example of oratorical effort.

In the sermons of the *Grand Carême*[2] we find the same courageous denunciation of sins and the same exaggeration in the portrayal of them—for instance, in the well-known sermons *Sur l'Enfant prodigue* (1701) and *Sur le petit Nombre des Élus* (1704). The second of these contains the highly eloquent passage cited by Voltaire[3], at which the preacher's

---

[1] *Sur la Mort du Pécheur et la Mort du Juste.* The "Advent" of 1699 comprised six sermons—for All Saints, the 1st (*Vérité de la religion*), 3rd and 4th Sundays in Advent, the Conception of the Virgin Mary, and Christmas Day.

[2] A *carême* should consist of nineteen sermons, three for each of the six weeks of Lent (except Wednesday in Holy Week), one for the Purification and one for Easter Day.

[3] In the article on *Éloquence* which he contributed to the *Encyclopédie.*

audience, moved by an involuntary transport, half rose in their seats.

Or, je vous demande, et je vous le demande frappé de terreur, ne séparant pas en ce point mon sort du vôtre, et me mettant dans la même disposition où je souhaite que vous entriez ; je vous demande donc : si Jésus-Christ paraissait dans ce temple, au milieu de cette assemblée, la plus auguste de l'univers, pour nous juger, pour faire le terrible discernement des boucs et des brebis, croyez-vous que le plus grand nombre de tout ce que nous sommes ici fût placé à la droite? croyez-vous que les choses du moins fussent égales? croyez-vous qu'il s'y trouvât seulement dix justes en nous? En trouveroit-il un seul?[1]

A general consideration of the sermons brings into prominence a third characteristic, namely, a most remarkable knowledge of human nature. It is not, perhaps, so deep or so thorough as Bourdaloue's, but it is singularly wide and various. Notable sermons in which this feature is conspicuous are *Sur l'emploi de notre temps* (1704), the second part of which is directed against worldly ambition; *Du pardon des Offenses* (1704?), against envy; *Sur la Médisance* (1704), which may be compared with the striking sermon on the same theme preached by Bourdaloue nine years earlier; *Sur l'Aumône* (1701); *Sur les Causes ordinaires de nos Rechutes* (Easter, 1704); and *Sur le Respect humain* (1704), this last an admirable homily of practical exhortation, without any oratorical display. The mastery with which Massillon lays bare the ruling passions of men and the motives which govern their actions, especially in that class which formed the great majority of his audience, must have been largely gained from the confessional. His sermon therefore *On Confession* (1701) has a peculiar interest and should be compared with Fénelon's *Lettre sur la direction*, referred to in the last chapter.

According to Brunetière, Massillon "discovered so many germs of virtue and sensibility" in human nature that "had it not been for the restraint of orthodoxy he would have been inclined to proclaim the natural goodness of man[2]." I can find no real evidence for this statement; rather Massillon in his view of

---

[1] Compare the version given by Goldsmith in English in *The Bee*, No. VII (*Works*, III, 106).

[2] *Op. cit.* p. 113.

human nature falls into line with the other great preachers, including Fénelon, and with all the great writers of the classical age. Listen to him in the sermon *Sur l'Injustice du Monde vers les Gens de Bien* (1701):

Et certes, mes Frères, pleins de passions comme nous sommes, dans la misérable condition de cette vie; chargés d'un corps de péché qui appesantit notre âme; les jouets éternels de notre inconstance et de l'instabilité de notre cœur; ne trouvant rien en nous qui favorise nos devoirs; vifs pour tout ce qui nous éloigne de Dieu, dégoûtés de tout ce qui nous en approche; n'aimant que ce qui nous perd, ne haïssant que ce qui nous sauve; foibles pour le bien, toujours prêts pour le mal; et en un mot, trouvant dans la vertu l'écueil de la vertu même....

Here again there is a touch of exaggeration, a defect which is due, partly no doubt to Massillon's southern temperament, but partly also to a cause, which is acutely set forth by Dejob. Massillon, he points out, is not, like Bossuet and Bourdaloue, profoundly imbued with theology, nor has he either the mental vigour or the unfailing good sense which in many men makes up for insufficient knowledge. As a consequence, he is sometimes over-severe and sometimes over-indulgent. The sermons, *Sur la Vérité d'un Avenir* (1704) and *Des Doutes sur la Religion* (reign of Louis XV), both directed against free-thinkers, betray a want of sureness in handling a difficult subject.

As a Provençal Massillon had a natural aptitude for eloquence; words came easily to him, and they came charged with emotion. It was no mere chance that Mascaron, Fléchier, and Massillon's friend and fellow-Oratorian, the Père Maure, all came from Provence, and that the same richly-endowed land gave to France her greatest political orator—Mirabeau. Among the most uniformly eloquent of Massillon's sermons is that *Sur la Mort*[1], and one naturally turns to it for an example of his powers. The following is at once a reminder of the essential brevity of life and a tribute to the reign of Louis XIV:

Hélas! mes frères, ce qui doit finir peut-il vous paraître long? regardez derrière vous; où sont vos premières années? que laissent-elles de réel

---

[1] It contains an allusion to events of 1712. Either this was added by Massillon later or the sermon was preached in 1712 or 1713 (see Blampignon, *op. cit.* pp. 491–493).

dans votre souvenir? pas plus qu'un songe de la nuit ; vous rêvez que vous avez vécu, voilà tout ce qui vous en reste ; tout cet intervalle, qui s'est écoulé depuis votre naissance jusqu'aujourd'hui, ce n'est qu'un trait rapide qu'à peine vous avez vu passer. Quand vous auriez commencé à vivre avec le monde, le passé ne vous paraîtrait pas plus long ni plus réel ; tous les siècles qui ont coulé jusqu'à nous, vous les regarderiez comme des instants fugitifs ; tous les peuples qui ont paru et disparu dans l'univers, toutes les révolutions d'empires et de royaumes, tous ces grands événements qui embellissent nos histoires ne seraient pour vous que les différentes scènes d'un spectacle que vous auriez vu finir en un jour. Rappelez seulement les victoires, les prises de places, les traités glorieux, les magnificences, les événements pompeux des premières années de ce règne ; vous y touchez encore ; vous en avez été la plupart, non-seulement spectateurs, mais vous en avez partagé les périls et la gloire : ils passeront dans nos annales jusqu'à nos derniers neveux ; mais pour vous ce n'est déjà plus qu'un songe, qu'un éclair qui a disparu, et que chaque jour efface même de votre souvenir.

This is only part of a superb flight[1], the effect of which must have been greatly enhanced by the sweet and resonant voice, the ascetic appearance, the modest bearing, the affectionate tone, of the preacher[2].

But an orator who has a ready flow of language runs the danger of being carried away by the current, and of forgetting that words are not argument. This is especially the case with southerners like Gascons and Provençals, whose emotions are easily roused and readily express themselves in speech. Massillon, though he wrote his sermons and learnt them by heart, did not wholly escape this danger; it betrays him, as we have seen, into exaggeration, and less often, for his sermons are as a rule well composed, into a want of proportion or even into irrelevance.

With his gift of natural and ready eloquence it was of an advantage to Massillon that he had been a Professor of Rhetoric and that he had learnt to discipline his emotional exuberance by the serious study of his art. As a result, he

---

[1] The whole passage is quoted by La Harpe; I was not aware of this when I selected it.

[2] A contemporary—M. Vuillart—who heard him preach the *carêmes* of 1699 (at Saint-Gervais) and 1700, speaks of his "onction," his "incomparable modestie," his "air modeste et mortifié" (Sainte-Beuve, *Causeries du Lundi*, IX, 37–40—an extract from *Port-Royal*, book III, c. xii and Appendix).

had at his command all the usual oratorical figures, but what most impresses his readers, and must have equally impressed his hearers, is his remarkable power of development and amplification. The passage quoted above from the sermon *Sur la Mort* is a good example of this power, and there are others in the same sermon, especially in the second part, where he rebukes in stern and forcible language those who shrink from thinking of death. Other sermons which are conspicuous for the same oratorical quality are those *Sur le mauvais Riche* (1704), *Sur la Samaritaine* (1701), *Sur la Pécheresse de l'Évangile* (1701), and these three sermons, especially *La Samaritaine*, are also admirable examples of his skill in handling a Gospel story so as to make it a real instruction in Christian morals. In all of them we have a "simple explanation of the Gospel," precisely as La Bruyère desired.

Sometimes, indeed, Massillon develops his point in too mechanical a fashion, as in the sermon *Sur les Fautes légères* (1704). In one place he apostrophises his "cher Auditeur" with an iteration that becomes tedious; a little further on he has a long-drawn-out metaphor representing charity as a celestial fire; and towards the end of the sermon he compares the first stage of moral disorder successively to the source of a stream, the little cloud seen by Elijah, the stone in David's dream which became a great mountain, a grain of hemp-seed, and a lump of leaven. The fact is that the subject, which is an excellent one for a homiletic discourse, is not suited to rhetorical treatment, but requires at once a more homely and a more subtle method. Yet the sermon concludes with a long passage which is an example both of fervent eloquence and of impressive exhortation: "Les crimes ne sont jamais les coups d'essai du cœur. David fut indiscret et oiseux avant d'être adultère, etc."— a passage which, as Sainte-Beuve points out, recalls Racine's

Ainsi que la vertu, le crime a ses degrés.

Sainte-Beuve adds that Massillon often remembers Racine and takes pleasure in paraphrasing him, and he quotes Mme de Maintenon as saying, after hearing Massillon preach at Saint-Cyr, "He has the same diction in prose as Racine in verse."

Massillon was not particularly successful in that difficult branch of the preacher's art—the funeral oration[1]. He had not Bossuet's power of transforming the panegyric of an individual into a great moral and spiritual lesson. His oration on the Prince de Conti, nephew of the great Condé (June 1709), the only sermon of his that was published with his authority in his lifetime, errs, not because it is uniformly laudatory, for that was almost inevitable, but because it is exaggerated in its praise. "Tant de valeur, tant de sagesse, tant de religion, tant de lumières"—the changes are rung on Conti's merits with wearisome repetition. It is true that he was greatly gifted but, as Saint-Simon says, "il avoit sa contre-partie. Cet homme si aimable, si charmant, si délicieux, n'aimoit rien. Il avoit et vouloit des amis, comme on veut et comme on a des meubles. ...Il étoit bas courtisan...avare, avide de bien, ardent, injuste[2]."

In the "Grand Dauphin," who according to Saint-Simon was characterless, Massillon had a more difficult task, but he did not shrink from it. He singles out two qualities for special praise—his kindliness—"bon pour ses amis"; "bon père"; "bon maître" (remembering Madame Choin, he cannot bring himself to say "bon mari")—and his respectful devotion to the king[3]. And he takes the opportunity of paying fine tributes to the Duc de Montausier, the Dauphin's governor, and to Bossuet, his tutor. Soon after this there is a fine passage on the unreality of human greatness:

> Tout ce qui doit passer ne peut être grand : ce n'est qu'une décoration de théâtre : la mort finit la scène et la représentation : chacun dépouille la pompe du personnage, et la fiction des titres ; et le souverain, comme l'esclave, est rendu à son néant et à sa première bassesse.

How many famous passages of prose and verse literature does this recall! But it is especially interesting because it foreshadows the famous opening words of Massillon's next funeral oration, that on Louis XIV—"Dieu seul est grand, mes frères."

---

[1] Massillon preached six funeral orations: for Conti, for the Dauphin, for Louis XIV, for the Duchess of Orleans, and for two ecclesiastics, Villars, Archbishop of Vienne, and Villeroy, Archbishop of Lyons.

[2] For the whole portrait see *Mémoires*, VI, 271–275.

[3] "Je ne songe au monde qu'à lui plaire et à apprendre mon métier" (the Dauphin to Mme de Maintenon).

The whole exordium is a piece of noble and moving eloquence. And the rest of the oration contains, as nearly everything of Massillon's does, some very fine passages, as for
instance that on the temptations to which Louis was exposed
in his youth, and that on the misfortunes, public and private,
which crowded on him in his old age. Considering the occasion,
the long portrait of the king is drawn with remarkable
impartiality, and the oration generally is, as M. Bourgeois
says, "one of the manifestations of the sentiment of opposition
which characterises the beginning of the eighteenth century."
Especially moving is the final appeal to God to look with pity
on "this desolate monarchy" and "to extend the wings of Thy
protection to this precious infant that Thou hast put at the head
of Thy people."

In 1718 Massillon was commanded by the Regent to preach
in Lent in the chapel of the Tuileries before the young king,
then eight years of age, and a select company of courtiers. This
course of ten sermons, known as the *Petit Carême*, the first of which
was preached on Candlemas and the last on Easter Day, has
always been the most widely read of Massillon's courses, and
it largely determined his popularity with the eighteenth-century
philosophers[1]. It was the *Petit Carême* which D'Alembert pronounced to be, "if not the masterpiece, at least the true model of
pulpit eloquence"; it was the *Petit Carême* that lay on Voltaire's
table by the side of *Athalie*, and that he had read to him at
meals; it was to the *Petit Carême* that Massillon owed his
reputation as an opponent of war and military glory, as a
sympathiser with the poor and the oppressed, and as a general
friend of humanity.

The fact that Massillon found favour with the eighteenth
century has led Brunetière to regard him unfavourably.
Brunetière disliked the eighteenth century, particularly its
sensibility and its belief in the essential goodness of man, and
he believed (with singularly little justification) that both these
characteristics are to be found in Massillon. One almost in-
voluntarily associates, he says, the *Petit Carême* with *Télémaque*,

---

[1] "Il nous semble qu'on a vanté trop exclusivement son Petit Carême"
Chateaubriand, *Le Génie du Christianisme*).

and the remark is just; not only were both written for the instruction of a prince of tender age, but the *Petit Carême* shews
traces of a close study of *Télémaque*[1]. Both alike contain severe
criticisms on the government of Louis XIV. Listen to this from
the sermon *Sur la tentation des grands*:

> Sa gloire, Sire, sera toujours souillée de sang : quelque insensé chantera
> peut-être ses victoires ; mais les provinces, les villes, les campagnes en
> pleureront : on lui dressera des monuments superbes pour immortaliser
> ses conquêtes ; mais les cendres encore fumantes de tant de villes autre-
> fois florissantes, mais la désolation de tant de campagnes dépouillées de
> leur ancienne beauté, mais les ruines de tant de murs sous lesquelles des
> citoyens paisibles ont été ensevelis, mais tant de calamités qui subsisteront
> après lui, seront des monuments lugubres qui immortaliseront sa vanité
> et sa folie. Il aura passé comme un torrent pour ravager la terre, et non
> comme un fleuve majestueux pour y porter la joie et l'abondance : son nom
> sera écrit dans les annales de la postérité parmi les conquérants, mais il
> ne le sera pas parmi les bons rois ; et l'on ne rappellera l'histoire de son
> règne que pour rappeler le souvenir des maux qu'il a faits aux hommes.
> Ainsi son orgueil, dit l'esprit de Dieu, sera monté jusqu'au ciel ; sa tête
> aura touché dans les nuées ; ses succès auront égalé ses désirs ; et tout
> cet amas de gloire ne sera plus à la fin qu'un monceau de boue qui ne
> laissera après elle que l'infection et l'opprobre.

The picture represents any monarch who "prefers his own
glory to the love and welfare of his people," but with a little
toning down it will serve for the Roi-Soleil.

That it was inspired by the memory of the wars of the
preceding reign is clear from a comparison with the famous
passage in the funeral oration for Louis XIV beginning,
"Monuments superbes, élevés au milieu de nos places publiques,
pour immortaliser la mémoire de nos victoires, que rappellerez-
vous à nos neveux?" These sentiments were counted to
Massillon for righteousness by Voltaire[2], but Brunetière regards them as a proof of exaggerated sensibility. He is no less
scornful of the passage in the sermon *Sur l'humanité des grands*

---

[1] See for parallel passages Bayle, *op. cit.* pp. 313–314.

[2] "De cinq ou six déclamations de cette espèce, il y en a trois ou quatre
tout au plus composées par un Gaulois nommé Massillon, qu'un honnête
homme peut lire sans dégoût ; mais, dans tous ces discours il n'y en a pas
un seul où l'orateur ose s'élever contre ce fléau et ce crime de la guerre,
qui contient tous les fléaux et tous les crimes" (*Dict. philosophique*,
GUERRE).

envers le peuple in which he assures the young king that, "Vous ne serez grand qu'autant que vous leur serez cher; l'amour des peuples a toujours été la gloire la plus réelle et la moins équivoque des souverains."

Another grievance which Brunetière has against Massillon is that he has put into his sermons "peu de doctrine et beaucoup de morale." M. Lanson goes much farther than his master; "Sa prédication est toute morale, toute philosophique, presque laïque. Si l'on excepte les formules traditionnelles, rien n'y sent le chrétien[1]." This is not even a distortion of the truth; it is absolutely opposed to it. In every sermon of the *Avent* and the *Grand Carême* a Christian accent, sincere and courageous, makes itself clearly felt. It is equally unmistakeable in the *Petit Carême*. Indeed, in the sermon for Palm Sunday, *Sur la Fausseté de la Gloire humaine*, Massillon carefully points out the insufficiency of a purely lay morality:

La probité humaine sans la crainte de Dieu est presque toujours fausse, ou du moins elle n'est jamais sûre. Je sais que le monde se vante d'un fantôme d'honneur et de probité indépendant de la religion: il croit qu'on peut être fidèle aux hommes sans être fidèle à Dieu ; être orné de toutes les vertus que demande la Société, sans avoir celles qu'exige l'Évangile ; en un mot, être honnête homme sans être chrétien.

The fact is that both the admirers and the critics of the *Petit Carême* have forgotten that its sermons were composed for the special edification of a boy-king, and that the preacher's aim was not to expound to him the mysteries of Christian dogma, but to impress upon him the principles of Christian morality, and to warn him against the temptations to which, in that corrupt court, surrounded by flatterers, he was so terribly exposed.

Sainte-Beuve, who regards the *Avent* and the *Grand Carême* as superior to the more celebrated *Petit Carême*, says that the latter belongs to a different epoch and in some measure to a different method of preaching. But I doubt whether the difference in method is more than can be accounted for

---

[1] So too Faguet says, "Le caractère distinctif de la prédication elle-même de Massillon est l'oubli un peu près complet du dogme et le souci constant de prêcher la morale" (*Hist. de la litt. française*).

by the special circumstances in which it was preached. Nor is
it easy to detect in it any relaxation (*amollissement*) of the
moral fibre, such as Sainte-Beuve suggests. Certainly there is
none in the sermon of which he says, "I know nothing finer
or truer"—the sermon *Sur les Malheurs des Grands qui
abandonnent Dieu*, in which Massillon attacks with no gentle
hand the passions, the *ennui*, and the strange uncertain tempers
(*bizarrerie*) of the great.

> Loin de la cour, ils croient vivre dans un triste exil; sous les yeux du
> maître, ils se plaignent sans cesse de l'assujettissement des devoirs, et de
> la contrainte des bienséances : ils ne peuvent porter ni la tranquillité d'une
> condition privée, ni la dignité d'une vie publique.

> L'ennui...semble réfugié chez les grands; c'est comme leur ombre qui
> les suit partout....Toute leur vie n'est qu'une précaution pénible contre
> l'ennui, et toute leur vie n'est qu'un ennui pénible elle-même[1].

If we turn from the substance of Massillon's sermons to
their form, there is more justice in Brunetière's criticisms.
The first count of his indictment is that, "il compose par le
dehors," that is to say, that, instead of allowing his sermon to
develop naturally, he constructs an elaborate framework with
many divisions and sub-divisions. To illustrate this, Brunetière
with the help of numerals and letters makes a careful analysis
of that much-admired picture of the sinner's death, to which
reference has already been made[2]. He could not have found a
better instance, for in this sermon Massillon's fault of exaggeration, which includes exaggeration in the use of rhetorical
figures, is unusually conspicuous. The enumeration of the
"changes," the "surprises," the "separations" which the sinner
experiences becomes tedious, as does the repetition of the
text—"Partez, âme chrétienne"—as a refrain. A similar use
of the text is made in *Sur l'Enfant prodigue* and *Sur
l'Impénitence finale*.

Of Massillon's abuse of antithesis Brunetière gives several
examples. He would have found a goodly crop of them in a
single page of the funeral sermon on Conti.

---

[1] Sainte-Beuve aptly quotes Saint-Simon's remark on the Regent that,
"il étoit né ennuyé.

[2] See above, p. 305.

Un prince ne devoit compter pour rien de *combattre*, s'il ne se rendoit digne de *commander*.

Persuadé que si la *naissance* peut donner les grandes dispositions, c'est l'*application* toute seule qui fait les grands hommes.

Il pense déjà qu'un prince n'est *aimable* qu'autant qu'il est *grand*, et que les traits qui le rendront immortel, doivent être plus gravés dans la *beauté* de ses actions, que dans les *charmes* de sa personne.

Other charges made by Brunetière are the abuse of periphrasis—that avoidance of the *mot propre* which was to become one of the crying faults of the classical decadence—and the use of inappropriate metaphor[1] and of vague and otiose epithets[2]. But, as M. Dejob points out, though a reader of the sermons may detect these blemishes, they would have passed unnoticed in the pulpit.

The fact of Massillon being the last of the great preachers disposes one to look for symptoms of decline in his oratory. He is admittedly inferior to Bossuet[3] and Bourdaloue, and that chiefly from a certain lack of simplicity, from a proneness to exaggeration, and from a too great love of rhetorical artifice. But it is difficult to say whether these marks of inferiority are due to his temperament and training, or, as in the somewhat analogous case of La Bruyère, to a consciousness that "all has been said," and that it only remains to say it differently. "Je leur trouve bien de l'esprit et du talent," said Massillon to the Superior General of the Oratory, after hearing several renowned preachers, "mais je ne prêcherai pas comme eux."

Finally, there is the question how far Brunetière is right in accepting the view of Voltaire and the other philosophers that he foreshadows, if he does not actually represent, the eighteenth-century spirit. The reasons would seem to be three, firstly that he concerned himself with morals rather than with

---

[1] "Tel est l'homme entre les mains de ses propres lumières."

[2] Brunetière quotes a short sentence (the last but one) from *Sur le mauvais riche* (*Œuvres choisies*, p. 268), in which there are eight adjectives which add little or nothing to the sense.

[3] Massillon sometimes preaches on the same subject as Bossuet, as for instance on *Le mauvais riche*, in which he emphasises the absence of positive vice in Dives and paints the torments of hell in lurid colours, with the result that his warning, being regarded as the exaggeration of a rhetorician, makes less impression than Bossuet's.

religion, secondly that he inveighed against the horrors of war, thirdly that he was a humanitarian. The first reason, as I have already tried to shew, is not founded on fact. The second is very dubious, for how could a Christian preacher, who had seen his country brought to the verge of ruin by a quarter of a century of continuous warfare, have failed to denounce war? The third reason chiefly rests on his sermon *Sur l'Humanité des Grands envers le Peuple*[1], in which he proclaimed that princes and great men are only great if they promote the welfare of others, and that a king's true glory is the affection of his subjects. This is the same recognition of the rights of the people that we find in Boisguillebert and Vauban and Fénelon and, less markedly, in La Bruyère, but it must be remembered that the sermon was preached in 1718, the year after the publication of the concluding volume of the Abbé de Saint-Pierre's *Projet de paix perpétuelle* and only a month before the appearance of his *Discours sur la Polysynodie*, in which the whole policy of Louis XIV was severely criticised.

---

[1] *Œuvres choisies*, pp. 60 ff.

CHAPTER X

THE QUARREL OF THE ANCIENTS
AND THE MODERNS[1]

THE writers whom I have been considering hitherto nearly all foreshadow, in one direction or another, the eighteenth century, but they belong in spirit to the seventeenth. Take La Bruyère. In two ways he was an innovator with a marked influence on the literature that came after him; he substituted the observation of manners for that of character, and he introduced the short pointed phrase which was to become the habitual style of the eighteenth century. Yet he gave his allegiance to the century in which he was born and died, and in the great Quarrel he was whole-heartedly on the side of the ancients. Dancourt, Regnard, and Dufresny, all influenced by La Bruyère, but possessing the dramatic instinct which he lacked, were too much intent on enjoying and observing the life that was immediately around them to look forward to the future. Dufresny's *Amusements sérieux et comiques* do, however, form a link between La Bruyère and Montesquieu. Lesage was only a lad of nineteen when our period opens, and his most important work, *Gil Blas,* had hardly begun to appear when our period ends. But both as man and artist he was essentially of the *grand siècle.* He thoroughly disliked the social degeneration, as he deemed it, of his times, and he built up his chief play and his chief novel with the logical and constructive art of his great predecessors.

[1] The best account of the Quarrel is still that of H. Rigault, *Histoire de la Querelle des Anciens et des Modernes,* 1856. See also G. Lanson, *Boileau,* 1892; F. Brunetière, *L'évolution des Genres dans l'histoire de la littérature, leçon* IV, 1898; J. Delvaille, *Essai sur l'histoire de l'idée de progrès jusqu'à la fin du XVIIIᵉ siècle,* book IV, esp. cc. v and vi, 1910; H. Gillot, *La Querelle des Anciens et des Modernes en France,* 1914; J. B. Bury, *The Idea of Progress,* cc. iii–v, 1920; J. G. Robertson, *Studies in the Genesis of Romantic Theory in the Eighteenth Century,* Cambridge, 1923.

The light society verse which poured forth in such abundance in the latter part of the reign of Louis XIV was but a continuation of the stream which had begun to flow in the middle of the seventeenth century. Even those who very occasionally rose to higher things—Mme Deshoulières, Chaulieu, La Fare, Hamilton—were, like the dramatists, too much children of their age and surroundings to be forerunners of a later age. All that can be said is that Hamilton hands on to Voltaire the art of Voiture, that is to say the art of writing well-turned and witty verse, which in an unpoetical age did duty for poetry. The one writer in verse of our period who aspired to be a poet in the grand style, Jean-Baptiste Rousseau, was as orthodox as Boileau in his devotion to the ancients.

Curiously enough it is among the writers of fiction that we come upon two works which bear the authentic stamp of the eighteenth century—the *Voyages et Avantures de Jaques Massé* by Tyssot de Patot and the *Voyages du Baron de Lahontan*. The former, as we saw, is a pure work of fiction, and the chief interest of the latter is in the imaginary dialogue between the Baron and a Huron chief which was added as a supplement to the travels either by Lahontan himself or by his editor.

Of the more important writers that have up to now come under our notice the two that are the best entitled to be regarded as precursors of the eighteenth century are Fénelon and Massillon. We have seen that they were so regarded by Voltaire and his contemporaries. But the philosophers were under an illusion when they imagined that in their denunciations of war and extravagant luxury and their sympathies with the sufferings of the people Fénelon and Massillon were prompted by humanitarian rather than by Christian principles. They were as faithful and loyal preachers of the Gospel as Bossuet himself. Moreover, if we turn from the social to the literary aspect, Fénelon in spite of his modern sympathies and his diplomatic letters to the Secretary of the Academy and to La Motte was too thoroughly saturated with the literature of Greece and Rome not to be at heart an ancient.

On these considerations I have postponed till now the account of the Quarrel of the Ancients and the Moderns, for though chronologically it marks the beginning of our period, it is the real starting-point of the eighteenth century[1].

At first sight this famous Quarrel appears as a futile and rather ridiculous controversy, in which the champions of the moderns matched a single nation and a single century against the whole of antiquity and were moreover singularly ill-equipped for their self-appointed task. But, looked at closer, the Quarrel is of considerable interest and great significance. Firstly, it throws considerable light on the attitude of critics and society and the general educated public towards the great literature of the age of Louis XIV; secondly, it had a marked influence, partly for good, and partly for evil, on the subsequent development of literature and criticism; thirdly and chiefly, it has behind it the difficult and much-debated question of human progress.

As W. P. Ker, with his customary insight, points out in his Introduction to the Essays of Dryden, the debate had been going on for a long time and was in fact the inevitable result of the Revival of Learning[2]. Rabelais, who began with a wholly uncritical reverence for the ancients, developed in the twelve years between the publication of *Gargantua* (1534) and that of his *Third Book* (1546) a growing conviction that their writings were not infallible repositories of truth, and that they must be carefully tested in the light of common sense and experience. Rabelais was a modern and a believer in human progress before his time[3], but a general reaction against excessive humanism in France set in after St Bartholomew, and was continued in the years of rapine and anarchy which preceded and followed the death of the last Valois king. It was a sign of this reaction, that the death of Ronsard (1585) was the prelude to a rapid decline in the popularity of his whole poetical school. It was another sign that Montaigne, who was

---

[1] "Dans le débat sur les anciens et les modernes j'aperçois le XVIIIe siècle qui apparaît et qui détruit le XVIIe siècle en s'en dégageant" (G. Lanson, *Hist. de la litt. franç.*).

[2] *Essays*, 1925, I, 19.

[3] See A. F. Chappell, *The enigma of Rabelais*, Cambridge, 1924, esp. c. v.

brought up on Latin from his cradle, whose great exemplar was Socrates, and who regarded the world of his day as greatly inferior to the ancient world, felt it no disrespect to meet his old friends, the great writers of antiquity, with frank criticism, and that he could write in his essay on education, "C'est un bel et grand agencement sans doute que le Grec et Latin, mais on l'achète trop cher."

In the next century, when France had sobered down under the wise guidance of Henri IV, Malherbe, the new dictator of French poetry, was but a cool lover of the ancients. "He loved the Greeks and Romans," says the Abbé Godeau, "but he did not idolise them[1]." Towards the poets, if we may believe his disciple and biographer, Racan, he was still cooler. He thought nothing of the Greeks and he was a declared enemy to the *galimatias* of Pindar. His favourite Latin poet was Statius, and after him Horace, Juvenal, Ovid, and Martial. But what of Virgil or Lucretius or Catullus? Descartes, who had been educated at the Jesuit college of La Flèche, professed a contempt, which was not altogether genuine, for ancient literature, as was perhaps natural in the man who liberated thought from the tyranny of Aristotle. Corneille's outward and enforced respect for the great Greek as a dramatic critic did not prevent him from violating his precepts, though it compelled him to justify their violation. The founder of French classical tragedy remained at heart an innovator and a modern. Chapelain, the principal author of *Les Sentiments de l'Académie sur la Tragicomédie du Cid*, who forms a link between Malherbe and Boileau, though he was well acquainted with Latin, Spanish, and Italian literature, seems to have known that of Greece chiefly at second-hand. He certainly had not read Aristotle's *Poetics* in the original. Passages in Corneille's *Trois Discours* suggest that his knowledge of Greek was no deeper than Chapelain's and the inspiration of his tragedies comes almost entirely from Latin sources. His first tragedy, *Médée*, owes far more to Seneca than to Euripides; *Horace, Cinna* and *La Mort de Pompée* are taken from Roman history; in fact his only incursion, besides *Médée*, into Greek tragedy was the unfortunate *Œdipe*. This preference was

[1] Malherbe, *Œuvres* (*Les Grands Écrivains de la France*), I, 383.

only natural, for Greek was always an exotic in France, and except during the golden age of her classical scholarship, her culture remained almost exclusively Latin. Even Plutarch, after Amyot's translation had made him almost a Frenchman, commanded a much readier sympathy for his Roman than for his Greek heroes.

Nor was the education of the day such as to promote a more thorough understanding of ancient literature. It is true that the reforms introduced by Henri IV into the University of Paris made the teaching more classical and gave a place to Greek in the programme. But the University did not recover its prestige; and although the teaching of its successful rivals, the Jesuits, followed the same severely classical lines, the latter insisted more upon translation and composition than upon the explanation of authors. In the Little Schools of Port-Royal, which were definitely organised in 1644, the importance of Latin was fully recognised and the range of authors was much wider, and in the higher classes the principal Greek authors (with the curious omission of Aeschylus and Plato) were read. It was to Claude Lancelot, one of the Port-Royal teachers, that Racine owed his knowledge of Greek literature and his sympathy with the Greek spirit.

The result of all this was that a knowledge of Greek became more and more restricted to a small body of scholarly students, who were often recluses or pedants, or, if they touched society at all, touched it only on its outer fringe. Thus even the cultivated Frenchman of the seventeenth century, with few exceptions, was dependent upon translations for his knowledge of Greek literature, while the general educated public owed its knowledge even of Latin literature to the same source. And what translations! *Les belles infidèles* of Perrot d'Ablancourt, the translator of Xenophon, Thucydides, and Lucian, have become a byword, but a far greater sinner was the Abbé de Marolles, who in nine years (1652 to 1661) dispatched all the Latin poets—"he did not pardon even Plautus or Lucretius," says Chapelain—in translations which were models of slovenly inaccuracy. No ancient author fared worse than Homer. He was translated into French prose by Du Souhait in 1614, and

T D   21

Rigault, who quotes a passage from the first book of the *Iliad*, says that the translator is "exact but diffuse and spun-out." He is not even exact. But Homer was rightly held in the highest honour by the partisans of the ancients as the fountain-head of Greek and Roman literature, and consequently he was singled out by the moderns as the chief target of their attacks. Thus in February 1635 Boisrobert, Richelieu's favourite and buffoon, read a discourse before the newly-constituted Académie Française, in which he made a scurrilous attack on the ancients in general and on Homer in particular[1].

After the death of Richelieu (December 1642) bad taste rioted in French literature for many years. It manifested itself in three ways; in the vulgarity of burlesque, in the pedantry of dull epics, and in the affectation of preciosity. The first two were merely passing fashions; the last, which crept into every kind of literature, was more elusive, more penetrating, and therefore more difficult to eradicate. All alike were distasteful to the lovers of the ancients—burlesque because one of its provinces was the travesty of classical poems, the epics because they were modelled on Tasso rather than on Homer or Virgil, preciosity because it substituted artificiality for nature and false sentiment for truth.

In 1656 a reaction against this all-pervading bad taste was marked by *The Provincial Letters*, but their popularity was shared with Thomas Corneille's sentimental melodrama, *Timocrate*, and when the great Corneille returned to the stage in January 1659, after an absence of seven or eight years, he produced *Œdipe*, which vied with his brother's play in romance and preciosity and had a brilliant success.

---

[1] Rigault conjectures that Tassoni's *Pensieri diversi*, which was trans-lated into French by Jean Baudoin, one of the original members of the Academy, suggested this attack. But there is no proof that Boisrobert had read Baudoin's translation, which, as Rigault admits, is not mentioned by Pellisson among his works. Moreover Tassoni's disparagement of Homer only occupies half-a-dozen lines of his comparison of the ancients with the moderns. This comparison forms the tenth book of the *Pensieri*—a book which was added in 1620 to the original edition of 1612. In the two chapters (xiv and xv) which he devotes to poets and orators he only mentions one Frenchman—Philippe de Commynes. See Rigault, *op. cit.* pp. 71–76.

Ten months later Molière inaugurated the campaign against bad taste with *Les Précieuses ridicules*. In the following year (1660) Boileau published his first satire. Then came in glorious succession *Les Fâcheux* (1661), which La Fontaine saluted as the proclamation of a new reign in comedy—the reign of Nature—*L'École des Femmes* (1662), which involved Molière in a war with *dévots, précieux,* and pedants, the first three acts of *Tartuffe* (1664), *Don Juan* (1665), in which Molière carried reprisals into the enemy's camp, Boileau's first collected satires (1666)[1], *Le Misanthrope* and *Andromaque* (both in 1667), Boileau's eighth and ninth satires and the first six books of La Fontaine's *Fables* (all in 1668), and *Britannicus* (1669). In prose the same great years from 1665 to 1669 were marked by La Rochefoucauld's *Maximes* (1665), and by the sermons of Bossuet and of Bourdaloue, who preached his first course at Paris in 1669. Meanwhile in 1664 a close literary alliance had been formed between Molière, Boileau, Racine, and La Fontaine, who in memorable meetings either at Boileau's lodgings or at the taverns of the *Mouton blanc* or the *Croix de Lorraine* discussed informally the principles and practice of their art. "They adored the works of the ancients," says La Fontaine in the partly imaginative and wholly charming account which he gives of their meetings at the beginning of *Les Amours de Psyché,* and they realised that in them they had models which had passed triumphantly the only infallible test of literary merit—the test of time. What was the secret, they asked, of their immortality? What were the specific virtues which preserved their writings from decay? In the first place—so we may suppose that the friends reasoned—they observed life for themselves and not merely at second-hand. Secondly, they recorded their observations in lucid and natural language, coloured by their own idiosyncrasies, and heightened in poetry by emotion and imagination. Thirdly, in their study of life they were guided by Reason, the faculty which distinguishes truth from falsehood. Fourthly, they spared no pains to bring their work to the highest point of perfection; they "polished and re-polished" it, and they subjected it to a

[1] I–VII.

severe criticism. Fifthly, they invariably chose the right form
for each kind of literature, the Greeks from an unerring instinct
and the Romans as their apt pupils.

Such were the leading principles which Boileau and his
friends detected in the ancient masterpieces, and which, while
preserving their artistic independence, they endeavoured to put
into practice in their own work. All four were now rapidly
rising in public reputation; they were in favour with the king,
with the more intelligent among the great nobles, and with
the higher *bourgeoisie*. In February 1669 Molière triumphed
over his enemies with the king's permission to play *Tartuffe* in
public. In 1673 Racine was elected to the Academy, though
his opponents must have numbered nearly half the whole body.
In 1674 he scored a fresh success with *Iphigénie*, and earlier
in that year a new edition of Boileau's works appeared, which
included the *Art poétique*, the poetical code of the new school.

Meanwhile, an attack in force had been made on the
ancients and on their champion, Boileau. Jean Desmarets de
Saint-Sorlin (1595–1676)[1], one of the original Academicians,
was a writer of "deplorable fecundity," to borrow Victor
Fournel's phrase. After tragedies, tragi-comedies, a comedy—
Les Visionnaires, the one work by which he is known—and
two unfinished prose romances, he embarked upon an epic,
when epics became the fashion, and in 1657 produced *Clovis*.
Hitherto a free-thinker, he was converted while writing it to
Christianity of a fanatical type, and believing his work to be
"the veritable poem of France," he constituted himself the
champion of the Christian epic and *le merveilleux chrétien* as
opposed to pagan poetry and mythology. *Clovis* was well
received, though without the enthusiasm which its author's
vanity had led him to expect, and in 1669 he produced another
Christian epic, *Marie-Madeleine*, with a preface, in which he
stated his theory as to the superiority of *le merveilleux chrétien*
to *le merveilleux païen*. In the following year (1670) he launched a
direct attack on the ancients under the title of *La Comparaison
de la langue et de la poésie françaises avec la langue et la poésie
grecques et latines*, in which he proclaimed their inferiority to

[1] See Rigault, *op. cit.* c. vii.

the moderns in poetry, and passed severe judgments on Virgil, Ovid, Horace, and, above all, Homer. He also enunciated the view, which was afterwards adopted by Perrault and Fontenelle, that since the days of the ancients the world had been progressing, and that while they represent the youth of the world, the moderns represent its maturity[1]. The treatise was reprinted in 1673 as an appendix to the third edition of *Clovis*, under the title of *Traité pour juger des poètes grecs, latins et français*, and he prefixed to his epic a *Discours*, in which he re-stated his view of Christian epics and *le merveilleux chrétien*. Boileau replied to this by introducing a long satirical allusion to *Clovis* in his *Art poétique* (1674)[2], and Desmarets countered with an anonymous volume of verse entitled *La defense du poëme héroïque avec quelques remarques sur les œuvres satyriques du Sieur D****[3] and with *La defense de la poësie et de la langue françoises*[4], published in his own name, in which he calls upon his friend Perrault to continue the good fight.

> Viens défendre, Perrault, la France qui t'appelle,
> Viens combattre avec moi cette troupe rebelle,
> Ce ramas d'ennemis qui, faibles et mutins,
> Préfèrent à nos chants les ouvrages latins.

In the same year (1674), Malebranche, in the second part of his *De la recherche de la vérité*, inveighed with sharp severity against the false respect, mingled with a silly curiosity, which makes men admire unduly things which are furthest removed from us, whether by age or distance.

> On recherche les médailles anciennes quoique rongées de la rouille, et l'on garde avec grand soin la lanterne et la pantoufle de quelque ancien, quoique mangées de vers....Il faut respecter l'antiquité, dit-on. Quoi! Aristote, Platon, Épicure, ces grands hommes se seraient trompés? On ne considère pas qu'Aristote, Platon, Épicure, étaient hommes comme nous, et de même espèce que nous; et de plus, qu'au temps où nous vivons, le monde est plus âgé de deux mille ans, qu'il a plus d'expérience, qu'il doit être plus éclairé, et que c'est la vieillesse du monde et l'expérience qui font découvrir la vérité.

---

[1] *Traité*, c. iv.   [2] III, 313–332.
[3] 1674 ; 2nd ed. 1675. See *Œuvres de Boileau*, ed. Berriat Saint-Prix, 4 vols. 1837, I, ccxvi–ccxviii.
[4] 1674.

We saw in a former chapter that Charles Perrault, to whom Desmarets's appeal was addressed, had been in earlier life a frequenter of *précieux* salons and a writer of *précieux* verse, that from 1663 to 1681 he had been employed by Colbert as his confidential agent in his great schemes for the advancement of national art and literature, and that latterly, having been released from these duties, he had returned to the world of letters and had renewed his opposition to Boileau and his friends. Moreover, since 1671 he had been an active member of the Academy[1]. On various counts, therefore, he was well qualified for the rôle which Saint-Sorlin had assigned to him.

He, however, shewed no hurry to respond to his friend's appeal, and before he appeared in the field, François Charpentier (1620–1702) published in 1683 a lengthy treatise, *De l'excellence de la langue française*, on the merits of the French language as opposed to Latin, in the course of which he made some remarks on the general question of the ancients and the moderns. If we have no Cicero or Livy, he argued, no Virgil or Horace, which is disputable, it does not follow that we may not have them in the future. Posterity will be our judge. If we have no great political orators, because our form of government does not need them, on the other hand, as the result of Christianity, we have great preachers. Repeating the argument of Saint-Sorlin, he declares that the so-called ancients are less ancient than we are, because the human race has added two thousand years to its life, and that consequently our age is more enlightened than theirs[2]. Further, he

---

[1] See above, p. 184.

[2] This had become by this time a commonplace. In the preface to his *Nouvelles conjectures sur la digestion* (1636), Cureau de La Chambre says, "Nous sommes dans la vieillesse du monde et ce que l'on appelle Antiquité en a été l'enfance et la jeunesse" (quoted by Gillot, *op. cit.* p. 285). The same ideas are expressed by Guillaume Colletet in a discourse read before the Academy, also in 1636 (see Brunetière, *Études critiques*, v, 185), by Descartes in the MS of a Latin fragment preserved and translated by his biographer, Adrien Baillet—"C'est un nom que nous méritons mieux qu'eux parce que le monde est plus ancien maintenant qu'il n'étoit de leur temps et que nous avons une plus grande expérience qu'eux" (*Vie de M. Descartes* [by A. Baillet], 2 vols. 1691, II, 531)—and by Pascal in his *Fragment d'un Traité du Vide*—"Ceux que nous appelons anciens étaient véritablement nouveaux en toutes choses, et formaient

points out the danger of excessive admiration for the ancients, because it discourages the French from cultivating and improving their own language. At last, on January 27, 1687, Perrault took occasion of a special meeting of the Academy, which was held to celebrate the king's convalescence, to read a short poem entitled, *Le siècle de Louis le Grand*[1]. It begins as follows:

> La belle antiquité fut toujours vénérable,
> Mais je ne crus jamais qu'elle fut adorable.
> Je vois les anciens sans plier les genoux :
> Ils sont grands, il est vrai, mais hommes comme nous ;
> Et l'on peut comparer, sans crainte d'être injuste,
> Le siècle de Louis au beau siècle d'Auguste.

This is a reasonable proposition, as Boileau afterwards recognised, but no sooner has Perrault stated it than he greatly extends his field of comparison by attacking first Plato (whom he accuses of being tedious) and then Aristotle and then, as was inevitable, Homer. "Vaste et puissant génie," he admits, but if he had lived in the *grand siècle*, how much more correct and more polished his work would have been. Menander, Virgil, and Ovid are all authors of merit, but in their own lifetime were they adored as they are now? Then follows an enumeration of the great modern poets who, when time has consecrated their writings, will have a glorious place in the Temple of Memory :

> Donc quel haut rang d'honneur ne devront point tenir
> Dans les fastes sacrés de siècles à venir
> Les Regniers, les Maynards, les Gombauds, les Malherbes,
> Les Godeaux, les Racans, dont les écrits superbes,
> En sortant de leur veine et dès qu'ils furent nés,
> D'un laurier immortel se virent couronnés?
> Combien seront chéris par les races futures,
> Les galants Sarrasins, et les tendres Voitures,
> Les Molières naïfs, les Rotrous, les Tristans,
> Et cent autres encore, délices de leur Temps.

l'enfance des hommes proprement, et comme nous avons joint à leurs connaissances l'expérience des siècles qui les ont suivis, c'est en nous que l'on peut trouver cette antiquité que nous révérons dans les autres." The fragment was written 1647–1651 but it was not printed till 1779. The same idea is expressed by Bacon in his *Novum Organum*, I, 84.

[1] See Rigault, *op. cit.* c. vii ; Bonnefon, *Rev. d'hist. litt.* XII (1905), 563 ff.

The enumeration of these "rare authors," all of whom are destined for apotheosis, is completed by eight lines in honour of Corneille.

It is easy to laugh at this list of immortals, none of whom, except Regnier, Malherbe, Molière, and Corneille, occupy more than a modest niche in the Temple of Fame. But it must be remembered that all, even Gombaud and Godeau, were highly praised in their day and that, except Regnier and Malherbe, who were dead when the Academy was instituted, and Rotrou, who died when he was forty, and Sarasin, who was an indiscreet buffoon, and Molière, who was disqualified by his profession, all had been members of the Academy. Nor must we blame Perrault for omitting Racine, La Fontaine, and Boileau, for he would have answered that it was not his intention to include living poets. But the contrast between the single and slightly contemptuous epithet given to Molière and the eight lines in praise of Corneille is significant. From literature Perrault turns to painting, sculpture, architecture, and music, and then follows a passage in which he expresses a belief in the inexhaustible power of Nature:

> A former les esprits comme à former les corps,
> La Nature en tout temps fait les mêmes efforts.
> Son être est immuable, et cette force aisée,
> Dont elle produit tout, ne s'est point épuisée.

This is not going so far as Desmarets, who had declared that the world was progressing, but it is at least a protest against the rival theory that it was degenerating. Ages, however, vary; some are enlightened, some are ignorant; but none has surpassed the age of Louis XIV. And so with a paean in praise of Louis's exploits in war and peace the poem ends.

It will be seen that the main purpose of Perrault's poem was to glorify the age of Louis XIV and to celebrate its achievements in art and letters. The attack on the ancients was subsidiary to this and moreover betrayed such gross ignorance that it was not worth answering. The three friends who "adored the ancients" behaved characteristically. La Fontaine wrote at once a charming epistle in verse to Huet, then Bishop of

Soissons (who had sat next to him at the meeting), in which he makes confession of his literary preferences:

Térence est dans mes mains, je m'instruis dans Horace,
Homère et son rival sont mes dieux du Parnasse.

But he also loves Ariosto and Tasso and Machiavelli and Boccaccio.

J'en parle si souvent que l'on est étourdi,
J'en lis qui sont du nord, et qui sont du midi.

Where in our days, he asks, shall we find a rival to Plato[1]? Racine complimented Perrault on his poem and pretended to regard it as a *jeu d'esprit*, a malicious thrust on his part, which, as was intended, went home. Boileau fussed and fumed, and at last, containing himself no longer, rose from his seat and openly protested, adding that as soon as he had leisure he would defend the ancients in writing[2]. For a time, however, he contented himself with writing a couple of epigrams, in which he compared Perrault and his supporters to Hurons and Topinamboux[3].

The next to take a hand in the Quarrel was Fontenelle, who had already given a foretaste of his views in one at least of his *Dialogues des Morts* (1683), namely the third, in which Montaigne maintains and Socrates denies that the human race has morally degenerated. "One is prejudiced in favour of antiquity," says Socrates, "because one is bitter against one's own age. In our own day we esteemed our ancestors more than they deserved, and now our posterity esteems us more than we deserve." Fontenelle's entry into the campaign took the form of a *Digression sur les Anciens et les Modernes*, which he appended, together with a treatise on the Eclogue, to a volume of Pastoral Poetry, published in January 1688[4]. Being of a more

---

[1] First printed separately on February 5, 1687, nine days after the meeting of the Academy. The epistle accompanied an Italian translation of Quintilian.

[2] Perrault, *Mémoires*, p. 137.

[3] The Topinamboux were a savage tribe who dwelt in northern Brazil.

[4] Rigault, *op. cit.* c. xi; Bury, *op. cit.* c. v (an admirable account, but, in my opinion, too favourable to Fontenelle).

philosophic mind than his friend Perrault and realising, no doubt, that a mere Battle of Books was bound to end in a stale-mate, he begins at once by stating in a simple but arresting form the contention of Perrault that Nature is unchangeable:

> Toute la question de la prééminence entre les Anciens et les Modernes étant une fois bien entendue, se réduit à savoir si les arbres qui étaient autrefois dans nos campagnes étaient plus grands que ceux d'aujourd'hui. En cas qu'ils l'aient été, Homère, Platon, Démosthène, ne peuvent être égalés dans ces derniers siècles. Mais si nos arbres sont aussi grands que ceux d'autrefois, nous pouvons égaler Homère, Platon, Démosthène.

Then he proceeds to explain what he calls "this paradox," and in the course of his explanation he says:

> La Nature a entre les mains une certaine pâte, qui est toujours la même, qu'elle tourne et retourne sans cesse en mille façons, et dont elle forme les hommes, les animaux, les plantes, et certainement elle n'a point formé Platon, Démosthène, ni Homère d'une argile plus fine ni mieux préparée que nos philosophes, nos orateurs, et nos poètes d'aujourd'hui.

Disposing easily, but far from satisfactorily, of the objection that some climates may be more favourable than others to the production of genius and intellect, he concludes that ancients and moderns—Greeks, Romans, Italians, Frenchmen—are equal by nature. But since the moderns have the mistakes of the ancients as well as their successes to profit by, it would be surprising if they did not surpass them. But we must make a distinction between eloquence and poetry, which depend chiefly on a vivid imagination, and scientific studies, like physics, mathematics, and medicine, which depend on experience. In the latter the moderns are necessarily superior to the ancients. But in eloquence[1] and poetry (though these are not important) it is possible that the ancients have reached perfection. Except, however, in tragedy, the Greeks are inferior to the Romans, and this is only natural, for the Romans are moderns in comparison with the Greeks. Indeed, with the exception aforesaid, the Romans in the age of Augustus seem

---

[1] By "eloquence" Fontenelle and Perrault understand all prose writing, including history, which aspires to be literature. So Wotton in his *Reflections upon Ancient and Modern Learning*, "By Orators I understand all those writers in prose who took pains to beautify and adorn their style."

to have reached perfection. Even in tragedy, however, the best
works of Sophocles, Euripides, and Aristophanes cannot hold
their ground before *Cinna, Horace, Ariane*[1], *Le Misanthrope,*
and a large number of tragedies and comedies of the good time,
"for one must honestly confess that the good time came to an
end some years ago[2]." Finally, he declares—and here everyone
will agree with him—that excessive admiration of the ancients
hinders all progress. "Si on s'allait entêter un jour de Descartes et le mettre à la place d'Aristote, ce serait à peu près
le même inconvénient." Here speaks the true and understanding disciple of Descartes.

Fontenelle's treatise has been highly praised, chiefly for its
treatment of the important and interesting question of human
progress. But there is little in it that is original. The neatly-
phrased passage with which it opens is merely another way
of putting Perrault's " La Nature est immuable." The statement
that the moderns are really the ancients was, as we have seen,
made in print by Cureau de La Chambre more than fifty
years before, and repeated first by Saint-Sorlin and then by
Charpentier. In his deprecation of excessive admiration of the
ancients, because it discourages progress, he is also following
Charpentier. On the other hand, we may give him the credit of
the comparison between the life of humanity and that of a
single man, for he can hardly have known Pascal's *Fragment
d'un Traité du Vide.* His argument is not very clear, but
apparently he means that humanity was in its youth during
the age of Augustus, when "things of the imagination, like
poetry and eloquence," reached perfection, and that now it is
in its virility and reasons with greater power and intelligence
than it ever did. Suddenly, however, he realises that at this
point the comparison breaks down, and he goes on to explain
that humanity, unlike individual man, will have no old age.
Moreover, it will always be as capable of poetry and eloquence
as it was in its youth, and more and more capable of science
and everything which befits the age of virility.

---

[1] A successful but second-rate tragedy by Fontenelle's uncle, Thomas
Corneille.

[2] Molière died in 1673, and Racine retired from the stage in 1677.

If Fontenelle's arguments are not altogether original, they are always put in a form calculated to attract intelligent, but ignorant and careless, readers, who would neither detect him when he is gliding over thin ice, nor would be conscious of his gross blunders in scholarship and taste. The worst of these is the assertion that Homer uses five different dialects, but almost as bad is the statement that the novels of La Calprenède and Mlle de Scudéry, "which are poems in prose," reveal the possibility of surpassing Virgil. His view that the ancients do not reason as well as the moderns is hardly less ridiculous, and I am afraid that, if his treatise were subjected to a searching analysis by Plato, there would not be much of it left. Writing, however, as a man of the world for men of the world and not for scholars, he scored a distinct success both in France and in other countries. To his opponents, indeed, his supercilious tone of superiority towards the ancients, marked though it is by outward courtesy and moderation, must have been galling. They must have detected too the underlying dogmatism and self-complacency. He is not even above calling attention to his own performances. He includes *lettres galantes* with *contes* and operas as new kinds of literature, "each of which has furnished us with an excellent author to whom antiquity has no one to oppose and whom posterity, it appears, will not surpass." And his final sentence is a puff direct of his singularly feeble eclogues. It is unfortunate that he should have called attention to what, except for his plays, are the two worst of his productions.

Perrault had now nearly completed the first volume of a long prose work on the great controversy, but before it appeared, François de Callières[1], a diplomatist with a taste for letters, who nine years later was to represent France at Ryswick, published in this same year (1688) a prose burlesque, under the title of *Histoire poétique de la guerre nouvellement déclarée entre les Anciens et les Modernes*[2]. It narrates how as the result of Perrault's poem

---

[1] "C'étoit un grand homme maigre, avec un grand nez, la tête en arrière, distrait, civil, respectueux,...fort instruit, fort modeste, parfaitement désintéressé" (Saint-Simon, I, 382 f.).

[2] An excellent English translation was published in 1705 under the

war had broken out in Parnassus between the Ancients and the Moderns. The first two books are occupied with the choosing of the chiefs, and the jealousies and disputes to which this gives rise are amusingly depicted and shew considerable critical insight. Homer is elected General of the Greek poets and Virgil of the Latin; Demosthenes of the Greek orators (i.e prose-writers) and Cicero of the Latin. Important commands under Homer are given to Sophocles and Euripides, to Aristophanes and Menander, and to Pindar, Theocritus, and Callimachus with Sappho for his colleague; under Virgil, to Statius, Horace (as General of the Satirists as well as of the Lyrics), Seneca the Tragedian, Terence, Ovid and Tibullus (jointly), and Catullus (as General of the Epigrammatists, in spite of Martial's claims); under Demosthenes, to Plato, Xenophon, and Lucian; while Cicero appoints Pliny (on account of his *Panegyricus*) as his Lieutenant-General and Quintilian as his Quartermaster-General. The elections of the moderns cause greater dissension. The French poets, in spite of the persistent claims of the epic writers headed by Chapelain, choose Corneille as their General. Under him serve Molière, Malherbe (in command of the Lyrics), the Comtesse de La Suze (in command of the Elegiacs), Racan (Pastoral Poetry), La Sablière (Madrigals), Voiture, and Sarasin. Corneille greatly affronts Saint-Sorlin, Chapelain, and Saint-Amant by sending them to the rear to guard the baggage. He appoints Scudéry Master-General of the Ordnance, and gives Brébœuf, who as translator of the *Pharsalia* had aspired to be Generalissimo, the command of the right wing. The Italian poets elect Tasso as their General, whereupon Ariosto retires in disgust. Tassoni, Petrarch, Guarini, Marini, and Lope de Vega have commands under him, the forces of Italy and Spain being united. Camões refuses to serve under anybody. He intends to command a separate army and asks no other favour

title of *Characters and Criticisms upon the Ancient and Modern Orators, Poets*, etc., followed by a verse translation of Perrault's poem, which is curiously ascribed to Fénelon. In the 3rd edition of his *Reflections*, Wotton accuses Swift of having plagiarised Callières in his *Battle of the Books*. Swift indignantly denied the charge and Craik points out that the resemblance between the two works is of the slightest (see H. Craik, *Life of Swift*, pp. 70–72).

but the liberty to engage the Ancients first. Chiefly owing to Balzac's assurance of his own merit, the French orators, *faute de mieux*, grant him the chief command, but they associate with him the blustering Gascon, La Calprenède, who had protested that Balzac was only a pedant and an upstart beggar. The Spanish orators choose Cervantes and the Italians, having no candidate of their own, agree to serve under him.

The battle begins with Camões's rash attack on Homer, who takes him prisoner and having bound him to his chariot drags him in triumph round the camp. Engagements then take place between various contingents of the two armies, the Ancients being successful in some and the Moderns in others; councils.of war and conferences are held; and Euripides and Horace are sent as ambassadors to two living poets (Racine and Boileau), who are on their way to the assistance of the Ancients. Finally the Muses appeal to Apollo to act as peacemaker. He gives audience to the eight chiefs, hears a complaint from Plato that Perrault had said he was tedious, listens to a controversy between Aristotle and Descartes, and bids all the combatants retire to await his decisions. They are as follows. Homer is confirmed in his title of the greatest poet that ever lived, and Virgil is to be acknowledged as next to him. Corneille and Racine are declared to be equal to Sophocles and Euripides, Boileau to Horace, and Molière to Aristophanes, Menander, and Terence. Among the orators Apollo assigns the first place to Demosthenes and the second to Cicero, continues the title of divine to Plato, and confirms the reputation of Xenophon and Lucian, of Pliny and Quintilian. He declares Aristotle to be one of the most immense and sublime geniuses that ever lived, but gives the Moderns liberty to criticise his Physics. He praises Balzac for having taken so much pains to perfect the style of the French language, so that he has enabled "the good writers that followed him to reach the highest point of perfection, which consists in a style that is less soaring and formal, and more easy and natural than his." He places the works of La Calprenède in the first rank of serious and heroic romances, and he puts Cervantes at the head of all the authors of comical romances, amorous histories, and gallant novels, and declares him to be the first of all the writers of his nation. He then considers the new poem by Perrault (which is freely quoted in the course of the narrative) and mingles praise with censure. Finally he summons Racine and Boileau and encourages them to persevere in the great work—the history of the reign of Louis XIV—upon which they are engaged, promises them immortal glory, and concludes with a fulsome panegyric "of that inimitable Prince."

Callières's burlesque had a great success, being applauded in both camps. The Academy, in particular, testified its approval by electing him a member in the following year. The success was deserved, for it is easy to agree with the English translator that it is "the justest piece of general criticism upon all those authors as well ancient and modern which are mentioned in it." There are of course omissions—notably Lucretius among the Ancients and Pascal among the Moderns. The ancient historians are left out altogether, probably by an oversight. Naturally, some of the Frenchmen—Voiture, Sarasin, Mme de La Suze—are over-rated, but then Boileau in his letter to Perrault is no less favourable to their "elegies." The author of *Les Héros de Roman*, however, would not have agreed with the praise of La Calprenède. But, on the whole, Callières shews himself to be a far more discerning and a far better instructed critic than either Perrault or Fontenelle. It is perhaps due to his acquaintance as a diplomatist with foreign countries that he includes Italian and Spanish authors, and even the Portuguese Camões, among the Moderns. That he should not have recognised English or any non-Latin literature was only to be expected. It was also to be expected that he should make French literature begin with Malherbe, and should refer slightingly to "poor old Ronsard," who had contracted an asthma by too much singing.

On October 30, 1688, the printing of the first volume of Perrault's *Parallèle des Anciens et des Modernes en ce qui regarde les arts et les sciences* was finished. It takes the form of dialogues, in which the speakers are an Abbé, whom it does not need the avowal of Perrault in the preface to his second volume to identify with Perrault himself, a President, who is represented as a foolish and fanatical admirer of the ancients, and whose only function is to provide themes for the Abbé's disquisitions, and a Chevalier, who passes for a wit but is really a fool, and whom Perrault, as he tells us, uses as a mouth-piece for views which appear paradoxical. The scene is laid at Versailles, than which there could be no spot more fitted to shew off the glories of Louis XIV and his age, and in the adornment of which Perrault had played so large a part.

The first dialogue, which is entitled *De la prévention en faveur des Anciens*, begins with generalities, and there is nothing particular to notice till we come to the now familiar comparison of the duration of the world to the life of a single man, with its corollary that the moderns are the true ancients[1]. Perrault makes it clear that he will depend on France to represent the moderns. He can do very well without Tasso and Ariosto, without Raphael, Titian, and Paul Veronese. With the help of France alone he will prove that there is no art and no science which the moderns have not brought to a higher point of perfection than the ancients.

The second dialogue, which concerns architecture, sculpture, and painting, is of no importance for our purpose. Perrault looks at these arts solely from the point of view of Colbert's *Contrôleur des Bâtiments* or Minister of Works. He only cites Roman examples of ancient architecture. Possibly he had never heard of the Parthenon, or even of the *Maison Carrée* at Nîmes. Certainly he ignores them, just as he ignores the great Gothic cathedrals which are the glory of France. His whole treatment of architecture is marred by pedantry and trivial criticism of details. But it is less ignorant and foolish than his remarks on sculpture and painting. We have a measure of these in the statement that Raphael's pictures are deficient in aerial perspective[2].

Perrault's second volume, containing the third dialogue, did not appear till 1692. Its subject, Eloquence (oratory, philosophy, history, letters, novels), is a wide one, and during the

---

[1] See above, p. 331.

[2] Wotton translates long passages, without criticising them, from Perrault's second dialogue (*Reflections*, c. vi).

four years which had elapsed since the publication of his first volume he had evidently read a good many ancient writers. But he read them in translations, and he consequently defends this practice almost at the outset. He gives two reasons for the superiority of the moderns in eloquence and poetry. The first is that they know the human mind better. The second is that thanks to Descartes—here he is following Fontenelle—they reason better. In his comparisons between individual writers and their works he invariably gives the advantage to the moderns. He ranks Pascal above Plato, Lucian, and Cicero, Voiture above Seneca and Pliny, La Bruyère above Theophrastus, and he considers the funeral orations of Bossuet, Fléchier and Bourdaloue hardly inferior to those of Pericles (as reported by Thucydides), Isocrates, and Lysias. He compares the speeches of Antoine Le Maître to those of Demosthenes and Cicero, and he even suggests the name of Mézeray—though this by the mouth of the irresponsible Chevalier—as a possible rival to Thucydides and Livy.

Poetry is the subject of the fourth dialogue[1]. Nearly a third of it is filled with meticulous and puerile criticisms of Homer. Though Perrault acknowledges that his genius is greater than Virgil's, he prefers Virgil because he is more modern and therefore free from the grossness, puerility, and extravagance of Homer. Passing rapidly over Pindar's *galimatias impénétrable* and the other Greek lyric poets, he comes to Horace, whose Odes he discusses at some length. Then he briefly dismisses Ovid, Catullus, Tibullus, and Propertius with a word of praise and with the criticism that their love-poems are less delicate than those of Voiture, Sarasin, Benserade and a hundred other moderns. He pronounces that in tragedy and comedy the French are supreme. He compares Boileau favourably with Horace in satire, but he blames him for his attacks on individual writers, and he proceeds to defend his victims—Chapelain, Cotin, Cassagnes, Saint-Amant, and particularly Quinault—with considerable spirit. After discussing Horace's *Ars Poetica* he praises the epigram, sonnet and other forms of

---

[1] The printing of the third volume, which contains this dialogue, was finished on September 2, 1692.

"menues poésies," with which Voiture, Sarasin, and an infinite number of other like geniuses "have delighted our age." He even says a word in favour of Burlesque, and lastly—and here posterity for once has abundantly ratified his verdict— he gives unqualified praise to the *Fables* of La Fontaine.

The above is a brief summary of Perrault's laborious and conscientious comparison of the literature of the Greeks and the Romans with that of his own nation during less than a century. It is evident that as regards the ancients he was singularly ill-equipped. He only read Greek in translations and his knowledge of Latin literature hardly went beyond Cicero, Virgil, Ovid, and Horace. The most noticeable omissions are Plutarch, who was read in France as widely as if he were a Frenchman, and Lucretius, who, as well as the other Latin poets, had been translated by the Abbé de Marolles. Perrault's preferences among the moderns are interesting, because they represent those of his party—the party which venerated Corneille as its hero, which kept up the *précieux* tradition and frequented *précieux* salons, and which numbered in the Academy a formidable body of supporters. Perrault, however, has had the wit—let us add, the magnanimity—to strengthen his case by the inclusion of the chief writers in the opposite camp—of Boileau and La Fontaine and La Bruyère. To one man, however—Racine—his magnanimity does not extend. He also includes Bossuet and Bourdaloue, but not La Rochefoucauld or Madame de La Fayette. It is further in his favour that he gives such high praise to Pascal, though doubtless he did not realise the influence that Pascal as well as the ancients had upon Boileau and his friends.

Perrault, as we have seen, claimed that the moderns knew more about the human mind than the ancients. He also claimed that they knew more about the human passions—at least in detail—as shewn in the ethical treatises, tragedies, and romances, produced in France in recent years. "In the tragedies of Corneille alone there are more delicate thoughts on ambition, vengeance and jealousy than there are in all the books of antiquity[1]." There is at any rate this much of truth in Perrault's contention;

[1] *Parallèle* (2nd ed. 1693), II, 29–31.

Descartes's *Traité des passions de l'âme* (1649) and similar works which preceded it had greatly helped to stimulate the growing interest in psychological analysis, and had influenced not only Corneille but the great writers of the next generation, whose psychological realism is the glory of French classical literature.

Perrault sent a copy of his *Parallèle* to his friend Huet, who, though a firm supporter of the ancients, had intimate relations with the opposite camp. Huet acknowledged the work in a long letter, dated October 10, 1692. Beginning with compliments, he proceeds to criticism, and with great frankness and some severity exposes his friend's blunders and defends Homer at length against his ignorant criticisms[1]. In 1693 La Bruyère, who had clearly shewn in *Les Caractères* to which party he belonged, was elected to the Academy[2], and by his aggressive *discours de réception* gave, as we have seen, great offence to the moderns. In March 1694 Boileau published his Tenth Satire[3], which had the effect of making the cause of the ancients still more unpopular with women. It contained a contemptuous hit at Perrault and at his Christian epic of *Saint-Paulin*, which, says Boileau, has twenty times fewer readers than even *La Pucelle*[4]. Perrault avenged himself by writing a preface to his *Apologie des femmes* (March 26, 1694), in which he attacked Boileau's satire in the name of morality and good taste. He sent a copy of his work to Antoine Arnauld[5], who acknowledged it in a remarkable letter dated May 5. The great Jansenist reproaches him with his language about Boileau and justifies the latter's new satire for its treatment not only of women, but of Chapelain, Pradon, and other poets[6]. In conclusion he expresses a fervent hope that the two opponents will become reconciled to one another in a spirit of Christian charity and peace[7].

[1] See Rigault, *op. cit.* pp. 217–219.
[2] Fontenelle had been elected, at his fifth attempt, in 1691.
[3] The printing was finished March 4, 1694.
[4] In editions later than 1698 the 14 lines which refer to Perrault were suppressed.
[5] Perrault's brother Nicolas was a strong Jansenist, and he himself and his brothers, Pierre and Claude, were on affectionate terms with Arnauld.
[6] Boileau, *Sat.* X, 449–460.   [7] Boileau, *Œuvres*, IV, 29–56.

For the moment the prospect of reconciliation seemed remote. A few weeks after Arnauld's letter, probably in June, there appeared a new edition of Boileau's works, which included his long-deferred defence of the ancients. It was prefixed to his translation of Longinus's *Treatise on the Sublime* (first published twenty years before) and was entitled *Réflexions critiques sur ce rhéteur où l'on répond à des objections faites contre quelques anciens*[1]. He could hardly have chosen a less attractive form or title, and the reflections themselves are quite beyond the comprehension of the unlearned reader. Eight out of the nine are wholly occupied with the exposure of Perrault's blunders about Homer (I–VI and IX) and Pindar (VIII). The only one which deals with the question from a wider point of view is the seventh. Taking as his text the words of Longinus, "That we must think of the judgment that posterity will pass on our writings," he declares "that it is only a long succession of years that can establish the value and true merit of a work....It is no longer a question at the present day, whether Homer, Plato, Cicero, Virgil are marvellous writers; it is an incontestable fact, since twenty centuries have agreed about it." Then he gives two examples of how contemporary judgments may be mistaken. Thirty years ago Balzac was regarded not only as the most eloquent man of his age, but as the only eloquent man. But suddenly it was perceived that the art upon which he had been employed all his life, namely, the epistolary art, was the art which he least understood. His letters are full of *esprit* and admirably written, but they have the two vices which are the most opposed to the epistolary art—affectation and bombast. Again, Corneille was regarded as a poet who could never be equalled again in France. But now his merit is reduced to eight or nine plays, and even in these one begins to detect faults. Thus, not only is it permissible to compare Racine with him, but there are plenty of people who prefer Racine. But as yet neither can be compared with Euripides or Sophocles, because they have not

---

[1] There is no imprint, but it must have been published later than March 4 (date of Satire X) and earlier than July 10, the date of a letter, citing it, by Arnauld (Boileau, *Œuvres*, I, clii).

been sealed with the approbation of many centuries. Finally he explains that he does not include among the approved writers third-rate ancients like Lycophron or Nonnus or Silius Italicus, but only the few marvels like Homer, Plato, Virgil, Cicero, etc. "There are plenty of ancients who are not admired, and plenty of moderns whom everyone praises. The antiquity of a writer is not a guarantee of his merit, but the long and constant admiration in which his works have always been held is a sure and infallible proof that we ought to admire him."

But in spite of this attack on Perrault the two opponents were really on the eve of a reconciliation. Boileau, who had been allowed to see Arnauld's letter to Perrault, wrote to the old man to express the pleasure that it had given him. He was especially touched, he says, by the reference to their friendship, and he declares that he is ready to bury the hatchet on one condition only—that the letter should be published. Perrault, who, as Boileau says, was a *galant homme*, accepted the condition, and on August 4, 1694, four days before the death of Arnauld, the two adversaries met and shook hands.

Perrault had not yet finished his task. Towards the end of 1696 he published his fourth and last volume, containing the fifth dialogue[1]. It is of little interest, for it is chiefly concerned with matters about which there was no dispute. Everybody agreed that in studies like astronomy, geography, navigation, and medicine which depend upon experience the moderns were superior to the ancients. Philosophy was more of an open question, and Perrault considers it at some length under the heads of metaphysics, logic, ethics, and physics, with a digression on Descartes's theory that animals are automata. Finally, the self-sufficient and dogmatic Abbé who represents Perrault formulates his conclusion, which is, that "in all the arts and all the sciences, with the exception of eloquence and poetry, the moderns are far superior to the ancients (as I think I have sufficiently proved) and that as regards eloquence and poetry,

---

[1] The printing was finished November 27, 1696, and the date of publication on the title-page is 1696. I do not know why the date is usually given as 1697.

although *there is no reason for judging differently*[1], we must for the sake of peace come to no decision."

Thus Perrault did not budge an inch from his position. But Boileau did not on that account renew the contest. Rather, in order to make their reconciliation public, he wrote in 1700 a friendly letter to Perrault, in which he suggests a compromise[2]. In his opinion, it is impossible to match the age of Louis XIV against all the other nations of the world and all the other ages together, but he is ready to prove its superiority to all the most famous ages of antiquity taken singly, and even to that of Augustus[3]. He admits, indeed, that the French have no epic poets or orators to be named with Virgil or Cicero, that their best historians are far below Livy and Sallust, and that in satire, in spite of Regnier, and in elegiac poetry, in spite of Voiture and Sarasin and the Comtesse de La Suze, the Latins are superior. But in tragedy and comedy the Latins have no one to compare with the great French dramatists, and though France has no writer of Odes as perfect as Horace, she has several poets whose works taken together may be put in the balance against the Latin poet's *Odes*. In physics again the Latins have neither a Descartes nor even a Gassendi, while in learning, astronomy, geography and navigation they are manifestly inferior to the French. So too in the arts; they have only Vitruvius to set against men like Poussin and Le Brun, Girardon and Mansart. In conclusion, Boileau makes a characteristic hit. You may, he says, criticise the *Iliad* and the *Aeneid* as much as you please, provided you do not compel me to read *La Pucelle* or *Clovis*.

Boileau's letter was written with a friendly rather than a critical intent. It must not therefore be examined too closely. But friendly though it is, it is far from being a confession of defeat. The only kind of literature proper in which Boileau admits the superiority of the moderns (as represented by

---

[1] The italics are mine.

[2] *Œuvres*, IV, 86 ff.

[3] The true Augustan age begins with Virgil—B.C. 39 (date of earliest eclogue)—and ends with the death of Ovid (A.D. 17), but Boileau makes extend from Cicero (c. B.C. 70) to Tacitus (c. A.D. 120).

France) is the drama. But that is as far as he will go in literature. He admits the general superiority of the age of Louis XIV, but he bases it on its achievements in the fine arts and in science, and it is only in physics that he ranks Aristotle below Descartes and Gassendi.

With this public expression of reconciliation between the two champions the great Quarrel died down. As a battle of books it had been thoroughly unsatisfactory. Perrault's knowledge of ancient literature was far too slight and superficial to be of any value, and his appreciation, both of modern and of ancient literature, was vitiated beyond remedy by his inability to understand poetry. His view that Homer can be judged in a prose translation as well as in the original Greek puts him hopelessly out of court. On the other hand, Boileau is hardly more effective. Whether he felt that Perrault's ignorance and self-sufficiency made it impossible to meet him fairly, or whether he underrated the influence that his skilful nonsense was likely to have upon less educated readers, he makes no real defence of his clients. In the *Réflexions* he crushes Perrault with his superior knowledge, but he is pedantic and rude, and he confines himself to details about two authors. The only real contribution to criticism is the assertion of the principle which he and his friends had always held, that it is for posterity to judge of the merits of a literary work.

The letter to Perrault then being written solely with a view to an amicable arrangement of their dispute, we must not expect either a complete survey or an attempt at serious criticism. But the preference given to what Boileau arbitrarily calls the Augustan age over the great period of Greek literature from Aeschylus to Aristotle not only confirms what has been said above, that the culture of the French classical age was essentially Latin, but it helps to fix the limitations of Boileau as a critic. His omissions cannot fairly be brought up against him, but one would have expected to find Catullus by the side of Horace as a lyric poet, and Tacitus with Livy and Sallust as a historian. The omission of Lucretius may be an oversight, but it is possible that Boileau did not appreciate him as much as his friend Molière, the pupil of Gassendi, did. The case for the moderns is similarly weakened by the absence of Pascal, whom Boileau admired beyond any ancient writer, of Bossuet and the other great pulpit orators, and of La Fontaine, whom Perrault had rightly placed far above Phaedrus. But, as I said, Boileau does not pretend to be complete and he carefully avoids mentioning any living writer by name.

For twenty years, counting from the reconciliation of 1694, the Quarrel slumbered. Then, with different protagonists and a more limited field of warfare, it broke out afresh. The champion of the ancients on this occasion was Mme Dacier (1654–1720)[1]. The daughter of Tanneguy Le Fèvre[2], "a man of learning and a gentleman" (Saint-Simon), who had excellent views on education, she had received from him a thorough instruction in Greek and Latin, and she had already distinguished herself as a translator of Florus, Callimachus, Anacreon, and Plautus when in 1683 she married André Dacier, an old pupil of her father's, who, like herself, had been active as a translator of the classics[3]. She was as sensible and modest as she was learned.

In 1711[4] she completed and published a work on which she had been engaged for many years, a translation of the *Iliad* into French prose. It was preceded by a long preface, in which she apologises for her temerity and recognises the impossibility of rendering the grandeur, the nobility, and the harmony of Homer's diction, especially in a language like the French, "which is always prudent (*sage*) or, rather, always timid." But a prose translation can at any rate give the ideas and, if it avoids a pedantic and over-scrupulous fidelity, also the spirit of the original. And it can do this better than a verse translation. Though Mme Dacier does not mention any names, her

[1] Sainte-Beuve devotes to her two of his most delightful *causeries* (*Causeries du Lundi*, IX), and Saint-Simon gives her a kindly and charming obituary notice (XVII, 134). See also XIX, 59.

[2] Professor at the Academy of Saumur; he died in 1672.

[3] Among his later translations were Plato, Plutarch, and Aristotle's *Poetics*, with a commentary (1692), which was translated into English in 1705. He was elected to the Académie Française in 1695 and was made Secretary in 1713.

[4] Rigault gives the date wrongly as 1699.

whole preface is a defence of Homer against the criticisms of Fontenelle, Perrault, and other moderns.

She hoped that her work would give those who did not read Greek a truer view of the great poet than translators like Du Souhait or ignorant critics like Perrault. But Fontenelle's friend and ally Houdar de La Motte, who was a modern of the moderns, had his own idea of how to present Homer to the French public. Accordingly at the end of 1713[1] he published a verse translation of the *Iliad*, abridged from twenty-four books to twelve[2] and generally embellished to suit the refined taste of his age. It is a most unhappy performance, and La Motte made it worse by prefixing to it a *Discours d'Homère*, in which he displays in Sainte-Beuve's words "une inintelligence totale du génie de l'antique poète." He protests—and so far of course he is quite right—against a blind and uncritical admiration for Homer, as he had already protested in his earlier *Discours de la poésie* (1707) against a blind and uncritical admiration for the ancients generally. But he goes further than this. He shews no respect for "the admiration of all the centuries," "for to appreciate is the business of Reason alone." This is Cartesianism with a vengeance. La Motte, like Perrault, knew no Greek and he resented the reproach that this put him out of court as a judge of Homer. He retaliates by declaring that no one, however great a scholar, is sufficiently master of Greek to feel Homer's beauties and defects. You can judge of Homer as of the other ancients as well in a translation as in the original. He resents Mme Dacier's assertion that the French language is inferior to the Greek in beauty and that it is too prudent and timid to give a true idea of Homer, and this moves him to an eloquent panegyric on his native tongue, on its elegance, its clarity, its dignity, its tenderness, its naïveté. The panegyric is well deserved, but La Motte forgets that Mme Dacier does not say that the French language was inferior to the Greek, but only that it was not capable of giving a true idea of Homer.

Mme Dacier was thoroughly roused both by the pitiable

---

[1] *Œuvres*, 5 vols. 1754, vol. II.

[2] As La Motte himself points out, they are much shorter than Homer's books.

travesty of Homer and by the preface which preceded it. In
1714 she published a stout volume of 500 pages entitled *Causes
de la corruption du goût*, in which she analyses La Motte's *Iliad*
book by book and attacks his discourse point by point. Her
position was sound, but she damaged her cause in the eyes of
the public by the vehemence and the personalities of her attack.
La Motte replied with his wonted courtesy and moderation
in *Réflexions de la critique* (1715)[1]. It contains little beyond a
repetition in an amplified shape of his former arguments, but
there is one gem which must not be overlooked, and that is the
pronouncement that *Clovis* and *Saint-Louis* (the epic of Père
Le Moyne) are "much better than the *Iliad*."

But we must go back to the year 1714. La Motte, whose
restless vanity impelled him to cultivate friendly relations with
distinguished men of letters, to whichever camp they belonged,
sent a copy of his *Iliad*, as soon as it was published, to Fénelon.
The Archbishop's letter of acknowledgment is delightfully
diplomatic[2]. He leads off with a true Gascon compliment—"je
viens de vous lire, Monsieur, avec un vrai plaisir"—and in what
follows he carefully abstains from a personal judgment. "On
dit," and "Votre parti conclut," are the forms in which he puts
both praise and criticism, and on the great question of the
Quarrel he shews an impartial indifference. In a letter to
La Motte of May 4, he writes more fully on the subject,
without, however, abandoning his neutrality. He does not, he
says, admire the ancients blindly. Even the greatest of their
orators and poets—and among these he does not include
either Aeschylus or Lucretius—have their imperfections. Like
Fontenelle he believes that men in all ages have more or less
the same intelligence and the same talents, but in some
countries, manners, government, and education are more
favourable to the progress of poetry than in others. The "noble
emulation" of the moderns to surpass the ancients cannot be
too highly praised, but it would be dangerous if it led them
"to despise or cease to study these great originals."

---

[1] *Œuvres*, vol. III. It was published in four parts, the printing of the
1st part being finished December 18, 1714. The 4th part was never finished.

[2] January 26, 1714.

In the chapter on Fénelon we saw that the last section of his letter to the Secretary of the Academy was concerned with the Quarrel[1]. It is in part a repetition of what he says in the letter to La Motte, in part a vindication of Homer, especially as a faithful painter of the morals and manners of his day. His heroes and still more his gods are no doubt far below the modern standard of *honnêtes gens*, but he has painted them as he saw them, with force, grace, feeling, and vivacity. The letter was read to the Academy, and La Motte wrote to Fénelon[2] that on the question of Homer both parties claimed him—as no doubt he anticipated—as an ally. In his answer Fénelon re-stated what was after all the fundamental maxim of the party of the ancients. "Il faut observer le vrai et peindre d'après nature[3]."

La Motte flattered himself with the belief that in essentials—for Homer's poetical qualities were nothing to him—Fénelon was on his side. But he had more genuine, if less distinguished, backers in the Abbé de Pons and the Abbé Terrasson. The Abbé de Pons (1683–1732)[4] was a little hunchback, who regarded La Motte as a rare genius. He was always to be found at the Café Gradot (where his hero La Motte, like Dryden at Will's, presided), ready to toss the ball of conversation to his friend on every conceivable subject. He had an excellent heart, says Trublet, he wrote with the same facility as he talked, and he was a courageous and conscientious critic. In the early months of 1714 he published without his name a *Lettre à M.* ✱✱✱ *sur l'Iliade de M. de La Motte.* The *Iliad,* he declares, is at the best a "beau monstre." Homer may be the first man of his rude age, but in the eyes of an enlightened age like that of Louis XIV his poem is very defective. It is far inferior for instance to Addison's *Cato*—the Abbé had read this recently in a translation—which is the work of a great poet, a poet who may be compared with Corneille. As surely as Descartes has overthrown Aristotle

---

[1] See above, p. 280.   [2] November 3, 1714.

[3] In his next letter (December 13, 1714) La Motte expressed a desire for a continuance of the correspondence, but twenty-five days later Fénelon died.

[4] See Sainte-Beuve, *Causeries du Lundi,* XIII, 142 ff. (another charming essay, kindly but critical); P. Dupont, *Houdar de La Motte,* 1898.

so surely will Homer fall before the lance of La Motte. Like La Motte he defends the French language against the depreciatory remarks of Mme Dacier. "A-t-elle mal servi... Corneille, Racine, Molière, Despréaux, La Fontaine?" The names do honour to De Pons's critical penetration, but did he reflect that Racine, Molière, Boileau, and La Fontaine were the very men by whose efforts the classical ideal had triumphed, and whose own writings had been nourished, not on a blind admiration of the ancients but on a careful study of their works?

The Abbé Jean Terrasson's contribution to the controversy did not appear till 1715[1] and was a far bulkier and more ambitious production than De Pons's[2]. It was in two volumes and was entitled *Dissertation critique sur l'Iliade d'Homère, où, à l'occasion de ce poëme, on cherche des règles d'une poétique fondée sur la raison et sur les exemples des anciens et des modernes.* The author (1670–1750), who was a native of Lyons, and who, like his three brothers, two of whom became preachers of distinction, had been educated at the Oratory, was an odd mixture of learning, intelligence, and imbecility. Seeing that he became professor of Greek and Latin philosophy at the Collège de France, it may be presumed that he knew Greek. He was also a geometer, and when Mme Dacier heard of his promised dissertation, she exclaimed, "Un géomètre! quel fléau pour la poésie qu'un géomètre!" She was right; in the name of geometry and logic Terrasson[3] condemned Homer and his admirers, and declared his intention of applying to literature the same spirit of philosophy and reason which had effected such progress in the natural sciences. He rejects Fontenelle's distinction between the natural sciences and literature, and declares that everything is an affair of experience. The superiority of the moderns to the ancients is "a natural and necessary effect of the constitution of the human mind." He follows Fontenelle in recognising the flaw in the comparison

---

[1] The privilege is dated June 25.

[2] Rigault, *op. cit.* pp. 417–426; Vial and Denise, *op. cit.* pp. 31–38.

[3] *Dissertation critique sur l'Iliade*, 2 vols. 1715. Half the book is taken up with *les mœurs*.

between humanity and individual man, and like Fontenelle he declares that the human race reached maturity in the time of Julius Caesar and Augustus[1].

Meanwhile a supporter of Mme Dacier had appeared in the person of Jean Boivin (1663–1746), generally known as Boivin *cadet*, professor of Greek at the Collège de France. But his *Apologie d'Homère et bouclier d'Achille* was so courteous and temperate in tone and so full of concessions that it earned more gratitude from La Motte than from Mme Dacier[2]. The public and the combatants were now getting tired of the controversy, and at last, on April 5, 1716, after some ineffectual attempts to bring about a reconciliation, Jean-Baptiste de Valincourt, the common friend of Mme Dacier and La Motte, invited them, with other representatives of the two parties, to supper. "We drank to the health of Homer," says Mlle Delaunay, who represented neutrality, "and all went off well[3]."

Brossette, the Lyons friend and correspondent of Boileau and J.-B. Rousseau ,writes to the latter on April 24, 1715, that he hears from La Monnoye that "all the young are furious (*déchaînée*) against Homer, and that if the Academy took any part in the quarrel the majority would certainly be for M. de La Motte against Mme Dacier." The champions of the moderns had in fact won the long-contested battle. They had shewn ignorance and partiality, their arguments had been often superficial and unsound, and they had proved themselves incapable of appreciating not only Homer, but any kind of poetry; but they had outwitted their opponents in tactics; they had kept their tempers and, except under severe provocation, had been

[1] "Jamais on n'a exprimé la confiance moderne...avec plus de résolution et plus d'intrépidité que l'abbé Terrasson" (Sainte-Beuve, *Causeries du Lundi*, IX, 505).

[2] We learn from Brossette's letter to J.-B. Rousseau (see below) that Boivin's book was published before April 24, 1715, and that Terrasson's appeared later.

[3] *Mémoires*, ed. F. Barrière, pp. 210–211. Dacier, after his wife's death, was very anxious to marry Mlle Delaunay and M. de Valincourt pressed her to accept him. But Mme de Lambert, "toute moderne," was against it. "Que ferez-vous d'un homme tout hérissé de grec?" The Duchesse du Maine, in whose service Mlle Delaunay was, also expressed her disapprobation. So the match never came off (*ib.* pp. 211–216).

uniformly courteous, they had asserted their opinions with courage and consistency, and they had glorified their age and their country. It was little wonder that the Academy, the salons, and the majority of the reading public, awarded them the victory. And up to a certain point the victory was real and permanent. The tyranny of the ancients was overthrown. They would no longer be regarded as the only possible models. The almost superstitious reverence, which had compelled Corneille to justify by ingenious quibbles his violations of the supposed rules of Aristotle, which had led La Fontaine to apologise for having departed from the dry brevity of Aesop, and La Bruyère to publish his *Caractères* as a modest appendix to Theophrastus, and which had seduced Boileau into so slavish an adherence to the *genres* of the ancients that he ignored La Fontaine's verse fables and Molière's prose-comedies—all this was gone for ever.

But if the victory of the moderns was assured, it was not complete. The ancients ceased to be gods, but they remained heroes. The contention of Perrault and La Motte that the moderns had surpassed the ancients at all points in art and literature as well as in science did not meet with general acceptance; nor did their argument that reason must prevail over the admiration of centuries. Three years (1719) after the reconciliation between Mme Dacier and La Motte there appeared a remarkable work of criticism, entitled *Réflexions critiques sur la poésie et sur la peinture.* It was originally in two volumes, but in the revised second edition (1733) some of the chapters were transferred to a third volume. After this it was frequently reprinted, and in 1770 it reached a seventh edition. There was a Dutch translation in 1740 and an English one in 1748[1]. The author, whose name first appears in the edition of 1740, was the Abbé Jean-Baptiste Du Bos (1670–1742), who was already favourably known for his learning and his services on diplomatic missions. The object of his book is to establish a new theory of aesthetic criticism, founded, not on reason, but on

[1] See the excellent thesis of A. Lombard, *L'Abbé Du Bos, un initiateur de la pensée moderne*, 1913. I have used the sixth edition, 3 vols. 1755, a beautiful specimen of typography.

sensibility[1], and it is not—at least in the first edition—till the end of his book that he devotes eight sections[2] to the question of the ancients and the moderns. In a powerful and well-reasoned section (II, 33) he defends the ancients against the attacks of "our geometer-critics," and incidentally he denies that the moderns reason better than the Greeks and Romans. He is scornful about those who pretend to judge the ancients without knowing Greek or Latin and he is excellent on the subject of translations (II, 35)[3]. And towards the end he asserts with confidence: "Tandis qu'on ne fera mieux, ni même aussi bien que les Anciens, les hommes continueront à les lire et à les admirer" (II, 38)[4].

The greater detachment and wider vision with which Du Bos handled the question of the ancients and the moderns was due partly to the fact that he approached it from a different angle from that of his predecessors, especially that of Perrault. The aim of his book was to establish a new theory of criticism, not to glorify the age of Louis XIV. Perrault in his exaggerated patriotism had presumptuously matched that age against the whole of antiquity, and Boileau in his letter of reconciliation had met him, not by widening the field of the moderns, but by narrowing the field of the ancients. French literature during the period of the Quarrel, when it had turned away from Italy and Spain and had barely begun to discover England, was extremely self-centred. Moreover, it not only ignored other literatures, but it ignored five centuries of its own. For Boileau as well as for Perrault, for Du Bos as well as for Fontenelle, French literature begins with Malherbe[5]. Both Boileau and

---

[1] Du Bos, who knew Locke personally as well as his writings, was no doubt influenced by his theory of sensation.

[2] See the passages quoted by Vial and Denise, *op. cit.* pp. 40–42.

[3] See *ib.* pp. 50–53.

[4] Attention may also be drawn to the remarkable sections (II, 12–20) in which he discusses the causes, moral and physical, of great ages of art and literature. In his treatment of climate (§§ 14–19) he foreshadows Montesquieu. Voltaire gives high praise to his book in his *Catalogue des écrivains du siècle de Louis XIV.*

[5] Boileau, however, having regard to the fashionable cult of Marot, does point out that in the epigram, the *rondeau*, and the epistle Marot, Saint-Gelais, and others are "generally esteemed" (*Réflexions*, c. vii).

Du Bos give Ronsard as an instance of a writer prematurely lauded by his contemporaries and then totally neglected[1]. His subsequent fate might have caused them considerable surprise. Neglected for 230 years, then recalled to the sympathetic notice of his countrymen, and finally established as a great and enduring classic, he certainly calls for some readjustment in their views as to the judgment of posterity.

The popularity of Du Bos's book from 1733 onwards is symptomatic of a reaction from the more extreme views of the moderns. Men like Marivaux, Vauvenargues, and Turgot, who were certainly modern in their sympathies, all recognised that distinction between science and *belles-lettres*, between knowledge and taste which Fontenelle proposed and Terrasson repudiated. "Poetry, painting, music, have a fixed point which is determined by the genius of languages, the imitation of nature, and the limited sensibility of our organs, which they reach by slow stages and beyond which they cannot go. The great men of the age of Augustus attained to it and they are still our models[2]." In the reign of Louis XVI there was a marked return to classicism, though to a classicism more pedantic and less intelligent than that of the age of Louis XIV. In the supplement to the *Encyclopédie* (1776), Marmontel refers to Perrault's contention that the moderns are really the ancients as "ce sophisme ingénieux," and he declares that, though it may possibly apply to the progress of sciences and arts, Perrault cannot seriously think that it applies to taste and genius[3].

If the result of the Quarrel was to break down the authority of the ancients, it did not make French literature altogether free. Rather, it substituted the authority of the moderns for that of the deposed ancients. Corneille, Racine, and Molière took the place of Homer and Virgil, of Sophocles and Euripides. Boileau reigned instead of Aristotle and Horace. Tragedy, in spite of the timid innovations of Voltaire, clung to the type

---

[1] Arnauld in his letter to Perrault (see above, p. 339) speaks of "les pitoyables poésies de Ronsard."

[2] Turgot, *Sur les progrès de l'esprit humain*, 1750, quoted by Vial and Denise, *op. cit.* p. 59.

[3] Vial and Denise, *op. cit.* pp. 74–75.

established by Corneille and perfected by Racine, and it was Racine whom Victor Hugo, Sainte-Beuve, and Stendhal alike singled out for attack, just as Perrault and La Motte had singled out Homer. Comedy fared better, because Molière worked on no stereotyped pattern, but it is noticeable that La Harpe in his *Lycée* gives only a few pages to Marivaux, and selects for special praise *Le Glorieux*, *Le Méchant*, and *La Métromanie*, all of which conform to the pattern of classical comedy as represented by *Le Misanthrope*. Indeed, in his classification by *genres* La Harpe is not a whit less strict than Boileau.

There was yet another authority, more tyrannical because less clearly defined, which restrained the freedom of literature. This was *le goût*. It was a mixture of reason and sensibility. At first, under the influence of Fontenelle and La Motte and other Cartesians, it was more reason than sensibility. Later, perhaps owing to the popularity of Du Bos's book, the element of sensibility increased, and in the *Encyclopédie* (1757) D'Alembert defines it as "le talent de démêler dans les ouvrages de l'art ce qui doit plaire aux âmes sensibles, et ce qui doit les blesser[1]." In the first half of the century *le goût* meant the collective taste of the narrow circle, half worldly and half lettered, which conversed and displayed its *esprit* in the salons of Mme de Lambert and her successors. Later this oligarchy was almost superseded by a monarchy, and *goût* came to mean in practice, if not in theory, the *goût* of Voltaire. Thus, while the Quarrel liberated French literature from one form of compulsion, it replaced it by others. The first critic who judged literature without references to rules or *genres* or *le goût* was Chateaubriand in his *Le Génie du Christianisme* (1802). It was a further evil that the claim put forward so insistently by the later partisans of the moderns, that it was the province of reason, and reason alone, to judge everything, had a sterilising effect on creative literature. The Reason of Descartes, as understood by Boileau, who treated it as the faculty of distinguishing truth from falsehood, had kept the emotions and the imagina-

[1] Art. *Goût* in vol. VII. The article is made up of contributions by Voltaire, Montesquieu, and D'Alembert.

tion under severe control, but the same Reason, as interpreted by Fontenelle and La Motte, tended to banish them from literature altogether. Thus inspiration was checked at its source, and the greatest minds in France became philosophers (in the eighteenth-century sense) rather than creative artists.

It is customary to say that the real significance of the Quarrel lies in its connexion with the idea of human progress. Granting this, it may be pointed out that the supporters of the moderns did not handle the question with much ability or success. The argument put forward by Perrault and Fontenelle that nature is immutable only proved that there was no reason why the moderns should not at least equal the ancients. The distinction between science and *belles-lettres*, suggested but not frankly accepted by Fontenelle, and accepted by Perrault under protest in the interests of peace, only carried them as far as the superiority of the moderns in everything that depends upon experience. And subsequent opinion, even that of eighteenth-century philosophers, tended to confirm this distinction. The analogy between humanity and the life of an individual was recognised by Fontenelle as faulty and misleading. So he first interpreted it in an arbitrary fashion by declaring that the age of Homer was the youth of the world and the whole period from the age of Augustus to that of Louis XIV its maturity, and then abandoned it by assuming that humanity, unlike individual man, would continue in its maturity and never become old or decrepit. Moreover, throughout the whole discussion the moderns concerned themselves solely with intellectual progress. Into the far more difficult question of whether the human race has progressed on the whole in virtue and happiness they did not enter[1]. This was left to the Abbé de Saint-Pierre.

While the Quarrel of the Ancients and the Moderns was occupying the attention of men of letters, a similar contro-

---

[1] Lord Bryce has some cautious and sagacious words on the subject (referred to by his biographer, Mr H. A. L. Fisher) in his Introductory Essay to Helmolt's *The World's History* (I, lviii). "What," he asks, "is the test of Progress?"

versy was going on in the artistic world. The protagonists
were André Félibien (1619–1695) and Roger de Piles (1635–
1709)[1]. Félibien's god was Poussin, De Piles's was Rubens, and
the two parties were known as "Poussinists" and "Rubenists."
The latter were also called "Colourists," for their watchword
was colour, as that of their opponents was drawing. In 1677
De Piles published his *Dialogue sur le coloris*, in 1681 his
*Dissertation sur les ouvrages des plus fameux peintres avec
la vie de Rubens*. In 1685 appeared the fourth volume of Félibien's *Entretiens sur la vie et les ouvrages des plus excellents
peintres anciens et modernes*, which contains the fullest life of
Poussin that we possess. Félibien had behind him the *Académie royale de peinture et de sculpture* and its Director, Le
Brun, who, in the eyes of his admirers, was the greatest
painter in the world. Among the more fervent of his admirers
was Charles Perrault, like him a protégé of Colbert and like
him a firm believer in Descartes. But Le Brun's power was
beginning to decline. His patron, Colbert, died in 1683, and
Colbert's successor in the *surintendance des bâtiments*, who was
Louvois, did not like Le Brun. No sooner had the decoration
of the Great Gallery at Versailles received its finishing touches
in 1684, than Louvois gave the commission to paint the Little
Gallery to Le Brun's rival, Mignard. In 1690 Le Brun died, and
Mignard, the bitter enemy of the Royal Academy, was made
its Director. In 1695 Félibien died. In 1699 his opponent,
Roger de Piles, was elected to the Royal Academy and in the
same year he published a new edition of his *Dialogue sur le
coloris*. During the two and twenty years which had elapsed
since the first edition a remarkable change had come over
artistic criticism. Then Rubens was hardly known in France,
now the leading French painters—Largillière, Rigaud, Des-
portes—had all felt the spell of his influence and that of his
pupil Van Dyck. Three years later (1702) Antoine Watteau,
a young lad of eighteen, a native of Valenciennes, ignorant of
all classical knowledge, and almost self-educated in art, came

---

[1] It is interesting to note that this champion of the moderns in art
painted portraits of Boileau and Mme Dacier.

to Paris. There, in the Luxemburg, he studied with passion Rubens's series of pictures representing the life of Marie de' Medici, and became, like Rubens, while preserving to the full his own individuality, a great colourist as well as a great draughtsman. In 1712 he was promised, if he continued to work, admission to the Academy, and in 1717 he was definitely admitted. He presented as his *ouvrage de réception* the *Embarquement pour Cythère*[1].

---

[1] See for the above L. Hourticq, *De Poussin à Watteau*, 1921.

CHAPTER XI

BAYLE[1]

BAYLE is little read now. Though his style is easy, agreeable, and lucid, it is not distinctive, and it hardly ever rises above

[1] *Œuvres diverses*, 4 vols. fo., The Hague, 1725–1727; 1727-1731; 1737. The edition of 1737 contains practically all Bayle's writings except the Dictionary and a few pieces published with it and some of his letters. Vols. I–III of the edition of 1725-1727 are in the *Bib. Nat.*, but vol. IV (tom. III, 2ᵉ *ptie*) is missing; so far as I know, this edition is not mentioned in any bibliography of Bayle. The usual edition is that of 1727-1731. That of 1737, though it has the imprint of The Hague, was printed at Trévoux.

Pensées sur la Comète, 12mo, P. Marteau, Cologne [Reinier Leers, Rotterdam], 1682; 1683 (much enlarged); *Œuvres*, III; ed. A. Prat, 2 vols. (1911–1912, *Soc. des textes français modernes*). See this last (pp. xv and xviii) for the full titles of the earlier editions. E.T. 2 vols. 1708.

Critique générale de l'Histoire du Calvinisme de M. Maimbourg, 12mo, Ville-Franche [Amsterdam, 1682]; 1683; 1684; 4 vols. 1685; *Œuvres*, II.

Nouvelles de la République des Lettres, 12mo, Rotterdam, 1684-1687; *Œuvres*, I.

Ce que c'est que la France Toute Catholique sous le règne de Louis le Grand, 12mo, Saint-Omer [Amsterdam], 1685; *Œuvres*, II.

Commentaire philosophique sur ces paroles de Jesus-Chri[s]t. Contrains-les d'entrer...Traduit de l'Anglais du Sieur Jean Fox de Bruggs par M.J.F., 12mo, Cantorbery, chez Thomas Litwell [Amsterdam], 1686 (1st and 2nd parts); 3rd part, 1687; *Supplément du Comm. phil.*, etc., Hambourg [Amsterdam], 1688; *Œuvres*, II.

Ce que c'est que la France Toute Catholique and the *Commentaire* with its additions were published (with alterations) by P. Marchand in one vol., Rotterdam, 1713.

La Cabale chimérique, 12mo, Cologne [Rotterdam], 1691; Rotterdam, 1691; 2nd ed. 1691; *Œuvres*, II.

Chimère de la Cabale de Rotterdam, 12mo, Rotterdam, 1691; *Œuvres*, II.

Projet et fragmens d'un dictionaire critique, 8vo, *ib.* 1692.

Additions aux Pensées sur les Comètes, 12mo, *ib.* 1694.

Dictionnaire historique et critique, 2 vols. fo., *ib.* 1697; *revue, corrigée et augmentée*, 3 vols. fo., *ib.* 1702; ed. P. Marchand, 4 vols. fo., *ib.* 1720 (prized by book-collectors, but less complete and correct than the following); 4 vols. fo., Amsterdam, 1730 (with the Life of Bayle by Desmaizeaux); 4 vols. fo., *ib.* 1740 (a copy of the preceding, but with some additions); ed. A.-J.-Q. Beuchot (the editor of Voltaire), 16 vols. 8vo, Paris, 1820. Vol. XVI contains

the Life and a full account of all previous editions. E.T. 4 vols. fo., 1701;
5 vols. fo., 1734–1738 (the work of French refugees whose knowledge of
English was insufficient for their task); *General Dictionary, Historical and
Critical: in which a new and accurate translation of that of Mr. Bayle is
included*, by J. P. Bernard, Thomas Birch, and John Lockman, 10 vols.
fo., 1734–1741.
    Continuation des Pensées diverses, etc., 12mo, Rotterdam, 1694; 2 vols.
12mo, *ib.* 1707.
    Réponse aux Questions d'un Provincial, 5 vols. 12mo, *ib.* 1704–1706;
Œuvres, III.
    Entretiens de Maxime et de Thémiste, 2 vols. 12mo, *ib.* 1707; *Œuvres*, IV.
    Lettres choisies de Bayle, ed. P. Marchand, 3 vols. 12mo, *ib.* 1714 (not
from the originals); ed. Desmaizeaux, 3 vols. 12mo, Amsterdam, 1729
(from the originals); *Œuvres*, IV (with 56 unpublished letters); *Nouvelles
lettres* (150, written to relations), 2 vols. 12mo, The Hague, 1739; *Œuvres
diverses* of 1737; *Choix de la correspondance inédite de Pierre Bayle*, ed.
E. Gigas, Copenhague, 1890 (of great interest). For other recently published letters see Bourgeois and André, *op. cit.* II, 338–339.

    Pierre Desmaizeaux, *La Vie de Monsieur Bayle*, 12mo, Amsterdam, 1712;
2 vols. 12mo, The Hague, 1732 (greatly enlarged). Desmaizeaux wrote soon
after Bayle's death a life of him for Lord Shaftesbury, which was translated
into English and printed in 1708 in vol. II of the translation of the *Pensées
sur la Comète* under the title of *Life of Bayle in a letter to a peer of Great
Britain*. The French edition of 1712 is a re-translation of this. It was
greatly expanded by Desmaizeaux and was printed in the 1730 edition of
the Dictionary and in subsequent editions. Pierre Desmaizeaux (1673–
1745) came from Geneva to England with Lord Shaftesbury in 1699 and
gained his living partly as a tutor—among his pupils was the second Earl
of Macclesfield, the astronomer and P.R.S.—and partly as a writer. Among
his English friends were Sir Hans Sloane, Addison, Anthony Collins,
Bishop Warburton, and Hume. He published the first authentic edition of
Saint-Évremond's writings in 1705, and he wrote lives of Saint-Évremond,
Boileau, Hales, and Chillingworth. He did not know Bayle personally,
but he took great pains to collect reliable information, and his book, which
includes letters and other original documents, though too voluminous, is
thoroughly trustworthy.

    G. G. Leibniz, *Théodicée*, Amsterdam, 1710 (*Œuvres*, 2 vols. 1842, II);
I. D'Israeli, *Curiosities of Literature* (1st ed. 1791), 9th ed. IV, 185–205;
W. G. Tennemann, *Geschichte der Philosophie*, 1819, XI, 251–279; Sainte-
Beuve, *Portraits littéraires*, 1835, I; *Nouveaux Lundis*, IX, 1–30 (article
on Matthieu Marais); L. Feuerbach, *P. Bayle*, Anspach, 1838; Leipzig,
1848; A. Sayous, *Histoire de la littérature française à l'étranger*, 2 vols.
1853, I, 211–374; C. Lenient, *Étude sur Bayle*, 1855; A. Vinet, *Moralistes
des XVIe et XVIIe siècles*, 1859, pp. 295–344; A. Deschamps, *La genèse du
scepticisme érudit chez Bayle*, Liège, 1878; J. Denis, *Bayle et Jurieu,
Mémoires de l'Académie de Caen*, Caen, 1886; E. Faguet, *Dix-huitième*

a certain modest level[1]. As for his subject-matter, his knowledge of history, philosophy, and theology, remarkable though it was for his day, is naturally out of date. Further, his writings, including his Dictionary, are largely controversial, and nothing ages so rapidly as controversy, unless it is vivified by genius. Finally, though he is not dull—for he has a lively mind—his lack of plan and his numerous repetitions and digressions make him often tedious and difficult to follow. There is much that is interesting, but the interest is spaced at long intervals.

But in the history of French thought he is of great importance. He is a link between the rationalism and scepticism, not always anti-Christian, of the sixteenth and seventeenth centuries, and the definitely anti-Christian rationalism of the eighteenth—between Rabelais, Montaigne, Bodin, Charron, La Mothe Le Vayer, Naudé, and Saint-Évremond on the one hand and Montesquieu, Voltaire, Diderot, and the other philosophers, most of whom pillaged him without acknowledgment, on the other[2].

siècle, 1890; J. F. Stephen, *The scepticism of Bayle* in *Horae Sabbaticae* (1892), pp. 174 ff. (first appeared in the *Saturday Review*); F. Brunetière, *Études critiques*, V (1893); L. P. Betz, *Pierre Bayle und die "Nouvelles de la République des Lettres,"* Zurich, 1896; J. Delvolvé, *Religion, critique, et philosophie chez Pierre Bayle*, 1906; H. E. Haxo, *Pierre Bayle and his Literary Taste*, Modern Language Association of America (reprinted from its publications), 1923. There are good accounts in Haag, *La France Protestante*, 2nd ed., and *La Grande Encyclopédie* (by F. Picavet). For full bibliographies see Deschamps and Delvolvé, the former being the rather more complete of the two. To both these writers I am greatly indebted.

[1] Voltaire notes the defects of his style, but not its merits—"sa manière d'écrire trop souvent diffuse, lâche, incorrecte, et d'une familiarité qui tombe quelquefois dans la bassesse" (*Le siècle de Louis XIV*). Contrast this with Boileau, as reported by Brossette: "Bayle est un grand génie. C'est un homme marqué au beau coin. Son style est fort clair et fort net. On entend tout ce qu'il dit" (Marais, *Mémoires*, ed. Lescure, 4 vols. 1863–1868, I, 21).

[2] Voltaire at any rate gives high praise to both his character and his writings. "Cet esprit si étendu, si sage et si pénétrant, dont les livres, tout diffus qu'ils puissent être, seront à jamais la bibliothèque des nations....C'était une âme divine" (Letter to Père Tournemine, 1735, quoted by Sainte-Beuve, *Port. litt.* I, 388). See also the *Catalogue des écrivains* in *Le siècle de Louis XIV*, from which the passage in the previous note is taken. For Voltaire's debts to Bayle see M. Lanson's notes to his edition of the *Lettres philosophiques*, especially those on c. xiii (on Locke).

That the deists and atheists of the eighteenth century found
in his works an arsenal well stocked with weapons for their
purpose is a commonplace, but it is by no means agreed what
Bayle's intention was when he forged them. Was he or was
he not conducting an insidious campaign against Christianity
and religion in general? The question has been answered, in
one way or another, with much confidence, but intercourse
with Bayle should at least teach us to be wary in forming our
conclusion. Critics have been too ready to judge of his work
as a whole, as if his thought never varied. But, as a matter of
fact, his thought, as with all serious thinkers, developed with
the years and under the influence of external events. It will
be well, therefore, to consider his work in the order of its appearance and in conjunction with the circumstances of his life.

Pierre Bayle (1647–1706) was born at Carlat, a small village
in the county of Foix, not far from Pamiers, on the slopes of
the Pyrenees. His father, of whom he was the second son,
was the Protestant minister of the village. Absorbed though
he was in the work of his ministry, he found time to educate
his son, teaching him Latin from an early age and Greek from
the age of twelve. From the first, the young Bayle shewed
an ardent desire for knowledge, being spurred by an eager
curiosity and a retentive memory[1]. His favourite authors were
Montaigne and Plutarch. At nineteen he was sent to a Protestant Academy at Puy Laurens near Castres, but during his
first vacation his health broke down from over-work, and he
did not return there till November 1668. Three months later
he migrated to Toulouse, where there was a Jesuit College of
repute and where he lodged with a Catholic priest. It was an
ordinary thing, says Desmaizeaux, for Protestants to study
with Jesuits, but probably Bayle took this step with the deliberate intention of settling the doubts which the reading of
many books of religious controversy had raised in his mind.
At any rate he was converted to Catholicism and joined the
Jesuit College as a student of philosophy. Eighteen months
later he returned to the religious faith of his family.

[1] At a later age he regretted that there had not been more method in
his studies.

There was no question of self-interest in this double conversion. As Bayle himself explained later, it was the absence
of a "juge parlant," of what another distinguished double convert, Chillingworth, calls an "infallible living guide," that led
him to abandon Protestantism; it was the "excessive worship
of creatures" and the impossibility (as philosophy had taught
him) of transubstantiation that brought him back to it[1]. In
other words, his distrust in the power of human reason to
adjudicate on the variations of the Protestant Churches had
driven him, as it has driven others, to Rome, and reason again
had brought him back to Geneva. But he returned with a
weakened faith and a changed attitude towards religion[2]. He
could not accept dogma when it was disproved by reason, but
neither did he trust in reason as the arbiter. He was left with
a still restless spirit of inquiry, a loyal attachment to his
religious party, and a torpid faith.

That he was perfectly disinterested in his second conversion
is shewn by the fact that as a "relapsed Catholic" he was
condemned, under a recent edict, to exile, and to a man who
had never been more than fifty miles away from his home
this was a severe penalty. His first migration was to Geneva,
where he spent four and a half years (1670–1675), studying
theology (at first as a candidate for the ministry) and Cartesianism. Then, after venturing to Paris, where he had to
support himself by a highly uncongenial tutorship, he gladly
accepted a professorship of philosophy in the Protestant
Academy at Sedan[3]. This he held for six years, but in 1681
Louis XIV, having determined on a policy of violence in
order to obtain religious unity, closed the Academy, and Bayle
had to find a new refuge and a new situation. Thanks to the
influence of Adrian Paets, a brother-in-law of Cornelis de Witt,
he was invited to Rotterdam and granted a pension, with permission to teach philosophy. He arrived there on October 31,

[1] *La chimère de la Cabale de Rotterdam, Œuvres diverses*, II, 759.

[2] Delvolvé, pp. 10–11, has some good remarks on this.

[3] The principality of Sedan was ceded by the Duc de Bouillon to
Louis XIII in 1642 under the promise that all the rights and privileges of
the Protestant Church should be preserved. See Bayle, *La France Toute
Catholique, Œuvres*, II, 344.

1681. It was to be his home for the remaining twenty-five years of his life. Before long he was joined by Pierre Jurieu, whose colleague and friend he had been at Sedan, and, through the influence of Paets, Jurieu was appointed professor of theology and Bayle professor of philosophy and history.

At Geneva he had, as we have seen, at first studied theology. But, when he had given up the idea of entering the ministry, he had turned to Greek, Latin, and history, with a view to obtaining an appointment as a lecturer. He had also attended lectures on the Cartesian philosophy, being chiefly attracted by its physics, but only as an "ingenious hypothesis." He admired equally "the atoms of Epicurus, which the great Gassendi has so ably established." He also studied Spinoza and classical philosophy. But as the result of his studies he wrote to his brother in May 1681: "The more I study philosophy, the more I find uncertainty: the difference between the sects only amounts to a greater or less degree of probability[1]." He was widely read in religious controversy, and was specially attracted by writers of a sceptical tendency. Montaigne, as we have seen, had been a favourite from early days, and to Montaigne he now added his disciple, Charron. In 1675 he writes to his brother that he regarded La Mothe Le Vayer and Gabriel Naudé "as the two best-read *savants* of the century," adding the criticism that "because they pose too much as *esprits forts* they often enunciate doctrines which have dangerous consequences[2]."

---

[1] Quoted by Delvolvé, p. 23.

[2] François de La Mothe Le Vayer (1588–1672) was a man of wide reading, but he had little originality or critical sense, and his style is cumbrous and involved. Though he was a professed sceptic in most matters, arguing on both sides of a question and coming to no conclusion, he made a point of stopping short on the threshold of religion. His best-known writings are *Cinq dialogues faits à l'imitation des anciens par Horatius Tubero*, Frankfort, 1506 [Paris, 1630]; *Petit discours chrestien de l'immortalité de l'âme*, 1637, and *De la Vertu des Payens*, 1642. His collected works were published fairly frequently from 1653 to 1684. Gabriel Naudé (1600–1653), the friend of Gassendi and Guy Patin, took his degrees at Padua and, returning to Italy five years later, spent eleven more years there. Like Le Vayer he was influenced by the Italian free-thinkers of the sixteenth century. He returned to Paris in 1642 to become the librarian, first of Richelieu and then of

We may now come to his first important treatise, generally known as *Pensées sur la Comète.* The comet in question was first observed in Western Europe on December 22, 1680. It had a very impressive tail, but its chief distinction is that it led Newton to determine that comets move in a regular orbit and that this orbit is a parabola. According to Voltaire and to Desmaizeaux, it caused a wide-spread panic, but M. Prat points out that this is a greatly exaggerated view, and he quotes letters from Mme de Sévigné and Bussy-Rabutin and notices from the *Mercure galant* to shew that the attitude, at any rate of the educated classes, was one of curiosity rather than terror[1]. Though the comet gave rise to a large crop of dissertations, Bayle, who was still living at Sedan, determined to add to the number by writing a letter to the *Mercure galant.* But the letter grew into a book, and, when he wished to publish it at Paris, he found that it was a long and troublesome job to obtain the necessary permission. Then came the move to Rotterdam, where Reinier Leers, a man of enterprise and intelligence, undertook to publish it. It appeared in March 1682, under the title of *Lettre à M. L.A.D.C. Docteur de Sorbonne, où il est prouvé par plusieurs raisons tirées de la Philosophie et de la Théologie que les Comètes ne sont point le présage d'aucun malheur.* Bayle took great pains to conceal his authorship. The book was not only anonymous, but it pretended to be the work of a Roman Catholic—a pretence, however, which can have deceived nobody. The familiar disguise of Pierre Marteau, Cologne, was assumed by the publisher, though everyone knew that "Cologne" was in Holland. That country was now of great importance in the publishing world, especially for works which could not have passed the censorship in a

Mazarin. His chief work is *Le Mascurat, ou Jugement de tout ce qui a été imprimé contre le cardinal Mazarin* (1649), a dialogue in which, under the pretext of a defence of Mazarin, he discusses with great freedom all sorts of subjects. See R. Kerviler, *La Mothe Le Vayer,* 1879; Sainte-Beuve, *Portraits littéraires,* II (for Naudé); and for both writers J.-R. Charbonnel, *La pensée italienne au* XVIe *siècle et le courant libertin,* 1919, pp. 49–65.

[1] *Pensées sur la Comète,* I, v–x.

Catholic country[1]. The book was immediately successful and in the following year Bayle published a new and definitive edition under the title of *Pensées diverses écrites à un Docteur de Sorbonne, à l'occasion de la Comète qui parut au mois de Décembre* 1680.

If the comet was the occasion of Bayle's book, it is very far from being its sole topic. Indeed in his penultimate chapter he naively exclaims, "What a strange collection of thoughts I have heaped together," and he compares the irregularity of his work to that of a town which has been built at various dates, with small houses next to large ones, and old ones next to new. It is true that like Charron he has arranged his book under numerous divisions and sub-divisions—reasons, proofs, objections, answers—but this does not make his argument any more consecutive. He begins by proving from numerous historical instances that comets have not generally been fore-runners of great calamities. If they are really presages of calamity, they must be miraculous interpositions of God made for the purpose of warning sinners of the evils that await them if they do not repent. But such warnings given to pagans would only have the effect of confirming them in their idolatry (§§ lvii–lx). And this eventually leads to four propositions. First: "Atheism is not a greater evil than Idolatry" (§ cxiv)[2]. Second: "Atheism does not necessarily lead to the corruption of morals" (§ cxxxiii). Third: "It is contrary to experience that the knowledge of God corrects the vicious inclinations of men" (§ cxxxiv). Fourth: "A society of Atheists would make for itself laws of good behaviour and honour" (§ clxxii).

In an age when atheists were regarded as enemies to society, when, for instance, Locke excluded them from his scheme of

---

[1] See Deschamps, *op. cit.* pp. 92–101, for some excellent pages on the position of Holland as "la grande officine littéraire de l'époque" and as a centre of European thought.

[2] This is the theme of Plutarch's treatise *On Superstition*, from which Bayle quotes a fairly long passage, and of an essay by Bacon, who quotes part of the same passage. Bayle might have found both references in La Mothe Le Vayer's *Cinq dialogues*, a book which was very familiar to him. See also for references to Plutarch's treatise, Shaftesbury's *Characteristics*, 3 vols. 1749, I, 28, and III, 88–89.

religious toleration, one may imagine how dangerous these propositions must have seemed, and Bayle was doubtless only saved from immediate attack because he was not regarded as holding them seriously[1]. But though his arguments are often faulty and his evidence one-sided, he is certainly serious in his main endeavour, which is to make morality independent of religion. In this he is a true disciple of Montaigne and Charron. But while Montaigne came in his later life to hold a fairly high opinion of human nature, Bayle believes firmly in the doctrine of original sin. "The more one proves the corruption of man, the more the reason is compelled to believe what God has revealed to us touching the corruption of Adam" (§ clx)[2].

It has been said that the *Pensées sur la Comète* might have been entitled "A treatise against superstition," for it even notices such minor forms of it as the common beliefs that it is unlucky to sit down thirteen at table or to upset a salt-cellar or to be married in May. But among this "strange collection of thoughts," there are many topics that have less relevance to the main subject. Thus Bayle attacks the vices of contemporary society with all the outspokenness of a Bossuet or a Bourdaloue, and like both these great preachers he is specially severe on *médisance* or evil-speaking. "Nowhere in the world is evil-speaking so rampant as in places where the two sexes are always together[3]." And in a section directed against those who observe religious ceremonies without amending their way of living, he pertinently says: "You abstain from eating meat in Lent, but do you abstain from back-biting your neighbour[4]?"

Some of the ideas which Bayle developed more fully later are to be found in germ in this, his first important work. First, there is his cherished idea of toleration. The banished Protestant would naturally approach it from the Protestant standpoint, but, as he is here wearing the mask of a Catholic,

---

[1] Voltaire examines Bayle's views in his *Dictionnaire philosophique*, art. Athée, Athéisme. He denies that idolatry is more dangerous than atheism, because "the sanctity of oaths is necessary" and atheists think they can swear falsely with impunity. This is practically Locke's view.

[2] Cp. the passages from Bayle's later writings quoted by Prat (II, 75 n.[1]).

[3] § clxviii. Naturally one thinks of Célimène's salon.

[4] § cxxxvii.

he skilfully argues against forced conversions on the ground that Protestants so converted would make bad Catholics[1]. In another section he briefly discusses miracles. Theology and philosophy, he says, alike teach us that we must not multiply miracles unnecessarily. We must, therefore, never have recourse to one when a natural explanation is possible, nor suppose that God has intervened in an extraordinary fashion if such intervention appears useless or contrary to His holiness[2]. For instance, the words "I will harden Pharaoh's heart" seem out of keeping with human ideas of God's justice, but if we had an express revelation to assure us that the words must be taken literally, "the Church would defer to it, imposing silence upon reason[3]." This excessive orthodoxy is, as M. Delvolvé remarks, disquieting, for it introduces in no ambiguous terms that conflict between reason and revelation which appears so frequently in Bayle's later writings.

Bayle's next book was of a different character. In 1682 Louis Maimbourg (1610–1686), whose attractive style and considerable learning had given him a high reputation as a historian and a controversialist, and who had recently been expelled from the Jesuit Order for his Gallican sympathies, published a one-sided history of Calvinism in the interests of Louis XIV's anti-Protestant policy. Bayle's reply, which he wrote in a fortnight, appeared in the following June. It was entitled *Critique générale de l'Histoire de Calvinisme de M. Maimbourg* and was in the form of letters to a friend. It had a great success. A second edition, greatly enlarged, was published in November (1682), and a third, with some further alterations, in May 1684[4]. He begins by complaining that most historians,

---

[1] § lxxxviii.

[2] § ccxxiii. Locke's view, though he never questioned the reality of divine miracles, is similar to Bayle's. See *A Discourse of Miracles* (*Works*, 10 vols. 1823, IX, 256–266).

[3] § ccxxv. Bayle strangely regards the hardening of Pharaoh's heart as an unnatural event rather than as the natural result of constant wrongdoing. He might have cited a stronger instance of God's apparent injustice in the moving of David to number Israel (2 Sam. xxiv, 1).

[4] *Œuvres*, II, 1–160. There are 30 chapters in the 3rd edition and only 27 in the 2nd, but the additional chapters are composed of matter transferred from earlier chapters of the 2nd edition. I have not seen a copy of the 1st edition.

whether contemporary or otherwise, are biassed and deliberately unfair. A flagrant instance are the historians of the
French wars of religion. For his part he will be a Pyrrhonist[1].
But, as a matter of fact, for the rest of the book, which is as
disorderly in structure as his former one, Bayle is a Pyrrhonist
neither in history nor in doctrine. It is true that he is not so
violent a partisan as most of the writers on his side and that
he displeased some of his co-religionists by his relative moderation, but on all disputed questions—on the conspiracy of
Amboise, on the responsibility for the first outbreak of the
war and for that of the second and third "troubles," on the
cause of the Massacre of St Bartholomew—he openly supports his own party. He is equally decided when he comes to
questions of morals and doctrine. He attacks with no sparing
hand the morals of the monks and clergy at the time of the
Reformation and he contrasts with "the horrible disorders of
the Roman Church" the austerity of the reformers[2]. Towards
the end of the book he severely criticises some of the chief
tenets of the Catholic religion—prayers for the dead, confession,
transubstantiation[3], and, above all, the infallibility of the Church,
to which he devotes one whole chapter[4] and parts of others[5].
For he realises that the question of toleration, which he has so
much at heart, is bound up with infallibility. If the Roman
Church is not infallible, her right to persecute at once falls
to the ground. But on what does her claim to infallibility rest?
On tradition? But tradition gives an uncertain note. "We do not
yet know what to believe either with regard to the Immaculate
Conception of the Virgin or with regard to her Assumption."
What is the truth about Grace? Was St Augustine a Jansenist
or a Molinist? Are Popes above councils, as the papal theologians maintain, or is the Gallican Church right in holding
that councils are above Popes[6]? Thus Bayle forestalls Bossuet,
who was to publish his famous *History of the Variations of the
Protestant Churches* six years later, by calling attention to the
variations of the Catholic Church. "Bons arguments pour le
Pyrrhonisme historique" is his comment, but it will be noticed

---

[1] *Lettres* I and II.   [2] *Lettre* IX.
[3] *Lettre* XXVIII.   [4] *Lettre* XXIX.   [5] Parts of XXIV and XXVI.
[6] *Lettre* XXIV, pp. 116–117.

that he is here using scepticism not, like Descartes and Pascal, as a philosophic method in order to arrive at the truth, but as a weapon of attack in order to obtain victory.

Maimbourg was greatly incensed by Bayle's reply and tried to get La Reynie, the Lieutenant of Police, to prohibit its circulation. But La Reynie, who found the book good reading, turned a deaf ear, and it was only after a formal command from Louis XIV that the work was condemned as "defamatory and calumnious" and ordered to be burnt at the Grève (March 9, 1683)[1]. This did not prevent Bayle from issuing, as we have seen, a third edition in 1684, or from publishing in the following January *Nouvelles Lettres de l'Auteur du Critique, etc.* A great part of the new volume is taken up with answering criticisms on the earlier one. Bayle does this with great moderation, though his inveterate love of argument betrays him into a good deal of repetition. The whole tone of the work is lighter than that of its predecessor, especially in the last nine letters (XIV–XXII), which are principally concerned with the motives which lead men and women to marry. As a sort of appendix Bayle discusses Nicole's recently published work, *Les Prétendus réformés convaincus de schisme* and points out that "in matters of religion the criterion (*la règle de juger*) is not in the understanding but in the conscience." "You cannot expect," he says, "simple folk to suspend their judgment till they have reached the certainty required by M. Descartes[2]." Thus, as M. Delvolvé points out, Bayle introduces the moral reason instead of the speculative reason as a criterion of faith, whence it follows that religious belief, being a question of conscience, should not have violence done to it[3].

This, however, was not the opinion of Louis XIV and his advisers, and by Louvois's orders the *dragonnades* were conducted more ruthlessly than ever, especially in Guienne and

---

[1] La Reynie, who had a sense of humour, made Maimbourg draw up the order himself, and had over three thousand copies distributed over Paris, which proved an excellent advertisement for Bayle.

[2] Pp. 333–334.

[3] See Delvolvé, *op. cit.* p. 66.

Languedoc. Bayle's elder brother, Jacob, was arrested and imprisoned, first at Pamiers, and then at Bordeaux, where, ten days before the arrival of an order for his release, he died (November 22, 1685)[1]. In the previous March Bayle had lost his father and, in May 1684, his younger brother, Joseph. The death of his remaining brother cut him to the quick, and all the more because he felt that his own position as a relapsed Catholic had led to his arrest.

His grief and indignation found vent in a short pamphlet, which he entitled *Ce que c'est que la France Toute Catholique sous le règne de Louis le Grand*[2]. As usual, he wrapped up his authorship in mystery. But the style alone, which is more concentrated and more eloquent than usual, would have diverted suspicion. In matter the pamphlet is a powerful indictment of the bad faith and violence of the Catholics in France, in which all alike are accomplices—prelates, priests, monks, courtiers, *bourgeois*, peasants. The one person who escapes is Louis XIV, for whom Bayle had a sincere admiration.

This vehement denunciation of a particular instance of intolerance was followed, in 1686, by a philosophic treatise directed against intolerance in general. It was entitled *Commentaire philosophique sur ces paroles de Jésus-Christ, Contrains-les d'entrer*, and with even greater mystification than usual it was alleged to be translated from English. The pretended place of publication was "Cantorbery[3]." It is divided into two parts. A third part, criticising a letter of St Augustine's against the Donatists, was published in 1687, and a supplement in 1688. Bayle begins by laying down as a principle that "every literal interpretation" (of a passage in Scripture) "which imposes the obligation to commit a crime is false," and the whole of the first part is taken up with reasons against accepting Our Lord's words literally. In the second part he examines the various arguments that have been put forward at different times in defence of persecution, and he compares the Protestant record in this respect favourably with that of

---

[1] The Edict of Nantes was formally revoked October 18, 1685.
[2] Saint-Omer [Amsterdam], 1685; *Œuvres*, II, 336-354.
[3] See bibliography above; *Œuvres*, II, 355-444.

the Catholics. He rightly stigmatises the burning of Servetus as "a hideous blot" on the Reformation, but he is hardly fair in regarding it as a "relic of Papacy," which would not be repeated[1].

Bayle, as one would expect, makes no exception to his theory of tolerance. Jews, Mahometans, Pagans, Socinians must all alike be exempt from persecution for their religious opinions. But if these opinions lead them to words or acts dangerous to public order, it is for the magistrates to protect society. This is more or less on the lines of Locke's famous letters on toleration, for though the English philosopher, less tolerant than Bayle, excepted Papists and Atheists, this was for political, not religious, reasons[2]. As in all Bayle's writings, his argument is constantly interrupted by long-winded digressions and does not follow any preconceived plan. But the gist of it is that persecution is a violation of the moral reason, and chapters VIII and IX of the second part, in which the rights of conscience are carefully examined, have a special importance[3].

Bayle's pen was always busy, but it was never so busy as at this period of his life. Simultaneously with his warfare on intolerance he was giving a fine example of tolerance as editor of the *Nouvelles de la République des Lettres*, a review which he founded in March 1684. It was modelled, with some deviations, on *Le Journal des Savants*, the earliest literary review, which was founded on January 5, 1665, by Denis de Sallo, a councillor of the Paris *Parlement* and a man of wide erudition and sound judgment[4]. It appeared every

---

[1] P. 415. See Acton on *The Protestant theory of persecution* (*The History of Freedom and other essays*, 1907) and Lecky, *Rationalism in Europe*, II, 39–57.

[2] Locke's first three letters were published 1689–1692 and the fourth after his death.

[3] Lecky regards the *Commentaire* "as one of the most valuable contributions to the theology during the seventeenth century and as forming more than any other work the foundation of modern rationalism" (*op. cit.* II, 60). But this is an exaggerated estimate. Feuerbach thinks that in form it is perhaps Bayle's worst writing.

[4] For what follows see E. Hatin, *Hist. de la Presse en France*, 2 vols. 1859, II, 151 ff.; Bourgeois and André, *op. cit.* IV, Nos. 1947 ff.; Hallam, *Literature of Europe*, III, 545–550.

Monday in the form of twelve quarto pages[1]. According to the preface of the first number, its object was to bring to notice every new event in the republic of letters, and its features were to be a list of new books with short reviews of the more important ones, *éloges* of distinguished men, and accounts of experiments in physics and chemistry. Sallo carried out this programme till March 30, when, owing to the machinations of the Jesuits, who detested him as a Gallican and therefore suspect of Jansenism, his privilege was withdrawn. However, the publication of the *Journal* was revived in January 1666, under the editorship of the Abbé Gallois, who began brilliantly, but soon became careless and unpunctual. He was succeeded in 1675 by the Abbé de La Roque, whose punctuality and business-like habits were his chief merits[2].

While *Le Journal des Savants* was addressed to serious readers, *Le Mercure galant* appealed to a wider and more frivolous public. Founded in 1672 by Donneau de Visé, it appeared for two years, and then, after an interval of three years, re-appeared in March 1677, as a monthly publication of about 150 to 200 12mo pages[3]. Its chief contents were notices of plays, reviews of *livres de galanterie*, original compositions (*histoires amoureuses* and a little poetry), obituaries of distinguished persons (not necessarily authors), and news of various description.

Bayle's idea for his new review was that, like *Le Journal des Savants*, it should deal almost exclusively with solid and serious works, but in a lighter and livelier manner. The first number, which was for March 1684, did not appear till the middle of May, but from July onwards the review was published regularly in the first days of the month after it

---

[1] There was also an Amsterdam edition in 12mo.

[2] From 1688 to 1701 the editor was Louis Cousin, known as a translator of the later Greek and Latin historians. In 1702 the Chancellor Pontchartrain bought the *Journal* for the State and entrusted it to an editorial committee.

[3] In 1690 Thomas Corneille joined Donneau de Visé as co-editor; on the latter's death a privilege was granted, as we have seen in chapter IV, to Charles Dufresny, who edited it from 1710 to 1713 (see above, p. 131).

was due[1]. It consisted of 120 pages 12mo of about the same size as *Le Mercure galant* and the Amsterdam edition of *Le Journal des Savants*, and from May onwards it was composed of (1) *Articles* or fairly long reviews, and (2) *Catalogue des livres nouveaux* or short notices. In either division there appeared from time to time extracts from letters of correspondents, or accounts of experiments or receptions at the Académie Française (those of La Fontaine, Boileau, and the younger Corneille). Among the books reviewed, theological works, especially those of a controversial nature, are the most numerous. The long controversy between Arnauld and Malebranche, arising out of the latter's *Recherche de la Vérité*, is followed with close attention, but on the whole pure philosophy occupies less space than theology. Other subjects of review are classical editions (almost entirely Latin), history, mathematics, hydrostatics, astronomy, medicine, and surgery. It is characteristic of Bayle that he is keenly interested in curious and abnormal cases. *Belles-lettres*, as we shall see, are very sparsely represented. Most of the articles were written by Bayle himself, a feat which testifies to the extent and versatility of his erudition. For mathematics and natural science he was greatly helped by the *Philosophical Transactions* of the Royal Society (founded 1665) and the *Acta Eruditorum* of Leipzig (founded 1682), which he read regularly. Friends and correspondents sent him complete articles, or gave him information in letters from which he made extracts. Among these helpers were Daniel Larroque, a Protestant minister, who in 1684 took refuge in England, where he lived, partly at Oxford and partly in London, till 1686[2]; Pierre Allix, the well-known preacher, who founded a church in London for Protestant refugees and was made a D.D. of Oxford and Cambridge; and another resident in England, the physicist, Denis

---

[1] See esp. L. P. Betz, *Pierre Bayle und die "Nouvelles de la République des Lettres,"* Zurich, 1896.

[2] See Gigas, *op. cit.* pp. 415 ff. for his letters to Bayle; Nos. ix to xi are of great interest. In No. x (July, 1686) he says, "Je regretterai toute ma vie le temps que j'ai passé hors d'Oxford." He returned to France in 1690, and soon afterwards abjured Protestantism.

Papin, who sent him French translations of papers which he had published in the *Philosophical Transactions*[1]. In France he had his old friend and colleague of the Sedan Academy, Jacques Du Rondel[2], and in Holland the Arminian theologian, Jean Le Clerc, who, young though he was, had already given proofs of that erudition which was to become even more extensive than Bayle's[3].

Bayle's choice of books for reviewing was necessarily determined by what publishers sent him. In a notice prefixed to the March number of 1686 he complains of the difficulty of getting books printed out of Holland. There were a few from France, none from Italy and Spain; of English books there was a "terrible dearth," and for Germany he had to depend on the two Frankfort fairs. But in spite of difficulties Bayle's venture proved a signal success. He received letters from all quarters, testifying how greatly the new review was appreciated and how eagerly the next number was looked for. Although its circulation was forbidden in France[4], it found plenty of readers there. Benserade wrote him a flattering letter on behalf of the Académie Française thanking him for a copy and asking him to send them the *Nouvelles* every month. "Nous demeurâmes tous d'accord de votre mérite[5]." Among his admirers were the great Condé, who became a regular subscriber, Malebranche, Melchisedech Thévenot, Mme de La

---

[1] 1686, pp. 570 ff. and 670 ff. (with illustrations).

[2] Gigas, *op. cit.* pp. 362–370.

[3] *Ib.* pp. 449–469. "Le plus grand mérite de Leclerc est d'avoir approché de Bayle, qu'il a combattu souvent. Il a beaucoup plus écrit que ce grand homme; mais il n'a pas connu comme lui l'art de plaire et d'instruire, qui est si au-dessus de la science" (Voltaire, *Siècle de Louis XIV*). In 1686 Le Clerc began to publish the first of the three reviews by which his name is best known. This was the *Bibliothèque universelle et historique* (1686–1693). It was followed by the *Bibliothèque choisie* (1703–1713) and by the *Bibliothèque ancienne et moderne* (1714–1727). All were published at Amsterdam. He was a friend of Locke's.

[4] Apparently early in 1685, at the instigation, it was suspected, of the Abbé de La Roque, the editor of *Le Journal des Savants* (Gigas, *op. cit.* p. xiii).

[5] May 18, 1685 (*Œuvres*, IV, 618); it is quoted by Betz, *op. cit.* pp. 101–102.

Sablière, and the traveller François Bernier[1]. The Royal Society was equally complimentary with the Académie Française and sent him, with a letter (May 13, 1686) by its Secretary and former President, Sir John Hoskyns, a copy of Francis Willughby's *History of Fishes*, which his friend and former tutor, John Ray, had just published, fourteen years after his early death in 1672[2]. Bayle acknowledged the compliment by reviewing not only Willughby's book[3] but also the first volume of Ray's *History of Plants*[4], which appeared soon afterwards. Charles Ancillon from Berlin, Jacques Lenfant from Heidelberg, Jean Chouet and Vincent Minutoli from Geneva, all sent reports of the success of the new review[5].

Criticisms, however, were not wanting, and they were passed on to Bayle by his friends. He was blamed for taking a side in controversial questions, for making reflections and criticisms on books, instead of merely giving an account of them, and for praising inferior authors too highly[6]. The second charge is singularly wide of the mark. "Lorsqu'il s'agit de rendre compte d'un livre, j'y apporte toute l'attention dont je suis capable," and he writes his review in easy and unpedantic language with remarkably little criticism[7]. His fault is that he is too good-natured, even to the extent of allowing authors to puff their own productions[8]. As to the first charge he could justly have pleaded that had he been entirely free from bias he would have failed to interest his readers. But even his Protestant bias, with which Malebranche gently reproaches him[9], is no[t]

[1] See Gigas, *op. cit.* p. 125 for a letter from P. Allix, and pp. 184–194 for letters from Bernier.
[2] *Œuvres*, IV, 622–623.   [3] June 1686, art. ix.
[4] November 1686, art. vii.
[5] See Gigas under the names of these correspondents.
[6] See Gigas, *op. cit.* pp. 125–126 and 447–448.
[7] A good example of his method is the review of Guy Patin's *Letters* (1684, pp. 107–118).
[8] A rather flagrant instance is that of Gregorio Leti and his *Life of Sixtus V* (July 1686, art. ix), which damaged the Pope's reputation, till Ranke 150 years later exposed Leti's untrustworthiness. In April 1684 (art. iv) Bayle had printed a laudatory review of his *Teatro Britannico*, written by Le Clerc, who was Leti's friend and later his son-in-law.
[9] Gigas, *op. cit.* p. 511.

very pronounced, and in the long controversy between Malebranche and Arnauld it is with Malebranche, *pace* Sainte-Beuve,
that his sympathies evidently lie[1].

Literature proper, as I have said, finds little place in the
Nouvelles, but that is partly because during the three years of
Bayle's editorship very little of any importance was published.
Except for funeral orations by Bourdaloue and Fléchier (which
Bayle notices) and two by Bossuet, the chief French productions
of these years were Fontenelle's *La Pluralité des Mondes* and
Histoire des Oracles[2], both of which he reviews at some length,
partly, no doubt, because the subject-matter interested him.
But it is a mistake to accuse Bayle, as some critics do[3], of an
absolute lack of literary taste. No doubt he was less interested
in pure literature than in theology or history or philosophy,
but there are judgments of his on all the great writers of his
age (except, I think, on Bossuet) which shew that he appreciated them at their true value[4]. His favourite poet among the
moderns seems to have been La Fontaine[5], and he declares
that neither the Greeks nor the Romans have produced anything as good.

> I do not know what we should do to moderate the transports of *Messieurs
> les Humanistes*, if they had to comment on an ancient author who dis-
> played as much delicate wit, so many natural beauties, so many lively and
> piquant charms as are to be found in this work[6].

The reference to *Messieurs les Humanistes* is interesting. It
shews that Bayle was more in sympathy with the Moderns
than with the Ancients, and we know from letters that he
was in friendly relations with Perrault who certainly regarded

---

[1] Sainte-Beuve says, "Les idéalistes comme Malebranche font les
affaires des sceptiques comme Bayle." See *Port-Royal*, 6th ed. V, 348–
450, for an account of the controversy.

[2] May 1686 and February 1687.

[3] For instance, Betz, *op. cit.* pp. 82–85.

[4] See H. E. Haxo, *Pierre Bayle and his Literary Taste* in the *Publications of the Modern Language Association of America*, XXXVIII, No. 4,
esp. pp. 849–853, where Bayle's judgments are cited.

[5] La Fontaine in turn thought highly of Bayle (see *Lettre à M. Simon
de Troyes*, 1686).

[6] April 1685.

him as an ally[1]. But even if Bayle had not been a sworn foe to absolute opinions, he was far too well versed in Greek and Roman literature to belittle the ancients as Perrault or Fontenelle did. A man who could say at eight and twenty that "the genius of the Greek language was a thousand times more delicate than that of the Latin" had the root of true criticism in him[2].

In February 1687 Bayle's health broke down and he had to give up the *Nouvelles de la République des Lettres*. The editorship was entrusted by the publisher to other hands and the review was continued with interruptions till 1718, but it lost the distinctive character which Bayle had impressed on it. His real successor, the successor of his choice, was Henri Basnage de Beauval (like his more distinguished brother, Jacques, a refugee in Holland), who believed he could best carry out Bayle's wishes by founding a new review. It appeared in September, 1687, under the title of *Histoire des Ouvrages des Savants*, and was carried on with success till 1709, the year before Basnage's death[3].

In the spring of 1688 Bayle began to lecture again, but his health was not fully restored till some months later. For the next three years he was engaged in an increasingly bitter controversy with his old friend, Jurieu, who since the death of Jean Claude in 1687 was regarded as the leader of the French Protestants[4]. Jurieu had already attacked the *Commentaire philosophique* with its doctrine of universal tolerance in an anonymous treatise, *Des droits de deux Souverains en matière de religion, le Conscience et le Prince* (1687), and Bayle had briefly replied in the preface to his *Supplément du Commentaire philosophique* (1688)[5].

---

[1] Du Bos to Bayle, 1696 (Gigas, *op. cit.* p. 248) and Perrault to Bayle, 1694 (*ib.* pp. 603–604).

[2] In the article in the Dictionary on Andromache, note H, he says that Homer is "trop grand parleur et trop naïf." "S'il vivoit aujourd'hui il feroit un poème épique où il ne manqueroit rien."

[3] The only other review of this period that need be mentioned is the well-known Jesuit *Journal de Trévoux*, the proper title of which is *Mémoires pour servir à l'Histoire des Sciences et des Beaux-Arts, recueillis par l'ordre de S.A.S. Monseigneur le Prince souverain de Dombes* (Louis-Auguste de Bourbon, who set up a printing-press at Trévoux). The first number appeared in 1701. See Hatin, *op. cit.* pp. 260–279.

[4] See Delvolvé, *op. cit.* pp. 143–217.

[5] *Œuvres*, II, 497 ff. Bayle says that he had completed in December

Then at the beginning of 1689 there appeared a short pamphlet entitled *Réponse d'un nouveau converti à la lettre d'un réfugié*[1], in which the Protestants were vehemently attacked for their past and present intolerance, and this was followed at the beginning of 1690 by *Avis important aux réfugiés sur leur prochain retour en France*[2], a much longer work, which was even more bitter in character. The refugees are warned that if they wish to return to France they must no longer indulge either in "satirical writings" abusive of France and her king (point I) or in "seditious writings" which inculcate the pernicious doctrines of the sovereignty of the people and the right of rebellion (point II). Both works were anonymous, but Jurieu came to the conclusion that Bayle was the author and consequently, nearly a year after its publication, attacked him[3] in unmeasured terms. A long duel ensued, to which Bayle's principal contributions were *La Cabale chimérique* (May 1691)[4] and *Chimère de la Cabale de Rotterdam* (September 1691)[5]. His last and not least formidable thrust was delivered in Latin—*Janua coelorum reserata cunctis religionibus* (1692)[6].

Was Bayle the author of the *Avis aux réfugiés*? He persistently denied it, and in the second part of the *Cabale chimérique*, which is very well written[7], he rebuts with great skill and evident enjoyment all Jurieu's arguments in favour of his authorship.

1687 a long treatise in three parts by way of answer, but that he had determined to suppress it. The state of his health shews that this was only one of his mystifications.

[1] *Ib.* pp. 561–572.

[2] *Ib.* pp. 577–633. There is a preface explaining that the writer of it had received the work for publication from an old friend, that he was greatly surprised and shocked by it, and that he intended to write a vigorous reply.

[3] *Examen d'un libelle contre la religion, contre l'État et contre la Révolution d'Angleterre*, 1690.

[4] *Œuvres*, II, 635–685.

[5] *Ib.* pp. 717–788. For a full list of the pamphlets see Delvolvé, *op. cit.* p. 196 n.[3] and Prat, II, xxii–xxiii.

[6] *Ib.* pp. 817–902.

[7] It even reminds one at times of *Les Provinciales*; indeed towards the end of the postscript there is a quotation from that masterpiece of controversy.

A simple denial would no doubt have carried more weight than this wealth of clever dialectic. But it seems incompatible with Bayle's high character for honesty and his long fidelity to his religious party that, fond though he was of assuming a mask, he should have chosen that of a violent and intolerant Catholic, and that he should have envenomed his attack on his fellow-Protestants with gross historical misrepresentations and even have adopted from time to time a tone of snuffling hypocrisy. In a letter to his friend, David Constant, professor of theology at Lausanne, he says that the public voice ascribed the *Avis* to Daniel Larroque, who, either just before its publication or shortly afterwards, abjured Protestantism[1]. Basnage de Beauval, whom Desmaizeaux consulted on the point when he was writing Bayle's life, agreed with this, but added that he believed Bayle wrote the preface. Desmaizeaux, though he included the *Avis* in Bayle's *Œuvres diverses*, accepted Basnage's opinion, but with his usual conscientiousness he notes that Moetjens, who published it, ascribed it to Bayle and that one Louis, Moetjens's proof-corrector, told somebody, who told Desmaizeaux, that the manuscript was in Bayle's handwriting throughout[2].

In spite of these two pieces of evidence, the second of which, being at third-hand, is of little or no value, I agree with M. Deschamps in accepting Basnage's opinion that Bayle was not the author of the *Avis*, but that he received it from Larroque for publication, had it printed, and wrote a preface

---

[1] October 24, 1690 (*Œuvres*, IV, 644). Jurieu and others at first believed that the author was Paul Pellisson, the historian of the Académie Française, who after his release from the Bastille, had abjured Protestantism, taken Orders and been rewarded with rich benefices. But, though he corresponded with Leibniz on the subject of tolerance, the *Avis* is very foreign to his amiable character.

[2] Desmaizeaux's defence of Bayle on the supposition that he wrote the *Avis* is lame and unconvincing. Equally unconvincing is Jean Chouet (in a letter to Bayle), who believed the writer to be a Protestant (Gigas, *op. cit.* p. 207). On the other hand, Vincent Minutoli, also in a letter to Bayle (Gigas, *op. cit.* p. 547), said that the author was all the more dangerous because he wrote "d'une manière fine et délicate," and Basnage de Beauval roundly called it an "ouvrage odieux.'

to it[1]. Even so, we must admit with Sainte-Beuve that, whether he wrote it or merely revised it and had it printed, "the whole affair is the sorriest episode of his life[2]."

The controversy over the *Avis* had hardly died down, when Jurieu launched a fresh and more dangerous attack on his opponent. Going back to the *Pensées diverses sur la Comète*, he based upon it a charge of atheism[3], with the final result that the magistrates of Rotterdam dismissed Bayle from his professorship and forbade him to teach even in private (October 30, 1690). Although this deprived him of a considerable source of income—the pay of his professorship was 500 florins—he bore the blow with philosophic calm. "Je n'aime point assez les conflits, les cabales, les entre-mangeries professorales, qui règnent dans toutes nos Académies. *Canam mihi et Musis*[4]." It was no doubt of the Dictionary that he was thinking, as a preparation for which he had already published *Projet et fragments d'un dictionnaire critique*[5].

In a long preface to the *Projet*, addressed to his friend, Jacques Du Rondel, he announces his intention. It was to compile the largest collection that he possibly could of the errors which are to be met with in existing dictionaries[6] and to add articles (*faire des courses*) on all sorts of authors, when

---

[1] Deschamps, *op. cit.* p. 171 n.[1]

[2] *Port. litt.* I, 386. The majority of modern writers on Bayle, from Gibbon downwards, regard him as the author of the *Avis*. M. Delvolvé even finds a striking agreement between its essential ideas and Bayle's doctrines (see *op. cit.* pp. 186–194). I ought in fairness to call attention to the fact that on the question of the authorship of the *Vindiciae contra tyrannos* there is a close similarity between the *Avis* and the article on Junius Brutus in the *Projet d'un dictionnaire*. But Bayle may have borrowed from the *Avis* without having written it.

[3] *Courte Revue des maximes de morale*, cited by Bayle in the *Additions aux Pensées diverses* (*Œuvres*, III, 161–186).

[4] Bayle to Minutoli (cited by Delvolvé, *op. cit.* p. 217).

[5] Rotterdam, May 1692. The copy in the Cambridge University Library was presented by Bayle to the "pensionnaire" Beyer, with an inscription in his handwriting. It formed part of Bishop Moore's library, which George I bought and gave to the University in 1715. Bayle began to publish the Dictionary in December 1690, but was interrupted by the controversy with Jurieu after the first leaf was printed.

[6] "Le but et l'esprit de ce dictionnaire...[est] de rassembler bien des mensonges et bien des fautes" (*Dict. hist.* art. Abel).

opportunity presented itself. For this "sketch" or "forerunner" of his great work he had chosen as specimens not the least bad articles, but those which he thought most open to criticism (*qui m'étaient les plus suspects*). They are twenty-two in number, the most important perhaps being those on Antoine Arnauld and Stephanus Junius Brutus (the pseudonymous author of the *Vindiciae contra tyrannos*). The long article on Erasmus is of little value.

The main work, the *Dictionnaire historique et critique*, appeared in 1697 in two volumes folio, and in 1702 Bayle published a second edition, revised and considerably enlarged, in three volumes. He still adhered to his project of making it the aim of his Dictionary to collect errors and untruths (*bien des mensonges et bien des fautes*), but he now divided his articles into two parts, of which one is "purely historical—a narrative of facts," the other "a Commentary—a mixture of proofs and discussions, and sometimes a tirade of philosophical reflections." Of these the notes—or, as he calls them, *remarques*—occupy by far the greater space and are of far greater interest than the text. For instance, the article "Anaxagoras" consists of 105 lines of text and $12\frac{1}{2}$ folio pages in double column of notes[1]. Note C which deals with the errors of Moreri is divided into nine heads, numbered I to IX. Moreri was Bayle's immediate predecessor and, though Bayle is never tired of pointing out his mistakes, he fully acknowledges his merits as a pioneer[2]. His dictionary—*Le Grand Dictionnaire Historique*, 1674 (one volume folio)—he says, "has shed light in places to which other books would never have penetrated." Its utility, indeed, is proved by numerous editions, which appeared at intervals till 1760, when the twentieth and latest was published in ten volumes folio, though by this time little of Moreri was left. "C'est une ville nouvelle, bâtie sur l'ancien plan," said Voltaire.

---

[1] The notes are distinguished by the letters of the alphabet, and in the margin are references to authorities in Arabic numbers.

[2] Louis Moreri died in 1680 at the early age of thirty-seven. The 2nd edition of his Dictionary was published in 1681. See R. C. Christie, *Selected Essays*, 1902, pp. 10–12.

Bayle's Dictionary is sometimes said to be a supplement to
Moreri. But it is only so in the sense that it makes a point of
correcting his mistakes and that it sometimes gives as a reason
for the brief treatment of a name that it has been fully treated
by his predecessor. Otherwise Bayle's choice of names is purely
arbitrary. As Faguet says, his work ought to be entitled, "What
M. Bayle knows." And what he knew was ancient and modern,
but not medieval, philosophy, mythology, theology, the history
of religions, and the history and religious controversies of the
sixteenth and seventeenth centuries. His knowledge of ancient
history, especially of Greek history, was not great. Polybius's
name does not occur in the index, and that of Thucydides only
twice. He would have been a better historian if he had studied
them. He was not much interested in literature from the purely
literary point of view, but he was well read in ancient literature
and quotes freely from it. He knew little about French medieval
literature, but on that of the sixteenth century he was better
informed than most of his contemporaries[1]. His notices of
Renaissance humanists and scholars are often full and good[2].
As might be expected from his method, or rather his want of
method, there are some disappointing omissions. Chief of these
are Plutarch, Montaigne, and Plato, from all of whom, however,
he quotes frequently in the notes, while the article on Aristotle
deals almost entirely with his life and hardly at all with his
writings[3].

With rare exceptions all the articles were written by Bayle
himself and they testify to the breadth and solidity of his
erudition—an erudition all the more remarkable when one
considers how few summaries and books of reference and
other short cuts to knowledge there were in his day. Moreover at Rotterdam, as he not unfrequently complained, he had
far less opportunity for consulting books than if he had
lived at Paris. The article on Euripides may be taken as a fair

---

[1] Cp. Faguet, *Dix-huitième siècle*, p. 22.

[2] E.g. Agricola, Amyot, George Buchanan, Budé, Daurat, Emilius
Paulus.

[3] He refers his readers to Moreri's long article.

example of his work. His main source is the edition, with a
life prefixed, which Joshua Barnes, Professor of Greek at
Cambridge, had recently published (1694), and some of his information is derived at second-hand from Barnes. But he cites
or refers to between thirty and forty authorities whom he has
consulted at first-hand. About half are Greek or Latin pagan
writers; the rest are either ecclesiastical writers (Eusebius,
Origen, Clement of Alexandria) or scholars of the Renaissance
(Coelius Rhodiginus, Lilius Giraldus, Erasmus, Gesner) or the
seventeenth century (Grotius, Balzac, Menage, Boileau, Sir
Thomas Browne). The whole article occupies eight pages, of
which only sixty-four lines are text, while the rest is filled with
thirty-two long notes. Moreover Bayle deals with his sources
with the accuracy and candour of a true scholar. He gives
full references, and if he quotes at second-hand, or if he has
not been able to consult some special authority, he frankly
says so.

The blemishes are as patent as the merits. We need not
waste time over the indecencies. He has defended them in
the last of four *Éclaircissements* which were published at the
end of the Dictionary from 1720 onwards, but the defence,
which is very long and is evidently written with his tongue in
his cheek, is worthless. "Lasciva est nobis pagina, vita proba,"
was true in his case, if not in Martial's, but it is no excuse.
He does not realise that his offence is, first, that when an
opportunity for indecency presents itself he seizes it with
both hands, and second, that he introduces it where it is unnecessary or even quite irrelevant. It should be added in
fairness that he has no immoral intent; his indecency is partly
that of a schoolboy, partly that of a recluse who is ignorant
of the ways of society, and especially of female society. A
somewhat similar fault is his love of old wives' stories and
other trivialities[1]. In fact, his curiosity about unimportant details

---

[1] The article "Achilles" is a good instance of the mixture of out-of-the-
way erudition with frivolity. It discusses among other things Achilles's
precocious love affairs and whether he was fed with lion's marrow. In the
article on St Augustine there is a long discussion on the exact meaning of
crapula.

and his readiness to accept scandalous reports are decided drawbacks to his merits as a critical historian. We must not, of course, judge him by the standard of modern historical research, but the easy credence which he gives to the stories of a malicious retailer of scandal like Brantôme or an uncritical, if honest, biographer like Suetonius, forbids us to recognise in him the "perfect critic" that he is sometimes represented to be. On the other hand, it is to his credit that he shews a growing distrust of that dishonest impostor, Varillas, whose great reputation had already begun to decline, till finally "un Varillas" became synonymous with an untrustworthy historian. We must remember too that in Bayle's day historical research was at a low ebb in France. Mézeray, whose conception of history was a purely literary one, was still the historian who best fulfilled the demands of the public[1]. The attempt of his predecessor, Scipion-Dupleix[2], to write history from the original sources had been premature, though its failure was due partly to its decided monarchical bias and partly to its lack of style and general dullness. It was not till 1690 that Lenain de Tillemont wrote in the preface to his *Histoire des Empereurs*, "L'auteur...a cru ne devoir songer qu'à chercher la vérité des faits et des temps....Il l'a recherchée dans les auteurs originaux[3]." It was not till 1696 that Père Daniel attempted in his *Histoire de France* to write from original documents, and declared in his preface that "la partialité et la prévention sont encore des défauts qui gâtent plusieurs Histoires au préjudice de la vérité[4]."

But it is time to turn to what is after all the main interest in Bayle's Dictionary at the present day, and that is his attitude towards the kindred subjects of philosophy and theology. It may at once be said that his Biblical articles are few in number and contemptible in quality. They are flippant, irreverent, and childish[5]. One article especially, that on David,

---

[1] His *Histoire de France*, in 3 vols., was published 1643–1651, and a new edition, with additions, in 1685.

[2] *Hist. générale de France*, 5 vols. 1621–1648; *Hist. de Louis le Juste* 1635–1648.

[3] Quoted by Vial and Denise, *op. cit.* p. 221.   [4] *Ib.* p. 222.

[5] See "Adam," "Cain," "Ève," "Élie," "Jonas."

gave great offence—and rightly so—for it shews not only an utter want of sympathy with what, in spite of its faults, is generally regarded as a singularly noble character[1], but a complete failure to take into account the conditions of his age and country—conditions which modern records of travel in Arabia have made so familiar to us[2]. The article had to be considerably modified for the second edition, but in the third edition of 1720 both versions were printed.

Though remarks bearing on Bayle's religious and philosophical opinions may be found scattered about the Dictionary, and often in places where you the least expect them, there are certain articles which stand out as the chief documents for them. In the articles on Leucippus and Epicurus, Bayle discusses the atomistic theory with considerable sympathy, but he characterises Epicurus's attempt to account for free-will by the swerving of the atoms as "pitoyable." He has a very long article on Spinoza, who died (1677) just twenty years before the publication of the Dictionary, and who resembled Bayle in his disinterested devotion to truth and his blameless life. But Bayle, while doing justice to his character, criticises very severely the "monstrous absurdities[3]," as he calls them, of "cet impie," "cet athéiste de système." In a long article on Pomponazzi he analyses that philosopher's arguments against the immortality of the soul, and he recurs to the same subject in a short article on Giacomo Zabarella of Padua (1533–1589), author of *De rebus naturalibus*[4].

The articles which called forth the strongest protests from his opponents may be divided into two groups, those which deal with the origin of evil and the kindred subject of free-will—"Manichéens," "Pauliciens," "Xenophane," "Zoroaste[5]"—and those

---

[1] The Dean of Ely (A. F. Kirkpatrick) quotes Carlyle, *Heroes and Hero-worship*, 2nd ed. p. 72 (*Cambridge Bible for Schools and Colleges*, Samuel II).

[2] Milman, *History of the Jews*, 4th ed. I, 306 (referring to Bayle).

[3] See esp. note N.

[4] M. Charbonnel thinks that Bayle owed something to both these Italian thinkers (*op. cit.* pp. 673–688).

[5] The articles on Xenophanes, Simonides, and Zoroaster were added in the 2nd edition. In the last article Bayle refers to the recently published *Historia religionis veterum Persarum* (Oxford, 1700) by Thomas Hyde, Bodley's Librarian and Professor of Arabic and Hebrew at Oxford, and formerly of King's College, Cambridge.

which discuss Pyrrhonism—"Pyrrhon," "Simonide" (Simonides of Ceos), "Zénon." They are of great importance for the solution of the very difficult question as to what Bayle's opinions really were, but we had better leave the consideration of them till we have finished the account of his life.

The years from 1697 to 1702 were chiefly occupied in writing new articles for the Dictionary or in making corrections in the old ones, and a new edition with nearly five hundred additions was brought out at the beginning of 1702. Early in 1704 he published *Réponse aux Questions d'un Provincial*, a duodecimo volume of miscellaneous learning addressed to an imaginary correspondent. Several of the answers (cc. XXXV–XLIV and LIV–LVIII) deal with sorcery and magic[1]. Later in the same year appeared *Continuation des Pensées sur la Comète*[2], in which, with a good deal of repetition, he answers the criticisms on his parallel between atheists and pagans. Then, in the following year, began the series of attacks by Jurieu, Jaquelot, and Le Clerc, whom Bayle believed to be leagued together against him. First came Jaquelot's *Conformité de la Foi avec la Raison*[3], which Bayle answered in a second and third *Réponse* (January 1706)[4]. In the same year Jaquelot counter-attacked with *Examen de la théologie de M. Bayle*, and Jurieu entered the lists with *Le Philosophe de Rotterdam accusé, atteint et convaincu*, to which Bayle disdained to reply. Before the end of the year, however, he had written a fourth *Réponse aux Questions d'un Provincial*[5], in which he examined some criticisms by Bernard, the editor of the *Nouvelles de la République*

---

[1] *Œuvres diverses*, III, 501–630.

[2] *Ib.* pp. 187–417.

[3] *Ou défense de la religion contre les principales difficultés répandues dans le Dictionnaire historique et critique de M. Bayle.* Isaac Jaquelot (1647–1708) was at this time minister of the French Church at Berlin. He was a fervent Christian rationalist, whom his enemies accused of being a Socinian. His chief work was his *Traité de l'existence de Dieu*.

[4] 2 vols. 12mo; *Œuvres*, III, 631–896. These volumes also contained an answer to the *De origine mali* (1702) of William King, Bishop of Londonderry and afterwards Archbishop of Dublin, which Bayle, however, only knew (as he candidly says) from Bernard's analysis of it in the *Nouvelles de la République des Lettres*.

[5] *Œuvres*, III, 897–988 (here numbered III).

des Lettres, on the second volume of the *Continuation des Pensées sur la Comète*. He was also engaged in writing *Entretiens de Maxime et de Thémiste*, the first part of which, directed against Le Clerc, was published in this year. But he was now a dying man. Already on July 23 he had written to Desmaizeaux that for the last six months he had been struggling against the inroads of tuberculosis, a malady which had been fatal to his mother and his grandmother[1]. He had no illusions as to the gravity of his condition. Talking hurt him, so he paid and received no visits. But he went on writing. It amused him, he wrote to Lord Shaftesbury, to refute M. Le Clerc and M. Jaquelot[2]. On the evening of December 27, 1706, he handed over to his publisher's proof-reader the copy of the second part of the *Entretiens de Maxime et de Thémiste*, which was directed against Jaquelot[3]. On the following morning, at about ten o'clock, he died. His friend, Basnage de Beauval, wrote a short *éloge* of him in the *Histoire des ouvrages et de la vie des savants* for December 1706, in which he speaks of him as "without pride (*faste*) and without ambition," as "a faithful and obliging friend," and as combining learning with genius[4].

The Marquis d'Argens in his memoirs tells a story of how a M. Jerson, a cousin of his informant, went to see Bayle three or four hours before his death but was refused admittance, and how Bayle shortly before he died wrote him a note regretting that he had not been admitted, and saying: "Je meurs en philosophe chrétien persuadé et pénétré des bontés et de la miséricorde de Dieu." D'Argens adds that the note was handed over to Basnage in the presence of his informant. Sayous thinks that the authenticity of this note is incontestable, but the story does not agree with Leers's account of the time of Bayle's death[5], and it is therefore safer not to rely on it.

---

[1] *Œuvres*, IV, 817. [2] Oct. 29 (*ib.* pp. 883–884).

[3] The two parts (I against Le Clerc, II against Jaquelot) were published together in 2 vols. 12mo (*Œuvres*, IV, 3–106) in 1707, as were the fourth *Réponse* (already mentioned) and also a fifth, numbered IV in *Œuvres*, III, pp. 1010–1084.

[4] Reprinted at the beginning of vol. IV of the *Œuvres diverses*.

[5] Sayous, *op. cit.* I, 358; Deschamps, *op. cit.* pp. 196–197. D'Argens's *Mémoires* were published in 1744, when he was forty.

What, then, were Bayle's real views on religion? According to some he was a complete sceptic, doubting everything and believing nothing. According to others his scepticism was a pretence, under cover of which he masked an insidious and carefully-planned attack on the existence of God and the immortality of the soul. M. Delvolvé has gone much further than this. In his well-informed and penetrating study, the most complete that we have, he has extracted from Bayle's writings an imposing body of positive doctrine, cosmological, psychological, and moral, of which the chief features are an animate atomism and a natural morality founded upon the needs of society[1].

The most hopeful method, it seems to me, of arriving at a just conclusion is to begin by recapitulating what we know about his predispositions and intellectual habits, and how these were shaped and developed by the pressure of external events. From his early youth he was distinguished by what he calls a "hungry curiosity," which led him to read widely but, from want of guidance, without system. The favourite authors of his youth were Plutarch and Montaigne. Then came his double change of religion and his exile as the penalty for the second change. At Geneva he studied theology, history, and philosophy (ancient and modern) and read much Greek and Latin literature. From Geneva he moved to Sedan, where he became professor of philosophy and literature, and from Sedan he moved to Rotterdam. There he published his first important book, the *Pensées sur la Comète*, in which he tilted at superstition and gave offence by his parallel between atheists and pagans. It was followed by a vigorous but temperate defence of Protestantism against the attacks of the Gallican ex-Jesuit Père Maimbourg. His next undertaking was the one of which, according to Basnage de Beauval, he was the fondest—for he was, as he said, a "nouvelliste à l'outrance"—the *Nouvelles de la République des Lettres*. Then, in the middle of his editorship came the revocation of the Edict of Nantes, and the death of his brother, to whom he was much attached, in prison. In a burst of indignation he delivered an impassioned attack on

---

[1] *Op. cit.* pp. 336–424.

intolerance and followed it up with a reasoned plea for universal tolerance. But the latter work offended many of his
fellow-Protestants and involved him in a long controversy with
his old friend Jurieu, which was greatly embittered by Jurieu's
belief that he was the author of the *Avis aux réfugiés*. Then
Jurieu, going back to the *Pensées sur la Comète*, publicly
charged him with atheism, and he was dismissed from his professorship. The dismissal had its compensations, for it enabled
Bayle to devote himself to his latest project, the *Dictionnaire
historique et critique*, but it left him more disposed than ever
to question the dogmas of orthodox religion, whether Catholic
or Protestant.

Bayle was a diligent searcher after truth, but he would probably have agreed with Lessing that he loved the search after
truth even better than truth itself. He had a passion for dialectic in the ordinary sense of the term. But he did not adopt
the dialectical method of Socrates and Plato, that is to say,
the art of argument by question and answer. What attracted
him especially was what Grote calls "the negative tendency,
the probing, testifying, and scrutinising force of Greek specu-
lation." Indeed, it may be said of Bayle, as truly as of the
great Greek thinkers, that his object was "to unmask not only
positive falsehood, but even affirmation without evidence, exaggerated confidence in what was only doubtful, and show of
knowledge without the reality—to look at a problem on all
sides, and set forth all the difficulties attending its solution[1]." It
is therefore interesting to note that Bayle has devoted a considerable space to Zeno of Elea, who was not only, according
to Aristotle, the inventor of dialectic[2], but who was a master
of destructive argument[3]. In this article Bayle not only states
Zeno's famous four arguments concerning motion, but suggests
six other possible ones and then he adds characteristically

---

[1] *A History of Greece*, ed. of 1862, VI, 48.

[2] The beginnings of the method, however, are to be found in his teacher,
Parmenides.

[3] "Do we not know the Eleatic Palamedes, who has an art of speaking
by which he makes the same thing appear to his hearers like and unlike,
one and many, at rest and in motion?" (Plato, *Phaedrus*, 261 C.)

that, judging of Zeno by himself, he is assured that, though
Zeno regarded his arguments as irrefutable, he believed in
motion like everybody else, and that if he failed to prove
the impossibility of motion "he fortified the hypothesis of
acatalepsy or the incomprehensibility of all things."

The article on Pyrrho is naturally short, for he wrote no
book, and our knowledge of him is almost entirely derived
from Diogenes Laertius's gossiping Life. Bayle accepts him as
the traditional representative of the utmost limits of scepticism
in ancient philosophy. One of his notes gave special offence,
because it puts in the mouth of an Abbé who is a philosopher
various objections to the essential truths of Christianity considered by the light of Reason[1]. Similarly in the article on
Simonides, in which there are quotations from Charron and
La Mothe Le Vayer, Bayle maintains in his own person that
Reason is incapable of comprehending the nature of God. In
the *Éclaircissement sur les Pyrrhoniens*, he defends himself on
the plea that philosophy and religion are two distinct and
independent spheres. The one is founded upon Reason, and the
other upon Faith[2].

Two other articles which gave a handle to his adversaries
were those on the Manicheans (whom he calls an "infamous
sect"), and the Paulicians, which deal with "the dogma of the
sin of Adam and all that depends upon it, among all mysteries
the most inconceivable to our reason, and the most inexplicable
according to its maxims." The pith of the short article on
the Manicheans may be found in note D, and especially in
an imaginary dialogue between Zoroaster and the Greek

---

[1] The dialogue between the "Abbé Pyrrhonien" and the "Abbé Papiste"
is severely criticised by Jaquelot in *Réponse aux Entretiens composez par
Mr Bayle*, Amsterdam, 1707.

[2] There are two interesting quotations in this *Éclaircissement*, one from
Saint-Évremond's immortal *Conversation du Maréchal d'Hocquincourt
avec le Père Canaye*—the passage in which the good father is enchanted
with the Marshal's repudiation of reason as a guide to religion, "Point
de raison! C'est la vraie religion cela"—and the other from the *Religio
Medici* in which Sir T. Browne says, "I can answer all the objections of
Satan and my rebellious reason with an odd resolution I learned of
Tertullian, *Certum est quia impossibile est.*"

philosopher, Melissus of Samos. In the same note is a statement
of Bayle's views on human nature:

L'homme est méchant et malheureux....L'histoire n'est qu'un recueil
des crimes et des infortunes du genre humain; mais remarquons que ces
deux maux, l'un moral et l'autre physique, n'occupent pas toute l'histoire,
ni toute l'expérience des particuliers: on trouve partout et du bien moral
et du bien physique; quelques exemples de vertu, quelques exemples de
bonheur; et c'est ce que fait la difficulté[1].

In the longer article, "Pauliciens," he gives it as his final
conclusion that it is best to "laisser courir comme de vaines
chicaneries les objections des philosophes et n'y opposer que
le silence avec le bouclier de la foi[2]."

In spite of the arguments which Bayle suggests in favour of
the Manichean theory of a good and evil principle—and it is
evident that he regards it with a good deal of sympathy—
Basnage de Beauval is no doubt right in saying that he was
far from adopting it. In the *Éclaircissement* he gives four reasons
why he does not spend much time over its refutation. His
third reason is that it is founded on "a supposition which is
repugnant to our clearest ideas," and his fourth that it contains
"monstrous absurdities." Finally he says that "the origin of
evil is one of the most inconceivable of Christian mysteries
and that it ought to be enough for every good Christian that
Faith is supported by the testimony of the word of God[3]."

This appeal to faith, comments Faguet with perfect truth,
is repeated by Bayle like a refrain. "One is always sure in
advance that every article on Platonism, Manicheism, Socini-
anism, the creation, original sin, or the immortality of the soul
will end with it." And he contemptuously describes it as "a
classical *ruse de guerre* which was in use before Montaigne[4]

---

[1] Quoted by Delvolvé, *op. cit.* p. 285 n.[3] Cp. "Xenophane," note D. For
the whole question see Delvolvé, c. viii.   [2] End of note M.

[3] The Protestant theologian, Isaac de Beausobre, in his *Histoire critique
de Manichée et du Manichéisme* (2 vols. Amsterdam, 1734–1739), says of
Bayle's article in the Dictionary, "il me semble qu'il auroit mieux fait ou
de l'omettre ou de le composer autrement," and that he amuses himself
"à pousser et à orner les arguments des Manichéens" (p. 3).

[4] Notably by Pomponazzi (see Bayle's article on him, notes F and G,
and H. Busson, *Les sources et le développement du Rationalisme dans la
littérature française de la Renaissance*, 1922, pp. 54–56).

and which since Montaigne has been practised so frequently that it deceives nobody and nobody even pays attention to it[1]."

But is it always a *ruse de guerre*? It was not so with Descartes. "His religious faith was sincere, but he separated the truths of religion from science and philosophy[2]." Similarly Gassendi, the reviver of classical atomism, who conscientiously performed his duties as a priest and of whom it has been said that he kept his philosophy and his religion in two water-tight compartments, claimed "to adjust his system to the level of Christianity as well as to that of reason." Even Montaigne, who like so many men of his day regarded religion as having no bearing on life, accepted, sincerely and without questioning, all the dogmas of the Church[3].

Saint-Évremond, says Bayle, ended his long life as he had lived—an *esprit fort*. But, if one reads his account of his religious views addressed to the Maréchal de Créquy, one realises that this is not the whole truth[4]. For instance, Bayle himself quotes from it a passage ending with "A bien considérer la Religion Chrétienne, on dirait que Dieu a voulu la dérober aux lumières de notre esprit, pour la tourner sur les mouvements de notre cœur." And elsewhere he quotes him as saying that "in matters which God has not willed to submit to argument…the silence of the sage is worth more than the discourse of the philosopher." "Je fais plus d'état de la foi du plus stupide païsan, que de toutes les leçons de Socrate[5]."

Bayle believed that he was treading the same path as Pascal, for he says of him, "Il distingua exactement toute sa vie les droits de la Foi d'avec ceux de la Raison." But Pascal's faith, unlike Bayle's, was a living and active principle. He did not regard Reason and Faith as entrenched in two hostile camps. Faith for him was an advance force of the same army as Reason. Its duty was to explore unknown territory, to devise new hypo-

---

[1] *Op. cit.* p. 23. Similarly Lenient, *op. cit.* p. 91, says that Bayle's recourse to Faith is "un piège ou un jeu d'esprit."

[2] A. Fouillée, *Descartes*, 1893, p. 18.

[3] *Essais*, I, xxvi and liv.

[4] See *Œuvres meslées*, 8 vols Amsterdam, 1798–1799, III, 51. This is the edition used by Bayle.

[5] *Ib.* II, 24.

theses, to test them by experience, and so to clear the way for a further advance[1].

Leibniz in his *Théodicée*, which was written as an answer to the difficulties propounded by Bayle and which is a model of courteous controversy, has some excellent pages on the antithesis between Faith and Reason. Drawing a distinction between what is contrary to Reason and what is above it, he insists that Faith is above Reason but not contrary to it[2]. He also discusses, and at great length, the arguments of Bayle about "the goodness of God, the liberty of man, and the origin of evil[3]."

Bayle's *Éclaircissement* on the parallel between atheists and pagans is feeble and disingenuous. Persons, he says, without religion are often better than those who have it, and he explains that when he speaks of the good morals of certain atheists he does not mean to attribute to them virtues. His parallel is only between atheists and pagans, not between atheists and Christians, and he is only concerned with *athées de théorie*, e.g. Diagoras (nicknamed "the atheist"), Vanini, Spinoza, not with *athées de pratique*. This sounds very harmless and commonplace. But in the original *Pensées sur la Comète* and in the *Continuation* he went much further than this. There he certainly compared atheists with Christians as well as with pagans, and his general aim clearly was to shew that religion, except for those to whom efficacious grace has been granted—for Bayle, when it suits him, can be a strong Jansenist—has no effect

---

[1] Bayle has a very meagre article on Pascal, but, in a notice of an Amsterdam edition of the *Pensées* in the *Nouvelles de la République des Lettres* for December 1684 (pp. 531 ff.), he praises highly his piety and calls him "one of the greatest geometricians, one of the most subtle metaphysicians, one of the most penetrating minds, that has ever existed." "His extraordinary humility and devotion are more mortifying to the free-thinkers than if you let loose on them a dozen missionaries" (quoted by L. Brunschvigg on p. 1 of his edition of the *Pensées*). On the whole subject of Reason and Faith see a remarkable sermon by Liddon on *The conflict of faith with the undue exaltation of intellect* (*Sermons preached before the University of Oxford*, 1st series).

[2] *Œuvres*, 2 vols. 1842, II, 25–72.

[3] *Ib.* pp. 73–308. It is worth noting that in the same number of the *Hibbert Journal* (Jan. 1928) there is a review of Prof. Galloway's *Faith and Reason in Religion* and Prof. N. P. Williams's *The Ideas of the Fall and Original Sin* (Bampton Lectures for 1924).

upon morals. But his original argument is as weak as his defence. It is easy to cite instances of individual atheists who were good men or individual pagans or Christians who were bad men, but if he really wanted to prove his case, it was incumbent on him to investigate (as Lecky did) the influence of Christianity upon morals by means of a comprehensive historical survey[1].

And this brings us to Bayle's limitations as a thinker and writer. Professor Saintsbury exactly hits the mark when he says that he lacked grasp. In detecting the fallacies of long-accepted theories, in exploding old or popular traditions, in countering the arguments of his opponents with fresh arguments of his own, he shews remarkable acuteness and sagacity. But he can seldom grasp a subject as a whole; his knowledge of philosophy, of history, of theology, is all piecemeal. Moreover, though he can criticise, he cannot construct. He is singularly deficient in that power of planning and of constructing according to plan which was so remarkable in the majority of his great contemporaries, above all in Bossuet. He says himself that he often began his work without knowing what he was going to write. Hence his digressions, his repetitions, his failure to bring an argument to a convincing conclusion.

Yet in criticising his defects we must not be blind to the real value of his thought. First and foremost is his noble love of tolerance. He was not only in advance of his time in the width of his tolerance, but he gave it a rational basis by insisting on the inviolability of the conscience as well in error as in truth[2]. Further he makes the conscience or moral reason a criterion of the truth of Scripture, applying it to passages which seem to impute injustice or cruelty to God, and the criterion only breaks down because he fails, as was inevitable in his day, to see that the historical books of the Old Testament are largely the record of a barbarous people.

[1] It will be remembered that La Bruyère in *Des esprits forts* denies the existence of atheists—"J'aurais une extrême curiosité de voir celui qui serait persuadé qu'il n'y a point de Dieu," and "L'athéisme n'est point."

[2] "The compelling of a man to anything against his own conscience, especially in matters of faith, is a doing ill." This passage from a rare pamphlet, *Liberty of Conscience*, published in 1644, exactly expresses Bayle's view (quoted by M. Creighton, *Persecution and Tolerance*, 1895, p. 114).

But, partly as a consequence of this failure to reconcile the moral reason and revelation, he was greatly perplexed by that question which perhaps most troubles thoughtful Christians at the present day—the origin of evil and its co-existence with an all-good and all-powerful God. His opponents accused him of being a Manichean and of making God the author of sin. But though he could not find a solution of the problem, he definitely repudiated that of the Manicheans, and he fell back on his old "refrain," that where Reason fails us, we must be content with Faith[1].

In this I believe he was sincere. His faith, no doubt, was weak and impotent, but it was genuine[2]. His scepticism too, which was the result of many causes—temperament, the influence of Montaigne, his wide and unmethodical reading, his love of arguing on both sides of a question—was genuine, and not a mere camouflage for an attack on Christianity and all forms of religion. Reason was the only approach to truth that he recognised, but seeing that it invariably led him to two diametrically opposite conclusions, he despaired of it as a means of arriving at truth. What wonder then that theologians like Le Clerc and Jaquelot, who believed that all the Christian mysteries were intelligible to reason, and who represented the liberal wing of Protestantism, combined with the more orthodox Jurieu to attack Bayle as the arch-enemy of their faith?

In spite of the attacks to which he was subjected, perhaps by reason of them, Bayle's reputation remained undiminished. Ever since he had begun to write the *Nouvelles de la République des Lettres*, he had been in active correspondence with the thinkers and writers of Holland, France, England, Switzerland, and Germany, and the success of his Dictionary had given him a position of international importance. The Danish dramatist, Holberg, describes how, when he was at Paris in 1714, he used to see a queue of young men waiting outside the

---

[1] For La Bruyère's views on this question see in *Des esprits forts* the *remarque* beginning, "Plusieurs millions d'années."

[2] In *La Cabale chimérique* written in 1691 he speaks of himself as a man who communicated four times a year and often attended public worship (*Œuvres*, II, 680, and see *ib.* p. 714).

Bibliothèque Mazarine for admission, in order to read Bayle's Dictionary. In the following year a pirated edition was published at Geneva, in 1720 the third authorised edition at Rotterdam, and two fresh editions followed in 1730 and 1740. That of 1730 contained Bayle's Life by Desmaizeaux. Editions of his *Œuvres diverses* appeared in 1725, 1727, and 1737. From about 1715 to 1750 may be regarded as the period of Bayle's greatest influence. For the greater part of it his fame was actively cherished by a Paris advocate named Matthieu Marais, who thought him "the greatest man in the world," and whose loyalty to him equalled that of Mlle de Gournay to Montaigne. His correspondence with him—it does not appear that they ever met—began in 1698 soon after the publication of the Dictionary, for the second edition of which he often furnished information, earning thereby Bayle's gratitude[1]. He died in 1737 and three years later appeared the last edition of the Dictionary that was published till 1820. By this time France must have been amply furnished with copies. M. Mornet has counted 288 in the catalogues of 500 private libraries[2]. Meanwhile, its rival as a biographical dictionary, Moreri, was from time to time brought up to date and the last edition of it was published in ten volumes in 1760. Before this the dictionaries of Chaufepié (4 vols. 1750–1756) and Prosper Marchand (2 vols. 1758–1759) had appeared as supplements to Bayle.

But Bayle's Dictionary was more important for its thought than for its information, and by 1750 its thought had been, so to speak, absorbed in the general stream. Voltaire, in his *Siècle de Louis XIV* (1751), pays Bayle a handsome tribute, but as a thinker he regards him as a back number. The passage is worth quoting.

Dialecticien admirable, plus que profond philosophe, il ne savait presque rien en physique. Il ignorait les découvertes du grand Newton. Presque tous ses articles philosophiques supposent ou combattent un cartésianisme

---

[1] See Lescure's introduction to Marais's *Mémoires*, 4 vols. 1863–1868, and Marais's correspondence with Mme Mérigniac (1707–1712), an equally ardent *bayliste* (*op. cit.* pp. 103–150). See also for Marais, Sainte-Beuve, *Nouveaux Lundis*, vol. IX.

[2] *La Pensée française au XVIIIe siècle*, 1926, p. 31.

qui ne subsiste plus. Il ne connaissait d'autre définition de la matière que l'étendue. Ses autres propriétés reconnues ou soupçonnées ont fait naître enfin la vraie philosophie. On a eu des démonstrations nouvelles et des doutes nouveaux : de sorte qu'en plus d'un endroit le sceptique Bayle n'est pas encore assez sceptique.

"Il ne savait presque rien en physique." That was Bayle's great drawback in an age which cared chiefly for scientific knowledge. The demand was met by the *Encyclopédie*, the first two volumes of which were published in the same year as the *Siècle de Louis XIV*.

CHAPTER XII

FONTENELLE[1]

FONTENELLE'S long life of nearly a hundred years did not end till past the middle of the eighteenth century, but he was thirty and had produced two important and successful works when our period opens, and by 1700 his position was assured. We have already met him as a protagonist of the Moderns in the great Quarrel, biassed, indeed, by his kinship with the two Corneilles and his friendship, as the result of this kinship, with a powerful section of the Académie Française but a thorough modern by temperament. His little treatise was not conspicuous either for scholarship, or depth, or originality, but its urbanity, its moderation, its lucidity, its happy turns of thought and expression, commended it in all quarters where society and literature joined hands.

Bernard Le Bouyer (pronounced and often written Bovier) de Fontenelle was born at Rouen in 1657. His father was an

---

[1] *Œuvres*, 6 vols. 12mo, 1742; 12 vols. 1758–1766; 8 vols. 8vo, 1790; 3 vols. 8vo, 1817.

Nouveaux Dialogues des Morts, 1683; *Lettres diverses du Chevalier d'Her✳✳✳*, 1683; *Entretiens sur la Pluralité des Mondes*, 1686; *Histoire des Oracles*, 1686; ed. L. Maigron, 1908 (*Société des textes français modernes*); *Poésies Pastorales, avec un Discours sur l'Églogue, et une Digression sur les Anciens et les Modernes*, 1688; *Éloges des Académiciens*, preceded by *Histoire du renouvellement de l'Académie Royale des Sciences en* 1699 *et les Éloges* (12) *historiques des Académiciens morts depuis le renouvellement*, 1708; vol. II (17 *éloges*), 1717; vol. III (11 *éloges*), 1722; *Suite des Éloges des Académiciens morts depuis* 1722 (20 *éloges*), 1733; 2 vols. (69 *éloges*), 1766.

L'Abbé Trublet, *Mémoires pour servir à l'histoire de la vie et des ouvrages de Mr de Fontenelle*, Amsterdam, 1759; D.-J. Garat, *Mémoires sur la vie de M. Suard*, 2 vols. 1820, I, 76–83 and 110–125; Charma, *Biographie de Fontenelle*, Caen, 1846; P. Flourens, *Fontenelle ou de la philosophie moderne relativement aux sciences naturelles*, 1847 (I have not seen either this or the preceding work); A. Vinet, *Histoire de la littérature française au XVIIIe siècle*, 1851; C.-A. Sainte-Beuve, *Causeries du Lundi*, III, 1851, a review of the preceding; É. Faguet, *Études sur le XVIIIe siècle*, 1890; F. Brunetière, *Études critiques*, V (1893), 197–201 and 234–246; A. Laborde-Milaà, *Fontenelle*, 1905; L. Maigron, *Fontenelle*, 1906; J. B. Bury, *The Idea of Progress*, 1920, pp. 98–118.

advocate of the Rouen *Parlement*, and his mother was Marthe
Corneille, sister of Pierre and Thomas. The younger Corneille
was his godfather. He was educated at the Jesuit college of
Rouen, where he greatly distinguished himself. Moreover, at
the age of fifteen he won two prizes, one for a French ode and
the other for a sonnet, from the Academy of the Palinods of
Rouen, thus following in the footsteps of both his uncles and
of Jacqueline Pascal. In accordance with the traditions of his
family he was called to the bar, but, after losing his first case,
he deserted law for the more congenial field of literature.

His *début* was made in 1677 in the pages of *Le Mercure
galant*, which had in that year been launched afresh under the
editorship of Donneau de Visé, with Thomas Corneille as his
chief assistant. Fontenelle's contribution was a poem entitled
L'Amour noyé[1], and it was sped on its way by a kindly avun-
cular puff. In 1678 and again in 1679 he collaborated with his
uncle in the production of a libretto for an opera, the uncle
furnishing the *scenario* and the nephew doing the rest. The
success of both operas, *Psyché* and *Bellérophon*, which were
produced under the name of Thomas Corneille, encouraged
Fontenelle to continue writing for the stage. So in the following
year (1680), becoming bolder, he composed unassisted a tragedy,
Aspar, and a comedy, *La Comète*. The tragedy was produced
in December and the comedy in the following January, and
both were failures. *Aspar* alone survives in Racine's two cruel
epigrams[2], from one of which we learn that Fontenelle, who
had come to Paris to witness its production, returned crestfallen
to his native Normandy[3].

[1] *Œuvres*, V, 238 ff. The note in *Le Mercure galant* says that he was living
at Rouen and adds, "plusieurs personnes qui l'ont vu à Paris avouent que
c'est un meurtre de le laisser dans le province" (Maigron, p. 20). Fontenelle's first visit to his uncles was made in 1674, but it was only a short one.

[2] *Œuvres*, ed. Mesnard, IV, 183–185 and 242–243.

[3]   "Mon aventure est étrange:
               On m'adorait à Rouen.
               Dans le *Mercure galant*
               J'avais plus d'esprit qu'un ange.
               Cependant je pars demain
               Sans argent et sans louange;
               Cependant je pars demain,
               Un bâton blanc à la main."

In spite of this double failure he did not abandon his
hopes of a literary career, but he realised that reason and not
imagination must be his mistress. He accordingly devoted himself to serious reading and study, with the result that he produced in 1683 a prose work, entitled *Nouveaux Dialogues des
Morts*[1]. Its dedication to "Lucian in the Elysian Fields" points
to the source of its inspiration. The dialogues, which are short,
though not quite so short as Lucian's, are divided into Dialogues
of the ancient dead, Dialogues of the modern dead, and Dialogues between the ancient and the modern dead. Each dialogue
is headed by a statement of the question discussed. The mere
names of the speakers reveal the author as a young man who
wishes to call attention to his learning and cleverness[2]. The
speakers, none of whom appear a second time, as they do in
Lucian, are chosen from a wide range of history, and some of
them must have been known to very few of Fontenelle's readers.
How many people have heard of Icasia, who by her pert remark
lost the hand of the Emperor Theophilus, or of Paulina, the
Roman matron, and her adventure with the pretended Anubis,
or of Straton, whose ingenuity won for him the throne of Tyre?
They all, however, as well as other not widely known personages, appear in Moreri's Dictionary, of which a second edition
had been published in 1681, and here no doubt Fontenelle
found them. Besides this parade of out-of-the-way learning, one
notices the ingenuity with which incongruous speakers are
brought together. Our curiosity is piqued by the collocation
of Augustus and Aretino, Hadrian and Margaret of Austria,
Apicius and Galileo, Paracelsus and Molière, Seneca and
Scarron, Plato and Margaret of Scotland, Lucretia and Barbe
Plomberge (Barbara Blomberg, the reputed mother of Don
John of Austria). It is chiefly in the dialogues of the ancients
with the moderns that these strange encounters occur. When
both speakers are moderns they are more often than not
contemporaries, as, for instance, Anne of Brittany and Mary

---

[1] It was published in two separate parts.
[2] "Il semble que cet ouvrage ne soit fait uniquement que pour avoir de
l'esprit," says Voltaire at the beginning of a severe criticism of the work
(*Œuvres*, ed. Beuchot, XXXIX, 201–206).

of England, Charles V and Erasmus, Queen Elizabeth and the
Duc d'Alençon, Mary Stuart and Riccio, Diane de Poitiers
and Anne Boleyn, Cortez and Montezuma.

Fontenelle flatters himself that he has reproduced the characters of his dead in such a way that "one can recognise them
for what they were in life." But, as M. Maigron says, "if he is
sincere, he is under a singular illusion"; all alike "are Cartesians—and children worthy of their father[1]." They have no
independent existence; they are puppets pulled by their show-
man's string, and the thoughts to which they give expression
are his and not theirs. But the dialogue-form enables Fontenelle to display to advantage his double rôle of *philosophe* and
bel esprit. The *bel esprit* delights in epigram and paradox, in
finding arguments on both sides and coming to no conclusion.
The *philosophe*, as the term was then beginning to be understood, questions the accepted findings of authority and tradition, and examines all questions by the light of reason.

Socrate et Montaigne, one of the best dialogues, the subject
of which is announced as "Si les anciens ont plus de valeur
que nous," has been referred to in a previous chapter as giving
a foretaste of the *Digression sur les Anciens et les Modernes*.
Socrates believes in progress—"Je croirais que le monde de-
vait avoir une vieillesse plus sage et plus réglée que n'a été
sa jeunesse"—Montaigne in degeneration—"De jour en jour
tout empire." But both give ground in the course of argument.
Socrates admits that nature remains much the same and that,
though the external fashions of man may change, his heart does
not. And Montaigne accepts this view with the reservation that
some ages may be better endowed than others. On somewhat
parallel lines is the dialogue between Erasistratus, a famous
Greek physician of the third century B.C. and Harvey (whom
Fontenelle disguises as Hervé), in which the merits of modern
discoveries in physics and medicine are discussed. Here again
the conclusion is that nature does not change. "You may make
new discoveries in anatomy, you may penetrate further and
further into the secrets of the structure of the human body, but
you will not make a dupe of nature; you will die as of old."

[1] *Op. cit.* p. 230.

Most of the dialogues end on a note of pessimism. Like Bayle, Fontenelle had a poor opinion of mankind. "Partout où il y a des hommes, il y a des sottises, et les mêmes sottises," says Montaigne, and even Socrates believes that only two or three dozen reasonable men are born throughout the whole world in the course of a century. "C'est une plaisante condition que celle de l'homme, si elle est telle que vous croyez," is Anselme's final remark to Joanna I of Naples. "Il est né pour aspirer à tout, et pour ne jouir de rien ; pour marcher toujours, et pour arriver nulle part." Most pessimistic of all is the dialogue between the two madmen, Guillaume de Cabestan, the Provençal troubadour, and Albert-Frederick of Brandenburg, King of Prussia (d. 1618). "All men alike," says Cabestan, "are fools, and they are never cured." "The follies of men have adjusted themselves so harmoniously that they have served to form the strongest links of human society; witness the desire for immortality, the false glory, and many other principles on which rests everything that goes on in the world."

If in his pessimism and his low estimate of human nature Fontenelle is of the seventeenth century, on the other hand in the undisguised libertinism of some of the dialogues he is distinctly of the eighteenth. And it is libertinism of the worst kind, for it is founded on a disbelief in the virtue of women. Conspicuous instances are the dialogues between Callirrhoe and Paulina, between the Duchesse de Valentinois (Diane de Poitiers) and Anne Boleyn, between Dido and Stratonice, and between Lucretia and Barbe Plomberge—all, be it observed, dialogues in which men take no part. In that between Plato and Margaret of Scotland Plato frankly disavows the belief in spiritual or platonic love which he held in his lifetime. "Vous êtes devenu libertin depuis votre mort," says Margaret in surprise. But this cynical attitude towards love and marriage did not prejudice the popularity of a book which had at least the merit of novelty and variety and of never being tedious. Translated into English and Italian in the same year, it laid the foundation of Fontenelle's reputation.

His next step was decidedly a retrograde one. If in the *Dialogues des Morts* the *bel esprit* and the libertine were balanced by the *philosophe*, in the *Lettres diverses de M^r le Chevalier d'Her***[1]* they riot unchecked. The new book catered for the readers of the *Mercure galant* and the popular *Recueils* of verse, and for the frequenters of the *précieux* salons. Its *préciosité* displays itself not so much in the language, though it is easy to find in it examples of the *précieux* style almost worthy of *Les Précieuses ridicules*, but in its perpetual striving after *esprit*, not only in the thought but in the choice of dilemmas and other situations. Yet the *préciosité* is not that of Mlle de Scudéry and her friends, for it has in it no element of prudery. The letters, says Faguet, "sont le plus souvent du pur Benserade," but the *feux* and the *flammes*, the *appas* and the *attraits* of Benserade's day have disappeared. The ladies are no longer cruel, the lovers no longer languish. "The languishing attitude has its uses," says the Count, "but it is fatal to be always languishing." The whole tone of the book is already that of the eighteenth century. It is at once immoral and indelicate—immoral in its views on marriage, and indelicate in its suggestions and *sous-entendus* and appeals to a prurient imagination. It often reminds one of Voltaire or Sterne at their worst. It was published without the writer's name and this anonymity contributed to its success[2].

In October 1684 the great Corneille died, and in the following January Bayle inserted in his *Nouvelles de la République des Lettres* an *éloge* from the pen of Fontenelle[3]. It was at once a pious tribute from a nephew to an uncle and the forerunner of many *éloges* from the same pen. Early in the following year (1686) its writer inaugurated what was to be the chief work of his life—the popularising and development of science—with a little book entitled, *Entretiens sur la Pluralité des Mondes*. It purported to be the report of a series of conversations on astronomy which Fontenelle held with a "belle Marquise" in

---

[1] This is the original title; in the 3rd edition of 1699 it was altered to *Lettres galantes*.

[2] It was included in his *Œuvres* in 1715.

[3] It was republished with many alterations in 1702 in the *Histoire de l'Académie française* by Pellisson and Olivet and became later the *Vie de Corneille*. It is full of inaccuracies and mis-statements.

the park of her château. The Marquise was a real person, Mme de La Mesangère, who lived in the neighbourhood of Rouen, but the conversations are purely imaginary. They are an attempt, and a most successful one, to make the results of one branch of science known to unscientific readers, and that not by means of a text-book or manual, but in a form which combines transparently clear exposition with something of the charm of fiction. The conversations are not those of a professor with a *femme savante*, but of a *bel esprit* with a *belle dame*. "Nous sommes en humeur," says Fontenelle, "de mêler toujours les folies de galanterie à nos discours les plus sérieux." Sometimes, indeed, he relapses into the insipid fatuities of the *Lettres galantes*, as for instance when the Marquise suggests that the planet Venus has an "air galant," and Fontenelle replies that its inhabitants, no doubt, consist only of Céladons and Silvandres, and that their most ordinary conversations are worth the most admired of Clélie's.

In 1666 that great organiser and administrator, Colbert, following the example of Richelieu with regard to the Académie Française, turned a private society of men of science, which met at regular intervals, into the Académie des Sciences. The only rule that he imposed upon it was that it should meet twice a week, and that one meeting should be devoted to mathematics and the other to physics. In 1671 Jacques Rohault (1620–1675), an enthusiastic disciple of Descartes, published his *Traité de physique*, which became the standard text-book on the subject both in France and England. In the following year Nicolas Lémery (1645–1715), who had lectured on chemistry at Montpellier for three years with great success, returned to Paris, and under the patronage of Condé opened a course of lectures, which, though he was only an apothecary, attracted enormous crowds. "Les dames mêmes, entraînées par la mode, ont l'audace de venir se montrer à des assemblées si savantes[1]." Among his more scientific hearers were Rohault, Bernier, and other distinguished men of science. In order to popularise the study he published his *Cours de chimie* (1675), which had as great a success as his lectures. Reprinted more

---

[1] *Éloge* by Fontenelle (*Œuvres*, VI, 369 ft.).

than thirty times, translated into many languages, it was the manual of chemists throughout the eighteenth century and was consulted for practical details even after Lavoisier had transformed the science. Another most popular lecturer at this time was Joseph Duverney (1648–1730), professor of anatomy at the *Jardin du Roi* (now the *Jardin des Plantes*), where he lectured for about half a century with equal zeal and success. He had as a colleague Joseph Tournefort (1656–1708), the distinguished botanist, who published his *Éléments de botanique* in 1694. To these we must add Joseph Sauveur (1653–1716), who was appointed Professor of Mathematics at the Collège Royal in the very year in which Fontenelle published his *Entretiens*. He is famous as one of the earliest investigators into the science of sounds, to which he gave the name of "acoustics[1]."

Another science which, thanks to Louis XIV and Colbert, was rapidly rising to distinction and popularity in France was astronomy. In 1667 the Paris Observatory was completed and in 1669 Giovanni Domenico Cassini (1625–1712)[2], professor at Bologna, who had a brilliant reputation, was induced to transfer his services to Paris, and eventually made France his home. In the new Observatory he added to his reputation by discovering four new satellites of Saturn[3]. It will be remembered that in *Les Femmes savantes* which was produced in 1672, three years after Cassini's appointment, astronomy is one of the sciences for which the learned ladies express an ecstatic interest. Philaminte loves Descartes's *mondes tombants* (almost certainly comets) and declares that she has plainly seen men in the moon. Trissotin bursts in on the company with the news that

> Un monde près de nous a passé tout du long,
> Est chu tout au travers de notre tourbillon;
> Et s'il eût en chemin rencontré notre terre,
> Elle eût été brisée en morceaux comme verre[4].

---

[1] For Tournefort and Sauveur see Fontenelle, *Œuvres*, VI, 228 ff. and 429 ff. Sauveur was tutor to the Duc de Bourbon with La Bruyère for his colleague (see above, p. 49).

[2] See Fontenelle, *ib.* pp. 316 ff.

[3] One in 1671, one in 1672, and two in 1684.   [4] Act IV, Sc. iii.

Twenty years later the astronomical studies of women have become more serious. Let Boileau be our witness:

> Qui s'offrira d'abord? Bon, c'est cette Savante
> Qu'estime Roberval et que Sauveur fréquente.
> D'où vient qu'elle a l'œil trouble, et le teint si terni?
> C'est que sur le calcul, dit-on, de Cassini,
> Un astrolabe en main, elle a dans sa gouttière
> A suivre Jupiter passé la nuit entière[1].

Thus in producing a popular work on astronomy Fontenelle was setting his sail to catch a favouring wind. Moreover, the slightly *précieux* setting that he gave to it was well suited both to himself and to his special public, the readers of *Le Mercure galant*.

The first conversation opens on a poetical note, a note seldom found in Fontenelle's verse or prose. He describes how one evening he and the Marquise walked in the park, with the white light of the moon shining through the branches of the black trees, and the stars of pure and dazzling gold against the deep blue of the sky, and how the spectacle set him dreaming and how he might have gone on dreaming, had it not been for the presence of so amiable a lady, and how, on his exclaiming that he cannot pardon the sun for obscuring from him all these worlds, she asks him in surprise what he means by "all these worlds." And when he explains that he believes that each star might be a world, she insists, in spite of his reluctance "to talk of philosophy in a wood at ten o'clock of the evening with the most amiable person of his acquaintance," that he should reveal to her the secrets of "his stars." So he proceeds to give her an explanation of the whole Copernican system. It is extraordinarily well done. Nothing could be more lucid than his exposition, nothing apter than his illustrations. And the Marquise is perfectly suited to the rôle assigned to her. She is quite ignorant of the fact that the earth turns round the sun and is not the centre of our universe, but she is anxious to learn all about the new system, and, though impatient of the least suspicion of pedantry, she is intelligent enough to follow easily her companion's lucid development of his marvellous story. It may seem strange that, more than

[1] *Sat.* X (1693), ll. 425-430. The *savante* is Mme de La Sablière.

seventy years after the evidence for the Copernican system had been greatly strengthened by the discoveries of Galileo, and more than sixty after the publication of Kepler's *Epitome Astronomiæ Copernicanæ*, an intelligent woman should still have believed that the sun revolved round the earth. But in the long and eloquent *remarque* which La Bruyère inserted in *Des Esprits forts* in 1692, six years after the publication of Fontenelle's book—beginning "Voyez, Lucile, ce morceau de terre"—he expounds the Ptolemaic system as if it were the accepted one, and only gives that of Copernicus as an alternative—"Voulez-vous un autre système[1]?"

The second and third conversations deal with the moon and with the question whether it and the planets other than the earth are inhabited. In his explanation of the revolutions of the moon and of how it receives and transmits its light Fontenelle is as lucid as ever. As regards the question of whether it is inhabited he is able to lay before the Marquise all the available evidence. With the help of gigantic, but unwieldy, telescopes[2] the astronomers of the Paris Observatory had mapped out the moon and given names to its mountains and craters and supposed seas. "In fine," says Fontenelle, with pardonable exaggeration, "the description of the moon is so exact that a *savant* who found himself there would not be more at a loss than I should be in Paris." But he recognises that the dark spaces that were at first supposed to be seas are perhaps only large cavities—they are now recognised as dry rock—for as there are no clouds round the moon and no exhalations or vapours, there can be no water. If it is inhabited, as he believes it is, the inhabitants must be quite different from men. But perhaps there may be exhalations and vapours which are imperceptible to us, and starting from this slender hypothesis he proceeds to develop his theory of the plurality of worlds in an attractive, if unscientific,

---

[1] The whole *remarque*, which fills ten pages, should be compared with the *Entretiens*, and one wonders whether, in spite of the enmity between the two men, it was suggested by Fontenelle's book. Bury, in referring to the *Entretiens*, points out that Milton's Raphael in book VIII of *Paradise Lost*, published in 1667, does not venture beyond a sympathetic explanation of the Copernican system (*The Idea of Progress*, p. 114).

[2] The largest was 136 feet in length.

fashion[1]. "The moon, according to all appearances, is inhabited"—this is how he now puts it—"then why should not Venus also be inhabited?" And so on for the other planets. These are described in turn in the fourth conversation. He has not much to say about Mercury, Venus, or Mars, but Jupiter with its four satellites and Saturn with its ring and five satellites[2] give him an opportunity to appeal to the Marquise's imagination. There is not much interest in the fifth conversation, which deals with the fixed stars, and still less in the sixth, which was published later as a supplement to the others, but at the beginning of the fifth there is a really eloquent passage. When the Marquise is told that the fixed stars are so many suns, each the centre of a system of revolving planets, she exclaims, "Voilà l'Univers si grand que je m'y perds, je ne sais plus où je suis, je ne sais plus rien....Cela me confond, me trouble, m'épouvante." And Fontenelle replies, "Cela me met plus à mon aise...je respire avec plus de liberté, je suis dans un plus grand air, et assurément l'Univers a tout une autre magnificence."

This wide outlook, touched with imagination, also appears in Fontenelle's bold prophecy about flying. "The art of flying is only just born, but it will come to perfection, and some day we shall fly to the moon." This shews a belief in human progress which is contrary to Fontenelle's usual point of view. He is more like himself when he indulges in one of his outbursts against the folly of the human race:

> Pourrions-nous bien nous figurer quelque chose qui eût des passions si folles, et des réflexions si sages; une durée si courte, et des vues si longues; tant de science sur des choses presque inutiles, et tant d'ignorance sur les plus importantes; tant d'ardeur pour la liberté, et tant d'inclination à la servitude; une si forte envie d'être heureux, et une si grande incapacité de l'être?

Les Entretiens sur la Pluralité des Mondes proved to be Fontenelle's most popular work. It has been reprinted at least

---

[1] Cf. La Bruyère in *Des Esprits forts*: "Mais la lune est habitée; i n'est pas du moins impossible qu'elle le soit."

[2] The sixth and seventh satellites were discovered in 1789 by Herschel, the eighth in 1848.

thirty-four times, though curiously enough there was only one edition between 1719 and 1811. It was translated into English in 1688 by both Afra Behn and John Glanvill.

In January 1686, not long before the publication of the *Entretiens sur la Pluralité des Mondes*, there appeared in the *Nouvelles de la République des Lettres* a short account of a civil war between two rival queens in Borneo. It purported to have been communicated by Fontenelle in Batavia to Henri Basnage at Rotterdam, and Bayle inserted it in his review under the belief that it was a *bona fide* narrative, whereas in reality it was a transparent and rather crude allegory, occasioned by the revocation of the Edict of Nantes, of the religious war between Rome and Geneva. The French government took it in bad part, and Fontenelle, in apprehension of the Bastille, wrote a retractation in verse.

Warned by this experience, he made his next incursion into the domain of religion and theology with greater prudence and greater seriousness. It happened that a Dutchman named Van Dale had published in 1683 a Latin work on the Oracles of the Pagans, in which he controverted the common belief that the oracles were due to the agency of demons and that they had entirely ceased at the birth of Christ[1]. The book shewed wide learning, but it was badly put together, badly written, and generally devoid of charm. Fontenelle, therefore, abandoned his original idea of translating it and determined, while preserving its principal contents, to give it an entirely new form. So he altered its arrangement, cut out everything that seemed superfluous, and added ornaments, elucidations, and reflections of his own, even to the extent of sometimes differing in opinion from the author. The result is a well-arranged and readable treatise which appeared in December 1686. Following Van Dale, it is divided into two parts or, as they are called, dissertations, in one of which it is maintained that the oracles were not given by demons, and in the other that they did not cease at the coming of Jesus Christ. Both these views

---

[1] It was the first book reviewed by Bayle in the *Nouvelles de la République des Lettres* (March 1684). It is in this review that occurs his well-known saying, "Les erreurs pour être vieilles ne sont pas meilleurs."

were in direct opposition to the opinion of the Church. As a
matter of fact the Fathers and ecclesiastical historians of the
early Church did not hold that the oracles completely ceased
at the coming of Christ, but only that a general decadence took
place[1]. Nor did they overlook the part played by fraud and
illusion. Indeed Eusebius, the chief authority with the Eastern
Church on the subject, brings forward many reasons, as
Fontenelle, after Van Dale, himself points out, for supposing
that the oracles were often due to the fraud of the priests[2].
But in the Western Church, ever since Augustine, the belief in
demons, or evil spirits, had been an article of faith.

What was Fontenelle's motive in re-shaping a learned Latin
work on the religion of the ancients so as to make it attractive
to the average reader? Did his unsparing criticism of the
alleged intercourse between the ancients and the unseen world
mask a covert attack on all religions, including that of Christ?
It will be easier to answer this question if we take into account
another little treatise, De l'Origine des Fables, which he wrote a
few months later on the growth of Greek fables and mythology[3].
He there points out that mankind in all ages is drawn to
fabulous stories, which have the double attraction of striking
the imagination by some trait of the marvellous and of satisfying
curiosity by the apparent explanation that they give of some
natural and well-known phenomenon. Moreover, two other
general principles have favoured the growth of fables, the love
of repetition and the blind respect for antiquity. "Our fathers
believed it; shall we claim to be wiser than they?" Examine
the errors of modern times and we shall find that they have
been established and preserved in the same way. Happily they

---

[1] Père Baltus points this out in his *Réponse à l'Histoire des Oracles de
Fontenelle*, Strasbourg, 1707 (*Hist. des Oracles*, ed. Maigron, p. 160 n.[1]).
For some later oracles see F. W. H. Myers, *Essays—Classical*, 1883,
pp. 60–67.

[2] *Hist. des Oracles*, 1re diss. c. ix.

[3] *Œuvres*, v, 351–372. It was not printed till 1724, but it was evidently
written between the *Histoire des Oracles* and the *Digression sur les
Anciens et les Modernes*. Fontenelle speaks in it of *le respect aveugle de
l'antiquité* and in one or two passages anticipates the *Digression*. Trublet
is surely wrong in saying that it was written between 1691 and 1699.

are not so great as those of the Greeks, "parce que nous sommes
éclairés des lumières de la vraie religion, et, à ce que je crois,
de quelques rayons de la vraie philosophie." We find very
similar ideas in the *Histoire des Oracles.* He there points out
the power which the marvellous has on the human mind[1],
and that "custom has on men a force which has no need of being
supported by reason[2]." In both treatises he expresses his
distrust in tradition. In *De l'Origine des Fables* he declares that
the stories which the earliest men told their children were often
false to begin with, but that they certainly became more and
more false as they passed from mouth to mouth. He says
much the same thing about the oracles.

> Leur premier établissement n'est pas fort difficile à expliquer. Donnez-
> moi une demi-douzaine de personnes, à qui je puisse persuader que ce
> n'est pas le Soleil qui fait le jour; je ne désespérerai pas que des Nations
> entières n'embrassent cette opinion.

This is, of course, merely an exaggerated illustration, not
meant to be taken seriously, of the gullibility of man and the
power of tradition. But some of Fontenelle's enemies detected
in it a malicious allusion to the "half-a-dozen persons" whom
Our Lord persuaded to be His disciples at the beginning of
His ministry. I do not believe that Fontenelle had any such
audacious parallel in his head, but the line of argument and
the general tone of the *Histoire des Oracles* and *De l'Origine
des Fables* fully justify the premonition of Pascal and Bossuet
(more far-sighted than most of their contemporaries) that
Cartesianism was a danger to the Church[3]. For Fontenelle was
a Cartesian in every fibre of his being. Not that he accepted
all the conclusions of the Cartesian physics, but he recognised
no authority but Reason. "Hors de la tradition, point de
vérité," said Bossuet, but Fontenelle disbelieved in tradition
as completely as he did in the marvellous, for neither could
pass the test of Reason. To their influence he attributed the
origin and growth of the fraudulent oracles and the childish

---

[1] P. 29.   [2] P. 70.

[3] "Je vois...un grand combat se préparer contre l'Église sous le nom de
la philosophie cartésienne," wrote Bossuet in 1687, five months after the
publication of the *Histoire des Oracles* (*Correspondance*, III, 372).

myths and immoral fables of the Greeks. But what of religions which owe their origin to similar beginnings? It is true that he makes an exception in favour of "the light of the true religion," and of "the chosen people, among whom the special care of providence has preserved the truth[1]." It is true also that throughout his life he was a practising Catholic. But, though he might choose himself to conform to the estab- lished religion of his country, he hinted with discretion in his writings that if an enlightened mind had the courage to apply to that religion the only reliable test, the test of Reason, it might be found that it rests on no firmer basis than the religion of the Greeks. Thus Fontenelle sowed the seed of free inquiry into religion, and it fell on soil which was favourable to its germination. In 1689 Richard Simon proceeded to examine the canon of the New Testament in the same Cartesian spirit and with the same weapons of philological and historical criti- cism which he had already applied to that of the Old Testament. In the same year Bossuet, the last great champion of ortho- doxy, began his controversy with Pierre Jurieu on the varia- tions of the Protestant Church[2], and though Jurieu himself was as orthodox from his point of view as Bossuet was from his, many of his fellow-Protestants, both in England and Hol- land, were Christian rationalists, latitudinarians, or even (at heart) Socinians. Thus, if the spirit of Descartes was at work within both the Catholic and the Protestant Churches, it was only to be expected that outside the Church the covert sug- gestions of Fontenelle should find a ready response. For at the close of the eighteenth century the *athées de pratique*[3], as Bayle calls them, men who led debauched lives and boasted of their impiety, but in sickness sent for a confessor, were being replaced by *athées de spéculation*, who lived soberly and subjected the dogmas of the Church to the test of honest and inquiring doubt.

If in the *Histoire des Oracles* the *bel esprit* that was one half of Fontenelle retired in favour of the *philosophe*, in the

---

[1] *De l'Origine des Fables.*

[2] *Six avertissements aux Protestants*, 1689–1691.

[3] *Œuvres*, IV, 414.

Poésies pastorales[1], which appeared in January 1688, it resumed full possession. The new volume was hailed with enthusiasm by Fontenelle's admirers. The women, says Le Cat in his *éloge*, knew all the eclogues by heart[2]. The *Mercure galant* congratulated him "on having permitted us to think that we might surpass the most wonderful achievements of the ancients." Perrault, as we have seen, made a special reference to the work in the poem, *Le Génie*, which he read before the Academy. As a matter of fact the eclogues are not only, like all Fontenelle's verse, thoroughly prosaic, but they are complete failures as pastorals. Pastoral poetry in spite of its conventions has a peculiar charm, but only in the hands of a true poet, and of one who is also a finished artist. Further, the pastoral poet must combine a warm sympathy with the loves and sorrows of humanity with an instinctive love of inanimate nature. He need not be a close observer of either man or nature, but his poetic imagination must react to both. Such qualifications are to be found in all great pastoral poetry, in the *Idylls* of Theocritus and the *Eclogues* of Virgil, in *Lycidas* and *Adonais*[3] and *Thyrsis*. Unfortunately Fontenelle, besides being incurably prosaic, had no feeling for nature and little sympathy with man, except as a reasoning being.

How poorly he was qualified to write pastoral poetry is revealed in the introductory *Discours sur la nature de l'Églogue*, in which he surveys the whole field of pastoral production. His criticisms are instructive. Theocritus keeps too close to nature; preferable to his "grossness" is the "delicacy" of Bion and Moschus. His fifth Idyll is inferior to the third eclogue of Virgil, because the latter's shepherds are more polished and more agreeable. But Virgil also comes in for criticism. The design of his *Pollio* is less happy than that of Calpurnius in his similar eclogue (the first) and that of his sixth eclogue than that of Nemesianus's third eclogue. Fontenelle admits the superiority of Virgil's style, but it does not occur to him that in pastoral poetry style, in the wide sense of poetical execution, is practically everything.

[1] *Œuvres*, v.   [2] See Maigron, *op. cit.* p. 49.
[3] In *Adonais* Shelley makes little use of the pastoral convention.

Fontenelle's incapacity to understand poetry, especially Greek poetry, is equally apparent in his other contributions to literary criticism. We have seen that he regarded Aeschylus as more or less a madman with a very vivid and ill-regulated imagination[1]. He can see no fun and no poetry in the *Birds* of Aristophanes[2]. His *Réflexions sur la Poétique*[3], written in 1685 but not published till 1742, is of little value. In it he formulates the absurd view that rhyme pleases the reader because it gives him a sense of a difficulty overcome, and in a short essay *Sur la Poésie en générale*[4], written after the death of Louis XIV, he expresses a similar opinion with regard to verse in general. In the same essay he discusses, rather ingeniously, the merits of the various kinds of poetical images, and at their head he places the metaphysical image, that is to say, images drawn from "the general order of the universe." After this it is only natural that he should give his preference to the poet who is also a philosopher.

The exact date at which Fontenelle migrated from Rouen to Paris is not known, but as the Abbé Trublet, who is generally well informed about all that concerns his hero, says in one place that he wrote all his works "perhaps down to the *Histoire des Oracles* (end of 1686) inclusively" at Rouen[5], and in another that he fixed his residence in Paris in 1687 or 1688, the natural inference is that he came to Paris in 1687 and that he was living there when he published his *Poésies pastorales* with the famous *Digression sur les Anciens et les Modernes*[5] by way of appendix.

Whatever its defects in modern eyes, his new work added to his already high reputation with a considerable and important section of the French public. They saw in him at once a charming poet, an admirable writer of prose, a progressive thinker, and a man of learning without a touch of pedantry. It was little wonder that he felt justified in becoming a candidate for the Académie Française at the next vacancy. But he was beaten by a

---

[1] *Œuvres*, III, 108.   [2] *Ib.* p. 113.
[3] *Ib.* pp. 119 ff.   [4] *Ib.* pp. 173 ff.
[5] This has been discussed sufficiently in the penultimate chapter. See pp. 329–332.

nobody, who was imposed upon the Academy by the king's brother, and later in the same year (1688) he was again defeated by one Jean de La Chapelle, whose reputation as a writer of tragedies was chiefly sustained by his excellent dinners. Two more defeats followed in 1689, one at the hands of a man of learning who had published nothing, and the other by François de Callières, whose share in the Quarrel of the Ancients and the Moderns has been related above[1].

Fontenelle's ill success may have been partly due to his comparative youth, but he had tenacious opponents in Boileau and Racine, who disliked him, firstly as Corneille's nephew, secondly as a *bel esprit*, and thirdly as the author of the *Digression sur les Anciens et les Modernes*. However, at the fifth attempt he was successful, and on May 5, 1691, he pronounced his *discours de réception*[2]. He had not forgotten or forgiven Racine's epigrams on *Aspar*, and his tribute to his illustrious uncle, "qui dans la plus noble espèce des productions de l'esprit *efface tous les autres noms*," was evidently meant as an insult to that uncle's rival and successor.

The ancients took their revenge two years later, when the newly-elected La Bruyère omitted Fontenelle's name from those Academicians whom he signalled out for especial praise. The *Mercure galant* replied, as we have seen, with an article attacking both La Bruyère's discourse and his *Caractères*, and La Bruyère countered with the portrait of Cydias[3]. It is too long to reproduce here in full, but I will give the passages which have special reference to Fontenelle's writings.

Ascagne est statuaire, Hégion fondeur, Æschine foulon, et Cydias bel esprit; c'est sa profession....Prose, vers, que voulez-vous? Il réussit également en l'un et l'autre....Fade discoureur, qui n'a pas mis plus tôt le pied dans une assemblée qu'il cherche quelques femmes auprès de qui il puisse s'insinuer, se parer de son bel esprit ou de sa philosophie, et mettre en œuvre ses rares conceptions: car, soit qu'il parle ou qu'il écrive, il ne doit pas être soupçonné d'avoir en vue ni le vrai ni le faux, ni le raisonnable ni le ridicule; il évite uniquement de donner dans le sens des autres et d'être de l'avis de quelqu'un: aussi attend-il dans un cercle que

---

[1] See pp. 332–335.　　　　　　[2] *Œuvres*, I, 109 ff.
[3] See above, p. 53. The portrait first appeared in the 8th edition (1693) of the *Caractères*, in the chapter *De la Société et de la Conversation*.

chacun se soit expliqué sur le sujet qui s'est offert, ou souvent qu'il a amené lui-même, pour dire dogmatiquement des choses toutes nouvelles, mais à son gré décisives et sans réplique. Cydias s'égale à Lucien et à Sénèque, se met au-dessus de Platon, de Virgile et de Théocrite; et son flatteur a soin de le confirmer tous les matins dans cette opinion. Uni de goût et d'intérêt avec les contempteurs d'Homère, il attend paisiblement que les hommes détrompés lui préfèrent les poètes modernes: il se met en ce cas à la tête de ces derniers, et il sait à qui il adjuge la seconde place. C'est, en un mot, un composé du pédant et du précieux, fait pour être admiré de la bourgeoisie et de la province, en qui néanmoins on n'aperçoit rien de grand que l'opinion qu'il a de lui-même.

The portrait is manifestly unjust, for it completely ignores the better and greater Fontenelle. But it no doubt represents with tolerable fidelity the Fontenelle of the Paris salons, as he appeared to a careful but morose and prejudiced observer. The love of differing from other people, for instance, which La Bruyère notes in Cydias was a real characteristic of Fontenelle. It arose partly from a desire to appear original, but partly also from a genuine distrust of tradition and popular opinion, and an equally genuine love of contradiction, which sometimes took the form of a temperately expressed, though none the less provoking, dogmatism.

After 1688 Fontenelle's literary activity slackened considerably. Two operas in 1689 and 1690 respectively, a tragedy in the latter year, the editing of a poetic anthology in 1692, and a short parallel between Corneille and Racine in 1693, the two last without his name, represent practically the sum total of his published work down to the close of the century. The anthology is interesting as evidence of his taste—or want of it. As Sainte-Beuve remarks, the school of Louis XIV has left absolutely no trace upon it, and in the fifth volume there are as many as 128 pieces by Benserade. The selection from each poet is preceded by a *petite vie*, which is like the *Éloges des Académiciens* in miniature[1]. In these productions we have Fontenelle the *bel esprit* and the original of Cydias. But his real work was of a more serious character. When he first came

---

[1] *Recueil des plus belles pièces des Poètes français depuis Villon jusqu'à Benserade*, 5 vols. Barbin. See Lachèvre, *op. cit.* III, and for Fontenelle's connexion with the work, Trublet, *op. cit.* pp. 72–74 and 292.

to settle in Paris, he often visited two of his fellow-students, Pierre Varignon and the Abbé de Saint-Pierre, both priests, who lived together in the *faubourg* Saint-Jacques[1]. Varignon, who became one of the leading mathematicians of his day, made himself known in 1687 by his *Projet d'une nouvelle Mécanique*. Saint-Pierre was principally occupied with the study of social man and the principles of government, but he found time to attend the lectures of Lémery and Duverney[2], with both of whom Varignon had close relations, as he also had with the astronomers and physicists, Duhamel and La Hire[3]. Thus Fontenelle, who had always had a liking and aptitude for mathematics, was brought into intercourse with the leading men in various branches of science, and his quick intelligence soon enabled him to follow the results of their studies and researches.

When the Peace of Ryswick gave Louis XIV once more leisure to turn his attention to home affairs, he took in hand a needed re-organisation of the Académie des Sciences. New regulations, or, as we should say, statutes, were drawn up by Pontchartrain, one of the Secretaries of State, and approved by the king and on February 4, 1699, they were read to the assembly by their president, the Abbé Bignon. One regulation was that the number of Academicians should be increased from sixteen to seventy, of whom ten should be honorary. Among the first honorary Academicians were Newton, Leibniz, Malebranche, Vauban, Renau, the naval engineer, and Fagon, the king's first physician. Fontenelle was appointed Secretary. It was an ideal choice, for, though he was a master of no science, he was well acquainted with all, and though he made no original contributions to knowledge himself, he could explain in lucid and literary language the contributions of his colleagues. Added to this he had the diligence, tact, and courtesy which help to make a perfect secretary[4]. In 1702 he

---

[1] A fourth friend was the Abbé de Vertot, whose *Histoire de la Conjuration de Portugal* appeared in 1689.

[2] See above, pp. 403–404.

[3] See Fontenelle, *Œuvres*, VII, 149–151.

[4] "Il lia une étroite amitié avec le secrétaire de l'Académie de Saturne,

justified his appointment by publishing the *Renouvellement de l'Académie des Sciences* (a brief notice of two pages), preceded by a remarkable *Préface sur l'utilité des Mathématiques et de la Physique*[1], to which I shall refer presently. In 1708 the *Renouvellement* was reprinted with 12 *éloges* of Academicians who had died since the re-organisation. The first three are quite short, but the fourth, that of Vincenzo Viviani, the pupil of Galileo, who died in 1703 at the age of 81, is much fuller. It is admirably done and the remaining eight are nearly all equally good. Best of all is Vauban, and Sylvain Regis, the opponent of Malebranche, and Denis Dodart, a distinguished physician and botanist and a writer on the history and theory of music, are both excellent. A second volume, containing 17 *éloges*, followed in 1717[2], a third with 12 *éloges* in 1722, and *Suite des Éloges des Académiciens morts depuis 1722* (20 *éloges*) in 1733. Fontenelle wrote only eight more, the last being that of Charles de Cisternay Du Fay (d. 1639), who distinguished himself in nearly every branch of science, but whose chief service perhaps was the resuscitation of the *Jardin du Roi*. After Fontenelle's death the whole number of 69 was published in two volumes in 1766[3].

These so-called *éloges* are really short biographies resembling those in the Supplements to the *Dictionary of National Biography*, in so far as they were written not long after the death of the "biographees," and in many cases from personal knowledge. "It has been so often said," remarks Faguet, "that these *éloges* are masterpieces that one could wish they

homme de beaucoup d'esprit, qui n'avait à la vérité rien inventé, mais qui rendait un fort bon compte des inventions des autres, et qui faisait passablement de petits vers et de grands calculs" (Voltaire, *Micromégas*, c. i).

[1] It will be remembered that, when the Academy was first founded, it had to divide its labours between mathematics and physics. Under the new regulations geometry, astronomy, and mechanics were constituted as departments of mathematics, and chemistry, anatomy, and botany as departments of physics.

[2] In the 1790 edition of Fontenelle's *Œuvres* the date of Parent's death is misprinted as 1719 instead of 1716.

[3] In the 1790 edition the *éloges* proper are followed by one on Claude Perrault, who died in 1688, and one on Mme de Lambert.

fell short of perfection, in order to be able to say something new. But one must accept the fact; they *are* masterpieces." I fully subscribe to this opinion. The only criticism
that Faguet has to make is that in what he calls the *grands
éloges*, as for instance in those of a Leibniz or a Malebranche,
one would welcome a more imposing tone, and a more outspoken admiration. One may say the same of the *éloge* of
Newton. But "outspoken admiration" was foreign to Fontenelle's nature and in one *éloge*, at least, that of Vauban, the
admiration is expressed with eloquence.

> Personne n'avait mieux que lui rappelé du ciel les mathématiques, pour
> les occuper aux besoins des hommes, et elles avaient pris entre ses mains
> une utilité aussi glorieuse peut-être que leur plus grande sublimité;

and the *éloge* ends with

> En un mot c'était un romain qu'il semblait que notre siècle eût dérobé
> aux plus heureux temps de la république[1].

But the biographies of the lesser men, of whom only about
half-a-dozen are known even by name at the present day, are,
as Faguet says, "marvels of truth and tact and taste." They
have two outstanding merits, one that they explain scientific
discoveries in language that is intelligible to the non-scientific
reader, the other that they portray these men of science in their
private life, as human beings with their virtues and their failings
—the latter touched on lightly and with tenderness. One loves
them for their modesty, their simplicity, their disinterestedness,
their devotion to their work. Many indeed were heroes, some
were even martyrs. The majority, as Fontenelle records with
evident admiration, were good Catholics, and a few were men
of real piety. Amid such general excellence it is difficult to
make a choice, but the lives of Sauveur[2], Renau[3], Varignon[3],
and Boerhaave[3] may be added to those of Vauban, Regis, and
Dodart as having a special charm and interest.

Fontenelle's sympathy with these representatives of science
sprang from his enthusiasm for science itself. If he did not

---

[1] With characteristic prudence Fontenelle omits all reference to the
dîme royale.

[2] *Œuvres*, VI.   [3] *Ib*. VII.

believe in the general progress of society, he at any rate
believed in the progress of science. In the *Préface sur l'utilité
des Mathématiques et de la Physique* he notes the great advance
that had been made during the last hundred years. In spite of
all the difficulties with which it had to contend,

On saurait s'étonner de la grandeur et de la rapidité du progrès des
sciences ; on en verrait même de toutes nouvelles sortir du néant, et peut-
être laisserait-on aller trop loin ses espérances pour l'avenir.

In this confident prediction of the future one is reminded of
the parting words of the priestess Bacbuc to Pantagruel and
his companions. And the latter part of the *Préface* is in the
same vein of eloquent enthusiasm. "Astronomy and anatomy,"
says Fontenelle, "are the two sciences which bring before us
most vividly two great characters of the Creator; the one His
immensity…the other His infinite intelligence." A little earlier
he compares the study of history unfavourably with that of
physics :

La physique suit et démêle, autant qu'il est possible, les traces de
l'intelligence et de la sagesse infinie qui a tout produit ; au lieu que
l'histoire a pour objets les effets irréguliers des passions et des caprices
des hommes, et une suite d'évènements si bizarres, que l'on a autrefois
imaginé une divinité aveugle et insensée pour lui en donner la direction.

Finally he points out that up to the present time nature had
only been studied in small pieces and he concludes with this
striking peroration :

Le temps viendra peut-être que l'on joindra en un corps régulier ces
membres épars ; et s'ils sont tels qu'on le souhaite, ils s'assembleront en
quelque sorte d'eux-mêmes. Plusieurs vérités séparées, dès qu'elles sont en
assez grande nombre, offrent si vivement à l'esprit leurs rapports et leur
mutuelle dépendance, qu'il semble qu'après avoir été détachées par une
espèce de violence les unes d'avec les autres, elles cherchent mutuellement
à se réunir.

In this passage we find clearly stated the idea of the solidarity
of the sciences, to which Brunetière insists that the name of
Fontenelle should be attached[1]. We are still far from complete
solidarity, but the advance in knowledge that has been brought

[1] *Op. cit.* p. 241.

about by the association of chemistry with physiology, physics, and biology, of botany with geology and physiology, of physiology with anatomy, and of physics with astronomy, amply proves the correctness of Fontenelle's prediction.

The *Éloges* represent Fontenelle at his maturest and best, not only in his thought but in his style. From the first he had abandoned the long periodic phrase of the seventeenth century for the short broken sentences which were to characterise the style of the eighteenth. But his earlier writings were disfigured by *préciosité* and a constant striving after *esprit*. In the *Histoire des Oracles* he dropped *préciosité* and contented himself with the natural *esprit* of his quick intelligence. His migration from his province to the capital and his intercourse with simple and clear-thinking men of science confirmed him in the cultivation of simplicity and lucidity and *netteté*, and his work as secretary of the Académie des Sciences with its routine of business-like reports almost completed the cure. He suffered, however, from occasional relapses, as in the *éloge* of Malezieu, where we come upon the following passage:

> Ce n'était point un mérite enveloppé qui perçât difficilement au travers d'un extérieur triste et sombre ; sa facilité à entendre et à retenir lui avait épargné ces efforts et cette pénible contention, dont l'habitude produit la mélancolie ; les sciences étaient entrées dans son esprit comme dans leur séjour naturel, et n'y avaient rien gâté ; au contraire, elles s'étaient parées elles-mêmes de la vivacité qu'elles y avaient trouvée[1].

This is neither simple nor lucid nor *net*.

The name of Malezieu recalls the Court of Sceaux[2], where Fontenelle was sometimes a visitor. But its lively entertainments, in spite of the *esprit* with which the Duchess seasoned them[3], could not have been much to his liking. He preferred the calm decorum of a true salon, where his conversational powers could have full scope.

Since the death of the Duchesse de Richelieu in 1696 and the decline of Ninon de Lenclos's salon a few years later, the salons had been more or less closed to men of letters, who

---

[1] Written in 1727. See *Œuvres*, VII.
[2] See above, p. 143.
[3] "Elle voulait que la joie eût de l'esprit" is Fontenelle's expression

in their default had resorted to the newly-instituted *cafés*[1].
But towards the close of the seventeenth century the Marquise
de Lambert, whose writings on education have been discussed
in an earlier chapter[2], opened in the Hôtel de Nevers (now
the *Cabinet des Médailles* of the *Bibliothèque Nationale*) a salon,
which was no doubt consciously modelled on that of Mme
de Rambouillet. By 1710 she had definitely organised it. On
two days of the week, Tuesdays and Wednesdays, she received
her friends, the Tuesdays being distinctly literary and scientific,
and the Wednesdays chiefly social. But the *gens du monde*
who cared for literature or science were perfectly welcome on
a Tuesday. On both days the general reception was preceded
by a dinner-party at noon, to which the hostess's more intimate friends were invited. Before long her salon acquired
great influence in the intellectual world, and her interest came
to be recognised as an indispensable passport to the Academy.
Her contemporaries accused her and her salon of *préciosité*.
Lesage satirised her in *Gil Blas* under the name of the Marquise
de Chaves, whose house at Salamanca was known as "le bureau
des ouvrages d'esprit[3]." Her old friend M. de La Rivière, the
son-in-law of Bussy-Rabutin, made it a special grievance against
her that "elle se livra au public, elle s'associa à Messieurs de
l'Académie, elle établit chez elle un bureau d'esprit[4]." Sainte-
Beuve touches on the question with his usual delicacy and
insight:

> Dès le commencement du dix-huitième siècle, une nouvelle maladie de
> l'esprit, un nouveau genre de précieux, et d'autant plus subtil qu'il se
> donnait des airs simples, s'introduisit et courut par Fontenelle et La Motte.
> Le salon de Mme de Lambert, la petite Cour de Sceaux, un peu plus tard

---

[1] See above, p. 154.

[2] See above, pp. 239–241. For Mme de Lambert and her salon see
Sainte-Beuve, *Causeries du Lundi*, IV; Ch. Giraud in *Journal des Savants*,
1880, pp. 112 ff.; G. Desnoiresterres, *Les Cours galantes*, 4 vols. 1859–1864,
vol. IV; and the notice prefixed to *Œuvres morales de la Mise de Lambert*,
ed. Lescure, 1883.

[3] Book IV, c. 8 (this part was published in 1715). Lesage repeated the
attack with more good nature twenty years later in *Le Bachelier de Sala-
manque* (1736) after Mme de Lambert's death.

[4] *Lettres choisies*, 2 vols. 1751, II, 205 (quoted by Sainte-Beuve).

l'hôtel de Brancas, en tenaient école à des degrés différents, et l'on y voyait comme des jeux d'esprit[1].

The Marquis d'Argenson, the author of the *Mémoires*, who dined with Mme de Lambert every Wednesday for fifteen years, found in her style "quelque affectation de précieux," and here again Sainte-Beuve comes to our aid. He notices in some of her expressions a search after novelty, which shews ingenuity but also a certain affectation, and he gives as examples "le *pensé* de M. de La Motte" and "les ajoutés de l'imagination[2]."

It was in this salon, the first of a long succession of literary salons which ended with that of Mme Necker on the very eve of the Revolution, that Fontenelle reigned, as he reigned later in those of Mme de Tencin (1726–1749) and Mme Geoffrin (1749–1766). He was in a very different position from that which he held at the time of La Bruyère's portrait. He was now a man over fifty, and a leading figure in the literary and scientific world of Paris. It was no longer necessary for him to attract attention by paradox and contradiction. He was recognised as an admirable conversationalist—all the more admirable, because he could listen as well as talk. Moreover, he liked society and was deservedly popular. He was gay, witty, and of a singularly even temperament. His ideal of happiness, as he tells us in his treatise, *Du Bonheur*[3], was tranquillity, and he realised his ideal with remarkable success. "He had never wept," says Mme Geoffrin, "he had never been angry, he had never run. One day I said to him, 'M. de Fontenelle, have you ever laughed?' 'No, I have never uttered ah, ah, ah.' That was his idea of laughter[4]." Mme de Tencin once said to him, pointing to his breast, "It is not a heart that you keep here, but brains like those in your head[5]." On which the Abbé de Trublet, who tells the story, aptly comments that some brains are worth a good deal more than some hearts. For Fontenelle, though he was never in love and never demonstrative in friendship, was a loyal and serviceable friend. The story of his generosity to his compatriot,

---

[1] *Causeries du Lundi*, XII, 483.　　[2] *Ib.* IV, 233.　　[3] *Œuvres*, V, 330 ff.

[4] Mme Necker, *Nouveaux mélanges*, 1801, pp. 164–173 (*Fragment après une conversation de Mme Geoffrin sur Fontenelle*).

[5] Trublet, *Mémoires*, p. 116.

M. Brunel, is well known. Soon after he came to Paris he saved a thousand crowns; it was the whole of his fortune. His friend wrote to him, "Send me your thousand crowns," and Fontenelle replied that he had destined them for a certain purpose. The friend answered, "I have need of them," and Fontenelle sent them[1]. When another old friend, the Abbé de Saint-Pierre, was expelled from the Académie Française for his criticisms on the government of Louis XIV, Fontenelle's was the only white ball.

There is one quality in his character, which his friends and contemporaries naturally did not notice, but which is worthy of our attention. He had an instinctive *flair* for every intellectual movement that promised to be more than a passing fashion, and almost from the inception of that movement he placed himself conspicuously in its vanguard. We have seen the part that he played in the revolt against the sacrosanct authority of the ancients, and how, when Mme de Lambert organised her salon, he at once became the most prominent figure in it. But, however great the charm of the eighteenth-century salon, it was not on the whole an advantage to literature, and in other ways Fontenelle is typical of the literary defects of the age of enlightenment. He reflects its insensitiveness to poetry and imagination, its lack of constructive power, its contempt for tradition and history. So too the practice of introducing indecent ideas under the cover of decorous language, which is so unpleasant a feature in the *Lettres persanes* and the novels of Voltaire, may be said to date from his *Lettres galantes*. Sometimes, as in the *préciosité* and the striving after *esprit* of his earlier writings, he is merely giving fresh life to a more or less discredited fashion, but even here he appears as something of an innovator, for his *préciosité* is more often displayed in his thought than in his language. So too, while in his unswerving devotion to the Cartesian reason he is but treading a well-worn track, in his hints that the Christian religion must logically come under the jurisdiction of this

[1] *Éloge* by Charles Le Beau, Secretary of the *Académie des Inscriptions et Belles-Lettres* (Fontenelle, *Œuvres*, I, 50 ff.). See also the portrait by Mme de Lambert in the same volume, pp. 45–49.

sovereign reason, he is helping to inaugurate a movement of momentous consequences.

Finally, of one movement, a movement which has gone forward uninterruptedly and without reaction to the present day, he may claim to be the absolute initiator. "In the share that he took in the development of science and in the formation of the scientific *esprit*—there," says his best modern commentator and critic, "lies his true title to glory and his greatest originality[1]." It was not only that he helped to make science popular—he had fellow-workers in this line—or that he wrote the first popular treatise on a scientific subject, but that he was the first to recognise the solidarity of science, and the brotherhood of men of science. Bacon, indeed, had proclaimed the unity of science, but by science he meant all knowledge. Fontenelle limited his vision to the natural sciences, and in these he had the great advantage over Bacon, that, through his own studies and his wide intercourse with scientific workers, many of whom were adepts in various branches of science, he was able to judge at first hand how far the separate sciences were mutually interdependent, and how far the discoveries in one were likely to assist research in another.

Fontenelle is reported to have said that his greatest merit was that he was not jealous of M. de La Motte. For La Motte's position in the literary world, and especially in the salon of Mme de Lambert, was almost equal to Fontenelle's. Like his friend he was applauded for his *esprit universel*, but he confined his "universality" to the field of literature. There was no kind of poetry and no form of drama that he did not attempt, but though he had great facility and considerable talent, not a single line of his has survived. If he had more warmth of feeling than Fontenelle he equally lacked imagination.

Born in Paris, Antoine Houdar de La Motte (1672–1731)[2]

---

[1] See Maigron, *op. cit.* pp. 392–404; the whole of chapter II on Fontenelle's scientific work (pp. 325–372) is of the highest excellence.

[2] *Œuvres*, 10 *tom.* 1754; Trublet, *op. cit.* pp. 329–414 (an article by the Abbé Goujet which Trublet revised for the *Grand Dictionnaire* of Moreri, 1759); P. Dupont, *Un poète-philosophe au commencement du XVIIIᵉ siècle, Houdar de La Motte*, 1898.

was a pupil of the Jesuits and later a law-student, though he never practised. After producing a comedy at Les Italiens, which was a failure (1693), he conceived the idea of entering La Trappe, but, after a two months' trial, M. de Rancé declined to admit him. In 1697 he returned to the theatre and scored a great success with an opera, entitled *L'Europe galante*. Other dramas—a heroic pastoral, opera-tragedies, opera-ballets, comedy-ballets, and comedies—followed, at about the rate of one a year, down to 1709. In 1707 he published a volume of *Odes avec un Discours sur la Poésie en générale*, and in 1710 he was elected to the Académie Française, the rival candidate being his enemy J.-B. Rousseau[1]. In the following year Mme Dacier published her prose translation of the *Iliad* and at the end of 1713 La Motte produced his abridgement in verse. But I have already recounted how the Quarrel between the Ancients and the Moderns was renewed over the body of Homer[2]. La Motte behaved throughout with his habitual amiability and courtesy, and in his last contribution to the controversy, *Réflexions sur la Critique* (1715), he sums up in a few words the opinion of all sensible men:

Il est hors de doute qu'il faut les (the ancients) estimer et les lire; il s'agit seulement de savoir s'il ne les faut pas peser au même poids que les modernes.

.   .   .   .   .   .

J'aime mieux croire que les anciens ont examiné; et je prétends seulement que ce droit n'est pas éteint pour nous.

And in his earlier *Discours sur la Poésie* he had said:

En un mot ce n'est point un préjugé légitime que je condamne, c'est un joug que je secoue.

It was the application to literature of the Cartesian right of free inquiry.

It was a merit of La Motte's that he had the courage of his opinions, but in his latest critical writings he allowed his love of paradox—for its own sake, and not merely as a help to serious argument—to carry him beyond the bounds of common sense. As, however, his campaign against poetry, in

---

[1] See above, p. 154.   [2] See above, pp. 345–347.

which he puts forward his worst paradoxes, did not take place till 1730[1], we need not concern ourselves with it here. He has an excuse in the condition of French poetry in his day, which, as we have seen, was at once prosaic and frivolous[2]. "Ce sont les poètes, me dit-il," writes Montesquieu in the *Lettres persanes*, "c'est-à-dire ces auteurs dont le métier est de mettre des entraves au bon sens, et d'accabler la raison sous les agréments," and, after a good word for the dramatic poets, he adds, "Voici les lyriques que je méprise autant que je fais cas des autres[3]." Finally it should be said that though La Motte, as his *Correspondance galante poétique* with the Duchesse du Maine shews, could write in the *précieux* style with the best, his ordinary prose, the prose of his critical discourses, is easy, lucid, and entirely free from affectation.

Of far more importance than La Motte in the history of thought is Fontenelle's fellow-Norman and fellow-student, Charles-Irénée Castel, Abbé de Saint-Pierre (1658–1743), the second son of the Marquis de Saint-Pierre, who came to Paris a year before Fontenelle[4]. But he was a preacher rather than a practical reformer, and of the two ideas with which his name is associated, the progress of human society to perfection and the abolition of war, the first did not become prominent till the second half of the eighteenth century, and the second, though an abridgement of the *Projet de Paix* was made by

---

[1] In 1730 La Motte published in 2 vols. his *Œuvres de théâtre, avec plusieurs Discours sur la Tragédie* and later in the same year, *Suite des Réflexions sur la Tragédie où l'on répond à M. de Voltaire* (see *Œuvres*, IV). In vol. I of *Œuvres de théâtre* will be found a comparison of the first scene of Racine's *Mithridate* with the same scene in prose and in vol. II an ode in prose. But some of the remarks on tragedy are quite sensible. One of his tragedies, *Inès de Castro* (1723), had a great success, running for forty performances.

[2] See above, c. v.

[3] *Lettre* CXXXVII.

[4] See above, p. 416. For Saint-Pierre generally see É. Goumy, *Étude sur la vie et les écrits de l'Abbé de Saint-Pierre*, 1859; G. de Molinari, *L'Abbé de Saint-Pierre, sa vie et ses œuvres*, 1857; Sainte-Beuve, *Causeries du Lundi*, XV (1861)—a notice of the two preceding works; J. Drouet, *L'Abbé de Saint-Pierre: l'homme et l'œuvre*, 1912; J. B. Bury, *The Idea of Progress*, 1920, c. vi. There is an incomplete edition of his writings, *Ouvrages de morale et de politique*, 16 tom., Rotterdam, 1733–1741.

Rousseau, can only be said to have received serious consideration in quite recent years. I do not, therefore, propose to include
him in my survey, and shall content myself with a brief mention of the few notices that we get of him during our period.
Though everyone recognised and respected his transparent
honesty and sincerity, he was generally regarded as a crank
and a bore, impervious to irony and wholly devoid of humour.
One of his peculiarities was that he made a practice of "running after"—the expression is his own—anyone who had
distinguished himself as a writer. Among the sufferers from
this habit was La Bruyère, who retaliated by introducing the
character of Mopse into the fifth edition (1690) of *Les Caractères*.

Je connais *Mopse* d'une visite qu'il m'a rendue sans me connaître. Il
prie des gens qu'il ne connaît point de le mener chez d'autres dont il n'est
pas connu; il écrit à des femmes qu'il connaît de vue; il s'insinue dans
un cercle de personnes respectables, et qui ne savent quel il est, et là, sans
attendre qu'on l'interroge, ni sans sentir qu'il interrompt, il parle, et souvent, et ridiculement[1].

It is not likely that the good Abbé was in the least disturbed
by this unflattering portrait or that in consequence he paid one
less visit to "persons of importance." It must be remembered
that he was not actuated by any desire for self-advertisement;
his object was partly to widen his field of observation, and partly
to interest people in his innumerable "projects" for the reform
of society. Nor does it appear that men of letters in general
greatly resented his intrusions, for early in 1695, though he had
published nothing, he was, thanks largely to the active canvassing
of himself and Fontenelle, elected to the Academy. No doubt
the moderns, who were now in a majority in that assembly,
regarded him as a useful addition to their party. In the same
year he bought the post of first almoner to Madame, whom he
found an excellent mistress. Writing of this to Mme de Lambert, he says:

Je n'ai fait qu'acheter une petite loge pour voir de plus près ces acteurs
qui jouent souvent sans le savoir, sur le théâtre du monde, des rôles très
importants au reste des sujets....Je vois jouer tout à mon aise les premiers

---

[1] *Du Mérite personnel.*

rôles, et je les vois d'autant mieux que je n'en joue aucun, que je vais partout, et que l'on me remarque nulle part[1].

From this convenient post of observation at the Palais-Royal he observed and reflected at leisure and collected material for his *Annales politiques*[2]. In January 1712 he went to Utrecht as secretary to the Abbé (afterwards Cardinal) de Polignac, one of the two French plenipotentiaries, and he remained in Holland till the peace was signed on April 11, 1713. Returning to France, he published in the same year the first two volumes of his famous *Projet pour rendre la Paix perpétuelle en Europe*, to which he added a third volume in 1717. In the following year appeared the *Discours sur la Polysynodie*, the work for which he was expelled from the Academy—not because it defended the creation of the six Councils in place of the suppressed ministries, but because it severely attacked the government of Louis XIV. Saint-Simon, in his account of the episode ("une fort plate chose"), does not spare his contempt for this action of the Academy, in which the Maréchal de Villeroy, whom he greatly disliked, played a leading part. He says of the Abbé that he had "de l'esprit, des lettres, et des chimères," and he adds that he was

fort rempli de lui-même, bon homme et honnête homme pourtant, grand faiseur de livres, de projets et de réformations dans la politique et dans le gouvernement en faveur du bien public[3].

---

[1] Goumy, *op. cit.* pp. 22–23.

[2] Published after his death in 2 vols. Londres (?), 1757; *ib.* 1758; Geneva, 1767; ed. J. Drouet, 1912. They cover the years 1658–1739.

[3] *Mémoires*, XIV, 389–390.

EPILOGUE

ALMOST at the beginning of his first *causerie* on the Abbé de
Saint-Pierre Sainte-Beuve writes as follows:

Le règne de Louis XIV avait trop duré: la dernière partie de ce règne
produisit un bon nombre d'esprits, très sensibles aux défauts, aux abus et
aux excès d'un si long régime, qui passèrent à une politique tout opposée
et rêvèrent une amélioration sociale moyennant la paix, par de bonnes lois,
par des réformes dans l'État et par toutes sortes de procédés et d'ingrédients
philanthropiques.

Among these "reforming spirits" he numbers Catinat, who
wrote nothing, Vauban, Boisguillebert, Fénelon, Saint-Simon
(up to a certain point), and Boulainvilliers, who published
nothing before 1727. Some, he says, were retrograde reformers,
and some were progressive reformers. In the latter class he
naturally includes the Abbé de Saint-Pierre. He might have
added the names of La Bruyère and Massillon, who, if they
had no specific reforms to propose and if on the whole they
were loyal admirers of Louis XIV, were at any rate keenly alive
to the price which the country had to pay for his conquests
in the crushing load of taxation and the sufferings of the large
majority of his subjects[1]. Unfortunately the reaction in politics did not last long. The Councils, which the Abbé de Saint-
Pierre defended so warmly in April 1718, were dissolved in
the following September, and the government of the Regent,
with Dubois at the helm, became every whit as despotic as
that of Louis XIV[2]. Thanks mainly to the good relations which
prevailed between France and England, and to the fact that
the first ministers of these two countries, Fleury and Walpole[3],
were lovers of peace, France was at peace for twenty years
from the Treaty of Utrecht, but in 1733 the war-party, which

---

[1] See above for La Bruyère, pp. 63–64, and for Massillon, pp. 313 and 316.

[2] "Je n'examine pas la théorie des Conseils. Elle fut, vous le savez,
l'objet idolâtre des esprits creux de la vieille Cour" (Letter of Dubois,
quoted in Lavisse, *Hist. de France*, VIII, ii, 18).

[3] Walpole became prime minister in 1721, Fleury first minister in 1726.

Fleury, who was now eighty, had no longer the energy to withstand, got the upper hand, and war was declared against Austria. During the next thirty years France had only eight years of peace.

If the spirit of revolt against the established political *régime* only smouldered in discontent and quickly died down, it was far otherwise in the sphere of religion. Here the spirit of free inquiry, which had manifested itself in the early days of the Renaissance, was becoming ever and ever bolder. The growth of rationalism in French literature in the sixteenth century has been recently traced in an admirable volume by the Abbé Busson[1], but, though much has been written on various aspects and phases of rationalism in the seventeenth century, this period, considered as a whole, awaits its historian. M. Busson's book carries the inquiry down to 1601. In the following year St François de Sales came to Paris and the Catholic revival may be said to have begun.

In the first half of the seventeenth century, especially from 1615 onwards, free-thought, rendered perhaps more aggressive by the activity of the new religious spirit, was represented by a group of men, chiefly young men, who proclaimed themselves disciples of Vanini, led debauched lives, and wrote a good deal of verse, which has been carefully collected and edited by M. Lachèvre in numerous volumes. When Pascal began to put into execution his design for an Apology for Christianity (1657), this more noisy and conspicuous type of free-thought was on the decline. Yet in July 1662, six weeks before his death, he could speak of "the ungodly and the atheists" as "abounding in Paris," and earlier in the same year Bossuet preached his famous sermons *Du mauvais Riche* and *Sur la Providence*. Atheism of this superficial and unphilosophic character continued for a time to be the fashion with dissipated nobles and other worldlings, but, though in their high-flown moods they sometimes made a childish and tasteless parade of impiety, as soon as they felt a twinge of gout they sent for their confessor.

[1] H. Busson, *Les sources et le développement du Rationalisme dans la littérature française de la Renaissance* (1533-1601), 1922.

Of far more importance than these "athéistes de pratique," as Bayle calls them[1], were the genuine rationalists or doubters, who led respectable lives, and, while they submitted the Old Testament records and the dogmas of the Christian religion to a searching scrutiny, often accepted as a matter of faith what they questioned in the name of reason, even conforming to the observances of their church, whether Catholic or Protestant. It may be remembered that Bayle criticised Le Vayer and Naudé, whom he greatly admired for their learning, for posing too often as *esprits forts*, but neither of these freethinkers and sceptics ever challenged accepted opinions with regard to religion or morals so boldly as Bayle did in the *Pensées sur la Comète* (1682).

As side issues arising out of this treatise against superstition, he defended atheism, argued that morality is not dependent on religion, and maintained that the test of a miracle is its utility and its conformity to our ideas of justice and goodness. The treatise also contains in germ his advocacy of toleration, and this he further develops in his next work, the *Critique générale de l'Histoire du Calvinisme*, while it forms the main subject of the *Commentaire philosophique* (1686). But Bayle, in pleading for tolerance, attacked dogma. It is on dogma, he argued, that the supreme authority of the Church rests. If dogma is founded on insecure foundations, her right to impose her will on reluctant consciences falls to the ground. Five or six months before the appearance of the *Commentaire philosophique* Bossuet delivered his funeral oration on Anne di Gonzaga, the Princess Palatine, which contains his celebrated attack on the *libertins*. A few short passages will shew how utterly he was opposed to Bayle's views.

Il a mis dans cette Église une autorité, seule capable d'abaisser l'orgueil et de relever la simplicité....C'est contre cette autorité que les libertins se révoltent avec un air de mépris. Mais qu'ont-ils vu, ces rares génies, qu'ont-ils vu plus que les autres?...Par où ont-ils deviné...que toutes les religions qu'on voit sur la terre soient également bonnes? Leur raison,

[1] *Œuvres*, III, 414, and see *Dict. hist.* art. ' Des Barreaux ' in which Bayle makes some very just and sensible remarks on Des Barreaux and his friends.

qu'ils prennent pour guide, ne présente à leur esprit que des conjectures et des embarras....Qu'est-ce donc après tout, Messieurs, qu'est-ce que leur malheureuse incrédulité, sinon une erreur sans fin, une témérité qui hasarde tout, un étourdissement volontaire, et, en un mot, un orgueil qui ne peut souffrir une autorité légitime?

Bayle would have resented, and did in fact resent, the imputation that he was a *libertin*, but Bossuet, with his habitual skill in diagnosis, has put his finger on the motive power of the free-thought of the age. It was a revolt against the autocracy of the Church, just as the views of the political reformers and philanthropists were a revolt against the autocracy of the State.

Fontenelle was not, like Bayle, steeped in theology and philosophy, nor, like Bayle, did he delight in written controversy. But equally with Bayle he mistrusted tradition and common opinion, while he viewed the miraculous with even greater suspicion. We need not suppose that he had any aim in the *Pluralité des Mondes* beyond popularising astronomy, but, as has often been pointed out, the change from the Ptolemaic to the Copernican system, in relegating this world of ours from the centre of the universe to a subordinate place in one of many solar groups, has made a radical difference in the conception of man's part in the scheme of creation. It is true that for the practical Christian the Fall of man and his Redemption remain the great central truth, but it is equally true that the new astronomy, and in more recent times the new geology, have made the Fall far more difficult of comprehension.

In the *Histoire des Oracles*, published like the former work in 1686, he openly expresses his distrust of tradition and miracle, and though he confines his criticism to the religions of Greece and Rome he leaves it to be inferred that the Christian religion is equally a subject for the scrutiny of the Cartesian reason. His book might fairly be regarded as an invitation to that combat which Bossuet foresaw between the Church and the Cartesian philosophy[1].

In this combat the Cartesian rationalist found a strong support for his opinions in the numerous books of travel which

[1] See above, p. 410 n.[3]

appeared throughout the seventeenth century, especially in those relating to New France. Samuel de Champlain was too good an observer to be biassed by imagination and sentiment, but the lawyer, Marc Lescarbot, who was in Canada from 1606 to 1608, and Gabriel Sagard, the Récollet father, who spent two years in the country of the Hurons, were enthusiastic in their praise of the innocence and simplicity of the Indians. The Jesuits too, who from 1633 onwards began rapidly to supplant the Récollets, though they warned intending missionaries not to believe too implicitly in the optimistic accounts of Lescarbot and Sagard, painted in their own annual *Relations* a hardly less attractive picture. "They wrote in perfect good faith," says Parkman[1], but on the evidence of their own reports and still more on that of their personal sufferings and heroic deaths, it is clear that, though the practices of the Indian tribes varied considerably, and though stationary settlers like the Hurons were less ferocious than wandering hunters like the Iroquois, all the tribes alike were in a high degree licentious, cruel, and superstitious. But, in spite of the facts, the legend of the "noble savage" continued to hold the field. M. Chinard quotes a pertinent passage from a *Relation* of 1694, when, as he says, the Jesuits had lost much ground in Canada:

Nous voyons dans les sauvages les beaux restes de la nature humaine qui sont entièrement corrompus dans les peuples policés. De toutes les onze passions ils n'en ont que deux, la colère est la plus grande; mais encore en ont-ils peu dans l'excès, lors de la guerre. Vivre en commun sans procès, se contenter de peu sans avarice, être assidus au travail, on ne peut rien voir de plus patient, de plus hospitalier, affables, libéraux, modérés dans leur parler: enfin, tous nos P.P. et les Français qui ont fréquenté les sauvages estiment que la vie se passe plus doucement parmi eux que parmi nous[2].

The *naïveté* and good faith of the Jesuit missionaries is shewn by their disregard of the handle which their optimistic accounts of these non-Christian savages gave to opponents of the Christian faith. We have seen in an earlier chapter to what

---

[1] *The Jesuits in North America*, 20th ed. 1885.
[2] Chinard, *op. cit.* p. 147.

use the free-thinking Baron de Lahontan, who went to Canada
as a soldier in 1683 and published his book twenty years
later, put the "noble savage." But another line of argument
was suggested to free-thinkers by tales of travel—of travel not
only in America, but in Africa, Asia, and the East and West
Indies—which they accepted with an inability to distinguish
truth from fable that is not unknown even in this critical age.
If, they argued, there are so many different religions, if there
is so much diversity in moral conduct, if what is a crime in
one country is a virtue in another, what becomes of the claim
to exclusive truth of the Christian religion and the Christian
moral code? The argument, so far as it relates to morals, had
been put forward, though not very seriously, by Montaigne
in his essay *On Cannibals*[1], and it is enforced by examples
drawn from a much wider acquaintance with books of travel
by La Mothe Le Vayer in his *Cinq dialogues*.

Another method of employing the increasing knowledge of
distant and little-known countries in the service of free-thought
was that of writing imaginary accounts of travel or, as they
are sometimes called, Extraordinary Voyages. Of two of these,
which appeared before our period, *La Terre Australe* (1676)
and *Histoire des Sévarambes* (1677), and of two which appeared during our period, *Histoire de l'île de Calejava* (1700)
and *Voyages et Avantures de Jaques Massé* (1710), I have spoken
in the chapter on Fiction, and it is not necessary to refer to them
further. By the time the two last were published free-thinking
had greatly increased. "Faith is extinguished in this country,"
bluntly says Madame in July 1699, "to such an extent that
you will not find a single young man who does not desire to be
an atheist[2]." But the strongest invective against the wide-spread
unbelief of the age is to be found in Massillon's Funeral
Oration on the Prince de Conti, which he delivered in 1707.
He says that Conti, though not a devout worshipper nor an
altogether orthodox believer, "did homage to the truth of
God's mysteries," and then he bursts forth with:

Dois-je le dire ici, Messieurs? dans un siècle, où la religion est devenue
le jouet, ou de la débauche, ou d'une fausse science : dans un siècle, où

---

[1] I, xxx.   [2] *Correspondance*, ed. Jaeglé, I, 202.

l'impiété est comme la première preuve du bel esprit: dans un siècle, où croire encore en Dieu, est presque la honte, ou de la raison, ou du courage: dans un siècle, où pour n'être pas confondu avec le vulgaire, il faut se donner l'affreuse distinction de l'incrédulité: dans un siècle, enfin, où tant d'hommes superficiels blasphèment ce qu'ils ignorent; se croyent plus habiles à mesure qu'ils sont plus téméraires; apprennent à douter de la religion avant de la connoître; s'érigent en docteurs de l'impiété avant que d'avoir été les disciples de la foi; et s'élèvent contre la science de Dieu, sans avoir même celle des hommes.

Something must be allowed for oratorical exaggeration, but even so it is a formidable indictment.

Hand in hand with the revolt against absolutism in politics and religion went the revolt against absolutism in literature. That is the real significance of the Quarrel of the Ancients and the Moderns, a significance which is partially concealed by the confused character of the attack and the languor of the defence. When Perrault read his famous poem to the Academy, he had two ostensible objects in view, to protest against the adoration of the ancients and to extol the age of Louis XIV. But he had, though unavowed, a third object—to mortify Boileau and Racine, who were regarded by the king and not a few competent judges as the chief living masters of French literature. The result was that in his eagerness to slight the real masters of the age he selects as its representatives against the ancients a number of poets who not only do not belong to the age, but who by no stretch of courtesy can be described as anything but second-rate. Fontenelle, who backed up Perrault with his *Digression,* had the wit to see that the really important point was whether the human race was progressing or deteriorating, but he too damaged the case against the infallibility of the ancients by indulging in comparisons between individual writers, for which his slender knowledge of ancient literature and the feebleness of his literary criticism quite unfitted him. Meanwhile Perrault gave several laborious years to the presentation of his case in elaborate detail. His *Parallèle* shews controversial skill and a certain literary ability, but it also reveals his ignorance of the ancients and his insensibility to the whole poetic side of literature. Perhaps Boileau did not think that it deserved a proper answer; at any rate his answer was long delayed and, when it came, ineffective. A reconciliation between the two chief combatants followed, and six years later (1700) Boileau announced it to the world in an open letter to Perrault. In this letter he conceded that the moderns had surpassed the ancients in some departments of literature, and this concession was practically an abandonment of the whole position. If the writers of a single age—the age of Louis XIV—were superior to the ancients (as he contended) in drama and their equals in lyric poetry, why should not the moderns in general be the equals or even the superiors of the ancients in other branches of literature? Fourteen years later the controversy broke out afresh, this time between Mme Dacier and La Motte. Mme Dacier was mostly in the right, but she lost her temper; La Motte was largely in the wrong, but he remained calm and courteous and the public were with La Motte. As a critic and translator of Homer he had failed egregiously, but when he claimed that the ancients were not sacrosanct, but that they must be subjected to criticism in the same way as the moderns, he was indubitably right.

Thus French literature was emancipated from the tyranny of the ancients. But it was not set free altogether. In the place of Greek and Roman classicism the arbiters of taste set up French classicism. Racine became their Homer, and Boileau their Aristotle. For all Voltaire's efforts to introduce more external action and spectacular effect into tragedy he did not advance beyond *Athalie*. Marmontel and La Harpe were still in tutelage to Boileau.

Perrault, Fontenelle, and La Motte fought their campaigns against the ancients under the Cartesian flag of Reason, and their excessive devotion to it led them to ignore the claims of imagination and emotion. As the result nearly all creative literature began to shew signs of decline. Poetry only survived in neatly turned *vers de société* and the empty virtuosity of Rousseau. The study of human nature, which had owed much to Descartes, also underwent a change. La Bruyère, believing that all the best about human conduct had been already said, directed his remarkable power of observation to man's outward appearance, to his bearing in society, and other external habits.

His book had a great success and a far-reaching influence. We have seen that it led in comedy to the creation of types rather than characters, and to lively and well-filled pictures of society rather than to well-constructed dramas. *Turcaret*, the masterpiece of the period, is a comedy of manners instead of a comedy of character, and though admirably constructed has no plot. Turcaret himself, a living embodiment of La Bruyère's Sosie, is not so much an individual as a type. Lesage owed still more to La Bruyère in the series of social sketches which he strung together under the title of *Le diable boiteux*, and even in *Gil Blas*, which inaugurated the one branch of creative literature that bore new fruit in the eighteenth century, the hero's readiness to adapt himself to every variety of social experience is one of the conspicuous features in his character.

But *Gil Blas* dates from 1715; during our period no regular novel, unless *Télémaque* is to be accounted one, appeared. Fiction was represented by fictitious voyages, apocryphal memoirs, and fairy-tales, and among the writers of the two latter were a considerable number of women. The fact is significant of the growing importance of women in literature, which was increased and consolidated by the establishment of Mme de Lambert's salon, the first of a long line of *bureaux d'esprit*. With Fontenelle and La Motte for its high priests it became a living influence in the literary world. Conversation took the place of the written word as an organ for the formation of taste, and gradually and imperceptibly a new tyranny was set up. *Esprit*, variety, and novelty were proclaimed as indispensable qualities; long works were discouraged as putting too much strain on the attention of the reader; and literature generally was shaped to meet the needs of a pleasure-loving and fashionable society.

But this is looking forward. Looking back at the literature of our period as a whole, one has to confess that it can shew very few works that rank among the world's masterpieces. Eliminating the *Oraison de Condé*, the *Histoire des Variations des Églises protestantes*, *Esther* and *Athalie*, the Twelfth Book of La Fontaine's *Fables*, the sermons of Bourdaloue, and the *Entretiens sur la Métaphysique et la Religion* (of which the first two and the last appeared quite at the beginning of our period) as written by men who belong to an earlier generation, we have nothing but *Les Caractères* of La Bruyère that will pass unchallenged as a great French classic. Fifty years ago one would unhesitatingly have added *Télémaque*, but, though it has recently received the honour of apotheosis in M. Cahen's admirable edition in *Les Grands Écrivains de la France*, it is no longer widely read, even, I fancy, in France. I have not forgotten Saint-Simon's *Memoirs*, which, in spite of certain dull and tedious stretches, is on the whole the most remarkable work that has been noticed in the above pages. But, as it was not begun till 1739 or 1740, was not completed till 1751 and did not appear in print (except in a few extracts) till 1788, it does not strictly belong to the literature of our period. Of what we may call minor masterpieces, we have *Turcaret* and Perrault's fairy-tales, and I should like to add Fontenelle's *Éloges*. In works which without being masterpieces still keep their place in the ranks of living literature, and are still read with pleasure, the period is fairly rich. It is represented by Fénelon's *Lettres spirituelles, Éducation des Filles*, and *Lettre à l'Académie*, Mme de Maintenon's *Lettres et Entretiens*, Bayle's *Pensées sur la Comète*, Fontenelle's *Pluralité des Mondes* and *Histoire des Oracles*, Massillon's sermons, Lesage's *Le diable boiteux*, Regnard's *Le Joueur* and *Le Légataire universel*, some of Dancourt's comedies, especially *Les Bourgeoises à la Mode*, a comedy or two by Dufresny and his *Amusements sérieux et comiques*, some half-a-dozen poems, the best of Mme d'Aulnoy's fairy-tales and her *Relation du Voyage d'Espagne*, and Hamilton's *Mémoires de Gramont*. Nearly all these have been reprinted in quite recent years. Bayle's Dictionary, on the other hand, was last printed more than a hundred years ago and is not likely to be reprinted. But it is of great historical importance, and it may be still dipped into with pleasure and profit.

It will be seen that the more creative kinds of literature are sparsely represented. There is a fair amount of comedy, but little of the first class, no tragedy, hardly any poetry, not much fiction, and no regular novel. The rest is composed of more or less occasional writings, including letters and treatises suggested by some special event or circumstance—writings, in short, which require no creative and little constructive effort. History, as we saw in the chapter on Bayle, was at a particularly low ebb. After the *Discours sur l'histoire universelle* (1681) and the *Variations* (1688) no work appeared till Montesquieu's *Considérations sur la Grandeur et la Décadence des Romains* (1734), which was at once history and literature. Yet the scientific side of history was shewing distinct signs of improvement in the hands of the Jesuit, Père Daniel, and the Port-Royalist, Tillemont de Nain. A great work too, partly antiquarian and partly historical, was being carried on by the Benedictines of Saint-Maur. The greatest of all, Jean Mabillon, though he lived till 1707, belongs to an earlier generation, and his *De Re Diplomatica* was published in 1681, but Montfaucon, Ruinart, Sainte-Marthe, and Martène were all born in the 'fifties, and of these Dom Ruinart published in 1699 what is still the only complete edition of the works of Gregory of Tours, and Dom Denis de Sainte-Marthe wrote a life of Gregory the Great in 1697, to be succeeded by an edition of his works (1705) for which the community of Saint-Maur was responsible[1]. To our period also belong the great contributions made to ecclesiastical history by Louis Ellies Dupin (1657–1719), whose *Nouvelle Bibliothèque des Auteurs ecclésiastiques* appeared in fifty-eight volumes from 1686 to 1704[2], and the Abbé Claude Fleury (1640–1723), who gave the last thirty years to his *Histoire ecclésiastique*[3], "the best history of the Church," said Voltaire, "that has ever been written."

The despotic government of Louis XIV with its strict censorship of the press was naturally unfavourable to the production of memoirs. Those that have been cited or referred

---

[1] "D'immenses travaux d'érudition dont la gloire égale presque celles des œuvres littéraires du siècle de Louis XIV, avaient mis à la portée des hommes studieux la plupart des documents historiques du moyen âge, surtout des monuments législatifs, les actes publics et ceux du droit privé, inconnus au siècle précédent." (Thierry, *Considérations sur l'histoire de France*, c. II).

[2] Also *Histoire des Juifs*, 1710, and *Histoire de l'Église en abrégé*, 1712.

[3] Vols. I–XX were published from 1691 onwards, the rest after Fleury's death.

to in the previous chapters—those of Mme de La Fayette, La Fare, Perrault, Mme de Caylus, and the Abbé de Choisy—were not published till after the king's death, and none of them throws much light on the latter part of his reign. Those of Mme de La Fayette, though they possibly formed part of a longer work now lost, only relate to the years 1688 and 1689. Choisy's unmethodical fragments of recollections are chiefly concerned with the early part of the reign, and except for a brief account of the disgrace and death of Louvois (1691) stop short at the year 1686. The death of Louis XIV was the signal for the gradual publication, chiefly at Amsterdam and often from pirated copies, of a whole series of memoirs. Thus La Fare's were published in 1716 (Rotterdam), Guy Joly's in 1718, those of Retz and the elder Brienne in 1717, of the younger Brienne in 1720, Segrais's and Mme de Motteville's in 1723, Gourville's in 1724, Choisy's in 1727, and Mlle de Montpensier's in 1728. In fact, almost the only memoirs that saw the light in the latter part of the reign of Louis XIV were those of Bussy-Rabutin, which do not go beyond the year 1666[1]. Villars did not even begin to write till just after his master's death[2]. The Life of Du Guay-Trouin (1673–1736), well written though it is, will perhaps not appeal to a reader who is not familiar with nautical terms and manœuvres, but it gives an admirable idea of the intrepidity of the French privateers, who, like the author, Jean Bart, Forbin, and others, did much damage to the shipping and commerce of the allies after the French had lost command of the seas. From the time when as a boy of eighteen he sailed up the estuary of the Shannon and sacked a mansion of Lord Clare's to when, twenty years later (1711), he seized Rio de Janeiro and compelled the Portuguese governor to pay a huge ransom for the town, Du Guay-Trouin's career was a succession of thrilling adventures[3].

This brief retrospect of the literature of the latter part of the

---

[1] I do not count the largely fictitious memoirs for which Courtilz de Sandras was responsible.

[2] The memoirs of Dangeau, Sourches, and Saint-Hilaire, though important as sources of information, have no literary value.

[3] *Mémoires*, Amsterdam, 1730; ed. H. Malo (*Chefs-d'œuvre méconnus*), 1922.

reign of Louis XIV shews, as I have said, a marked falling off in the creative or, what is practically the same thing, the imaginative element. La Bruyère as a moralist is on a par with his predecessors, but his portrayal of human nature owes almost everything to observation and little to imagination. The same may be said of the comic dramatists who trod so closely in his footsteps.

This tendency of French literature to desert imagination for reason was no new thing. It had made itself felt all through the seventeenth century and during our period, as we have seen in the last three chapters, it had become accelerated under the pressure of the Cartesian philosophy. Before long La Motte opened a campaign against poetry, and in spite of Lesage, Prévost, and Marivaux fiction was regarded with no great favour[1]. The sovereignty of reason was greatly promoted by the growing interest in science and the spread of education among the lower classes. The Abbé Du Bos in the letter to Bayle cited in the second chapter[2] notices the increase of education among servants, an observation which suggests that the Frontins and Lisettes of the comedy of our period are truer to nature than is often supposed. Mme de Staal-Delaunay's story of how she had to spend the night in a wretched tavern in Normandy—it was in the year 1709—and how her room was only separated by a thin partition from one occupied by soldiers and carters, and how she was reassured by hearing them dispute about the antipodes and the roundness of the earth, is cited by Brunetière as evidence of this educational progress and of the introduction of "the ferment of democracy" into literature to which it ultimately led[3].

From our period, too, dates the interest in English thought and literature which was to be so marked a feature of the eighteenth century[4]. At the beginning of the year 1685 the

---

[1] Voltaire, who had a contempt for novels, said in 1733 that the public was losing its taste for fiction.

[2] See above, p. 43. "Pas un petit bourgeois n'eût reçu un laquais, même une cuisinière, qui ne sût lire et écrire."

[3] *Études critiques*, V, 227.

[4] The translations of English works into French made between 1715 and the Revolution fill 21 pages of Lanson's *Manuel bibliographique*.

only works written in English by Englishmen of which French translations existed were the *Arcadia*, Greene's *Pandosto*, Bacon's *Essays*, Hall's *Characters of Virtues and Vices*, and the *Religio Medici*. There were also translations of the principal Latin works of Bacon and Hobbes. It was the revocation of the Edict of Nantes which, so to speak, introduced England and English literature to France. This was done partly by communications to the international reviews published in Holland, and partly by translations[1]. In 1685 a beginning was made with a translation of the first two volumes of Burnet's *History of the Reformation*. In the next decade translations appeared of Halifax's *Advice to a Daughter* (1697), of most of Temple's writings, and of some of Locke's—the second ot the *Two Treatises of Government* (1691; 7th ed. 1695), *Some Thoughts concerning Education* (1695), and *The Reasonableness of Christianity* (1696). These last two were the work of Pierre Coste, the editor of Montaigne, as was the translation of *An Essay concerning Human Understanding* which appeared in 1700. Locke resided in Holland from 1683 to 1689 and made friends there with Leclerc, who in 1710 published a translation of some of his writings under the title of *Œuvres diverses*. Clarendon's *History of the Rebellion* appeared in a French version in 1704, Shaftesbury's *Letter concerning Enthusiasm* in 1708, and Collins's *Discourse on Free-thinking* and Addison's *Cato* in 1714. The last was translated by Abel Boyer, who in 1702 had published an English-French and French-English dictionary. In the same year, 1714, a translation of the *Spectator* (1711–1714) was begun and in 1715 appeared Steele's *Œuvres diverses*. Mention should also be made of the observations on this country by two Protestants, Henri Misson[2] of Valbourg and Georges-Louis Lesage[3] of La Colombière in Burgundy. The

---

[1] See above, pp. 371–376, and J. Texte, *J.-J. Rousseau et les origines du cosmopolitisme littéraire*, 1895, c. i.

[2] *Mémoires et observations faites par un voyageur en Angleterre*, The Hague, 1698. Sometimes attributed to Maximilien Misson, the editor of Leguat's *Voyages et Avantures* (G. Atkinson, *The Extraordinary Voyage in French Literature*, p. 144).

[3] *Remarques sur l'Angleterre faites par un voyageur dans les années 1710, 1711*, Amsterdam [Rouen], 1715.

latter, who spent eleven years (1700–1711) in England, also wrote an account of Newton's philosophy under the title of *Le Mécanisme de l'Esprit*[1].

"Between the phrase of the seventeenth century and the phrase of the eighteenth century," says M. Lanson, "there is the same contrast as there is between the societies of the two centuries[2]." The style—to use a more general term—of the age of Louis XIV is the style of a great age, of an age which loved magnificence, order, and decorum, which thought logically and acted with energy and decision. It is ample, eloquent, and stately. It employs a phrase which is built up with the help of rhythmical and skilfully connected periods into a logical and harmonious whole. Its greatest exponent is Bossuet. But by the side of the full-dress style of the great masters there was an easier and more familiar style, which copied the language of the court and society. M. Lanson gives as instances the epistolary prose of Bussy-Rabutin and the critical prose of Père Bouhours, both of whom are referred to with approval by La Bruyère, and above all the historical prose of Racine, the prose of the *Abrégé de l'histoire de Port-Royal*, "the prose which of all the prose styles of the seventeenth century most resembles Voltaire at his best[3]." The *Abrégé* was probably written in 1697, but, as we have seen, there are other works of our period which anticipate the new prose with its "phrase courte, sèche, nerveuse, hachée, sautillante, qui semble ne vouloir parler qu'à l'esprit." La Bruyère, with his love of variety, uses sometimes the long periodic phrase and sometimes the short broken phrase. Fontenelle and Hamilton are consistent in their use of the short phrase, but interpreting La Bruyère's recommendation to introduce *esprit* into style in too literal a sense, they do not always escape the pitfall of conscious *esprit*—preciosity. It needed the nervous vigour and sure touch of Montesquieu and Voltaire to bring to perfection the style of the eighteenth century.

[1] Geneva, 1700. [2] *L'Art de la Prose*, p. 140. [3] Lemaître, *Racine*.

INDEX